CULTURALLY DIVERSE MENTAL HEALTH

CULTURALLY DIVERSE MENTAL HEALTH

The Challenges of Research and Resistance

Edited by

Jeffery Scott Mio
Gayle Y. Iwamasa

Brunner-Routledge
New York and Hove

Published in 2003 by
Brunner-Routledge
29 West 35th Street
New York, NY 10001
www.brunner-routledge.com

Published in Great Britain by
Brunner-Routledge
27 Church Road
Hove, East Sussex
BN3 2FA
www.brunner-routledge.co.uk

Brunner-Routledge is an imprint of the Taylor & Francis Group.
Printed in the United States of America on acid-free paper.

10 9 8 7 6 5 4 3 2 1

Library of Congress Cataloging-in-Publication Data

    Culturally diverse mental health : the challenges of research and
    resistance / edited by Jeffery Scott Mio, Gayle Y. Iwamasa.
       p. cm.
    Includes bibliographical references and index.
    ISBN 0-415-93357-9 (hardback) — ISBN 0-415-93358-7 (pbk.)
    1. Cultural psychology. 2. Minorities—Mental health services
I. Mio, Jeffery Scott, 1954– II. Iwamasa, Gayle.

RC455.5. E8 C783 2003
362.2dc21   2002152052

Contents

SECTION 3
DIVERSE NONETHNIC POPULATIONS

FOREWORD

In the late summer of 1968, a group of Black psychologists stormed the American Psychological Association's Annual Convention to demand an accurate understanding of Black psychology. Not surprisingly, this first challenge from ethnic psychologists was met largely with resistance and defensiveness by the White mainstream psychologists—the Black psychologists were accused of, among other things, contaminating psychology with racism. Several years later, in 1976, Robert Guthrie wrote a pioneering book, *Even the Rat Was White: A Historical View of Psychology,* that documented the hitherto ignored contributions of Black psychologists. The spirit of this book was clearly before its time; it garnered hardly any attention at the time of its publication. Now, of course, this book is regarded as a groundbreaking contribution to psychology, and Guthrie has even been honored by the National Archives of American Psychology.

Despite the chilly reception from mainstream psychology, these early efforts to discuss culture nevertheless grew in strength and numbers. This first challenge to psychology has since gathered a groundswell of support and has grown into a movement of significance—it has even been hailed as the fourth force in psychology. Yet, despite this growing acceptance and popularity, this fourth force in psychology continues to be stymied by concerted resistance from different fronts.

One of the hallmarks of a paradigm shift is that it engenders antagonism and rejection from proponents of the prevailing power structure. Hence, it is natural and expected that a paradigmatic shift in thinking such as that of the multicultural movement be met with forceful resistance from the old guard. An astute response to this resistance would be to clarify, analyze, and understand its conceptual and emotional underpinnings. Such a response has been undertaken in this book by Jeffery Mio and Gayle Iwamasa. The first half of this book offers a rigorous examination of the various forms of resistance to multiculturalism at different levels and settings, from the individual to the organizational level, from the fields of counseling and psychology to politics and the government. Particularly noteworthy is the attention paid to the more advanced and insidious forms of resistance, such as modern forms of racism (see Chapter 1: "Modern Forms of Resistance to Multiculturalism: Keeping Our Eyes on the Prize" and Chapter 3: "Resistance to Multiculturalism: The 'Indian Problem'").

At the same time, a successful call for change needs to offer hope and solutions. This is accomplished in the latter half of the book where concrete ideas for change and constructive action are offered. This book goes far beyond the norm in this area—it not only includes chapters on the four main ethnic minority populations in America, it also offers perspectives on other diverse populations that are often overlooked in the research literature and in mainstream thinking, such as South Asian Americans, biracial and multiracial individuals, lesbians, gays, and bisexuals, the aging population, and the deaf.

A call for change is also a call to action. It is fitting that the two halves of the book are bridged by the inspiring and hopeful chapter written by Mio and Roades, "Building Bridges in the 21st Century: Allies and the Power of Human Connection across Demographic Divides." This chapter reminds us that in order to come to a place of reconciliation and mutual enrichment, it is imperative that we be courageous enough to leave our safety zones, to reach out to individuals who are different from us, and to experience them up close. This chapter chronicles outstanding individuals who have paved the way in this regard, who have traversed seemingly impossible boundaries, and who have created positive change in the process. The authors of this chapter remind us that *all* of us can be allies for change and that even seemingly insignificant acts of personal courage can effect social change.

The call to multiculturalism does not take place in a vacuum—the need to address multiculturalism in America has never been more urgent. At this point in time, the population of People of Color in America is growing at such a fast rate that it is estimated that most Americans will be people of color by the year 2050. In fact, this has already become a reality in California, where "minorities" are now numerically the majority. The phrase, "the browning of America" is already part of the popular parlance. At the same time, the events of September 11 have created a backlash of hatred, discrimination, and racism against Muslims, Middle Easterners, and those who look like them. These are just a few of the demographic and political realities that provide the impetus for knowledge, awareness, and sensitivity to the challenge of living and working in a multicultural society. In particular, psychologists, therapists, educational specialists, and all professionals in the helping fields are faced with this challenge of learning how to work effectively and sensitively with people who do not look like them or think like them.

The road to effective and authentic cross-cultural communication will not be a smooth one—there will be more mishaps and stumbling blocks than successes along the way. However, this is a challenge that we cannot ignore. Given the multicultural future that we face, this is a road that we need to keep walking on, despite mistakes or setbacks along the way. This book, *Culturally Diverse Mental Health,* is a timely resource for this place and time in America. It provides excellent, state-of-the-art thinking on cross-cultural understanding as we progress on this road of multicultural understanding—it not only points us toward positive interactions and constructive action, it also helps us recognize blind spots that may lurk in the form of modem racist attitudes and beliefs. This book is an important contribution to the mental health literature; it should be required reading for all psychologists, therapists, clinical supervisors, students in training, and their teachers. At the same time, mental health professionals are not the only ones who will benefit from the book. We believe that the first section of the book contains vital information for those who work in the fields of human resources, business, social policy, politics, education, and economics—it will undoubtedly challenge the thinking, attitudes, and assumptions of anyone who wields influence over others' lives. The second section of the book is particularly useful as a specific reference guide to different diverse groups.

The future of multiculturalism is here and we need to use all available tools and knowledge to help us grapple with it. It is our hope that leaders in psychology, business corporations, governments, and other organizations of power will read this book and become aware of their potential resistance to multiculturalism and, in turn, lead the way to true multicultural sensitivity in America.

Joseph L. White, Ph.D.
Professor Emeritus of Psychology and Psychiatry
University of California, Irvine

Anne Chan
Doctoral Candidate in Counseling Psychology
Stanford University

Joseph L. White, Ph.D., Professor Emeritus of Psychology and Psychiatry at the University of California, Irvine, is former Chair of the Psychology Licensing Board in the State of California and holds membership in the American Psychological Association, the American Psychological Society, the California Psychological Association, Association of Black Psychologists, the American Association for Higher Education, and the American Counseling Association. He is the author of several journal articles and three books, *The Psychology of Blacks: An Afro-American Perspective* (1984, 1990, 1999), *The Troubled Adolescent* (1989), and *Black Man Emerging: Facing the Past and Seizing a Future in America* (1999).

Anne Chan, M.A., received her master's degree in marriage and family counseling at California State University-Hayward. She is currently a doctoral student in counseling psychology at Stanford University and is an associate member of the American Psychological Association, and the Asian American Psychological Association.

CONTRIBUTORS

Patricia Arredondo, Ed.D., is an Associate Professor of Counseling/Counseling Psychology at Arizona State University. The three foci of her research are multicultural competency models, organizational diversity climate studies, and Latino perspectives in education, research, and practice. She can be reached at empower@asu.edu

Audrey K. Bangi, M.A., is a doctoral student in the Clinical-Community Psychology program at DePaul University in Chicago, IL. Her research interests include examining women's health issues and conducting evaluations of community-based HIV/AIDS prevention programs for urban ethnic minority youth. She can be reached at abangi@depaul.edu

Lori Barker-Hackett, Ph.D., is an Associate Professor of Psychology in the Behavioral Sciences Department at California State Polytechnic University, Pomona. She is also a staff counselor and supervisor at the institution's Counseling and Psychological Services Department. Her research is on multicultural education and diversity training. She can be reached at labarker@csupomona.edu

John M. Chaney, Ph.D., is Professor of Clinical Psychology at Oklahoma State University and Clinical Associate Professor of Psychiatry at the University of Oklahoma Health Sciences Center. Dr. Chaney's research interests focus on children's adjustment to chronic medical illness and on implicit racism affecting academic achievement among Native Americans. He can be reached at jchaney@okstate.edu

Theodora B. Consolacion, M.A., is in the Social Psychology Ph.D. program at University of California, Davis. Her research focus is on Asian-American mental health, gay/lesbian/bisexual issues, and ethnic and sexual identities. She can be reached at tbconsolacion@ucdavis.edu

Martha R, Crowther, Ph.D., M.P.H. is an Assistant Professor of Psychology and coordinator of the PhD/MPH program at The University of Alabama in Tuscaloosa. Her research, teaching, and clinical interests are in geropsychology and cultural competence in research training. She can be reached at crowther@bama.ua.edu

Michael D'Andrea, Ph.D., is a Professor in the Department of Counselor Education at the University of Hawaii. His research interests include White privilege and antiracism, which fuels his social activism. He can be reached at michael@hawaii.edu

Cynthia de las Fuentes, Ph.D., is an Associate Professor of Psychology at Our Lady of the Lake University in San Antonio, TX. Her teaching and scholarship focus on diversity, especially Latino psychology, feminist psychology, and ethics. She can be reached at delac@lake.ollusa.edu

Juanita M. Dimas, Ph.D., is the Cultural and Linguistic Program Manager at the Alameda Alliance for Health serving Alameda County, CA. The primary focus of her work is health disparities and culturally competent health care delivery. She can be reached at jdimas@alameda-alliance.com

G. Rita Dudley-Grant, Ph.D., M.P.H., is Director of Program Development at Virgin Islands Behavioral Services, a comprehensive system of care for adolescents in the Virgin Islands. Her research interests are in the areas of ethnic minority psychology, Buddhism, spirituality, and psychology in psychotherapy and Caribbean family psychology. She can be reached at ritadgrant@attglobal.net

Robert Geffner, Ph.D., is the Founder and President of the Family Violence and Sexual Assault Institute (and Executive Editor of the *Family Violence & Sexual Assault Bulletin*) located in San Diego, CA. He is a Clinical Research Professor of Psychology at the California School of Professional Psychology, Alliant International University, in San Diego. He is Editor-in-Chief of Haworth's Maltreatment and Trauma Press. He can be reached at bgeffner@pacbell.net

Joseph P. Gone, Ph.D., is an Assistant Professor in the Department of Psychology (Clinical Area) and the Program in American Culture (Native American Studies) at the University of Michigan in Ann Arbor. His research interests include cultural psychology and American Indian mental health. He can be reached at jgone@umich.edu

Christine C. Iijima Hall, Ph.D., is a psychologist and the Director of Employee Services for the Maricopa Community College District in Arizona. Her research, publications, and lectures have focused on ethnic minority and women's issues. Dr. Hall is one of the pioneer researchers in multiracial identity. She can be reached at christine.hall@domail.maricopa.edu

Kristin A. Hancock, Ph.D., is Professor of Psychology at John F. Kennedy University's Graduate School of Professional Psychology. She is past Chair of APA's Committee on Lesbian, Gay, and Bisexual Concerns (CLGBC), past President of Division 44 of APA, and co-chaired the Division 44/CLGBC Joint Task Force that developed APA's Guidelines for Psychotherapy with Lesbian, Gay, and Bisexual Clients. She can be reached at khancock@jfku.edu

Michele Harway, *Ph.D.*, is a Professor at Antioch University, Santa Barbara. Her work has focused on domestic violence research, research on women's development, and on training mental health professionals to recognize domestic violence perpetrators. She can be reached at mharway@antiochsm.edu

Arpana G. Inman, Ph.D. is an Assistant Professor in the Counseling Psychology Program, within the Department of Education and Human Services at Lehigh University, Bethlehem, PA. Her scholastic and research interests are in the areas of South Asian American concerns, women's issues, and multicultural supervision and training. She can be reached at agi2@lehigh.edu

David C. Ivey, Ph.D., is an Associate Professor and Director of Graduate Programs in Marriage and Family Therapy at Texas Tech University. His research interests involve the study of clinical judgment in marriage and family therapy, gender issues in marriage and family therapy, and the training of mental health practitioners. He can be reached at david.ivey@ttu.edu

Gayle Y. Iwamasa, Ph.D., is an Associate Professor in the Clinical Community Psychology Program in the Department of Psychology at DePaul University. Her research and clinical interests are in multicultural mental health across the lifespan. She can be reached at giwamasa@depaul.edu

Shalonda Kelly, Ph.D., is an Assistant Professor in the Clinical Department of the Graduate School of Applied and Professional Psychology at Rutgers, The State University of New Jersey. The primary foci of her research are racial, ethnic, and cultural issues, and couple relationships. She can be reached at skelly@rci.rutgers.edu

Mary P. Koss, Ph.D., is Professor of Public Health and Psychology at University of Arizona in Tucson. Her current research focuses on the RESTORE Program, which uses restorative justice principles to bring cultural competency to the adjudication of selected sexual offenses. She can be reached at mpk@u.arizona.edu

Irene W. Leigh, Ph.D., a deaf psychologist, is currently a Professor in the Clinical Psychology doctoral program at Gallaudet University in Washington, DC. Her research and publications have focused on deaf people and issues related to identity, multiculturalism, parenting, attachment, depression, and cochlear implants. She can be reached at irene.leigh@gallaudet.edu

J. Douglas McDonald, Ph.D., is an Associate Professor of Psychology at the University of North Dakota (UND) and Director of the UND Indians into Psychology Doctoral Education (INPSYDE) Program. His primary research interests lie in investigating the relation between cultural orientation and adaptive functioning and success among American Indians. He can be reached at justin_mcdonald@und.nodak.edu.

Jeffery Scott Mio, Ph.D., is Professor of Psychology in the Behavioral Sciences Department at California State Polytechnic University, Pomona, and Director of the M.S. in Psychology Program in that department. His research interests include multicultural education and the development of allies. He can be reached at jsmio@csupomona.edu

Bianca Cody Murphy, Ed.D., is Professor of Psychology at Wheaton College in Norton, MA. Her research areas include lesbian health and mental health. She can be reached at bmurphy@wheatonma.edu

James M. O'Neil, Ph.D., is Professor of Family Studies and Educational Psychology at the University of Connecticut. His teaching and research interests are men's gender role conflict, the new psychology of men, and violence against women. He can be reached at james.o'neil@uconn.edu

Laurie A. Roades, Ph.D., is an Associate Professor in the Behavioral Sciences Department at California State Polytechnic University, Pomona. Her research interests include gender and mental health and allies across demographic groups. She can be reached at laroades@csupomona.edu

Daya Singh Sandhu, Ed.D., is Professor and Chair of the Educational and Counseling Psychology at University of Louisville. He has special interest in multicultural counseling, school counseling, career counseling, and the role of spirituality in counseling and psychotherapy. He can be reached at daya.sandhu@louisville.edu

Stanley Sue, Ph.D., is Professor of Psychology, Psychiatry, and Asian American Studies at the University of California, Davis. His research examines ethnicity, mental health, and treatment. He can be reached at ssue@ucdavis.edu

Karen L. Suyemoto, Ph.D., is an Assistant Professor in Clinical Psychology and Asian American Studies at the University of Massachusetts, Boston. Her general interests are on cultural diversity and antiracist practice. Her current research interests are in ethnic and racial identities in multiracial and Asian-American people, particularly as they interface with education. She can be reached at karen.suyemoto@umb.edu.

Nita Tewari, Ph.D., is a Staff Psychologist in the University of California, Irvine's Counseling Center. She is currently serving as the Division on Women Co-Chair for the Asian American Psychological Association. Her interests lie primarily in South Asian/Indian Americans, but she also works with ethnically diverse populations in general. She can be reached at ntewari@cox.net

Antonette M. Zeiss, Ph.D., is Clinical Coordinator and Director of Training in the Psychology Service at the VA Palo Alto Health Care System. She is former President of AABT, former President of Section II of Division 12 of APA, and Chair of APA's Committee on Aging. Her research and scholarly interests include treatment of depression, psychotherapy with older adults, and sexual dysfunction. She can be reached at antonette.zeiss@med.va.gov

RESISTANCE TO MULTICULTURAL PSYCHOLOGY

As most of us who teach multicultural issues know, this topic stirs up issues that are not present when we teach other topics in psychology, such as social psychology, cognitive psychology, developmental psychology, or physiological psychology. These other topics seem to stir up feelings of wonder or discovery about how psychologists conceive of these topics. However, multicultural psychology often challenges people's fundamental worldviews, and this challenge stirs up feelings of resistance and defensiveness. The first section of this book addresses this resistance.

In Mio's chapter, resistance to multiculturalism is conceived as a type of modern form of racism. Traditional racism was overt and sometimes even proudly practiced in some areas of the country. Modern forms of racism are subtle, covert, and often unconscious. Mio uses a cognitive dissonance perspective to both understand modern forms of racism and also address the resistance coming from these forms of racism.

D'Andrea's chapter reports on his longitudinal study examining White resistance to multiculturalism across a wide range of settings. He has conversed with or observed over 1,500 White individuals in settings such as faculty meetings, professional conferences, White supremacy rallies, and diners. He has categorized these individuals into having five types of dispositions: Affective–Impulsive Disposition, Rational Disposition, Liberal Disposition, Principled Disposition, and Principled Activistic Disposition. D'Andrea offers intervention strategies for individuals with each of these forms of disposition.

McDonald and Chaney see resistance against including issues dealing with American Indians as a modern form of the "Indian Problem." Historically, the White European-American culture attempted to wipe out American Indians through direct genocide and then through policies designed to eliminate traditional cultural practices. They see resistance to American Indian issues as stemming from ethnocentrism, where the worldview of the White culture does not understand the worldview of American Indians. This clash of worldviews resulted in justification of the Indian Reservation system and boarding schools through the religiously endowed Manifest Destiny doctrine. Modern forms of this ethnocentric view have been the society's offensive use of sports teams using American-Indian nicknames and a refusal to see these as offensive, and through psychology's complicity in the superiority of Whites through application of scientific racism.

Suyemoto and Dimas address issues of multicultural individuals and resistance both coming from the majority culture and also ethnic minority cultures. From a broader perspective, despite the fact that we are in an era of sensitivity to issues of diversity, only 28 articles published in APA journals and APA division-sponsored journals in the last 5 years have dealt with multicultural individuals. This represents only 0.13% of all such articles published. Exclusion of multicultural issues by the majority group results from issues related to a dilution of a "pure race" ideology, as evidenced by antimiscegenation laws that were in existence even as late as last year. Resistance from ethnic minority groups results from challenges to their conception of in-group versus out-group members and also a diminution of political power.

Arredondo suggests that because of the political nature of diversity initiatives in organizations, there is a need for support of the management. Diversity initiatives are fundamentally about change in the organization, and there are many ways of resisting this change. Arredondo contends that there are at least three paradigms of resistance: (a) reactions occur at the cognitive, emotional, and behavioral levels; (b) reactions are dynamic; and (c) reactions of resistance may be directed toward the facilitator of the change. Arredondo offers ways of conceptualizing these forms of resistance and addressing such resistance.

Finally, Mio and Roades discuss the issue of allies. Allies are individuals who cross demographic boundaries to advocate for groups on the downside of power. With respect to race and ethnicity, allies are White individuals who advocate for ethnic minority causes. However, allies can cross many different demographic boundaries, such as those dealing with gender, sexual orientation, religion, and ability. Mio and Roades identify historical and current figures who have made profound differences by their courage to advocate for those on the downside of power.

CHAPTER 1

Modern Forms of Resistance to Multiculturalism

Keeping Our Eyes on the Prize

JEFFERY SCOTT MIO

In his Pulitzer Prize–winning book, *Eyes on the Prize*, Juan Williams tells the story of Emmett Till. Till was a 14-year-old African-American boy from Chicago visiting relatives in Money, Mississippi, in the summer of 1955. He told some African-American boys down there that he had a White girlfriend. These boys challenged him to talk to a White woman who was in the store with him. Not one to back down from a dare, Till left the store and said, "Bye, Baby" to the woman. The woman's husband, Roy Bryant, was outraged by this. He and a friend, J. W. Milam, went searching for Till. They found him at his uncle's (Mose Wright's) house around midnight that night.

> Till's body was found three days later. The barbed wire holding the cotton-gin fan around his neck had become snagged on a tangled river root. There was a bullet in the boy's skull, one eye was gouged out, and his forehead was crushed on one side. (Williams, 1987, p. 43)

Bryant and Milam were put on trial for the murder of Emmett Till. The evidence against them was overwhelming. The NAACP and the Black press wanted to make sure that this trial received national attention. Charles Diggs, a congressman from Michigan, attended the trial to observe the proceedings. However, a defense attorney contended that the body was so mutilated that it could not be identified as that of Emmett Till. Williams (1987) wrote:

> At the end of the five-day trial, John C. Whitten, one of the five defense attorneys, made his simple pitch to the all-white, all-male jurors: "Your fathers will turn over in their graves if [Milam and Bryant are found guilty] and I'm sure that every last Anglo-Saxon one of you has the courage to free these men in the face of that [out-side] pressure." (p. 52)

As those who are familiar with this case know, it took the jury a little over an hour to acquit Bryant and Milam for the murder of Emmett Till. The jury bought the argument that, because the face of Till was so mutilated that he could not be definitively identified, it was uncertain that he was in fact murdered.

The picture of Till's face was truly horrific. Moreover, after the subsequent trial, Bryant and Milam admitted that they murdered Till. They said that they *had* to kill Till because he refused to apologize for talking fresh to Bryant's wife, and he refused to beg for mercy.

In his book, Williams (1987) also documented other examples of overt racism in resistance to civil rights in this country. Such examples included the 1957 resistance to integration at Central High School in Little Rock, Arkansas, where the National Guard was called out in order to protect a handful of African-American students attempting to attend high school; the 1963 incident involving Bull Connor, police chief in Birmingham, Alabama, who unleashed police dogs and fire hoses on African Americans attempting to peacefully demonstrate against segregation; and the 1964 tragedy where Andrew Goodman, Michael Schwerner, and James Chaney were found murdered near Philadelphia, Mississippi, during "Freedom Summer," where Whites joined with African Americans to register African Americans to vote.

Overt, obvious forms of racism are generally a thing of the past, at least in terms of public complicity in the acts. Certainly, there are incidents of overt racist acts, such as the horrific murder of James Byrd, Jr., who was dragged behind a pickup truck in Jasper, Texas, by two racist White men (Sartwell, 1998). However, this act was not publicly condoned, and in fact, these men were convicted and sentenced to death for their heinous act. Morris Dees of the Southern Poverty Law Center (Dees, 1991) continually fights against organized racism in the country (e.g., Ku Klux Klan, the Aryan Nations National Church), but again, such racist groups are considered "fringe" elements in this society whose ideas are not acceptable. As many have written, the problem of today is not these kinds of overt forms of racism but covert forms of racism (Jones, 1997; Mio & Awakuni, 2000; Ridley, 1995). The remainder of this chapter discusses such forms of covert racism and suggests ways of intervening.

MODERN FORMS OF RACISM

Jones (1997) identified three forms of present-day racism: (a) symbolic racism, (b) modern racism, and (c) aversive racism. These forms of racism serve to resist efforts to increase multiculturalism in our society. As a result, majority people benefit because this keeps their power in place.

Symbolic Racism

Sears (1988) presented the term symbolic racism as an indication of White hostility toward Blacks. Users of symbolic racism employ popular symbols of "traditional values" in order to appeal to otherwise unaware individuals to agree with positions against

African Americans (or other target groups). For example, those who use this form of racism may first discuss the importance of the "Protestant work ethic" upon which the United States was built, then convince people that providing welfare to people violates this work ethic, so welfare should be withdrawn. Similarly, as Milloy (1999) pointed out, "gang" is used symbolically to refer to a group of ethnic minority youths (particularly African Americans and Latinos), whereas when a group of White youths get together, as in the killers in the Columbine High School massacre, they are referred to as a "clique." Gangs, of course, violate the "traditional value" of individualism, where people should defend themselves, whereas cliques are social groups that are acceptable in the broader society. As Milloy pointed out, members of a gang are referred to as "animals" and are demonized, whereas members of a clique are not. Instead, the Columbine killers were referred to as being "full of academic promise" and one of them was even referred to as "a gentleman who drove a BMW."

An example of how this form of symbolic politics can be applied to a nonethnic group occurred here in California during the 2000 elections. Proposition 22 was popularly known as "The Defense of Marriage Initiative." If passed, this proposition would legally forbid recognition of marriage between same-sex partners. The appeal to the "traditional value" of marriage was first presented, then the antigay purpose of the initiative was presented as a "logical" extension of the traditional value. Proponents of the measure contended that if same-sex partners were allowed to marry, the entire institution of marriage would be demolished, because we would then allow adults to marry children, animals, and multiple partners.[1]

Modern Racism

McConahay (1986) introduced the term "modern racism." This form of racism suggests that racism is a thing of the past, and that modern cries of racism are merely pushing a "liberal agenda," or crying wolf. So-called victims of racism are not really advancing up the economic and social ladders, but they are given breaks to allay guilt or avoid the problems of legal repercussions of accusations of racism. Thus, any gains by these so-called victims are fundamentally unfair because they are undeserved. Although symbolic racists are somewhat or quite conscious of their racism and try to conceal it via symbolic manners, modern racists are not consciously racist and in fact feel that racism is unpalatable. However, since they feel that racism is a thing of the past, they feel they could not possibly be racist, and that their views are merely based upon facts of modern society.

For example, many believe that those being assisted by affirmative action programs are receiving an unfair advantage. If racism no longer exists, we should not have programs that take race, culture, and ethnicity into account in hiring or college admissions decisions. In taking such factors into account, those not in the disadvantaged groups are themselves disadvantaged by the hiring and admissions decisions. They are, in essence, victims of reverse discrimination.

If we were to take a strictly legal perspective (leaving aside the moral arguments in favor if it), affirmative action could be justified by law as it is generally practiced.

Affirmative action was initially designed to address past wrongs (Cheatham, 1999). This may necessarily have a negative impact upon those who did not have had a direct involvement in the past wrongs. However, *any* legal remedy can have this impact. Even conservative newspaper columnist George F. Will recognized this when he wrote of then Los Angeles Police Chief Daryl Gates in the aftermath of Rodney King's arrest:

> Gates can be called The Eight Million Dollar Man. Just in the last year that sum has been awarded to victims of Los Angeles police misconduct. There will be two commas in the sum awarded to the man whose savage beating by some of Gates's men was recorded by a citizen with a video camera. . . . Gates sees no racial aspect to the videotaped beating. But when three white men club and stomp a black man while a dozen other white men watch, well, people will talk. They did when Jamaal Wilkes, who is black and a former star with the Lakers, was handcuffed because his auto registration was about to—yes, about to—expire. Joe Morgan, who is a black and a Hall of Fame second baseman, was thrown to the ground and handcuffed when cops decided he looked like a drug dealer. (Later the cops said "oops!" and a court said: Pay Mr. Morgan $540,000.) (p. A17)

Certainly, Los Angeles residents did not brutalize victims held by the police, but the citizens of Los Angeles paid in the form of higher taxes and reduced city services because of Chief Gates's renegade police force.

Another reason for affirmative action's existence about which modern racists may not be fully aware is that the criteria for "qualifications" may not be completely captured by the "objective" measures that purport to measure one's qualifications. In my own classes on multiculturalism, I point out that one reason why being a woman may be part of what qualifies a person to be a police officer is that if the police are investigating a rape case, a female rape victim may open up more and provide better information to a female officer than a male officer. So too, if one is studying ethnic minority populations, the ethnic minority subjects may open up more and give more accurate data to ethnic minority researchers than White researchers. Ethnic minority students may also have more insight into answers given by ethnic minority subjects. Thus, ethnicity may be a very important dimension of "qualifications" that one sets when searching for graduate students. Identifying gender or ethnicity as qualities that candidates must possess for the actual job or admissions qualifications would be illegal, but considering these qualities as important may be essential. As Justice Lewis Powell said in the landmark Supreme Court case *Bakke vs. Regents of the University of California* (1978), although the inclusion of race in evaluating the qualifications of applicants must be done with scrutiny and must only be conducted when it involves a compelling state interest, race or ethnicity may be used as one of the many factors weighed in admissions decisions. Moreover, diversity *is* a compelling state interest.

Aversive Racism

Gaertner and Dovidio (1986) presented the notion of aversive racism. Those who are aversive racists feel that racism is bad, and if they were accused of being racist, that would be at odds with their self-concept. However, the clash between the existence of racism in this society with notions of egalitarianism create a conflict in the aversive racist's mind. Therefore, they become avoidant of interactions with African Americans (or other ethnic minorities) in order to avoid their discomfort. Aversive racists hold negative views toward African Americans but are not consciously aware of these attitudes.

Dovidio (2001) presented some compelling data in support of the aversive racist view (see also Dovidio & Gaertner, 2000). He measured White research participants with an aversive racism scale and had them make hiring decisions regarding Black and White job candidates who had clearly strong, ambiguous, or clearly weak qualifications for the job. The strong job candidate of both races had high qualifications on two measures of ability (for this example, I will use "experience" and "letters of recommendation"), the candidates with ambiguous qualifications were strong on one of the qualifications and weak on the other, and the weak job candidates had low qualifications on both measures. Therefore, there were four types of generic job candidates: (a) strong on criterion A and strong on criterion B; (b) strong on criterion A and weak on criterion B; (c) weak on criterion A and strong on criterion B; and (d) weak on criterion A and weak on criterion B. When asked to make hiring decisions, research participants judged to be aversive racists recommended hiring both the White and the Black job candidates who were strong on both criteria, and they recommended not hiring both the White and the Black job candidates who were weak on both criteria. However, they tended to recommend the White job candidate over the Black job candidate in *both* of the ambiguous situations. When asked which of the criteria was more important, these aversive racists were able to protect themselves from feeling like they made a racist decision because they rated the criterion on which the White candidate was stronger as the more important of the two criteria. Figures 1.1 and 1.2 are depictions of Dovidio's findings.

Using the proposed illustrations, if the White candidate had a lot of experience but a somewhat poor letter of recommendation, whereas the Black candidate did not have a lot of experience but had a good letter of recommendation, aversive racists would recommend the White candidate be hired and "experience" would be judged to be the more important criterion. However, if the White candidate did not have a lot of experience but had a good letter of recommendation, whereas the Black candidate had a lot of experience but a somewhat poor letter of recommendation, aversive racists would recommend the White candidate be hired and "letter of recommendation" would be judged to be the more important criterion. As Dovidio and Gaertner (2000) have written:

> The aversive-racism framework further suggests that contemporary racial bias is expressed in indirect ways that do not threaten the aversive racist's nonprejudiced self-image. Because aversive racists consciously recognize and endorse egalitarian values, they will not discriminate in situations in which they recognize that discrimination would be obvious to others and themselves—for example, when the appropriate response is clearly dictated. However, because aversive racists do possess negative feelings, often unconsciously, discrimination occurs when bias is not obvious or can be rationalized on the basis of some factor other than race. (p. 319)

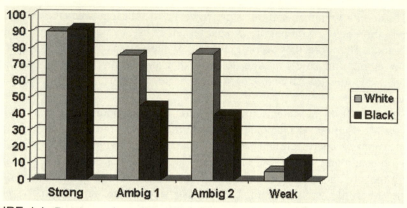

FIGURE 1.1. Representation of Dovidio's data on aversive racism—Probability of being hired. In Ambiguous 1, the White candidate was strong on Criterion A and weak on Criterion B, whereas the Black candidate was weak on Criterion A and strong on Criterion B. In Ambiguous 2, the White candidate was weak on Criterion A and strong on Criterion B, whereas the Black candidate was strong on Criterion A and weak on Criterion B.

COVERT RACISM:
HIDDEN RESISTANCE TO MULTICULTURALISM

Ridley (1995) proposed a taxonomy of three different kinds of racism: (a) overt, intentional racism; (b) covert, intentional racism; and (c) covert, unintentional racism. These three forms of racism can occur at both the individual and institutional levels.

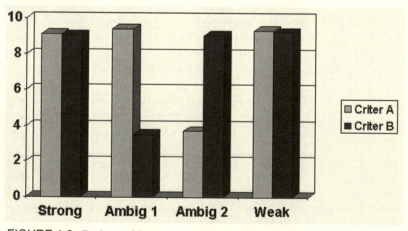

FIGURE 1.2. Ratings of importance of both of the criteria in Dovidio's study.

Overt, Intentional Racism

As discussed, blatant racism is generally not tolerated in modern society, at least at the institutional level. This form of racism was addressed earlier in our discussion of Williams' (1987) documentation of the civil rights movement in America. Certainly, overt, intentional racism still exists in some individuals. However, such blatant overt, obvious racism generally does not occur at the institutional level. Where racism does occur at the institutional level, it is at the covert level for the most part.

Covert, Intentional Racism

Covert, intentional racism is racism that is hidden or "deniable." A good example of covert, intentional racism at the institutional level (Mio & Awakuni, 2000) is when Mayor Richard J. Daley of Chicago had a number of schools built in Chicago in the 1960s, ostensibly to address overcrowding needs. However, after he died, it was discovered that Chicago had 25% more schools than it really needed, and this put the cost of public education at an unmanageable level. Many analysts believed that Mayor Daley really had these schools built in order to keep African-American children out of predominantly White schools. Thus, if the schools were built out of a truly intentionally racist motivation, deniability at the overt level could be maintained by the overcrowding argument.

Because Mayor Daley was the head of the Chicago institution of government, his maneuver could be considered a covert, intentional racist maneuver at the institutional level. However, his maneuver also could be considered an example of covert, intentional racism at the individual level for him personally. One often hears someone denying his or her apparent racism by saying, "Some of my best friends are Black [or whatever the target group is]." Those who engage in symbolic racism may also be considered to be covert, intentional racists. For example, when former Ku Klux Klan leader David Duke was running for governor of Louisiana in the early 1990s, he was clearly using conservative Republican issues as a cover for his racist platform. At the public level, he denied that he was racist, but his efforts were a thin disguise of his underlying racism.

Covert, Unintentional Racism

Covert, unintentional racism is perhaps both the most troubling and the most prevalent of the forms of racism that Ridley (1995) identified. This is because these kinds of racists truly do not want to be racist, yet they do not understand that many of the views they hold are racist in nature. This is because their views are based upon traditions, stereotypes, and institutionalized policies, so they are unaware of the racist (or at least biased) origins of such views. As I have stated elsewhere (Mio & Awakuni, 2000), an example of a covert, unintentional racist view I held when I was in high school was made clear during a discussion with Rico, a friend of mine. Vince Ferragamo, a classmate of mine who later became a professional football quarterback, was graduating. I wondered who was going to be the quarterback for my high school the following year. Rico suggested that an excellent quarterback would be an African American in his class. I said, "He can't be a quarterback . . . he's Black!" I did not know *why* Blacks could not be quarterbacks, I just knew that football analysts at the time said that they could not be quarterbacks. I did not realize that the analysts were *really* saying that Blacks were not smart enough to be quarterbacks. As there were no African-American quarterbacks in the National Football League nor major colleges at the time, there was no evidence to contradict the analysts' assertion. I naïvely accepted their analysis, not realizing how racist this position was. Now, I am more aware of such matters, and I cannot be as easily fooled. However, every now and then, a situation that is subtly or covertly racist presents itself and my first reaction is to accept it. Upon further analysis, I recognize the underlying racism involved, and I wonder how many people blindly accept the racist statement without such awareness.

The preceding example is of covert, unintentional racism at the individual level. An example of covert, unintentional racism at the institutional level is how tenure is decided in many universities across this country. Many universities essentially weigh some combination of research and teaching as the most important elements in tenure decisions, with some lesser weighting for service to the department and/or the university in the form of serving on committees. As most ethnic minority faculty members know—particularly in psychology and other social sciences—many community entities ask ethnic minority professors to make presentations and contribute somehow to the larger society. This places such professors in a quandary. Quite often they are hired to perform such community activities, making presentations in the community on racism or related topics. However, these kinds of activities are not weighed in tenure decisions because they do not fit in the research, teaching, or committee service categories. Therefore, the professor asked to perform these activities must make a choice between serving the community versus receiving tenure. I would venture to guess that most college administrators are not intentionally racist nor would they support intentionally racist policies. However, rules for tenure tend to be biased against ethnic minority professors. Of course, the way to address this problem is to perhaps broaden our conception of what constitutes "service" and give that category a heavier weighting. However, major research institutions will probably still insist that research—specifically, publications and grants—should be the primary criterion upon which tenure is decided. (By the way, in my opinion, this stance is also biased against developmental researchers who rely upon longitudinal studies. This is particularly true because merely receiving permission to collect data on children often takes very long to receive, because it must go through, typically, school system reviews and parental approval regimes before the study is allow to proceed.) Thus, in order to be truly free of bias, universities need to develop categories that explicitly take into account community service for tenure.

MODERN FORMS OF RACISM AS RESISTANCE
TO MULTICULTURALISM

If one has ever been called a racist, one knows that one's first response is often to deny it. Energy is expended to prove one's "innocence" of this charge; it simply does not feel good to be thought of as a racist. Put in cognitive dissonance terms (Festinger, 1957), if one does not feel racist but is being called a racist, dissonance occurs. Dissonance causes tension, and the individual is motivated to reduce this tension. One way to reduce this tension is to identify situations or instances where one has not acted in a racist manner, and another way to reduce this tension is to avoid situations that might arouse the tension in the first place.

As Dovidio and Gaertner (1998) stated, "Aversive racists recognize prejudice is bad, but they do not recognize that they are prejudiced" (p. 25). In identifying situations where they have not acted in racist manners, aversive racists—or any contemporary racists—can preserve their self-image as nonracists. Because this can successfully reduce the tension caused by the two dissonant positions, contemporary racists subsequently are no longer motivated to explore why they were accused of racism in the first place. Hence, their [covert, unintentional] racist views are not modified or changed.

As discussed, Gaertner and Dovidio (1986) also indicated that aversive racists avoid situations that may arouse their dissonant views. In my opinion, this avoidance is at the root of resistance to multiculturalism. It can be conceived as being maintained by the traditional behavioral principle of negative reinforcement (see Sue, Sue, & Sue, 2000): (a) Cognitive dissonance is aroused when a contemporary racist is placed in a multicultural situation; (b) anxiety, tension, and/or discomfort is aroused by the dissonance; (c) relief from these negative emotions comes when one escapes from the dissonant situation; and (d) one avoids the dissonant-arousing situations in the future. As Festinger (1957) indicated, we are motivated to reduce cognitive dissonance, thus we are motivated to avoid dissonant-inducing situations.

A common complaint by those who conduct multicultural programs and also the participants in these programs is that we are always "preaching to the choir." Those who are interested in multiculturalism attend multicultural programs. The people who typically "need" to attend such programs tend to avoid these programs, much to the frustration of the attendees who work with this second set of people. As an example, on my own campus there is an annual event called the Cross-Cultural Retreat (CCR), which occurs over the weekend on or near the Martin Luther King, Jr. holiday. The CCR is open to students, staff, and faculty, and draws between 150 and 200 participants each year. The goals of the CCR are to help increase multicultural understanding and awareness in various areas of diversity.[2] Over the course of the last six CCRs I have attended, only about five professors per year have attended. The president of my university is one of the only Asian presidents of a 4-year university in the country, and when he arrived on campus 10 years ago, one of his two major initiatives was to encourage the campus to be more sensitive to multicultural issues. The other initiative was to increase the technology infrastructure of the university. Although professors did not directly state that they did not want to increase their multicultural sensitivity, many stated that they "wanted things like they used to be." To my knowledge, none of the professors on campus objected to receiving new computers every 3 years or so, so I could only conclude that what was being resisted was the multicultural initiatives on campus. To the extent that most of my colleagues have not deemed it important enough to commit themselves for a weekend to attend the CCR, avoidance of multiculturalism seems prevalent.

ADDRESSING RESISTANCE TO MULTICULTURALISM

As others (Cialdini, 1993; Myers, 1999) have indicated, there are three kinds of cognitive dissonance: forced compliance, "we come to like the things for which we suffer," and threat of punishment. These subsets of cognitive dissonance can be used to conceptualize how resistance to multiculturalism can be addressed.

Forced Compliance

In their classic experiment, Festinger and Carlsmith (1959) had research participants perform menial tasks, then essentially lie to another individual, telling the other individual that the task was interesting. Half of the participants received $1 for lying, and the other half received $20 for lying. Those who received $1 later reported that the task was *more* interesting than those who received $20. According to Festinger and Carlsmith, they did so because they were underjustified—the $1 was not enough inducement to get them to lie, so there was some degree of cognitive dissonance to be reduced. This reduction happened when they convinced themselves that the menial task was actually more interesting than it really was, so their "lie" was not a lie at all; it was a reflection of how they truly felt about the task. Other studies ensued that supported this essential finding (e.g., Brehm & Cohen, 1962). Since participants felt that they had some free choice in making their decisions (they could have refused to lie to the next participant, because $1 is not enough compensation to lie to another individual), their attitude changed in the direction counter to their original attitude. This line of research has thus also been called the "counterattitudinal advocacy paradigm."

In applying the counterattitudinal advocacy paradigm to addressing resistance to multiculturalism, for those who are resistant or potentially resistant to multiculturalism, it might be helpful if they were given assignments that required them to advocate positions counter to their opposition. For example, Mio and Awakuni (2000) discussed an Asian student who did not believe that affirmative action programs should be continued. After his term paper, where he advocated for the continuation of affirmative action programs, this student told me that he had changed his mind and saw the value in such programs.[3] Undoubtedly, his change of mind was also derived from class discussions we had and oral presentations from students on both sides of the issue. However, I contend that at least part of his change of heart was based upon the counterattitudinal advocacy process through which he went. Incidentally, those students who are initially strongly in favor of affirmative action and are required to write a paper in favor of its abolishment have not changed their attitudes (by anecdotal report). It is obvious to them that the overwhelming amount of literature in the area is in favor of affirmative action and those writing against affirmative action tend to be opinion papers and not based upon research.

We Come to Like the Things for Which We Suffer

Aronson and Mills (1959) discussed the aspect of cognitive dissonance where those who suffered for something cherished the reward for the suffering more than their counterparts who did not suffer for the same reward. In their classic experiment, they recruited undergraduate students for a seminar course to discuss college life. Half of the participants had to undergo an extensive interview process before they were admitted into the course; the other half was simply allowed to sign up for the course. Students participated in the semester-long course by just sitting around and talking about their experiences in college. At the end of the semester, they evaluated the course. Those who were made to feel that it was very difficult to get into the course rated the course more positively in the standard course evaluations given at the end of the term than those who simply signed up for the course.

In applying this principle to addressing resistance to multiculturalism, one would have to get individuals in situations where there is a lot of "suffering" in dealing with multicultural issues. This seemed to have occurred in Jane Elliott's *A Class Divided* (Peters, 1985; see Mio & Awakuni, 2000). Elliott was a third grade teacher who divided students into brown-eyed students and blue-eyed students. One day, the brown-eyed students were made victims of discrimination and the next day, the blue-eyed students were made victims of discrimination. The original film made about this exercise was called "Eye of the Storm." In *A Class Divided*, there was a 15-year reunion of the students in "Eye of the Storm." They watched the film together and discussed the impact that exercise had on them. Although all of the students discussed how painful it was to participate in the exercise, they all felt it was worth it and applied the lessons learned from the exercise to their everyday lives. They felt that the pain reinforced the lessons of nondiscrimination more than if they had simply been told not to discriminate against others. However, because of modern ethical evaluations of studies (particularly on children), Elliott's powerful technique could probably not be implemented in today's classrooms.

Threat of Punishment

In their classic study, Aronson and Carlsmith (1963) had boys playing in a playroom. This playroom had a multiplicity of toys, but the most attractive toy of all was a robot. The boys were told that they could play with any toy they wanted except the robot. Half of the boys were told that if they played with the robot, the experimenter would be disappointed that they did not follow directions. The other half of the boys were told that if they played with the robot, they would be punished severely. Although both groups of boys did not play with the robot immediately after these instructions, when they came back weeks later with no instructions on which toys to play with, only the boys who received the minor threat did not play with the robot. Over half of the boys who received the severe punishment threat played with the robot. Aronson and Carlsmith reasoned that when the boys with the minor threat did not play with the robot the first time, they internalized this value because the threat was not great enough to truly prevent them from playing with the robot. The boys who received the severe punishment threat did not internalize the value of not playing with the robot; they did not play with it the first time because they did not want to be punished. This reasoning is essentially the one used in the forced compliance paradigm, only instead of a minor versus a major reward as the conditions under which one complies with a request, the threat of punishment paradigm used a minor versus a major threat as the conditions of compliance. Major rewards or punishments are clearly sufficient justifications for compliance with tasks that are either distasteful or against one's preexisting beliefs, whereas minor rewards or punishments are insufficient justifications for compliance with such tasks. Therefore, in order to reduce the dissonant effects of complying, attitudes are changed to bring people more in line with their actions.

As mentioned, on our campus we hold a weekend retreat called the Cross-Cultural Retreat (CCR). This event costs money and requires that people dedicate nearly an entire weekend of their time to attend (Friday afternoon until Sunday midday). The CCR forces individuals to examine issues regarding diversity, such as racial/ethnic, religious, language, class, sexual orientation, and ability differences. As the CCR is held near the Martin Luther King, Jr. holiday, racial/ethnic differences are at the core of the retreat. Many of the people who attend the CCR are from University Housing Services. They are applying to be residence hall advisors, and one of the requirements is for them to attend the CCR. Thus, although there is an implied threat of the students not receiving the job as a residence hall advisor if they do not attend the CCR, since it is their choice to apply for this job and they know that attendance at the CCR is compulsory, the "threat" is not perceived to be very great. As indicated from the ratings of the CCR, most people feel that it is a valuable experience (social desirability notwithstanding). Certainly, many who attend the CCR may already have positive attitudes toward multicultural issues, but others who attend are clearly confronting these issues for the first time in their lives at more than a superficial level.

CONCLUSIONS

Many people might think that the passage of the Civil Rights Act of 1964 and the Voting Rights Act of 1965 have solved the problem of racism in our country. Nationally, many commentators and news guests on news and information programs assert that racism is a thing of the past. These voices tend to be from the conservative end of the political spectrum, and they tend to lead a charge to eliminate programs that take into account issues of race and ethnicity. However, events such as the violence after the first Rodney King trial, "English Only" movements throughout the country, and the government's actions against Wen Ho Lee, the Taiwanese-born worker accused of passing nuclear secrets to mainland China (which do not even make sense, given the tensions between Taiwan and mainland China), remind us that issues of racism are still barely underneath the surface. However, often such racism is undetectable because of modern forms of racism. People either conceal their racism or are unaware of their own racism because of the ways in which we can fool others or ourselves about racist tendencies.

One way of identifying or at least addressing modern racism is to apply cognitive dissonance principles to racism. Although some people who engage in concealing their racism may never change their views, most people are motivated not to be racist (Dovidio & Gaertner, 1998; Gaertner & Dovidio, 1986). In fact, racist attitudes may create cognitive dissonance in them. Therefore, we must develop ways where people can behave in nonracist manners so that their attitudes will follow. This will not only lead to a more just society, but also it will allay the anxiety in those who feel that racism is aversive yet may harbor hidden or unconscious racist attitudes. Leon Festinger's Theory of Cognitive Dissonance presents three avenues of such intervention: forced compliance, coming to like the things for which we suffer, and threat of punishment. As I have outlined, these interventions can be used to get people to engage in behaviors that value multiculturalism, thus causing their attitudes to change in a manner consistent with such behaviors. This in turn will alert people to be able to detect resistance to multiculturalism and to defeat such resistance. Because the principles of this country are based upon equality for all, the defeat of resistance to multiculturalism will keep our eyes on this prize.

END NOTES

1. I cannot provide a specific reference for this so-called "logical extension," but this point was made a few times in a debate on the "Defense of Marriage Initiative" on the CNN program "Crossfire."
2. The topics of the Cross-Cultural Retreat (CCR) vary from year to year. Recent topics have included race/ethnicity, gender, sexual orientation, religion, skin color, language, and social class. Typically two or three areas are covered during the weekend retreat.
3. My assignment for students in this class is that those who are leaning in the direction of continuing affirmative action should write a term paper advocating its continuance, and those who are leaning in the direction of discontinuing affirmative action should write a paper advocating its abolishment. Those who are strongly in favor or against affirmative action should write a paper advocating the opposite stance.

REFERENCES

Aronson, E., & Carlsmith, J. M. (1963). Effect of severity of threat on the devaluation of forbidden behavior. *Journal of Abnormal and Social Psychology, 66,* 584–588.

Aronson, E., & Mills, J. (1959). The effect of severity of initiation on liking for a group. *Journal of Abnormal and Social Psychology, 59,* 177–181.

Bakke v. Regents of the University of California, 438 U.S. 265 (1978).

Brehm, J. W., & Cohen, A. R. (1962). *Explorations in cognitive dissonance.* New York: Wiley.

Cheatham, H. E. (1999). Affirmative action. In J. S. Mio, J. E. Trimble, P. Arredondo, H. E. Cheatham, & D. Sue (Eds.), *Key words in multicultural interventions: A dictionary* (pp. 7–8). Westport, CT: Greenwood.

Cialdini, R. B. (1993). *Influence: Science and practice.* Boston: Addison Wesley Longman.

Dees, M. (1991). *A season for justice: The life and times of civil rights lawyer Morris Dees.* New York: Charles Scribner's Sons.

Dovidio, J. F. (2001, January). *Why can't we get along?: Interpersonal biases and interracial distrust.* Invited address delivered at The National Multicultural Conference and Summit II, Santa Barbara, CA.

Dovidio, J. F., & Gaertner, S. L. (1998). On the nature of contemporary prejudice: The causes, consequences, and challenges of aversive racism. In J. Emberhardt & S. T. Fiske (Eds.), *Confronting racism: The problem and the response* (pp. 3–32). Thousand Oaks, CA: Sage.

Dovidio, J. F., & Gaertner, S. L. (2000). Aversive racism and selection decisions: 1989 and 1999. *Psychological Science, 11,* 319–323.

Festinger, L. (1957). *A theory of cognitive dissonance.* Stanford, CA: Stanford University Press.

Festinger, L., & Carlsmith, J. M. (1959). Cognitive consequences of forced compliance. *Journal of Abnormal and Social Psychology, 58,* 202–210.

Gaertner, S. L., & Dovidio, J. F. (1986). The aversive form of racism. In J. F. Dovidio & S. L. Gaertner (Eds.), *Prejudice, discrimination and racism* (pp. 61–90). Orlando, FL: Academic Press.

Jones, J. M. (1997). *Prejudice and racism* (2nd ed.). New York: McGraw-Hill.

McConahay, J. B. (1986). Modern racism, ambivalence, and the Modern Racism Scale. In J. F. Dovidio & S. L. Gaertner (Eds.), *Prejudice, discrimination and racism* (pp. 91–126). Orlando, FL: Academic Press.

Milloy, C. (1999, May 2). A look at tragedy in Black, White. *Washington Post,* p. C1.

Mio, J. S., & Awakuni, G. I. (2000). *Resistance to multiculturalism: Issues and interventions.* Philadelphia: Brunner/Mazel.

Myers, D. G. (1999). *Social psychology* (6th ed.). New York: McGraw-Hill.

Peters, W. (1985). A class divided. In D. Fanning (Producer), *Frontline.* Boston: WGBH.

Ridley, C. R. (1995). *Overcoming unintentional racism in counseling and therapy: A practitioner's guide to intentional intervention.* Thousand Oaks, CA: Sage.

Sartwell, C. (1998, June 21). White America needs its bigotry. *The Los Angeles Times,* M5.

Sears, D. O. (1988). Symbolic racism. In P. A. Katz & D. A. Taylor (Eds.), *Eliminating racism: Profiles in controversy* (pp. 53–84). New York: Plenum.

Sue, D., Sue, D. W., & Sue, S. (2000). *Understanding abnormal behavior* (6th ed.). Boston: Houghton Mifflin.

Will, G. F. (1991, March 13). L.A. police: Time for an accounting. *The Washington Post,* A17.

Williams, J. (1987). *Eyes on the prize: America's civil rights years, 1954–1965.* New York: Viking.

CHAPTER 2

Expanding Our Understanding of White Racism and Resistance to Change in the Fields of Counseling and Psychology

MICHAEL D'ANDREA

Racism is a complex problem that continues to have an adverse impact on the lives of millions of Persons of Color in the United States. Over the past three decades, our understanding of this complex problem and the toxic psychological and spiritual effect it has on both the victims as well as its perpetrators has greatly increased. One of the significant advancements that has occurred in our understanding of White racism relates to new knowledge that has been generated by numerous social scientists in different disciplines. This new knowledge helps to illuminate the various ways that this complex and pervasive problem continues to be perpetuated in nearly every aspect of our society.

Among the most respected scholars in this area, Jones (1997) has done much to help expand our constructions of White racism. In his analysis of this social pathology, Jones clearly explains some of the ways in which racism extends far beyond individual acts of racial bigotry and describes how it is embedded in organizational and institutional policies and practices that frame the infrastructure of our entire society.

Researchers in other fields and disciplines support Jones' (1997) findings. These investigators not only describe the ways in which White racism continues to be perpetuated in our nation's justice (Braithwaite & Taylor, 1992), economic (Meyers, 1995), and educational systems (Black, D'Andrea, Daniels, & Heck, 2002; Scheurich & Young, 1997), but also outline how this multifaceted problem is manifested in the mental health professions as well (Kiselica, 1999; Rollock & Gordon, 2000; Thompson & Neville, 1999). Some of the notable ways that racism is currently perpetuated in the mental health professions include but are not limited to: (a) the disproportionate number of White mental health practitioners, researchers, and trainers who continue to far outnumber Persons of Color working in the fields of counseling and psychology (Daniels et al., 2000); (b) the large numbers of counselors and psychologists who have not acquired the types of multicultural counseling competencies that are necessary to work effectively and ethically with non-White persons in our society (D'Andrea & Daniels, 2001a; Sue, Arredondo, & McDavis, 1992); (c) the continued use of culturally biased tests and assessment procedures among persons from racially diverse client populations (Artiles & Trent, 1994; Paniagua, 2001); and (d) the ongoing utilization of counseling and psychotherapeutic theories in our professional training programs and clinical settings that reflect a monocultural and ethnocentric view of mental health and psychological well-being (Kiselica, 1999).

Given the adverse effect that these and other forms of institutional racism have on many Persons of Color who seek mental health-care services in this country, it is disconcerting to note the high level of resistance that many mental health professionals continue to exhibit when they are challenged to deal with the various forms of racism that exist in the fields of counseling and psychology. In light of the demographic changes that are taking place in our society and the moral imperative to deal with this complex problem in our own ranks, I have repeatedly argued that it is vital that the fields of counseling and psychology direct time, energy, attention, and resources to effectively eradicate all forms of White racism with great earnestness (D'Andrea & Daniels, 2001a, b; D'Andrea, Daniels, & Locke, 1996). This position has been supported by other experts in the field who have emphasized that failure to do so will inevitably undermine the credibility and viability of this nation's mental health-care system given the cultural transformation that is occurring in the demography of our nation (Locke, Myers, & Herr, 2001).

This transformation is marked by the fact that the United States is rapidly shifting from a country that has been comprised of a majority of people who have historically come from White, western European backgrounds to a nation that will soon be made up of a majority or persons from non-White, non-European, non-English speaking groups and backgrounds (D'Andrea & Daniels, 2001a). Given: (a) the unprecedented nature of this demographic transformation; (b) the interracial tensions that exist in the United States; and (c) the ethnocentric and racially biased practices that dominate the mental health professions (D'Andrea & Daniels, in press), it has been suggested that counselors and psychologists will increasingly be viewed as irrelevant entities at best and as disrespectful and antagonistic "handmaidens of the status quo" (Sue & Sue, 1999, p. 231) at worst unless they demonstrate a greater commitment to ameliorating the problem of racism within their own ranks.

With this backdrop in mind, this chapter is designed to serve a twofold purpose. First, it attempts to expand the reader's understanding of the psychological responses that White people in general and White counselors and psychologists in particular demonstrate when confronted with the problem of racism in this country. To accomplish this I briefly discuss the results of a 16-year study of White racism that I have conducted with my colleague, Dr. Judy Daniels.

This investigation led us to identify five distinct psychological dispositions of White racism that were exhibited by more than 1,500 persons who were included in this study. The first four psychological dispositions that we identified in our research were characterized by unique types of resistances that the vast majority of White persons included in our sample group exhibited when they were confronted with the issue of racism. The fifth psychological disposition represents what we believe is the goal in developing a more sophisticated, mature, and effective psychological disposition toward White racism within the context of the increasingly multicultural, multiracial society in which we all live and work.

Second, this chapter outlines several practical strategies that counselors and psychologists can use to effectively address the different resistances they are likely to encounter when working to ameliorate the problem of racism within our society in general and the fields of counseling and psychology in particular. The antiracist strategies that are described in this chapter have been tested and found to be useful in addressing the problem of White racism in various settings in which counselors and psychologists commonly work.

INVESTIGATING THE PROBLEM OF WHITE RACISM IN THE UNITED STATES

Rather than focusing on the ways that White racism adversely impacts People of Color (which has been the primary focus of most research that has been done in this area in the past), Dr. Daniels and I have spent a great deal of time studying those persons who are fundamentally responsible for perpetrating this problem in our society. Thus, from 1984 to the present time, we have undertaken the task of investigating the different reactions that a large number of White persons from different geographical, economic, and cultural–ethnic backgrounds in the United States exhibited when presented with questions about the state of race relations in the United States in general and the problem of White racism in our nation in particular.

To date, this study includes observations of more than 1,500 White persons who reside in the northeastern, southeastern, midwestern, southwestern, and far western parts of the United States. The persons who comprised this sample group came from a broad range of socioeconomic backgrounds and included unemployed White persons, doctors, lawyers, state legislators, law enforcement personnel, ministers, business persons, teachers, counselors, psychologists, social workers, university professors, and undergraduate and graduate students in counseling and psychology training programs at various public and private universities (D'Andrea & Daniels, 1999a). Although we intentionally studied the ways in which these persons responded to various issues related to racism and the state of race relations in our nation, much of our research was specifically directed toward assessing the reactions that White counselors, psychologists, faculty members, and students in counseling and psychology training programs had to these issues.

There were two primary reasons for directing attention to these persons. First, as mental health professionals ourselves, we are genuinely interested in learning about the different cognitive, affective, and behavioral reactions that White counselors, psychologists, faculty members, and counseling and psychology students have to the problem of racism in the United States. Second, we hoped our findings would generate new ideas about the types of interventions that mental health professionals might be able to use to deal more effectively with the problem of White racism in different sectors of our society and the mental health professions.

By using a naturalistic inquiry approach in our study of White racism (Erlandson, Harris, Skipper, & Allen, 1993), we were able to collect a substantial amount of data from the persons in our large sample group by acting as participant-observers in a broad range of settings. These settings included: graduate and undergraduate psychology/counseling classes; staff meetings at various universities in which we have been employed; meetings and workshops that were held at state conferences and national conventions sponsored by the American Counseling Association (ACA) and the American Psychological Association (APA); discussing the issue of White racism with White persons in various public settings; interacting with White persons at Ku Klux Klan demonstrations; talking about this problem with White elected officials in state legislatures; and soliciting reactions from White ministers, rabbis, priests, and members of religious congregations about the problem of White racism and the state of race relations in their religious settings.

The fundamental research question that guided our work was stated as follows: "What are the different cognitive, affective, and behavioral reactions that White persons have to racism in the United States?" (D'Andrea & Daniels, 1999a, p. 95). By keeping this fundamental research question in mind when conducting our study, we hoped to gather information from multiple sources that would help us develop a more comprehensive understanding of the various ways White persons respond to the problem of racism in the United States. Acting as participant-observers in the various settings that were mentioned, we intentionally interjected questions about racism and asked the persons with whom we interacted to talk about their thoughts and feelings regarding the state of race relations in the United States. Because we thought that note-taking would detract from the research participants' willingness to honestly express their thoughts and feelings about these issues, we refrained from recording their reactions when directly interacting with these persons and recorded their reactions to our questions at a later time.

By using these research methods, we were able to record a variety of cognitive, affective, and behavioral reactions that individuals in our sample group had to the complex problem of racism in our society. Ultimately, our investigation resulted in the construction of five distinct psychological dispositions of White racism. This includes the Affective-Impulsive, Rational, Liberal, Principled, and Principled Activistic Dispositions of White racism.

THE PSYCHOLOGICAL DISPOSITIONS OF WHITE RACISM

Characteristics of the Affective-Impulsive Disposition

Persons operating from the Affective-Impulsive Disposition of White racism are characterized by a cognitive style that reflects simple, openly hostile, and illogical ways of thinking about individuals who come from different racial groups. Some of the statements that these individuals used to describe their thinking about racial issues included such base remarks as: "Niggers are lazy, good for nothings" and "I don't like those Asian gooks because they are only trying to take over America by buying all kinds of land and stuff" (D'Andrea & Daniels, 1994, p. 77). These and other statements commonly made by persons operating at the Affective-Impulsive Disposition represented what we referred to as a "delay in one's ability to accurately conceptualize similarities and differences among persons from diverse racial/cultural backgrounds" (D'Andrea & Daniels, 1999c, p. 225).

Individuals operating from the Affective-Impulsive Disposition were also frequently observed to demonstrate marginal impulse control when reacting to Persons of Color. This resulted in a variety of behaviors that ranged from physical violence (e.g., participating in the physical harassment and beatings of non-White persons) to destroying or defacing property (e.g., burning African-American churches, painting obscene racial graffiti on buildings, participating in cross burnings) to making openly demeaning and hostile comments about Persons of Color. Locke's (1992) discussion of *overt and intentional* forms of racism accurately describes much of the heightened resistance, anger, and hostility that persons operating from the Affective-Impulsive Disposition typically displayed in terms of their genuine unwillingness to deal constructively with the problem of racism in our country. It is also important to point out that these individuals did not appear to be ashamed or embarrassed by overtly expressing their negative thoughts and feelings about Persons of Color, even though such racist expressions are generally viewed as being inappropriate and unacceptable within the broader context of our contemporary society.

Characteristics of the Rational Disposition of White Racism

Persons operating from the Rational Disposition manifested a cognitive style that was marked by what William Perry (1970) calls *dualistic thinking*. Individuals who exhibited this sort of thinking generally described their thoughts about racism and race relations in dichotomous terms. For instance, in discussing the state of race relations in the United States, Rational Disposition individuals tended to analyze interracial conflicts from a "someone is right and someone is wrong." The sort of dualistic thinking that Rational Disposition persons typically exhibited was in sharp contrast to multiple perspective and relativistic thinking abilities that were exhibited by persons operating from the more complex psychological dispositions that are described later in this chapter.

Rational Disposition persons were cognitively distinguishable from individuals operating from the Affective-Impulsive Disposition of White racism as they generally appeared to be more knowledgeable of racial differences, more aware of some of the historical forms of oppression that negatively impact Persons of Color in the United States, and more cognizant of some of the ways in which racial discrimination has been a central part of this country's history. However, they appeared to be similar to persons exhibiting an Affective-Impulsive Disposition in their adherence to numerous racial stereotypes about People of Color.

These stereotypes were commonly used to justify separatist beliefs that were frequently manifested by persons who manifested a Rational Disposition. For example, numerous persons manifesting this psychological disposition indicated that they would not buy a home in a racially integrated neighborhood out of fear that their land value would deteriorate. Others expressed opposition to interracial dating and marriages because they thought these relationships were likely to fail because they violated social taboos in our society.

Behaviorally speaking, persons operating from the Rational Disposition exhibited greater impulse control in dealing with the interracial issues in comparison to those individuals who operated from an Affective-Impulsive Disposition. This is not to suggest that individuals with a Rational Disposition do not exhibit strong negative reactions toward People of Color. In fact, many Rational Disposition persons exhibited behaviors that clearly reflected their dislike and lack of support for persons who have historically suffered as a result of racist practices in our nation. This was particularly apparent when we engaged these individuals in discussions about racial quotas and affirmative action policies and practices. Unlike persons exhibiting an Affective-Impulsive Disposition who manifested their hatred of non-White persons in more overt and violent ways, individuals operating from a Rational Disposition usually demonstrated subtler forms of racist behaviors. This included taking part in petition drives that supported the elimination of affirmative action practices in their local communities (Feagin & Vera, 1995).

Another interesting behavioral characteristic that was observed among individuals who manifested this disposition involved the naive and simplistic manner in which they spoke about racial issues. Frequently, phrases such as, "I think there is only one race—the human race," and "when I work with Black persons, I don't see the color of their skin, I only see them as people" were often expressed by individuals identified as operating from this psychological disposition.

In conjunction with these behavioral characteristics, persons operating from the Rational Disposition typically demonstrated "a superficial affective niceness" when it came to discussing issues related to racism (D'Andrea & Daniels, 1994, p. 79). This affective superficiality was frequently replaced with expressions of hostile emotionality, however, when individuals operating from a Rational Disposition of White racism were confronted with dissonant concepts involving racial issues. Such emotional hostility was exhibited by several White southern ministers who expressed anger at the suggestion that Jesus may have been a Person of Color given the geographical location in which he lived (D'Andrea & Daniels, 1994, 1999b).

Characteristics of the Liberal Disposition of White Racism

The Liberal Disposition is marked by more complex ways of thinking about racism and human rights. This includes demonstrating: (a) a more in-depth understanding of the various ways that White racism is manifested in our society (e.g., individual, institutional, cultural forms of racism); and (b) an increased awareness and respect for the different values, attitudes, behaviors, and worldviews that persons from diverse racial/

cultural backgrounds exhibit in their lives. The increased awareness and respect for racial/cultural differences that are commonly manifested among Liberal Disposition persons coincide with the development of a new cognitive ability that enables these individuals to more accurately understand the perspectives of others. Perry (1970) describes this developmental advancement as a cognitive milestone in which individuals exhibit an increased capacity for multiple perspective-taking.

It was interesting to note that the Liberal Disposition of racism emerged as the modal disposition from which the majority of White counselors, psychologists, faculty members, and undergraduate and graduate students in professional counseling and psychology training programs appeared to be operating (D'Andrea & Daniels, 1999a, b). Upon studying these individuals more closely, we noted several curious contradictions in the way many persons in the fields of counseling and psychology commonly responded to White racism. In this regard we noted that the vast majority of White counselors, psychologists, faculty members, and students we studied readily expressed an interest in learning about various multicultural and diversity topics, including issues related to counseling women, poor persons, individuals with physical challenges, and older clients. However, these persons rarely indicated a desire to study the problem of racism and the adverse impact that this social pathology has on the lives of millions of persons in our society. When pressed to talk about their interest in dealing with the problem of racism as mental health professionals, most of these persons indicated that they were not particularly motivated to address this issue in either their professional or personal lives.

The pervasive sense of apathy and indifference that the majority of White counselors, psychologists, faculty members, and students in counseling and psychology training programs typically manifested regarding this problem appeared to be fueled by multiple factors. One of the most important factors that contributed to this apathy and indifference related to the desire of many Liberal Disposition persons to avoid dealing with the negative interpersonal repercussions that normally occur when individuals take an antiracist stance in their lives. The importance of avoiding negative reactions from others was explicitly stated by numerous persons in the fields of counseling and psychology who were identified as operating from the Liberal Disposition (D'Andrea & Daniels, 1999b). When explaining why they thought they were not very active in dealing with this problem, many persons operating from this psychological disposition indicated that they felt that they would not be taken very seriously or would be met with defensive reactions by many other White individuals in the field. Other practitioners specifically reported that they did not care for the "negative emotionality" and "argumentative attitude" that commonly ensues when the topic of White racism is raised for discussion in professional circles.

Another important factor that contributed to the lack of antiracist advocacy noted among Liberal Disposition persons in the fields of counseling and psychology involves the resistance they demonstrated in dealing with their own White privilege. Several persons have pointed out that the process of developing an antiracist disposition inevitably requires White people to acknowledge the ways in which they personally and professionally benefit from various forms of White privilege that continue to be perpetuated in our society (Daniels et al., 2000; McIntosh, 1989; Scheurich & Young, 1997). Because acknowledging these issues causes much discomfort for White persons who are operating from the Liberal Disposition, it is easier (and certainly less challenging) to avoid situations that might force them to confront the ways in which they personally or professionally benefit from perpetuation of the different forms of racism in the United States (D'Andrea & Daniels, 1999b, c).

Characteristics of the Principled Disposition of White Racism

Major advancements are noted in the cognitive abilities manifested among individuals operating from the Principled Disposition. These cognitive abilities enabled these persons to discuss the complex interrelationships that exist between various forms of White privilege, White superiority, and White racism (D'Andrea, Daniels, & Locke, 1996). Persons operating from this disposition were also noted to be very knowledgeable about the historical and social-political underpinnings of White racism in the United States (D'Andrea & Daniels, 1999c). Jones (1997) and Carter (1995) provide a detailed description of the cognitive capacities that were commonly manifested by persons operating from the Principled Disposition. For instance, it was Carter (1995) who stated that "the unpleasant and uncomfortable histories and perspectives of peoples who have been oppressed by Whites can be comprehended and understood, as well as the present consequences of long-term racial inequities that accompany racial disparities in the U.S." (p. 7).

The advanced cognitive abilities that mark this psychological disposition complement a host of emotional characteristics that persons functioning from the Principled Disposition routinely exhibited when addressing the problem of White racism. This included a heightened passion and excitement that these individuals demonstrated when discussing the possibility of ameliorating racism in society. The passionate excitement that many Principled Disposition persons manifested in this regard was frequently accompanied by a sense of idealism regarding the possibility of effectively dealing with this problem in the future. This idealism appeared to fuel a level of optimism and hopefulness that was clearly not evident among persons operating from the other psychological dispositions that were described earlier in this chapter.

Having said this it was ironic to note that a number of persons, who exhibited many of the cognitive characteristics associated with the Principled Disposition, expressed a heightened sense of cynicism regarding the state of race relations in the United States in general and the possibility of ameliorating the complex problem of White racism in particular. As a researcher who has studied this problem for the past 20 years, I have developed a new hypothesis about the sort of cynicism that permeated the psychological status of numerous individuals who otherwise appeared to be operating from the Principled Disposition of White racism. My sense is that the genesis of much of this cynicism is rooted in what might be referred to as a heightened sense of *frustrated idealism*. I have developed this hypothesis as a result of interacting with individuals who, although clearly exhibiting many of the cognitive characteristics associated with the Principled Disposition, expressed a deep sense of disappointment and frustration with the unwillingness of many White persons to address the ways that racism continues to be manifested in society.

The cognitive and affective characteristics associated with the Principled Disposition were accompanied by a host of behavioral reactions to racism that were not commonly manifested by individuals operating from the other dispositions that are described in this model. Unlike persons exhibiting characteristics associated with the Affective-Impulsive, Rational, and Liberal Dispositions, Principled Disposition individuals not only exhibited overt disgust for all forms of racism but often felt compelled to address this social pathology in personal and professional ways. Consequently, these persons were much more likely to express concern about the state of race relations in our nation and to initiate discussions about racism with their friends, colleagues, and students than would individuals who were operating from the other dispositions described in the preceding.

When focusing on those counselors, psychologists, faculty members, and students in counseling and psychology training programs who were identified as operating from the Principled Disposition, we noted that they frequently acknowledged that progress had been made in terms of the mental health profession's commitment to multiculturalism (D'Andrea & Daniels, 2001b). Most of these persons agreed, however, that the profession could do a much better job of dealing with the various forms of racism that continue to exist in the United States. Nevertheless, the majority of these persons fell short in acknowledging the various ways that individuals in the fields of counseling and psychology unintentionally contribute to the perpetuation of racism by continuing to use a monocultural-ethnocentric and racist epistemology in our professional training programs, research endeavors, and clinical practices (Daniels et al., 2000; Sue & Sue, 1999).

Characteristics of the Principled Activistic Disposition of White Racism

Less than one percent of the White persons we studied were identified as operating from the Principled Activistic Disposition. This included only a handful of White counselors, psychologists, faculty members, and students in professional counseling and psychology training programs who were included in our study. When discussing their thoughts about racism, these persons demonstrated more abstract, comprehensive, and systemic thinking abilities in comparison to individuals operating from the Principled Disposition. The systemic thinking ability that characterized Principled Activistic Disposition persons was manifested in a more in-depth understanding of the various ways that White racism continues to be embedded in our educational, economic, media, political, and social institutions. As a result of developing this cognitive ability, Principled Activistic persons exhibited a much greater understanding of the types of individual, institutional, and cultural changes that need to occur in order to successfully ameliorate the problem of racism in our nation.

Although Principled Activistic Disposition persons were more knowledgeable of the intricacies and complexity of White racism than those operating from the Principled

Disposition, they did not appear to be overwhelmed with the magnitude of the problem nor made cynical by the time and resources that are required to effectively deal with this social pathology. Unlike the cynical attitude that was commonly reflected in the affective reactions of many Principled Disposition individuals, White persons functioning at the Principled Activistic Disposition consistently demonstrated a much greater sense of hopefulness and optimism in terms of dealing with the problem of racism in the future (D'Andrea & Daniels, 1999c).

Principled Activistic Disposition persons were further distinguished from individuals operating from the other dispositions in this model by the level of commitment they expressed in working to combat this complex social problem. These persons were commonly viewed as being social–political activists who consciously and consistently addressed the various ways that racism and other forms of cultural oppression continue to be perpetuated in our contemporary society. This activism included but was not limited to addressing the types of racism that African Americans, Asian Americans, Latinos, and Native Americans routinely experience in their lives, as well as confronting other types of oppression that physically challenged persons, poor people, women, and gays and lesbians continue to experience in this country.

INTERVENTION STRATEGIES

Recommendations for Dealing with Persons Operating from the Affective-Impulsive Disposition

Although less than 5% of the persons that were included in our study were found to be operating from the Affective-Impulsive Disposition, individuals functioning from this psychological disposition represent a serious threat to Persons of Color. This threat is often manifested in obscene and threatening remarks as well as more serious forms of physical violence that are directed to non-White persons in our society.

It is important to point out that none of the counselors, psychologists, faculty members, or students in the counseling and psychology training programs we studied were noted to be operating from this psychological disposition. Although it is unlikely to find many mental health professionals who are operating from this disposition, counselors and psychologists will predictably encounter persons who do exhibit Affective-Impulsive Disposition characteristics in their work. For this reason, mental health practitioners need to be prepared to deal with these individuals in ways that help them develop more positive responses to the problem of racism.

From a developmental-ecological perspective this may necessitate using intervention strategies that are intentionally designed to foster more complex cognitions, less hostile feelings, and more respectful behaviors when relating to persons from diverse racial backgrounds; and promote positive ecological changes that reinforce the psychological development of persons operating at the Affective-Impulsive Disposition. What follows is a brief description of some of the ecological interventions that mental health professionals can use to promote the kinds of environmental changes that will help foster positive outcomes among persons who are operating from the Affective-Impulsive Disposition of White racism.

Advocating for Antiracist Laws and Institutional Policies

Developmentally speaking, individuals operating from the Affective-Impulsive Disposition reflect what Kohlberg (1981) describes as a "preconventional" state of moral development and a personality style that Loevinger (1976) describes as being dominated by impulsive and self-protective tendencies (D'Andrea & Daniels, 1994). We have noted that when working with persons who are operating at these early developmental stages, it is vital to have ecological protectors in place that are intentionally designed to constrain these individuals from expressing the sort of unreflective, disrespectful, aggressive, and hostile reactions that are often manifested toward Persons of Color. This includes the establishment and implementation of laws and institutional policies that protect the rights and dignity of non-White persons.

Given the important role that such laws and policies can play in curbing the negative and violent behaviors that Affective-Impulsive persons commonly exhibit toward Persons of Color, mental health professionals are encouraged to work with elected officials, administrators, and organizational policymakers to institutionalize antiracist laws and policies in their communities, schools and universities, and workplaces. Such laws and policies need to be explicitly stated and made readily available to all persons in these settings. Punitive consequences for violating these laws and policies also need to be clearly and explicitly stated as a way to deter individuals from exhibiting the sort of behaviors that Affective-Impulsive Disposition individuals frequently manifest in their dealings with persons from different racial–cultural groups.

Training and Education Services

To strengthen the potential impact that these anti-racist laws and policies might have among Affective-Impulsive Disposition persons, counselors and psychologists should encourage lawmakers, administrators, and policymakers to support the development and implementation of ongoing antiracist training and education programs in schools and universities, employment, and community settings. The sexual harassment training and education programs that are used to combat sexism in a variety of ecological settings (e.g., schools/universities, employment settings, government agencies) are good models to follow in this regard.

In addition to providing information that is aimed at increasing individuals' understanding of the different ways that racism may be manifested in various environmental settings, antiracist training and education programs should also clarify the types of punitive actions that will be taken if the institution's policies regarding respect for racial differences are violated. This clarification is particularly important for persons operating from an Affective-Impulsive Disposition as they are more inclined to control their racist impulses when they know what punitive actions are likely to be taken against them for intentionally violating antiracist laws and policies.

Individual Consultation Services

Individuals operating from the Affective-Impulsive Disposition are unlikely to seek individual counseling voluntarily for issues related to racism (D'Andrea & Daniels, 1999b). When persons exhibiting this disposition are found in counseling settings it is usually because they have been required to receive such services as part of a court order or have been referred to a counselor by a school administrator or employer for exhibiting inappropriate and racist behaviors in educational or employment settings. Rather than using traditional counseling and psychotherapeutic approaches (e.g., humanist-existential, psychodynamic, client-centered approaches) with these clients, mental health practitioners would do well to use individual consultation and racial awareness enhancement activities that are designed to serve four purposes. This includes activities that are aimed at: (a) educating these individuals about the negative (legal and organizational) consequences for exhibiting racist attitudes and behaviors; (b) helping to reduce any confusion as to why their behaviors are perceived by others to be racist; (c) offering specific suggestions about the ways in which these clients might change some of their racist attitudes and beliefs; and (d) making appropriate referrals to other school, employment, or community-based organizations that might further assist these individuals in developing a more sensitive and respectful racial disposition.

Recommendations for Dealing with Persons Operating at the Rational Disposition

There are several things that mental health professionals can do to stimulate the development of persons who are functioning at this psychological disposition. This includes using: (a) counseling approaches and psychoeducational interventions that enable these persons to cognitively restructure the ways they have learned to construct meaning of White racism; (b) antiracist training and educational services; and (c) community service projects that serve as developmental prompts.

Counseling and Psychoeducational Interventions

Counseling approaches and psychoeducational interventions that are designed to enhance cultural–racial understanding in clinical and classroom settings are particularly useful in restructuring and expanding the stereotypic thinking that characterize persons operating from the Rational Disposition. Although these interventions have much potential to promote the development of these individuals' disposition toward racism, it is important to keep in mind that the unexamined racial myths and stereotypes that such persons carry with them are often embedded in a highly self-protective attitude when it comes to dealing with racial issues. This self-protective attitude is commonly linked to what Feagin and Vera (1995) call zero-sum thinking. Such thinking reflects the belief that gains achieved by non-White persons in this country (e.g., job gains for Persons of Color) automatically result in losses for White people (e.g., job losses for White people).

Given the self-protective attitude and zero-sum thinking that characterize individuals operating from the Rational Disposition, counselors and psychologists are encouraged to help these persons discover some of the potential benefits they are likely to derive from thinking about and responding to non-White persons in more understanding, respectful, and effective ways. This can be done, in part, by: (a) discussing the ways in which our society is being affected by the rapid cultural–racial changes that are occurring in this nation's demography (D'Andrea & Daniels, 2001a) and (b) emphasizing the importance of developing the kinds of multicultural competencies that will be necessary to work effectively within the context of a diverse 21st century society (Sue et al., 1992). When using these cognitive restructuring techniques with Rational Disposition persons it is important to emphasize the social, economic, and professional benefits that White people are likely to derive from becoming more culturally competent and respectful of the racial diversity of our country.

Training and Educational Services

White students in counseling and psychology training programs who operate from the Rational Disposition commonly exhibit negative reactions and overt resistance to learning about the different ways that White racism continues to be embedded in our contemporary society. These resistances are frequently manifested in multicultural counseling courses where this complex and controversial topic is typically explored in greater depth (Kiselica, 1999). Even the use of the term "White racism" leads many students operating from this disposition to react in negative and resistant ways (D'Andrea & Daniels, 1999b).

These negative reactions can be overcome, however, when faculty members use instructional strategies that address the dualistic and zero-sum thinking that is associated with the Rational Disposition. To be effective with students who may be operating from this psychological disposition, it is useful to provide information that helps them: (a) learn about the challenges mental health professionals will face in the future as the United States continues to undergo major cultural–racial changes in its demography (Atkinson, Morten, & Sue, 1998), and (b) understand that their overall effectiveness as professionals will largely depend on their willingness to develop a broad range of multicultural competencies that will enable them to work in more effectively, ethically, and respectfully with Persons of Color. By emphasizing these professional benefits, faculty members in counseling and psychology training programs provide the sort of developmental incentive that motivates many students who may be operating from the Rational Disposition to learn more about the problem of racism in a less defensive and resistant manner.

Community Service Projects

Another way that counselors and psychologists can help individuals move beyond the stereotypic thinking that characterizes the Rational Disposition is to have them work in settings that are comprised of persons who are routinely subjected to various forms of racism. The use of community service projects is particularly useful in this regard. Working with other researchers to study the impact of such services, we have noted that persons functioning from the Rational Disposition began to manifest more complex ways of thinking about the problem of White racism as a result of taking part in various community service projects that involve Persons of Color from diverse socio-economic backgrounds. This included: (a) individuals who participated in a community service project that provided free meals to poor African-American youths and their families (D'Andrea & Daniels, 2000); (b) persons who volunteered to work in voter registration campaigns that targeted communities comprised of poor persons of color (D'Andrea, Daniels, & Locke, 1996); and (c) individuals who participated in a community project that provided mental health and social support services to non-White homeless children and their mothers in Hawaii (Daniels, D'Andrea, Omizo, & Pier, 1999).

Because many middle-class White persons operating from the Rational Disposition typically have limited contact with Persons of Color, community service projects represent excellent opportunities for them to learn firsthand about many of the day-to-day racial difficulties non-White persons commonly experience in their lives. One of the important roles that mental health practitioners and faculty members in professional training programs can play in these community service projects is to use their interpersonal group process skills to assist White students and clients in talking about their thoughts and feelings as participants in these activities. By taking time to help Rational Disposition persons process their reactions to these kinds of community service projects, they are able to gain new insights and develop more complex cognitions about racism and the adverse impact it has on People of Color.

This sort of development was reflected in numerous statements we have heard Rational Disposition persons express in groups that were designed to help individuals reflect on their community service experiences. Two specific statements that White counseling students have made in groups that we worked in this regard are provided to clarify how these persons developed a more complex psychological disposition toward White racism: "I never realized the types of difficulties these people experience every day of their lives," and "I used to think that people are just people and that if you have problems it is up to you to take care of them. But by taking part in this project, I am beginning to think differently about things. I mean I can see where being poor and Black adds a lot of pressure to a person's life that I didn't think of before" (D'Andrea & Daniels, 1999b, p. 70).

Recommendations for Dealing with Persons Operating at the Liberal Disposition

There are several psychological interventions that offer much promise in promoting the development of persons who are functioning at the Liberal Disposition of White racism. This includes using individual and group intervention strategies that are aimed at fostering these persons' affective development and behavioral responsivity to this complex social pathology.

When working to stimulate the affective development of Liberal Disposition persons, we have found it useful to begin by encouraging them to talk about the different feelings they have experienced as a result of being discriminated against, stereotyped, or oppressed in some way in the past. Such discussions can take place in individual or small group counseling settings as well as in larger consultation, training, and classroom situations.

Given the sensitivity and personal nature of such issues, some individuals may initially be apprehensive to openly discuss these experiences. What we have found to be helpful in respectfully dealing with this apprehensiveness is to ask individuals to write short narratives or personal essays that describe some of the times that they have felt discriminated against, stereotyped, or oppressed in their lives. We let these persons know that there are two purposes for doing this activity. This includes providing them: (a) an opportunity to reflect on some of the feelings they experienced when they were unfairly treated in the past; and (b) a chance to discuss any feelings they were comfortable sharing about the unfair experiences they personally encountered in their lives.

By taking the time to have these individuals write down some of their personal experiences and encouraging them to share whatever thoughts and feelings they had to these personal events in a nonthreatening and supportive environment, we found that many Liberal Disposition persons were more willing to discuss some of the negative experiences they encountered in ensuing class meetings and group counseling sessions. We also noted that, by communicating a genuine sense of empathy for their experiences, counselors and psychologists are able to gain a level of trust that enables them to challenge persons operating at the Liberal Disposition to stretch their thinking about racism. Once this trust was gained, we found that it was easier and more effective to ask Liberal Disposition persons to consider how non-White persons might experience similar thoughts and feelings as a result of routinely being subjected to various forms of racism. We have found this antiracist counseling and development approach to be particularly effective in stimulating a greater sense of racial empathy among numerous White women and White gay and lesbian persons who appeared to be operating from the Liberal Disposition. This approach was noted to have limited success, however, when used among White males who participated in various group and classroom settings in which we served as group leaders and instructors (D'Andrea & Daniels, 1999b, c).

Stimulating Behavioral Responsivity to Racism

When working with persons who are operating from the Liberal Disposition, we have found that it is very important to initially direct time and energy toward fostering their affective and empathic responsivity to racism before trying to stimulate new behavioral responses to this social pathology. By taking time to foster greater emotional receptivity to the types of pain, anger, and frustration that People of Color commonly experience as a result of being subjected to various forms of racism in the United States, White persons are more likely to discuss the types of actions that are willing to undertake in combating the problem of racism.

Having conducted numerous antiracist workshops and teaching multicultural counseling courses that included White persons who manifested many of the characteristics that are associated with the Liberal Disposition, we have used a simple technique that has proven to be effective in stimulating other professionals' and students' behavioral responsivity to racism. We frequently use this instructional technique to bring closure to our antiracim workshops and multicultural counseling courses. It is intentionally designed to encourage workshop participants and students to consider some of the specific actions they might be willing to take to help ameliorate the problem of racism in the future. Thus, in the final 30 minutes of our antiracism workshops and multicultural counseling courses, we take time to ask the participants to take a couple of minutes to reflect on the various issues that were discussed during the day/semester as we summarize the key topics that were covered. Then we ask the workshop participants and students to think of one thing they might be willing to do to help deal with the problem of racism in the future. In doing so we emphasize that it does not matter how large or small their proposed actions may be. Rather, it is their willingness to commit themselves to undertaking some specific action that really counts. Finally, we ask those individuals who may be willing to share their action plans with the rest of the participants/students in the final phase of the workshop/course to briefly describe what they plan to do in the future.

Using this instructional strategy in our professional development workshops and multicultural courses we have been consistently impressed with the types of actions Liberal Disposition persons indicate they are willing to initiate to address the problem of racism in the future. Some of the strategies that a number of persons agreed to implement in this regard include: trying to initiate discussions about racism with friends or colleagues at work; including the topic of White racism in future counseling and psychology courses; writing a letter to the editor of a local newspaper that discussed the importance of dealing with the problem of racism in the community in which one workshop participant lived; being willing to express displeasure when another person tells a racist joke in their company; agreeing to set time aside to talk about the frustration and sadness that one White counseling student experienced each time a family member made racist comments in her company; and having another workshop participant make a commitment to implement a racism prevention project for elementary school students that she had already developed but not found time to initiate (D'Andrea & Daniels, 2002).

Recommendations for Dealing with Persons Operating at the Principled Disposition

In designing interventions that are aimed at fostering the development of individuals functioning at the Principled Disposition, it is useful to utilize activities that are primarily aimed at helping these persons acquire new skills that can be used to help ameliorate the problem of racism. These interventions should secondarily address some of the unique affective needs that are commonly manifested by individuals who are operating from this psychological disposition.

Antiracist Consultation and Training Services

These services represent excellent strategies to promote the development of persons operating from the Principled Disposition. In providing these services, counselors and psychologists are encouraged to present information that describes the various ways that other antiracist advocates have effectively addressed racism in different environmental settings (e.g., school, university, business, and community settings). In doing so, counselors and psychologists should: (a) examine the types of problems that other White persons have encountered when addressing this social pathology; (b) identify the personal and professional qualities that characterize those White persons who have been successful in dealing with racism in various ecological settings; (c) give examples of the ways in which other individuals have dealt with persons who operate at different psychological dispositions of White racism; and (d) describe the kinds of interventions that are effective in addressing the negative impact that racism has on People of Color.

Individual and Group Support Services

As was discussed earlier in this chapter, Principled Disposition persons typically exhibit a genuine desire to address the complex problem of racism in their personal and professional endeavors. However, in doing so, they frequently put themselves in a precarious position in terms of the way other White persons and People of Color relate to them. In this regard many persons exhibiting the Principled Disposition reportedly experience a general sense of isolation from family members, friends, and colleagues as a result of their antiracist advocacy (D'Andrea & Daniels, 1999b; Kiselica, 1999).

Research findings also indicate that these persons are frequently met with suspicion by many Persons of Color who are skeptical about their "real agenda" and "motives" for working to reduce the level of racism that exists in our society (D'Andrea & Daniels, 1999b). The sense of isolation and skepticism that these persons encounter when trying to deal with this complex social problem often undermines their motivation to pursue antiracist work in the future, and nurtures a disabling sense of cynicism that was manifested by many Principled Disposition persons we studied.

In light of these factors, persons operating from the Principled Disposition are commonly in need of ongoing support and encouragement from other persons in order that they might remain energized in pursuing the arduous task of effectively dealing with the complex problem of racism. One way of dealing with this need is to develop support groups for White persons who are interested in making personal connections with other White antiracist activists.

Given the lack of support that Principled Disposition persons often encounter within their own White communities as a result of taking a strong stand against racism, it is also important that non-White mental health professionals articulate their support for such efforts. However, to promote the sense of trust that many non-White persons need to develop before they are comfortable and willing to publicly support the work that Principled Disposition persons undertake, it is helpful to convene multicultural meetings in which White and non-White antiracist advocates have the opportunity to discuss their interests and strategies in dealing with this complex social pathology, and build supportive and trusting networks in the process.

Recommendations for Dealing with Persons Operating at the Principled Activistic Disposition

Two specific recommendations are offered to support the development of persons who were identified as operating from the Principled Activistic Disposition of White racism. This includes encouraging their participation in leadership training and consultation services that specifically address issues of racism and social justice, and building the sort of supportive and trusting antiracist networks that were described in the preceeding (D'Andrea & Daniels, 1999b).

Given the level of commitment and understanding these persons have regarding the problem of White racism, they appear to be personally and professionally invigorated by participating in activities where they can utilize their knowledge, enthusiasm, and skills to combat this complex social problem. For this reason, Principled Activistic Disposition persons should be encouraged to use their knowledge and skills to provide leadership training workshops and offer consultation services to other White persons who are interested in learning how to deal more effectively with this social pathology in the different settings where they work.

Because individuals operating from this disposition are commonly viewed as controversial figures when it comes to dealing with the problem of racism in our society, they are often misunderstood, criticized, subjected to hate mail, and in some cases verbally and even physically attacked by other White persons. Such criticisms and attacks can tax the personal resources of persons operating from this psychological disposition (D'Andrea & Daniels, 1999b, c). It is important, therefore, that Principled Activistic Disposition individuals form the kind of supportive antiracist networks that will enable them to periodically share their experiences, thoughts, and questions regarding the challenges they face with other persons who are equally knowledgeable, respectful, and sympathetic to their commitment in this area. In this way, Principled Activistic Disposition persons will be better able to avoid the sort of burnout that frequently occurs when committed individuals work hard to help ameliorate the problem of White racism over an extended period of time. A description of the evolution of the National Institute for Multicultural Competence (NIMC) (D'Andrea et al., 2001) provides a good example of some of the ways that several individuals in the fields of counseling and psychology were able to build this sort of supportive network.

CONCLUDING REMARKS

This chapter summarizes some of the essential findings of more than 16 years of research Dr. Judy Daniels and I have conducted into the psychology of White racism. The five psychological dispositions that are described in the preceding pages provide a broad overview of the different cognitive, affective, and behavioral responses that more than 1,500 White persons typically exhibited when confronted with issues related to the problem of White racism in our nation.

After carefully analyzing the negative, defensive, and apathetic reactions that were commonly manifested by the persons who were included in our large sample group, we have concluded that many White persons in the public at large and in the fields of counseling and psychology are not sufficiently committed, personally or professionally, to help ameliorate the complex problem of racism at this point in time.

Other multicultural theorists have noted that the low level of motivation and lack of racial empathy combined with the high level of apathy that most White counselors and psychologists demonstrate when they are called upon to eradicate the various forms of racism that continue to be embedded in many of our professional training programs, research strategies, and clinical practices represent significant barriers to making progress in this area (Sue & Sue, 1999). Although such reactions are indeed frustrating for those White persons who are genuinely committed to ameliorating racism in the United States, they should not be viewed as insurmountable barriers that cannot be overcome in the future.

However, as anti-racist advocates strive to overcome the barriers and resistances that continue to be manifested in the fields of counseling and psychology, they are encouraged to think about the ways that they would approach individuals who exhibit characteristics that are associated with the different psychological dispositions of White racism that were identified in our study, and consider the benefits of using any of the intervention strategies that are described in the preceding section. In closing, it is hoped that the information presented in this chapter stimulates an increased understanding of the complex components that underlie the psychology of racism and provides the reader with helpful guidelines that can be used to ameliorate this complex and pervasive social problem in the future.

REFERENCES

Artiles, A. J., & Trent, S. C. (1994). Over representation of minority students in special education: A continuing debate. *Journal of Special Education, 27,* 410–437.

Atkinson, D. R., Morten, G., & Sue, D.W. (1998). *Counseling American minorities* (5th ed.). Boston: McGraw-Hill.

Black, R., D'Andrea, M., Daniels, J., & Heck, R. (2002). *Examining racial/ethnic biases in special education diagnoses in Hawaii.* Unpublished manuscript. University of Hawaii, Honolulu, HI.

Braithwaite, R. L., & Taylor, S. E. (Eds.) (1992). *Health issues in the Black community.* San Francisco: Jossey-Bass.

Carter, R. T. (1995). *The influence of race and racial identity in psychotherapy: Toward a racially inclusive model.* New York: Wiley.

D'Andrea, M., & Daniels, J. (in press). *Multicultural counseling: Empowerment strategies for a diverse society.* Pacific Grove, CA: Brooks/Cole.

D'Andrea, M., & Daniels, J. (2002, March). *Dealing with racism: Counseling and development strategies.* A workshop presented at the annual meeting of the American Counseling Association, New Orleans, LA.

D'Andrea, M., & Daniels, J. (2001a). The changing demographic structure of our society: Future challenges facing the counseling profession. In E. Herr, D. C. Locke, & J. Myers (Eds.), *The handbook of counseling* (pp. 529–540). Thousand Oaks, CA: Sage.

D'Andrea, M., & Daniels, J. (2001b). Expanding our thinking about White racism: Facing the challenge of multicultural counseling in the 21st century. In J. G. Ponterotto, J. M. Casas, L. A. Suzuki, & C. M. Alexander (Eds.), *Handbook of multicultural counseling* (2nd ed., pp. 289–310). Thousand Oaks, CA: Sage.

D'Andrea, M., & Daniels, J. (2000). Youth advocacy. In J. Lewis & L. Bradley (Eds.), *Advocacy in counseling: Counselors, clients, and community.* Alexandria, VA: American Counseling Association.

D'Andrea, M., & Daniels, J. (1999a). Exploring the psychology of White racism through naturalistic inquiry. *Journal of Counseling and Development, 77,* 93–101.

D'Andrea, M., & Daniels, J. (1999b). Assessing the different psychological dispositions of White racism: A comprehensive model for counselor educators. In M. Kiselica (Ed.), *Addressing the problem of racism and prejudice in counselor education* (pp. 59–88). Alexandria, VA: American Counseling Association.

D'Andrea, M., & Daniels, J. (1999c). Building on our knowledge of racism, mental health, and mental health practice: A reaction to Thompson and Neville. *The Counseling Psychologist, 27,* 224–238.

D'Andrea, M., & Daniels, J. (1994). The many faces of racism: A cognitive developmental framework. *Thought and Action, 10,* 73–90.

D'Andrea, M., Daniels, J., Arredondo, P., Ivey, M. B., Ivey, A. E., Locke, D. C., O'Bryant, B., Parham, T., & Sue, D. W. (2001). Fostering organizational changes to realize the revolutionary potential of the multicultural movement: An updated case study. In J. G. Ponterotto, J. M. Casas, L. A. Suzuki, & C. M. Alexander (Eds.), *Handbook of multicultural counseling* (2nd ed., pp. 222–254). Thousand Oaks, CA: Sage.

D'Andrea, M., Daniels, J., & Locke, D.C. (1996, April). *Dealing with racism: Counseling strategies.* Preconvention workshop presenter at the meeting of the American Counseling Association, Pittsburgh, PA.

Daniels, J., Arredondo, P., D'Andrea, M., Locke, D. C., O'Bryant, B., Parham, T., & Sue, D. W. (2000, March). *Social justice counseling, research, and training: Our responsibility and potential.* A paper presented at the annual meeting of the American Counseling Association, Washington, DC.

Daniels, J., D'Andrea, M., Omizo, M. M., & Pier, P. (1999). Group work with homeless youngsters and their mothers. *Journal for Specialists in Group Work, 24,* 164–185.

Erlandson, D. A., Harris, E. L., Skipper, B. L., & Allen, S. D. (1993). *Doing naturalistic inquiry: A guide to methods.* Newbury Park, CA: Sage.

Feagin, J. R., & Vera, H. (1995). *White racism: The basics.* New York: Routledge.

Jones, J. M. (1997). *Prejudice and racism* (2nd ed.). New York: McGraw-Hill.

Kiselica, M. (Ed.). (1999). *Confronting prejudice and racism during multicultural training.* Alexandria, VA: American Counseling Association.

Kohlberg, L. (1981). *The philosophy of moral development.* San Francisco: Harper & Row.

Locke, D. C. (1992). *Increasing multicultural understanding: A comprehensive model.* Thousand Oaks, CA: Sage.

Locke, D. C., Myers, J. E., & Herr, E. L. (Eds.) (2001). *The handbook of counseling.* Thousand Oaks, CA: Sage.

Loevinger, J. (1976). *Ego development.* San Francisco: Jossey-Bass.

McIntosh, P. (1989, July/August). White privilege: Unpacking the invisible knapsack. *Peace and Freedom,* pp. 8–10.

Meyers, S. L. (1995). Racial discrimination in housing markets: Accounting for credit risk. *Social Science Quarterly, 76,* 543–561.

Paniagua, F. A. (2001). *Diagnosis in a multicultural context: A casebook for mental health professionals.* Thousand Oaks, CA: Sage.

Perry, W. G. (1970). *Forms of intellectual and ethical development in the college years.* New York: Holt, Rinehart, & Winston.

Ridley, C. R. (1995). *Overcoming unintentional racism in counseling and therapy: A practitioner's guide to intentional intervention.* Thousand Oaks, CA: Sage.

Rollock, D., & Gordon, E. W. (2000). Racism and mental health into the 21st century: Perspectives and parameters. *American Journal of Orthopsychiatry, 70,* 5–13.

Scheurich, J. J., & Young, M. D. (1997). Coloring epistemologies: Are our research epistemologies racially biased? *Educational Researcher, 26,* 4–16.

Sue, D. W., Arredondo, P., & McDavis, R. J. (1992). Multicultural counseling competencies and standards: A call to the profession. *Journal of Counseling and Development, 70,* 477–486.

Sue, D. W., & Sue, D. (1999). *Counseling the culturally different: Theory and practice* (3rd ed.). New York: Wiley.

Thompson, C. E., & Neville, H. A. (1999). Racism, mental health, and mental health practice. *The Counseling Psychologist, 27,* 155–223.

CHAPTER 3

Resistance to Multiculturalism

The "Indian Problem"

J. DOUGLAS McDONALD

JOHN M. CHANEY

*If the Great Spirit had desired me to be a white person, he would have
    made me so in the first place.*
*He put in your heart certain wishes and plans; in my heart he put other
    and different desires.*
Each person is good in the sight of the Great Spirit.
It is not necessary that eagles should be crows.

Sitting Bull (Teton Sioux)

This chapter is our attempt to highlight similarities in the way in which mainstream psychology and the majority culture inconsistently value true multiculturalism. In our view, true multiculturalism involves genuine recognition, active acceptance, and participation in diversity—not mere tolerance of American-Indian worldviews, beliefs, and behavior. In and among many historical venues, from federal removal policies to the doctrine of mandatory boarding school attendance, the majority culture has callously referred to this conundrum as the "White Man's Burden" or the "Indian Problem."

Our intent is to present in an open and frank manner the issues that we see hindering the full realization of multiculturalism in psychology, particularly related to Native Americans. Although some of our opinions and analogies may impress the reader as inflammatory, we do not wish to engage in a fingerpointing invective or assign culpability. Rather, it is our hope that by speaking plainly about the historical underpinnings and contemporary roadblocks to achieving legitimacy for cultural diversity, we can promote its recognition as a fundamental feature of mainstream psychology and escape the *ghettoization* (Trimble, January 2001, personal communication) of ethnic/multicultural psychology, as it exists today.

We will use the terms "Native American," "American Indian," "Native," and "Indian" synonymously. We wish it were possible to answer the question most often posed by culturally sensitive non-Indians, "What do you want to be called?" in this chapter. Inasmuch as we would like to, we cannot, for time and space do not permit such a discussion (for a thorough discussion of this topic, see Trimble & Jumper-Thurman,

2002). In general, however, the use of the term "Indian" should be reserved for those belonging to the cultural group. Outsiders using that term may be viewed as disrespectful. Further, many issues regarding American Indians and our relationship with the majority culture are shared with other ethnic/cultural/racial groups, as well as those representing other diverse walks of life. Because these perspectives are represented in other chapters in this volume, we spend minimal time clarifying these distinctions. As American Indians writing this chapter, we speak from our campfire, and let our brothers and sisters speak from theirs.

We would also like to clarify that the words and ideas portrayed in this chapter are not exclusively ours. Our elders and mentors have passed them down to us, and we honor them above ourselves and ask their forgiveness should we misspeak. At the same time, it is important to clarify that we as authors are only two of millions of American Indians, and do not presume to speak for all members of the 700+ different Native American tribes and groups in the United States (only a fraction of whom are "formally" recognized by the federal government). Further, we relate more from our hearts than from numbers. We believe that much of the misunderstanding of Indians by non-Indians is a function of mainstream psychology's firm allegiance to the significance of databanks to the exclusion of understanding the value of riverbanks. But, we are getting ahead of ourselves.

HORSES AND ELK:
A LESSON IN DIFFERENCES AND SIMILARITIES

While high-country fishing with his father in the Shoshone Wilderness area of Wyoming around 1995, one of the authors (JDM) almost got bucked off his horse when an elk wandered too close. In response to the exasperatingly snarled question, "What's wrong with this horse? They're just elk—'bout the only difference between them is that elk have horns!" The wise Oglala elder smiled and replied, "These horses aren't used to being around elk." As usual, the wisdom of the response was embedded in its simplicity, akin to the manner in which immense data files today are "zipped" into manageably smaller ones.

Just as most horses are not accustomed to being around elk, and will—despite their vast similarities as a species—experience a significant startle response, so do many majority culture members respond to American Indians. Moreover, horses accept the presence of elk, deer, or other nonpredators if: (a) they are gradually and consistently exposed to them; (b) they maintain a numerical superiority; and (c) their resources (i.e., grass, water) are not significantly threatened by the elks' presence. In other words, elk are allowed to stay only and as long as they "keep their place" vis-à-vis horses. Fortunately for elk, horses do not possess sufficiently developed frontal lobes, adequate stereoscopic vision, or opposable thumbs, otherwise they would probably annihilate as many elk and deer (and their resources) as European-Americans did Indians.

EXPLANATIONS FOR RESISTANCE TO MULTICULTURALISM

Ethnocentrism

The majority culture's resistance to unconditional acceptance and inclusion of American Indians is emblematic of the type of monocultural ethnocentric in-group/out-group value system that typically leads to discrimination. Tajfel (1978) discussed this cultural groupthink as a part of social identity theory, and suggested that when sharp, distinctive boundaries are maintained between groups, conflicts arise. Perhaps more importantly, social dominance theory (Sidanius, 1993) extends this concept to predict that the larger and stronger in-group ultimately bestows upon its own ideology a superior status and utilizes this self-referenced value system to justify oppression of the perceived inferior out-group. As Sue and Sue (1999) point out, it is not so much a problem that we as humans tend to prefer like-minded others, it is when the more powerful group assumes superiority, privilege, and the right to impose their standards on others *without sufficient warrant* that problems arise. An excellent and more thorough discussion of this topic is presented in Jones (1997).

Value Differences

Not surprisingly, the barriers separating American Indians and the majority culture, as well as American Indian psychology from mainstream psychology, are defined by and consist of differences in value systems. Because value systems are an integral component of any group's subjective culture, they serve much like an information-processing schema to punctuate, classify, quantify, and clarify our experiences, as well as to inform appropriate behavioral responses in accordance with the standards of the group. Although the value orientations of Native Americans can vary greatly both between and within tribes and groups, it is fairly safe to say that most American Indians experience and assign different meanings to the world, life, and certainly cognition and behavior compared to majority culture members in general, and psychologists more specifically (Trimble & Jumper-Thurman, 2002).

Numerous value system differences (e.g., time orientation, harmony with nature) exist between Native American and mainstream cultures. The implications of these differences have been described in detail elsewhere (Sue & Sue, 1999; Trimble & Jumper-Thurman, 2002). One of the more meaningful distinctions for our discussion is the differential emphasis placed on collectivistic (we) versus individualistic (me) philosophies within the Native-American and mainstream cultures. Simply put, the collectivistic person is best characterized as an interdependent member of a larger group and derives a sense of self "through individual contribution toward collective success" of the group (Earley, Gibson, & Chen, 1999; p. 615). An individualist emphasizes personal achievement, personal fate, and independence from the group (Triandis, 1990). Although people in both cultures (actually all cultures) possess individualistic and collectivistic tendencies, as a general rule Native American culture functions largely from a collectivistic perspective; mainstream culture emphasizes individualistic values to a substantially greater degree.

The types of misunderstandings produced by the nexus of these distinctive worldviews are numerous and run the gamut (Triandis, 1990). In our opinion, the lack of genuine appreciation for the collectivistic approach preferred by Native Americans has led to two primary misperceptions of the tribal nature of Indian life. First, because collectivistic values are poorly understood in individualistic terms, the tribal lifestyle of Native people is frequently romanticized and subsequently dismissed as an idealistic utopian existence. Our tribal ancestors did not enjoy a utopian lifestyle and experienced their share of hardships. The fundamental difference is that, unlike the mainstream individualist culture, the tribal (collectivistic) way of life does not designate a class of people to do most of the suffering or a privileged class to be exempt from the suffering. Further, the tribal approach to life existed and flourished for centuries on this continent and should not be reduced to something that is seen as cute or lovable; it is time-tested and therefore viable. Second, because Native people are more group process-oriented in nature, the mainstream culture often mistakenly sees this as a lack of self-reliance or the inability to make independent decisions, requiring the assistance of a more task-focused (and assumed superior) approach to the problem.

In spite of these differences in worldviews, we—as with elk and horses—must occupy the same living space. Paradoxically, a fundamental difference between humans and our four-legged brethren is our uniquely human reasoning skills, which allow us to achieve monumental feats on the one hand and result in lucid, but unjustifiable, rationalizations for excluding many individuals from mainstream society on the other (see Gergen, 2001). The major tenets of both social identity and social dominance theories describe unfortunate byproducts of this human capacity for higher-order cognitive functioning that help us to understand why humans, unlike horses, can and have been stubbornly resistant to change—particularly with respect to inclusion of culturally dissimilar others. As near as we can tell, the inane pursuit of cultural superiority in this country (despite the lack of any supporting evidence) merely constitutes an obstinate 500-year extinction burst that is maintained on an intermittent schedule of reinforcement in the form of periodic demonstrations of American "superiority," usually following a good war. The painful, yet intriguing, punch line to this ironic situation is that American Indians—as with the elk—were here first! After thousands of years on this continent the in-group became the out-group seemingly overnight.

HISTORICAL FOUNDATIONS OF THE RESISTANCE TO AMERICAN-INDIAN MULTICULTURALISM

One need not be a scholar of American history or search with much perseverance to locate many—often bloody—examples of this country's distaste for accepting culturally different individuals, particularly American Indians, as equals. Indeed, this country was built on the backs of slaves and in the bloody footprints of our ancestors. The earliest contacts by British and Spanish explorers are rife with examples of exploitation of local and regional tribes, despite the culturally mandated generosity and hospitality with which these European newcomers had been greeted.

Happy Columbus Day:
The "Thanks a Lot" Massacres by Columbus et al.

Christopher Columbus, the heralded "Discoverer of America" (which by the way is still an item on the *more culturally sensitive* 3rd Edition of the Wechsler Intelligence Scale for Children), was only the first of many early "discoverers" to extend one hand in peace while concealing a weapon in the other. Interestingly, the original intent of most of the early European explorers did not include genocide of local tribes as the primary agenda. Most were interested in enticing the locals to work toward mining of vast, mythical gold mines, or—as with the British and French—the establishment and advancement of colonization. Unfortunately for all involved the local tribes in modern-day Mexico, Canada, and New England did not share the invaders' enthusiasm for such endeavors, and grew weary of expending their own stores, supplies, and other resources keeping these demanding "guests" alive.

Whether it was Columbus killing off the Taino; the British Roanoke, Puritan, and Jamestown settlers exploiting the Algonquians and Pequots; Cortez manipulating and then destroying the Aztecs; or the Plymouth pilgrims attacking the welcoming Wampanoags, the values and behaviors were consistent. The "New World's" inhabitants were deemed unworthy of inclusion, and were systematically exterminated or driven off. It mattered not that these tribes taught, nursed, and otherwise sustained these groups. If they refused to fully "comply" (the early Euro-invader concept of multiculturalism), they would suffer grievously. Positive tribal group behavior was violently and diabolically punished on a continuous reinforcement schedule.

Happy Thanksgiving: Manifest Destiny and the "Indian Wars"

John O'Sullivan's articulation of the rationale behind the American zeal for expansion was expressed as *Manifest Destiny*. This ethnocentrically privileged ideology was made official by the Supreme Court when, in 1823, it ruled that the United States' *right of discovery* superceded the Native Americans' *right of occupancy*. According to this philosophy, it seemed that God himself (especially the Christian God) sanctioned the broadening of European-American borders. God (and God's ambassadors) would apparently embrace the indigenous inhabitants, as long as they unconditionally submitted to this multicultural olive branch. In the name of God, others were punished who thought, felt, worshipped, or otherwise espoused a different preferred worldview. Unfortunately—again—American Indians held views dissimilar from their oppressors. In response, these self-ordained newcomers, disguised under the banner of a Christian God and authorized by the federal government, proceeded to annihilate the American Indian in the name of Manifest Destiny, and the American crusades were born and reared in a bassinet of blood.

The Reservation Era

Ultimately, the armies, missionaries, and diseases of first the Europeans, and then the new Americans, decimated the Native-American population from several million to only several thousand. Entire tribes, clans, languages, and ancient ways of life were eliminated, disbursed, or at best displaced. Treaties were "negotiated" often with any tribal member willing to sign, and reservations, health care, and education were promised in return for ending hostilities and relegation to tiny plots of land. Readers are encouraged to pick up a map of any state, particularly in the Great Plains region, and note the size of the local reservations. These tribes were traditionally accustomed to ranging unrestricted across the vast expanses of those maps. Now, they were killed or otherwise punished for leaving the boundaries of these areas to hunt or protect their families. The sharp edges of the vanquishers' boundaries were encapsulated by definable, mapable boundaries. Whereas majority culture members were free to pursue their individualized versions of the American Dream, American Indians' collective mandate was simple and clear: assimilate, stay in your place, or die.

The Boarding School Experience: "Kill the Indian, Save the Man!"

Without much debate, it is safe to say that compulsory attendance for our children in government-run boarding schools represented one of the more diabolic attacks on Native-American culture in the history of this continent (Duran & Duran, 1995). Beginning in the 1870s, this policy (which amounted to nothing short of war waged by the United States government against Native-American children) merely represented a highly sanitized refinement of a systematic, yet unspoken, cultural genocide program that had existed for nearly a century. This policy called for children as young as 5 years old to be forcibly taken from their parents and often transported thousands of miles away from their homes. They were subjected to emotional and physical atrocities such as being punished for speaking their tribal languages, cutting off their braids, being forced to work to maintain the underfunded schools (thus, violating child labor laws), and being made to wear Western-style clothing and to destroy their native clothing (Tafoya & Del Vecchio, 1996). Parents were not able to visit their children, nor were children able to visit their families on weekends or holidays because of the distances they were taken. Many children died in the boarding schools, so these children were taken from their parents and often disappeared forever.

This federally imposed *social evolution* of the Indian through education was consistent with the view that "a wild Indian requires a thousand acres to roam over, while an intelligent man will find a comfortable support for his family on a very small tract" (Adams, 1995, p. 20). In other words, cloaked under the guise of educating the native savage by means of a privileged Christian hegemony, Indian children were separated from their families; stripped of their traditional names, customs, and language; and educated in more sedentary ways of life in an attempt to make more land available for White development and alleviate the burden on the federal government of feeding and clothing Native people. Unfortunately, much like contemporary atrocities perpetrated against Native Americans, financial gain was the fuel that pushed the boarding school movement, although its vision emanated from the inoculated gaze of a self-ordained cultural superiority and belief in a divinely appointed right to wield dominion over this continent and proselytize its inhabitants.

Majority Culture as Iktomi

One pan-Indian generalization that is valid fairly consistently across tribes is the existence of a *Trickster* within their oral tradition. The Trickster may take the form of a coyote, owl, human, spider, or other creature that contributes wisdom to the purpose of the story. The Lakota version of Trickster is Iktomi—which translates literally as "spider," although he may take any form. Iktomi always has a hidden agenda in his dealings with others, is selfish by nature, and seldom is straightforward or altruistic. The majority culture's dealings with American Indians have often been Iktomi-like in nature, particularly regarding acceptance and multicultural coexistence. Whether it was early settlers gaining the trust of and then exploiting coastal tribes or the federal government forcing treaties later broken by their authors, the majority culture's Iktomi message has been clear: Indian people are acceptable so long as they "stay in their place." More specifically:

1. "You can continue to live here, but . . . " only on these reservations (or urban Indian communities for those not even "fortunate" enough to be placed on a reservation). Again, readers are encouraged to peruse a Plains state map and note the tiny plots of land—usually unsustainable and isolated—where reservations were typically designated for tribes accustomed to roaming vast geographic areas. They were not allowed to leave or, in the case of many Oklahoma agricultural tribes, they were conspired against and defrauded of their land once it was discovered that they had been placed on top of immense oil reserves (Debo, 1940). Moreover, the Indians were often punished for practicing cultural traditions on their own land for fear of an "Indian uprising." The interested reader is encouraged to see Amendment I of the United States Constitution regarding limitations of Congress to make laws regarding the establishment of religion, or prohibiting the free exercise thereof, abridging the freedom of speech, or the right of the people peaceably to assemble. It is a fascinating document.
2. "We promise to educate your people, but . . . " in church, or reservation/Bureau of Indian Affairs (B.I.A.) boarding schools where you will assimilate to a proper Christian belief system in every manner or suffer harsh, sadistic punishments and even death. Apparently separation of church and state did not apply when it came to educating Indians.
3. "We will provide your health care, but . . . " it will be regulated by a severely underfunded and understaffed arm of the Public Health Service (Indian Health Service).

True egalitarian coexistence has never been an option for this continent's first inhabitants. The American Indian's "place" within the mainstream has been relegated to a stereotyped or dehumanized misrepresentation. Guthrie (1998, p. 8) describes this process as the "Noble Savage" phenomenon, whereby indigenous peoples must be characterized as brutish, yet stoic and strong (but still defeatable), in order to be perceived as socially palatable. The cowboys always win in the movies and the cigar shop/dime store wooden Indians (always a fully head-dressed Chief, interestingly) still exist at many establishments.

A much more harmful contemporary illustration of this dehumanization phenomenon that is difficult for mainstream culture to appreciate is the *cartoonization* of Native Americans and our symbols as school and sports team mascots. We are often astonished by the lack of awareness and sensitivity to this issue on the part of our professional and academic colleagues, not to mention alumni and administrators of universities that bear Indian monikers. To illustrate, one of us (JDM) is on the faculty at an academic institution (University of North Dakota) that has received national notoriety for its *Fighting Sioux* nickname and the Indian-head logo that accompanies it (see Dohrman, 2001). Specifically, when it appeared that the UND President was sympathetic to possibly changing the name and logo, the North Dakota State Board of Higher Education removed his ability to make this decision. The reason? A new $100 million hockey arena heavily subsidized by a well-heeled alumnus benefactor who threatened to let it stand, half-finished, if the university changed the nickname/logo. The majority of North and South Dakota tribes, particularly the Lakota, Dakota, and Nakota "Sioux" (a non-Indian word derived from the French for "snake"), as well as UND faculty members were outraged, but to no avail. One small, and meaningful, consolation from this situation was the passage of a resolution by the UND Psychology Department against the name and logo. It is unfortunate that university administrations capitulate to financial and political extortion tactics like these, even though universities who have demonstrated the courage to make the change from Indian mascots (e.g., Stanford, St. John's) have not experienced financial downturns from alumni contributions as a result (Spindel, 2000).

In addition to the *money talks* justification for the continued exploitation of Indian symbols, one of the more infuriating rationales offered by defenders of this practice involves eloquent clarifications of how we (Native Americans) misconstrue the intent of these mascots—*to honor us*. However, despite the fact that many of us are insulted and express these sentiments, we are reminded that it is *we* who do not understand and that we *should* feel honored by these stereotypical and unflattering caricatures of our people. Further, if we fail to appreciate the magnanimous nature of such big-hearted gestures, then it is we who are being ungrateful for the generosity extended to us. Such anesthetized responses serve to highlight the manner in which the mainstream culture arrogantly assumes the authority to dictate to us our experiences and even their *correct* meaning. In other words, "It doesn't matter how it makes you feel, that's not the way we mean it. And, since our way of thinking is the privileged version, we get to make up the rules. So get over it." Again, constructive coexistence is allowable, but it is entirely conditional.

MANIFESTATIONS OF PSYCHOLOGY'S RESISTANCE TO MULTICULTURALISM

Scientific Racism

The process of *conditional muticulturalism* demonstrated throughout history has been clearly paralleled within the field of psychology. Pioneering anthropologists were the first to attempt to scientifically reduce American Indians to living museum exhibits. Not to be outdone, early psychologists were concerned with empirically demonstrating the racial and cultural inferiority of American minorities using groundbreaking mental measures to demonstrate their own professional version of social identity and dominance theories. Thomas and Sillen (1972) refer to the use of scientific methodology to perpetuate cultural, racial, and ethnic stereotyping as *scientific racism* (see also Sue & Sue, 1999). We have seen a number of noteworthy cases of scientific racism dating back to Cyril Burt's fabricated data demonstrating the inferiority of African-American brains (Dorfman, 1978) and more contemporary efforts such as Hernstein and Murray's (1994) work of "science fiction," *The Bell Curve*.

Perhaps, nowhere has mainstream psychology's scientific racism been more evident than in Indian country. Some studies (Garth, 1927; Hunter & Sommermier, 1922) sought to demonstrate the positive correlation between degree of White blood and higher IQ test scores. Still others (Paschall & Sullivan, 1925) went a step further to suggest the degree of Indian blood present in other races was a predictor of lower intelligence. Even when empirical evidence was found to the contrary, it did not escape the clutches of a cultural superiority interpretation. For example, when an 1895 study demonstrated the superiority of Native Americans' sensory perception relative to Caucasians, the findings were claimed as further evidence of White superiority, attributing the slower reaction times of Whites to the fact that they belonged to a more deliberate and reflective race (Gossett, 1963). Either way, Indians could not win.

One of the most disturbing features of scientific racism today is that, although the more blatant examples have largely disappeared, modern and more subtle illustrations persist. These examples are seen in the continued practice of *race comparative* research that applies established theoretical and methodological approaches to ethnic minority individuals (McDonald, 2000; McLoyd & Randolph, 1984), despite the fact that practically all of these paradigms are derived from data gathered on Anglo-American samples (Sue, 1999). As another example, the proposed national *standardization* of testing and curricula in the schools will, in all likelihood, exclude perspectives unpopular with the dominant culture's view of education. As such, this proposed initiative stands as a frightening manifestation of scientific racism representing a "xenophobic movement . . . reminiscent of the assimilation hysteria" experienced by Native people in boarding schools (Forbes, 2000; p. 7).

In our opinion, mainstream psychology continues to grapple with issues of scientific racism primarily as a function of the persistent adherence of many psychologists to an ethnocentrically narrowed view of human nature imbedded deeply in psychology's European roots—to the exclusion of alternative and equally valid perspectives. This situation seems to parallel the challenge faced by a great many individuals in the majority culture: On the one hand, they should "know better"; but they struggle to escape the vestiges of historical cultural influences—resulting in an all-too-eager susceptibility to accept evidence confirming deeply ingrained, and perhaps unconscious, suspicions regarding the inferiority of ethnic minority individuals.

The Arbitrary Valuing of Variance in Mainstream Psychology

Generating and capitalizing on variance is such a fundamental feature of contemporary psychology that its central importance requires practically little or no mention. Even the most elementary introductory statistics text teaches us that limited variability (i.e., restricted ranges of scores) on any measure(s) limits the probability of producing reliable results from statistical analyses. As a result, most graduate psychology training programs emphasize this principle through three common research rules of thumb: (a) gather data on as many subjects as possible; (b) utilize as many measures (and items on those measures) as possible; in hopes to (c) generate as much variance on these measures as is necessary to produce statistically significant results.

The popular consensus being, if one implements these rules and sets the appropriate alpha level (which is often about as "scientific" as using a "divining rod" to find water), then one will demonstrate "truth" if indeed statistical significance is achieved. It seems that in most aspects of psychology variance is the wood that keeps our quantifiable, empirical fire warm. If range (and ultimately variance) is restricted, we worry that the wood may be unreliable or maybe we do not have enough. Plenty of variance, and we feel warm and content in the interpretation of our findings.

Interestingly, however, variance is not universally desirable across all realms of contemporary psychology. Specifically, whereas statistical variance is enthusiastically embraced, range and variance in worldviews and the potential array of diverse behaviors that they inform are not. To illustrate, it is not uncommon for Indian graduate students to be pressured to cut their braids, shed their accents, dress "professionally," conform to the majority culture's concept and value of "time," and accept the sacrament of linear thinking. These ethnocentric conformist demands resonate with an eerie tone reminiscent of those experienced by their parents in the boarding schools.

Perhaps even more unsettling, the standards for admission into the academic psychology community reflect a similar monadic philosophy characterized by an extremely narrow definition of *merit* that places almost exclusive emphasis on individual achievement. Although merit, like any other value judgment, is a social contrivance possessing no inherent properties independent of subjective evaluation, the naïve observer would walk away from most faculty discussions on the topic convinced that merit is easily definable, universally applicable, and occurs naturally in the environment, much like hydrogen.

Based on our experience as faculty members over the past 10 years, most graduate programs, psychology departments, and graduate schools continue to evaluate potential students according to traditional standards of merit comprised mainly of Graduate Record Examination (GRE) scores and to a lesser extent undergraduate grade point average and letters of recommendation from impressive, identifiable writers. These practices continue despite empirical findings indicating that GRE scores are dismally poor predictors of academic success beyond the first year of graduate school (Sternberg & Williams, 1997) and that other factors (e.g., achievement motivation, leadership abilities) may be more influential to the academic success of Native-American students (Fore & Chaney 1998; Huffman, Sill, & Brokenleg, 1986). Put simply, "standardized" tests such as the GRE play a pivotal role in determining who gets into graduate school (or not, in the case of many minority students), but may have little or nothing to do with the abilities required to get out. Likewise, the definition of merit utilized for hires and promotions at the faculty level similarly reflects a singular focus in its emphasis on publication record and research grant activity. Absent from this definition, however, is the potential contribution to training made by an ethnic minority faculty member's rich and diverse life experiences—despite the fact that these unique perspectives and divergent worldviews may provide for innovative research and clinical opportunities (Hall, 1997).

Through propagation of these ethnocentrically biased practices, psychology merely continues to re-create itself in its own image, in much the same way historical accounts of the American Indian fraudulently "recapture and represent the past" (Roseneau, 1992, p. 64). This recapitulation of institutionalized restrictions results in the creation of a self-reflexive Ouroborus that bites its own tail (Schopenhauer, 1907) and further serves to galvanize mainstream psychology's resistance to multiculturalism. Unfortunately, it would seem that the primary difference between many graduate psychology programs and Indian boarding schools is that, with the former, students are figuratively dying to get in; with the latter, they literally died to get out.

HELPING THE HORSE RUN ON ALL FOUR LEGS

A horse can easily walk, fight, mate, and run on four good legs. Injure even one leg and its ability to accomplish any of these survival activities is significantly compromised. The relationship between Indians and mainstream psychology has been like the wounded horse. First, the horse had use of only one leg (exclusion and blatant scientific racism, circa 1800s–World War II) and then two (several Indian psychologists, graduate students, circa World War II–1990s). Currently it is walking on three legs. Although the exact number of Indian psychologists is difficult to determine, American Psychological Association data indicate that American-Indian psychologist membership finally eclipsed 100 in the year 2000 (APA, 2001). Hopefully, this figure will double by decade's end. However, there are several crucial aspects of this relationship that must develop before the horse can become sound, and true multiculturalism is realized in mainstream psychology.

First, American-Indian psychologists should set their sights on the target of achieving a representative ratio in the communities they serve. Nationally, there should be proportionally at least as many American-Indian psychologists in the field as there are American-Indian people in the country (around 2%). Regionally, in states with higher concentrations of Indian citizens (e.g., California, Oklahoma, New Mexico, Arizona, and all Plains states), the numbers should similarly reflect the demographics of the state. Not only should there be a representative ratio of Native-American licensed psychologists in a given geographic region, there should also be an equivalent representation of Native-American professionals occupying academic and Masters-level practitioner positions, as well as health and academic administration slots—to name but a few.

Second, increasing Indian representation in terms of training is also crucial. Positive role modeling and culturally inclusive curricula are essential to American-Indian and non–American-Indian college students. Hiring identifiable and accessible American-Indian faculty and staff will be essential to accomplish this (Hall, 1997). Although the representation of American-Indian faculty and students in graduate psychology training programs is increasing (American Psychological Association, 2001; National Science Foundation, 2000), current numbers remain insufficient to achieve the stated goals.

Finally, and perhaps most importantly, in order for parity to be reached on all fronts, a "paradigm shift" must take place specifically within the culture of academia, and within the tribe of psychology more generally. Directors of training programs, psychology departments, and university administrators can demonstrate sincere commitments to increase recruitment, retention, and successful production of American-Indian psychologists, as well as recruitment of American-Indian faculty and staff by being bold enough to think differently and take risks. Although glacially slow to adapt at times, mainstream psychology is a dynamic culture. Some *Pillars of Truth* (as described by Matsumoto, 1994) must indeed be shaken and the courage to think differently shouldered. American-Indian graduate faculty and graduate students should be valued for their ability to bring alternative perspectives on research, assessment, diagnosis, and treatment to the field of psychology. Sometimes dramatic progress is made when the status quo shifts ever so slightly to accommodate another worldview.

When the day dawns that mainstream psychology recognizes the legitimacy of the Native-American perspective, the horse will indeed run true and sound. On that day we will not only be content, but also enriched to open and close all conventions and meetings with homage to those we honor and cherish, whether it is Crazy Horse or B. F. Skinner. We will embrace the idea that human experience is as much influenced by riverbanks as it is by databanks, and that exclusive reliance on traditional scientific worldviews is an inadequate guide for living life. On that day psychology may take its place as a truly "spiritual science."

CONCLUSION

In conclusion, we would like to share a gift with our readers. This gift is actually a prayer offered to the U.S. Senate in 1975 by Fools Crow, the famous Lakota medicine man. This prayer epitomizes the honorable, yet ironic, reality that a group so marginalized and subjugated may still wish for peaceful coexistence with their oppressors.

> In the presence of this house, Grandfather, Wakan-Tanka (Creator) and from the directions where the sun sets, and from the direction of cleansing power, and from the direction of the rising sun, and from the direction of the middle of the day, Grandfather, Wakan-Tanka, Grandmother, the Earth who hears everything, Grandmother, because you are a woman, for this reason you are kind, I come to you this day. To tell you to love the red men, and watch over them, and give these men the understanding because, Grandmother, from you comes the good things, good things that are beyond our eyes to see have been blessed in our midst. For this reason I make my supplications to you again. On this day, on this great Island, Grandfather, upon which I stand I make this prayer to you, for those of us who are here in this house. Give us a blessing so that our words and actions be one in unity and that we be able to listen to each other, in so doing, we shall with good hearts walk hand in hand to face the future. This is what I want for all of us. For this reason, Grandfather and Grandmother, I make this Thanksgiving prayer. You give me this Sacred Pipe with which I pray to say thank you. So be it. In the presence of the outside, we are thankful for many blessings. I make my prayer for all people, their children, all women and all men. I pray that no harm will come to them. And that on the great island, there be no more war. That here be no ill feelings among us. From this day on may we walk hand in hand. So be it. (Mails, 1979, p. 218)

So be it indeed. Not only for the nation in general, but for the field of psychology in particular. *Hecetu-aloh, Kola Waste, Mitakuye Oyasin!* ("That's the (right) way it is, good friend, we are all related!")

REFERENCES

Adams, D. W. (1995). *Education for extinction: American Indians and the boarding school experience 1875–1928.* Lawrence, KS: University Press of Kansas.

American Psychological Association. (2001). *Ethnic minority professionals in psychology* (4th ed.). Washington, DC: Author.

Brislin, R. (2000). *Understanding culture's influence on behavior.* Fort Worth, TX: Harcourt College Publishers.

Brown, J. E. (1991). *The spiritual legacy of the American Indian.* New York: Crossroads.

Debo, A. (1940). *And still the waters run: The betrayal of the Five Civilized Tribes.* Princeton, NJ: Princeton University Press.

Dorfman, D. (1978). The Cyril Burt question: New findings. *Science, 201,* 1177–1186.

Dohrman, G. (2001, October). Face-off: A bullying North Dakota alumnus built the school a $100 million rink but tore its campus asunder. *Sports Illustrated,* 44–49.

Duran, E., & Duran, B. (1995). *Native American postcolonial psychology.* Albany, NY: State University of New York Press.

Earley, P., Gibson, C., & Chen, C. (1999). "How did I do?" versus "How did we do?": Cultural contrasts of performance feedback use and self-efficacy. *Journal of Cross-Cultural Psychology, 30,* 594–619.

Faragher, J., Buhle, M., Czitrom, D., & Armitage, S. (2000). *Out of many: A history of the American people.* Englewood Cliffs, NJ: Prentice Hall.

Forbes, J. (2000). The new assimilation movement: Standards, tests, and Anglo-American supremacy. *Journal of American Indian Education, 39*, 7–28.

Fore, C., & Chaney, J. (1998). Factors influencing the pursuit of educational opportunities in American Indian students. *American Indian and Alaska Native Mental Health Research, 8*, 46–55.

Garth, T. R. (1927). The will-temperament of Indians. *Journal of Applied Psychology, 11*, 512–518.

Gergen, K. J. (2001). Psychological science in a postmodern context. *American Psychologist, 56*, 803–813.

Gossett, T. (1963). *Race: The history of an idea in America.* Dallas, TX: Southern Methodist University Press.

Guthrie, R. (1998). *Even the rat was white: A historical view of psychology* (2nd ed.). New York: Harper & Row.

Hall, C. (1997). Cultural malpractice: The growing obsolescence of psychology with the changing U.S. population. *American Psychologist, 52*, 642–651.

Hernstein, R. J., & Murray, C. (1994). *The bell curve: Intelligence and class structure in American life.* New York: Free Press.

Huffman, T., Sill, M., & Brokenleg, M. (1986). College achievement among American Indian college students. *Journal of American Indian Education, 25*, 32–38.

Hunter, W., & Sommermier, E. (1922). The relation of degree of Indian blood to scores on the Otis Intelligence Test. *Journal of Comparative Psychology, 2*, 257–277.

Jones, J. (1997). *Prejudice and racism* (2nd ed.). New York: McGraw-Hill.

Mails, T. E. (1979). *Fools Crow.* New York: Avon Books.

Matsumoto, D. (1994). *Cultural influences on research methods and statistics.* Pacific Grove, CA: Brooks-Cole.

McDonald, J. D. (2000). A model for conducting research with American Indian participants. *Guidelines for research in ethnic minority communities* (pp. 12–15). Washington, DC: American Psychological Association.

McLoyd, V., & Randolph, S. (1984). The conduct and publication of research on Afro-American children. *Human Development, 27*, 65–75.

National Science Foundation. (2000). *Women, minorities, and persons with disabilities in science and engineering* (Report No. 00-327). Arlington, VA: Author.

Paschall, F. C., & Sullivan, L. R. (1925). Racial factors in the mental and physical development of Mexican children. *Comparative Psychology Monographs, 3*, 46–75.

Roseneau, P. (1992). *Post-modernism and the social sciences.* Princeton, NJ: Princeton University Press.

Schopenhauer, A. (1907). *The will in nature.* London: Bell.

Sidanius, J. (1993). The psychology of group conflict and the dynamics of oppression: A social dominance perspective. In S. Iyengar & W. McGuire (Eds.), *Explorations in political psychology* (pp. 183–219). Durham, NC: Duke University Press.

Spindel, C. (2000). *Dancing at halftime: Sports and the controversy over American Indian mascots.* New York: New York University Press.

Sternberg R., & Williams, W. (1997). Does the Graduate Record Examination predict meaningful success in the graduate training of psychologists? *American Psychologists, 52*, 630–641.

Sue, S. (1999). Science, ethnicity, and bias: Where have we gone wrong? *American Psychologist, 54*, 1070–1077.

Sue, D. W., & Sue, D. (1999). *Counseling the culturally different: Theory and practice* (3rd ed.). New York: Wiley.

Tajfel, H. (1978). *Differentiation between social groups: Studies in the social psychology of intergroup relations.* London: Academic Press.

Tafoya, N., & Del Vecchio, A. (1996). Back to the future: An examination of the Native American holocaust experience. In M. McGoldrick, J. Giordano, & J. K. Pearce (Eds.), *Ethnicity & family therapy* (2nd ed., pp. 45–54). New York: Guilford.

Thomas, A. & Sillen, S. (1972). *Racism and psychiatry*. New York: Brunner/Mazel.

Triandis, H. (1990). Theoretical concepts that are applicable to the analysis of ethnocentrism. In R. Brislin (Ed.), *Applied cross-cultural psychology* (pp. 34–55). Newbury Park, CA: Sage.

Trimble, J., & Jumper-Thurman, P. (2002). Ethnocultural considerations and strategies for providing counseling services to Native American Indians. In P. Pederson, J. Draguns, W. Lonner, & J. Trimble (Eds.), *Counseling across cultures* (5th ed., pp. 53–91). Thousand Oaks, CA: Sage.

CHAPTER 4

To Be Included
in the Multicultural Discussion

Check One Box Only

KAREN L. SUYEMOTO
JUANITA M. DIMAS

Although the United States has a long history of legal, institutional, and social exclusion of racial minority groups,[1] the dominant dialogue about race in the United States has been a Black/White dialogue, with its accompanying policies of the "one-drop" rule, where any evidence (familial or physical) of African-American heritage classifies one as Black—one drop of Black blood affects all the rest. Although this dialogue has recently been expanding to include consideration of the experience of other racial/ethnic minorities, the categorical ideology implicit in the one-drop rule continues to permeate the discussion (reflected in the "check one box" approach to demographic forms). This categorical approach persists despite the scientific consensus that there is no biological basis for race (Goodman, 2000; Krieger, 2000; Spickard, 1992) and despite a variety of social realities that challenge the ideology. For example: 5% of the U.S. population reported mixed ancestry in the 1990 census, and 7% reported mixed ancestry in a 1995 study (Waters, 2000); the number of interracial couples has more than quadrupled in the past 30 years, from 310,000 to 1,348,000. (This does not reflect couples who may have multiracial children and be unmarried, whether heterosexual or gay/lesbian couples; U.S Bureau of the Census, 1999.) Demographic trends suggest that contacts between diverse ethnic groups will continue to rise, increasing the number of intermarriages, and the proportion of children from such unions. Sociologists estimate that up to 90% of Black Americans have White ancestors (Wehrly, 1996), the majority of Latinos/as and American Indians are of mixed racial and ethnic heritage (Amaro & Zambrana, 2000; Mihesuah, 1996), and interracial marriage is becoming the norm for some racial/ethnic minority groups such as American Indians and Japanese-American women (Jaimes, 1995; Kitano, Fujino, & Sato 1998; Nagel, 1997).

The categorical approach and the effects of the dominance of the Black/White dialogue has also shaped the research, theory, and practice within psychology and mental health, leading to a relative exclusion and marginalization of multiracial individuals and families who do not "fit" into the boxes created by this approach. Of 21,383 articles in American Psychological Association (APA)–published or APA division–published journals in the last 5 years, 28 (0.13%) have addressed multiracial issues.[2] This exclusion is currently being challenged by researchers and theoreticians, who are primarily from multiracial families themselves. For example, both of the authors of this chapter come to the area of psychological and mental health research addressing multiracial issues through our own personal and family experiences; one of us is multiracial Japanese-European American (KLS) and the other is multiethnic Mexican-American and Irish-American (JMD). In the last decade several exceptional interdisciplinary books have been published addressing the multiracial experience, including Root's two edited volumes, *Racially Mixed People in America* (1992) and *The Multiracial Experience* (1996), and Zack's edited *American Mixed Race* (1995). Although many of the contributors to these volumes have been mental health researchers and practitioners, there continues to be a relative dearth of specific psychological and mental health literature directly addressing the experience of individuals and families with multiple heritages (an exception is Wehrly's *Counseling Interracial Individuals and Families, 1996*, and her—with Kenney and Kenney—*Counseling Multiracial Families, 1999*). In addition, although the importance of books such as these cannot be ignored, there continues to be resistance to the general inclusion of multiracial issues and needs in mental health research and treatment literature.

The continued minimal attention paid to individuals and families with multiple heritages within mental health needs to be acknowledged, explored, and addressed. Acknowledging and addressing this marginalization is necessary if we are to continue our journey toward cultural competence and adequately serving the mental health needs of the U.S. population. An in-depth exploration of the possible reasons behind the continued resistance to inclusion may help us not only to better understand but also to challenge the constructions of race, ethnicity, racism, and ethnocentrism. In addition, we may better understand how these variables have been socially constructed within the context of our history and society; and how all people (monoracial, multiracial, monocultural/monoethnic, and multicultural/multiethnic) may be affected by these constructions. These understandings could lead to changes in our approach to mental health and psychology for both monoracial and multiracial individuals.

This chapter attempts to begin such an exploration. We take an ecological perspective by addressing the societal contexts within which psychology is imbedded, from the perspective of the mainland United States. We address the issue of psychology's, and in particular, multicultural psychology's, resistance to the discussion of multiracial issues, and the effects that this resistance has had. And we conclude with a call to action for the field of psychology and multicultural psychology. It is not our purpose here to address the psychology of multiracial individuals, nor the effects of the field's resistance on individuals. Instead, we take a systems approach, where our subject is the field of psychology.

DEFINITION OF TERMS

Although it is important to define terms such as race, ethnicity, multiracial, and multicultural, it is extraordinarily difficult to agree on meaning, because these concepts are socially constructed and tightly tied to history and power. Even within the process of cowriting this chapter, we encountered confusion in the terminology that we tried to use with each other, requiring extensive discussion. Because we believe our difficulties to be reflective of the difficulties in the greater dialogue in the field, we decided that it would be useful to discuss our process here.

Initially, we assumed we were discussing the same things. It soon became clear, however, that we were not. Our initial need for clarification was on the definition of multiracial, whether this was a valid concept, and whether multiethnic might not be more accurate. We were, of course, both speaking from our own cultural and racial contexts, one of which (Latina) consciously emphasizes ethnicity far more than race, and the other of which (Japanese-American) continues an incorporation of ideas of racial purity in addition to ethnic socialization. And we struggled, also, with identifying which were our personal definitions, and which were the dominant, socially constructed ideas that we were trying to approach or critique. As our discussions on terminology continued, we needed to revisit our previous decisions, reflecting an ongoing iterative process of tentative defining, critique, contextualizing, and redefining. Ultimately, we did not find terms that either of us was truly happy with, but for the sake of continuing our discussion, we agreed on "good-enough for now" terms, with the understanding and recognition of our different opinions. Oftentimes our different opinions were even within ourselves, and not just between us.

Given the extensive discussions we had in approaching this chapter, it became clear that we need to emphasize that *all* definitions of race and ethnicity are socially constructed. Race is not a biological concept; it is a social construct (Goodman, 2000; Root, 1998b; Spickard, 1992). And it is a social construct whose primary use currently and historically appears to be the creation of in-groups and out-groups and a hierarchy of power and privilege (Omi & Winant, 1994; Pinderhughes, 1989; Root, 1998b). In contrast, although ethnicity is also a social construct, the boundaries are more permeable and the primary purpose appears to be to create and maintain communities and commonalities (Pinderhughes, 1989; Root, 1998b), except when ethnocentrism again introduces the issues of power and supremacy. Ethnicity is frequently confounded with race, although it is clear that they are different concepts with different social consequences and purposes.

Part of our difficulty in discussing race and monoracial and multiracial experiences is that different groups and individuals construct these concepts somewhat differently, in terms of their basic definitions, their acceptance of the "reality" of the categories within their own self-defined in-group, and their differentiation of race and ethnicity (see the following). To discuss the multi*racial* versus mono*racial* experience is to accept, at least temporarily and in the language used, the predominant and oppressive reality of the social construct "race." And yet to discuss instead multi*ethnic* versus mono*ethnic* denies the social reality of the importance of race shared by many individuals particularly in relation to groups (such as White or Asian) that more actively focus on race rather than, or in addition to, ethnicity. It also denies the social reality of racism where the acceptance of the idea of race by the dominant (White) group is imposed on all other groups of color (Krieger, 2000; Spickard, 1992).

In sum, we would like to emphasize the *socially constructed* nature of the basic ideas of race and ethnicity, and the associated ideas of "monoracial," "monoethnic," "multiracial," and "multiethnic." We explicitly state that we believe these concepts have no foundation in any biological or physical "reality" (Goodman, 2000; King, 1981; Krieger, 2000; Spickard, 1992). And we acknowledge the tension that discussing these ideas as if they are real contributes to their maintenance and, therefore, to the foundation of exclusion we are attempting to critique (Kitzinger, 1995).

Given all of these difficulties, we still need to communicate through a shared understanding of the language we are using. Therefore, we offer the following definitions:

Ethnicity: cultural patterns (variable system(s) of meanings including values, beliefs, behavior, roles, affective styles, attitudes, etc.) shared by a group frequently unified by a common national or geographical origin (Atkinson, Morton, & Sue, 1998; Fry, 1999; Pinderhughes, 1989; Wehrly, 1995).

- Monoethnic: enacting and/or claiming only one group's shared cultural patterns
- Multiethnic: enacting and/or claiming more than one group's shared cultural patterns

Race: a socially constructed concept of categorization and distinction within social relationships based on physical characteristics (Atkinson, Morton, & Sue, 1998; Helms & Cook, 1999; Spickard, 1992; Young, 1999).

- Monoracial: being identified (by self and/or by others) as belonging to only one "racial" group
- Multiracial: being identified (by self and/or by others) as belonging to more than one "racial" group

REASONS FOR THE RESISTANCE
TO THE MULTIRACIAL DISCUSSION

Despite the emphasis on diversity, multiculturalism, and equal rights, there continues to be resistance to the recognition and inclusion of multiracial individuals and issues. Why do we continue to construct racial group definitions in absolute terms focusing on exclusion? Why would minority groups themselves be reluctant to construct their group definition in a more inclusive manner? Why would multicultural psychology continue to be drawn toward the traditional (and imposed) racial categorizations? Part of the resistance to including multiracial individuals and issues is likely related to an attempt to maintain intimacy and connection with others through drawing boundaries.

Thus, an in-group is created that is unified by experiences deemed important to the individuals coconstructing the boundaries. Identifying others who are similar helps us create our own group-referenced identities and meanings, helping us organize our experiences and social interactions (Suyemoto, 2002). And yet, the creation of an in-group necessitates the simultaneous creation of an out-group—being able to define what is "like-me" also requires the articulation of "not-like-me." In terms of the multiracial experience, this becomes problematic when the boundaries become rigid and closely drawn, continually placing multiracial people in the "not-like-me" category.

In addition to this general shared reason for resistance, we suggest that the dominant White European-American group and minority groups (both together as people of color and specifically) have different and group-specific reasons for resisting the inclusion of multiracial individuals and issues. Part of the *dominant* group or society's resistance may result from: (a) an internalization of the historical categorical approach with the related development and maintenance of an exclusionary ideology that focuses more on drawing boundaries to keep some people out, than on loosening boundaries to enable broad inclusion; (b) the maintenance of power and privilege accorded to the dominant group; and (c) an interaction with the resistance from minority groups. Part of *minority* groups' general resistance result from: (a) privileging of "pure race" ideologies by the dominant group and a related acceptance of the racial hierarchy; (b) a process of reclaiming identity and/or power; and (c) a variety of group-specific reasons. Part of multicultural psychology's resistance may be due to the developmental stage of the field; we are not yet able to dismantle the construct of race, and continuing to use the terminology of race reifies the concept itself.

REASONS FOR THE RESISTANCE
BY THE DOMINANT U.S. SOCIETY

Historical Legacy

The primary reason for the resistance to including multiracial individuals and issues by the dominant White European-American society is the internalization and acceptance of the historical categorical approach of pure race ideology. This categorical approach has permeated the basic thinking about race for both dominant and minority groups as well as for specific fields, such as psychology. As such, it is worthwhile to consider the origins and enactments of this ideology in more depth.

The first question many people of mixed descent are asked is "What are you?" The importance of the question for the speaker is "How do I classify you?" and it implies that only one classification will be allowed. Although it is part of our cognitive make-up to categorize and classify, the inability to accept multiple and fluid categorizations and the social meanings imposed on the categorizations themselves are embedded in our history and issues related to power. Racial categorization becomes relevant when two or more distinct groups are in contact *and* are in conflict over power and resources (Spickard, 1992). The "discovery" of America and the indigenous people therein provided the context and reason for the early conversations about race and equality that have contributed to our current conversations in the U.S. mainland today. Although these conversations were initially tied to religious ideologies, even at that time they were used to justify exploitation and enslavement (Omi & Winant, 1994).

The *scientific* classification of human races began in the 18th century with Linnaeus' classification system of all living organisms, including human beings. Soon after, the subdivision of races as Caucasoid, Negroid, and Mongoloid was added and organized hierarchically by European and American scholars, scientists, and politicians with Caucasians at the top, followed by Asians, American Indians, and Africans (Spickard, 1992). Race was seen as a biological reality with each race being distinctly separate "with physical features, gene pools, and character qualities that diverged entirely one from another" (Spickard, 1992, p. 14; Omi & Winant, 1994) despite the acknowledgment that over time there was some mixing of the groups (Spickard, 1992). This "scientific" racial hierarchy reflected sociopolitical views of the superiority of the culture, physical abilities, and moral qualities of Caucasian/Europeans (Omi & Winant, 1994; Spickard, 1992). Miscegenation (interracial marriage) was discouraged not only on grounds that separate "species" should not mate, but also because it was seen as the dilution of the superior race by inferior stock (Nobles, 2000; Omi & Winant, 1994; Spickard, 1992). Because of this particular view of miscegenation as dilution, individuals who were the products of miscegenation were inevitably classified by descent from the "lesser" stock, reflected in the "one-drop" rule in the United States.

Approaches to the sociohistorical understanding and categorizing of race and "mixed race" are reflected in the U.S. census categories, which have changed in different administrations (Nobles, 2000; Spickard, 1992). The term "Mulatto" first appeared in the 1850 census and continued to 1930 in an attempt to support U.S. polygenist theorists who purported that human races were distinct and unequal species, with "separate origins, permanent racial differences, and the infertility of racial mixture" (Nobles, 2000, p. 1740). Although the existence of multiracial individuals had led European scientists away from the theory of polygenism, the "Mulatto" category was included in the U.S. census to provide "statistical data to prove that Mulattos, as hybrids of different racial species, were less fertile than their pure-race parents and lived shorter lives" (Nobles, 2000, p. 1740). The instructions of the 1870 census made even clearer the official and institutionalized idea of the "one-drop-rule" of hypodescent:

> Be particularly careful in reporting the class *Mulatto*. The word here is generic, and includes quadroons, octoroons, and all persons *having any perceptible trace* of African blood. Important scientific results depend upon the correct determination of this class in schedules 1 and 2 [emphasis added]. (U.S. Bureau of the Census, 1989, p. 26; in Nobles, 2000, p. 1740)

Regardless of the "biological" heritage (e.g., the Caucasian "blood quantum"), Mulattos were never considered to be "mixed Whites." White was always pure and superior; only other groups could be mixed (Nobles, 2000). While originating in the 1800s, these ideas continue, as evidenced by the 1982 case of Susie Phipps, a descendent of an 18th century White plantation owner and a Black slave who was denied the legal right to change her racial classification from Black to White (Omi & Winant, 1994).

After the Mulatto category was removed in the 1930 census, the one-drop rule previously used to categorize "Mulattos" now became the basis of categorization of all multiracial African Americans as "Negroes": "A person of mixed white and Negro blood should be returned as a Negro, no matter how small the percentage of Negro blood. Both black and mulatto persons are to be returned as Negroes, without distinction" (U.S. Bureau of the Census, 1930, cited in Nobles 2000, p. 1741). The category "Other Mixed Races" was used to report other mixed race individuals and "Mexicans" and "Indians" were treated similarly to Blacks (Nobles, 2000). Until the most recent 2000 census, multiracial individuals were restricted to choosing only one box or remaining in the "Other" category, continuing the institutionalization of the strict categorical approach.

In the 20th and 21st centuries, most scientists reject the notion of biological racial types, although the ideology remains strong among general social beliefs (King, 1981; Omi & Winant, 1994; Spickard 1992). In addition, the sociohistorical constructions that grew from the initial erroneous "scientific" categorical approach continue to plague our social reality. This approach has shaped our governmental policies as well as our social institutions and continues to be reflected in our social and political structures today (Nobles, 2000) providing an ideological foundation of exclusion, rather than inclusion (Bradshaw, 1992). The 2000 U.S. census is the first time multiracial individuals had inclusive, rather than exclusive options. It was not until 1967 that the Supreme Court struck down antimiscegenation laws. Even recently there has been resistance to removing the last states' antimiscegenation laws, regardless of their inability to be enforced given the Supreme Court ruling (Greenberg, 1999; Sengupta 2000a, b). Thus, to date in the United States there has been only one generation grown to midlife without legal restrictions to intermarriage. Because "social flexibility regarding the rules that govern race relations and perceptions about race would threaten existing social structures by implying that inclusion should replace exclusion as the guiding principle" (Bradshaw, 1992, p. 78), multiracial inclusion and recognition continue to be resisted by the dominant White European-American group.

Power and Privilege

The categorical and hierarchical approach to race has resulted in defining "American" as "White" (Omi & Winant, 1994). This equation has led to the privileging of White European Americans in a variety of ways, including the privilege of not considering race as an important variable at all (McIntosh, 1997; Pinderhughes, 1989). The shifts of the U.S. census illustrate how racial categories have been used primarily as a social and political tool in the guise of a scientific approach. Clear racial boundaries have been necessary for the maintenance of White privilege, resulting in laws and institutions that are explicitly aimed at maintaining these boundaries. These laws and institutional definitions have included defining African Americans for the purpose of separating slaves from nonslaves or those subject to Jim Crow laws versus those privileged by them; defining American Indians by blood quantum or eligibility for "card-carrying" status; defining Asian immigrants as aliens and therefore ineligible to own land; enacting legislation such as "Operation Wetback" in the 1950s that allowed many Mexican Americans to be arrested, detained and, sometimes, deported; and the antimiscegenation laws in effect from the 1600s through 1967. Although the social and political dialogue has focused on the Black–White issue, the one-drop rule has permeated views of all White-minority mixes, as the concern has continually been with the mixing of White/Caucasian with "inferior" races (Waters, 2000). Breaking down a monoracial categorical approach would confront White Americans with their own privilege through exposing the hierarchical approach (Bradshaw, 1992). Race would then be shown as a social construct, rather than a biological given, and the systemic and structural aspects of racism and oppression would be exposed, defying the myth of meritocracy and equality.

The Interaction with Minority Groups' Monoracial Ideologies

Although the dominant categorical and monoracial ideology may have been constructed and imposed by White Europeans/Americans centuries ago, the effects of these imposed ideologues have permeated minority groups' own definitions of race and racial belonging, as described in the following sections. Although it should not be forgotten that monoracial hierarchical ideologies began with and continue to benefit the dominant White group, we must recognize that currently both the dominant White group and specific minority groups contribute to the maintenance of these ideologies and the resistance to the inclusion and recognition of multiracial issues and experiences.

REASONS FOR THE RESISTANCE BY MINORITY GROUPS

Over time, it has not been only the dominant White groups' ideologies, laws, and institutions that have contributed to maintaining racial "purity" and clear categorical boundaries. It has also been the ideologies and definitions created by the minority racial groups themselves. Minority groups may accept categorical approaches and resist the inclusion of multiracial issues for many reasons, including: (a) privileging pure race and racial hierarchy; (b) reclaiming identity and power; and (c) a variety of group-specific reasons.

Privileging Pure Race and Racial Hierarchy

The imposition of racial ideologies by the dominant group through the offering of privileges or benefits to a minority group based on race definitions is one contributor to the development of rigid in-group boundaries for some minority groups. A minority group may be encouraged to create rigid boundaries in order to restrict privileges to a select group of individuals. For example, American Indians are often conscious of blood quantum criteria for the purpose of Bureau of Indian Affairs benefits. In contrast, a minority group may rigidly define racial in-group criteria because there is a group perception that access to the privileges offered to or accessed by multiracial individuals creates a different experience than that which unifies the group. This is related to an internalization of the racial hierarchy and accompanying power dynamics.

The race hierarchy stratifies minority groups themselves such that those higher in the hierarchy (e.g., Asian Americans) are offered more access and benefits, leading to between-minority prejudice and concern with racial definitions. The rejection of those "lower" in the hierarchy contributes to the minority group's need to maintain clear racial boundaries. What is problematic here is that the imposed concept of race, with its categorical approach, is then used by the oppressed minority group to maintain its boundaries. Although the cohesion of the group may be maintained, the possibility of challenging the underlying social construct of race is lost and the hierarchy maintained.

Reclaiming Identity and Power

A minority group may also create rigid in-group boundaries as part of the attempt to either reclaim a positive group identity, or to maintain or fight for social and political gains. In the case of creating or reclaiming a positive group identity, members of the racial in-group may create fixed boundaries because of the fear that the multiracial person's experience may be too far afield, too different to be encompassed within the in-group construction without a loss of intimacy or identity. For some multiracial individuals, this can be problematic, because they may see their experience as more similar to the in-group and have that view refuted. Because the boundaries between in-group and out-group may be drawn differently by various individuals or groups, a multiracial individual may also find her- or himself defined as an outsider by all of the groups she or he self-identifies with—for example, a multiracial Asian–European American may self-define as "in" both groups but be rejected by the European-American group owing to being classified as Asian and simultaneously be rejected by the Asian-American group owing to being classified as European American (Root, 1998a, b).

A racial minority group may also draw narrow boundaries around racial definitions because of a fear of losing any little power that has been won at great expense (Kitzinger, 1995). Although it is true that we cannot deconstruct race and racial categorizations by drawing narrow boundaries and denying self-identified claims to belonging, it is also true that, for now, racism is a social reality relying on the construct of race. Some resources and rights have been fought for and won by oppressed racial groups; and racial categorizations are still used to ensure the distribution of those few rights and resources. Thus, to "dilute" the definition of the group or blur the boundary between groups (particularly between the oppressed and privileged groups) may result in the loss of explicit recognition, whereas the social reality of oppression is maintained (e.g., fears that the new census policy of allowing people to check more than one box may lead to decreased numbers of people being "counted" as minorities and an accompanying decrease in allocated resources; Krieger, 2000). In other words, if we abandon the concept of race, or if we begin to blur the boundaries by including the "mixed" category, we would likely be ignoring the social reality of "racism" and its impact.

Reasons for the Resistance Within Specific Minority Groups

These possible explanations explore the general experience of minority groups as a whole (i.e., People of Color) in relation to the dominant White group, focusing on *racial* exclusion being situated primarily in the power and privilege associated with racial categorizing and the sociohistorical "reality of racism." However, specific racial minority groups have their own racial *and* ethnic constructions, and specific and particular reasons for their own resistance to the recognition and inclusion of multiracial people and experiences. The resistance to the acknowledgment and inclusion of multiracial individuals and issues within specific racial minority groups is related to a number of variables, including: (a) in-group definitions of race and ethnicity: to what extent an in-group definition depends on variables such as "blood heritage," claimed identity, shared physical characteristics, and shared cultural patterns; (b) history of contact that made racial categorization relevant, including the interaction of in-group definitions of race and ethnicity with histories of immigration, colonization, appropriation, and enslavement; (c) the creation of a sizable multiracial population; and (d) the social-historical-political position of the specific group in the mainland United States, and the sociopolitical consequences of inclusion of multiracial issues. These group-specific resistances contribute to the general resistance experienced socially and within psychology. By way of example, in the following sections we discuss how and why some of the major specific U.S. ethnic minority groups resist the acknowledgment and inclusion of multiracial individuals and issues. Some patterns begin to emerge, where we see that issues of racial purity and historical hierarchy play different roles within each racial/ethnic group discussed, thus affecting their unique resistances to the multiracial discussion. For example, European-American and Asian-American communities place great value on the ideal of racial purity; American Indian communities tend to value affiliation over racial purity, whereas there is an imposed need to prove racial purity; Latinos/as actively defy the concept of racial purity by placing a greater value on ethnicity rather than race, but have a value on colorism implying an acceptance of the racial hierarchy; and African Americans presume no racial purity, but have a high regard for purity of affiliation with the in-group exclusively. Each group's internal value systems, as well as history and place within society's hierarchical structure, have influenced the type of multiracial unions that are most predominant and most accepted. Perhaps reflecting the historical hierarchy position, each of the other minority groups tends to accept unions with White more easily than unions with African Americans, who are historically relegated to the bottom of society's structure.

We would like to emphasize that the following sections are generalizations, which is true whenever we discuss the psychological or sociological experiences of racial or ethnic *groups* (versus individuals). We recognize that there is considerable heterogeneity within "racial" groups (particularly in relation to ethnicity) and across individuals. There is also considerable heterogeneity regarding type of multiracial populations within each specific racial/ethnic group. For instance, the multiracial dialogue tends to assume *bi*raciality, or mixture of two groups, rather than allowing for the possibility of *multi*raciality. In addition, the dialogue tends to assume a minority–White combination, rather than minority–minority (e.g., Asian–Black) combinations. Although we attempt to avoid either of these *assumptions* within our discussions, we do attempt to place our discussions within predominant relevant social-historical-political contexts of each group, such as immigration issues for Asian Americans, and history of slavery for African Americans. Although these contexts may not apply to all individuals within the larger racial/ethnic group (particularly those whose generational status is outside the norm within their group; e.g., recent immigrants from Africa, later and more acculturated Asian-American individuals), these experiences have and continue to have significant effects on the larger group, and provide a larger context within which to consider the group's experiences.

American Indians

The majority of American Indians[4] in the United States are of mixed racial heritage (Fernández, 1992; Mihesuah, 1996). Before European contact, American Indians did not embrace a concept of race; membership in a tribe was based on social relationships (kinship, marriage, adoption) and cultural similarities and enactments (Jaimes, 1995; O'Nell, 1996). Meaningful categorizations were historically between various tribal groups, based on language, culture, geography, tradition, etc. The ideology of race, and particularly the importance and hierarchical valuing of "pure" race was part of European values introduced through invasion and colonization (Jaimes, 1995). European racial theories led to U.S. federal Indian policies which in turn influenced (if not dictated) tribal definitions of belonging within the constraints of the policies.

The current treatment of multiracial individuals within the American-Indian community is intertwined within the more general questions of who really is American Indian and how this is determined. Possible bases include blood quantum cut-offs, tribal enrollment, reception of government benefits, particular physical characteristics ("looking Native"), genealogical heritage, cultural knowledge and practice, political involvement, reservation upbringing or residence (Jaimes, 1995; Nagel, 1997; O'Nell, 1996). When exploring these many possible bases and their implications for multiracial individuals, it is most important to remember that each of these has strong ties to the history of genocide and colonization of the American-Indian peoples by the Europeans and European Americans, and continuing current conditions and oppression.

Historically, physical characteristics were often used to determine blood quantum and define membership within tribal rolls when these were first established by U.S. governmental agents (Nagel, 1997). Blood quantum continues to be used by the U.S. government to officially determine who is a "real" Indian, and who should be eligible for benefits as an Indian. And American Indians have, under pressure from the U.S. government, adopted the use of blood quantum for determining tribal membership and listing on the rolls (Jaimes, 1995; Nagel, 1997; O'Nell, 1996). The power of the U.S. government to impose its racial ideologies and political agendas becomes clear if one examines how the inclusiveness or exclusiveness of in-group definition changes with governmental policy. For example, the Flathead tribe's inclusion criteria became more stringent in response to U.S. government efforts in the mid-1900s to terminate support and recognition of the tribe because it was viewed as assimilated, partly because of the inclusion of multiracial Flathead individuals (O'Nell, 1996). Race in terms of physical presentation, distinction, and recognition becomes important because of its implicit link to the imposed ideology of blood quantum and because it is through physical characteristics that those with less "blood" are distinguished.

Thus, the resistance to including multiracial individuals and issues within American-Indian communities is a resistance rooted in: (a) the imposition of blood quantum; and (b) the colonization and seizing of American-Indian lands and resources leading to a current situation of impoverishment and minimal support from the U.S. government with an associated lack of resources that makes competition for survival somewhat inevitable. In addition, the extreme history of attempts at genocide (e.g., Trail of Tears, war, smallpox-infested blankets) and cultural eradication (e.g., boarding schools) and the current controversies and barriers for Nations seeking federal recognition make American Indians fearful of losing their identities altogether (O'Nell, 1996). Given the internalization of the importance of race and blood, this fear may be physically embodied in multiracial individuals who do not "look Native."

Although there continues to be resistance to the recognition and full acceptance of multiracial American Indians, particularly those who do not look American Indian and who do not reside on a reservation (Jaimes, 1995), within the American-Indian communities, belonging and recognition are rarely simply issues of blood quantum and physical characteristics. Cultural actions and knowledge can speak louder in American-Indian communities than physical appearance and there is active recognition that the effects of governmental policies on tribal definitions and approaches to "race" may be actively contradictory to the values of the tribe (O'Nell, 1996). Thus, those individuals who are clearly culturally knowledgeable are more likely to be accepted in spite of any resistance to the ideology of multiracial issues.

Latinos/as

The primary reason for the Latino/a resistance to the multiracial discussion is not so much a resistance against the recognition and acceptance of a multiracial category or populations, but rather a resistance to the larger conceptualization of "race." Latin America and the United States have vastly different definitions of race that derive from different histories of race relations dating from the first European colonizers. These differences in historical experiences have led to different current day attitudes toward "race" that then come into conflict when the U.S. conceptualization is imposed on Latinos/as in the United States.

Similar to the American-Indian history within the United States, discussions of race in Latin America began when Europeans arrived in the Americas. However, there was not an initial conflict for power and resources based along absolute racial lines. For example, the ruling classes of both Spaniards and certain indigenous groups in Mexico mixed to combine forces against the largest and most powerful indigenous group of the times, Aztecas (Fernández, 1992). Unlike the U.S. history of hypodescent and exclusion, the mixed offspring of the unions of these ruling classes were freely included by both groups. However, similar to the U.S. history, indigenous peoples were overrepresented in the more populous lower social levels; and similarly, there was rape of women of lower social class levels, and this resulted in the first "illegitimate" mestizos (Fernández, 1992). This is an early example of how class carries more social meaning than race in Latin America, although the two constructs are strongly intertwined. The large mixed population of Latin America increased when slaves were introduced in the 18th century. Today, Latinos/as as a group are predominantly racially mixed (Amaro & Zambrana, 2000; Fernández, 1992). For example, it is estimated that 80% to 85% of Mexico's population is mixed, and because of the social-historical-political irrelevance of the concept of race, the Mexicano census last inquired about racial categorization in 1921 (Fernández, 1992).

Given the great degree of racial mixing for centuries, it is almost impossible to draw lines between "racial" groups. For example, within single-family units there is often a wide spectrum of color evidenced in the various family members: one child can be very black, another very white, and the others all shades in between. No questions are asked, no impropriety presumed, and no consideration for implied ancestry focused upon. However, Latino/a communities do see and perpetuate a social construction of race related to privilege. In contrast to U.S. constructions of race, it is more narrowly defined as a value placed on color, where lighter is generally more positively regarded. Although the recognition of color exists, and one can see stratification of darker individuals at lower social levels and lighter individuals at higher social levels, the glass ceilings of segregation are not as low or as solid as in the United States. There is more room to prove oneself, although admittedly it is more difficult the darker you are. For examples, a full-blooded Indian, Juarez, was elected President of Mexico; a Japanese-Peruvian, Fujimori, was elected President of Perú; and a Black mestizo, Chavez, was elected President of Venezuela.

What happens when the dominant U.S. conceptualizations of race are imposed on Latino/a history and attitudes of race, culture, class, and color? Racial categories used in the United States tend to have clear social demarcations between groups, especially in reference to who is White and who is not. However, traditionally, Latinos/as do not have such clear boundaries between racial groups. So when U.S. categories are imposed on Latinos/as, categorizations are made with very unclear boundaries, leading to much confusion. The implications of this imposition can be found in results from the 2000 U.S. census. Because of the confounding of race and ethnicity, and ignoring the sociopolitical meaning of race and ethnicity, Latinos/as mark "Hispanic" on the one place that inquires about ethnicity. But more than any other group, Latinos/as marked "other" in the race category, despite instructions to "mark that all apply," because the provided list did not apply to them (Wallman, 2000). Many Latino/as do not identify with the U.S. racial categories that are offered.

Although Latinos/as traditionally have little consideration for "race," Latinos/as in the U.S. are treated by the dominant White European-American group as a racial minority group with its concomitant experiences of discrimination. Thus, U.S. Latinos/as experience the realities of racism stemming from the institutionalized conceptualization of race in the United States. The Latino/a resistance to the inclusion of the multiracial discussion stems from a fear of loss of culture, identity, and power, rather than a loss of racial purity. Thus, the Latino/a resistance to acknowledging multiracial individuals and issues is a resistance to acknowledging and accepting U.S. racial categories—categories that do not reflect the Latino/a experience. Similarly, there is the fear that to be counted as multiracial would dilute the visibility of a critical mass of Latinos/as. In addition, although Latinos/as can often identify as "mixed White," as previously discussed, U.S. social definitions have not included "mixed White" as a possibility, because White is only pure. In the United States, Latinos/as have been treated as "non-White," and thus the White option among the provided racial categories is not a viable option for Latinos/as because they are not allowed to identify with the dominant power group of the United States. Although traditionally Latinos/as have identified ethnically as Latino/Hispanic or with their specific nationality, rather than racially, there is a growing movement throughout the Americas to identify as "mestizo" or racially mixed (Amaro & Zambrana, 2000). However, the conceptualization of "mestizaje" or "mix" and the meaning of such, is different in Latin America than in the United States, and it has been suggested that the Latin-American conceptualization will influence the U.S. discussions of Latino/a mixed race (Amaro & Zambrana, 2000; Fernández, 1992).

Asian Americans

Interracial marriage among Asian Americans varies considerably according to the particular ethnic group, gender, and generation (Lee & Yamanaka, 1990). Although some research has found that Japanese Americans (particularly women) marry across race lines more frequently than they marry within (see Kitano et al.'s 1998 review), other ethnic groups' outmarriage rates are considerably lower, such as Vietnamese-American men, who marry interracially about 5.5% of the time (Lee & Yamanaka, 1990). United States-born and more acculturated individuals (e.g., those of later generations) are more likely to marry interracially (Lee & Yamanaka, 1990).

Unlike American Indians and Latino/as, Asian Americans do have a clear history of racial distinction and definition within their own culture. Like White European-American groups, Asian-American groups value the idea of racial purity (Root, 1990, 1998a), and within the cultures of their specific countries of origin a distinction is made between "pure" racial members and those of mixed race (e.g., the history of exclusion within Japan and Vietnam of Amerasian individuals; Root, 1998a; Valverde, 1992). Asian-American families also have strong preferences for marriage within the specific racial and ethnic group (Lee & Yamanaka, 1990). Finally, unlike American Indians and many Latinos/as, although Asian Americans have (and continue to) experience significant discrimination in the United States, they are for the most part not a colonized people within the mainland United States, with the possible exception of Pilipino Americans.[5] They continue to have a clear cultural origin referent (the Asian country of origin—although globalization and "Westernization" have affected these cultures) and are not struggling with reconstruction or integration of a decimated people and culture. Thus, the resistance to including multiracial individuals and issues within the Asian-American ethnic minority in-group is not only an effect of the dominant and imposed race ideology of the dominant White majority, as is the case for American Indians and Latino/as, but also related to the original cultural values.

However, this does not mean that the resistance to including multiracial individuals and issues is unaffected by the dominant ideology and the history of racism and oppression for Asian Americans. Like other minority groups, Asian Americans (particularly first-generation Asian Americans) fear the loss of their culture and values in the face of a more dominant and powerful ideology that actively denigrates or ignores their cultural traditions (Root, 1998a; Uba, 1994). Also like other minority groups, the historical and current legal, institutional, and social racism directed against Asian Americans within the United States leads to a bonding within the group and a suspicion of outsiders. Finally, in some cases multiracial Asian Americans are symbolic of U.S. involvement in foreign affairs that may be contested within the Asian countries and communities (e.g., Vietnam; Root, 1998a; Valverde, 1992).

Thus, the resistance to including multiracial individuals and issues within the Asian-American community is related to the valuing of racial and ethnic purity, as well as to experiences with racism and discrimination. Unlike all other minority groups, multiracial Asian-Americans may need to negotiate extreme exclusion from the Asian American group even if they are culturally knowledgeable and claim a primary Asian identity (Root, 1990, 1998a). In some areas, however, the significant numbers of multiracial Asian Americans are challenging Asian-American communities to re-evaluate their inclusion criteria, leading to a more open dialogue about the drawbacks and benefits of recognizing and including multiracial individuals as Asian American (King & DaCosta, 1996; Root, 1998a).

African Americans

In the U.S. mainland, the race dialogue and multiracial discussion tend to focus primarily on African Americans, as evidenced in the history and continued adherence to the one-drop rule of hypodescent. As a result of being the oppressed (rather than the privileged) group within the dichotomous Black–White dialogue, African-American communities tend to be more aware than the dominant White society of the sociopolitical meaning of race rather than the pseudoscientific construct. As a sociopolitical construct, race is subject to interpretation, and therefore, with which group one chooses to identify carries great importance among African Americans. To be in a mixed relationship or to claim mixed heritage can go against the group's sense of identity and solidarity. Thus, although African-American communities may readily accept a multiracial individual who identifies as African American, to actively identify as multiracial can be seen as a rejection of the African-American community and culture, and lead to rejection from the one group that might otherwise welcome the affiliation (e.g., see *Ebony* Magazine, July 1997, regarding Tiger Woods' identifying with his multiple heritages). Although this is true for all U.S. minority groups, it is particularly true for African Americans, given the African-American history in the United States.

African Americans have come to the United States over time, from many different countries, and by many different means. However, unlike all other groups, the
majority of today's African Americans are descendants of African Americans who
were brought to this country from other lands through slavery (Hines & Boyd-Franklin,
1982), which actively stripped them of their ethnic and national heritages, disallowing
any revitalization or reclaiming of the original and specific ethnic culture from the old
world. What exists now are some cultural ways that have survived and adapted to the
U.S. context, as well as new ways that were created for the new context. Given the
extreme oppression of slavery, time, and geographical distance from the old world, the
primary definitions of race and attitudes about mixing are greatly shaped by an internalization of and/or reaction to the dominant White culture's definitions of race and
attitudes toward mixing, and the related imposed social position. As a result of the
cultural stripping, and the dominant U.S. system of categorization, including laws of
hypodescent, race has become the primary construct among the majority of African
Americans, confounding race and ethnicity (Helms & Cook, 1999). This is contrary to
the experience in the Latino/a and Asian-American communities where there is an
ongoing revitalization of the culture from the homelands, and American Indians who
still carry echoes from their land and communities.

It is difficult to talk about African-American community's position on race without discussing the social-historical-political position within the dominant U.S. society, beginning with slavery, and continuing through the various mutations of societal
discrimination. Black slave women were often raped by White men, perhaps partly in
an active attempt to "replenish their slave 'stock'" (Helms & Cook, 1999, p. 49),
because children were legally accorded the status of their mothers (in direct violation
of English law according children the status of their fathers; Helms & Cook, 1999).
The legal and personal rejection of multiracial children by their White fathers, soon
institutionalized in the dominant U.S. one-drop exclusion rule, led the African American community to use the one-drop rule as an *inclusion* criteria for acceptance to the
African-American community (Daniel, 1992; Shipler, 1997). If a child has any Black
heritage, the child is Black, in keeping with the historical cultural reliance on the
kinship network (Hines & Boyd-Franklin, 1982). To acknowledge the child as mixed
would be to remember the source of the mixing. Memory is long, and for many African Americans today, Black–White unions and offspring can be a reminder of the
historical oppressions of slavery, rape, women being forced to bear the children of
White men, and Black men being lynched for looking at White women. Skin color
continues to serve as an immediate visual marker that the dominant White society sees
to label one as Black (see previous discussion regarding historical counting of African
Americans in the U.S. census), and as such, skin color carries great importance (Hines
& Boyd-Franklin, 1982), with often conflicted and divisive meaning for African Americans. Light skin is acknowledged to originate from White heritage, either from times
of slavery or more recently, and carries historical and contemporary social privileges
that are both desired and resented. Dark skin is more stigmatizing, but also represents
deeper cultural roots. Sociopolitical context can dictate whether light or dark skin is
desirable with African-American communities. The conflicted and shifting meaning

of skin tone may be explained by the Triple Quandry, where African Americans need to simultaneously negotiate three cultural frameworks, mainstream, African-American, and minority status (Boykin, 1982, 1985). It is because of the primary social role of race that skin color matters, and it is the presence of racial mixture in context of a racist society that makes for the conflicted meanings of skin color (Shipler, 1997).

Given the generally accepted understanding of the sociopolitical meaning of race and the experiences of racism, there is great importance on "proving" one's Blackness by showing group solidarity through ones actions and ideologies, in order to re-claim social power. Racial pride has been a means of combating pervasive racism. To claim one's White heritage can be experienced as claiming the heritage of the oppressor, and of giving up power (Daniel, 1992). The resistance to including multiracial issues in order to maintain group solidarity was reflected in many Black organizations opposing the inclusion of a "biracial" box in the 1994 census (Shipler, 1997), and asserting pressures to mark only one box in the 2000 U.S. census, arguing that ". . . it would exacerbate the undercounting of Blacks, diluting their perceived power in politics and the marketplace. Since society sees the vast majority of Black-White people as simply 'Black,' the argument holds, they should be tallied as such; otherwise, the figures will distort a social reality" (Shipler, 1997, p. 145). Therefore, the resistance to the inclusion of the multiracial discussion is a form of political and social resistance to race and power.

MULTICULTURAL PSYCHOLOGY AND THE RESISTANCE TO THE MULTIRACIAL DISCUSSION

Psychology as a science has learned the importance of measurement and categorization in order to perform "objective" scientific methodologies. Similarly to the U.S. census, which has also been purported to be an "objective" entity, the identification of categories to be considered within the field of psychology has been influenced by social-historical-political forces. The racial/ethnic groups that have traditionally been considered in multicultural psychology are the same as those used in the U.S. census— mark one box only. And like the U.S. government, psychology has been reactive to society's experiences rather than proactive in the identification and definition of the chosen categories. For example it has only been relatively recently, following the civil rights revolution of the 1960s and 1970s, that the field has started theorizing, analyzing, or considering unique developmental and clinical issues by gender and/or race/ethnicity. These changes occurred only after there was a critical mass of researchers and clinicians representative of these groups (e.g., Carol Gilligan, Joe White, Martha Bernal; National Multicultural Conference and Summit [NCMS], 1999; NMCS II, 2001).

The reasons for resistances to including mixed race are similar to those that were at the root of resistances to including gender and race/ethnicity in the 1970s—lack of awareness and discussion, assumptions that the issues are the same as with other groups, and fears that to include that population would confound empirical data. An additional resistance for the inclusion of mixed race groups is that, unlike gender and the more "obvious" races, mixed-race individuals are difficult to identify and label on face value. Given that there is resistance to the recognition and inclusion of multiracial individuals and issues within minority groups, as well as within the dominant group, the creation of a recognized "critical mass" and the building of allies becomes even more difficult.

Multicultural psychology specifically may also resist the recognition and inclusion of multiracial individuals and issues because it is itself still fighting for recognition and full acceptance. Multicultural issues are still relatively marginalized within psychology as a whole, as evidenced by the fact that of the 21,383 articles in APA published and APA division-published journals in the last 5 years, only 1180 (5%) focused on issues related to racial/ethnic groups.[6] Just as specific minority groups may resist recognition of multiracial individuals because of fear of loss of identity or power, the field of multicultural psychology may resist this inclusion for similar reasons. In addition, recognition and exploration of multiracial issues quickly lead to a more general consideration of the social construction of race, which leads to complex contextualized constructs that do not lend themselves particularly well to traditional methodologies, as they cannot be easily defined and quantified, which could further marginalize multicultural psychology. This also leads to the consideration of the need for and benefits of deconstructing race completely. Unfortunately, we are not yet ready as a field or a society to fully deconstruct race because we are far too rooted in the soil of racism; therefore, deconstructing race would be too easily used to denigrate or dismiss the effects of racial inequalities, which is likely another reason for resisting recognition of multiracial issues.

We hope and expect that, similar to previous resistances, the field of psychology (and particularly the area of multicultural psychology) will begin to loosen its resistances with increased exposure and information. This will happen as the mixed-race population continues to grow within the ranks of psychology, when it is repeatedly demonstrated that the psychology of mixed race people is not necessarily the same as for other groups already considered, when the existence of the resistance is named and its foundations understood, and when the negative effects of the resistance are more clearly understood and accepted. The goals of this chapter are to contribute to decreasing this resistance, particularly through addressing the latter two issues. We have thus far named the resistance and explored the social-historical-political contexts in which it is founded. The final section considers some of the effects of the resistance.

THE EFFECTS OF THE RESISTANCE

The racial/ethnic identity literature is one example of an area of multicultural psychology that still mostly does not address or incorporate the experience of people with multiple heritages. The majority of racial/ethnic identity models were developed to describe the experience of monoracial individuals. Although the models vary in the specific description of stages, most models (see Helms & Cook, 1999; Sue & Sue, 1999; and Wehrly, 1995, for overviews and summaries) propose a series of stages or statuses. These models are usually divided into models for People of Color and models for White people. Research and theory addressing multiracial issues and experiences have identified and discussed several problematic aspects of these approaches, including: (a) the problematic assumption of a single achieved identity status, rather than multiple identities experienced sequentially or simultaneously that individuals may negotiate developmentally and/or contextually (Root, 1990; Suyemoto, 2000); (b) the problematic assumption that individuals can reject the dominant White European culture or White European identification without rejecting a part of themselves or their families (Root, 1990, 1997; Suyemoto, 2001); (c) the problematic assumption of acceptance by the racial/ethnic minority group during the immersion/emersion stage (Root, 1998a, b); and (d) the problematic assumption that racial identity and ethnic identity are in accord, or are the same thing; that is, that there is a connection between race and culture, between White racial privilege and European cultural identification. This conceptualization does not allow for the possibility of European-American ethnic identification without White race, as in the case of someone who is a visible minority but identifies culturally as European-American (which may have ethnic privilege but not racial privilege) *or* of White racial privilege without European ethnic identification and privilege, as in the case of someone who looks White but identifies culturally with a minority or oppressed group.

These criticisms have been discussed explicitly in the context of the identity development experiences of multiracial people (Root, 1990, 1997, 1998a, b), and research into the identity development of multiracial individuals specifically attends to these issues, often by using one of the multiracial-specific models for identity development (e.g., Kich, 1992; Poston, 1990; Root, 1990) or developing alternative models or interpretations (e.g., Root, 1998b; Wijeyesinghe, 2001). However, these critiques point to difficulties in the monoracial models themselves that not may not only affect the application of these models to multiracial individuals but also may have implications for monoracial or seemingly monoracial people as well. And the critiques point to the fact that conceptualization of race and ethnicity is categorical, which should move us to examine the assumptions within that approach. Yet this is rarely the case. Instead, multiracial racial/ethnic identity development models and critiques continue to be separated and distinguished from monoracial identity development in chapters and journal articles, where it is discussed at all.[7]

The separation of multiracial issues within multicultural applied psychology is not limited to racial and ethnic identity development; in most explorations related to race and ethnicity, monoracial categories and approaches are utilized. Although there may be positive consequences of separating the experience of multiracial individuals from monoracial individuals (e.g., the unique experiences of multiracial individuals are explored and highlighted), this continued separation also reflects the resistance to the recognition and inclusion of multiracial issues and has the following negative effects.

First, it maintains the mythical distinction between monoracial and multiracial, continuing the marginalization of multiracial individuals, both individually within their identified or chosen in-group(s), and generally within the field of applied psychology.

On the individual level, this marginalization supports the idea that multiracial individuals are not really part of their own referent racial/ethnic group(s), especially if they assert or explore a multiracial identity (Nakashima, 1992). This has detrimental effects on both monoracial and multiracial individuals. Monoracial individuals are allowed to maintain rigid in-group definitions that may contribute to prejudice and/or racism and may re-enact the oppression they may be trying to undo. Multiracial individuals must address the negative effects of this marginalization. If we treat multiracial people as wholly different and separate in our thinking and research, then we should not be surprised when we find that those multiracial individuals who do have difficulty with racial/ethnic identity development attribute it to the social construction of the categories of race and the difficult experiences associated with social exclusion, the feeling of difference, and the lack of social acceptance or in-group belonging (Gibbs & Hines, 1992; Hershel, 1995). Nor should we be surprised that the normative (i.e., statistically usual) experience of racial/ethnic identity development in multiracial individuals often can be characterized by the feeling of difference and a struggle for social acceptance and belonging (Kich, 1992).

On the general level, continuing the separation (and, frequently, the resulting marginalization) of multiracial issues in multicultural psychology allows us to maintain racial boundaries and the categorical approach, contributing to the maintenance of race as a valid construct. This means that race is treated as something that affects people (a relatively one-way equation) and so we continue to explore "racial differences." This can be contrasted to the consideration of how people (all people, both those in the dominant White European-American group and those in the various minority groups) actively contribute to the construction of race. This latter approach enables a greater consideration of the interaction between the individual and the social group and context. Using identity again as an example, both identity and acculturation were foci within sociology and anthropology long before they were adopted into psychology's frame. Psychology has tended to focus almost exclusively on the individual's process, whereas sociology and anthropology focus primarily on the social process. We suggest that there needs to be more of a blending between the two processes. Including multiracial issues encourages this blending through breaking down the categorical approach, enabling questions such as: (a) Where are the boundaries between races and who gets to define them? (b) Who belongs and who does not, and who gets to decide? (c) What affects the boundaries and belonging criteria and how have these changed with time? (d) How do all of these questions and answers affect individuals' mental health in specific contexts? These questions then lead to the overarching philosophical question: How is race constructed, coconstructed, and reconstructed, by whom, and for what purpose? Although the social reality of racism may necessitate the exploration of racial differences and experiences related to the construct of race, the inclusion of multiracial issues may encourage us to continually remind ourselves that race is a construct in the service of racism.

Second, the continued separation of multiracial from monoracial suggests that multiracial individuals' are more similar to each other, across specific racial/ethnic groups, than to the primary referent group(s). This implies that the particular aspects of one's specific racial/ethnic heritage(s) are somehow less salient for multiracial individuals than for monoracial individuals, who are most frequently considered in terms of their specific racial/ethnic group, rather than as monoracial People of Color or monoracial White people. We agree that meanings of race, ethnicity, and many other issues vary considerably for different racial/ethnic groups because of different historical, cultural, and current social constructions of the meaning of race and ethnicity for these groups. Given this assumption, the separation of multiracial individuals from their specific referent group(s) seems to imply that these individuals would not be similarly affected by the particular historical, cultural, and current meanings of the specific racial/ethnic in-group(s). Our analysis above also indicates that the meaning of being multiracial may vary from group to group, leading to an even stronger argument for including multiracial issues within their specific referent group. The separation of multiracial individuals and issues from their specific racial and ethnic referents also has implications on both the individual and general levels.

On the individual level, the continued separation of multiracial from monoracial is not in agreement with many multiracial individuals' own experiences and identification. Although multiracial individuals may not want to choose only one identity at all (Stephan, 1992; Suyemoto, 2000), they may choose a specific racial/ethnic in-group over a cross-race/ethnicity multiracial identity or identify more strongly with single or multiple specific racial/ethnic in-groups rather than a mixed multiracial group (Suyemoto, 2000). And even if they do choose a multiracial identity label, this does not necessarily mean that they see themselves as separate from their multiple racial/ ethnic referent groups. Choices for identity should be open to the individuals themselves, with the possibility of multiple simultaneous or contextual choices available (Root, 1990). Our models and research should not *inherently* discourage or encourage certain types of identification.

On the more general level within the field, separating multiracial individuals and issues from their specific cultural and racial referent groups contributes to the confounding of race and ethnicity. This confound is problematic within all areas of multicultural psychology and has led more recently to the consideration of specific ethnic groups' experiences, a greater emphasis on culture, and a call for within group designs, rather than comparative approaches. Separating multiracial individuals from their racial/ethnic referent groups suggests that the most important issue is *racial* purity, and that individuals share experiences primarily because of race and, perhaps, racism. Yet most of the measures and aspects of racial/ethnic identity, for example, have more to do with shared *ethnic* experiences (Phinney, 1990). Including multiracial issues and individuals within the consideration of specific "racial" groups acknowledges the importance of this shared ethnicity and enables questions that explore the separation of race and ethnicity by considering how the racial experiences of multiracial individuals may be similar to as well as different from the ethnic experiences of these same individuals and the racial and ethnic experiences of monoracial individuals within the group.

LOOKING TO THE FUTURE

The resistance to the recognition and inclusion of multiracial individuals and issues *is* decreasing and will likely continue to do so as the multiracial population in the U.S. increases. Waters (2000) states: "By the year 2050, under medium assumptions of immigration and intermarriage, 21% of the population will be of multiple ancestry. Asians and Hispanics will be the most mixed, at 35% and 45% multiple ancestry, respectively" (p. 1736). This shift will inevitably affect our thinking about race and ethnicity, about racial and ethnic groups and belonging. There is already evidence that the shift is occurring at the general social level, indicating a lowering of the resistances of the dialogue. This shift can be seen in the 2000 U.S. census, high school records, high school and university and community groups, university courses, and chapters in books such as this one. An example of how the dialogue is changing, given the general population changes, is reflected in the fact that Berkeley High School (Berkeley, California) has been including a "multiracial" category on school forms for well over a decade. This is reflective of the local community, and a shift away from the need to categorize in a simple, prescribed manner.

Psychology, and especially applied and multicultural psychology, should be breaking the path in decreasing the resistance to inclusion and addressing the needs of multiracial individuals, not only as an ethical duty to our clients (who will be very different in the coming decades—will we be prepared?), but also because we have the potential to be leaders in shifting detrimental and oppressive views within the larger social context, rather than followers in shifts that take place only under great duress.

Resistance to including multiracial individuals and issues affects both multiracial and monoracial individuals and groups. It affects mental health and general conceptualizations that contribute to our psychological understanding of groups and individuals. This resistance is clearly related to the history of the construct of race and categorization, both for the dominant White European-American groups, and for the racial and ethnic minority groups. Given that we are, as a field and as a society, not yet developmentally ready to dispense with the concept of race altogether—or even with the categorical approach to that concept—there may be many benefits to separating the multiracial experience at times and considering the unique perspectives of both monoracial and multiracial individuals. However, it is clear that this considered separation is different from resistance to inclusion or marginalization.

The resistance to the recognition and inclusion of multiracial issues in psychology has contributed to a relative lack of literature exploring these experiences. Racial and ethnic identity development is likely the area with the most inclusion, and even there the research is relatively constrained and the issues continue to be separated as discussed. As a field, we need to recognize our resistance and explicitly encourage research and theory, including multiracial experiences. We propose that: (a) researchers using racial and ethnic categories or exploring race and ethnicity acknowledge the use and limitations of a monoracial approach; (b) we reconsider our language regarding race and ethnicity; (c) as a field, psychology needs to consider its approach to race and acknowledge the categorical ideology that has informed our ideologies thus far;

(d) psychology and psychologists consider a "both/and" approach, considering the unique experiences of monoracial and multiracial individuals (acknowledging and labeling *both* groups as such, rather than constructing multiracial individuals as deviant) while incorporating monoracial *and* multiracial experiences into explorations of race and ethnicity; and (e) psychology considers the sociohistorical context of the construction of race and race categories, including an awareness of how our own constructs and methodologies contribute to that construction. These changes need to affect counseling and therapy as well as research, as we have historically pathologized the multiracial "condition." We have little to no preparation to address the real issues in the real and complex contexts in which they exist.

The goal of this chapter is to continue the process that has been bravely started by others (e.g., Root, 1992, 1996, 1998b). Because this is still a fledgling area of study, and the greatest diversity occurs in the student body rather than the faculty ranks, much of the work to date has been in the form of dissertations. Unlike some other fields, such as medicine or public health, there has been little pressure or perceived need for psychology to respond to, or even be aware of some of the changes that are occurring on a societal level in regard to mixed race populations. Psychology is an "academic" discipline, whereas medicine and public health are "applied" or "professional" disciplines. As such, the applied/professional disciplines are much more directly involved with communities, whereas academic disciplines tend to be more involved in theorizing and laboratory research. Applied/professional disciplines are directly subject to the pressures of advocacy groups demanding consideration of their needs and experiences. Applied and professional disciplines are also dependent on data produced by other entities that are also subject to direct societal pressures, such as the U.S. census data. Traditionalists may argue that psychology's distance from these pressures protects the scientific purity or objectivity, despite the growing acceptance that it is not possible for science to be objective. The cost of psychology's distance from communities is the possibly decreased relevance of its work to society's populations, in other words, low validity and generalizability. As part of the field of psychology, we urge our field to recognize and address the resistances to the inclusion of multiracial issues. We offer this chapter as an invitation to begin the dialogue.

END NOTES

1. For example, American Indian histories of extermination, broken treaties, and confusion regarding extension of U.S. citizenship and rights; history of exclusionary immigration policies toward Asian immigrants; the Japanese-American concentration camps during World War II; initial reluctance/refusal to recognize Amerasian children of U.S. service men; Manifest Destiny and the seizing of American Indian and Mexican lands; U.S. colonization of Puerto Rico; slavery and Jim Crow laws (see Takaki, 1993).
2. Searching PsychInfo through 1998 restricted to journals listed as APA publications or listed specifically by APA division publications on the APA website. Only two of these articles actually use the PsychInfo Thesaurus term "interracial offspring" as a major descriptor. The remaining 26 have one of the following terms in their title, abstract, or descriptors: multiracial, biracial, interracial, mixed race, interracial offspring. Therefore, this 28 is likely

an *overestimation*, because it likely includes articles written about interracial marriage or relationships, as a result or including "interracial" in the search criteria.

3. The authors would like to thank Claudia Fox Tree-McGrath for the resources and guidance she provided that aided in this section.

4. Group naming language is always problematic. Many of the sources cited here use the terminology "Indian," although this term may be less preferred by many who may protest that it reflects more of the European-American history of naming. Native Americans is another alternative, although this is problematic because of considerations that anyone who is born in the United States is native to this country. Indigenous peoples or First Nation peoples are other alternatives, although very infrequently used within the sources cited. We chose American Indians as a general term, because most of our sources (both written and interpersonal) seem to prefer that term. We do, however, recognize the problematic nature of any pan-group label and the general issues of labeling for many of the groups we are discussing.

5. Although people traditionally associated East Asians with the term "Asian," more recently the term "Asian" has been applied to South Asians, including Indians, Pakistanis, and Bangladeshis, among others, because of sociopolitical factors and geographic accuracy. Moreover, the terms "Asian/Pacific Islanders" and "Asian/Pacific Americans" have been more widely used. These terms include individuals from the Macronesian, Micronesian, and Melanesian Islands, such as Maylasians, Pilipinos, Tahitians, and Guamanians, among others, as part of the "Asian racial" group. We use the term Asian American here to signify the constructed "racial" group.

6. Only 272 articles listed one of the thesaurus terms in the major descriptor field ("American Indians," "Hispanics," "Asians," "Blacks," "interracial offspring," "racial and ethnic group," or "minority group"). The remaining 908 included thesaurus and nonthesaurus terms (e.g., Native American, Latino/a, Asian American, African American) in title, abstract, keywords, or descriptors.

7. Two examples of leading texts in the field of multicultural psychology are Ponterotto, Casas, Suzuki, and Alexander's first edition (1995) of the *Handbook of Multicultural Counseling*, where there are separate chapters on each of the five major racial/ethnic groups and a separate chapter on multiracial racial/ethnic identity development; and Sue and Sue's third edition (1999) of *Counseling the Culturally Different*, where there is minimal mention of multiracial individuals or issues within each of the chapters addressing the four major VREG (visible racial and ethnic groups) or within the two chapters on identity development, and no separate chapter. Another example would be this book, where the resistance to multiracial issues is explored in one chapter and mental health issues related to multiracial populations in another—both separated from "monoracial" minority groups and issues.

REFERENCES

Amaro, H., & Zambrana, R. E. (2000). Criollo, Mestizo, Mulatto, LatiNegro, Indígena, White, or Black? The US Hispanic/Latino population and multiple responses in the 2000 census. *American Journal of Public Health, 90,* 1724–1727.

Atkinson, D. R., Morten, G., & Sue, D. W. (Eds.). (1998). *Counseling American minorities* (5th ed.). New York: McGraw-Hill.

Boykin, A. W. (1982). Triple Quandary. Unpublished manuscript, Howard University, Washington, DC.

Boykin, A. W. (1985). The triple quandary and the schooling of Afro-American children. In U. Neisser (Ed.), *The school achievement of minority children* (pp. 57–92). Hillsdale, NJ: Lawrenece Erlbaum.

Bradshaw, C. K. (1992). Beauty and the beast: On racial ambiguity. In M. P. P. Root (Ed.), *Racially mixed people in America* (pp. 77–90). Newbury Park, CA: Sage.

Daniel, G. R. (1992). Passers and pluralists: Subverting the racial divide. In M. P. P. Root (Ed.), *Racially mixed people in America* (pp. 91–107). Newbury Park, CA: Sage.

Fernández, C. A. (1992). La raza and the melting pot: A comparative look at multiethnicity. In M. P. P. Root (Ed.), *Racially mixed people in America* (pp. 126–143). Newbury Park, CA: Sage.

Fry, L. (1999). Ethnicity. In J. S. Mio, J. E. Trimble, P. Arredondo, H. E. Cheatham, & D. Sue (Eds.), *Key words in multicultural interventions: A dictionary* (p. 110). Westport, CT: Greenwood.

Gibbs, J. T., & Hines, A. M. (1992). Negotiating ethnic identity: Issues for Black-White biracial adolescents. In M. P. P. Root (Ed.), *Racially mixed people in America* (pp. 223–238). Newbury Park, CA: Sage.

Goodman, A. H. (2000). Why genes don't count (for racial differences in health). *American Journal of Public Health, 90,* 1699–1702.

Greenberg, D. (1999). *White weddings: The incredible staying power of the laws against interracial marriage* [On-line serial]. Available: http://slate.msn.com/HistoryLesson/99-06-14/HistoryLesson.asp#Bio [2001, July 15].

Helms, J. E., & Cook, D. A. (1999). *Using race and culture in counseling and psychotherapy.* Boston: Allyn and Bacon.

Hershel, H. J. (1995). Therapeutic perspectives on biracial identity formation and internalized oppression. In N. Zack (Ed.), *American mixed race: The culture of microdiversity* (pp. 169–181). Lanham, MD: Rowman & Littlefield.

Hines, P. M., & Boyd-Franklin, N. (1982). Black families. In M. McGoldrick, J. K. Pearce, & J. Giordano (Eds.), *Ethnicity and family therapy* (pp. 84–107). New York: Guilford.

Jaimes, M. A. (1995). Some kind of Indian: On race, eugenics, and mixed-bloods. In N. Zack (Ed.), *American mixed race: The culture of microdiversity* (pp. 133–153). Lanham, MD: Rowman & Littlefield.

Kich, G. (1992). The developmental process of asserting a biracial, bicultural identity. In M. P. P. Root (Ed.), *Racially mixed people in America* (pp. 304–321). Newbury Park, CA: Sage.

King, J. C. (1981). *The biology of race.* Berkeley: University of California Press.

King, R. C., & DaCosta, K. M. (1996). Changing face, changing race: The remaking of race in the Japanese American and African American communities. In M. P. P. Root (Ed.), *The multiracial experience: Racial borders as the new frontier* (pp. 227–244). Thousand Oaks, CA: Sage.

Kitano, H. H. L., Fujino, D. C., & Sato, J. T. (1998). Interracial marriages: Where are the Asian Americans and where are they going. In L. C. Lee & N. W. S. Zane (Eds.), *Handbook of Asian American psychology* (pp. 233–260). Thousand Oaks, CA: Sage.

Kitzinger, C. (1995). Social constructionism: Implications for lesbian and gay psychology. In A. R. D'Augelli & C. J. Patterson (Eds.), *Lesbian, gay, and bisexual identities over the lifespan: Psychological perspectives* (pp. 137–161). New York: Oxford University Press.

Krieger, N. (2000). Counting accountably: Implications of the new approaches to classifying race/ethnicity in the 2000 census. *American Journal of Public Health, 90,* 1687–1689.

Lee, S. M., & Yamanaka, K. (1990). Patterns of Asian American intermarriage and marital assimilation. *Journal of Comparative Family Studies, 21,* 287–305.

McIntosh, P. (1997). White privilege: Unpacking the invisible knapsack. In V. Cyrus (Ed.), *Experiencing race, class, and gender in the United States* (2nd ed., pp. 194–197). Mountain View, CA: Mayfield.

Mihesuah, D. A. (1996). *American Indian stereotypes and realities.* Atlanta: Clarity Press.

Nagel, J. (1997). *American Indian ethnic renewal: Red power and the resurgence of identity and culture.* New York: Oxford University Press.

Nakashima, C. L. (1992). An invisible monster: The creation and denial of mixed-race people in America. In M. P. P. Root (Ed.), *Racially mixed people in America* (pp. 162–178). Newbury Park, CA: Sage.

National Multicultural Conference and Summit. (1999, January). Newport Beach, CA.

National Multicultural Conference and Summit II. (2001, January). Santa Barbara, CA.

Nobles, M. (2000). History counts: A comparative analysis of racial/color categorizations in US and Brazilian censuses. *American Journal of Public Health, 90*, 1738–1745.

O'Nell, T. D. (1996). *Disciplined hearts: History, identity, and depression in an American Indian community.* Berkeley, CA: University of California Press.

Omi, M., & Winant, H. (1994). *Racial formation in the United States* (2nd ed.). New York: Routledge.

Phinney, J. S. (1990). Ethnic identity in adolescents and adults: A review of literature. *Psychological Bulletin, 108*, 499–514.

Pinderhughes, E. (1989). *Understanding race, ethnicity and power: The key to efficacy in clinical practice.* New York: The Free Press.

Ponterotto, J. G., Casas, J. M., Suzuki, L. A., & Alexander, C. M. (Eds.). (1995). *Handbook of multicultural counseling.* Thousand Oaks, CA: Sage.

Poston, W. S. C. (1990). The biracial identity development model: A needed addition. *Journal of Counseling and Development, 69*, 152–155.

Root, M. P. P. (1990). Resolving "other" status: Identity development of biracial individuals. *Women and Therapy, 9*, 185–205.

Root, M. P. P. (Ed.). (1992). *Racially mixed people in America.* Newbury Park, CA: Sage.

Root, M. P. P. (Ed.). (1996). *The multiracial experience.* Thousand Oaks, CA: Sage.

Root, M. P. P. (1997). Multiracial Asians: Models of ethnic identity. *Amerasian Journal, 23*, 29–41.

Root, M. P. P. (1998a). Multiracial Americans: Changing the face of Asian America. In L. C. Lee & N. W. S. Zane (Eds.), *Handbook of Asian American Psychology* (pp. 261–287). Thousand Oaks, CA: Sage.

Root, M. P. P. (1998b). Reconstructing race, rethinking ethnicity. In A. S. Bellack & M. Hersen (Eds.), *Comprehensive clinical psychology* (pp. 141–160). New York: Pergamon.

Sengupta, S. (2000a, November 12, 2000). Marry at will. *New York Times*, Section 4, p. 2.

Sengupta, S. (2000b, November 5, 2000). The color of love: Removing a relic of the Old South. *New York Times*, Section 4, p. 5.

Shipler, D. K. (1997). *A country of strangers: Blacks and Whites in America.* New York: Alfred A. Knopf.

Spickard, P. R. (1992). The illogic of American racial categories. In M. P. P. Root (Ed.), *Racially mixed people in America* (pp. 12–23). Newbury Park, CA: Sage.

Stephan, C. W. (1992). Mixed-heritage individuals: Ethnic identity and trait characteristics. In M. P. P. Root (Ed.), *Racially mixed people in America* (pp. 50–63). Newbury Park, CA: Sage.

Sue, D. W., & Sue, D. (1999). *Counseling the culturally different: Theory and practice.* (3rd ed.). New York: Wiley & Sons.

Suyemoto, K. (2000). Self-identification and self-reported effects of multiracial Japanese Americans. Poster presented at the International Congress of Psychology, Stockholm, Sweden.

Suyemoto, K. L. (2002). Constructing identities: A feminist, culturally contextualized alternative to "personality." In M. Ballou & L. S. Brown (Eds.), *Rethinking mental health and disorders: Feminist perspectives* (pp. 71–98). New York: Guilford.

Takaki, R. (1993). *A different mirror: A history of multicultural America.* Boston: Little, Brown.

Uba, L. (1994). *Asian Americans: Personality patterns, identity, and mental health.* New York: Guilford.

United States Bureau of the Census. (1989). *200 years of census-taking: Population and housing questions, 1790–1990.* Washington, DC: US Bureau of the Census.

United States Bureau of the Census. (1999, January 7). *Interracial married couples: 1960 to present*. Available: http://www.census.gov/population/socdemo/ms-la/tabms-3.txt [October 30, 2000].

Valverde, K. C. (1992). From dust to gold: The Vietnamese Amerasian experience. In M. P. P. Root (Ed.), *Racially mixed people in America* (pp. 144–161). Newbury Park, CA: Sage.

Wallman, K. (November, 2000). *Recognizing diversity in our nation's population: Revisions to the federal standards for data on race and ethnicity.* Paper presented at the 128th Annual Meeting of the American Public Health Association, Boston, MA.

Waters, M. D. (2000). Immigration, intermarriage, and the challenges of measuring racial/ethnic identities. *American Journal of Public Health, 90*, 1735–1737.

Wehrly, B. (1995). *Pathways to multicultural counseling competency*. Pacific Grove, CA: Brooks/Cole.

Wehrly, B. (1996). *Counseling interracial individuals and families*. Alexandria, VA: American Counseling Association.

Wehrly, B., Kenney, K. R., & Kenney, M. E. (1999). *Counseling multiracial families*. Thousand Oaks, CA: Sage.

Wijeyesinghe, C. L. (2001). Racial identity in multiracial people: An alternative paradigm. In C. L. Wijeyesinghe & B. W. Jackson, III (Eds.), *New perspectives on racial identity development: A theoretical and practical anthology* (pp. 129–152). New York: New York University Press.

Young, L. W., Jr. (1999). Race. In J. S. Mio, J. E. Trimble, P. Arredondo, H. E. Cheatham, & D. Sue (Eds.), *Key words in multicultural interventions: A dictionary* (p. 219). Westport, CT: Greenwood.

Zack, N. (Ed.). (1995). *American mixed race*. Lanham, MD: Rowman & Littlefield.

CHAPTER 5

Manifestations of Resistance to Diversity and Multiculturalism in Organizations

PATRICIA ARREDONDO

SITUATION #1

The University of Higher Learning (UHL) was picketed by a coalition of students and faculty, challenging the administration's failure to appoint a senior Scholar of Color to a deanship. Over the years, UHL had touted its strategy, *Talented Scholars of Color,* a recruitment and retention program for attracting junior and senior Faculty of Color. After some early success, the university had recently seen its Faculty of Color lured away to other institutions. Among reasons cited for leaving were: lack of mentorship, second-class status, the gap between word and deed with respect to UHL's diversity agenda, and excessive expectations for these faculty to be spokespersons for the university's underrepresented students. In short, faculty reported feeling devalued for their accomplishments as academics and researchers, stating that their colleagues and administrators saw them only as Affirmative Action hires.

At a loss for how to proceed, and mindful of the negative press brought to the university by the picketing behavior, the administration decided to offer a senior Scholar of Color a special appointment to the President's office. The objective was to have this individual serve as an advisor to the president and provost regarding the crisis at hand, and to develop strategies to keep other Faculty of Color from leaving. When he declined the appointment, the provost declared that the university's diversity initiative would never advance if Faculty of Color did not assume "their share of the responsibility. This has to be a two-way street."

SITUATION #2

Andrea felt fortunate when she was selected for her first-choice APA-internship site in the greater Boston area. She traveled from a midwest university known for its multicultural and diversity emphasis. In fact, she had field experiences with ethnic and linguistic minority clients through practicum assignments; her program had a two-semester multicultural requirement; and her advisor was an openly gay man. Andrea was also active in the student chapters of various professional organizations, eager to learn about how these sociopolitical systems operated.

Though she had only been to Boston for national conferences, Andrea knew of Boston's reputation as a liberal, education-oriented city, and expected the same at her internship. Among the first things she noticed was the lack of evidence of multiculturalism in the agency setting. Although the clinic had many Latino clients, she noticed that no one at the reception desk spoke Spanish, there was no bilingual signage nor literature describing the agency's services, only English-language parent's magazines were in the waiting area, all staff were "traditional and White" with the exception of two African-American social workers and a White lesbian counselor, and there were no evening hours.

Andrea also noticed the absence of certain items on the clinic's intake forms, such as years in the United States, ethnic group affiliation, contact with extended family, and language preference. When she inquired about these items, she was told that therapists could gather that information informally. When Andrea introduced such data into case presentations, she was often told that her clients had real issues and that there was not time to look at the "soft stuff" regarding family and years in the United States. Discouraged, Andrea wondered about her options to introduce multicultural competencies to the agency. "They really need some guidelines," she lamented, "there seems to be a denial that these cultural and linguistic differences exist."

SITUATION #3

A diversity education workshop was introduced to the faculty of a large urban institution. Although the consultants/facilitators had advised against mandatory attendance, the administration decided it needed to send a message to everyone. Several conditions did not occur, leading to overt resistance by some faculty. First, the senior administration did not schedule a session for itself, and second, the workshop was to take place between semesters, a time deemed private by most faculty. Attendance was poor, leading to a cancellation of the remaining sessions.

BACKGROUND

Organizational resistance to multiculturalism and diversity comes in many forms (Arredondo, 1996; Carter, 2000; Ridley, 1995). As the preceding situations describe, resistance is communicated overtly and covertly, through verbal and nonverbal behavior, through organizational practices, and by individuals. In an organization, these resistant behaviors manifest in structural forms. An example is drawn from Situation #2. Even though Andrea was in an agency serving linguistic minorities and immigrants, they did not have mechanisms in place to address the particular language and cultural needs of these clients.

In her study of hospitals serving acute patient populations, primarily ethnic minorities, Garcia-Caban (2001) describes differences among institutions that have adapted their systems to be more responsive to cultural diversity and those who have not. She found that leadership and administration prepared in cultural competency related to systems change, location of the hospitals, and the payer's regulations were motivating factors for many structural adaptations that were made. Ultimately, these changes contributed to more culturally competent care.

Resistance may come from different sources, ranging from designated leaders, perceived "like-minded" colleagues, identifiable foes, and individuals often perceived as "powerless." In my study of multiple organizations with diversity initiatives, I found that it was not unusual for nonmanagement personnel or Participants of Color and other underrepresented groups to be the most critical of a diversity initiative. Through data acquired primarily in focus groups, I learned that this occurs for several reasons: (a) White nonmanagement personnel believe that preferential treatment may go to ethnic minorities. (b) Ethnic minorities believe they are undervalued and that a diversity initiative is more lip service. (c) Underrepresented groups—including gays, lesbians, and persons with disabilities—are critical because they see the diversity focus primarily for women and ethnic minorities. (d) In college environments, students, particularly Students of Color, generally see themselves as a commodity and actually more versed in issues of diversity than their professors and administration. The mindset of any individual or groups can lead to opposition to a diversity initiative or training, in spite of the good intentions organizational leadership may be vocalizing.

The increased attention to diversity initiatives in organizations, including colleges and universities, healthcare organizations, mental health agencies (American Council on Education, 2000; Arredondo, in press; Carter, 2000) and other settings in the private sector where counselors and psychologists may be employed, introduces many opportunities for individuals and organizations. First, for counselors and psychologists schooled in programs based on multicultural and diversity competencies (Arredondo, 1996; Arredondo et al., 1996; Pope-Davis & Coleman, 1997), there may be roles to assume as internal or external consultants to an organizational diversity or cultural competency process. Our skill sets grounded in clinical practice, assessment strategies, and developmental psychology theories are also assets.

For organizations and institutions, there is an opportunity as well as a mandate to attend to diversity, multiculturalism, and cultural competency. This is motivated by: national demographic trends based on Census 2000 data; accrediting bodies and funding entities demanding evidence of diversity strategies; competition for the most talented culturally competent students and professional employees; and for providing relevancy in educational and workplace settings. In effect, there are many internal and external motivators for engaging in a diversity initiative, but there are also a number of manifestations and acts of resistance to slow down or sabotage a process of change. To focus on diversity, multiculturalism, or cultural competency systematically is to move toward organizational change.

ABOUT ORGANIZATIONAL DIVERSITY INITIATIVES

Diversity initiatives have been launched in private industry, human service agencies, healthcare institutions, and governmental sectors since the early 1980s. Educational institutions, particularly colleges and universities, are among the latest to become proactively engaged with this focus. The context for these initiatives is threefold: (a) Diversity management initiatives are voluntary and are different from compliance policies such as affirmative action and equal employment opportunity (Arredondo, 1996; Bowen, Bok, & Burkhart, 1999; Thomas, 1991, 1996). (b) Diversity initiatives are driven by demographic trends about the future workforce in terms of retention rates of high school students, types of technology and other skilled labor that is required to fuel the future economy; and demographic diversity based on age, ethnicity, gender, degrees earned, and other data that reflect population trends (Judy & D'Amico, 1997). (c) Globalization through technology, cross-national mergers, and population migration internationally, suggest that culture, diversity, and cultural competency are as important to an organization's continuity/permanence as is its fiscal management. The former affects the latter.

Definitions and Basic Assumptions

The context for diversity management initiatives as voluntary and distinctive from Affirmative Action and Equal Employment Opportunity compliance strategies is fundamental to the direction an organization takes. Simultaneously, there is language often related to an initiative that also introduces different assumptions and expectations. For the sake of clarity, a few of these terms and definitions are cited: (a) *Diversity* typically refers to people differences and intersecting social identities for individuals and groups (e.g., White women, African-American management, and persons with disabilities). In organizations, the terms are usually used in reference to people, and in a diversity initiative, the concept may be defined as "underrepresented groups." (b) *Multiculturalism or cultural pluralism* is more often used in reference to umbrella cultural groups (e.g., Latinos, Arabs, and Jews). Embedded in this concept is language as another manifestation of multiculturalism. In the counseling literature, multiculturalism has been used inconsistently. At times, it refers to Persons of Color or ethnic minority groups in the United States. Others indicate that multiculturalism is inclusive of Whites. A third perspective is that women, persons with disabilities, and gays and lesbians are also cultural groups and therefore part of the definition of multiculturalism. (c) *Cultural competency* is another concept with multiple meanings. Emanating from cultural awareness and valuing diversity paradigms, it has been used through typologies to describe organizations on a continuum from monocultural to multicultural or from cultural destructiveness to cultural proficiency (Cross et al., 1989; Issacs & Benjamin, 1991). In the multicultural counseling literature, the concept of cultural competency is often interchanged with multicultural competence or ethnic-specific competence and therefore equated with individual and interpersonal awareness, knowledge, and behavioral skills (Arredondo et al., 1996; Sue, Arredondo, &

McDavis, 1992). (d) *Diversity management* refers to a strategic organizational change process that promotes people development through equitably functioning systems and practices. In other words, because people/human diversity is present in all organizations, diversity management initiatives examine institutional practices as they differentially affect various constituencies, particularly underrepresented groups, and implement strategies to address discrepancies or voids.

These basic definitions also reflect the bias of this consultant. Depending on the settings and the clients/students/customers, terms can be customized for use. The important point, however, is to ensure that organizational representatives have a clear understanding about what these terms mean to them and how they want to operationalize them within their particular context. Most participants in an organization are laypersons, not educated about diversity and multiculturalism or organizational development. Often their only information is through previous experiences with diversity training, not always the most positive, and through an erroneous association to Affirmative Action. Clarity for the purpose of communication and goal setting is essential from the beginning of an initiative.

Premises of Diversity Initiatives

In addition to clarifying principal terms, there are also premises about organizational diversity initiatives (DI) that must be recognized. For if these basic premises are not acknowledged, there will surely be misunderstandings and covert/overt resistances as a process unfolds. Many of these premises also hold true for diversity or multicultural training, although the latter tend to be single events and not by design developmental in nature. Therefore, they cannot be expected to create the same kinds of organizational change as diversity management initiatives.

Diversity initiatives:

1. Are about *change,* about culture change in an organization and people development; deliberate, systematic attention to diversity means changes in the infrastructure (systems and practices) and growth opportunities for employees
2. Introduce flux and transformation into an organization (Morgan, 1997)
3. Are often perceived as a threat to individuals or groups who believe that others will benefit at their expense and who fear loss of power
4. Typically give more attention to historically disenfranchised or underrepresented groups such as ethnic, racial, and sexual minorities, the physically disabled, and women
5. Are often perceived as another manifestation of Affirmative Action and therefore negatively
6. Raise expectations among constituents that some things will change
7. May become the scapegoat for dissatisfied employees
8. Must be more than an education and training project
9. Will not be perceived as legitimate without active involvement of senior level administration

10. Must be built upon an organizational business plan with long-term objectives
11. Require a systemic work plan with measurable outcomes
12. Must be led internally by an individual with credibility and in collaboration with a consultant who has a tried and proven track record

These basic assumptions are typically challenged during the life of an initiative. Often times leadership is unaware of sequelae when they launch an initiative. Situation #1 offers an example about how one program (*Talented Scholars of Color*), although well intentioned, could not meet the needs or objectives with respect to the retention of Faculty of Color. A program and an initiative are not one and the same. Administration may have believed they were being proactive; however, that was not the perception of its constituents. Because individuals in authority have the power to define reality (Sue et al., 1998), and because of historic and pervasive institutional racism, resistance to organizational diversity is easily reinforced.

The lack of a proactive initiative may both raise and dampen expectations. For example, referring back to Situation #1, the provost encountered resistance from an unanticipated source, a senior Faculty of Color. Expectations about support for talented Scholars of Color across the institution never occurred. The program could not be self-sustaining because participants had many academic responsibilities in addition to trying to guide the program's evolution. By design, they lacked sufficient institutional resources to advance it. Academics of Color report that they are not surprised when a program designed to address diversity is scrapped. For them, it is a reminder of work environments that are racist, operate based on cultural double standards, and do not value People of Color (Turner & Myers, 2000).

BASIC ASSUMPTIONS ABOUT RESISTANCE

Resistance to organizational change is not a new phenomenon. The psychological literature discusses the tendency of individuals to resist change. "It's human nature" is often the adage invoked. In an article published 30 years ago, Greiner (1972) cited six trends to obstructing organizational change. These included: (a) putting the individual before the organization; (b) promoting an informal versus a formal organization; (c) recommending behavioral solutions (e.g., team building) before making a diagnosis; (d) overemphasizing process before task; (e) directive and non-collaborative consultants; and (f) an "off the shelf package" versus a customized approach. He cautioned that introducing organizational development too quickly is never a good idea.

The introduction of computers into work settings was often met with fierce resistance. Primarily affected were women in clerical roles, often the most unrewarded. In universities, even today, not all faculty are equally enamored with computers and still rely on secretaries to do their word processing. Resistance to learning how to work with a computer is quite different than resistance to diversity, multiculturalism, and cultural competency. Again, depending on one's definition, there may be a suggestion of not valuing women, Persons of Color, or other underrepresented groups in the workplace. The word often becomes "resentment" versus resistant with diversity initiatives. Certain individuals are resented because of their perceived benefits through diversity. Depending on experience, consultants and organizational personnel can anticipate resistance for a number of reasons.

The introduction of resistance:

1. May be perceived as a symptom in response to the unfamiliar and unpredictable
2. Is a symptom of both conscious and unconscious processes at work for individuals
3. Is a result of a sense of disequilibrium in the organization and for individuals
4. Is a predictable reaction to imposed change and a sense of paradox
5. Manifests differently based on the culture and norms of the organization (e.g., high or low in power distance, lack of trust, and competitive versus conflict-avoidant)
6. Results from a perceived and/or real loss of power
7. Can manifest in passive-aggressive and scapegoating behavior
8. Affects individual and group self-esteem and self-efficacy for individuals and groups of particular social identities
9. Can be managed

With diversity initiatives, fear, covert and overt racism (Ancis & Szymanski, 2001; Ponterotto & Pedersen, 1993; Ridley, 1995), sexism and homophobia, and other expressions of prejudice may quickly emerge. These may be fueled by contributing factors that include the type of industry, its economic strength, the "legitimacy" and leadership of the endeavor, previous experiences with diversity initiatives, successful and unsuccessful change-oriented initiatives, and perceived beneficiaries of the initiative. Not to be understated is the organization's historical experience with "culturally different" individuals and groups. If a diversity initiative is introduced in a historically White, heterosexual, male-dominated organization where Anglo harmony reigns (Homan, 2000), initial reactions of resistance may be heard with statements such as: "Why do we need this? We're not prejudiced. Talent rises to the top," and "This is a color-blind organization, a meritocracy. Everyone has the same chance."

In an educational institution, specifically a counseling or psychology program, resistance may take the form of: (a) not having a multicultural requirement nor a multicultural counseling course or assuming one course with a multicultural focus is sufficient; (b) expecting that Faculty of Color will serve on Affirmative Action committees and advise the Students of Color; (c) discouraging students from conducting qualitative research with underrepresented groups (e.g., gays and lesbians); and (d) not providing culturally relevant supervision.

In mental health agencies similar to Situation #2, we introduced a diversity focus into management practices. Through these endeavors and others, we observed behaviors that point to operating assumptions and interpersonal dynamics. Specifically, when there is no organizational management vision to focus on diversity/people development, and where there are other administrators in conflict about making it an organizational priority, there will be a loss of focus and impetus at many levels.

PARADIGMS OF RESISTANCE

The paradigms to be discussed are the loss and change process, internal/external personas, and the ethnocentric and racial identity development models. These paradigms have three features: (a) They address both conscious and unconscious processes and interpersonal dynamics that impact individuals' reactions at three levels: cognitive, emotional, and behavioral. (b) A second feature of these models is their dynamic nature. Basically, they speak to an object, or stimulus in this case, the initiative or training that precipitates an imbalance or cognitive dissonance in the organization because of stated expectations about individual and institutional change. Individuals, work groups, and other cohorts will likely experience a range of dynamic responses (e.g., fear, loss of power), some of which have already been outlined. (c) An initiative presupposes a set of interactions between an internal diversity coordinator/practitioner and possibly a consultant with the workforce and/or student body, and among different constituents of the organization such as students, clerical staff, faculty, and management or administration, and so forth. Oftentimes, the coordinator or consultant becomes the messenger of plans and expectations related to the initiative, thereby inducing differential types of anxiety and dissonance. Thus, another level of resistant reactions must be recognized—those directed to the facilitators of the change process. (This is addressed in the next section.)

This discussion is based on the author's subjective social construction, informed by psychological principles related to change processes in general, and from extensive organizational consulting work in particular. The latter have provided live experiences that have led to the descriptive examples used here. There are some examples that are specific to a type of organization. In other cases, similar manifestations of resistance show up across different settings and come from like groups of individuals, such as White male faculty. The discussion primarily addresses the third paradigm.

Defense Mechanisms

Throughout the ensuing discussions, there are also references to defense mechanisms. These are widely used to express resistance both covertly and overtly. Defenses are a means of coping for those who begin to feel defensive as well as for others who indeed feel hostility to anything at work that refers to diversity. Because of the numbers of individuals who invariably participate in diversity training, most examples derive from those settings.

The most common defense mechanisms are denial, displacement, projection, personalization, rationalization, and idealization. For example, a White manager who perceives ethnic minority individuals only through stereotypic lenses will rationalize that "Asians are great technically but would not make good managers." Others caught up with their sense of self-righteousness about being fair-minded may strike out against others to express frustration and anger through joking and other demeaning comments. In addition, there is personalization; one hears a comment or a fact and believes he or she is responsible for another's lack of ability and overcompensates through patronizing behavior. The discussion about paradigms offers examples of other defenses at work.

Loss and Change Model

Several loss and grief models come to mind when trying to explain resistance to diversity initiatives and training. The central premise is that individuals experience a sense of loss that introduces upset and change in different forms. The stage model that seems most applicable comes from the work of Elizabeth Kübler-Ross (1975) who described the reactions of survivors when a loved one died. The five stages in her model are: denial, anger, bargaining, sadness, and acceptance. For the purposes of this discussion, the organizational status quo of White privilege (Ancis & Szymanski, 2001; McIntosh, 1989) represents the loss and the diversity initiative or training a contributing factor or even the reason for the loss. Examples for each stage will be introduced.

Stage One: Denial

Statements representing this stage may include:"Whites still outnumber minorities," and "We all get along. What's the big deal?" They manifest as thoughts that may or may not be expressed to a peer, a supervisor and/or the trainer. There is usually a sense of shock that sets in when one really pays attention to some of the Census 2000 figures and trends. These speak to Latinos becoming the largest ethnic minority group in the United States, the aging of the baby boomers (Judy & D'Amico, 1997), and the settlement of new immigrants in previously all-White rural areas.

Denial is a way of distancing oneself from these changes and an attempt to continue to maintain the status quo, minimally within one's own mindset. "If I don't acknowledge it, I can't see it; it doesn't exist" or vice versa.

Stage Two: Anger

Sentiments of anger run very deep. They are exhibited in statements such as: "This is a waste of time. I have more important things to do." "They shouldn't get any more special treatment." "Why don't they just learn English?" "This is reverse discrimination." These statements or thoughts may be symptoms of personal biases and prejudices that have gone unchallenged or a fear of being uneducated about persons different from oneself. A number of examples include the terms "they" and "them." Use of these terms typically signal resentment, distancing, or disparagement.

Individuals also may become angry because they feel judged by others for their negative attitudes and privilege (Helms & Cook, 1999). Self-judgment may also provoke the anger. In training, hostility is often directed to the instructor or to the material. Individuals overtly challenge the legitimacy of the material as well as the messenger. They minimize its value and substance and sometimes try to undermine the class.

"This is just another version of Affirmative Action" or "Do you really think this is important?" Such statements have actually been voiced to instructors. An unsuspecting trainer may become the scapegoat for angry participants.

Stage Three: Bargaining

Statements that represent bargaining include: "Why can't we continue to think of ourselves as a melting pot?" "I don't mind doing the training as long as it helps my career," and "Sure, bring in more Students of Color but why do they need special programs?" These statements acknowledge ambivalence but perhaps also a shift because there is some acceptance that organizational change will occur and because personal change is also expected.

In university settings, faculty may reluctantly admit international students or Students of Color. Bargaining may occur in the actual training session or within the organization with one's manager, almost in the form of asking permission or making a plea that things not change too much, such as: "I agree we can promote a few more women but not too many" and "I believe in diversity but we have to be careful not to lower our standards."

Stage Four: Sadness

Sadness is a complex stage, and reactions are typically less overt, such as: "I learned some things about myself that make sense." "I didn't know others had been excluded for so long." "I didn't realize that White privilege really exists." The statements may be private thoughts about anticipated loss and changes that seem far too real and irreversible. Other reasons for sadness may come from commonly used videos in diversity training. These simulations tend to demonstrate the range of human emotions of hurt and disillusionment as a result of prejudice or another unwarranted disrespectful behavior. In the actual training, sentiments of sadness may be provoked by role-taking exercises that allow a participant to see something from another's perspective. If presented effectively, this can bring about a positive insight/reaction through which the learner may discover that there is a rationale for this training after all and that there is a responsibility for change one can assume.

Stage Five: Acceptance

Learners do not usually embrace diversity training; therefore, acceptance might be perceived as a major step in moving away from remaining stuck in the resistance, as evidenced in statements such as: "I learned some things about myself that make sense, especially how I use stereotypes that harm my relationships with others." "I guess this training is necessary after all." "This is just one more thing I'll have to deal with." Questioning and challenging behavior may still persist after one has seemingly accepted the change. From a developmental perspective, this is the growth process in action. Reinforcement and support for change and accountability must come from institutional administration. Acceptance is dependent on a personal sense of control—individuals must be able to determine that they can choose to be part of the process, learn, and benefit in different ways.

Internal/External Personas

Central to the resistance process is the *self* with both internal and external dimensions or personas. Social learning theory is a useful paradigm to explain this phenomenon. All personas are impacted by socialized, internalized messages and societal forces that set forth norms or expectant behaviors, attributions, and other stereotypes. For example, through modeling one may have internalized a sense of White male superiority and be strongly influenced by this in her or his public workplace and social interactions (e.g., only White men are leaders). However, the latter may be self-moderated or adapted because of societal standards that promote the equality of the sexes. In public, one may behave differently from the internalized thinking. Thus, situations dictate the persona that is "politically correct." This model also reflects the interaction of cognitive, affective, and behavioral processes when there is ongoing resistance to diversity.

Cognitive

The cognitive dimension involves both conscious and unconscious memories that hold one's biases, personal prejudices, and other viewpoints about persons different from oneself. This learned thinking has a strong influence on emotional and behavioral reactions, and if unchecked, as noted, these can lead to negative interpersonal outcomes. The external persona is motivated by politically correct (PC) values. However, the person may worry too much about what others think and have fear of failure for not living up to expected "PC" behavior.

Perfectionists or persons considered to be "superachievers" often have low frustration tolerance when it comes to participating in diversity training. They may actively or covertly begin to blame others because they cannot "get" the material as easily as happens with other types of training. Diversity training is not like any other workshop most individuals have taken because it generates considerable cognitive dissonance. What is taught may be disconcerting but because ethnocentrism has prevailed, individuals representing the majority group often feel a loss of control and exposed. They do not want to appear stupid.

Affective

Mental messages and cognitive dissonance influence affective reactions, primarily anxiety, fear, and personalization. These tend to be the most prevalent and primary feelings among trainees and for many good reasons. Individuals experience a sense of frustration because they lack the skill to do something new and are treading in a field that is very different from what they know. Many fears that set in include fears about competence, about being judged, and of not supporting the diversity program.

Behavioral

In training, resistance can manifest through attempts to avoid active participation in the class. We have had participants share aloud that the only reason they are there is to "fulfill a requirement." As the workshop continues, resistant participants may begin to question the relevance of the training for their jobs and wonder aloud if "we're making this a bigger issue than it really is." Body language may also be a clue to individuals' resistance. The way someone sits or looks may communicate the message: "Just try to teach me," or "I think this is a waste of my time."

Not all behavior may manifest as resistance because of different motivating emotional forces. The preceding examples suggest behavior influenced by anger and frustration. For those motivated by guilt or a fear of being judged adversely, the behavior might be oversolicitous or self-righteous, in an attempt to compensate for negative feelings or to be perceived unfavorably. A different external persona is revealed. "It must be terrible to be judged because of your race or sexual orientation." If someone who fits one of these dimensions is in the class or is the instructor, he or she may be put on the spot, thereby assuaging the speaker's guilt feelings. Manipulation of an instructor is commonly demonstrated by individuals who want an external persona to be stroked. Instructors must be cautious around individuals who appear too eager or willing to accept everything that is said.

Ethnocentrism and Racial Identity Models

Psychological models about ethnic/racial identity development are particularly relevant to understanding resistance. Examples from White identity and minority identity models are used for this discussion. The models, like those previously discussed, involve disequilibrium, stimulating varying cognitive, affective, and behavioral responses.

White identity development models (Hardiman, 1982; Helms, 1984, 1990) have principally addressed White–Black relations or dynamics. These stage models contextualize individuals' behavior in terms of the U.S. sociopolitical and historical structures that have perpetuated a dominant-subordinate attitude toward persons of African descent. Thus, when diversity initiatives or training are introduced into an organization, there is an automatic assumption that there will be a focus on racism and Blacks. These assumptions may arise from individuals at different stages of White identity development. For example, at UHL, the administration as a whole might be in what is termed the Pseudo-Independent (Helms, 1992) or Redefinition (Hardiman, 1982) stages. Through the establishment of the *Talented Scholars of Color* program, they are expressing some responsibility for racism and are now attempting to change the status quo. However, as the example demonstrated, personal emotions erupted when a crisis occurred, and these emotions seemed to suggest that individuals actually might still be in the Disintegration (Helms, 1990) or Acceptance stages (Hardiman, 1982). These statuses suggest that the White individuals may still have many unresolved beliefs and feeling about Blacks such that they emerge through frustration and blaming behavior.

Other proposed models of White identity consciousness are inclusive of all White-ethnic/racial minority groups (Pontertoto, 1988; Sabnani, Ponterotto, & Borodovsky, 1991). Specific to Situation #2, it is possible to posit that the administration and Andrea's peers were in the Pre-Exposure or Pre-Exposure–Pre-Contact stages. By denying the importance of language preference and ethnic group affiliation for their Latino clientele, they seemed to suggest their naivete about "racial issues and their inherited White privilege as White people in America" (Ponterotto & Pedersen, 1993, p. 74) and their obliviousness to cultural and linguistic issues. The third case demonstrates how faculty privilege readily asserts itself. Granted, the administration sabotaged itself by offering the training at an ill-advised time, still the faculty had the privilege of ignoring the invitation. In some situations, we have heard faculty state that they are too busy with their publications; going to training will not count toward tenure or merit raises.

Through diversity-related training, participants become even more aware about the concepts of White privilege, worldviews about gender roles and race relations, and about the reality of multiple social identities and how these may benefit or limit particular individuals and groups in this country. New awareness can stimulate growth from one stage of racial identity development to another, from Conflict to Pro-Minority/Antiracism (Sabnani et al., 1991).

Minority Identity Development

Another model that applies particularly to ethnic minority and underrepresented individuals is the Minority Identity Development model (Atkinson, Morten, & Sue, 1998). Using this stage model with five dimensions of "relationships," it is possible to recognize why ethnic/racial minority individuals may express mistrust and dismiss diversity training or an initiative. For example, Puerto Rican women in the "resistance and immersion" stage would be more self-appreciating of their ethnic/racial identity and group and appreciating of others of the same group. Their attitude toward the dominant group, usually Whites, would be group-depreciating. With respect to other ethnic/racial minority groups, the Puerto Rican women may have feelings of empathy as well as ethnocentrism.

For a contrasting perspective, we will use an Asian-American associate professor in math. Let's say he is at the "conformity" stage. He would likely distance himself from diversity training and an initiative asserting that *everything is all right*. Underneath may lie a group-appreciating view toward the dominant group (Whites), and a self and group-depreciating feeling toward other Asians. In terms of other ethnic/racial minority groups, he would likely engage in discriminatory or other avoidant behavior.

Extension of Identity Development Models to Organizations

There can be similar application of these stage models to resistance expressed in diversity training. These are based on the premise that all persons have ethnocentric and survival thinking that shapes personal emotions and actions. The mindset or worldview

(Sue, 1977) is a representation of values, standards, and life experiences that serve as a reference point when choices or decisions are to be made. It is particularly relevant to the examination of resistance to diversity training because ethnocentric thinking embodies many other deeply rooted barriers to working with changes and differences related to people perceived as different. Literature on neglecting the cultural factor in psychology highlights several reasons that perpetuate culturally encapsulated thinking (Wrenn, 1962). These include: one-way tendencies in the United States, our emphasis on medical/biological versus sociopolitical and historical factors, fear of working with those viewed as "different" because of lack of contact and/or previous experiences, cultural universality versus cultural variability, and ethnocentric thinking (Bronstein & Quina, 1988). Thus, historically, the aura of the White/right way has been advanced with ethnic minority individuals typically viewed as outsiders. Helms and Cook (1999) present the concepts of VREG (visible racial ethnic groups) and ALANA (African, Latino/Latina, Asian and Pacific Islander, and Native American) to underscore the labeling because of phenotype and other visible physical differences.

A number of ethnic identity models have emerged in the psychology literature since the early 1970s (Ramirez, 1998). These theorists suggest that Persons of Color and of minority status in the United States are affected by contexts that introduce oppression, minimal self-efficacy, and modeling that reinforces negative self-messages (e.g., through the media, societal sources of power). Thus, in work settings with cues of Anglo dominance and White privilege, there are different emotional and behavioral reactions based on one's ethnic identity status. These reactions will demonstrate either passive or active resistance or a combination of both.

CHALLENGES FOR THE DIVERSITY PRACTITIONER

Resistance to organizational diversity may be aimed at multiple targets but one of these is always the diversity practitioner. Internal and external practitioners or consultants receive similar and different messages of resistance based on their social identity, including age, gender, ethnicity, and credentials. For internals, position and seniority are also considerations. Because there is still great confusion about diversity management and a tendency to view it as affirmative action, practitioners need to be prepared with multiple sources of knowledge, experiences, and personal strengths. The combination of these dimensions contributes to greater proficiency as one tries to communicate with different constituencies and to manage different forms of resistance.

Typical Resistance Aimed at Practitioners

The examples provided come from personal experiences of this practitioner and from others who participated in a practitioner supervision group over a 7-year period of time. The consultants ranged in age from 35 to 55 and 60% were women. The group was multicultural with individuals from African, European, Jewish, Latino/a, and Chinese heritage. The consultants tended to work in teams, one way to balance gender, ethnic, and sexual orientation differences. At times, this proved very useful, as they could support and counterpoint resistances aimed at one of them. For the purposes of this discussion, all of the resistances are termed "microaggressions" because they represent overt hostile to passive-aggressive behavior. Quite often the behavior is verbal, indicating that there are witnesses.

Microaggressions

Intellectualism or Academic Snobbery

This has typically occurred in higher education settings, primarily emanating from faculty and faculty who are administrators. Examples are: criticizing the focus on cultural differences; indicating this perpetuates stereotypes; challenging the methodology followed in an organizational study; questioning the content of surveys; wondering what the "rewards and recognition" category has to do with diversity; including demographic information; questioning the efficacy of materials used in diversity training; indicating that they do not support educational objectives; and asserting that disciplinary content supersedes discussions about cultural differences and that the latter can be learned elsewhere. The affect in most of these comments ranges from condescending to swearing.

Nonverbal Behavior

Resistance also manifests through body language including eye contact or lack thereof, facial and hand gestures, sitting posture, and other behaviors (e.g., reading the newspaper or not participating in any discussion or written tasks during the contact period). According to communications experts, 93% of our face-to-face communication is nonverbal suggesting that people have many ways to communicate a message or sentiment from disapproval to disgust. Nonverbal forms of resistance are fairly easy to detect. Examples of such resistance include: hostile staring or glaring at the presenter; sneering or snickering when facts or data are reported; sitting in ways that communicate inattention or lack of interest; stone face—no reactions even if others laugh at a comment or at a video scene; continuously shifting in one's seat; overtly monitoring the time; coming back late from a break during a training session; and shaking one's head as a gesture of disapproval. There are many other examples that may come to mind to anyone who has ever taught or made a group presentation.

Racism

Ridley (1995) discusses overt and covert forms of racism (see Mio, this volume). These are manifested in institutions and individuals. Practitioners, particularly Practitioners of Color, have often had comments directed to them, challenging their credentials, appearance, and rationale for involvement with diversity consulting. White men and women have also had their motivation called into question, and at times, have been criticized for being part of the affirmative action "problem."

In a previous discussion, it was indicated that ethnic/racial identity status is relevant to understanding individuals' resistances to diversity. In our experience, racist comments are related to one's status. For example, an African-American consultant was questioned about her hairstyle during the middle of a presentation. A participant wanted to know if hers was an Afrocentric style. In another instance, the same practitioner, who is a lawyer by training, was told that her skills would be better applied in the field of law and not in teaching about diversity. Individuals' comments could be characterized as reflecting Helms' independence status.

White male practitioners have been directly questioned, particularly by other White men: "Why are you doing this kind of work?" The persons inquiring are generally quite incredulous about the participation of White men, assuming it is only White women and Persons of Color who consult to diversity initiatives. On other occasions, Persons of Color challenge White women as they are well represented among diversity consultants. Individuals have been told that, as White women, "they cannot know the experience of Persons of Color" and should not try to speak about them.

Diversity practitioners face many ironies and biases. If the practitioner is an employee working without an outside consultant, they are exposed to certain vulnerabilities if senior leadership is not there to back their actions. This is also a reason why internal credibility of the internal practitioner is essential. They must have a reputation for being performers and also be well positioned with decision-making power within the organization.

External consultants, like the individuals in the peer supervision group, may serve as a group target for hostilities. Because of their outsider and usually "expert" status, they are often perceived as not trustworthy and only as troublemakers. Employees have been heard to remark about how a consultant is "making work for everyone" or "does not know the company well enough" or "is making too much money."

MANAGING AND FACILITATING RESISTANCE

As the examples have shown, diversity practitioners require multiple skills in order to manage resistances that assuredly emerge in a consultation process or diversity training. These skills are technical, multicultural/interpersonal, and experiential. The textbook of recommendations is only a set of guidelines that may be followed; it is only through multiple and varied experiences that a consultant learns how to manage and facilitate resistance to diversity.

Situations of Resistance

Over the years, both internal and external diversity consultants have sought guidance about how to facilitate diversity-related programs, including how to manage individual and institutional barriers. Members of boards of directors for colleges and social service agencies have sought ideas on how to "convince" other board members of the institutional benefits (e.g., economic, academic, public relations) of addressing diversity. Diversity coordinators can expect internal resistance from management personnel, nonmanagers, support staff, and in some instances, union representatives. These people should be included on diversity committees. Still, Persons of Color may question the merits of having White men on the committee.

External consultants also become targets of resistance. Although they are typically engaged by senior-level staff based on their credentials and references, other personnel may not appreciate this or not be fully brought into the organizational decision making. Challenges also depend on the culture of the organization and the nature of the business. Within engineering and financial institutions, there are more questions about the effects of training on the bottom line and its relevance to workplace tasks. Individuals' approach to business is typically task-oriented, not one that examines the interpersonal and cultural dynamics. In higher education, there is a great value on academic freedom; thus, faculty on a committee want to be certain that consultants know this basic premise. Furthermore, we have found that faculty is more particular than any other client about the competence of the diversity practitioner. Practitioners with higher education experience as faculty or administrators are viewed more favorably.

Multidimensional Skills to Recognize and Manage Resistance in Context

All work environments are culture-bound and have a worldview that may be more implicit than explicit. Some work settings are more conflict-avoidant, leading to passive-aggressive behaviors. Others are characterized by consensus building or by a norm of "agree to disagree." In the latter, employees will readily raise questions with their boss or a consultant. It may not signal resistance but simply reflect a discussion style that is normative in the organization. These possibilities cannot escape a well-prepared diversity practitioner; he or she must be sufficiently adept to discern whether a question or comment is a clarification or an attempt to disrupt the process.

Whether the comment reflects a factual inquiry or resistance, the explanations cannot be abstractions. Rather, a consultant must provide responses that are relevant in that particular setting. In hospitals and nursing homes, for example, nurses might inquire in a challenging manner about how diversity training will help their work with patients speaking a variety of languages or presenting with culture-specific healthcare needs. *Can generic training really bring the desired information?* In a university setting, we have had administrative staff wonder if the initiative will truly be "inclusive" and honest: *Are they really going to value our opinions by responding to them, or is this just window dressing?*

Communication Skills: Culturally and Contextually Proficient

Diversity practitioners must possess technical skills that are best described as primarily interpersonal communication. These derive from counseling preparation and are ones that can transcend and be adapted in different contexts. To recognize and manage resistance, practitioners require excellent listening, clarifying, facilitating, reframing, reflecting, tracking, perspective-taking, and summarizing skills. All will be pressed into service during diversity consulting and training exchanges.

Practitioners must also keep in mind that consulting and counseling processes have similar and different expectations. In counseling, promoting insight and awareness building and offering interpretations are normative practices. Although these strategies may be introduced in diversity management initiatives, it is important for the practitioner to recognize the nature of the relationship she or he has with employees (e.g., faculty, staff, management personnel). A practitioner perceived as "playing" psychologist receives less cooperation. Authenticity is key; listening to comments and questions and responding in the most accurate manner possible is essential. Again, the context influences how communication processes occur.

Cross-cultural proficiency is another competence for recognizing and managing resistances to diversity. That is, the diversity practitioner must have the flexibility to modify the intervention to resistance on the spot, recognizing that what may be needed are different listening skills, reframing a situation rather than reflecting back, using visuals and/or a fact sheet to respond to a challenge, and terminology or language that is readily understood in that specific work environment. Cross-cultural proficiency involves cognitive, affective, and behavioral skills. However, it is the affective domain that is often triggered. Resistance at times becomes personalized. At the UHL, the provost responded to the African-American faculty member in what might be described as a reactive manner, personalizing his comments by indicating that Faculty of Color had to assume "their share of the responsibility."

Why does personalization occur so readily? The negative association between diversity and affirmative action is one of the reasons. Participants still free-associate to "quotas" when they hear about diversity initiatives. Additionally, it is not uncommon for employees, particularly in a diversity training, to assert that they have "no intention of changing their attitudes." There still seems to be a prevailing perception in most work environments that diversity-related training is about telling individuals what's wrong with their belief system about women and ethnic minorities, especially if they are White men. Personalization is a manifestation of resistance and it behooves practitioners to be well in touch with their hot buttons as well. To react rather than respond to a participant's personalization typically reduces one's credibility.

MULTICULTURAL COMPETENCIES—GROUNDING GUIDELINES FOR APPLICATION

In order to recognize and manage different forms of resistance from individuals in different client organizations, there must be a grounding in multicultural counseling competencies (MCC) (Arredondo et al., 1996; Guidelines on Multicultural Education, Training, Research, Practice, and Organizational Change, 2002; Sue, Arredondo & McDavis, 1992). All versions of MCC provide important concepts that can be utilized by diversity practitioners to facilitate situations of resistance. Central concepts include worldviews, ethnic/racial identity, institutional racism, White privilege, and power distance. A framework of great practical value to exploring conflicting perspectives is that of worldviews. One of the definitions most often used is that worldviews encompass our beliefs, values, and assumptions and these in turn influence our thinking, feelings, and behaviors. The MCC suggest that self or personal understanding, as well as recognition and understanding of others' (individuals' and groups') worldviews, including those of an institution, are foremost.

Situation #1 offers at least three operating worldviews, all embodying resistances. The students believed that administration was not upholding the principles of diversity when it did not appoint an African American as the new dean. They believed the person passed over was the best candidate and that the appointment would have endorsed the institution's mission for valuing diversity. The administration, through its *Talented Scholars of Color* program, presumed it was promoting diversity. However, this was not the perspective held by faculty who believed they were viewed as Affirmative Action hires despite their academic accomplishments. As they indicated, there was a "gap between word and deed with respect to UHL's diversity agenda" and between expectations held for the diversity initiative.

As a starting point, a diversity practitioner could make an assessment of the three worldviews operating. All parties want to improve something in the name of diversity, but are coming from three different worldviews. Self-protection sets in and groups retreat to prevailing thoughts and feelings of mistrust. Moreover, this situation is a telling example of how programs cannot exist without institutional systems to support them. Administrators at times view hiring practices and issues of representation as the primary approaches to promote diversity. This is insufficient. The institutional climate must provide more through systems and behaviors such as participation, fairness, equity, rewards, and recognition (Arredondo & Woy, 1998).

Situation #3 described the failure of a mandatory diversity workshop for university faculty. In this institutional setting, there is low power distance and considerable privilege for faculty based on their position. There is a governance structure in place reinforcing this status quo and these dynamics. The challenge for a practitioner, called in after the fact, would be to determine how to create a win–win situation for the faculty and administration. Again, the concept of worldviews could be applied in this dilemma. Faculty perceive themselves as autonomous, well educated, and experts on many issues. Diversity may not happen to be one of them, yet they are now put in a learner mode. Unless it is mandated by law, such as with sexual harassment training, most faculty balk at diversity-related education. Administrators, on the other hand, see themselves as stewards of the institution and its mission and values. They likely see diversity training as a means to promote their mission relative to diversity. These different perspectives have to be acknowledged by a practitioner as a way of facilitating communication and creating understanding between faculty and administration.

One of the reminders to practitioners is the well-used statement "clinician know thyself." It has been stated that clinicians need to be aware of their hot buttons in order to be as neutral, unbiased, or nonreactive in their communication. All practitioners have biases about their field of work, their objectives, and how they attempt to achieve them. When organizational resistance is encountered, this can derail even the best laid plans. Consequently, practitioners must be open-minded, excellent listeners, and flexible. They must know when to bend and when to hold tight in the midst of disagreements with participants. One resistance is not the end of the world; thus, the recovery skills of the practitioner must be well honed. A checklist (Fig. 5.1) for attributes and behaviors is provided.

The Diversity Practitioner Self-Assessment

Directions: Please rate yourself on the following descriptions. There are no right or wrong answers. The self-assessment will help you to determine areas where you feel greater competency and confidence, and areas in need of development or continued improvement. The ratings are 4 (high) to 1 (low).

1. _____ Enjoy being involved with change-related processes.

2. _____ Understand the organization's motivators for pursuing a diversity agenda.

3. _____ Can describe the organizational culture.

4. _____ Can describe the organizational enablers and barriers to the diversity agenda.

5. _____ Are knowledgeable about the history of workforce diversity in the United States.

6. _____ Can articulate some of the best practices for organizational diversity.

7. _____ Can communicate with ease about the company's diversity agenda to different groups in the company.

8. _____ Seen by others (peers, supervisors, direct reports) as a credible representative/spokesperson for the company's diversity initiative.

9. _____ Consider self a risk-taker.

10. _____ Tend to be a supportive colleague/supervisor/direct report.

11. _____ Recognize important dimensions of personal identity.

12. _____ Do not fear conflict.

13. _____ Can facilitate disagreements or conflicts.

14. _____ Enjoy "thinking out of the box."

15. _____ Consider self a team-player.

16. _____ Recognize personal hot buttons.

17. _____ Can anticipate pitfalls to diversity goals in specific situations.

18. _____ Can recognize forms of resistance to the diversity agenda.

19. _____ Participate in external activities that promote more learning about diversity.

20. _____ Recognize communication strengths and limitations.

FIGURE 5.1.

SUMMARY

Dealing with resistance to organizational diversity initiatives is not the responsibility of only one person. It is a management responsibility. From the beginning, leadership must endorse a diversity initiative signaling that it is a priority. Too often, the diversity coordinator or manager becomes the scapegoat and the primary focus of resistance. Additionally, the diversity initiative also becomes the target for other unresolved issues in the organization. For the diversity practitioner, awareness, knowledge, and skills with regard to negotiating organizational culture are essential. Based on the author's experience, there are many lessons that have been learned and every good reason to be able to anticipate the pitfalls when resistances do manifest. For administrators, psychologists, and counselors, this domain of organizational change through diversity represents a learning experience, one that can be generalized to a number of work settings.

REFERENCES

American Council on Education and American Association of University Professors. (2000). *Does diversity make a difference?: Three research studies on diversity in college classrooms.* Washington, DC: American Council on Education and American Association of University Professors.

Ancis, J. R., & Szymanski, D. M. (2001). Awareness of White privilege among White counseling trainees. *The Counseling Psychologist, 29,* 548–569.

Arredondo, P. (1996). *Successful diversity management initiatives.* Thousand Oaks, CA: Sage.

Arredondo, P., Toporek, R., Brown, S. P., Jones, J., Locke, D. C., Sanchez, J., & Stadler, H. (1996). Operationalization of the multicultural counseling competencies. *Journal of Multicultural Counseling & Development, 24,* 42–78.

Arredondo, P., & Woy, J. R. (1998). *Faculty, administrators, and staff survey.* Boston: Empowerment Workshops, Inc., unpublished document.

Atkinson, D., Morten, G., & Sue, D. W. (1998). *Counseling American minorities* (5th ed.). Boston: McGraw-Hill.

Bowen, W. G., Bok, D., & Burkhart, G. (1999). A report card on diversity: Lessons for business from higher education. *Harvard Business Review, January-February,* 139–149.

Bronstein, P. A., & Quina, K. (1988). *Teaching a psychology of people.* Washington, DC: American Psychological Association.

Carter, R. T. (2000). *Addressing cultural issues in organizations.* Thousand Oaks, CA: Sage.

Cross, T., Bazron, B., Dennis, K., & Issacs, M. (1989). *Toward a culturally competent system of care. Vol 1: Monograph on effective services for minority children who are severely emotionally disturbed.* Washington, DC: CASSP Technical Assistance Center, Georgetown University Child Development Center.

Garcia-Caban, I. (2001). Improving systems of care for racial and ethnic minority consumers: Measuring cultural competence in Massachusetts acute care hospital settings. Unpublished doctoral dissertation. Brandeis University, Waltham, MA.

Greiner, L. E. (1972, June). Red flags in organizational development. *Business Horizons,* 1–8.

Guidelines on multicultural education and training, research, organizational change, and practice for psychologists (2002). Washington, DC: American Psychological Association, Public Interest Directorate. Available: www.APA.org/p1/multiculturalguidelines

Hardiman, M. (1982). *White identity development: A process oriented model for describing the racial consciousness of White Americans.* Unpublished doctoral dissertation, University of Massachusetts, Amherst.

Helms, J. E. (1984). Toward a theoretical model of the effects of race on counseling: A Black and White model. *The Counseling Psychologist, 12,* 153–165.

Helms, J. E. (1990). *Black and White racial identity. Theory, research and practice.* New York: Greenwood.

Helms, J. E., & Cook, D. A. (1999). *Using race and culture in counseling and psychotherapy.* Needham Heights, MA: Allyn & Bacon.

Homan, M. S. (2000). *Promoting community change* (2nd ed.). Pacific Grove, CA: Brooks/Cole.

Issacs, M., & Benjamin, M. (1991). *Toward a culturally competent system of care: Vol 2: Programs which utilize culturally competent principles.* Washington, DC: CASSP Technical Assistance Center, Center for Child and Mental Health Policy, Georgetown University Child Development Center.

Judy, R. W., & D'Amico, C. (1997). *Workforce 2020.* Indianapolis, IN: Hudson Institute.

Kübler-Ross, E. (1975). *Death: The final stage of growth.* Englewood Cliffs, NJ: Prentice-Hall.

McIntosh, P. (1989, July/August). White privilege: Unpacking the white knapsack. *Peace and Freedom,* pp. 8–10.

Morgan, G. (1997). *Images of organization* (2nd ed.), Thousand Oaks, CA: Sage.

Ponterotto, J. G. (1988). Racial consciousness development among White counselor trainees: A stage model. *Journal of Multicultural Counseling and Development, 16,* 146–156.

Ponterotto, J. G., & Pedersen, P. B. (1993). *Preventing prejudice.* Newbury Park, CA: Sage.

Pope-Davis, D. B., & Coleman, H. L. K. (1997). *Multicultural counseling competencies: Assessment, education and training, and supervision.* Thousand Oaks, CA: Sage.

Ramirez, M. (1998). *Multicultural/Multiracial Psychology: Mestizo Perspectives in Personality and Mental Health.* Northvale, NJ: Jason Aronson.

Ridley, C. R. (1995). *Overcoming unintentional racism in counseling and therapy.* Thousand Oaks, CA: Sage.

Sabnani, H. B., Ponterotto, J. G., & Borodovsky, L. G. (1991). White racial identity development and cross cultural counselor training: A stage model. *The Counseling Psychologist, 19,* 76–102.

Sue, D. W. (1977). Barriers to effective cross-cultural counseling. *Journal of Counseling Psychology, 24,* 420–429.

Sue, D. W., Arredondo, P., & McDavis, R. J. (1992). Multicultural competencies/standards: A call to the profession. *Journal of Counseling and Development, 70,* 477–486.

Sue, D. W., Carter, R. T., Casas, J. M., Fouad, N. A., Ivey, A. E., Jensen, M., LaFromboise, T., Manese, J. E., Ponterotto, J. G., & Vazquez-Nutall, E. (1998). *Multicultural counseling competencies: Individual and organizational development.* Thousand Oaks, CA: Sage.

Thomas, R. R. (1991). *Beyond race and gender: Unleashing the power of your total work force by managing diversity.* New York: Amacom.

Thomas, R. R. (1996). *Redefining diversity.* New York: Amacom.

Turner, C. S. V., & Myers, Jr., S. L. (2000). *Faculty of color in academe. Bittersweet success.* Needham Heights, MA: Allyn & Bacon.

Wrenn, G. C. (1962). The culturally encapsulated counselor. *Harvard Educational Review, 32,* 442–449.

CHAPTER 6

Building Bridges in the 21st Century

Allies and the Power of Human Connection Across Demographic Divides

JEFFERY SCOTT MIO
LAURIE A. ROADES

> *In a multiracial society no group can make it alone. It is a myth to believe that the Irish, the Italians, and the Jews . . . rose to power through sepa-ratism. It is true that they stuck together. But their group unity was always enlarged by joining in alliances with other groups such as political ma-chines and trade unions. To succeed in a pluralistic society, and an often hostile one at that, the Negro obviously needs organized strength, but that strength will only be effective when it is consolidated through constructive alliances with the majority.*
>
> The Words of Martin Luther King, Jr., 1964/1987, p. 22

As the quote indicates, it has long been known that groups on the downside of power need allies with power to gain equality and justice. Members of oppressed or disen-franchised groups are clearly the first to recognize and give voice to inequalities and clearly provide most of the energy and work aimed at correcting these situations. The civil rights and feminist movements obviously were begun by and achieved primarily through the efforts of African Americans and women, respectively. However, mem-bers of dominant groups frequently either hold much of the real decision-making power to create change or are able to be heard by their colleagues in ways that are different from that of the group directly affected by these efforts. Thus, allies can play a very real role in helping to create change and advance social justice in our society.

We are reminded of an ABC *Nightline* program (Kaplan, 1989) discussing a prime time program, *Black in White America* (Nunn, 1989). *Black in White America* was reported, produced, and edited by African-American professionals who worked for the ABC network. This program highlighted areas of despair, concern, progress, and hope within the African-American community in the United States. The *Nightline* program was a discussion among the on-camera correspondents (Carole Simpson, Charles Thomas, and George Strait) who participated in *Black in White America*, that program's producer Ray Nunn, filmmaker Spike Lee, Spelman College president Johnnetta Cole, and San Jose State University English professor Shelby Steele. Professor

Steele objected to a subtext that there is rampant racism in the United States and that African Americans cannot make it unless White Americans offer them a helping hand. He believed that this was a prescription for dependency and antithetical to self-empowerment. He accused Ray Nunn, the program's producer, of naïvely reducing all of the problems in the African American community to racism. Nunn clarified his position by stating that he knew he could produce a quality program and that his AfricanAmerican colleagues could report and edit such a quality program. After all, they had produced numerous other quality news segments in their respective careers, so their capabilities were never in question. However, the reality was that the head of the ABC News Division was Roone Arledge, a White man, who had the power to schedule programs. Arledge became an ally to Nunn and the African-American professionals involved in the project by assigning them the project and providing a full hour of expensive prime time scheduling for the program to be aired. Arledge's decision to empower Ray Nunn and his colleagues to make the program they did is a clear case of how a group of individuals on the downside of power benefited from an ally with power.

For a number of years, Peggy McIntosh (1986, 1988, 1995; McIntosh & Hu-DeHart, 1998) has been discussing her unearned White privilege. She reports coming to this understanding of privilege while battling with her male colleagues who refused to give up some of their male privilege in order to allow attention in their curricular discussions for the accomplishments and viewpoints of women. "Since I have had trouble facing white privilege, and describing its results in my life, I saw parallels here with men's reluctance to acknowledge male privilege" (McIntosh, 1995, p. 77). She likens this privilege to an invisible knapsack of assets she can use every day, the equivalent of which does not exist for ethnic minorities. Some examples of these assets or privileges are:

- I can avoid spending time with people whom I was trained to mistrust and who have learned to mistrust my kind or me.
- I can turn on the television or open to the front page of the paper and see people of my race widely and positively represented.
- I can talk with my mouth full and not have people put this down to my color.
- I am never asked to speak for all the people of my racial group.
- If my day, week, or year is going badly, I need not ask of each negative episode or situation whether it has racial overtones (McIntosh, 1995, pp. 79– 81).

McIntosh serves as an ally by using her White privilege to benefit People of Color in order to help produce a more equitable society. For example, whenever she is invited to give a speech, she insists upon a Person of Color having equal time and equal status in the presentation (McIntosh & Hu-DeHart, 1998). She also reports having refused to write a chapter for a book because the editor of the book declined her request to have a Person of Color contribute a responding chapter. The editor "didn't want to dilute the quality of the book" (McIntosh & Hu-DeHart, 1998). Of course, from her perspective, this responding chapter would have *enhanced* the quality of the book. Thus, although a short-sighted decision by an editor made the quality of a book poorer, McIntosh's behavior surely left the quality of our society richer.

THE DEFINITION OF AN ALLY

So, what exactly *is* an ally? We define an ally as an individual in a sociopolitical demographic group on the upside of power who actively advocates for individuals or classes of individuals in a different sociopolitical demographic group on the downside of power. In our society, this most obviously includes Whites advocating for People of Color and men advocating for women. However, these are not the only alliances that can be formed. McIntosh (1995) lists several other groups who might be privileged on the basis of age, ethnicity, physical ability, nationality, religion, or sexual orientation/ identity.

We believe that an important part of the definition of an ally includes both active advocacy, as well as public advocacy. Those who do not actively and publicly advocate for others may be perceived by the outgroup as part of the mountain of opposition that must be confronted. Even if a nonactive advocate votes for or otherwise behaves in a manner desired by the group on the downside of power, this nonactive advocate may be perceived as merely capitulating or yielding to "political correctness." The behavior may not even be seen by members of the outgroup. Therefore, this nonopen advocate may not be perceived to be a reliable ally in the future. Active allied behavior, in contrast, reveals a consistent, philosophical consciousness of a position. The ally demonstrates a clear understanding and commitment to particular positions and acts accordingly.

Second, allies must be willing to advocate their positions publicly. This willingness by an ally to take a supportive stance even when not politically expedient demonstrates commitment and assurance to those in the outgroup that she or he believes in and will act in a trusted manner. To speak out only when there is no risk of disagreement or possible cost does not demonstrate a firm commitment. However, to risk rejection in front of a majority group, or to identify with a group out of power in front of one's own dominant group or those who might disagree indicates a willingness to ally oneself and work toward change. As we know, active advocates who speak out publicly can change the entire tenor of a social situation.

As an illustration of the importance of public and active advocacy, we will describe a situation that occurred in an academic department. (The name of the department has been changed and the description of the event altered slightly in order to mask the identity of the department.) This department, pseudonymed "Humanities and Social Sciences," offered two separate degrees, one in the humanities and one in the social sciences. Although the department operated under one budget, the two degree programs and curricula were almost completely separate. Although the Social Sciences division of the department had a balance between male and female faculty members, the Humanities division was entirely male. A few years ago, the Humanities division received approval to fill two new faculty positions. Both positions had a male and female candidate with essentially equal qualifications for each of the two final spots. Despite the fact that well over 60% of the undergraduate majors in the humanities were female and there were no female faculty members within the division, this all-male faculty justified placing the male candidate in the top spot for both of the new positions. Moreover, the justification for one position—which benefited the male candidate—would have favored the female candidate for the other position, yet the reasoning was exactly reversed for the second position.

It had essentially been the policy of the department to allow each division to have nearly complete control over hiring decisions into its program. However, many of the female faculty from the Social Sciences division questioned the consistency of the reasoning applied in this case, and argued strenuously in favor of at least one of the positions being offered to a female candidate. These faculty members found their arguments to be either trivialized or dismissed by their male colleagues. It was not until a single male colleague from the Social Sciences division advocated the same position as his female colleagues that the male Humanities faculty members seemed more open to the merits of the arguments.

In analyzing the situation, it appears that the male ally's statements had essentially the same content and logic, but they were more likely to be seen as coming from an "objective," neutral third party with nothing personal to gain from the decision. Therefore, it could only be concluded that it was his maleness that made the difference. It is disappointing that this was the situation, but it is a reality that women face in many situations. It is only when a man gives his "stamp of approval" that people move beyond the belief that women are simply advocating positions because they are women, instead of because it is the right thing to do.

This incident prompted us to begin developing a set of male privileges akin to the McIntosh set of White privileges. The following are a few such male privileges:

- I can always assume that my opinion will be listened to and respected.
- I can look at nearly every major company in the world and know that my gender will be represented at the very top levels.
- I know that if I am promoted to the top levels of my company, it won't be attributed to my company "needing that gender at the top to show progress."
- If I am upset, I know that people won't attribute it to "that time of month" and discount the reasons for my being upset.
- If I do any housework at all, I will get credit for being "such a good husband," even if it is only 15% of the total work.
- If I do any child rearing at all, I will get credit for being "such a good father" (Mio, 2000).

Ethnic minority individuals, gays and lesbians, and other individuals outside "power" groups face the problem of their voices being ignored as well (Parham, 1990). Allies, however, can help break down this "we/they" dichotomy. Allies make it somewhat harder for members of the group in power to identify someone or a position as "other" and thereby discount it. Often, it is only through understanding allies, with whom listeners more closely identify, that important positions seem to be heard.

THE ACKNOWLEDGMENT OF THE NEED FOR ALLIES

For years, in attending multicultural workshops, presentations, conference sessions, and the like, we have heard of the need for allies in combating oppression (e.g., Herron, 1989; Kivel, 1996). Some of the "pioneers" of multicultural counseling have indicated the need to get White colleagues to become advocates for multiculturalism or at least to understand the importance of the field (Carter, 1995; Lee, 1994; Sandhu, 1995). Some individuals have written specifically on the need for allies (e.g., Kivel, 1996; Rose, 1996; Tatum, 1997).

An example of the long-time recognition of the importance of developing White allies in the area of multiculturalism came in an interview with Clemment E. Vontress by Courtland C. Lee (1994). Vontress said that "since the majority of counselor educators are White, it would be a very good thing if they were interested enough, effective enough, and devoted enough real research to finding out about [multiculturalism]" (p. 72). Such recognition is an acknowledgement that ethnic minority researchers alone cannot shoulder the entire burden of being advocates for multiculturalism.

Tatum (1997) discussed how allies can help when one is trying to educate people about the realities of race relations. She reported that her White students often feel paralyzed about issues of racism, believing that they cannot do anything about such a monumental problem. However, when she brings in a White colleague who discusses the important role of being an ally, her White students feel empowered to do something about racism. Moreover, they learn that the role of allies is not necessarily to help victims of racism but to challenge their White colleagues to assist them in speaking out against racism.

Rose (1996) wrote about an incident that occurred in one of her workshops and how the *failure* to become an ally can come at a cost. A female police officer discussed an incident that took place a few years earlier in which a female colleague of hers was driven out of the police force because she had reported being sexually harassed by one of her male colleagues. He had retaliated by committing "pranks" like putting used condoms in her desk and deleting reports she had written from her computer. This escalated to the point where this female officer was wounded in the field because she could not call for back-up help because her radio had been jammed. This female officer subsequently left the police force. The female colleague who described this incident said that "If one male, just one, had spoken up, it would have made all the difference in the world" (p. 46).

Rose (1996) went on to discuss how she had addressed a male member of the audience who was with the police force at the time of the incident. He had intellectualized his sadness and inaction, but Rose sensed subtle changes as she ever so gently pushed him to examine more closely his feelings about the incident. She finally broke through his defenses:

I asked, "What did you lose?" This man was at least 6'3", a large white soldier of
the law, standing with his hands stuffed into his pockets. Little by little his chin
began quivering. His eyes were beginning to fill with tears. I had expected him to
be defensive, to give excuses, or to remain detached and academic. To see him
choosing to do otherwise was deeply affecting for the people in the room. I never
learned his name, but I will love this man forever. He said, and I quote, "I lost the
ability to be soft, I lost the ability to be kind, and I lost the ability to be just." (pp.
46–47)

Clearly, being an ally is important not only for those who are oppressed but also
for those whose demographic group is in control. In helping the world to be more just,
we help to create a world in which we ourselves want to live.

BUILDING BRIDGES, MAKING A DIFFERENCE

Allies have existed across time and continent. They have been men and women, young
and old, famous and not famous, who have built bridges across demographic groups
and have greatly enhanced the worlds in which they lived. As examples, we present allies—both by name and issue—who have made differences on the world, national, and
local stages. These allies, not belonging to the groups for which they advocate, have helped
to change the lives not only of people they have touched, but also of our larger society.

Allies on the World Stage

F.W. de Klerk

As most people are aware, F. W. de Klerk, President of South Africa in the late 1980s
and early 1990s, released Nelson Mandela from prison. Mr. Mandela had been imprisoned for years because of his advocacy of Black South African freedom from the
oppressive apartheid policies of his country. (Ironically, one of President de Klerk's
relatives was directly responsible for designing the South African apartheid system.)
Then-President de Klerk recognized that it was time (long past time, actually) to dismantle apartheid, lifting legal restrictions, and allowing Black South Africans the types
of freedoms enjoyed by White South Africans. According to Patrick Sibaya, a Black
South African psychologist (personal communication, August 22, 1999), de Klerk took
these steps despite horrific pressure from the White South African community, including
threats of personal injury and death. Clearly, this helped to transform an entire nation.

Oskar Schindler, Chiune Sugihara, and Corrie ten Boom

We should all know of the horrific atrocities committed against Jews during the Holocaust as a result of antisemitism. We may be less familiar, however, with the courageous activities of non-Jewish allies who worked to protect and save Jewish lives
during World War II. Perhaps one of the best-known allies was Oskar Schindler whose

heroism was made popular by the film *Schindler's List* (Spielberg, Molen, & Lustig, 1994) and described in his wife Emilie's memoirs (Schindler, 1996).

Chiune Sugihara is not as well known as Oskar Schindler, but he has been recognized as the "Japanese Schindler" (Levine, 1996). The Japanese consul in Kovno, Lithuania in 1940, Sugihara saved an estimated 10,000 Jews by writing travel visas to any Jew who asked. He wrote so many that his right hand would cramp, leaving him to write with his left hand. He then made up stamps approving such visas. Sugihara was ordered by the Japanese government to leave Kovno, but issued visas from the moving train even as he was leaving, and he continued to issue visas from his other posts, including Nazi-occupied Prague, despite orders from Japanese authorities to stop such activity. Ultimately, he was fired from his position upon his return to Japan.

Corrie ten Boom is yet another example of a courageous ally to Jews during World War II whose story became widely known through the book and movie depicting her life, *The Hiding Place*. Born in 1892, ten Boom grew up in a Christian home in Haarlem, Holland (ten Boom, 1971). She and her family, although not Jewish and not personally at risk, helped hide Jews in their home until they could be moved to "safe houses," eventually building a hidden room into the back of Corrie ten Boom's bedroom for use if and when the Nazis searched their home. On February 28th, 1944, their house was raided and, although those in hiding were not found, ten Boom and her family members were arrested and sent to prisons and concentration camps (ten Boom, 1971). She was released almost a year later, but had lost her members of family following their arrest. Clearly, she and her family could have avoided this tragedy had they chosen not to become involved. However, they believed in what they were doing, and her family's efforts saved the lives of numerous individuals.

Mother Teresa

Few individuals have been more recognized for their efforts on behalf of the poor than Mother Teresa, a Catholic nun. Born Agnes Gonxha Bojaxhiu in Skopje, Yugoslavia, Mother Teresa was sent to India by her religious order in 1928 (Chawla, 1996; Vardey, 1995). She taught and worked in the convent's school until she felt a "call" to work with the poor, receiving final permission in 1948 to leave her convent and begin this new work. In 1950, she founded the Missionaries of Charity, working to care for the dying, lepers, and the poor throughout the remainder of her life (Chawla, 1996; Vardey, 1995). Mother Teresa was awarded the Nobel Peace Prize in 1979, with her efforts as an ally having brought international attention to the plight of the poor and dying.

Allies on the National Stage

Morris Dees

Morris Dees is a White man who has clearly served as an ally for African Americans and other ethnic minorities, and who has made a difference in the national landscape. Morris Dees and Joe Levin, Jr., cofounded the Southern Poverty Law Center in 1971. The Center defends individuals against civil rights abuses. In 1987, the Center won a landmark civil rights case against the United Klans of America, Inc. (UKA) for $10 million for its encouragement of hate that motivated its followers to murder a young African-American man, Michael Donald. The UKA forfeited its 7,400-square-foot headquarters as payment for this suit. Beulah Mae Donald, Michael's mother, assumed ownership of this building. Less than a year later, she passed away. "The pain of losing her Michael was too much for her heart to bear" (Dees, 1991, p. 332). The Southern Poverty Law Center is now housed in this former Ku Klux Klan building.

Marian Wright Edelman

Children make up a group we often forget to see as disenfranchised or relatively powerless in our society. They have no right to vote and are dependent on adults, both in their families and in our society, to recognize and meet even their most basic needs. Marian Wright Edelman, however, has long been known as an advocate—an ally—for children. Most people know her as the founder of the Children's Defense Fund, an organization that draws attention to and lobbies on behalf of the needs of all children, paying "particular attention to the needs of poor and minority children and those with disabilities" (Children's Defense Fund website, 2002). She serves as president of the Children's Defense Fund, writing and speaking across the country to draw attention to the needs of children, encouraging and demanding that adults actively work to make our society more responsive to their needs (Edelman, 1993).

John Shelby Spong

The Right Reverend John Shelby Spong, retired Episcopal bishop of Newark, New Jersey, is yet another national, even international, figure who has served as an ally for numerous groups, as described in his autobiography *Here I Stand* (Spong, 2000). A White, heterosexual male who grew up in North Carolina while racial segregation laws were in full force, he went on to fight racism against African Americans in the communities and congregations he served. Later, as bishop, he worked to ensure that he provided visible opportunities for ethnic minorities and women to serve congregations and that a very reluctant denomination see the gifts these leaders had to offer. However, he is probably best known for his efforts in working to open the religious community and our society to lesbians and gays. He has tirelessly withstood attacks from critics as he has written, spoken, and acted to educate others across the country and the world and to affirm the rights and abilities of lesbians and gay men.

Americans with Disabilities Act

In 1977, during the Carter Administration, the White House Conference on Handicapped Individuals called for an extension of the Civil Rights Act of 1964 and the Voting Rights Act of 1965 to the disabled population (Pelka, 1997). Legislation began working its way through Congress in the ensuing years. However, momentum for this extension was halted during the Reagan Administration. During the presidential campaign of 1988, both Democratic nominee Michael Dukakis and Republican nominee George Bush endorsed legislation extending civil rights to persons with disabilities. After the election of President George Bush, the Americans with Disabilities Act (ADA) was revived. Most of those in favor of it were not disabled themselves, as the bill was shepherded through the Senate by Senators Ted Kennedy, Tom Harkin, and, later, John McCain, and through the House of Representatives by Congressperson Stenney Hoyer. On July 12, 1990, the ADA passed the House of Representatives by a vote of 377 to 28, and was passed by the Senate the next day with a vote of 91 to 6. President Bush signed the bill into law on July 26, 1990.

Allies on the Local Stage

Although stories of well-known, public allies often inspire us, most of us feel that we cannot make an impact on the world or national stage by what we do. However, as was stated in the award-winning documentary, *"Eyes on the Prize"* (Hampton, 1986) regarding how the civil rights laws in this country were changed, ". . . the change began, first with small acts of personal courage." We can all contribute to the overall fight for justice by making our own acts, large and small, of personal courage.

Our previous discussions of McIntosh insisting on equal status of ethnic minorities in her presentations and writings, the male faculty member advocating for a position taken by female faculty members, and Tatum reporting how energized her White students feel when a White ally makes a presentation to her classes are all ways in which individuals can make a difference at a local level. Below are just a few additional examples of allies who have been active on a local level within their communities.

Steven Cozza

Steven Cozza is an Eagle Scout of the Boy Scouts of America (BSA). When he learned that the BSA discriminated against gay scouts and adults, he founded a movement called "Scouting for All" (Scouting for All website, 2001). He first began his campaign at the age of 12 at the local level, asking people in his scouting troop and his community to sign a petition to send to the national BSA headquarters trying to rescind its policy against gays in scouting. (This ultimately became a national campaign.) Because he began his campaign before achieving Eagle Scout status, there was a very real risk of him being rejected in his application for such status. In fact, there was precedent for this, because one individual who qualified for Eagle Scout status was denied such status by the national headquarters of the BSA because he was gay; another individual who was already an Eagle Scout and disclosed that he was gay was dismissed from scouting. Although not gay himself, Cozza was appalled when he discovered that the BSA discriminated against gay individuals, despite the fact that scouting literature indicates that one should not discriminate against anyone on the basis of race, creed, or religion. Other adult advisors who agreed with Cozza and joined him in his campaign to allow scouting for all were asked by the national headquarters to discontinue their association with BSA.

In the year 2000, the Supreme Court of the United States found that the Boy Scouts of America, being a private organization, was within its rights to deny gay individuals access to the BSA. Although this settled the legal case, a national campaign still exists to pressure the BSA to voluntarily lift its ban against gays, as its access to members depends greatly upon public institutions such as schools and community centers.

Men Against Rape

Men have also begun serving as allies to women in an effort to end violence against women, a topic long thought of as a "woman's issue." Students on a number of U.S. college campuses have organizations specifically aimed at men working with and educating other men to stop sexual assault (e.g., the University of Rochester, Tulane University, and the University of Texas). For example, the Men Against Sexual Assault organizations at the University of Rochester (University of Rochester Men Against Sexual Assault website, 2001) and the University of Texas (University of Texas Men Against Sexual Assault website, 2002) work to provide information to men and women about sexual assault via group presentations and their extensive web pages. They have members who work as liaisons to other student and campus organizations with a particular focus on getting men involved in this issue. Tulane Men Against Rape (Tulane Men Against Rape website, 2002) recognizes the important role men have in ending violence against women by providing education through presentations and training sessions and by helping to develop strong, supportive male role models. Washington State University even has a program where men in fraternities volunteer to be available at any time of the night to escort women from buildings on campus to their cars, apartments, or residence halls (personal knowledge). These male allies help further the work initially begun by women to end violence in their lives and help provide a unique voice likely to be heard by their male colleagues.

Although these are just a few examples of allies making a difference on a local level, the possibilities are most likely unlimited. We know of heterosexual students who have attended gay pride parades and graduation ceremonies to support their gay and lesbian friends and colleagues. We know a heterosexual faculty member who developed a gay/lesbian course on her campus and numerous White faculty who serve as speakers on issues of racism. Individual actions can and do have an effect upon the entire environment. Marian Wright Edelman (1993) reminds us that "one or a few positive people can set the tone in an office or congregation or school. Just doing the right and decent thing can set the pace for others to follow in all kinds of settings" (p. 68).

CONCLUSIONS

It is difficult to think about where to start if one wants to make a difference. There are many areas to address and, even for those individuals who want to become involved, most of these issues seem far beyond the reach of a single person. How does one person fight racism or sexism or homophobia? Clearly, change cannot come about all at once, and little in the world is likely to change instantaneously. Many of us, however, have heard the environmental saying or seen the bumper stickers encouraging us to "Think Globally; Act Locally." We believe that this is applicable to allied behavior. What we do individually, in our relationships, workplaces, and communities can make a difference. Everyone who has heard the story of Rosa Parks refusing to give up her seat on the bus knows that social change can begin with even a single act of personal courage.

Edelman (1993) reminds us that each of us is empowered to help create change, perhaps to serve as an ally to others.

> And do not think that you have to make big waves in order to contribute. My role model, Sojourner Truth, slave woman, could neither read nor write but could not stand slavery and second-class treatment of women. One day during an anti-slavery speech she was heckled by an old man. "Old woman, do you think that your talk about slavery does any good? Why I don't care any more for your talk than I do for the bite of a flea." "Perhaps not, but the Lord willing, I'll keep you scratching," she replied.

> A lot of people think they have to be big dogs to make a difference. That's not true. You just need to be a flea for justice bent on building a more decent home life, neighborhood, work place, and America. Enough committed fleas biting strategically can make even the biggest dog uncomfortable and transform even the biggest nation. . . . Be a flea for justice wherever you are and in whatever career you choose in life and help transform America by biting political and business leaders until they respond. (pp. 59–60)

Who is it then who can and should come forward to make a difference? Levine (1996) attempted to understand what motivated Sugihara to risk his career and even his life for the benefit of people who he seemed to have no personal reason to save.

> Sugihara grew up middle class in a most homogeneous society. There simply *were* no Jews with whom to empathize. Sugihara's earliest exposure to Jews—from high school readings of The Merchant of Venice to a military training that pointed to Jews as fomenters of communism—were altogether negative. We know of no reason for him to have had any positive identification with the people he saw outside his consulate. (p. 4)

Little historical evidence exists to explain Sugihara's acts of heroism. In his own memoirs (Sugihara, cited in Levine, 1996), Sugihara only stated, "I acted according to my sense of human justice, out of love for mankind" (p. 14). Levine found this to be quite unsatisfying and even banal. However, after an exhaustive examination of Sugihara's life, Levine ultimately concluded, "Sugihara's ordinariness is perhaps what is so extraordinary about this story. In illustrating for us how a common person can perpetrate a most uncommon act, he empowers us all as he challenges us to greater responsiveness and responsibility" (p. 284).

Thus, the search for allies lies within us all. We all have the ability, and responsibility, to become allies for groups other than our own. We began to address many challenges during the 20th century, but many challenges remain. As we move further into the 21st century, let us each reach across the aisles that separate us to build bridges and work to create that "more perfect union" and world.

REFERENCES

Carter, R. T. (1995). Pioneers of multicultural counseling: An interview with Janet E. Helms. *Journal of Multicultural Counseling and Development, 23,* 73–86.
Chawla, N. (1996). *Mother Teresa.* Rockport, MA: Element.
Children's Defense Fund. (2001). Retrieved January 13, 2002, from http://www.childrens defense.org
Dees, M. (1991). *A season for justice: The life and times of civil rights lawyer Morris Dees.* New York: Charles Scribner's Sons.
Edelman, M. W. (1993). *The measure of our success: A letter to my children and yours.* New York: HarperPerennial.
Hampton, H. (Producer). (1986). *Eyes on the prize.* Boston: WGBH.
Herron, K. (1989, January). Experiential exercises in antiracism work. Workshop delivered at the 1st Annual YWCA Racial Justice Committee Conference, *Learning and unlearning racism: Yesterday, today, and tomorrow.* Washington State University, Pullman, WA.
Kaplan, R. (Executive Producer). (1989). *Nightline.* New York and Washington: American Broadcasting Company.
King, C. S. (1987). *The words of Martin Luther King, Jr.* New York: Newmarket.
Kivel, P. (1996). *Uprooting racism: How White people can work for racial justice.* Philadelphia: New Society.
Lee, C. C. (1994). Pioneers of multicultural counseling: A conversation with Clemment E. Vontress. *Journal of Multicultural Counseling and Development, 22,* 66–78.
Levine, H. (1996). *In search of Sugihara.* New York: The Free Press.
McIntosh, P. (1986, April). *White privilege and male privilege: A personal account of coming to see correspondences through work in women's studies.* Paper presented at the Virginia Women's Studies Association Conference, Richmond, VA.
McIntosh, P. (1988). *White privilege and male privilege: A personal account of coming to see correspondences through work in women's studies* (Working Paper Number 189). Wellesley College, Wellesley, MA.
McIntosh, P. (1995). White privilege and male privilege: A personal account of coming to see correspondences through work in women's studies. In M. L. Andersen & P. H. Collins (Eds.), *Race, class, and gender: An anthology* (2nd ed., pp. 76–87). Belmont, CA: Wadsworth.
McIntosh, P., & Hu-DeHart, E. (1998, February). White privilege: Unpacking the invisible knapsack and proposing to distribute the contents: From the perspective of a White woman and a woman of color. Paper presented at the *". . . then what is 'white?': An interactive conference for exploring issues related to white racial identity in the United States"* Conference, Riverside, CA.
Men Against Sexual Assault. (n.d.). Retrieved January 12, 2002, from http://www.utexas.edu/students/utmasa/
Men Against Sexual Assault at the University of Rochester. (2001). Retrieved January 12, 2002, from http://sa.rochester.edu/masa/
Mio, J. S. (2000, August). Allies and allied behavior: Men being allies for women. In L. A. Roades (Chair), *Allies across diverse demographic groups—Their development and ex-*

periences. Symposium presented at the 108th Annual Convention of the American Psychological Association, Washington, DC.

Nunn, R. (Producer). (1989). *Black in White America*. New York: American Broadcasting Company.

Parham, T. A. (1990, August). Do the right thing: Racial discussion in counseling psychology. In J. G. Ponterotto (Chair), *The White American researcher in multicultural counseling: Significance and challenges*. Symposium presented at the 98th Annual Convention of the American Psychological Association, Boston, MA.

Pelka, F. (1997). *The disability rights movement*. Santa Barbara, CA: ABC-CLIO.

Rose, L. R. (1996). White identity and counseling White allies about racism. In B. B. Bowser & R. G. Hunt (Eds.), *Impacts of racism on White Americans* (2nd ed., pp. 24–47). Thousand Oaks, CA: Sage.

Sandhu, D. D. (1995). Pioneers of multicultural counseling: An interview with Paul B. Pedersen. *Journal of Multicultural Counseling and Development, 23*, 198–211.

Schindler, E. (1996). *Where light and shadow meet: A memoir*. New York: Norton.

Scouting for All. (2001, July 23). www.scoutingforall.org/mediacenter/steven.shtml

Spielberg, S., Molen, G. R., & Lustig, B. (Producers), & Spielberg, S. (Director). (1994). *Schindler's list* [Film]. (Available from MCA Universal Home Video, Universal City, CA.)

Spong, J. S. (2000). *Here I stand: My struggle for a Christianity of integrity, love, and equality*. New York: HarperCollins.

Tatum, B. D. (1997). *"Why are all the Black kids sitting together in the cafeteria?" and other conversations about race*. New York: Basic Books.

ten Boom, C. (1971). *The hiding place*. Westwood, NJ: Barbour and Company.

Tulane Men Against Rape. (n.d.). Retrieved January 12, 2002, from http://www.tulane.edu/~tmar/

Vardey, L. (1995). Introduction. In Teresa, M. & Vardey, L. (Compiler), *A simple path* (pp. xvii–xxxiii). New York: Ballantine Books.

DIVERSE ETHNIC MINORITY POPULATIONS

At the heart of most books on diversity is ethnic minority populations. This book is no exception. This book has chapters on the four main traditionally conceptualized ethnic minority populations—Blacks/African Americans, Latinos, Asian/Pacific Islanders, and American Indians—plus a chapter on biracial individuals.

Barker-Hackett's chapter begins this section. For years, one of the central questions within the African-American population is that of identity. As most of us know, old terms such as "colored" and "negro" were replaced by more modern terms such as "Black" and "African American." Barker-Hackett discusses the history of more formal racial identity development models and how these models related to African-American mental health issues. As the Afrocentric view began taking hold, mental health was inextricably interwoven with one's identity with one's African roots. However, Barker-Hackett feels that African-Americans need to develop a uniquely African-American perspective, not an Afrocentric one.

Kelly further explores the experience of African Americans by focusing specifically on heterosexual relationships among African Americans. Her chapter reviews the existing literature on the particular issues and challenges that face African-American couples as they endeavor to remain together in the face of discrimination and economic difficulties. She also takes a strength-based approach and summarizes the literature on culture-specific protective factors displayed by many African-American couples. This chapter concludes with a summary of therapy issues clinicians should consider in working with African-American couples.

The chapter by de las Fuentes discusses Latinos, particularly individuals of Mexican descent. Although this chapter discusses many issues general to Latinos, such as immigration and acculturation, language, and Latino values, de las Fuentes illustrates these issues via case illustration with Mexican and Mexican-American clients. To the extent that those of Mexican descent constitute the majority of Latinos living in the United States (about 70%), these case illustrations seem appropriate. Values discussed in these case vignettes include gender relations and expectations, the influence of family and religion, the use of *curanderos* (folk healers), different types of disorders, and the relation between clients and therapists.

Asian Americans and Pacific Islanders are one of the most heterogeneous ethnic groups. Sue and Consolacion summarize the mental health literature on Asian Americans and Pacific Islanders. In particular, the roles of culture and minority status are summarized as they affect mental health. Sue and Consolacion review the existing literature on major disorders among Asian Americans and Pacific Islanders and also discuss the role of somatization. The chapter concludes with a discussion of treatment issues.

The Tewari, Inman, and Sandhu chapter discusses an important subgroup within the Asian/Pacific Islander population—South Asians. This is a diverse subgroup, but within the United States, this subgroup is dominated by Indians and Pakistanis. In fact, according to the latest U.S. Census data, Indians are now the third largest Asian/Pacific Islander group, trailing only Chinese and Pilipinos in numbers. The U.S. psychological literature discussing Asian/Pacific Islander issues and values is based by far upon East Asian populations. There are similarities and differences between South Asians and East Asians, and Tewari and coworkers discuss many of these. Similarities include the acculturation process, collectivistic thinking, and family structure. Differences include reasons for immigration, income levels, the British influence upon South Asians, and religion.

Gone's chapter focuses on American-Indian mental health and the challenges facing clinicians who provide services to this population. The chapter begins with a review of the historical context of the treatment of American Indians by the U.S. Government. Tribal Nations and the Indian Health Service are explained, providing readers with a context to understanding the complexities of the issues facing American Indians and those who wish to improve mental health services for them. Gone concludes by reviewing the role of the scientific method in terms of mental health research and provides suggestions and recommendations for steps needed to address the mental health needs of American Indians.

Finally, Hall's chapter examines the most dominant mental health issue for biracial individuals—that of biracial identity. Hall examines the history of biracial individuals in the United States. This history includes a great deal of racism from the dominant culture, with laws forbidding interracial marriages. Moreover, the discussion about biracial individuals was exclusively centered around Blacks and Whites. Although there is now a growing number of biracial individuals, until recently these individuals have been made to feel marginalized. Presently, biracial individuals have been both more accepted by the dominant culture and more accepted by themselves, as evidenced by the formation of social groups and networks (e.g., the Multiracial International Network), and the notion of "multiethnic" as a formal category. The discussion has also expanded to include multiethnic individuals that are not just a result of Black–White unions.

CHAPTER 7

African Americans in the New Millennium

A Continued Search for Our True Identity

LORI BARKER-HACKETT

I recently attended a special graduation ceremony for African-American students at a large West Coast university. The theme of the graduation was "Defining Ourselves." The program stated, "Defining ourselves, as opposed to being defined by others, is the most difficult task facing African Americans today." I was intrigued by the theme and anxious to hear how the graduates would define themselves. The ceremony was an eclectic and exuberant celebration. The graduates danced down the aisle to an African beat. They showed a video that featured graduates sending thank you messages to family members and friends. Each graduate received a certificate and a kente cloth sash, a hand-woven multicolored cloth traditionally from Ghana. The student speaker talked of her experiences at the university, expressing the anger and frustration she felt as one of few Blacks in a predominantly White university. The ceremony ended with a shower of red, black, and green balloons that poured over the graduates as they stood proudly on the stage.

I left the ceremony feeling proud and excited, but a bit unsettled. Where was their definition of self? Was it in the music? In the dance? In the messages to family members and friends? In the speech? In the kente cloths? Are these the things that define what it means to be Black in America today? These questions remain unanswered.

Like those graduates, I feel one of the most critical challenges facing African Americans today is to develop a true sense of who we are. In other words, the main task for African Americans—both individually and collectively—is to find our true identity.

The struggle for identity began during the slave trade. One of the main goals of slave traders and slave owners was "dis-Africanization" (Mazrui, 1986), a process designed to destroy the identity of African slaves in order to keep them in submission and to reduce emotional connection to the homeland and the desire to escape. Tactics used included forbidding African slaves to speak their native languages, forbidding them to practice their religious ceremonies and rituals, changing their African names to European names, and breaking up families and tribes.

Since the days of slavery, African Americans have been in a continuous struggle to understand and rebuild a sense of who we are. This search for an identity is evident in the various terms used to identify ourselves. We changed from "Negroes," to "Coloreds," to "Blacks," and now "African Americans." Lake (1997) gives a historical overview of the various terms used to refer to African Americans as well as the psychological and sociopolitical implications of these changes. She states, "The degree of dissension over a name for people of African descent and the number of labels we have chosen over the decades is directly related to the instability of our identity as a people" (p. 267). The labels a group uses to identify itself not only reflect how they see themselves, but also affects the attitudes of others toward that group (Fairchild, 1985; Lake, 1997). Lake (1997) prefers the term African American because it locates Africans in America in time and space. The term African recognizes our African ancestry and the term American refers to our current citizenship status. Fairchild (1985) believes that the term adds dignity and self-respect to those who adopt it, and consequently to their sense of psychological well-being. In addition, he feels that it may serve to attenuate the hostilities of Whites toward African Americans.

Evidence for the importance of identity for African Americans is also seen in struggles over who is Black enough. This is sometimes referred to as the "Blacker than Thou" debate (Cross, 1971) where African Americans argue among themselves as to who is true, who is genuine. We accuse each other of "acting White" or being "too ghetto." We worry about being accepted by other Blacks. We have issues about hair. If we straighten it we're accused of trying to be White. If we wear it natural we're too Black. If we date or marry someone from a different race we're a sell-out. We question each others' interests. Some activities are seen as acceptable and others unacceptable. For example, we say things like, "Black people don't ski," or "Black people don't swim."

The underlying theme in all these examples is identity. Who are we? What does it mean to be Black? Can some people be more Black than others? What's the standard? Who decides? All of these questions illustrate the fact that African Americans are struggling to gain a sense of who we are. A large literature exists on African-American identity. This chapter now focuses on this literature as a first step in examining this issue.

AFRICAN-AMERICAN IDENTITY: THEORY AND RESEARCH

Some authors (e.g., Sellers, Smith, Shelton, Rowley, & Chavous, 1998; Smith & Brookins, 1997) trace the beginnings of research on African-American identity to the classic study by Kenneth and Mamie Clark in 1939. In this study Clark and Clark (1939) asked African-American children to select the doll or picture that was the prettiest or smartest. They found that African-American children tended to associate more positive images with White dolls or pictures. The Clarks concluded that Black children have low self-esteem and negative feelings about their Blackness, and that these were the result of racism and discrimination suffered in the United States. Although subsequent studies have challenged the Clarks' original conclusions, their work influenced future work on racial identity.

Although the Clark and Clark study is of historical importance, it was the work of William Cross that more specifically addressed the issue of identity development for African Americans. In 1971 Cross published an article on the "Negro-to-Black conversion experience," where Blacks move from self-hatred to self-acceptance. Cross called this process "nigrescence," or the process of becoming Black. Cross proposed five stages that African Americans go through in the development of their identity. Briefly, the first stage is the *Pre-Encounter* stage, in which individuals view and think of the world as being non-Black, anti-Black, or the opposite of Black and act in ways that devalue their Black identity and idealize Whiteness. In the *Encounter* stage, individuals experience a startling personal or social event that motivates them to challenge their previous frame of reference and allows them to be receptive to a new interpretation of identity. In the third stage, *Immersion–Emersion*, the person idealizes Blackness, totally immerses him- or herself in Black culture, and rejects all non-Black values. Cross' fourth stage is *Internalization*. At this stage the person internalizes aspects of his or her immersion–emersion experience, achieves a feeling of inner security, feels more satisfied with and confident in his or her Black identity, and demonstrates increased comfort with and acceptance of other cultures. Cross' fifth and final stage is *Internalization–Commitment* in which the person's confidence in his or her Blackness leads to a sense of commitment to his or her community along with a plan of action for how to change that community. Later, these last two stages (Internalization and Internalization–Commitment) were combined into one fourth and final stage—*Internalization*.

Cross' model has had a major impact on the field. Parham (2001) states, "Studies involving racial identity have dominated the literature on multicultural counseling for some time" (p. 162). Studies include the development of scales to measure racial identity development (e.g., Parham & Helms, 1981); tests of the validity of Cross' model (e.g., Helms, 1989); application of Cross' model to other populations, such as Whites (e.g., Helms, 1995), and gays and lesbians (e.g., Walters & Simone, 1993); the relationship between racial identity and other variables, such as self-esteem (e.g., Parham & Helms, 1985a), demographic factors (e.g., Parham & Williams, 1993), affective states (e.g., Parham & Helms, 1985b), and the counseling process (e.g., Helms, 1985); and the development of other theories of racial/ethnic identity (e.g., Sellers et al., 1998). Most recently (July 2001), the *Journal of Multicultural Counseling and Development* published a special issue titled "Psychological Nigrescence Revisited," in which contributing authors give a historical overview of research on nigrescence theory, critically analyze its current status, and outline challenges for future research.

In 1991, Cross reviewed the first 20 years of racial identity research. His review of the literature resulted in a number of revisions to his original model. The basic ideas reflected in the original five stages were maintained. However, substantive changes were made to some of the stages, especially the Pre-Encounter and Internalization stages. The Pre-Encounter stage now includes two distinct identities—Pre-Encounter

Assimilation and Pre-Encounter Anti-Black. The *Pre-Encounter Assimilation* identity is characterized by adoption of a pro-American or mainstream identity. An individual at this stage views race as unimportant and race is not considered to be an important part of his or her identity. In contrast, the person with a *Pre-Encounter Anti-Black* identity sees being Black as very negative. One reason may be because the person internalized the negative stereotypes propagated about Black people by mainstream society (e.g., lazy, dumb, ugly). At the extreme, internalization of these negative stereotypes can lead to self-hatred. The Immersion–Emersion stage was also divided into two separate identities—Intense Black Involvement and Anti-White. *Intense Black Involvement* is similar to the original conceptualization of Immersion–Emersion in that there is an intense love and enthusiasm for everything Black. Yet, this identity also involves rage at White society for deceiving Black people, as well as rage and guilt toward oneself for believing them. The *Anti-White Immersion—Emersion* identity involves extreme negative attitudes toward White society, which may be expressed through daydreams and fantasies about hurting White people. Cross believes that these two can evolve as unique, separate identities. In other words, a pro-Black attitude does not automatically correlate with an anti-White attitude.

Cross' (1991) revised model also includes changes to the Internalization stage. Originally Cross saw movement through the stages as a self-actualization process where the person progresses to higher, healthier levels of psychological functioning. Cross now emphasizes the importance of Black acceptance and pride, rather than self-actualization. He no longer sees Internalization as synonymous with mental health. A person can achieve a sense of pride in his or her Blackness but still have problems in psychological functioning. The achievement of Internalization simply means a positive identification with one's racial group.

Although positive Black self-acceptance is the defining feature of the Internalization stage, Cross now proposes three distinct internalized identities—Black Nationalism, Biculturalism, and Multiculturalism. *Black Nationalism* is characterized by social and political activism, with a focus on empowerment, economic independence, Black history, and culture. An individual who typifies a *Bicultural* internalized identity is someone who integrates the positive aspects of both Black and American identities. Finally, someone with an internalized *Multicultural identity* has at least two other identities that are just as important as his or her positive Black identity. Thus, the person may consider his or her gender, sexual orientation, and/or religion to be equally as important as his or her race. The Multicultural identity also includes acceptance of others from diverse backgrounds.

Other modifications have been made to the theory over time. Cross initially proposed these as distinct stages occurring in progressive order. Parham (1989) suggests that an individual may not progress through each stage in nice orderly fashion; rather, a person may cycle back and forth through stages over his or her lifespan. For instance, someone who has reached the final stage of Internalization may have an experience that throws him or her back into the Encounter or Immersion–Emersion stages. It is also no longer assumed that each person begins his or her developmental process at the Pre-Encounter stage with pro-White/anti-Black sentiments. Adolescents who are raised in homes with parents who teach them to have a positive sense of their Blackness, or individuals who grow up in a predominantly Black environment may begin with a pro-Black orientation (Parham, 1989). Other developments in the theory relate to the conceptualization of the stages. It has been suggested that, rather than seeing each stage as separate and distinct, they should be seen as statuses (Helms, 1995) or differing worldviews (Helms, 1986).

A number of criticisms have been raised against Cross' model. One question is whether or not it is still relevant today. Cross developed the model during the late 1960s and early 1970s to describe a process he saw occurring among militant African-American college students at an exclusive Northeastern university (Cross, 1978). The question was raised as to whether the same stages apply to Black urban youth (Krate, Leventhal, & Silverstein, 1974). Cross' model has also been criticized for assuming a homogeneity of African-American experience and failing to recognize the many differences that exist between individual African Americans (Celious & Oyserman, 2001; Sellers et al., 1998), and for focusing only on the reactions of African Americans to racism and oppression (Akbar, 1989; Nobles, 1989). The validity of the stages has also been questioned. Some of them (e.g., Pre-Encounter) are not well-supported by empirical evidence (Cross, 1995; Helms, 1989).

Although Cross' model is arguably the most influential, there are at least 11 other models of racial/ethnic identity (Cross, Parham, & Helms, 1991). One of the more recent is the Multidimensional Model of Racial Identity (MMRI; Sellers et al., 1998). This model examines the significance of race in the overall self-concept of African Americans as well as the qualitative meanings they attribute to being members of that racial group. The Sellers et al. model includes four dimensions of African-American racial identity: salience, centrality, regard, and ideology. Racial *salience* "refers to the extent to which one's race is a relevant part of one's self-concept at a particular moment or in a particular situation" (p. 24). In other words, the significance of one's race varies across individuals and across situations. For example, being the only African American in a class may make race salient for one person but not have an impact on another student in the same situation. *Centrality* is the extent to which a person defines him or herself with regard to race, that is, whether or not race is a core part of the person's self-concept. Unlike salience, centrality is stable across situations. The evaluations that one has about being Black are the essence of *regard*. Sellers et al. identify two different types of regard—private and public. *Private regard* refers to the positive and negative feelings individuals have about their own Blackness as well as their feelings about Blacks as a group. *Public regard* is the extent to which individuals feel African Americans are viewed positively or negatively by society as a whole. Sellers et al.'s fourth dimension is *ideology*, or the individual's beliefs about how members of the race should act.

Sellers et al. (1998) also identify four ideological philosophies that are manifested across four areas of functioning. Someone with a *nationalist* ideology believes that African Americans should be in charge of their own destiny with little input from other groups. The *oppressed minority* ideology emphasizes the similarities between African Americans and other oppressed groups and sees coalition building as the most appropriate strategy for social change. Someone with an *assimilationist* ideology emphasizes the similarities between African Americans and the rest of American society and believes that African Americans should enter, as much as possible, into the mainstream. Individuals with a *humanist* ideology emphasize the similarities between all human beings and de-emphasize distinguishing characteristics such as race, gender, and class. These individuals are often concerned with larger human issues such as the environment, hunger, and peace.

Sellers and his colleagues use their model to explain the processes by which an individual's beliefs about race influence his or her attitudes and behavior in different situations. First, racial centrality and situational cues interact to determine the significance, or salience, of race for that person in that situation. In other words, both the characteristics of the person and the characteristics of the situation interact to determine how important race is at a particular time. Then, the individual's ideology and regard beliefs influence his or her interpretation of the event. This interpretation then determines the person's particular behavioral response. Let's illustrate this process with an example. Say Student A is a person for whom race is a core part of his overall self-concept (high centrality). Student A is the only African-American student in a sociology class and the class is having a discussion about gangs (situational cues). For Student A, the discussion heightens his awareness that he is the only African American in the class (high racial salience). Student A believes that the other students in the class and the professor have a negative view about gangs (public regard). Student A has strong feelings about the topic because he grew up in a neighborhood with a lot of gang activity (private regard). Student A interprets the discussion personally and gets very angry when he hears the professor and his fellow classmates making negative, stereotypical remarks about gang members and their behavior (appraisal/construal). Student A decides to drop the class.

Another student in the situation described in the preceding may have a very different response. Student B might also be high in race salience, but his private regard may be more negative and his ideology more assimilationist, so instead of dropping the class, he may decide to just sit quietly or may even agree with the negative, stereotypical comments being made by others. The Sellers et al. model increases the richness of our understanding of racial identity. The concepts they propose break racial identity down into more specific dimensions and increase understanding of the variable impact racial identity may have for different people in different situations.

A basic assumption of most African-American racial identity models is that African Americans face identity issues and conflicts that other groups do not because of their unique history in this country (i.e., slavery) and the racism, discrimination, and oppression they have experienced (e.g., Sellers et al., 1998). Because of this unique status it is believed that models and measures of racial identity must be specific to African Americans. Not everyone agrees with this perspective. One of the main proponents of ethnic identity as a general phenomenon is Phinney (1992). Phinney stated, "It is clear that each group has its unique history, traditions, and values; yet the concept of a group identity, that is, a sense of identification with, or belonging to, one's own group, is common to all human beings" (p. 158). Phinney (1990, 1992) identifies four key aspects of ethnic identity she believes are generalizable across ethnic groups. These are: (a) self-identification as a group member; (b) a sense of belonging, and attitudes toward one's group; (c) ethnic behaviors and practices; and (d) ethnic identity achievement.

Is there something unique about the African-American experience? Are there experiences common across ethnic groups? I would say that the answer to both questions is Yes. Yes, there are things unique to the experience of African Americans, as well as other groups, that should be acknowledged and explored. At the same time, we can expand our knowledge about race/ethnicity and its functions by looking for commonalities and similarities between groups. We must take both the emic (culture specific) and the etic (universal) perspectives.

Many measures have been designed to capture race. [See Burlew and Smith (1991) for an overview.] For example, Cross and his colleagues developed their own measure called the Cross Racial Identity Scale (CRIS; Vandiver, Fhagen-Smith, Cokley, Cross, & Worrell, 2001). Milliones (1980) also developed a scale based on Cross' stages called the Developmental Inventory of Black Consciousness (DIBC). However, the most widely used and cited measure based on Cross' model is the Racial Identity Attitude Scale (RIAS) by Parham and Helms (1981). Sellers et al. developed the Multidimensional Inventory of Black Identity (MIBI) to operationalize the MMRI (Sellers, Rowley, Chavous, Shelton, & Smith, 1997). In contrast, Phinney (1992) constructed the Multigroup Ethnic Identity Measure (MEIM) as a general measure of ethnic identity applicable across groups.

Other scales have been developed to look at separate, yet possibly related constructs. For example, Grills and Longshore (1996) developed a measure of *Africentrism*. Africentrism is defined as "the degree to which a person adheres to the *Nzugo Saba*, or the seven principles of Kwanzaa—*Umoja* (unity), *Kujichagulia* (self-determination), *Ujima* (collective work and responsibility), *Ujamaa* (cooperative economics), *Nia* (purpose), *Kuumba* (creativity), and *Imani* (faith) [see Thumbutu (1999) for more elaboration of these terms]. Landrine and Klonoff (1994, 1996; Klonoff & Landrine, 2000) developed the African American Acculturation Scale to measure eight theoretically derived dimensions of African-American culture. Individuals who score high on the scale reflect a traditional cultural orientation, or are immersed in African-American culture. Those who score low reflect an acculturated orientation, or low immersion in African-American culture. Although there is some evidence for a correlation between acculturation and racial identity (Pope-Davis, Liu, Ledesma-Jones, & Nevitt, 2000), the relationship between racial identity and these other constructs is not entirely clear.

Erikson (1950/1963) stated that one of the major developmental tasks for human beings is the establishment of an identity. For African Americans, a core aspect of their identity development process is discovering and deciding how their racial background fits into their overall sense of self. Racial identity theory and research have increased our understanding of this process. The theories have broken down racial identity into various stages and dimensions and the research has helped us understand how it is related to other aspects of our lives. Although much more work needs to be done, racial identity theory and research have helped us understand better who we are as African Americans.

Another step in addressing the question of identity is to examine the meaning of the current label we use to identify ourselves—African American. This means looking at both terms and exploring what it means to be African, what it means to be American, and what it means to be both. The next part of this chapter examines the Afrocentric worldview, the European-American worldview, how these two combine to form an African-American worldview, and how each of these has impacted the study of African-American identity.

The Afrocentric Worldview

Sue (1978) defined a worldview as "the way in which people perceive their relationship to nature, institutions, other people, and things. Worldview constitutes our psychological orientation in life and can determine how we think, behave, make decisions, and define events" (p. 458). What are the core components of an Afrocentric worldview? The following is a synthesis from a variety of sources that describes the basic tenets of an African-centered worldview (Casas & Mann, 1996; Mazama, 2001; Myers, 1985, 1988; Nobles, 1991; Parham, 1996; Parham, White, & Ajamu, 1999).

African people are a deeply spiritual people. Humans and spirit are one. "Spirit" is the energy that infuses all things in the universe, it is what connects us to God, the Creator of the universe. This spirituality relates to two other core concepts in the African perspective—interconnectedness and harmony. If all things in the universe are connected, then it is important to live in harmony with them, with nature. Interconnectedness and harmony also extend to social relationships. African cultures are collectivistic rather than individualistic. [See Triandis (1995) for an in-depth discussion of individualism and collectivism.] In collectivistic cultures the welfare of the group takes priority over the welfare of the individual and one's identity is rooted in the group as a whole. In African cultures, one's worth is evaluated based on his or her contributions to the community. This connectedness with others also extends to the self-concept, which has been described as the "extended self" (Nobles, 1976). The extended self includes all of the ancestors, the yet-unborn, all of nature, and the entire community. It is embodied in the statement, "I am because we are; we are, therefore, I am" (Mbiti, 1970).

The Afrocentric perspective also emphasizes holism, or a unity of being between the material and spiritual. It also encompasses a diunital philosophy, or unity of opposites, where the existence of opposing forces is seen as the natural order of things, such as male/female, good/evil, and life/death. Feelings are legitimate and emotional vitality is a central part of one's experience and expression. There is a more fluid and cyclical sense of time in African cultures. Time is elastic and is based on the occurrence of events rather than mathematical units. The focus in an Afrocentric worldview is more on the past (e.g., connection to one's ancestors) and on the present, or "being in the moment." African culture is based on an oral tradition. History is not written, it is passed down from generation to generation through the sharing of stories.

In summary, the Afrocentric worldview emphasizes spirituality, harmony with nature, collectivism, an extended sense of self, holism, a diunital philosophy, emotional vitality, a fluid and cyclical sense of time, an orientation toward the past and the present, and an oral tradition. Now we turn toward an examination of the Afrocentric worldview in psychology.

The Afrocentric Perspective in Psychology

Afrocentrism is a philosophical perspective that places African values and ideals at the center of life. The Afrocentric paradigm contends that our main problem as African people is our adoption of the Western/European worldview. Psychologists who adopt this paradigm believe that the key to mental health is the renunciation of Western values and beliefs and the adoption of an African worldview (Mazama, 2001). African Psychology, therefore, is defined as "the dynamic manifestation of the unifying African principles, values, and traditions whereby the application of knowledge is used to resolve personal and social problems and promote optimal human functioning" (Parham, 1996, p. 182).

The Afrocentric perspective was reflected in the theme of the 31st Annual Convention of the Association of Black Psychologists in 1999, "From Sankofa to Ma'at: Healing Ourselves." The word "Sankofa" suggests that in order to move forward we must look back, and reflects the idea that healing and growth for African Americans lies in returning to our African roots. Afrocentric psychologists look to African concepts, values, and principles to help the community develop a greater understanding of itself and to develop more effective ways for intervening with its members. All models of helping in psychology are based on European culture. Afrocentric psychologists reject these European approaches as inappropriate for their community and argue that new models must be developed based on traditional African culture.

Akbar (1981), Baldwin (1981), and Azibo (1989) offer three of the most cited theories on the Afrocentric perspective in psychology. Akbar (1981) proposes a classification of mental disorders specifically for African Americans. He describes four main categories of mental disorder among African Americans. The *Alien Self Disorder* includes those individuals who act contrary to their nature by rejecting their Africanness. They are materialistic and ignore the impact of racism and oppression. In essence, they adopt the perspective of and try to assimilate into the dominant (European) culture. The *Anti-Self Disorder* is similar to the Alien Self Disorder but has the added dimension of hostility toward one's own group and, by implication, toward oneself. These individuals identify with the oppressor by adopting the hostility and negativism of the dominant group. His third category is the *Self Destructive Disorders*. These are individuals who have found legitimate paths to survival blocked and have therefore turned to socially and personally destructive means to get their needs met. Examples include pimps, prostitutes, and drug pushers. Finally, Akbar includes *Organic Disorders*. He recognizes that some mental disorders have a physiological basis, but argues that these interact with social and environmental phenomenon. For example, poverty may lead to poor nutrition, which may lead to abnormal development for a fetus or child, which then results in an organic disorder.

Like Akbar, Azibo (1989) suggests alternative categories of mental disorder for African Americans. Azibo first makes a distinction between two concepts—*genetic Blackness* and *psychological Blackness*. Genetic Blackness refers to phenotypic racial features and psychological Blackness refers to African-centered psychological and behavioral functioning. (i.e., looking Black and acting Black). Azibo uses these two concepts to define various personality disorders for Black people. For example, Azibo's second category of personality disorders, *Psychological Misorientation,* involves operating without an African-centered belief system. This would be genetic Blackness minus psychological Blackness, where the person looks Black but does not act Black. Baldwin's (1981) theory emphasizes the importance of an identity that represents one's true, innate African core. This core interacts with the world, and when one's African self-consciousness is affirmed, one experiences harmony, but when it is suppressed or inhibited, one experiences disharmony or psychological problems.

These three theories illustrate the basic premise of Afrocentric psychology, that all people of African descent share a common psychological and biological core. This core is built on Afrocentric values, such as collectivism and harmony. As a result of the oppression and domination of Europeans, Blacks have gotten away from their true African selves and the only path to mental health is to center one's beliefs and behavior around Afrocentric values. Any identification with Eurocentric values is defined as psychological disorder for the Black person. Afrocentric psychologists believe these values should be incorporated into theory, research, and practice with African Americans. The assumption is that psychologists need to work from this perspective, rather than a Eurocentric one, if they are to truly understand and be effective in working with African Americans.

The European-American Worldview

Like the term African American, the term European American implies a blending of two cultures. In order to understand what it means to be American we must begin by looking at a Eurocentric, or Western worldview, since American culture has its roots in Western Europe. The basic tenets of the Eurocentric, or Western worldview were also gleaned from a variety of sources (Akbar, 1991; Baldwin, 1981; Myers, 1988; Parham, White, & Ajamu, 1999; Sue et al., 1996; White & Parham, 1990). Whereas in the Afrocentric worldview the emphasis is on "being," in the Eurocentric worldview the emphasis is on "doing." One's worth is evaluated based on his or her individual achievements, primarily economic success and material possessions. Therefore, Western cultures tend to be very materialistic and individualistic. In individualistic cultures the emphasis is on the self as a separate and unique being. The statement "I think, therefore I am" embodies this notion. Individual needs, wishes, and desires take precedence over those of the group. Independence and competition are valued. For example, in Western cultures, when a child reaches the age of 18, he or she is expected to be self-sufficient and to separate from the family. This might be accomplished by going away to college or by getting a job to support oneself financially. In collectivistic cultures often children stay at home until they are married, and children are expected to contribute economically to the family.

The idea of separateness extends into the spiritual realm. In the Eurocentric perspective, the material and spiritual are seen as separate entities and dichotomous (either/or) logic is used. Rather than being motivated to maintain harmony with nature, one is motivated to obtain mastery and control over it. Objectivity and rationality are valued. Knowledge is seen as a commodity external to oneself and is gained through counting, measuring, and observation. Time is also a commodity; it is seen as linear, concrete, precise, and measurable, and the focus is primarily on the future.

When we first think of what it means to be American we may conjure up images of John Wayne, Elvis Presley, or Bill Gates. (Notice that these are all White males.) These men symbolize the idea that to be American means to be powerful, independent, unique, creative, innovative, and rich. It is the idea that anyone can grow up to be President, even a poor boy from a broken home in Arkansas. All it takes is a little hard work and determination. In other words, American culture is based on the Protestant work ethic, which includes the ideas of hard work, self-control, personal initiative, resourcefulness, and future planning (White & Parham, 1990). It is the idea of "pulling oneself up by the bootstraps." Bill Gates and Bill Clinton are viewed as the ultimate American success stories because they started out with very little (or at least the same as everyone else) but used their ingenuity, talent, skill, and effort to gain money, power, and prestige. These examples also illustrate that American culture is based on the Western European values of materialism, independence, individualism, and competition.

Besides the Protestant work ethic, materialism, and individualism, American ideals also include freedoms, such as freedom of speech and religion. Americans believe in individual rights and fairness and justice for all, and unlimited educational and economic opportunities (Phinney & Onwughalu, 1996). Many people seek these ideals when they immigrate to this country. They come seeking "The American Dream." According to Hoschild (1995), the American Dream rests on four central tenets. They are: (a) equal opportunity; (b) the promise of success; (c) individual control over one's destiny; and (d) personal virtue conferred on the successful. America is seen as the land of unlimited opportunity. All one has to do is work hard and take advantage of those opportunities. That is why Americans are not very impressed with royalty in other countries. It is because those individuals (e.g., Prince Charles) did not do anything to gain their fame and fortune, it was simply handed to them at birth. Instead, Americans revere movie stars such as Tom Cruise and athletes such as Michael Jordan.[1] They are seen as possessing special virtues that allowed them to gain recognition and success.

There is really no need to summarize the impact of the European-American perspective on psychology. In essence, the field of psychology *is* European-American psychology because of the field's long history of focusing its theory, research, and practice on European (White) males. [See Robert Guthrie's (1997) book, *Even the Rat Was White: A Historical View of Psychology.*] It is only within the last 30 years that the field openly acknowledged the need to be more inclusive of those from diverse backgrounds.

The African-American Worldview

As mentioned, the term "African American" implies that Black people of African descent who were born and raised in the United States represent a blending of the two cultures. However, the whole is more than the sum of its parts in that African-American culture has many unique characteristics. All one has to do is look at the language, style of dress, food, music, literature, etc., to see how unique African-American culture is. One can see within these cultural manifestations elements of both African and European-American cultures as well as the impact of sociocultural and historical factors such as slavery, racism, discrimination, and oppression. These three forces combine to create African-American culture. The blending of these three forces can be seen in rap music where you hear the layering of complex rhythms that echo back to African drums, the Eurocentric values of individualism and materialism in the MC's[2] audacious bragging about his or her material possessions (e.g., Jay Z's "Big Pimpin'" on a yacht, wearing lots of gold, and drinking champagne), and stories about the pain, suffering, and violence associated with growing up Black in American society. (The Furious Five say, "It's like a jungle sometimes, it makes me wonder how I keep from going under.")

The uniqueness of the African-American worldview is evident in the six psychological themes for African Americans outlined by White and Parham (1990). Two of these are part of the more general Afrocentric worldview—emotional vitality and interrelatedness—but the remaining four can be viewed as unique to the African-American experience. The third psychological theme is *realness*, which reflects the idea that life is full of hardship, pain, sorrow, and struggle. These are considered a normal part of life that can not be avoided. The challenge is to survive these tragedies and keep on going. The fourth psychological theme is *resilience*. Once one has survived life's struggles he or she is able to go on and experience the renewal of joy, laughter, and sensuousness. Trouble will pass and freedom will emerge on the other side. White and Parham also discuss the *value of direct experience*. This is the idea that the best teacher is practical life experience. This is why older folks in the Black community, who may not have had a lot of formal education, are still valued for their life experience. This practical wisdom is reflected in sayings passed down from one generation to another, such as "Hard head make a soft behind," and "You don't get to be old being no fool." The final theme is *distrust and deception*. The racism and oppression experienced by Blacks in this country have led to a basic distrust of White people. This, in turn, has led Blacks to be somewhat deceptive in dealing with Whites. For example, during slavery Blacks sang spirituals to pass messages to one another. When slaves sang "Swing Low, Sweet Chariot" the slave master thought they were singing about going to heaven, but the slaves were talking about going up North to freedom. One can see the influence of both the Afrocentric worldview and the history of racism in White and Parham's six psychological themes for African Americans.

The African-American Perspective in Psychology

Although Afrocentric psychologists feel the key to a healthy identity is identification with traditional African core values and beliefs, the African-American perspective posits that a healthy identity is achieved through integration of both African and European-American worldviews. The evolving perspective of White and Parham in their second and third editions of *The Psychology of Blacks* presents an interesting contrast between these two perspectives. For example, in both books they describe the goal of mental health for African Americans as *identity congruence,* but their definition of this changes. In the second edition White and Parham (1990) state, "Each Black adolescent must attempt to set up some workable balance between Afro-American and Euro-American values within his or her own life space. Complete denial of either frame of reference will restrict choices and personal growth, interpersonal relationships and economic opportunities" (p. 47). In the more recent edition (Parham, White, & Ajamu, 1999) they define identity congruence (i.e., mental health) as "strong awareness of and identification with African cultural heritage, strong sense of motivation directed at ensuring collective survival of African people and related institutions, and the active resistance of any force (i.e., racism) that threatens the survival and maintenance of one's people and oneself" (p. 43). It is clear that they have moved from the African-American to the Afrocentric end of the continuum.

These two worldviews may conflict. W. E. B. DuBois (1903/1982) described this when he wrote, "One ever feels his twoness—an American, a Negro: two souls, two thoughts, two unreconciled strivings; two warring ideals in one dark body" (p. 45). White and Parham (1990) called it the "duality dilemma" in which young African Americans are exposed to two different sets of values and are confronted with being a part of, yet apart from, American society. Again, the Afrocentrists argue that the answer to this conflict is to let go of European-American values and beliefs and reconnect with one's African roots. However, those who take the African-American perspective have a different view. For example, Dr. Lisa Henry (personal communication, 1999), in her work on racial identity development, asserts that younger African Americans are forging a new identity that is distinctly American. She rejects the idea of the Afrocentric psychologists that the road to self-acceptance among African Americans lies in rediscovering our African roots. Instead, she believes that African Americans need to understand the influence that growing up in American society has had on them.

I became vividly aware of my "Americanness" the first time I traveled in Europe. Although I had traveled a lot before, most of the places I visited had a similar history where slavery occurred on the same soil (e.g., Brazil, the Caribbean). In most of those places, as in this country, it seemed the first thing people responded to was my Blackness. However, in Europe, the first thing people reacted to was my nationality. They saw me as American first and being Black was somewhere farther down the list. This became clear when I overheard some Greeks refer to my friends (also Black) and me as "the American girls." When I looked around to see about whom they were talking, one of my friends said, "They're talking about us." I was dumbfounded. American? Me? In the United States we would have been "the Black girls." My Americanness also became apparent in interactions with friends we made in different countries. It was clear that our sense of humor, our tastes in food, our cultural traditions, our interpersonal relationships, and even our life goals and aspirations were very different. Although I never identified myself that way before, it became apparent that in many ways I am indeed American. The same was true in my visits to Africa. Although we shared the same skin color and the same historical roots, it was clear that my experiences as an American made me very different from my African brothers and sisters.

The African-American perspective says African Americans are a blending of both African and European-American cultures. What evidence is there in the literature for the African-American perspective? Phinney and Devich-Navarro (1997) interviewed African-American adolescents about their sense of being American and gave them measures of American identity. African-American adolescents in their sample expressed a wide range of views, from strong identification with being American to denial of being American at all. In another study, Phinney, Cantu, and Durtz (1997) found that ethnic identity (i.e., positive identification with one's ethnic group) was negatively related to American identity. In contrast, American identity was positively correlated with attitudes toward other groups. In other words, adolescents who expressed a strong, positive degree of attachment to being African American had a weaker sense of being "American." However, if they had a strong sense of being "American," they also felt more positively toward other ethnic groups. In yet another study, Phinney and Onwughalu (1996) compared African immigrants with African-American students and the perceived applicability of American ideals (i.e., rights, freedoms, and opportunities). Although African-American students perceived themselves as more "American," African students perceived American ideals, such as freedom of speech and religion, as more applicable to them. That was the reason many of the African students immigrated to the United States, to take advantage of the opportunities available here, such as greater access to education. African-American students expressed a stronger sense of being American than the African students, but saw such opportunities as less available to them. Another group of researchers (Barlow, Taylor, & Lambert, 2000) studied African-American women and their perceptions of being "American." African-American women believed themselves to be American, but believed that European Americans did not perceive them as such, and perceived themselves as less "American" than European Americans.

In summary, the African-American perspective acknowledges the influence of both African and European-American cultures on Blacks in the United States. Although aspects of both cultures are evident, the whole is more than the sum of its parts, resulting in a unique culture all its own.

A CULTURAL CONTINUUM MODEL
OF AFRICAN-AMERICAN IDENTITY

It is interesting that all three perspectives presented in the chapter—Racial Identity theory, the Afrocentric paradigm, and the African-American paradigm—assume a homogeneity of experience, that is, one "Black experience" and/or one particular path to mental health. Although most of the authors presented here agree that African Americans are a heterogeneous group, many of them fail to account for this in their conceptualizations. African Americans' experiences and identity may differ based on additional demographic characteristics such as socioeconomic status, gender, and skin color (Celious & Oyserman, 2001).

I suggest an alternative perspective where African-American identity occurs along a continuum. At one extreme lies an Afrocentric identity, where one identifies most strongly with being African and shapes his or her identity around more traditional African values (e.g., collectivism). At the other end lies an identity where the individual primarily identifies with being American and espouses more traditional European-American values (e.g., individualism). An individual can fall anywhere along the continuum between those two extremes. Where he or she falls differs based on factors such as family background, life experiences, and other demographic characteristics (e.g., socioeconomic status). Other authors agree that African-American identity occurs along a continuum. For example, White and Parham (1990) state, "One can think of Black Americans as being spread along a cultural spectrum, the majority representing a combination of both African and American culture" (p. 21).

The concepts of individualism and collectivism are used as an example. Afrocentric psychologists say it is impossible for someone to fall in the middle and simultaneously espouse both individualistic and collectivistic views. The cultural continuum model proposes otherwise. An individual may be more individualistic or collectivistic depending on the topic or the situation. For example, when it comes to career goals, an African-American person may be more individualistic and may choose to move away from his or her family in order to take a promotion or better-paying position. Nonetheless, when it comes to voting behavior, that same person may vote for a candidate whose policies he or she believes are more favorable toward the African-American community as a whole.

The Afrocentric definition of mental health includes a value judgment about what kind of identity African Americans "should" have. From this perspective, a healthy African American is one who primarily identifies with African culture. Even some within the African-American perspective have very specific ideas about what it means to be "Black." We need to broaden this perspective and accept that mental health means many different things. For one individual, a healthy identity might mean being more Afrocentric, and he or she might wear Afrocentric clothing and hairstyles and belong to racially oriented organizations. However, for another person a healthy identity might mean wearing suits and ties and competing in the workplace. I agree that either extreme is unhealthy—total denial of one's Africanness or total denial of one's European-Americanness. One must find a balance somewhere between the two. How that is accomplished can vary widely. Such within-group diversity needs to be acknowledged, accepted, and respected.

Practical Implications of the Cultural Continuum Model

Since identity is one of the most critical issues facing African Americans, it is important to address these issues in psychotherapy (e.g., Allen, 1999; Baker & Bell, 1999, Sue & Sue, 1999). Carter (1995) says,

> Racial identity has a powerful effect on psychotherapeutic interactions on a covert and an overt level. . . . In therapy, each participant's racial identity and worldview combine to form particular types of relationships that result in varying processes, such as therapist and client strategies, affective responses, and outcomes. (p. 5)

When one views racial identity from a cultural continuum perspective, it means working with African-American clients without making assumptions about what "healthy" means. The goals of therapy are different for each person. The therapist must work with each individual to help him or her resolve identity issues in the most appropriate manner for him or her. This means assessing where he or she falls along the identity continuum. Determine what values the client currently espouses, how those values developed, and identify areas of conflict and distress. Which values seem to be egodystonic and which egosyntonic? Which ones are functional and which dysfunctional? It is important to do this assessment because if the therapist makes incorrect judgments about the client's racial identity this could be detrimental to the therapeutic relationship. For instance, if the therapist discusses topics and acts in a manner that is more Afrocentric when the client identifies more with the European-American end of the continuum, this could alienate the client.

The cultural continuum model of ethnic identity sees limitations in the European-American, Afrocentric, and African-American perspectives for their homogeneous view of African Americans and limited definitions of mental health. The cultural continuum model proposes that positive resolution of ethnic identity issues can vary widely from person to person, with some falling closer to the Afrocentric end, some the European-American end, and most somewhere in between.

CONCLUSION

In this chapter I have argued that the most critical issue facing African Americans in the new millennium is identity. During the slave trade concerted efforts were made to destroy the identity of African slaves. Despite the fact that more than 100 years have passed since the abolition of slavery, African Americans continue to struggle to regain a sense of who we are. Leading thinkers in the field agree that the main task for our community is to find our true sense of self. How we accomplish this is open for debate. Afrocentric psychologists believe the answer lies in returning to traditional African values and beliefs. Those who represent the younger generation suggest that we forge a new, distinct identity as Americans. They believe that we must accept the impact American culture has had on our values, beliefs, and behaviors. So what is the answer?

I believe it lies everywhere in between. There is no single path to mental health for African Americans; there is no one correct identity. What is healthy for one individual may not be for another. Psychologists need to broaden their perspective and develop a true appreciation and respect for the heterogeneity that exists in our community.

Racial identity development is a continuous process, one that continually moves African Americans forward toward greater growth and development. All voices and perspectives are needed. We needed both Martin Luther King, Jr. and Malcolm X. Today we need both Na-im Akbar and Lisa Henry. We are all working toward the same goal—the well-being of African Americans, individually and collectively.

END NOTES

1. African-American athletes and celebrities, such as Michael Jordan and Oprah Winfrey, are often used by European Americans as examples to support their believe that racism no longer exists and that all African Americans have to do is work hard to get ahead. This just further illustrates the effect of the Protestant work ethic on American culture.
2. "MC" stands for Master of Ceremonies and is the term used to refer to the lead or solo rapper.

REFERENCES

Akbar, N. (1981). Mental disorder among African Americans. *Black Books Bulletin, 7,* 18–25.
Akbar, N. (1989). Nigrescence and identity: Some limitations. *The Counseling Psychologist, 17,* 258–263.
Akbar, N. (1991). The evolution of human psychology for African Americans. In R. L. Jones (Ed.), *Black Psychology* (3rd ed., pp. 99–123). Berkeley, CA: Cobb & Henry.
Allen, I. M. (1999). Therapeutic considerations for African American students at predominantly White institutions. In Y. M. Jenkins, *Diversity in college settings: Directions for helping professionals* (pp. 37–49). New York: Routledge.
Azibo, D. A. (1989). African-centered theses on mental health and a nosology of Black/African personality disorder. *Journal of Black Psychology, 15,* 173–214.
Baker, F. J., & Bell, C. C. (1999). Issues in psychiatric treatment for African Americans. *Psychiatric Services, 50,* 362–368.
Baldwin, J. A. (1981). Notes on an Africentric theory of Black personality. *The Western Journal of Black Studies, 5,* 172–179.
Barlow, K. M., Taylor, D. M., & Lambert, W. E. (2000). Ethnicity in America and feeling "American." *Journal of Psychology, 134,* 581–601.
Burlew, A. K., & Smith, L. P. (1991). Measures of racial identity: An overview and a proposed framework. *Journal of Black Psychology, 17,* 53–71.
Carter, R. T. (1995). *The Influence of Race and Racial Identity on Psychotherapy: Toward a Racially Inclusive Model.* New York: Wiley.
Casas, J. M., & Mann, D. (1996). MCT Theory and implications for research. In D. W. Sue, A. E. Ivey, & P. B. Pedersen, *A theory of multicultural counseling and therapy* (pp. 139–154). Pacific Grove, CA: Brooks/Cole.
Celious, A., & Oyserman, D. (2001). Race from the inside: an emerging heterogeneous race model. *Journal of Social Issues, 57,* 149–165.
Clark, K. B., & Clark, M. P. (1939). The development of consciousness of self and the emer-

gence of racial identification of Negro pre-school children. *Journal of Social Psychology, 10*, 591–599.

Cross, W. E. (1971). The Negro-to-Black conversion experience. *Black World, 20*, 13–27.

Cross, W. E. (1978). The Thomas and Cross models of psychological nigrescence: A review. *Journal of Black Psychology, 5*, 13–31.

Cross, W. E. (1991). *Shades of Black: Diversity in African American identity*. Philadelphia: Temple University Press.

Cross, W. E. (1995). The psychology of nigrescence: Revisiting the Cross model. In J. G. Ponterotto, J. M. Casas, L. A. Suzuki, & D. M. Alexander (Eds.), *Handbook of multicultural counseling* (pp. 93–122). Thousand Oaks, CA: Sage.

Cross, W. E., Parham, T. A., & Helms, J. E. (1991). The stages of Black identity development: Nigrescence models. In R. L. Jones, *Black Psychology* (3rd ed., pp. 319–338). Berkeley, CA: Cobb & Henry.

DuBois, W. E. B. (1903/1982). *The Souls of Black folk*. New York: Signet.

Erikson, E. H. (1950/1963). *Childhood and Society* (2nd ed.). New York: Norton.

Fairchild, H. (1985). Black, Negro, or Afro-American? The differences are crucial. *Journal of Black Studies, 16*, 47–55.

Grills, C., & Longshore, D. (1996). Africentrism: Psychometric analyses of a self-report measure. *Journal of Black Psychology, 22*, 86–106.

Guthrie, R. V. (1997). *Even the Rat was White: A historical view of psychology* (2nd ed.). Boston: Allyn & Bacon.

Helms, J. E. (1985). Cultural identity in the treatment process. In P. Pedersen (Ed.), *Handbook of cross-cultural counseling and therapy* (pp. 239–245). Westport, CT: Greenwood.

Helms, J. E. (1989). Considering some methodological issues in racial identity research. *The Counseling Psychologist, 17*, 227–252.

Helms, J. E. (1995). An update of Helms's White and people of color racial identity models. In J. G. Ponterotto, J. M. Casas, L. A. Suzuki, & D. M. Alexander (Eds.), *Handbook of multicultural counseling* (pp. 181–198). Thousand Oaks, CA: Sage.

Hoschild, J. L. (1995). *Facing up to the American dream: Race, class, and the soul of the nation*. Princeton, NJ: Princeton University Press.

Klonoff, E. A., & Landrine, H. (2000). Revising and improving the African American Acculturation Scale. *Journal of Black Psychology, 26*, 235–261.

Krate, R., Leventhal, G., & Silverstein, B. (1974). Self-perceived transformation of the Negro-to-Black identity. *Psychological Reports, 35*, 1071–1075.

Lake, O. (1997). Cultural hierarchy and the renaming of African people. *The Western Journal of Black Studies, 21*, 261–271.

Landrine, H. & Klonoff, E. A. (1994). The African American Acculturation Scale. *Journal of Black Psychology, 20*, 104–127.

Landrine, H. & Klonoff, E. A. (1996). *African American acculturation: Deconstructing race and reviving culture*. Thousand Oaks, CA: Sage.

Mazama, A. (2001). The Afrocentric paradigm: Contours and definitions. *Journal of Black Studies, 31*, 387–405.

Mazrui, A. (1986). The dis-Africanization of the Diaspora. In *The Africans: A triple heritage*. Boston: Little, Brown.

Mbiti, J. S. (1970). *African religions and philosophies*. Garden City, NY: Anchor Books, Doubleday.

Milliones, J. (1980). Construction of a Black consciousness measure: Psychotherapeutic implications. *Psychotherapy: Theory, Research, and Practice, 17*, 175–182.

Myers, L. J. (1985). Transpersonal psychology: The role of the Afrocentric paradigm. *Journal of Black Psychology, 12*, 31–42.

Myers, L. J. (1988). *Understanding the Afrocentric worldview: Introduction to an optimal psychology*. Dubuque, IA: Kendall/Hunt.

Nobles, W. W. (1976). Extended self: Rethinking the so-called Negro self-concept. *Journal of Black Psychology, 2*, 15–24.

Nobles, W. W. (1989). Psychological nigrescence: An Afrocentric review. *The Counseling Psychologist, 17*, 253–257.

Nobles, W. W. (1991). African philosophy: Foundations for Black psychology. In R. L. Jones (Ed.), *Black psychology* (3rd ed., pp. 47–63). Berkeley, CA: Cobb & Henry.

Parham, T. A. (1989). Cycles of psychological nigrescence. *The Counseling Psychologist, 17*, 187–226.

Parham, T. A. (1996). MCT Theory and African American populations. In D. W. Sue, A. E. Ivey, & P. B. Pedersen (Eds.), *A theory of multicultural counseling and therapy* (pp. 177–191). Pacific Grove, CA: Brooks/Cole.

Parham, T. A. (2001). Psychological nigrescence revisited: A foreward. *Journal of Multicultural Counseling & Development, 29*, 162–164.

Parham, T. A., & Helms, J. E. (1981). The influences of a Black student's racial identity attitudes on preference for counselor's race. *Journal of Counseling Psychology, 28*, 250–256.

Parham, T. A., & Helms, J. E. (1985a). Attitudes of racial identity and self-esteem of Black students: An exploratory investigation. *Journal of College Student Personnel, 26*, 143–147.

Parham, T. A., & Helms, J. E. (1985b). Relation of racial identity attitudes to self-actualization and affective states of Black students. *Journal of Counseling Psychology, 22*, 431–440.

Parham, T. A., White, J. L., & Ajamu, A. (1999). *The psychology of Blacks* (3rd ed.). Upper Saddle River, NJ: Prentice-Hall.

Parham, T. A., & Williams, P. T. (1993). The relationship of demographic and background factors to racial identity attitudes. *Journal of Black Psychology, 19*, 7–24.

Phinney, J. (1990). Ethnic identity in adolescence and adulthood: A review of research. *Psychological Bulletin, 108*, 499–514.

Phinney, J. (1992). The Multigroup Ethnic Identity Measure: A new scale for use with diverse groups. *Journal of Adolescent Research, 7*, 156–176.

Phinney, J. S., Cantu, C. L., & Durtz, D. A. (1997). Ethnic and American identity as predictors of self-esteem among African American, Latino, and White adolescents. *Journal of Youth and Adolescence, 26*, 165–185.

Phinney, J., & Devich-Navarro, M. (1997). Variations in bicultural identification among African American and Mexican American adolescents. *Journal of Research in Adolescence, 7*, 3–32.

Phinney, J., & Onwughalu, M. (1996). Racial identity and perception of American ideals among African American and African students in the United States. *International Journal of Intercultural Relations, 20*, 127–140.

Pope-Davis, D. B, Liu, W. M., Ledesma-Jones, S., & Nevitt, J. (2000). African American acculturation and Black racial identity: A preliminary investigation. *Journal of Multicultural Counseling and Development, 28*, 98–113.

Sellers, R. M., Rowley, S. A. J., Chavous, T. M., Shelton, J. N., & Smith, M. (1997). Multidimensional Inventory of Black Identity: Preliminary investigation of reliability and construct validity. *Journal of Personality and Social Psychology, 73*, 805–815.

Sellers, R. M., Smith, M. A., Shelton, J. N., Rowley, S. A. J., & Chavous, R. M. (1998). Multidimensional model of racial identity: A reconceptualization of African American racial identity. *Personality and Social Psychology Review, 2*, 18–39.

Smith, E. P., & Brookins, C. C. (1997). Toward the development of an ethnic identity measure for African American youth. *Journal of Black Psychology, 23*, 358–377.

Sue, D. W. (1978). Worldviews and counseling. *Personnel and Guidance Journal, 56*, 458–462.

Sue, D. W., Ivey, A. E., & Pedersen, P. B. (1996). *A theory of multicultural counseling and therapy*. Pacific Grove, CA: Brooks/Cole.

Sue, D. W., & Sue, D. (1999). *Counseling the culturally different: Theory and practice* (3rd ed.). New York: Wiley.

Thumbutu, T. M. (1999). Kwanzaa. In J. S. Mio, J. E. Trimble, P. Arredondo, D. Sue, & H. E. Cheatham (Eds.), *Key words in multicultural intervention: A dictionary* (p. 168). Westport, CT: Greenwood.

Triandis, H. C. (1995). *Individualism and collectivism.* Boulder, CO: Westview.

Vandiver, B. J., Fhagen-Smith, P. E., Cokley, K. O., Cross, W. E., Worrell, F. C. (2001). Cross's *nigrescence* model: From theory to scale to theory. *Journal of Multicultural Counseling & Development, 29,* 174–200.

Walters, K. L., & Simone, J. M. (1993). Lesbian and gay male group identity attitudes and self-esteem: Implications for counseling. *Journal of Counseling Psychology, 40,* 94–99.

White, J. L., & Parham, T. A. (1990). *The psychology of Blacks: An African American perspective* (2nd ed.). Englewood Cliffs, NJ: Prentice-Hall.

Zak, I. (1973). Dimensions of Jewish-American identity. *Psychological Reports, 33,* 891–900.

CHAPTER 8

African-American Couples

Their Importance to the Stability of African-American Families and Their Mental Health Issues

SHALONDA KELLY

The importance of marital and couple relationships in America cannot be overstated. Almost every person develops intimate couple relationships at some point across the lifespan. Moreover, even with the rising divorce rates in America, nearly half of all marriages are life-long. American society and media commonly portray couple relationships as the wellspring for lifetime companionship, romance, support, sexual fulfillment, and individual well-being (Halford, Kelly, & Markman, 1997). For the heterosexual couples that are the focus of this chapter, media portrayals mirror empirical findings; on most happiness and mental health indices, people in happy marriages generally fare better than other members of society, both inside and outside of the United States. (Stack & Eshleman, 1998; Williams, Takeuchi, & Adair, 1992). For example, young married adults have higher rates of well-being than those who do not marry, even when accounting for premarital rates of mental health (Horwitz, White, & Howell-White, 1996). Happy couple relationships are also associated with positive familial adjustment. For example, children in two-parent families exhibit fewer rates of disorder as compared to those in divorced and step-parent families (Dawson, 1991), and marital satisfaction can buffer the effects of having severely mentally retarded children (Floyd & Zmich, 1991).

Just as happily married persons are likely to have greater well-being than other groups, unhappy marriages often have complex and bidirectional associations with familial distress and pathology (Grych & Fincham, 2001). For example, distressed couples commonly experience domestic violence (Mio et al., this volume), drug or alcohol abuse (McCrady & Epstein, 1995), and spousal depression or anxiety (Carter & Schultz, 1998), to the extent that conjoint treatments have been developed for these problems. In addition, spousal conflict and divorce are associated with child emotional and behavioral problems (Marcus, Lindahl, & Malik, 2001).

Although few studies investigate marriage among African Americans, national survey data demonstrate similar patterns with this population. In a five-site epidemiological study in the United States, rates of psychiatric disorder were higher for separated/divorced and widowed African Americans as compared to married African Americans. Notably, never-married African Americans did not have a higher risk of mental illness as compared to the married group. In addition, despite a few differences, these patterns were similar for Whites (Williams et al., 1992) and for separated versus married Mexican Americans (Warheit, Vega, Auth, & Meinhardt, 1985). In the National Survey of Black Americans, marital separation was associated with decreased life satisfaction, and divorce was associated with decreased life and family life satisfaction (Broman, 1988). In this same survey, working African-American parents who were married or cohabited reported greater life satisfaction than their never-married, separated, divorced, or widowed counterparts, and being married or cohabiting also predicted reduced effects of parental role strain on life satisfaction (Beale, 1997). Finally, National Opinion Research Center data indicate that higher percentages of married African Americans report being "very happy" as compared to their never-married, separated/divorced, and widowed counterparts (Creighton-Zollar & Williams, 1987).

Similar to other findings (Bryant & Beckett, 1997), these combined data show that married African Americans consistently report greater mental health and happiness than their non-married counterparts, with qualifications. First, findings were more consistent for those who were married as compared to separated and divorced, than as compared to never married or widowed. This inconsistency may result from an increasing tendency for Americans to cohabit. Given that one-fourth of all Americans and 35% of African Americans aged 15 to 44 have ever cohabited (Taylor, Tucker, Chatters, & Jayakody, 1997), it is likely that some never-married persons reap mental health benefits from cohabitation, perhaps owing to increased support and intimacy. Moreover, associations between marital status and mental health remain significant when the effects of age, gender, SES, and household size moderators are controlled (Creighton-Zollar & Williams, 1987, 1992; Williams et al., 1992).

THE PRIMARY ISSUES FACED BY AFRICAN-AMERICAN COUPLES, PUT IN PERSPECTIVE

Though all couples face similar challenges, African-American couples may have more difficulties with marriage. Many predictors of marital happiness are similar across racial and ethnic groups (McLoyd, Cauce, Takeuchi, & Wilson, 2000). For example, frequency of conflict, the wives' affairs, perceived interferences by the wives' friends, and the wives' feelings of marital unhappiness predict marital instability for African-American and White couples (Orbuch, Veroff, & Hunter, 1998), and familial predictors of marital distress are similar for White and Latino couples, such as low family cohesiveness (Lindahl & Malik, 1999). Despite interethnic similarities, U.S. Census Bureau data from 1970 to 2000 (Fields & Casper, 2001) show alarming statistics for African Americans in particular. In this period, the percent of married women in all ethnic groups combined dropped from 62% to 55%, whereas the corresponding drop for African-American women was from 54% to 36%. Similarly, although the percent of unmarried U.S. women rose from 38% to 45%, for the subgroup of African-American women, the corresponding rise was from 46% to 64%. Unlike with other groups, for unmarried African-American women, the greatest percentage change was the increase within the never-married subgroup. For African-American men, the gaps are smaller but very similar in comparison with men of other ethnic groups (Fields & Casper, 2001). Beyond these widening differences in married and never-married rates, census data also show that only 48% of African-American family households in 2000 were married-couple households, as compared to 68%, 80%, and 83%, for Hispanic, Asian and Pacific Islander and White non-Hispanic family households, respectively (Fields & Casper, 2001).

Marriage trends suggest that African Americans choose to marry less often than other groups; however, divorce is also a large problem. America's divorce rate has been rising such that currently one-half of all first marriages end in divorce (Lawson & Thompson, 1994). Yet although Whites experienced an increase from 56 to 153 divorces per every 1,000 women from 1970 to 1990, the comparative increase for African-American women was from 104 to 358 (Tucker & Mitchell-Kernan, 1995). Almost no data compare African-American couples with couples of other ethnic minority groups (McLoyd et al., 2000). Yet as compared to Whites, African Americans report significantly less happiness in their marriages (Oggins, Veroff, & Leber, 1993), they separate sooner (Taylor et al., 1997), and are less likely to remarry after divorce (Lawson & Thompson, 1994). Whereas 66% of White women remarry within 10 years of divorce, only 32% of African-American women do so (Cherlin, 1992), and African-American women are more likely to express dislike for marriage after experiencing it (Lawson & Thompson, 1994). Combined, the marriage and divorce rates reveal that African Americans primarily face difficulties in maintaining stable units as opposed to issues in meeting and forming a relationship.

These statistics should not lead readers to assume that African-American couples or families are pathological. First, as found with never-married African Americans and Spanish-speaking Mexican Americans, those who are not married do not necessarily experience poor mental health (Warheit et al., 1985; Williams et al., 1992). Like other ethnic minority groups, African Americans typically endure greater stress than Whites, yet they also typically have resources to cope with and compensate for these stressors (Ramseur, 1998), such as with extended family supports. Second, these statistics may be associated with oppression, and thus their accompanying problems are not endemic to being African American. For example, research conducted on minorities tends to overattend to pathology and oppression, which are maladaptive, as opposed to ethnicity and coping, which are adaptive (Bowman, 1992). Thus, this chapter addresses both ethnic strengths and weaknesses. Third, when social class and external stressors are controlled, African Americans tend to experience similar levels of self-esteem and overall mental health as compared to Whites (Neighbors, Jackson, Bowman, & Gurin, 1983). Fourth, leading models of mental health typically do not take into account the mental health needs of African Americans (Ramseur, 1998), and the instruments used to assess African Americans' mental health are typically neither made for nor normed on this population. From this, the interpretability of many adverse findings about the mental health of African Americans (as well as other minority groups) can be called into question (see Okazaki & Sue, 1995; Ramseur, 1998).

Based upon longitudinal data, Veroff and colleagues (Orbuch et al., 1998; Veroff, Douvan, & Hatchett, 1995) postulated ways that racial and cultural contexts may explain differing marital statistics across racial groups. First, couples' relationships are embedded in their cultures, which provide norms and expectations that influence couples' perceptions of and responses to interpersonal events. Second, some phenomena may be important to couples in one culture, but not to couples in another culture. For example, husbands' participation in child care is associated with well-being for African-American but not White wives (Orbuch et al., 1998). Third, the risk factors for marital instability may differ for ethnic groups, such as with life cycle transitions. For example, African-American women have a higher likelihood of entering into marriage as a parent as compared to White women (Orbuch et al., 1998). Further, African-American couples' pattern of conflict over the life cycle differs from that of Whites and Mexican Americans (McLoyd, Harper, & Copeland, 2001). Fourth, couples of different ethnic backgrounds may organize their interactions differently in major areas, such as gender and power. Finally, some variables that predict marital stability may manifest themselves differently within and across cultures (Orbuch et al., 1998). Thus, major factors that impact the stability of African Americans' marriages are summarized in the following pages.

UNIQUE ISSUES FACING AFRICAN AMERICANS THAT CAN IMPACT THEIR COUPLE RELATIONSHIPS

Economic hardship deters marriage and promotes marital dissolution, and since 1959, African Americans have historically had substantially higher poverty rates than all other ethnic groups measured by the census, with the exception of Latinos (Dalaker, 2001). Since 1954 their unemployment rates have been twice those of Whites, even in times of economic growth (McLoyd, 1990). The decline in blue collar manufacturing jobs historically held by African-American men exacerbates this issue, and renders them less appealing as potential husbands (Taylor et al., 1997). In fact, African-American men with employment instability are less likely to marry as compared to their employed counterparts (Kiecolt & Fossett, 1995). For married African-American couples, financial dissatisfaction partially accounts for marital problems (Broman, 1993). Although African Americans' strength of egalitarian relationships may help them to cope with the economic "glass ceiling," additional strengths may be needed to counter their financial difficulties. For example, African-American men's employment difficulties are associated with decreases in their own family satisfaction, which are correlated with other quality of life indices (Bowman, 1992). In addition, marital disruption related to Black men's economic situation results in more female-headed single parent families (McLoyd, 1990). Although many female-headed families thrive, single mothers are more at risk than other family heads for stress, economic loss, and emotional problems in themselves and their children (McLoyd, 1990).

African-American couples' socioeconomic situation is often accompanied by an emotional component that may also result in marital problems. For example, although African-American women tend to be more educated than their male counterparts and often obtain jobs more quickly, they make less money than White men, African-American men, and White women (Aborampah, 1989). Conversely, African-American men are more likely to be unemployed as compared to other men (Chapman, 1988). At times, these different challenges may lead African-American spouses to compete and resent each other because of accompanying beliefs that the other partner has it "easier" in the labor market (Aborampah, 1989; Boyd-Franklin, 1989). Additionally, African-American men's decreased economic opportunities coexist with a societal expectation that men are primary providers (McLoyd, 1990), which sometimes elicits anxiety and further contributes to marital instability (Veroff et al., 1995).

There is also a sex-ratio imbalance where African-American women outnumber the men (Aborampah, 1989; Orbuch et al., 1998). The imbalance also contributes to the rise in African-American single parent families (Taylor et al., 1997), because when the community sex ratio is fairly even, the likelihood that African-American women are or have ever married is higher (Kiecolt & Fosset, 1995). The decrease in number of men per 100 women has been attributed to higher male mortality, imprisonment, and drug abuse (e.g., Lawson & Thompson, 1994). For example, over 200,000 of the nearly 500,000 regular crack users are African American, and the vast majority of these users are males in the marriageable age range of the twenties through the fifties (Lawson & Thompson, 1994). In addition, substance abuse is associated with marital instability for African-American men (Veroff et al., 1995). African-American singles and couples who do not suffer these ills at times may cope maladaptively with the sex-ratio imbalance, such as with jealousy, competition, and man sharing by the women, and commitment problems for the men (Aborampah, 1989; Lawson & Thompson, 1994).

These findings suggest that the combination of economic powerlessness experienced by many African-American husbands and the sex ratio that favors them may make it all too easy for competition and extramarital relations to ensue. Such problematic coping mechanisms have been noted to exist more frequently in societies with unbalanced male–female sex ratios, because viable alternatives exist for the gender that is in short supply (Taylor et al., 1997). Data also support the assertion that the less available gender may take on more importance in couple relationships. For example, African-American husbands reported receiving more affirmation from their wives than their wives reported receiving from them, as well as more affirmation than White husbands reported receiving from their wives (Oggins et al., 1993). Also, unlike with White couples, African-American wives' understanding of their husbands and their use of a collaborative style with their husbands was predictive of future levels of marital well-being (Acitelli, Douvan, & Veroff, 1997; Orbuch et al., 1998). These data further indicate that alternative positive coping mechanisms exist; in this situation, African-American women may benefit from attending to the societal experiences of their husbands in a supportive fashion (Acitelli et al., 1997).

Societal pressures that include racism also negatively impact African-American couple relationships in several ways. As early as 1950, Erikson (1950) noted the entertainment industry's extensive dissemination of negative African-American caricatures and stereotypes that serve to strip them of positive identities. Since the 1960s, African Americans have faced strong White resistance to the advancement and equality of African Americans embedded in racially hostile practices and policies, such as with a drastic increase in arrest rates (Edsall & Edsall, 1991) and housing discrimination (Lawson & Thompson, 1994). In turn, African-American couples may experience psychological depletion and decreased marital quality as a result of the "carry home effects" of discrimination and lack of opportunity (Lawson & Thompson, 1994; Oggins et al., 1993). Clinicians note that African-American couples sometimes displace their racism-related anger and frustration toward each other (Boyd-Franklin & Franklin, 1998). Because of these pressures, African Americans' perceptions of their own group and society are very important.

One racism-related perception that impacts African-American couples is the belief in negative in-group stereotypes. Racism is theorized to affect African-American couples when they internalize the negative images of themselves portrayed by society (Jewell, 1983), which may also be aggravated by an increase in social ills that are often a byproduct of racism. For example, African-American women who did not live with their fathers reported that their mothers either avoided intimate relationships or had a series of transitory relationships (Boyd-Franklin, 1989). According to Boyd-Franklin (1989), these experiences seemed to convey to these grown daughters that "Black men are no good" or that "They won't be there for you when you need them" (p. 226), especially in regard to financial support. Empirical analyses have also documented the deleterious effects of negative racial in-group perceptions; even low endorsement of negative stereotypes indicating that African Americans are cognitively inferior to and more sexual than Whites differentiates distressed from non-distressed African-American couples (Taylor & Zhang, 1990). Similarly, a more recent study found modest support for the deleterious effects of internalized stereotypes on the dyadic trust and adjustment of African-American couples (Kelly & Floyd, 2001). Further, data show that the endorsement of a number of negative racial and cultural perspectives, indicative of anti-White and/or hostile pro-Black attitudes, is consistently associated with increased individual distress, and decreased dyadic trust and relationship quality (Kelly, 2002). These associations appear to be worse for low SES African-American couples as compared to those of higher SES couples (Kelly, 2002; Taylor, 1990).

STRENGTHS OFTEN FOUND WITHIN AFRICAN-AMERICAN COMMUNITIES, FAMILIES, AND COUPLES

The African-American community is also the repository for culturally related strengths that can compensate for the aforementioned issues. These include role flexibility, egalitarianism, extended familialism, and a religious and/or spiritual orientation. Bryant and Beckett's (1997) review of empirical studies conducted in the 1960s through the 1980s demonstrates that African-American couples have long been more egalitarian as compared to White couples in terms of family structure, power, engagement in household chores, and child care. African Americans have also reported more liberalized views of women's roles as compared to Whites (Crovitz & Steinmann, 1980), perhaps because African-American women had long histories of working outside of the home before it became commonplace in America. Yet satisfied African-American couples are also traditional in some ways. For example, as with findings regarding most Americans, husband-led African-American couples reported more happiness in their relationships than egalitarian or wife-led couples (Gray-Little, 1982). However, when they reported similar (i.e., more egalitarian) levels of decision-making power and "giving in" during disagreements, their marital quality was higher than if they reported large differences between the partners in decision making and "giving in" (Gray-Little, 1982).

Recent data support this historical trend. In a study of 80 married African-American couples, both spouses were more likely to reject than accept male-dominance ideologies, and each indicated having some decision-making authority in a variety of areas presented to them (Bryant & Beckett, 1997). Still, across SES levels, the men tended to endorse male dominance more strongly than their wives, whose endorsement of male-dominance ideologies was likely to decrease as their SES levels increased (Bryant & Beckett, 1997). Also, the areas in which the spouses reported having the highest levels of authority tended to be fairly traditional. Thus, although African-American couples tend to be more egalitarian than White couples and tend to reject male-dominance ideologies, some traditional preferences also remain.

African Americans' role flexibility goes beyond the couple to the extended family. The extended family can include blood kin, such as uncles, as well as "fictive" kin, who are unrelated by blood but are like family in terms of involvement and function (e.g., a "church family" or "play mama," Boyd-Franklin, 1989). Traceable to Africa, the extended family is a source of support and help for African Americans (Hines & Boyd-Franklin, 1996). The extended family engages in reciprocal assistance with money, goods, and services, and it may serve a mediating, judging, or networking function. It is also common for extended family members to share their homes with each other, ranging from short-term stays to help family members recover from housing or financial problems, to an indefinite number of years in the case of informal adoption (see Boyd-Franklin, 1989). Ethnographic research has long found that extended family networks increase the economic viability of African-American families. Additionally, surveys show that kin proximity, subjective closeness, and frequency of kinship interaction contribute to the physical and emotional well-being of African Americans (Taylor, Chatters, & Jackson, 1997).

Religious institutions and spiritual beliefs are additional sources of strength for African Americans, and are central within the African-American community. Religion refers to "institutional expressions of spirituality" (Frame & Williams, 1996, p. 41), which for most African Americans, refers to the church. African-American churches provide mutual aid, serve educational functions, and develop formal and informal programs designed to support and improve the welfare of African Americans (Ellison, 1997). Churches also confer status roles on African Americans, such as deacons, which can compensate for any lack of occupational and educational status in American society (Boyd-Franklin, 1989). Churches further serve a political function in encouraging organizational leadership skills, resistance, and activism (Taylor, Mattis, & Chatters, 1999). Beyond religious institutions, African Americans' spirituality can be defined as "an inner journey toward a relationship with a transcendent Being" (Frame & Williams, 1996, p. 41). Both religious and nonreligious African Americans tend to have a generalized spiritual orientation that is part of their daily experiences, to the extent that they often discuss psychological problems in the context of spirituality and religion (Frame & Williams, 1996).

Consistent with the foregoing clinical observations, data have demonstrated greater levels of religiosity and spirituality within African Americans as compared to other ethnic groups. Across five national probability samples consisting of 46,725 Whites and 9,802 African Americans, African Americans reported significantly higher levels of religious involvement and spirituality as compared to Whites (Taylor et al., 1999). In another sample, African Americans reported significantly higher levels of religiosity as compared to Mexican Americans and Whites, although the profiles of African Americans and less acculturated Mexican Americans supported theory that ethnic minority populations may seek meaning in religion to compensate for a disadvantaged status (Neff & Hoppe, 1993). Moreover, African Americans endorsed more meaning, control, and self-esteem enhancing attributions to God than did Whites (e.g., "In God's eyes I am a worthwhile person," "God oversees all the events in a person's life," and "Everything in life happens for a reason in God's eyes," respectively, Blaine & Crocker, 1995, p. 1034). Unlike with White participants, for African Americans, religious belief salience (e.g., "Being a religious person is important to me," Blaine & Crocker, 1995, p. 1034) was associated with predictors of individual well-being. Moreover, unlike with White participants, after controlling for religious belief salience, African Americans' meaning-enhancing attributions to God and their private collective self-esteem (e.g., "I feel good about the social groups I belong to") were significantly associated with their individual well-being (Blaine & Crocker, 1995).

African Americans' religious beliefs and practices are also associated with their familial and couple well-being. Participation in church and other religious activities predicts increases in African Americans' positive self-ratings of their family role performance, and reports of church participation are associated with reports of having very close family ties (Ellison, 1997). Moreover, married African Americans are likely to report that religion is important in their lives; they regularly seek spiritual support and have high levels of religiosity as compared to nonmarried African Americans (Taylor et al., 1999). In explaining the marital results, researchers have highlighted the socially integrative functions of churches; they provide doctrine regarding ideal marital roles and socialize couples in ways that positively impact their marital and family lives (Taylor et al., 1999). These functions of the church are likely to be particularly important for African-American couples, who attend church more often than White couples.

CONDUCTING THERAPY WITH AFRICAN-AMERICAN COUPLES

It is crucial that clinicians understand how to utilize the preceding contextual information in treating Black couples. First, one cannot assume that each factor applies to
African-American couples who seek treatment, and therapists must use one of the
many methods are available to assess these factors. One can use questionnaires to
assess their racial identity, level of acculturation, or Afrocentricity (Vandiver, Cross,
Worrell, & Fhagen-Smith, 2002), to indicate how each views and participates in his or
her ethnic traditions, and in the larger American culture. Therapists can also ask sensitive yet direct questions about how each partner identifies culturally, according to
their level of comfort (Hines & Boyd-Franklin, 1996). For example, the therapist can
ask, "Are there aspects of your race or culture that you think are important for me to
know in working with you?" Another alternative is to probe each of the aforementioned racial/cultural factors individually, such as with the question, "Do you have any
spiritual or religious beliefs that are important?" Irrespective of the method used, therapists must assess these areas in a way that they feel comfortable, and raise the issue of
race and culture to engender an atmosphere in which anything can be discussed (Boyd-
Franklin, 1989).

In a related vein, despite potential similarities enjoyed by couples in which both
partners are African American, it is as crucial for therapists to notice and address
cultural differences within these couples as it is to address them with interracial couples.
This is because each partner has the choice of how much to participate in African-
American culture versus mainstream American culture, and these choices impact their
chosen gender roles, friends, leisure activities, values, and more. Based upon these
cultural decisions and values, Jones and Chao (1997) have noted three common ethnically and culturally related problems within African-American and other couples: "(a)
discrepant levels and kinds of ethnic identifications; (b) ignorance or denial in one or
both partners of the significant impact of ethnic/cultural differences and/or external
oppression; and (c) discrepant ideas about coping with external oppression" (p. 160).
Therapists must also note that these common problems can be so subtle that couples
may not know that they are operating. For example, partners' differing levels of ethnic
identification could be manifest in their differing levels of comfort with other groups.
In such a situation, a husband may feel anger at his wife regarding her time spent with
a White coworker. Yet he may not think to convey this to her or discuss why his anger
is related to her higher comfort with Whites as opposed to those of her own racial
group, or convey how this conflicts with his extensive pride in his race and heritage.
Such cultural mismatches may create much conflict and distress (Jones & Chao, 1997).

To alleviate cultural conflicts within the couple, Jones and Chao (1997) suggest
that therapists engender three cultural factors within couples: "(a) a conscious awareness by both partners of the role that culture plays in relationships; (b) the ability of
both partners to experience ethnic and cultural energies as an expansion rather than a
threat to the self; and (c) the paradoxical ability of both partners to develop their own
uniqueness because of the other partner's different cultural background" (pp. 169–
170). Toward these ends, they propose that therapists help couples to develop shared

meanings and spiritual understandings that transcend their culture and develop common rituals together (Jones & Chao, 1997). Therapists may also identify underlying value differences within the couple's conflicts, and explore the extent to which the differences are related to racial, ethnic, or cultural perspectives held by either partner. For example, with an African-American couple dealing with the husband's decreased household responsibilities in the face of his unemployment, the therapist can elicit discussion of and empathy for the husband's loss of the traditional provider role that he values, and his fears that housework would diminish his manhood. The therapist can also encourage the couple to contrast the provider value with the wife's value of the African-American tradition of flexible and egalitarian family roles, toward connecting the partners and engaging them in problem solving toward alternatives that can satisfy both values. This approach recognizes that it is essential to assist the couple in labeling and anticipating conflicts that may result when they make different choices in participating in in-group versus mainstream cultural activities (Jones & Chao, 1997).

African Americans' racial and cultural perspectives not only impact how they relate to their partners, but these perspectives also impact how African Americans perceive and treat their therapists. These reactions can be based upon the therapist's race alone, irrespective of how the therapist presents. For example, African Americans' racial identity attitudes are associated with preferences regarding the race of their therapist (Parham & Helms, 1981). Clinical observations also suggest common responses that African Americans may have toward Therapists of Color and White therapists. Therapists of Color who see African-American couples may receive questions as to their competence, responses conveying distance/dissimilarity, or responses conveying feelings of similarity and/or connection (Boyd-Franklin, 1989). White therapists commonly elicit one or both of the partners' strong anger at Whites because of oppression, reluctance to see a White therapist, or an ingratiating style and excessive deference. Such racial salience also makes it important for White therapists to understand the issue of White privilege (McIntosh, 1998), in order to truly empathize with and respect these sensitivities.

Knowledge of status and SES issues can also prepare the therapist for poor African Americans' reluctance to use therapy. Poor African-American families can consist of the working poor, the unemployed, the underemployed, and welfare recipients (Boyd-Franklin, 1998). African-American couples in each of these groups are likely to feel very powerless because of frequent intrusions of outside agencies, such as schools, clinics and hospitals, child welfare and social service agencies, and court systems. Often, they seek treatment from a therapist because of an agency mandate, as opposed to their own desire to seek this type of help (Boyd-Franklin, 1998). Particularly among poorer African Americans, cultural biases against therapy may also exist, wherein therapy is seen as being only for rich, "crazy," or White persons. Indeed, the word "therapy" may be perceived negatively; therefore, therapists may use the word "counseling" to improve the couple's openness to treatment (Boyd-Franklin, 1998).

Beyond SES issues, there is a community-wide reluctance for African Americans to participate in therapy. First, they are aware that the mental health field has traditionally held a pathological and deficit view of them (Jones, Brown, Davis, Jeffries, &

Shenoy, 1998). African Americans also generally do not share life details with those outside of their family network. Third, unlike with some groups, therapists do not automatically have credibility within the African-American community. Rather, some African Americans may ignore degrees and assess the feeling or "vibes" that they get from the therapist in regard to respect, sincerity, and trustworthiness (Boyd-Franklin, 1998). For example, at the end of the first couples therapy session, an African-American middle-class wife told her doctoral level therapist that she could receive therapy because of her feeling that the therapist understood and respected her concerns. Thus, for several reasons, a "healthy cultural suspicion" of the therapist and therapy situation may exist, particularly when therapists are unduly intrusive (Boyd-Franklin, 1998).

Therapists must prioritize conveying respect to African Americans, because they may be sensitive to being devalued by society, and may feel vulnerable with therapists and each other in regards to their status and achievement. Suggestions for conveying respect include avoiding the use of language that can convey the partners are defective in some way, professional jargon, and the assumption of familiarity (such as using their first names) without asking permission (Wright, 2001). Because African Americans are less likely than other groups to have therapy experience, the therapist can provide nonthreatening psychoeducation about the therapy process, and convey clear expectations regarding the therapist's and couple's roles. The therapist must also ensure that his or her practice or agency is deemed beneficial by the community, because the community's perception can also facilitate the therapist's ability to obtain clients from this population. Consistent with this notion, therapists who use approaches that involve problem solving and advocacy, such as multisystems, structural, and cognitive behavioral therapies, have experienced successes in treating African Americans because they deal with the particular concerns that are expressed by this population (Boyd-Franklin, 1998).

Therapists can also utilize African-American couples' cultural strengths in combating their problems. Particularly with poorer couples and families, therapists who operate from a strengths-based perspective are more likely to combat the common over-attendance to failures. For example, therapists can openly acknowledge and validate the importance that African Americans place on their kinship networks (Hill, 1998). Studies commonly show that it is key for all persons to have a positive sense of their own ethnic identity. Thus, helping couples to identify and share positive information about their racial and ethnic backgrounds can increase their feelings of self-worth and further convey respect (McGoldrick, Giordano, & Pearce, 1996; Wright, 2001). In addition, therapists can analyze African-American couples' relationships according to which common or typical strength of African Americans might be missing within the couple relationship, and then use therapeutic techniques to engender it. For example, if the couple reports to the therapist that they are isolated and do not have any community supports, the therapist can view and convey this fact as a loss of one of their strengths. Accordingly, rather than just treating the nuclear family, the therapist can then assist the couple with rebuilding any positive community ties that they may have once held, or to build new ones.

Another way to utilize African-American couples' strengths is to extend opportunities for elders, other respected family members and clergy to collaborate in treatment (Boyd-Franklin, 1989). For example, if the couple deems it appropriate, talking with their pastor and forming an alliance with him or her can enhance treatment outcomes and provide additional therapeutic leverage. Therapists should also identify the supports offered by local African-American churches, given that many provide couples ministries and programs to develop their parishioners. Therapists may also need to do home visits and to visit institutions in the African-American community so as to reach the couple's natural support systems. Therapists can help to identify community role models for the couple, and to discuss with them the valued roles that the couple may play in the community. Therapists can also use spiritual themes in conducting therapy with African-American couples (Frame & Williams, 1996). For African-American clients who do not go to church, therapists may determine the role of each partner's spirituality in their emotional and psychological lives and then build upon it as a coping mechanism (Boyd-Franklin, 1998). Clearly, methods of using the strengths of African Americans can increase the therapeutic alliance, motivation, and coping skills of these couples.

Therapists must be aware that when African-American couples fail to engage in their strengths and become impacted by oppression and negative media-driven stereotypes, they may have problems with developing healthy gender roles. For African-American men who have difficulties in fulfilling their provider, husband, or parent roles, therapists can predict their potential dissatisfaction and possible lack of involvement in their families (Bowman, 1992), and label it as role discouragement, rather than lack of interest. Accordingly, therapists can also focus upon building African-American men's skills and providing reinforcement when they enact their husband and parent roles. In a related fashion, knowledge of the sex ratio imbalance and its historical context can help therapists to understand that for some African-American men, sexual prowess may compensate for lack of societal status, even when they are relatively happy in their relationship (Majors & Billson, 1992). Therapists can address such a tendency by helping these men compare their values of being sexually potent with their values of being good husbands, while highlighting some of the power and status that they can experience as husbands. Simultaneously, therapists can assist African-American wives in further supporting and reinforcing their husbands' sense of power and status in times of economic stress.

Given the negative media images about African Americans, one issue for some African-American women is a concern about their attractiveness relative to White women. Thus, some African-American women may feel particularly threatened in regard to infidelity, their femininity, and their attractiveness (Jewell, 1983). Therapists may encourage African-American women to compare themselves with local examples of in-group beauty, which are likely to be more favorable than when they compare themselves to mainstream media images. Further, therapists can help their husbands to understand the potential double assault of infidelity on the bonds of marital trust, and on the women's sense of their own adequacy and worth.

Last, therapists' self-exploration in regard to race, ethnicity, and culture is essential. Presentation of issues germane to many African-American couples and tips on working with them do not imply that issues related to race and culture all reside within the couple. In fact, many data show that clinicians have significant diagnostic and treatment biases about African Americans (e.g., Atkinson, Brown, Parham, Matthews, Landrum-Brown, & Kim, 1996). Thus, therapists of all ethnicities must also assume that in living in a society that perpetuates racism, they have developed areas of discomfort around this sensitive issue. Therefore, *all* therapists can benefit from the following:

- Exploring and identifying their personal racial and cultural issues
- Learning basic knowledge about the racial and cultural backgrounds of their clients
- Learning about institutional and structural aspects of racism, as well as White privilege and power (see also Pinderhughes, 1989)
- Developing and assessing the appropriateness of hypotheses related both to the norms of their clients' subgroups as well as to mainstream norms
- Open discussion of racial and cultural factors in supervision
- Consideration of other groups in addition to African Americans and Whites, so as to have a broader, less polarized understanding of racial and cultural issues

CONCLUDING COMMENTS

The literature is unequivocal about the importance of couple relationships for all Americans, and for African Americans in particular. Although married African-American couples tend to be better adjusted than African Americans having other marital statuses, there is a decline in African-American marital relationships that outstrips the marital decline of other groups. Historical, clinical, and empirical approaches each indicate that pernicious factors related to oppression impact these couples, such as poverty, a sex ratio imbalance, and stereotypical, negative images that some African Americans develop about their own racial group. Given these factors, it is laudable that not only do African Americans cope with these factors in ways similar to other groups, but they also utilize particular community-related strengths in overcoming them, such as egalitarianism, a tendency toward extended families, and strong religious and spiritual beliefs and practices.

Beyond the identification of positive and negative factors important to many African-American couple relationships, therapists can develop an understanding of how these factors manifest themselves as therapeutic issues within the couple. The diversity in African-American communities necessitates that therapists determine which of the factors operate both upon and within each African-American couple encountered in treatment. Once the issues germane to each couple are assessed, therapists are encouraged to use African Americans' relevant strengths in addressing each couple's issues, and to engage in the relevant strategies delineated to significantly improve their treatments for African-American couples.

Finally, researchers and policymakers can help to strengthen African-American couple relationships. It is first important to reiterate that comparisons with Whites are often conducted with a deficit perspective, and few comparisons across ethnic minority couples have been done (McLoyd et al., 2000). Thus, policymakers can encourage more studies that examine common strengths of African-American and other ethnic minority couples so that researchers can contribute to an understanding of the mechanisms and conditions by which they operate. Moreover, researchers can work with clinicians to develop and validate ethnically and culturally effective therapy approaches that consider the strengths of African Americans. It is likely that tandem enhancement-oriented efforts like these can support and increase the viability of African-American couples. These successes may also spill over into African Americans' familial relationships, such that future generations may be similarly strengthened.

REFERENCES

Aborampah, O. (1989). Black male-female relationships. *Journal of Black Studies, 19,* 320–342.

Acitelli, L. K., Douvan, E., & Veroff, J. (1997). The changing influence of interpersonal perceptions on marital well-being among Black and White couples. *Journal of Social and Personal Relationships, 14,* 291–304.

Atkinson, D. R., Brown, M. T., Parham, T. A., Matthews, L. G., Landrum-Brown, J., & Kim, A. U. (1996). African American client skin tone and clinical judgments of African American and European American psychologists. *Professional Psychology: Research and Practice, 27,* 500–505.

Beale, R. L. (1997). Multiple familial-worker role strain and psychological well-being: Moderating effects of coping resources among Black American parents. In R. J. Taylor, J. S. Jackson, & L. M. Chatters (Eds.), *Family life in Black America* (pp. 132–145). Thousand Oaks, CA: Sage.

Blaine, B., & Crocker, J. (1995). Religiousness, race, and psychological well being: Exploring social psychological measures. *Personality and Social Psychology Bulletin, 21,* 1031–1041.

Bowman, P. J. (1992). Coping with provider role strain: Adaptive cultural resources among Black husband-fathers. In A. K. H. Burlew, W. C. Banks, H. P. McAdoo, & D. A. Azibo (Eds.), *African American psychology: Theory, research, and practice* (pp. 135–151). Newbury Park, CA: Sage.

Boyd-Franklin, N. (1989). *Black families in therapy: A multisystems approach.* New York: Guilford.

Boyd-Franklin, N. (1998). Application of a multisystems model to home and community based treatment of African American families. In R. L. Jones (Ed.), *African American mental health* (pp. 315–328). Hampton, VA: Cobb & Henry.

Boyd-Franklin, N., & Franklin, A. J. (1998). African American couples in therapy. In M. McGoldrick (Ed.), *Re-visioning family therapy: Race, culture, and gender in clinical practice* (pp. 268–281). New York: Guilford.

Broman, C. L. (1988). Satisfaction among Blacks: The significance of marriage and parenthood. *Journal of Marriage and the Family, 50,* 45–51.

Broman, C. L. (1993). Race differences in marital well-being. *Journal of Marriage and the Family, 55,* 724–732.

Bryant, S. A., & Beckett, J. O. (1997). Effects of status resources and gender on role expectations of African American couples. *Smith College Studies in Social Work, 67,* 348–374.

Carter, M. M., & Shultz, K. M. (1998). Panic disorder with agoraphobia: Its impact on patients and their significant others. In J. Carlson & L. Sperry (Eds.), *The disordered couple* (pp. 29–56). Bristol, PA: Brunner/Mazel.

Chapman, A. B. (1988). Male-female relations: How the past affects the present. In H. P. McAdoo (Ed.), *Black families* (pp.190–200). Newbury Park, CA: Sage.

Cherlin, A.J. (1992). *Marriage, divorce, remarriage.* Cambridge, MA: Harvard University Press.

Creighton-Zollar, A., & Williams, J. S. (1987). The contribution of marriage to the life satisfaction of Black adults. *Journal of Marriage and the Family, 49,* 87–92.

Creighton-Zollar, A., & Williams, J. S. (1992). The relative educational attainment and occupational prestige of Black spouses and life satisfaction. *The Western Journal of Black Studies, 16,* 57–63.

Crovitz, E., & Steinmann, A. (1980). A decade later: Black–White attitudes toward women's familial role. *Psychology of Women Quarterly, 5,* 170–176.

Dalaker, J. (2001). *Poverty in the United States: 2000.* Washington, DC: U.S. Census Bureau.

Dawson, D. (1991). Family structure and children's health and well-being: Data from the 1988 National Health Interview Survey on child health. *Journal of Marriage and the Family, 53,* 573–584.

Edsall, T. B., & Edsall, M. D. (1991). *Chain reaction: The impact of race, rights and taxes on American politics.* New York: Norton.

Ellison, C. G. (1997). Religious involvement and the subjective quality of family life among African Americans. In R. J. Taylor, J. S. Jackson, & L. M. Chatters (Eds.), *Family life in Black America* (pp. 117–131). Thousand Oaks, CA: Sage.

Erikson, E. H. (1950). *Childhood and society.* New York: Norton.

Fields, J., & Casper, L. M. (2001). *America's families and living arrangements: March 2000.* Washington, DC: U.S. Census Bureau.

Floyd, F. J., & Zmich, D. E. (1991). Marriage and the parenting partnership: Perceptions and interactions of parents with mentally retarded and typically developing children. *Child Development, 62,* 1434–1448.

Frame, M. W., & Williams, C. B. (1996). Counseling African Americans: Integrating spirituality in therapy. *Counseling and Values, 41,* 16–28.

Gray-Little, B. (1982). Marital quality and power processes among Black couples. *Journal of Marriage and the Family, 44,* 633–646.

Grych, J. H., & Fincham, F. D. (Eds.). (2001). *Interparental conflict and child development.* Cambridge, UK: Cambridge University Press.

Halford, W. K., Kelly, A., & Markman, H. J. (1997). The concept of a healthy marriage. In W. K. Halford & H. J. Markman (Eds.), *Clinical handbook of marriage and couples interventions* (pp. 3–12). New York: Wiley.

Hill, R. B. (1998). *The strengths of African American families: Twenty-five years later.* Lanham, MD: University Press of America.

Hines, P. M., & Boyd-Franklin, N. (1996). African American families. In M. McGoldrick, J. Giordano, & J. K. Pearce (Eds.). *Ethnicity and family therapy* (2nd ed., pp. 66–84). New York: Guilford.

Horwitz, A.V., White, H. R., & Howell-White, S. (1996). Becoming married and mental health: A longitudinal study of a cohort of young adults. *Journal of Marriage and the Family, 58,* 895–907.

Jewell, K. S. (1983). Black male/female conflict: Internalization of negative definitions transmitted through imagery. *The Western Journal of Black Studies, 7,* 43–48.

Jones, A. C., & Chao, C. M. (1997). Racial, ethnic, and cultural issues in couples therapy. In W. K. Halford & H. J. Markman (Eds.), *Clinical handbook of marriage and couples interventions* (pp. 157–176). New York: Wiley.

Jones, R. T., Brown, R., Davis, M., Jeffries, R., & Shenoy, U. (1998). African Americans in behavioral therapy and research. In R. L. Jones (Ed.), *African American mental health* (pp. 413–450). Hampton, VA: Cobb & Henry.

Kelly, S. (2002). *Construct and discriminant validity of selected instrumentation on racial perspectives.* Manuscript submitted for publication.

Kelly, S., & Floyd, F. J. (2001). The effects of negative racial stereotypes and Afrocentricity on Black couple relationships. *Journal of Family Psychology, 15,* 110–123.

Kiecolt, K. J., & Fossett, M. A. (1995). Mate availability and marriage among African Americans: Aggregate- and individual-level analysis. In M. B. Tucker & C. Mitchell-Kernan (Eds.), *The decline in marriage among African Americans* (pp. 121–135). New York: Sage.

Lawson, E., & Thompson, A. (1994). The historical and social correlates of African American divorce: Review of the literature and implications for research. *Western Journal of Black Studies, 18,* 91–103.

Lindahl, K. M., & Malik, N. M. (1999). Marital conflict, family processes, and boys' externalizing behavior in Hispanic American and European American families. *Journal of Clinical Child Psychology, 28,* 12–24.

Majors, R., & Billson, J. M. (1992). *Cool pose: The dilemmas of Black manhood in America.* New York: Simon & Schuster.

Marcus, N. E., Lindahl, K. M., & Malik, N. M. (2001). Interparental conflict, children's social cognitions, and child aggression: A test of a mediational model. *Journal of Family Psychology, 15,* 315–333.

McCrady, B. S., & Epstein, E. E. (1995). Marital therapy in the treatment of alcohol problems. In N. S. Jacobson & A. S. Gurman (Eds.), *Clinical handbook of couple therapy* (pp. 369–393). New York: Guilford.

McGoldrick, M., Giordano, J., & Pearce, J. K. (1996). *Ethnicity and family therapy* (2nd ed.). New York: Guilford.

McIntosh, P. (1998). White privilege: Unpacking the invisible knapsack. In M. McGoldrick (Ed.), *Re-visioning family therapy: Race, culture, and gender in clinical practice* (pp. 147–152). New York: Guilford.

McLoyd, V. C. (1990). The impact of economic hardship on Black families and children: Psychological distress, parenting, and socioemotional development. *Child Development, 61,* 311–346.

McLoyd, V. C., Cauce, A. M., Takeuchi, D. T., & Wilson, L. (2000). Marital processes and parental socialization in families of color: A decade review of research. *Journal of Marriage and the Family, 62,* 1070–1106.

McLoyd, V. C., Harper, C. I., & Copeland, N. L. (2001). Ethnic minority status, interparental conflict, and child adjustment. In J. H. Grych & F. D. Fincham (Eds.), *Interparental conflict and child development* (pp. 98–125). Cambridge, UK: Cambridge University Press.

Neff, J. A., & Hoppe, S. K. (1993). Race/ethnicity, acculturation, and psychological distress: Fatalism and religiosity as cultural resources. *Journal of Community Psychology, 21,* 3–20.

Neighbors, H., Jackson, J., Bowman, P., & Gurin, G. (1983). Stress, coping, and Black mental health: Preliminary findings from a national study. *Prevention in Human Services, 2,* 1–25.

Oggins, J., Veroff, J., & Leber, D. (1993). Perceptions of marital interaction among Black and White newlyweds. *Journal of Personality and Social Psychology, 65,* 494–511.

Okazaki, S., & Sue, S. (1995). Methodological issues in assessment research with ethnic minorities. *Psychological Assessment, 7,* 367–373.

Orbuch, T. L., Veroff, J., & Hunter, A. G. (1998). Black couples, White couples: The early years of marriage. In E. M. Hetherington (Ed.), *Coping with divorce, single parenting, and remarriage: A risk and resiliency perspective* (pp. 23–43). Mahwah, NJ: Lawrence Erlbaum.

Parham, T. A., & Helms, J. E. (1981). The influence of Black students' racial identity attitudes on preference for counselor's race. *Journal of Counseling Psychology, 28,* 250–257.

Pinderhughes, E. (1989). *Understanding race, ethnicity and power: The key to effective clinical practice.* New York: The Free Press.

Ramseur, H. P. (1998). Psychologically healthy African American adults. In R. L. Jones (Ed.), *African American mental health* (pp. 3–31). Hampton, VA: Cobb & Henry.

Stack, S., & Eshleman, J. R. (1998). Marital status and happiness: A 17-nation study. *Journal of Marriage and the Family, 60*, 527–536.

Taylor, J. (1990). Relationship between internalized racism and marital satisfaction. *Journal of Black Psychology, 16*, 45–53.

Taylor, J., & Zhang, X. (1990). Cultural identity in maritally distressed and nondistressed Black couples. *The Western Journal of Black Studies, 14,* 205–213.

Taylor, R. J., Chatters, L. M., & Jackson, J. S. (1997). Changes over time in support network involvement among Black Americans. In R. J. Taylor, J. S. Jackson, & L. M. Chatters (Eds.), *Family life in Black America* (pp. 293–316). Thousand Oaks, CA: Sage.

Taylor, R. J., Tucker, M. B., Chatters, L. M., & Jayakody, R. (1997). Recent demographic trends in African American family structure. In R. J. Taylor, J. S. Jackson, & L. M. Chatters (Eds.), *Family life in Black America* (pp. 14–62). Thousand Oaks, CA: Sage.

Tucker, M. B., & Mitchell-Kernan, C. (1995). Trends in African American family formation: A theoretical and statistical overview. In M. B. Tucker & C. Mitchell-Kernan (Eds.), *The decline in marriage among African Americans* (pp. 3–26). New York: Sage.

Vandiver, B. J., Cross, W. E., Jr., Worrell, F. C., & Fhagen-Smith, P. E. (2002). Validating the Cross Racial Identity Scale. *Journal of Counseling Psychology, 49*, 71–85.

Veroff, J., Douvan, E., & Hatchett, S. J. (1995). *Marital instability: A social and behavioral study of the early years.* London: Praeger.

Warheit, G. J., Vega, W. A., Auth, J. B., & Meinhardt, K. (1985). Psychiatric symptoms and dysfunctions among Anglos and Mexican Americans: An epidemiologic study. In J. R. Greenley (Ed.), *Research in community and mental health* (Vol. 5, pp. 3–32). Greenwich, CT: JAI Press.

Williams, D. R., Takeuchi, D. T., & Adair, R. K. (1992). Marital status and psychiatric disorders among Blacks and Whites. *Journal of Health and Social Behavior, 33,* 140–157.

Wright, E. M. (2001). Substance abuse in African American communities. In S. L. A. Straussner (Ed.), *Ethnocultural factors in substance abuse treatment* (pp. 31–51). New York: Guilford.

CHAPTER 9

Latinos and Mental Health

At Least You Should Know This

CYNTHIA DE LAS FUENTES

Latinos[1] represent the largest growing ethnic minority group in the United States whose ethnic heritages have origins in Mexico, Puerto Rico, Cuba, the Caribbean, Central America, and South America. According to the 1990 U.S. Census Bureau, there were over 22 million Latinos living in the United States. The 2000 Census data reported this population increased to over 35 million, exceeding population growth predictions by 5 years. These numbers do not sufficiently account for the many undocumented workers and their family members who have immigrated to this country.

Although many Latinos have been in what is now the United States since before Pilgrims arrived on the East Coast (Shorris, 1992), most Latinos immigrated to the United States in the last century. In terms of national origins, in 1990 Latin-American and Caribbean peoples had surpassed Europeans as the largest immigrant populations in the United States by a wide margin (Rumbaut, 1994). Mexicans account for just over one fourth of all immigrants arriving since 1970 (Rumbaut, 1994), and one-third of all immigrant Latinos. Most Latinos in the United States are under the age of 30 and tend to have large families. In addition, according to the 2000 U.S. Census, most Latinos in the United States speak another language in the home (about 17 million). Immigration and high fertility rates account for the fact that this ethnic population is one of the fastest growing in the United States. By midcentury one in four persons in the United States, or approximately 96 million people, are predicted to be Latino (Zavala, 1999).

Ethnic and historical heritages of Latinos are diverse and the sociopolitical histories of Latinos are as varied as the diversity within Latino cultures. For example, in Mexico, the history of indigenous peoples' contact with the Europeans includes a conquest by the Spanish and French, a legacy of slavery, and *mestizaje* (a blending of indigenous and European people, cultures, values, beliefs, and languages). Much of the territory now known as the Southwestern and Western United States was Mexican; it was taken by the United States through several wars and treaties.

Latinos also emigrate from islands. Puerto Rico, a colony of Spain for 400 years, is now a colony of the United States. In a 1917 Act of Congress all Puerto Ricans were made citizens of the United States. They are conflicted about three political options: Statehood (or annexation), Commonwealth (colonial status), and independence (Bernal, 1997). About 3.5 million Puerto Ricans live on the island of Puerto Rico, whereas another 2.5 million live in the United States. An island neighbor, Cuba, is the closest communist country to the United States. A massive migration of over 1 million Cubans, starting in the early 1960s and continuing through today, began because of a national revolutionary movement that culminated in 1959. Those who immigrated early tended to be wealthy and educated. Today, continued immigration is thought to be the result of the U.S. government's policies that attempt to destabilize Castro's government (Bernal, 1997).

The purpose of this chapter is to bring together some of the literature that is most important to better understand Latino mental health and improve the delivery of services to Latinos living in the United States. The topics and issues reviewed here focus on a context for understanding some of the Latino peoples we see in therapy. Although I cannot adequately review all of the contemporary issues relevant to Latinos in the United States, I will focus on the dominant cultural and familial values and beliefs that shape the lives of Latinos, their experiences of acculturation and acculturative stress, and concerns related to the competent delivery of services to Latinos. Examples from my own clients are used to illustrate certain concepts. Their names and identifying characteristics have been changed to protect anonymity and confidentiality.

ORGANIZING PRINCIPLES

Juan José is an officer in the police department. Marissa, his wife of 12 years, left him 5 months ago and took their children to live with her parents. The couple is in their midthirties and their children, two girls and a boy, are ages 12, 11, and 4, respectively. Marissa is a stay-at-home mother; Juan José moonlights as a security guard at a "gentlemen's club" on the outskirts of town to support their lifestyle. Although he was resistant to the idea, Juan José agreed to come to marital therapy as a condition Marissa put on him while she considered whether to reunite with him. Why did Marissa not leave him 2 years ago when she discovered he was having an affair with an exotic dancer?

It took several months for Marissa to confront Juan José with the evidence of his affair. She first confided her suspicions to her mother, an aunt, and one of Juan José's sisters, to whom she was close. Although their recommendations varied, the two older women urged her to pray, light candles to the *Virgen de Guadalupe* and ask for guidance, "be a better wife," and to *aguantar* (to tolerate), because they feared that if she confronted him, he would leave her. They confided to her their own stories of unfaithful husbands and how they had learned to ignore infidelity and pray that he would never leave them or their children. "*Así son los hombres*" ("That is how men are"), they lamented. Her sister-in-law recommended she tell Juan José's mother, who, she promised, would shame him into "being the righteous Hispanic man he is supposed to be."

Over the next 2 years Marissa did all of those things and more. She became angry, pleaded, tried guilt, shame, and sexy lingerie, talked to their parish priest, went to prayer meetings and a *curandera*, read self-help books, and went on Prozac. She was depressed because Juan José would assure her that the affair had ended, but Marissa would eventually be confronted with his lies. She would confront him and he would become explosive: yelling, punching walls, throwing things, and storming out of the house shouting that he would not be told what to do in his house. Finally, at her father's invitation, Marissa returned home.

Understanding the cultural organizing principles, values and beliefs, and pride and shame issues of a family or individual who presents for therapy is crucial to competent and ethical practice. Cultural characteristics influence the ease or difficulty with which a family or an individual adapts. There are several generally agreed upon organizing principles of Latino cultural values that greatly influence the ways in which families live their lives and cope with and manage cultural adjustment and stress (Marín & Marín, 1991; McGoldrick, Giordano, & Pearce, 1996).

Perhaps the most powerful organizing principle of Latino cultures is that of *la Familia. Familismo* is a relational orientation toward the family that emphasizes the needs of the family and the group as more important than the needs of any individual family member. Large extended families are a considerable source of support, strength, and resilience for Latinos, and close friends (*compadres*) are often considered part of this extended family network (Ginorio, Gutierrez, Cauce, & Acosta, 1995). In the preceding illustration, this familial interdependence diminished Marissa's feelings of isolation and pain as she struggled with her marital crisis.

Latino mental health beliefs lead Latinos to seek out solutions to their problems that include relatives, *compadres*, and spiritualists. The primacy of the family and the role of religion are such that Latinos are more likely to first seek help from these networks. Badillo Ghali (1982) found that some Latinos have a greater tolerance for mental illness or "deviant behavior" than other ethnic groups and rely on the family for support and resolution of the problem. This may be why some research has found more serious psychopathology in Latinos at the time of admission to mental health facilities (Koss-Chioino, 1995; Wallen, 1992).

If the central organizing principle for Latinos is the family, then the roles and the norms regarding the members and the genders becomes the next most important organizing principle. These roles and norms shape women's and men's behavior, cognitive and emotional styles, and perhaps most importantly, the pride or shame a family experiences by their individual member's adherence to them. For example, Latinas are traditionally socialized in ways that include strict rules for conduct and interpersonal relationships. Women and girls often are overprotected and sheltered in an attempt to shape them into socially "respectable" women. For many Latinas the greatest role they can strive for is to become a mother, but not merely a mother, a *marianista*. The concept of *marianismo* includes the tradition of following of the ways of the Virgin Mary, the ultimate mother. Women who adhere to this gender role are valued in the culture and are generally considered to be morally and spiritually superior to men (Falicov, 1998). This role requires subservience to fathers and husbands and controlling of sexual desire. A woman or girl is expected to remain a virgin until marriage, and once she marries, sex is considered an act of obligation sanctified by God for the purpose of procreation, and the pleasure of her husband. The message women and girls hear from this is that if they engage in sexual behavior prior to marriage, then they are whores. This Madonna–whore dichotomy leaves little room for exploration between the two positions and is used to protect the family's honor and enhance women's and girls' marital prospects (Vásquez & de las Fuentes, 1999).

Latino boys and men traditionally are given far more social and familial latitude. Although they are also socialized along a similar continuum as are girls and women, the focus is on different values and behaviors. For some Latino families, the continuum for men is that of *caballero–macho*. The *cabellero* identity encompasses values of being a gentleman, a respectable family leader, a role model, a primary wage earner, and later in life, deserving of the respectful title of *Don*. On the other hand, the *macho* identity focuses on sexual and physical virility. A *machista* is proud of his sexual potency and may be unfaithful to his spouse. In some of these Latino families, a *"casa chica"* (a mistress) is the norm (Falicov, 1998). The *macho* sometimes is physically abusive, toward women and children, and toward himself through the abuse of drugs and alcohol. For some Latino families, the identity of the *caballero* is upheld as ideal and any deviation from this is a shameful slide.

> At first Juan José denied that his affair had caused problems in his marriage, because he swore to Marissa that he would never leave her or the children and he provided well for them. He rationalized that this should be enough to keep Marissa *tranquila* ("calmed down"). In the first session, he reported that Marissa *no tiene las manos limpias* ("Her hands are not clean"), because she goes out once a month with her girlfriends and stays out until after midnight. "A good wife and mother shouldn't do that." He denied being "macho" because he respected and visited his mother regularly, he did not hit his wife or children, and he gave Marissa enough money to run the household.

Religion and spirituality can be sources of support and resilience when the individual and family can depend on their faith and religious community. Fatalism in Latino communities is often understood to be linked to religiosity with common *dichos* (sayings) such as *Si Dios Quiere* ("If God is willing"). Although there have been many pre-Columbian religions practiced in the New World since the Spanish conquest, Catholicism has been a pervasive force in the lives of many Latinos (Cervantes & Ramírez, 1992). Adherence to traditional Catholic values, especially the religious values regarding *marianismo* and the practice of *aguantar*, or tolerance, may prevent some Latinos from seeking psychological treatment (Acosta, Yamamoto, & Evans, 1982), favoring instead the support of family, and religious and lay persons in their churches.

Perhaps as a legacy of the hybridizing of native religions with Catholicism, *curanderia* (folk healing) is practiced by many Latinos. *Curanderismo* has been described as a set of folk and medical beliefs, rituals, and practices that address the psychosocial and spiritual concerns of some Latinos, especially Mexicans and Mexican Americans (Cervantes & Ramírez, 1992). For many Latinos, Catholicism and *curanderia* coexist in their lives and are manifested in such ways as regular church attendance while also using poultices and specific superstitious practices to ward off troublesome spirits.

> Marissa had consulted with her parish priest and a *curandera*. Marissa found the advice they gave her to be very helpful for her piece of mind. Interestingly, both the priest and the *curandera* recommended that she seek support and solace from the women in her family; and both recommended that she pray for advice and patience to *La Virgen de Guadalupe*. Whereas the priest offered marital counseling, the *curandera* offered a "break-up-my-man-and-his-mistress" candle, a tonic for her *"nervios"* (nerves), and smudge sticks to cleanse her home (*limpia*) from a jinx that may have been placed on them or it.

Many researchers have found that Latinos' mental health beliefs focus on an integration of health, illness, and religion (Abad, Ramos, & Boyce, 1974). Others have found that some Latinos believe this integration between physical and emotional illness is linked to both biomedical as well as supernatural etiologies, including predestination, spiritual influences, black magic, and strong emotional upsets (Guarnaccia, De La Cancela, & Carrillo, 1989). Mental health service providers should know that the polarization between mind and body more common to White Americans is not as evident in Latino cultures, thus, mental illness and mental stress are often presented in more psychosomatic manners.

Simpatia is a strong cultural value that involves being polite, avoiding ill-mannered behavior in all situations, and preventing interpersonal discord (Triandis, Marín, Lisansky, & Betancourt, 1984). One who is not simpatico or who communicates disrespect is considered to be *mal creado* ("ill-bred"). Simpatia is an aspect of *respeto* (respect) that is shown to persons in positions of authority. For example, children are expected to be polite and obey adults, and to use the formal, second-person pronoun of *usted* (you) when addressing adults until permission is granted to do otherwise. Likewise, between adults it is considered disrespectful and condescending to use first names before familiarity is established. These values have implications for the therapist–client relationship. For example, a client may appear to agree with his therapist's interventions, all the while not quite understanding them or their purpose in the change process, and as a result may not follow through on them. Clients may also passively accept the therapist's suggestions, not intending to follow through with them while not wanting to appear impolite or lacking in respect of the therapist's authority.

> When Judith and Diego attended their first marital therapy session they arrived several minutes late. At the conclusion of the session, when the therapist attempted to schedule a second session the following week, the couple became silent, exchanged eye contact, and accepted the appointment. The following week they called to cancel their appointment. It was not until the therapist returned their call to reschedule that she learned that Diego could not keep a daytime appointment because of his work. Although knowing that they would be unlikely to keep the original appointment they accepted it anyway because they did not want to seem ungrateful or impolite by asking for a more convenient day and time. Fortunately, the clinic was open for evening hours and the therapist and couple were able to reschedule.

ACCULTURATION

If a culture's organizing principles influence and shape an individual's and a family's lifestyles, the choices they make, and the pride and shame they feel as a result, then acculturation becomes a very significant moderating variable when working with Latinos in the United States. Acculturation refers to a transition (or blending) of values, norms, languages, and behaviors between two or more cultural groups (Atkinson, Morten, & Sue, 1998). Acculturation in Latinos is often referred to as the process by which they adopt the culture of a majority group. Acculturation can be defined and practically studied as a manifestation of behavioral, affective, and cognitive aspects of personality functioning. For example, the behavioral aspects of acculturation in Latinos might be manifested as language choice and facility with Spanish, music preferences, and decisions regarding ritual and customary preferences (e.g., celebrating a *Quincenera*, a formal party and church service for a girl's 15th birthday).

> Eliza and Chris were a lesbian couple who came in for couple's counseling. Chris, a 38-year-old fourth-generation Mexican-Anglo[2]-American woman, had been sexually "out" to her family and friends since she was in her twenties. Eliza, a 32-year-old second-generation Mexican-American, was a single mother with a 6-year-old son, Gabriel. Her family did not know that she and Chris were living together as a couple. Eliza and Chris struggled about when and how to tell Gabriel and Eliza's family. As a more acculturated woman, Chris was more "individualistically" oriented in her relationships with others. She needed Eliza to demonstrate her commitment by coming out to her family, thereby making the primacy of their "couplehood" explicit. Eliza, on the other hand, was more concerned about the impact her disclosure would have on her family, the selfishness she feared she would exhibit at causing them stress and shame for her own gain, and the disruption she would experience in her relationships with them. They had many heated arguments about this dilemma and even considered ending their 4-year relationship.

Understanding acculturation in Latinos is important to successful clinical intervention. For example, in the preceding situation with Eliza and Chris, a "cultural family genogram" (Hardy & Laszloffy, 1995) was used to help them understand why they were experiencing this particular conflict. Through the process of this exercise, this couple learned how acculturation and cultural transition has affected each of them and their families differently. They discovered which organizing principles and pride and shame issues they valued and maintained and which were in transition. Not only did this awareness help Eliza and Chris to see how their culturally based values, beliefs, and behaviors contributed to their conflict it also helped them to appreciate and understand each other better.

Clinicians need to know that there is some empirical evidence suggesting that less acculturated individuals favor a short-term psychotherapy relationship provided by a directive, active therapist, producing tangible outcomes and that more acculturated individuals are more likely to expect and appreciate a longer-term psychotherapeutic relationship by a less directive therapist with goals focused on broad personal developmental issues (Atkinson, Casas, & Abreau, 1992). In addition research on acculturation has also found that it is a critical variable in: (a) the content and extent of client self-disclosure (Castro, 1977); (b) client dropout rates (Miranda, Andujo, Caballero, Guerrero, & Ramos, 1976); (c) psychotherapy outcome (Miranda & Castro, 1977); and (d) preferences for ethnically and linguistically similar counselors (Sanchez & Atkinson, 1983).

ACCULTURATIVE STRESS

Acculturative stress has been defined as the affective reaction to stressors that occur as a result of the process of adjustment and acculturation. Barriers to social acceptance, lack of ethnic and cultural resources, immigration and migration issues and prejudice and discrimination have all been identified as acculturative stressors. For example, once they arrive in the United States, many immigrant Latinos face a life of poverty. Good paying jobs are scarce, housing is often substandard and unaffordable, and difficulties with English fluency often keep immigrant Latinos on the periphery of the acculturation process (Garcia-Preto, 1996). This is more true for dark-skinned (*morenos*, *negros*, or *prietos*) Latinos who are more highly segregated from Whites than are lighter-skinned (*güeros* or *rubios*) Latinos (e.g., Denton & Massey, 1989). The darker the skin, the harder it is for them to find housing (Yinger, 1991), and the more likely they are to earn low wages (e.g., Telles & Murguia, 1990). In addition, lack of fluency in English lowers their potential to earn higher wages and to attain higher paying jobs (e.g., Bean & Tienda, 1987).

As families establish roots in the United States and face the reality that returning to their countries of origin is unlikely, they may present in family therapy for different reasons: The birth of new generations of children and grandchildren whose values are different from their own, the intermarriage of these generations with American Whites, Blacks, Asians, and Indians, and difficulty maintaining the language may all contribute to distress in a family system that is in cultural transition. Furthermore, reinforcing cultural traditions, including culturally bound problem-solving skills, becomes more difficult. Parents in particular struggle with the dilemma of raising a generation exposed to White American values emphasizing individual strivings over family attachments and obligations.

> Tina and her mother, Carmen, came to therapy because of a conflict Tina and her father were having about whether she will go to college out of town. Tina received a scholarship at a major university 4 hours away from her hometown. Tina's father, Julio, forbade her to accept the scholarship because it was too far away from home and there was a good junior college in their hometown. He argued that she was not mature enough to live on her own and that after she earns her associates degree, he will permit her to go to the university. Tina threatened to go anyway, and her father threatened to disown her for disobedience and disrespect. Caught in the middle, Carmen somatized her anxiety. She complained of frequent bouts of *empacho* (best understood as intense stomach upset with cramping) and *ataques de nervios* (panic attacks).

Families in cultural transition often experience stress and conflict because of the acculturation process. For example, older family members (e.g., parents and grandparents) may not culturally and linguistically transition as quickly as children and adolescents, and may resist changes in their traditional values. Parents may become confronted with different childrearing and discipline practices and beliefs held by the institutions, such as schools and churches, in their new communities (Strier, 1996). In addition, the loss of familiar language, food, and people, leave many immigrant families feeling isolated and unsupported. These factors and conditions may lead an individual or family to experience acculturative stress. Acculturative stress involves a "particular set of stress behaviors that occur during acculturation, such as lowered mental health status (especially confusion, anxiety, depression), feelings of marginality and alienation, heightened psychosomatic symptom level, and identity confusion" (Berry, 1990, pp. 246–247).

ETHNIC IDENTITY

Although acculturation is largely related to the acquisition of dominant cultural attitudes, values, and beliefs by the minority person, ethnic and racial identity development focuses on the attitudes, beliefs, and feelings this person may have about his or her own group in comparison to the dominant group (Barón & Constantine, 1997; Phinney, 1990). In addition, "the ways in which ethnic minority individuals internalize the identity components of ethnicity and race have been found to have psychological importance" (de las Fuentes, Barón, & Vasquez, in press). Mental health service providers should know that because ethnicity, race, and general minority status are highlighted in the dominant U.S. society, ethnic minorities' identity development status has been found to be related to successful client–therapist matching (Parham & Helms, 1981), degree of self-regard, self-esteem, self-actualization, and degree of felt anxiety (Parham & Helms, 1985a, b).

There is a strong reciprocal relation between immigration and ethnicity—today's immigrants are influencing tomorrow's ethnic identities (de las Fuentes & Vasquez, 1999; Fernandez-Kelly & Schaufler, 1994). This dynamic process most clearly can be seen in the ethnic identity development of the second generation. Unfortunately, social science researchers have focused on adult immigrants, who are more visible and more easily studied (Portes, 1994), and research including the second generation has diluted its very uniqueness. For example, psychological and sociological studies most frequently use pan-ethnic labels such as "Hispanic" and the information gathered hides the second generation because children of domestic and immigrant Latinos are treated as the same population (Portes, 1994).

National origin is very important to Latinos, providing a sense of pride and identity that is reflected in the stories they tell, their music, and their poetry (McGoldrick et al., 1996). Feelings of grief and loss over having to leave their homeland are more pronounced when they have left relatives behind, and are unable to return to their home either because they are political exiles or are undocumented workers or residents.

In therapy, asking the question, *"¿De donde viene su familia?"* ("What is your country of origin?") and listening to the client's immigration narrative not only helps build rapport, but also gives the therapist an opportunity to learn about the country and people the client left behind, the culture, and the reasons for leaving (McGoldrick et al., 1996). A therapist might then explore issues about how long the family has lived in the United States, who made the decision to immigrate, how others felt about the decision, who immigrated first, who was left behind, and how all of this has influenced the family processes. In addition to seeking out information about stressors and concerns, it is likewise important for a therapist to inquire about what the family has learned as a result of this process and what strengths and resources they discovered within themselves and their networks. Assisting clients to reflect on cultural differences, what they appreciate and enjoy from each culture (as well as what they do not), may lead them to negotiate the acculturative process (Garcia-Preto, 1994).

ASSESSMENT WITH LATINOS

Assessment with Latinos is a growing area of inquiry and a continuing challenge for psychologists who provide assessment services to Latino populations. I would like to refer the reader to Paniagua's (1998) *Assessing and Treating Culturally Diverse Clients: A Practical Guide* (2nd ed.) for a nice review of the issues regarding appropriate assessment with Latinos. To summarize some of the concerns, there are three major issues that continue to emerge in developing a culturally appropriate assessment practice with Latino populations: (a) The issue of the validity of the instruments for Latino populations; (b) the dearth of normative data; and (c) the issue of language and translation and the appropriate approach in serving monolingual and bilingual language minorities. With regard to the issue of normative data for commonly used objective instruments, psychometricians have made serious attempts to norm their instruments using a stratified random sample, sometimes oversampling for certain ethnic groups. However, one of the primary criticisms surrounding this process is that the representation of Latinos and other People of Color remains a small minority of the sample population. The diagnostician is still stuck with making generalizations about his or her client on a sample that is predominantly White.

TYING IT ALL TOGETHER:
BEST PRACTICES IN THE TREATMENT OF LATINOS

In general, the clinician should view Latinos presenting for therapy as members of a family (even when coming alone), making family therapy skills, as well as cultural competence, very important. Because a primary organizing principle for Latinos is *Familismo*, presenting problems in therapy typically regard problems, conflicts, and concerns about one or more members of the family. It is not surprising, therefore, that marital conflict, parent–child conflict, and academic problems in children are the most common presenting problems presented by Latinos at the community counseling clinic in which the author practices.

Reflecting back on the topics reviewed, assessing level of acculturation in the individual (or within a family) who presents for therapy is strongly advised also (Paniagua, 1998). Determining the levels of acculturation of the family, or the discrepancy between individual family members, may facilitate an understanding about the nature of the complaint brought into therapy. In the case of Tina, who was struggling with her father over whether she would go to a university out of town or stay in her hometown, the therapist understood this conflict to be related to acculturative stress. Tina's desire to move out of town was not consistent with her parents' cultural expectations about her living at home until marriage. As reported by her mother, Tina's father told her, "A good girl moves out of her father's house into her husband's." During the course of treatment, the therapist fully explored the parents' traditional beliefs with those of the daughter's, which were in transition to the American culture's belief of parent–adolescent separation and individuation at age 18. In situations like these, it is important that the family understand that being more acculturated does not mean a rejection of the family (Paniagua, 1998).

Finally, knowledge of Spanish language and its use in psychotherapy with bilingual speakers is essential, because it is through language that cultural issues are often expressed. According to the 2000 Census, over 17.3 million people over the age of 5 in the United States speak Spanish in their homes (US Census Bureau, 2001). Most first-generation Latino Americans speak Spanish in their homes and teach their children Spanish as their first language (Dillard, 1987), thereby making the United States the fifth largest Spanish-speaking country in the world (Zavala, 1999).

Spanish-speaking Latinos are among those who traditionally have been underserved by community medical and mental health services (McNeill et al., 2001; Seijo, Gomez, & Freidenberg, 1995). According to Altarriba and Santiago-Rivera (1994), developing cultural sensitivity includes an understanding of the client's language by which customs, values, and social and cultural beliefs are expressed. Bamford (1991) and Padilla et al. (1991) found that the inability of psychotherapists to communicate in the dominant language of their clients compromised the quality of services delivered to those clients, and Altarriba and Santiago-Rivera (1994) found that language differences may serve as barriers to cultural understanding, causing a great deal of misinterpretation by the therapist.

A bilingual school psychology supervisee complained to her supervisor that the school in which she was completing a practicum had recently suspended a fifth grader because of suspicion of sexual inappropriateness with another student. The supervisee learned that one of the students' parents, a Spanish speaker, called to speak with a school counselor complaining that her son was being picked on by another student. The counselor, who had minimal understanding of Spanish, took the mother's complaint of "molestar" (best understood as "being bothered by") as "molested."

Research has shown that for Spanish-dominant Mexican Americans ethnic and language matching improves the outcome of therapy and decreases client-initiated terminations (Sue, Fujino, Hu, Takeuchi, & Zane, 1991). Spanish-speaking clients also are more positive about their treatment experience when the therapist is bilingual (Marcos, Alpert, Urcuyo, & Kesselman, 1973; Padilla & Salgado de Snyder, 1988). Fisher, Jome, and Atkinson (1998) argued that these and similar studies suggest that "ethnic and language similarity between client and therapist raises client expectation for success" (p. 555). They emphasized the importance of developing a shared worldview in therapy, recognizing that "showing respect and acceptance for clients' meanings may serve to maintain a positive relationship, as well as to demonstrate the counselor's acceptance of a client's interpretation of distress (which likely increases credibility)" (p. 551).

CONCLUSION

One of the first challenges of bringing cultural awareness of Latinos into the therapy room is that it may conflict with theoretical underpinnings of the conduct of psychotherapy with which the therapist has been trained. Being competent and proficient in the treatment of Latinos challenges traditional schools of thought, which often consider certain processes and dynamics to be universal. Assumptions about family functioning, the etiology and maintenance of problems, and how treatment is facilitated may have to change to accommodate new cultural understandings. Beliefs and behaviors that would have been judged as dysfunctional or "inappropriate" in the past must now make way for awareness of cultural heritage, beliefs, and practices.

Although the areas reviewed herein are certainly not exhaustive, I have focused on those areas I believe are particularly important in the competent delivery of psychological services to Latinos. A problem I encountered while writing this chapter was my concern about inadvertently stereotyping our peoples and cultures. In discussions with my colleagues, one of us would invariably deny having had a particular experience or belief system, whereas another affirmed it, produced literature or a case, thus illustrating the point. Obviously, Latino people are truly many "peoples" who have different cultures, practices, beliefs, and transition (acculturation) processes. This is especially so in an increasingly global environment where hybridizations and cultural beliefs and practices are the norm rather than the exception for Latino Americans.

END NOTES

1. Here I will use the term "Latino" or "Latina" to describe Spanish-speaking peoples whose descendants come from "Latino America." Although many people in the United States identify as "Hispanic," there is a social and political movement to avoid the term "Hispanic" because of its origins. The term "Latino" is not without its limitations, however, because it may not adequately describe a people, and still identifies with the linguistic origins of the

conqueror. For a more in-depth analysis of this matter, see Earl Shorris' (1992) book, *Latinos: A Biography of the People.*
2. The term "Anglo" is traditionally used in the Southwestern United States to describe White European Americans and distinguish them from Latinos, including White Latinos. Although rather offensive to some (Irish Americans), it remains in common usage and is used in this vignette, because that is how the client identified herself.

REFERENCES

Abad, V., Ramos, J., & Boyce, E. (1974). A model for delivery of mental health services to Spanish-speaking minorities. *American Journal of Orthopsychiatry, 44*, 584–595.

Acosta, F. X., Yamamoto, J., & Evans, L. A. (1982). *Effective psychotherapy for low income and minority patients.* New York: Plenum.

Altarriba, J., & Santiago-Rivera, A. L. (1994). Current perspectives on using linguistic and cultural factors in counseling the Hispanic client. *Professional Psychology: Research & Practice, 25*, 388–397.

Atkinson, D. R. , Casas, J. M., & Abreu, J. (1992). Mexican American acculturation, counselor ethnicity and cultural sensitivity, and perceived counselor competence. *Journal of Counseling Psychology, 39*, 515–520.

Atkinson, D. R., Morten, G., & Sue, D. W. (1993). *Counseling American minorities: A cross-cultural perspective* (4th ed.). Madison, WI: Brown & Benchmark.

Badillo Ghali, S. (1982). Understanding Puerto Rican traditions. *Social Work, 27*, 98–102.

Bamford, K. W. (1991). Bilingual issues in mental health assessment and treatment. *Hispanic Journal of Behavioral Sciences, 13*, 377–390.

Barón, A., & Constantine, M. G. (1997). A conceptual framework for conducting psychotherapy with Mexican American college students. In. M. C. Zea & J. Garcia (Eds.), *Psychological interventions with Latino populations* (pp. 108–124). Needham Heights, MA: Allyn & Bacon.

Bean, F. D., & Tienda, M. (1987). *The Hispanic population of the United States.* New York: Russell Sage.

Bernal, G. (Summer 1997). Reflections on the legacy of 1898 and ethnic minorities. *Variability.* Washington, DC: American Psychological Association Minority Fellowship Program.

Berry, J. W. (1990). Psychology of acculturation: Understanding individuals moving between cultures. In R. W. Brislin (Ed.), *Applied cross-cultural psychology* (pp. 232–253). Newbury Park, CA: Sage.

Castro, F. G. (1977). *Level of acculturation and related considerations in psychotherapy with Spanish speaking/surnamed clients* (Occasional Paper No. 3). Spanish Speaking Mental Health Research Center, University of California, Los Angeles.

Cervantes, J. M., & Ramirez, O. (1992). Spirituality and family dynamics in psychotherapy with Latino children. In L. Vargas & J. Koss-Chioino (Eds.), *Working with culture: Psychotherapeutic interventions with ethnic minority children and adolescents.* San Francisco: Jossey-Bass.

de las Fuentes, C., Barón, A., & Vasquez, M. J. T. (in press). Teaching Latino Psychology. In P. Bronstein & K. Quina (Eds.), *Teaching a psychology of people.* Washington, DC: American Psychological Association.

de las Fuentes, C., & Vasquez, M. J. T. (1999). Immigrant adolescent girls of color: Facing American challenges. In N. G. Johnson, M. C. Roberts, & J. Worell (Eds.), *Beyond appearance: A new look at adolescent girls* (pp. 131–150). Washington, DC: American Psychological Association.

Denton, N. A., & Massey, D. S. (1989). Racial identity among Caribbean Hispanics: The effect of double minority status on residential segregation. *American Sociological Review, 54,* 790–808.

Dillard, J. M. (1987). *Multicultural counseling.* Chicago: Nelson-Hall.

Falicov, C. J. (1998). *Latino families in therapy: A guide to multicultural practice.* New York: Guilford.

Fernandez-Kelly, M. P., & Schaufler, R. (1994). Divided fates: Immigrant children in a restructured U.S. economy. *International Migration Review, 28,* 662–689.

Fisher, A. R., Jome, L. M., & Atkinson, D. R. (1998). Reconceptualizing multicultural counseling: Universal healing conditions in a culturally specific context. *The Counseling Psychologist, 26,* 525–588.

Garcia-Preto, N. (1994). On the bridge. *Family Therapy Networker, 18,* 35–37.

Garcia-Preto, N. (1996). Latino families: An overview. In M. McGoldrick, J. Giordano, & J. K. Pearce (Eds.), *Ethnicity and family therapy* (2nd ed., pp. 141–154). New York: Guilford.

Ginorio, A. G., Gutierrez, L., Cauce, A. M., & Acosta, M. (1995). Psychological issues for Latinas. In H. Landrine (Ed.), *Bringing cultural diversity to feminist psychology: Theory, research and practice* (pp. 241–264). Washington, DC: American Psychological Association.

Guarnaccia, P. J., De La Cancela, V., & Carillo, E. (1989). The multiple meanings of ataques de nervios in the Latino community. *Medical Anthropology, 11,* 47–62.

Hardy, K. V., & Laszloffy, T. A. (1995). The cultural genogram: Key to training culturally competent family therapists. *Journal of Marital and Family Therapy, 21,* 227–237.

Koss-Chioino, J. D. (1995). Traditional and folk approaches among ethnic minorities. In J. F. Aponte, R. Young Rivers, & J. Wohl (Eds.), *Psychological interventions and cultural diversity* (pp. 145–163). Boston: Allyn & Bacon.

Marcos, L. R., Alpert, M., Urcuyo, L., & Kesselman, M. (1973). The effect of interview language in the evaluation of psychopathology in Spanish American schizophrenic patients. *American Journal of Psychiatry, 130,* 549–553.

Marín, G., & Marín, B. V. (1991). *Research with Hispanic populations.* Newbury Park, CA: Sage.

McGoldrick, M., Giordano, J., & Pearce, J. K. (Eds.). (1996). *Ethnicity and family therapy* (2nd ed.). New York: Guilford.

McNeill, B. W., Prieto, L. R., Niemann, Y. F., Pizarro, M., Vera, E. M., & Gómez, S. P. (2001). Current direction in Chicana/o psychology. *The Counseling Psychologist, 29,* 5–17.

Melville, M. B. (1980). Introduction. In M. B. Melville (Ed.), *Twice a minority: Mexican American women.* St. Louis: Mosby.

Miranda, M. R., Andujo, E., Caballero, I. L., Guerrero, C., & Ramos, R. A. (1976). Mexican American dropouts in psychotherapy as related to level of acculturation. In M. R. Miranda (Ed.), *Psychotherapy with the Spanish-speaking: Issues in research and service delivery* (pp. 35–50). Los Angeles: Spanish Speaking Mental Health Research Center, University of California, Los Angeles.

Miranda, M. R., & Castro F. G. (1977). Culture distance and success in psychotherapy with Spanish-speaking clients. In J. L. Martinez (Ed.), *Chicano psychology* (pp. 249–262). New York: Academic Press.

Padilla, A. M., Lindholm, K. J., Chen, A., Duran, R., Hakuta, K., Lambert, W., & Tucker, G. R. (1991). The English-only movement. *American Psychologist, 46,* 120–130.

Padilla, A. M., & Salgado de Snyder, N. (1985). Counseling Hispanics: Strategies for effective intervention. In P. Pedersen (Ed.), *Handbook of cross-cultural counseling and therapy* (pp. 157–164). New York: Praeger.

Padilla, A. M., & Salgado de Snyder, V. N. (1988). Psychology in Pre-Columbian Mexico. *Hispanic Journal of Behavioral Sciences, 10,* 55–66.

Paniagua, F. A. (1998). *Assessing and treating culturally diverse clients: A practical guide* (2nd ed.). Thousand Oaks, CA: Sage.

Parham, T. A., & Helms, J. E. (1981). The influence of Black students' racial attitudes on preferences for counselor's race. *Journal of Counseling Psychology, 28*, 250–257.

Parham, T. A., & Helms, J. E. (1985a). Attitudes of racial identity and self-esteem of Black students: An exploratory investigation. *Journal of College Student Personnel, 26*, 143–147.

Parham, T. A., & Helms, J. E. (1985b). Relation of racial identity attitudes to self-actualization and affective states of Black students. *Journal of Counseling Psychology, 32*, 431–440.

Phinney, J. S. (1990). Ethnic identity in adolescents and adults: Review of research. *Psychological Bulletin, 108*, 499–514.

Portes, A. (1994). Introduction: Immigration and its aftermath. *International Migration Review, 28*, 632–639.

Rumbaut, R. G. (1994). The crucible within: Ethnic identity, self-esteem, and segmented assimilation among children of immigrants. *International Migration Review, 28*, 748–794.

Sanchez, A. R., & Atkinson, D. R. (1983). Mexican-American cultural commitment preference for counselor ethnicity, and willingness to use counseling. *Journal of Counseling Psychology, 30*, 215–220.

Seijo, R., Gomez, H., & Freidenberg, J. (1995). Language as a communication barrier in medical care for Hispanic patients. In A. Padilla (Ed.), *Hispanic psychology: Critical issues in theory and research* (pp. 169–181). Thousand Oaks, CA: Sage.

Shorris, E. (1992). *Latinos: A biography of the people.* New York: Norton.

Strier, D. R. (1996). Coping strategies of immigrant parents: Directions for family therapy. *Family Process, 35,* 363–376.

Sue, S., Fujino, D. C., Hu, L., Takeuchi, D. T., & Zane, N. W. S. (1991). Community mental health services for minority groups: A test of the cultural responsiveness hypothesis. *Journal of Consulting and Clinical Psychology, 59*, 533–540.

Telles, E. E., & Murguia, E. (1990). Phenotypic discrimination and income differences among Mexican Americans. *Social Science Quarterly, 71*, 682–696.

Triandis, H. C., Marín, G., Lisansky, J., & Betancourt, H. (1984). Simpatia as a cultural script of Hispanics. *Journal of Personality and Social Psychology, 47*, 1363–1375.

Vásquez, M. J. T., & de las Fuentes, C. (1999). American-born Asian, African, Latina, and American Indian adolescent girls: Challenges and strengths. In N. G. Johnson, M. C. Roberts, & J. Worell (Eds.), *Beyond appearance: A new look at adolescent girls* (pp. 151–173). Washington, DC: American Psychological Association.

U.S. Census Bureau. (2001). Overview of race and Hispanic origin: Census 2000 brief. Available: http://www.census.gov/prod/2001pubs/c2kbr01-1.pdf

Wallen, J. (1992). Providing culturally appropriate mental health services for minorities. *Journal of Mental Health Administration, 19*, 288–295.

Yinger, J. (1991). *Housing discrimination study: Incidence of discrimination and variations in discriminatory behavior.* Washington, DC: U.S. Department of Housing and Urban Development, Office of Policy Development and Research.

Zavala, A. E. (1999). *Anuario Hispano-Hispanic yearbook.* McLean, VA: TYIM Publishing.

CHAPTER 10

Clinical Psychology Issues Among Asian/Pacific Islander Americans

STANLEY SUE
THEODORA B. CONSOLACION

Clinical psychology is a field that encompasses the study, treatment, and prevention of psychopathology. It deals with issues concerning assessment; the nature, distribution, and correlates of abnormal behaviors; and psychotherapeutic and prevention interventions. As a field, clinical psychology was established in the United States over a century ago. Much research has accumulated over this time concerning issues in the field. However, research on ethnic minority groups in general and Asian/Pacific Islander (API) Americans in particular has not been well developed. The API-American population is composed of at least 43 distinct groups and the largest groups include Chinese, Filipino, South Asians, Koreans, and Japanese. In this chapter, we examine the research on clinical psychology issues of API Americans and suggest directions for future research and practice with this population. Specifically, we address issues such as the prevalence of mental disorders among this population, correlates of these disorders, adequacy of mental health services, and recommend future tasks that are important in ensuring that the mental health needs of API Americans are adequately met.

Underlying our entire discussion is the influence of culture and minority group status on API Americans. Such influences provide the backdrop that molds the clinical issues concerning this population. One cannot begin to understand clinical psychological issues involving API Americans without the appreciation of how expressions and causes of psychopathology, valid assessment strategies, and effective treatment are shaped by culture and minority group status.

Culture and Minority Group Status

Culture can be defined as the behavior patterns, symbols, institutions, values, and human products of a society (Banks, 1987). A number of cultural differences have been noted between API Americans and individuals with European-American backgrounds. These differences include an interdependent rather than an independent self-construal, concern over loss of face, educational achievement aspirations, family involvement, filial piety, indirectness in communications, hierarchical rather than egalitarian social relations, and mind–body integration (Sue & Sue, 1999; Yee, Huang, & Lew, 1998; Ying, Lee, Tsai, Yeh, & Huang, 2000). These differences have a significant effect on behavior and on the appropriate means to intervene and study the API-American population. They may also create identity and personality conflicts for individuals caught between the conflicting demands of API-American versus European-American cultures. In addition to cultural factors, minority status has a substantial impact on API Americans. By minority status, we are referring to the fact that API Americans comprise about 4% of the population of the United States and have experienced much prejudice and discrimination both currently and historically. As noted by Young and Takeuchi (1998), API Americans have encountered stereotypes, anti-Asian violence, segregation, language difficulties, etc. For example, many recent immigrants have difficulty communicating in English. These conditions can act as stressors that impact mental health. Another important consequence of cultural differences and minority group status is that research and intervention tools, methodologies, strategies, and theories—primarily derived from work with European Americans— may have limited validity with API Americans. Therefore, analyzing clinical psychological issues for API Americans within the context of culture and minority group status is very important for effective mental health care.

RATES OF PSYCHOPATHOLOGY

General indicators of well-being have suggested that Asian/Pacific Islander Americans are adapting well into the mainstream American society. High educational achievements, family income levels, and occupational attainments coupled with relatively low rates of divorce and crime have reinforced the popular view that API Americans are a successful minority group. It is beyond the scope of this chapter to examine the general success of the population—a success that has been in dispute for decades. The primary focus of this chapter is on mental health. Is there evidence that API Americans have low rates of psychopathology or mental disorders? Until recently, the question could not be answered with a strong degree of confidence. In the past, few research studies had been conducted, and the few available studies used research assessment tools that potentially were culturally biased. Even the nosological system (e.g., the *Diagnostic and Statistical Manual-IV* of the American Psychiatric Association) from which diagnoses were made was considered culturally biased by some mental health researchers (Dana, 1998).

Sufficient research has been conducted over the past four decades to come to some preliminary conclusions. First, the overall prevalence rates of mental disorders among API Americans does not appear to dramatically differ from those of other Americans. Second, marked differences exist in the rates of psychopathology, reflecting the heterogeneity among API-American populations (U.S. Surgeon General, 2001).

For example, particular groups such as Southeast Asian refugees have exceedingly high rates of mental disorders. Moreover, level of acculturation is another important individual differences factor in mental health issues. Third, cultural background does influence the expression and nature of psychopathology exhibited by API Americans. Let us examine the bases for these three conclusions.

Depression

When an examination is made of the rates of mental disorders, some interesting findings have been discovered. The prevalence of depression among Asian/Pacific Islander Americans appears to be at least as high as that among European Americans; in the case of anxiety, high discrepancies in the rates have been found; with respect to substance abuse, prevalence rates have been fairly low.

In the depression research with API Americans, the rates have been found to range from high to moderate. High rates have been found among researchers using the Center for Epidemiology Studies of Depression Scale (CES-D) on community respondents. In comparison with established norms found among European Americans, Kuo (1984) found that Chinese, Japanese, Filipino, and Korean Americans in Seattle reported slightly more depressive symptoms. In addition, Ying (1988) found that Chinese Americans in San Francisco, especially those who were immigrants and from a lower socioeconomic background, were significantly more depressed than European Americans and than the Chinese Americans in Kuo's study. Hurh and Kim (1990) examined the self-reports of depression among Korean Americans and compared the findings with those of Kuo. Their findings revealed that Korean immigrants in Chicago exhibited more depression than the Chinese, Japanese, and Filipinos in Kuo's study. Because API Americans in Kuo's study exceeded the level of depressive symptoms among European Americans, the rates found by Ying and by Hurh and Kim suggested that API Americans may have much higher rates than other Americans. Studies of college students using measures other than the CES-D also suggest high rates. In direct comparisons of European-American students with a sample consisting of only Korean-American students (Aldwin & Greenberger, 1987) and a sample of API-American students (Okazaki, 1997), self-reports of depression were significantly higher among the Korean- and API-Americans students than among European Americans.

In the most rigorous study to date of the mental health of Chinese Americans, Takeuchi and his colleagues (Sue, Sue, Sue, & Takeuchi, 1995; Takeuchi et al., 1998) collected data on 1,747 immigrant and native-born respondents using a strata cluster, three-stage probability sampling method. Interviews of the respondents in English, Cantonese, or Mandarin were conducted in order to ascertain demographic characteristics and background, stressors experienced, available social supports, help-seeking sources, and mental health. To assess mental health, the investigators used the Composite International Diagnostic Interview. Findings indicated that the lifetime prevalence of major depression for Chinese Americans was 6.9%. This figure is lower than the 17.1% lifetime prevalence rate for Americans in the National Comorbidity study (NCS) (Kessler et al., 1994) but higher than the 4.9% lifetime rate found in the

Epidemiologic Catchment Area (ECA) study of Americans (Robins & Regier, 1991). The lifetime prevalence rates for dysthymia (5.0%) also fell between the rates in the NCS (6.4%) and ECA surveys (3.2%). Thus, the available evidence suggests that depression is at least as prevalent among API Americans as it is among European Americans. Furthermore, some studies even show higher rates among API Americans.

Anxiety

Research findings on anxiety have been much more variable, with some studies showing high rates, whereas others show low rates of anxiety. In general, research involving college students reveal that Asian/Pacific Islander Americans have higher rates of anxiety than European-American students. In early studies using the Omnibus Personality Inventory (OPI), API-American college students reported experiencing greater anxiety as well as loneliness and isolation than European-American students (see Sue & Frank, 1973; Sue & Kirk, 1973, 1975). Sue and Zane (1985) also found Chinese-American students to have high levels of anxiety on the OPI, especially among recent immigrants. Studies using other measures of anxiety have also demonstrated that API-American students have higher levels of anxiety than European-American students (Okazaki, 1997; Sue, Ino, & Sue, 1983). In contrast to the studies of college students, those that sample adults in the community have found very low rates of anxiety among API Americans. Data from the Epidemiologic Catchment Area (ECA) study of households revealed that API Americans were, in fact, less likely than European Americans to have anxiety disorders, as well as somatization, manic episodes, bipolar disorder, schizophreniform, panic, drug and alcohol abuse, and antisocial personality (Zhang & Snowden, 1999). However, the API-American sample was very small and may not have been representative of the larger population in general. Interestingly, in the major study (CAPES) of Chinese Americans by Takeuchi and his colleagues (see Sue et al., 1995; Takeuchi et al., 1998), the lifetime prevalence rates for Chinese Americans compared with other Americans from the NCS and ECA surveys were (CAPES versus NCS and ECA, respectively): 1.7% versus 5.1% and unknown (for generalized anxiety disorder), 1.6% versus 5.3% and 5.6% (for agoraphobia), 1.1% versus 11.3% and 11.3% (for specific phobia), 1.2% versus 13.3% and 2.7% (for social phobia), 0.4% versus 3.5% and 1.6% (for panic disorder), and 0.7% versus unknown and 1.5% (for panic attack). Thus, the rates of anxiety disorders were markedly lower for Chinese Americans than for other Americans found in the NCS and ECA surveys.

Why are the rates of anxiety found in research on API Americans so discrepant? Sue et al. (1995) have proposed that findings on API Americans often vary because of the (a) relatively small numbers of API Americans in the United States, which makes it difficult to find representative samples to study; (b) heterogeneity among API Americans, which may affect results depending on the sample studied; and (c) the ever-changing nature of the population owing to immigration which further affects the ability to find representative samples. Furthermore, there is evidence that API Americans are more situation-oriented than are European Americans (Zane, Sue, Hu, & Kwon, 1991). For example, most of the research results indicating high levels of anxiety among API Americans were obtained from studies of college students, whereas those with low rates of anxiety were found in studies of community samples. Perhaps some of the variability in the anxiety scores results from the fact that among API Americans anxiety levels highly depend on the situation and context. All of these factors may account for some of the discrepancies in the findings. However, it is also possible that different psychological measures of a construct such as anxiety may elicit different kinds of responses from API Americans or may be differentially susceptible to cultural response sets. The findings pointing to high rates of anxiety have largely come from studies using self-report questionnaires, whereas those revealing low rates have utilized interview methods (the ECA and CAPES projects). At this time, the conflicting results are difficult to explain; further research addressing this issue is needed.

Substance Abuse

In term of substances, the impression among many Asian/Pacific Islander Americans is that tobacco use is high. However, many different indicators suggest that substance use among API Americans is relatively low. In a study of alcohol, tobacco, marijuana, and cocaine use with different API American groups, Sasao (1994) employed multiple methods, including telephone surveys, community forums, archival data analysis, and service utilization statistics. The telephone survey involved 1,783 community residents of Chinese, Japanese, Korean, Filipino, and Vietnamese descent in California. Substance use (including alcohol, cigarettes, marijuana, and cocaine) revealed in the telephone survey was largely below that of other groups in United States. On the indicators of substance use, low rates were also found. In the archival phase of the study involving California state records, among ethnic/racial groups API Americans exhibited the lowest mortality rates owing to alcohol and drug related causes. They also had extremely low arrests rates for felony and misdemeanor drug offenses. Sasao also conducted a survey of about 1,000 high school students in the San Gabriel Valley of California, which had a high proportion of API Americans. They had the lowest drug use compared to Latinos, European-American, and other students.

Sasao's findings are consistent with those from other studies. Reviewing the research on substance use and addictive behaviors among API Americans, Zane and Huh-Kim (1998) came to several conclusions. First, API Americans tend to have relatively low rates of alcohol consumption, although rates varied according to the particular API-American group. For example, Native Hawaiians have consumption rates similar to European Americans. Men are far more likely to drink, and factors such as acculturation level, generational status, and place of birth are important to consider. Second, tobacco use among API Americans was also low although cigarette smoking was high in certain groups such as the Vietnamese. Women tended to have low rates of smoking, as well as more acculturated API Americans. Third, use of drugs appears to be fairly low among API Americans. In view of the findings concerning low rates of substance abuse, Ja and Yuen (1997) caution against the development of a model minority image of API Americans in substance use and point to the seriousness of substance abuse among many API Americans. A major concern is that focus on the low apparent rates of substance use may be used to justify the lack of attention and aid to those API Americans who seriously suffer from alcoholism or drug abuse.

In summary, some research has been conducted on the prevalence of depression anxiety and substance abuse. Research data suggest that rates of depression are at least as high among API Americans as other Americans. In the case of anxiety, results have varied markedly from extremely high to extremely low rates, for reasons that cannot be determined at this time. Only among substance use do we consistently find that API Americans appear to have low rates.

Posttraumatic Stress Disorder

The Southeast Asian refugee populations dramatically illustrate that the various Asian/ Pacific Islander-American groups dramatically differs in psychopathology. The refugee groups have been at risk for mental disorders, especially posttraumatic stress disorders (PTSD) and depression. Many of the Southeast Asian refugees were repeatedly exposed to catastrophic stressors and life-threatening events (Bemak, Chung, & Bornemann, 1996; Chun, Eastman, Wang, & Sue, 1998), including deprivation of food and shelter, physical injury and torture, forced detainment in camps, and witnessing of torture and killing of family members. Given these experiences, a number of investigators have found high rates of PTSD, depression, and anxiety (Du & Lu, 1997; Marsella, Fried-man, & Spain, 1993). Kinzie, Leung, and Boehnlein (1997) estimate that these disorders affect about 20% of the refugees in the community and 50% to 70% of refugees in a psychiatric clinic.

In addition to these premigration traumatic experiences, postmigration problems include acculturation difficulties, culture shock, and separation from family members (Mollica, Wyshak, & Lavelle, 1987). The experience and expression of anger and the loss of cultural ties were associated with PTSD (Abe, Zane, & Chun, 1994). Some differences were found among the different refugee groups. Refugee groups from Cambodia and Laos appear to have more serious adjustment problems than those from Vietnam, who generally came to the United States before the other refugee groups. Thus, these findings indicate the high complexity surrounding the mental health issues concerning API Americans.

Cultural Features: Somatic Problems

The *Diagnostic and Statistical Manual-IV* (DSM-IV) of the American Psychiatric Association (American Psychiatric Association, 1994) has recognized that cultural influences are important in the rate, distribution, and nature of mental disorders. The manifestation of symptoms, meaning of symptoms, explanations for the causes, and perceived prognosis are culturally conditioned. DSM-IV also identified culture-bound syndromes or those recurrent, locality-specific patterns of aberrant behavior and troubling experience that may or may not be linked to a particular DSM-IV diagnostic category. Many of these patterns are indigenously perceived to be "illnesses," or at least afflictions, and most have local names. Although disorders conforming to the major DSM-IV categories can be found throughout the world, the particular symptoms, course, and social response are often influenced by local cultural factors. In contrast, culture-bound syndromes are largely limited to specific societies or cultural areas and are localized, folk, diagnostic categories that frame meanings for certain repetitive and troubling sets of experiences and observations. For Asians/Pacific Islanders, some culture-bound syndromes have been specified. Many Asians/Pacific Islanders exhibit symptoms of neurasthenia, a condition that is characterized by fatigue, weakness, poor concentration, memory loss, irritability, diffuse aches and pains, sleep disturbances, and gastrointestinal problems (cf. Lin, 1989; Ware & Kleinman, 1992; Zheng et al., 1997) and other culture-bound syndromes that are somatic in nature. It has been argued that culture-bound syndromes such as neurasthenia, *hwabyung* (Lin, 1989; Lin et al., 1992), and *koro* (Edwards, 1984) are culturally recognized and sanctioned expressions of psychiatric disorder, mainly depression and anxiety (Chun, Enomoto, & Sue, 1996). Thus, the greater likelihood of encountering somatic complaints among API-American clients is supported by most of the research findings.

One of the more contentious issues concerns the question of whether API Americans are more likely than European Americans to exhibit somatic symptoms in emotional disturbances. Clinical folklore as well as some cross-cultural research has suggested that API Americans tend to exhibit somatic complaints when experiencing mental health problems. Various explanations have been proposed to account for the somatic expression of problems. First, the Confucian philosophy of many Asians are consistent with a collectivistic tradition that discourages open displays of emotions in order to maintain social and familial harmony or avoid exposing personal weakness. In this view, API Americans consciously or unconsciously are thought to deny the experience and expression of emotions (Chun et al., 1996). Second, API Americans, compared to European Americans, tend to have a holistic and integrated view of the functioning of the mind and body. What affects the mind also affects the body, and vice versa. One would therefore expect to find a positive correlation between somatic and psychological symptoms. Third, mental illness is highly stigmatizing in API cultures that emphasizes the importance of "face" or one's appearance to others. It may be more socially acceptable for psychological distress to be expressed through the body.

The evidence regarding somatic symptoms is not consistent. Some researchers have found that somatization is more prevalent among people in non-Western cultures, including ethnic Asians living in Asia and in the United States (Chin, 1998; Chun et al., 1996; Kirmayer, 1984). Gaw (1975) concluded that somatization is frequent among Chinese Americans living in the Boston Chinatown area, regardless of age or socioeconomic status. Some researchers believe that neurasthenia is a condition found among Asians, and it is recognized in China. It is an official category in the International Classification of Diseases (Version 10) but not in the DSM-IV (U.S. Surgeon General, in press). Some studies, however, have failed to find a greater prevalence of somatization among API Americans (Akutsu, 1997). For example, the Epidemiological Catchment Area (ECA) study data, analyzed by Zhang and Snowden (1999), revealed that API Americans reported significantly lower rates of somatization compared to European Americans. As mentioned, however, the ECA data on API Americans involved only a very small sample whose representativeness is unknown.

In summary, there is evidence that significant mental health problems exist among API Americans and that rates of disturbance appear to be within the range of those found among other Americans. Only in substance use do API Americans consistently demonstrate lower prevalence rates. Nevertheless, rates show great variability depending on the particular API group. In the case of Southeast Asian refugees, high rates of mental disorders have been discovered. There is evidence that cultural factors play an important role in the symptoms displayed and in the nature of mental disorders. Furthermore, it is also clear that a number of questions remain, such as the inconsistency of research findings for anxiety among API Americans and the phenomenon of somatization.

Lastly, there are also emerging issues that are now beginning to be recognized among API Americans. They include sexism (Homma-True, 1997; Root, 1998b), family violence (Lum, 1998), gay and lesbian issues (Aoki, 1997), children/youth/elderly (Huang, 1997; Kao & Lam, 1997; Lee & Zhan, 1998), and multiracial API Americans (Root, 1998a). Many of these issues have been suppressed in the past, perhaps because of an unwillingness to discuss them owing to shame and stigma. In any event, they are now topics of widespread interest and concern.

MENTAL HEALTH SERVICES AND TREATMENT

In general, disparities in the provision of mental health care to ethnic minority populations have been examined in one of four ways. First, are there barriers to accessing mental health services? The barriers may include a whole host of factors such as economic (e.g., one cannot afford services), geographic (e.g., one must travel great distances to receive services), or cultural (e.g., the services are culturally inappropriate for some groups). Second, and related to the first point, are individuals utilizing services? In this case, the services fail to be a resource for these individuals. Third, what is the quality of care received from the mental health service? Fourth, what is the outcome of treatment service? Do clients improve when they utilize mental health services?

Access and Utilization

In the case of API Americans, there is evidence that they tend to avoid using services and that there are cultural barriers to access such services. Clinicians have for many years pointed to the low utilization of services (Homma-True, 1997; Lee, 1997). The shame and stigma in using services, English language limitations on the part of many API Americans, cultural unfamiliarity with services, cultural differences in conceptions of mental health treatment, and cultural bias of traditional mental health services have all been proposed as reasons for the underutilization of services (Akutsu, 1997; Chin, 1998).

The convergent evidence points to the fact that API Americans show low rates of service utilization. All studies (Brown, Stein, Huang, & Harris, 1973; Cheung, 1989; Snowden & Cheung, 1990; Sue, 1977; Sue, Fujino, Hu, Takeuchi, & Zane, 1991) except for one (O'Sullivan, Peterson, Cox, & Kirkeby, 1989) demonstrate that API-Americans tend to be underrepresented in psychiatric clinics and hospitals compared to their populations. The underrepresentation occurs among student or nonstudent populations, men or women, young or old, inpatients or outpatients, and among the different API American groups. In a review of the utilization of state and county mental hospitals, private psychiatric hospitals, Veteran Administration psychiatric services, residential treatment centers for emotionally disturbed children, non-federal psychiatric services in general hospitals, outpatient psychiatric clinics, multiservice mental health programs, psychiatric day/night services, and other residential programs throughout the nation, Matsuoka, Breaux, and Ryujin (1997) discovered that utilization of services by API Americans was low, regardless of their population density in various states of the United States. In addition, Zhang, Snowden, and Sue (1998) found that API Americans were unlikely to seek services of any kind for mental health problems, including help from friends and family members.

Studies also demonstrate that the phenomenon of low utilization is associated with greater severity among API-American clients (Brown et al., 1973; Sue, 1977). Durvasula and Sue (1996) examined API-American outpatients using multiple indicators of disturbance. The indicators revealed that they had a higher proportion of severe diagnosis, lower level of functioning scores, and a higher proportion of psychotic features among those diagnosed with mood disorders. Thus, API Americans tend not to utilize services and those who do are severely disturbed. In all likelihood, only the most severely disturbed benefit from services and those with milder problems avoid using services.

API Americans' underutilization of mental health services is a dire problem for our society as noted by Sue and Kim (in press). First, API Americans pay taxes for services as do other Americans. If such services are culturally inappropriate for this population, then they are not receiving appropriate services. Second, services in a multicultural society must be diverse and flexible to accommodate all ethnic groups residing in the United States. Third, API Americans' mental health needs are not being addressed, despite the rapid population growth of this community.

Treatment Outcomes

Do API Americans fare well in treatment? Unfortunately, rigorous mental health outcome studies for this population have not been conducted (U.S. Surgeon General, 2001). Some researchers have used indirect evidence of treatment effects. For example, length of treatment can be considered as an indirect indicator of treatment outcome because it has been consistently associated with treatment change (Luborsky, Chandler, Auerbach, Cohen, & Bachrach, 1971; Pekarik, 1986). In the Seattle study of 17 community mental health facilities, Sue (1977) found that African Americans, American Indians, API Americans, and Latino Americans terminated treatment after one session at a higher rate than European Americans. Whereas about half of the ethnic minority clients failed to return after the first session, less than 30% of the European-American clients did so. The difference in dropout rates was evident even after controlling for the possible influences of social class, age, marital status, referral source, diagnosis, and type of treatment. Not surprisingly, European-American clients were found to average more treatment sessions. Findings from other studies are mixed. In the follow-up of the Sue study in Seattle, O'Sullivan et al. (1989) did not find any consistent differences in dropout rates between ethnic minorities and European Americans. Length of treatment at various inpatient facilities did not show consistent differences between ethnic groups and European Americans (Snowden & Cheung, 1990). Thus, although some differences have emerged in length of sessions, they have not been consistent. The results perhaps reflect the influence of specific and local factors (e.g., regional, community, and service system differences), or time period differences (e.g., between 1977 and 1991, culturally responsive community programs were developed).

Few studies have directly examined psychotherapy outcomes for API-American clients. Zane (1983) assessed outpatients at a community mental health center after the first and fourth sessions and found that API clients evinced significant improvement on both client self-report (Symptom Checklist) and therapist-rated (Brief Psychiatric Rating Scale) outcome measures. One study (Lau & Zane, 2000) compared patterns of the cost-utilization and outcomes of API-American outpatients using ethnic-specific services (ESS), developed to meet the unique cultural and linguistic needs of the ethnic client, to those API clients using mainstream services. It has been assumed that this type of service configuration provides more accessible, culturally responsive mental health care, which in turn, encourages utilization and enhances outcomes. Previous studies have found that ESS increase utilization of mental health services, but there has only been inconsistent evidence that ESS result in better outcomes. Consistent with earlier studies, cost-utilization of ESS for API clients was higher than that for mainstream API clients. Better treatment outcome was found for clients of ESS compared to their mainstream counterparts, even after controlling for certain demographics, pretreatment severity, diagnosis, and type of reimbursement. Moreover, a significant relationship between cost-utilization and outcome for clients of ESS was found, whereas for mainstream clients, this relationship was not significant. There is evidence that these services result in positive treatment outcomes for adults (Takeuchi, Sue, & Yeh, 1995) as well as children (Yeh, Takeuchi, & Sue, 1994). The findings strongly suggested that mental health services with an ethnic-specific focus provided more effective and efficient care for API Americans.

Outcome studies often have aggregated across different API-American groups with the exception of research on Southeast Asians. Mollica et al. (1990) reported improvement in depression among Cambodian clients following 6 months of psychotherapy, whereas no significant improvements in depression or anxiety were found for Vietnamese or Hmong/Laotian clients. In a pilot study of nine patients, Kinzie and Leung (1989) successfully decreased depression in Cambodians suffering from PTSD but the intervention primarily relied on drug therapy (using clonodine and imipramine) supplemented by group socialization therapy.

In terms of differential outcome, two studies have examined clinical outcome among API outpatients using the Global Assessment Scale (GAS), a measure of general psychosocial functioning as rated by the client's therapist. Zane and Hatanaka (1988) found no differences between API and European Americans on posttreatment GAS adjusting for pretreatment GAS. Sue et al. (1991) obtained similar results as API outpatients showed similar improvement compared with European-American clients. Other studies have found some evidence of differential outcome. Zane (1983) found that by the fourth session, there were no differences in therapist-rated outcome and in self-reported symptoms of depression and anxiety. However, API Americans reported greater anger than European Americans and were less satisfied with services and with their progress in treatment. The analyses controlled for both pretreatment level of severity and demographics that could have been confounded with ethnicity. Lee and Mixson (1985) had clients at a university counseling center rate the effectiveness of counseling and their therapists and indicate the reasons why they sought treatment. Despite presenting a similar number of concerns prior to treatment, API Americans rated both their counseling experience and therapists as less effective than did European Americans.

Any conclusions about the effectiveness of treatment for API clients would be premature given the limited data, but several empirical trends should be noted. First, some evidence suggests that certain API groups improve with psychotherapy and/or adjunct treatments. Second, with respect to differential outcome, divergent trends are found, and these are associated with the type of outcome measure used. Studies reporting no differential outcome between API and European Americans relied on a measure of general psychological functioning (e.g., GAS), whereas differential outcomes were found in studies that used client satisfaction measures and/or specific symptom scales. It is possible that the null results may reflect the unreliability and insensitivity of the global outcome measure used. The GAS essentially constitutes a one-item measure and is highly reliable if raters are extensively trained in its use (Endicott, Spitzer, Fleiss, & Cohen, 1976). Yet, there appeared to be no such training conducted with therapists in either study. In sum, API-American clients appear to be deriving less positive experiences from therapy than European Americans, but it is unclear if this difference in client satisfaction actually reflects ethnic differences in actual treatment outcomes (e.g., symptom reduction).

Some research evidence show that ethnic similarities between client and therapist are important in treatment outcomes. Sue et al. (1991) examined the effects of ethnic similarity-dissimilarity between clients and therapists in psychotherapy in the Los Angeles county mental health system. They found that African-American, API-American, Mexican-American, and European-American clients had lower premature termination rates, a greater number of sessions, or better treatment outcomes when matched with ethnically similar therapists. It was suggested that ethnic similarity may be beneficial for many clients. However, individual differences in the effects of match appear to be important as well. Cultural matching between client and therapist may be valuable for some, but not all clients. For example, ethnic and language match was important especially for unacculturated clients. The findings were not clear-cut when treatment outcome was examined for European and African Americans. What do these findings mean? Again, treatment outcomes as measured by the GAS failed to show consistent or significant differences. However, the fact that ESS were associated with lower dropout rates is important. A great deal of concern has been generated over the tendency for ethnic minority clients to prematurely drop out of treatment and to average fewer treatment sessions (Sue, 1977), especially because treatment outcome has consistently demonstrated a direct relationship with the number of sessions in treatment (Orlinsky, Grawe, & Parks, 1994). The fact that clients stay in treatment longer may mirror the greater rapport, comfort, or cultural consistency of the ethnic specific services.

Finally, cognitive match—that is, therapist–client similarity in thought processes—has also been found to be associated with better treatment outcomes for API Americans. Cognitive match was found to be significantly related to treatment outcome and clients' perceptions of the sessions. In various comparisons, therapist–client matches on goals for treatment and on coping styles were related to better adjustment and more favorable impressions of the sessions.

Psychotropic Medication

Interestingly, some recent research on the use of psychotropic medications with API American clients has revealed some important ethnic differences. Because of heredity, diets, and other factors that may affect rates of metabolism, API Americans often show at substantially lower dosages the same clinical responses to psychotropics as do European Americans (Lin & Cheung, 1999). Lin and Shen (1991) assert that pharmacokinetic and pharmacodynamic profiles of various psychotropic medications may be different in API than in non-API patients, leading to differences in dosage requirements and side-effect profiles. Studies of neuroleptics, tricyclic antidepressants, lithium, and benzodiazepines with API Americans have reported this effect (Chin, 1998; Lin, Cheung, Smith, & Poland, 1997). These findings strongly suggest that, in the treatment of mental disorders, medication levels may vary according to ethnicity. In the case of API Americans, care must be taken not to overmedicate. Initial doses of medication for API Americans should be as low as possible with gradual increases in order to obtain therapeutic effects (Du & Lu, 1997).

Toward the Establishment of Effective Interventions

A variety of programs and interventions are needed in order to appropriate serve API Americans. They can be classified according to three interrelated foci: (a) Mental health services, (b) community education, and (c) community-oriented interventions. As mentioned, mental health care providers should receive training on working with API clients. They should acquire cultural competency, which includes the development of cultural knowledge, awareness, and skills appropriate for the client (Sue & Sue, 1999). Obviously, Asian language proficiency at mental health service agencies may be difficult to find. However, providers should have a referral network or transla- tors available that can provide bilingual services to clients. Recruitment of API- American providers is also needed. Because of the heterogeneity of the API population, Asian-American providers may not match culturally with some API-American clients. Nevertheless, there is no question that there is a severe shortage of API providers, and an increase in such providers is critically important. Another mental health service with demonstrated value is ethnic-specific programs. At San Francisco General Hos- pital, there is a psychiatric ward especially designed for API-American clients (wards also exist for other groups such as African Americans, Latinos, and lesbians/gays). Clients can elect to enter or not enter these wards. The purpose of these wards is to have services that provide a linguistic and/or cultural milieu that may better match the client and affect positive treatment outcomes. For example, the Asian-American ward has bilingual and bicultural staff, hospital announcements and notices written in English and various API languages, and ethnic foods or drinks available. These services and programs are important, particularly in those communities with large numbers of API Americans.

Many API Americans do not understand what psychotherapy or mental health treatment is or they hold negative stereotypes and stigmas about mental disorders. In this case, community education may be of immense value. Schools, media (radio, television, ethnic newspapers, etc.), community forums, and other institutions, coor- dinated with mental health agencies, inform API-American communities of mental health issues and means of enhancing mental health. As noted by Sue and Kim (in press), educational messages should make several points: (a) Personal and interper- sonal problems are common; (b) much can be done to prevent or overcome problems; (c) there is nothing to be ashamed, if one has mental health problems; and (d) indi- viduals should seek services for mental health problems when they confront problems that they cannot handle.

Last, in terms of community-oriented interventions, prevention programs may accomplish a great deal. Prevention can come in the form of stress reduction or the enhancement of resources. Immigrants in particular are often under considerable stress because of limited English proficiency, culture conflicts, and lack of knowledge. Com- munity program that can enhance acculturative and language learning as well as pro- viding resources to assist immigrants would be very helpful in reducing stress and in reducing stress-related mental disorders. Because of a cultural as well as a generation gap between parents and children, child-rearing classes for parents and school-based adjustment programs for API youths are needed.

REFERENCES

Abe, J., Zane, N., & Chun, K. (1994). Differential responses to trauma: Migration-discrimi- nants of post-traumatic stress disorder among Southeast Asian refugees. *Journal of Com- munity Psychology, 22,* 121–135.

Akutsu, P. D. (1997). Mental health delivery to Asian Americans: Review of the literature. In E. Lee (Ed.), *Working with Asian Americans: A guide for clinicians* (pp. 464–476). New York: Guilford.

Aldwin, C., & Greenberger, E. (1987). Cultural differences in the predictors of depression. *American Journal of Community Psychology, 15,* 789–813.

American Psychiatric Association. (1994). *Diagnostic and statistical manual of mental disorders: DSM-IV.* Washington, DC: Author.

Aoki, B. K. (1997). Gay and lesbian Asian Americans in psychotherapy. In E. Lee (Ed.), *Working with Asian Americans: A guide for clinicians* (pp. 411–419). New York: Guilford.

Banks, J. A. (1987). *Teaching strategies for ethnic studies* (4th ed.). Boston: Allyn & Bacon.

Bemak, F., Chung, R. C.-Y., Bornemann, T. H. (1996). Counseling and psychotherapy with refugees. In P. B. Pedersen, J. G. Draguns, W. J. Lonner, & J. E. Trimble (Eds.), *Counseling across cultures* (4th ed., pp. 243–265). Thousand Oaks, CA: Sage.

Brown, T. R., Stein, K. M., Huang, K., & Harris, D. E. (1973). Mental illness and the role of mental health facilities in Chinatown. In S. Sue & N. N. Wagner (Eds.), *Asian-Americans: Psychological perspectives* (pp. 212–231). Palo Alto, CA: Science & Behavior Books.

Cheung, F. K. (1989). *Culture and mental health care for Asian Americans in the United States.* Paper presented at the 97th annual meeting of the American Psychiatric Association, New Orleans, LA.

Chin, J. L. (1998). Mental health services and treatment. In L. C. Lee & N. W. S. Zane (Eds.), *Handbook of Asian American psychology* (pp. 485–504). Thousand Oaks, CA: Sage.

Chun, C.-A., Enomoto, K., & Sue, S. (1996). Health care issues among Asian Americans: Implications of somatization. In P.M. Kato & T. Mann (Eds.), *Handbook of diversity issues in health psychology* (pp. 347–365). New York: Plenum.

Chun, K. M., Eastman, K. L., Wang, G. C. S., & Sue, S. (1998). Psychopathology. In L. C. Lee & N. W. S. Zane (Eds.), *Handbook of Asian American psychology* (pp. 457–483). Thousand Oaks, CA: Sage.

Dana, R. (1998). *Understanding cultural identity in intervention and assessment.* Thousand Oaks, CA: Sage.

Du, N., & Lu, F. G. (1997). Assessment and treatment of posttraumatic stress disorder among Asian Americans. In E. Lee (Ed.), *Working with Asian Americans: A guide for clinicians* (pp. 275–294). New York: Guilford.

Durvasula, R., & Sue, S. (1996). Severity of disturbance among Asian American outpatients. *Cultural Diversity and Mental Health, 2,* 43–51.

Edwards, J. W. (1984). Indigenous *koro,* a genital retraction syndrome of insular Southeast Asia: A critical review. *Culture, Medicine and Psychiatry, 8,* 1–24.

Endicott, J., Spitzer, R. L., Fleiss, J. L., & Cohen, J. (1976). The global assessment scale: A procedure for measuring overall severity of psychiatric disturbance. *Archives of General Psychiatry, 33,* 766–771.

Gaw, A. C. (1975). An integrated approach in the delivery of health care to a Chinese community in America: The Boston experience. In A. Kleinman, P. Kunstadter, E. R. Alexander & J. L. Gale (Eds.), *Medicine in Chinese cultures: Comparative studies of health care in Chinese and other societies* (pp. 327–349). Washington, DC: J. E. Fogarty International Center, U.S. Department of Health, Education, & Welfare Public Health Services, NIH.

Homma-True, R. (1997). Asian American women. In E. Lee (Ed.), *Working with Asian Americans: A guide for clinicians* (pp. 420–427). New York: Guilford.

Huang, L. N. (1997). Asian American adolescents. In E. Lee (Ed.), *Working with Asian Americans: A guide for clinicians* (pp. 175–195). New York: Guilford.

Hurh, W. M., & Kim, K. C. (1990). Correlates of Korean immigrants' mental health. *Journal of Nervous and Mental Disease, 178,* 703–711.

Ja, D., & Yuen, F. K. (1997). Substance abuse treatment among Asian Americans. In E. Lee (Ed.), *Working with Asian Americans: A guide for clinicians* (pp. 295–308). New York: Guilford.

Kessler, R. C., McGonagle, K. A., Zhao, S., Nelson, C. B., Hughes, M., Eshleman, S., Wittchen, H.-U., & Kendler, K. S. (1994). Lifetime and 12-month prevalence of DSM-III-R psychiatric disorders in the United States: Results from the national comorbidity survey. *Archives of General Psychiatry, 51,* 8–19.

Kinzie, J. D., & Leung, P. (1989). Clonidine in Cambodian patients with posttraumatic stress disorder. *Journal of Nervous and Mental Disease, 177,* 546–550.

Kinzie, J. D., Leung, P. K., & Boehnlein, J. K. (1997). Treatment of depressive disorders in refugees. In E. Lee (Ed.), *Working with Asian Americans: A guide for clinicians* (pp. 265–294). New York: Guilford.

Kirmayer, L. J. (1984). Culture, affect and somatization. *Transcultural Psychiatric Research Review, 21,* 159–217.

Kuo, W. H. (1984). Prevalence of depression among Asian-Americans. *Journal of Nervous and Mental Disease, 172,* 449–457.

Lau, A., & Zane, N. (2000). Examining the effects of ethnic-specific services: An analysis of cost-utilization and treatment outcome for Asian American clients. *Journal of Community Psychology, 28,* 63–77.

Lee, E. (1997). Overview: The assessment and treatment of Asian American families. In E. Lee (Ed.), *Working with Asian Americans: A guide for clinicians* (pp. 3-36). New York: Guilford.

Lee, L. C., & Zhan, G. (1998). Psychosocial status of children and youths. In L. C. Lee & N. W. S. Zane (Eds.), *Handbook of Asian American psychology* (pp. 137–163). Thousand Oaks, CA: Sage.

Lee, W. M. L., & Mixson, R. J. (1985). *An evaluation of counseling services by college students of Asian and Caucasian ethnicity.* Unpublished manuscript.

Lin, K.-M., & Cheung, F. (1999). Mental health issues for Asian Americans. *Psychiatric Services, 50,* 774–780.

Lin, K.-M., Cheung, F., Smith, M., & Poland, R. E. (1997). The use of psychotropic medications in working with Asian patients. In E. Lee (Ed.), *Working with Asian Americans: A guide for clinicians* (pp. 388–399). New York: Guilford.

Lin, K.-M., Lau, J. K., Yamamoto, J., Zheng, Y. P., Kim, H. S., Cho, K. H., & Nagasaki, G. (1992). *Hwa-byung*: A community study of Korean Americans. *Journal of Nervous and Mental Disease, 180,* 386–391.

Lin, K.-M., & Shen, W. W. (1991). Pharmacotherapy for Southeast Asian psychiatric patients. *Journal of Nervous and Mental Disease, 179,* 346–350.

Lin, T.-Y. (1989). Neurasthenia in Asian cultures [Special issue]. *Culture, Medicine and Psychiatry, 13.*

Luborsky, L., Chandler, M., Auerbach, A. H., Cohen, J., & Bachrach, H. M. (1971). Factors influencing the outcome of psychotherapy: A review of quantitative research. *Psychological Bulletin, 75,* 145–185.

Lum, J. L. (1998). Family violence. In L. C. Lee & N. W. S. Zane (Eds.), *Handbook of Asian American psychology* (pp. 505–525). Thousand Oaks, CA: Sage.

Marsella, A. J., Friedman, M. J., & Spain, E. H. (1993). Ethnocultural aspects of PTSD. In J. M. Oldham, M. B. Riba, & A. Tasman (Eds.), *American Psychiatric Press Review of Psychiatry: Vol. 12* (pp. 157–181). Washington, DC: American Psychiatric Press.

Matsuoka, J. K., Breaux, C., & Ryujin, D. H. (1997). National utilization of mental health services by Asian Americans/Pacific Islanders. *Journal of Community Psychology, 25,* 141–145.

Mollica, R. F., Wyshak, G., & Lavelle, J. (1987). The psychosocial impact of war trauma and torture on Southeast Asian refugees. *American Journal of Psychiatry, 144,* 1567–1572.

Mollica, R. F, Wyshak, G., Lavelle, J., Truong, T., Tor, S., & Yang, T. (1990). Assessing symptom change in Southeast Asian refugee survivors of mass violence and torture. *American Journal of Psychiatry, 147,* 83–88.

Okazaki, S. (1997). Sources of ethnic differences between Asian American and White American college students on measures of depression and social anxiety. *Journal of Abnormal Psychology, 106,* 52–60.

Orlinsky, D. E., Grawe, K., & Parks, B. K. (1994). Process and outcome in psychotherapy: Noch einmal. In A. E. Bergin & S. L. Garfield (Eds.), *Handbook of psychotherapy and behavior change* (4th ed., pp. 270–376). New York: Wiley.

O'Sullivan, M. J., Peterson, P. D., Cox, G. B., & Kirkeby, J. (1989). Ethnic populations: Community mental health services ten years later. *American Journal of Community Psychology, 17,* 17–30.

Pekarik, G. (1986). The use of termination status and treatment duration patterns as an indicator of clinical improvement. *Evaluation and Program Planning, 9,* 25–30.

Robins, L., & Regier, D. A. (1991). *Psychiatric disorders in America: The epidemiologic catchment area study.* New York: Free Press.

Root, M. P. P. (1998a). Multiracial Americans: Changing the face of Asian America. In L. C. Lee & N. W. S. Zane (Eds.), *Handbook of Asian American psychology* (pp. 261–287). Thousand Oaks, CA: Sage.

Root, M. P. P. (1998b). Women. In L. C. Lee & N. W. S. Zane (Eds.), *Handbook of Asian American psychology* (pp. 211–232). Thousand Oaks, CA: Sage.

Sasao, T. (1994). Using surname-based telephone survey methodology in Asian American communities: Practical issues and caveats. *Journal of Community Psychology, 22,* 283–295.

Snowden, L. R., & Cheung, F. K. (1990). Use of inpatient mental health services by members of ethnic minority groups. *American Psychologist, 45,* 347–355.

Snowden, L. R., & Hu, T.-W. (1997). Ethnic differences in mental health services use among the severely mentally ill. *Journal of Community Psychology, 25,* 235–247.

Sue, D. W., & Frank, A. C. (1973). A typological approach to the psychological study of Chinese and Japanese American college males. *Journal of Social Issues, 29,* 129–148.

Sue, D., Ino, S., & Sue, D. M. (1983). Nonassertiveness of Asian Americans: An inaccurate assumption? *Journal of Counseling Psychology, 30,* 581–588.

Sue, D. W., & Kirk, B. A. (1973). Differential characteristics of Japanese-American and Chinese-American college students. *Journal of Counseling Psychology, 20,* 142–148.

Sue, D. W., & Kirk, B. A. (1975). Asian Americans: Use of counseling and psychiatric services on a college campus. *Journal of Counseling Psychology, 22,* 84–86.

Sue, D.W., & Sue, D. (1999). *Counseling the culturally different: Theory and practice* (3rd ed.). New York: Wiley.

Sue, S. (1977). Community mental health services to minority groups: Some optimism, some pessimism. *American Psychologist, 32,* 616–624.

Sue, S., Fujino, D. C., Hu, L.-T., Takeuchi, D. T., & Zane, N. W. S. (1991). Community mental health services for ethnic minority groups: A test of the cultural responsiveness hypothesis. *Journal of Consulting and Clinical Psychology, 59,* 533–540.

Sue, S., & Kim, S.-Y. (in press). Mental Health Policy Implications for a Growing Asian Pacific America. In LEAP Asian Pacific American Public Policy Institute and UCLA Asian American Studies Center (Eds.), *The State of Asian Pacific America: Policy Issues to the Year 2020.* Los Angeles: Asian Pacific American Public Policy Institute.

Sue, S., Sue, D. W., Sue, L., & Takeuchi, D. T. (1995). Psychopathology among Asian Americans: A model minority? *Cultural Diversity and Mental Health, 1,* 39–51.

Sue, S., & Zane, N. W. (1985). Academic achievement and socioemotional adjustment among Chinese university students. *Journal of Counseling Psychology, 32,* 570–579.

Takeuchi, D. T., Chung, R. C.-Y., Lin, K.-M., Shen, H., Kurasaki, K., Chun, C.-A., & Sue, S. (1998). Lifetime and twelve-month prevalence rates of major depressive episodes and dysthymia among Chinese Americans in Los Angeles. *American Journal of Psychiatry, 155,* 1407–1414.

Takeuchi, D. T., Sue, S., & Yeh, M. (1995). Return rates and outcomes from ethnicity-specific mental health programs in Los Angeles. *American Journal of Public Health, 85,* 638–643.

U.S. Surgeon General. (2001). *Mental health: Culture, race, and ethnicity. A supplement to mental health: A report of the Surgeon General.* Rockville, MD: U.S. Department of Health and Human Services.

Ware, N. C., & Kleinman, A. (1992). Culture and somatic experience: The social course of illness in neurasthenia and chronic fatigue syndrome. *Psychosomatic Medicine, 54,* 546–560.

Yee, B. W. K., Huang, L. N., & Lew, A. (1998). Families: Life-span socialization in a cultural context. In L. C. Lee & N. W. S. Zane (Eds.), *Handbook of Asian American psychology* (pp. 83–135). Thousand Oaks, CA: Sage.

Yeh, M., Takeuchi, D. T., & Sue, S. (1994). Asian-American children in the mental health system: A comparison of parallel and mainstream outpatient service centers. *Journal of Clinical Child Psychology, 23,* 5–12.

Ying, Y.-W. (1988). Depressive symptomatology among Chinese-Americans as measured by the CES-D. *Journal of Clinical Psychology, 44,* 739–746.

Ying, Y.-W. Lee, P. A., Tsai, J. L., Yeh, Y.-Y., & Huang, J. S. (2000). The conception of depression in Chinese American college students. *Cultural Diversity & Ethnic Minority Psychology, 6,* 183–195.

Young, K., & Takeuchi, D. T. (1998). Racism. In L. C. Lee & N. W. S. Zane (Eds.), *Handbook of Asian American psychology* (pp. 401–432). Thousand Oaks, CA: Sage.

Zane, N. (1983, August). *Evaluation of outpatient psychotherapy for Asian and Non-Asian American clients.* Paper presented at the 91st annual convention of the American Psychological Association Conference, Anaheim, CA.

Zane, N., Enomoto, K., Chun, C.-A. (1994). Treatment outcomes of Asian- and White-American clients in outpatient therapy. *Journal of Community Psychology, 22,* 177–191.

Zane, N., & Hatanaka, H. (1988, October). *Utilization and evaluation of a parallel service delivery model for ethnic minority clients.* Paper presented at the Professional Symposium: Recent Trends and New Approaches to the Treatment of Mental Illness and Substance Abuse, Oklahoma Mental Health Research Institute.

Zane, N. W. S., & Huh-Kim, J. (1998). Addictive behaviors. In L. C. Lee & N. W. S. Zane (Eds.), *Handbook of Asian American psychology* (pp. 527–554). Thousand Oaks, CA: Sage.

Zane, N. W., Sue, S., Hu, L.-T., & Kwon, J.-H. (1991). Asian-American assertion: A social learning analysis of cultural differences. *Journal of Counseling Psychology, 38,* 63–70.

Zhang, A. Y., & Snowden, L. R. (1999). Ethnic characteristics of mental disorders in five U.S. communities. *Cultural Diversity and Ethnic Minority Psychology, 5,* 134–146.

Zhang, A. Y., Snowden, L. R., & Sue, S. (1998). Differences between Asian and White Americans' help seeking and utilization patterns in the Los Angeles area. *Journal of Community Psychology, 26,* 317–326.

Zheng, Y.-P., Lin, K.-M., Takeuchi, D., Kurasaki, K. S., Wang, Y., Cheung, F. (1997). An epidemiological study of neurasthenia in Chinese-Americans in Los Angeles. *Comprehensive Psychiatry, 38,* 249–259.

CHAPTER 11

South Asian Americans

Culture, Concerns, and Therapeutic Strategies

NITA TEWARI
ARPANA G. INMAN
DAYA SINGH SANDHU

Demographically, Asian Americans currently constitute the fastest growing racial/ethnic group in the United States (Lott, 1998). Within this subgroup, South Asians are the fourth largest ethnic subgroup, approximating a population of 2,963,999 in the United States (U.S. Census Bureau, 2000). Typically, individuals from South Asia have included those who are from India, Pakistan, Bangladesh, Sri Lanka, Nepal, Bhutan, and the Maldives. As the South Asian and South Asian American population continues to increase, it becomes important to examine how their experiences may be similar or different from other Asian-American groups. This chapter focuses on the specific experience of South Asians and South Asian Americans, the unique challenges faced within the context of immigration and acculturation, and the therapeutic issues pertinent for this group.

SOUTH ASIAN GROUPS

The term "South Asian" denotes a common identity, bringing together diverse populations on the basis of a shared culture and history (Shankar & Srikanth, 1998). They comprise a heterogeneous group, diverse in socioeconomic statuses, languages, religious practices, cultural values, beliefs, and acculturation levels. Among South Asian Americans, Asian Indian Americans are the majority group representing about 1,678,795 of the total South Asian population in the United States, followed by Pakistanis, and others of South Asian ancestry (U.S. Census Bureau, 2000).

Although historically, Pakistan and Bangladesh were part of India, with the independence of India from the British in 1947, there occurred a religious split resulting in separate Muslim (Pakistan, Bangladesh) and Hindu (India) countries. Of the several South Asian countries, India continues to be most diverse. For example, in terms of religion, India consists of Hindus (82%), Muslims (12%), Christians (2.5%), Sikhs

(2%), Buddhists (0.7%), Jains (0.5%), Zorastraians/Parsi (0.01%), and Jews (0.005%) (Daniel, 2001). A small number of individuals in India are also followers of the Bahai faith. On the other hand, Pakistanis and Bangladeshis are primarily Muslim, whereas Sri Lankans are mostly Buddhist. India is also unique with respect to language, as India has 14 major languages and approximately 400 dialects, all of which are derivatives of the Sanskrit language. The primary languages spoken by South Asians include Hindi in India, Urdu in Pakistan and Bangladesh, and Singhalese in Sri Lanka, with English (owing to Britain's colonization) spoken in most countries.

Additionally, each state in India has its own unique style of clothing, customs, and food that is specific to each region. Despite the distinct religious and regional diversity within and between the various South Asian countries, there is considerable overlap among the South Asian cultures. Having examined the distinctions within the South Asian cultures, it becomes relevant to examine how this group is similar or different from other Asian-American groups.

Similarities Among South Asian and Asian/Pacific Islander American Groups

Considering that most Asian and Pacific Islander Americans have immigrated to America, the first similarity relevant to these cultural groups is the issue of acculturation. Cross-cultural researchers have used the concept of acculturation when studying the impact of adjusting to a culture different from one's own, as is the case with many Asian Americans (Berry, 1980). Several of these groups have been in the United States for at least three to four generations, thus it is likely that many have thought about their ethnic, racial, and cultural identities and what it means to be South Asian American/Asian American as they have maintained their lives in America.

Second, South Asian and Asian Pacific Islander Americans both share similar values related to discipline, self-control, strong work ethics, the value of higher education (especially careers based in engineering or medicine), a commitment to family and community, preservation of their culture, religion, and respect for the decisions and wisdom of elders as well as humility in one's actions. Furthermore, it is not uncommon among these cultures for elders to emphasize their desires for younger generations to marry within the culture (e.g., region, religion, socioeconomic status, etc.).

A third similarity is the emphasis on a patriarchal family structure. Struggles of gender roles and behavioral expectations have been common among South Asian and Asian-American women and men attempting to adapt to the American culture. Specifically, common struggles among these groups of women have included being the primary child caregivers; the expectation that they respect the wishes of husbands, family members, and in-laws; the expectation that they become the carriers of customs and traditions, wearing clothing customary to their culture; and the expectation that they sacrifice their careers in relation to their husbands' or families' priorities. Men, on the other hand, have traditionally been the primary breadwinners and caretakers of the family, with sons typically being valued more than daughters.

Fourth, with regard to the workplace and living in a diverse society, many Asian Americans have faced different forms of discrimination—overt, covert, and institutional. The stereotype of being considered a "model minority" has been at a cost to these groups as evidenced by hate crimes perpetuated on the South Asian community by the "Dot Busters" in New Jersey; and the killing of Vincent Chin in Detroit. The combined values, experiences, and pressures faced by many men and women illustrate the similarities between the Asian subgroups in terms of their culture, struggles, and adaptation process to the American culture.

As a result of these pressures and struggles, Asian Americans and South Asian Americans have needed to seek support from different sources. However, the stigma of seeking professional help and avoiding shame to the self and family has resulted in an underutilization of therapeutic services by a majority of Asian Americans. Thus, a fifth similarity is the resistance to therapy as a form of emotional support. A lack of specific knowledge regarding the counseling process has resulted in a lack of trust toward mental health practitioners. This stigma has also impacted availability of South Asian and Asian-American culturally competent counselors.

Finally, even though there is much common ground among the subgroups as illustrated by the preceding similarities, it is important to recognize that the concerns, pressures, and experiences of both groups are spoken of broadly. Despite the similarities between these groups, the diverse immigration histories, acculturation processes, ethnic identity, and generational levels need to be taken into account when researching and working with South Asian Americans

Differences Between South Asian-American and Asian Pacific Islander Groups

Although Asians in Asia as a whole may share similar cultural values, Asians in the United States are quite distinct from each other. First, Asian Americans in the United States have experienced differing relationships between their home countries and the United States. For example, importation of Chinese laborers to build railroads, the colonization of the Philippines by the United States, the Japanese attack on Pearl Harbor and the resultant internment camps for Japanese Americans, and the United States involvement in Vietnam and Korean Wars are some of the different historical experiences of East Asian groups. In contrast, there has been no comparable military action associated with South Asia (Shankar & Srikanth, 1998).

Second, although the experience of discrimination has been similar among Asian-American groups, the South Asian immigrant group to the United States has had different immigration experiences. Several other Asian groups (e.g., Southeast Asians) have had refugee experiences and/or other notable differences in immigration patterns (e.g., political unrest, trauma) compared to most South Asians who came to the United States on their own terms. Although early South Asian immigrants experienced discrimination in terms of serving as indentured servants (Gupta, 1999), South Asians— especially Asian Indians—typically came to the United States in large waves after the

Immigration Act of 1965 under fairly decent financial conditions, with good mental and physical health, seeking higher education, and wanting to experience the "American Dream."

Third, there are many economic and educational differences among Asian sub-groups. Reports and data on income and education in the 1980s have indicated that many Indians have higher incomes and education levels than some of their Asian counterparts, such as Southeast Asian-Americans (Agarwal, 1991; Sandhu, 1997; Tanaka, Ebreo, Linn, & Morera, 1998). Historically, the impact of this pattern in-cludes categorically limiting or excluding South Asians from any "underrepresented" or "minority" category from need-based financial support or affirmative action. The assumption that these averages apply to all South Asians results in a marginalization of the impoverished South Asians and also the less educated relatives of the 1965 immigrants.

A fourth difference between South Asian and other Asian groups is religious philosophies. Hinduism, Islam, Sikhism, and Jainism are religions primarily practiced in India and other regions of South Asia, whereas Buddhism and Christianity are prac-ticed primarily in East and Southeast Asia. One of the key differences of South Asian (Hindu) religions includes a polytheistic versus monotheistic beliefs as well as the belief in an afterlife.

A fifth difference is the British influence in India and other parts of South Asia. This influence has familiarized South Asians with the English language, because many of the schools were forced to teach English in addition to the native languages (Hindi, etc.). As a result of the British rule, many Indians were exposed to a culture different than their own, leaving many middle- to upper-class individuals to adjust to a Euro-pean way of life. Such experiences have influenced preimmigration and postimmigration adjustment for South Asian immigrants.

Sixth, despite the fact that South Asians are a significantly growing ethnic group within the Asian-American group, they are often unnoticed within the literature. In reviewing the psychological literature, studies on South Asian Americans appear to be limited compared to other Asian groups. Although Indian Americans are the fastest growing South Asian immigrant group in America, with a 106% growth rate over the last decade (U.S. Census, 2000), Durvasula and Mylvaganam (1994) noted that Asian Indians have been neglected in the American mental health literature and in the Asian-American studies literature, a trend continuing in the 21st century.

Seventh, most Asian Indians (and probably most South Asians) agree that an important distinction between the East Asian, Southeast Asian, and the South Asian groups is that of phenotype. Many South Asians do not look physically similar to their other Asian counterparts (Tewari, 1998). Asian Indians as a race have long been cat-egorized as Caucasian, with their facial features being viewed as "Anglo-Saxon or Caucasian," whereas other Asians (e.g., Japanese, Chinese, etc.) have been described as having Mongoloid features and are labeled as Mongoloid by race (Gupta, 1999; Lott, 1998). Such physical differences have deterred South Asians from using the older term "Oriental," or the more current term "Asian," to describe themselves. In consider-ing the experience of South Asians, it is important to note that their differences or similarities may be more or less heightened for this group depending on their level of acculturation, socioeconomic status, immigration history, racism experienced, and other such factors.

THEORETICAL AND EMPIRICAL RESEARCH ON SOUTH ASIAN AMERICANS

South Asian-American Theoretical Research

The theoretical literature on South Asians in the United States has focused on providing a window into the cultural values of this ethnic group and how they might differ from the dominant culture. Furthermore, authors have theorized on the impact of acculturation on South Asians' adherence to their own cultural values and accommodation to the dominant culture and discussed the particular factors that either mitigate or create acculturative stress for this ethnic group. This section of the chapter addresses aspects relevant to these two areas.

Worldviews, Values, and Beliefs

Ibrahim, Ohnishi, and Sandhu (1997) believe that one's cultural identity and worldview are impacted by one's educational level, social class, identification with one's ethnicity and culture, generation in the United States, and experiences with racism, sexism, and exclusion, variations of which must be considered within the context of a person's total experiences. Thus, understanding the value orientations and worldviews of South Asians becomes an important foundation to their experience. Although the term "South Asian" subsumes countries composed of people and communities with many religions, *jatis* (castes), regional and language groups with varying social and cultural characteristics, many scholars believe there are universal value orientations and worldviews among South Asians (Ibrahim et al., 1997; Sodowsky & Carey, 1987; Sodowsky, Kwan, & Pannu, 1995). These authors have identified some general characteristics among South Asians (Table 11.1).

In understanding generational differences in South Asians, Juthani (cited in Prathikanti, 1997) identified some specific and different value orientations for first- and second-generation Asian Indian Americans (Table 11.2). Understanding the degree to which clients hold on to their culture of origin and adhere to their cultural values plays an important role in developing culturally relevant psychological services (Inman, Constantine, & Ladany, 1999; Kim 1998).

Acculturation

Ramisetty-Mikler (1993), in her overview on sociocultural issues in counseling Indian Americans, discussed important factors distinguishing Eastern (i.e., Indian) and Western (i.e., American) cultures. She focused on several cultural orientations that create

TABLE 11.1. General Characteristics Among South Asians

Primacy of the family over the individual
The importance of religion
A custom of arranged marriages
Nonconfrontation or silence as a virtue
Respect for older persons and elderly persons
Moderation in behaviors
Devaluation of individualism
Harmony between hierarchical roles
Filial piety
Structured family roles and relationships
Humility
Obedience
High regard for learning; modesty regarding sexuality
Not demonstrative with heterosexual affection
Less need for dating
Strong sense of duty to family
Protection of honor and "face" of family
Marrying within as opposed to outside ethnic group
Self-respect, dignity, and self-control
Respect for age
Awareness and respect for the community
Fatalism

conflicts in the process of adjustment. With "Perception of Time," she noted that Asians tend to stress the past and future and perceive the present as transitory, whereas Americans value the present and look forward to the future. With "Family Structure and Kinship," she noted that interdependence and obligation are valued within Asian cultures and that it is not uncommon for children to reside with their parents until marriage, or for married sons to live with their parents. On the other hand, autonomy and self-sufficiency are emphasized in American culture, with young adults encouraged to move out of their homes to develop independence from the family. The Asian "Ethics and Value System" is said to value the community and group cooperation, with jobs seen as sources of identity, and education and achievement as status symbols reflective of the family rather than the individual. Confronting such distinct value orientations are likely to cause social and psychological adjustment difficulties. Several authors have identified factors that mitigate and/or create stress for these immigrant groups in this acculturative process (Prathikanti, 1997; Ramisetty-Mikler, 1993; Sodowsky & Carey, 1988).

Network System

Sodowsky and Carey (1987, 1988) and Ramisetty-Mikler (1993) discuss the importance of a strong ethnic network within the South Asian community. Specifically, they note that ethnic social supports established in the community have offered a strong

TABLE 11.2. Value Differences Between First- and Second-Generation
South Asians

First-Generation South Asians	Second-Generation South Asians
Expectation of self-sacrifice for the good of the family	Expectation of family assisting in self-actualization
Authoritarian and hierarchical decision making	Endorsement of democratic decision making
Elders accorded more respect than juniors	Idealization of youth and subtle devaluation of old age
Males accorded more overt authority than females	Endorsement of little difference in authority based on gender
Expectation of filial piety	Expectation of separation and autonomy from parents
Indirect expression of anger as the norm	Direct expression of anger
Accommodation and tolerance in face of conflict	Confrontation and negotiation in the face of conflict
Emphasis on academic achievement/ professional career	Exploration of career options based on interests and talents
Little emphasis on sports and extracurricular activities	Emphasis on becoming a well-rounded person
Modesty in dress with limited exposure of body parts	Being comfortable displaying body in public
Few open displays of heterosexual affection	Being comfortable with open displays of heterosexual affection
Discouragement of dating and adolescent sexual expression	Acceptance of dating and sexual expression
Expectation of arranged marriage within the same ethnic group	Selection of own mate and acceptance of interethnic marriage
The importance of preserving religious/ethnic identity	Importance of creating a multicultural identity

moral and resource support for many of these immigrants in the United States. However, although such groups provide support by organizing religious and cultural activities, Ramisetty-Mikler (1993) argues that Asian Indians' "strong sense of group identity might, in turn, hinder a person from completely assimilating and adapting to the host culture" (p. 41).

Religion

Religious teachings have served as important spiritual philosophies guiding South Asians' pre- and posttransition to America. For example, Hindus believe in polytheism and read varying scriptures, including the *Vedas, Mahabharata, Ramayana,* and *Bhagavad-Gita,* instead of having just one holy book (e.g., the Bible in the Western world). Swamis or religious leaders are held in high regard and sought after at times of stress. Furthermore, the Hindu religion professes a belief in reincarnation, destiny, *karma* (where one's past impacts the present, and present impacts future lives), *dharma* (duty), and *moksha* (transcending, merging with God), which guide the lives of South

Asian Americans. The choice of deity and scripture worship is often regionally dependent (McLean, 2001). The belief in rebirth is an important aspect of the psychology of many Indians, who believe that one's time on earth is not final, and that life is continuous with the possibility of reentry onto Earth in different forms. Finally, South Asians who are Muslim do not believe in the worship of icons, but in *Allah* (God) as the unseen force, and follow the teachings of the holy book *Quran*. Like Christians, Muslims believe that the present life is only a trial preparation for the next realm of existence. Muslim life is guided by the "five pillars of Islam" and includes: belief in Allah, five prayers a day, going on a pilgrimage (*hajj*), fasting, and giving *zakat* (supporting the needy). Religious adherence varies by sect (e.g., Sunni and Shias) and should be noted whether it serves as a support at times of stress.

Families

Families are another resiliency factor; Indians are described as being family oriented; formal with respect to elders; dependent; and responsible toward parents, older siblings, and other family members. Although the Indian family system is considered a form of security and is often the core source of support for Indian family members, family role adaptations and conflicts also can be major sources of stress given the interdependent nature of the family system and the independent nature of the American culture.

Intergenerational Conflicts

Sodowsky and Carey (1987), Ramisetty-Mikler (1993), and Prathikanti (1997) discuss intergenerational conflicts as a major source of stress (see Table 11.2). Prathikanti (1997) noted that Asian Indians respond variably to the challenges of acculturation by selectively adapting to some sociocultural norms (e.g., speaking the English language, career goals) while holding on to other cultural values (e.g., family relations, marriage) to facilitate goal attainment. Ramisetty-Mikler (1993) suggested that most immigrant families try to maintain their traditional patterns, but may change in gender role expectations and assignments based on their length of stay in North America. For example, families may become more egalitarian; couples may share decisions and labor responsibilities, or children may be allowed more freedom in America. However, there is often a fear among parents that children may become "Americanized" (e.g., Dasgupta & Dasgupta, 1996).

Discrimination

As with most immigrants, discriminatory experiences have played a significant role among South Asians. Authors have discussed perceived prejudice in social and professional settings (being of a minority status) and negative stereotyping (math geniuses, snake worshippers, bride burners) as factors negatively impacting Indians (Ramisetty-Mikler, 1993; Sodowsky & Carey, 1988). A recent example is that resulting from the aftermath of September 11, 2001, when several South Asians were detained at airports because of their physical characteristics. Thus, differences in clothing style, accents, physical appearance, perceived negative stereotyping, non–majority status, and feelings of isolation may be continued sources of stress. Such acculturative stress can lead immigrants to become defensive and develop feelings of inferiority or prejudice against the majority culture (Ramisetty-Mikler, 1993).

Duration of Stay

Sandhu, Kaur, and Tewari (1999) explain that Asian and Pacific Islanders who choose to stay in the United States permanently often experience greater acculturative stress than those who come to America for a short period of time and intend to returning to their homeland (e.g., international students or sojourns). Thus, length of stay, adjustment experiences, and the other factors discussed become important variables in understanding the South Asian-American experience. Overall, authors suggest that there is no "one" Indian personality, and challenge social scientists and psychologists to understand this growing minority group.

SOUTH ASIAN EMPIRICAL RESEARCH FINDINGS

The empirical research reviewed in the literature on South Asian Americans has primarily been conducted on Asian Indian Americans and has focused on acculturation, ethnic identity, values, and worldviews. This section outlines the current empirical research in these areas.

Acculturation and Ethnic Identity

Acculturation and ethnic identification have been conceptualized as important processes facing South Asian Americans. In acculturating to a pluralistic society such as the United States, one is likely to experience a heightened awareness of one's ethnic identity as one is confronted with incongruent sets of cultural values, beliefs, and behavioral norms (Inman, 2001). Thus, the impact of these two processes has received considerable attention in the literature.

In an earlier article on Indian immigrants, Sodowsky and Carey (1988) researched the relation between acculturation-related demographics and the cultural attitudes of Indians. They found that Indians reported a high level of English proficiency and a preference for Indian food and dress at home but a preference for American dress and food outside the home. The majority labeled themselves as "mostly or very Indian," preferring Indian clothes and food, as well as thinking in an Indian language. Examined parental attitudes revealed that parents believed that their children should adhere to Indian cultural values, customs, religions, and rituals. Many parents also believed their children should not be allowed to date or go to dances with American peers of the opposite sex.

Tiwari (1995) examined the relationship among acculturation, self-esteem, and gender among 169 Asian Indians and Asian Indian-Americans (students and nonstudents) in California using Krishnan and Berry's (1992) Acculturation Attitudes Scales, a scale developed for Indian Americans. Her results indicated a significant difference between students and nonstudents. Among students, females were found to have higher self-esteem scores and integration attitude scores and lower assimilation and marginalization scores than males. Among nonstudents, the opposite was found for the two genders. Tiwari's (1995) study reflected acculturative and self-esteem differences in gender and generational status among Indian Americans.

Bufka (1998) conducted a study on family factors, acculturation, and identity in second-generation Asian Indians. She found the second generation to be more acculturated than the first with the first generation perceiving more prejudice. Her results also indicated that the greater the family cohesion, the stronger the individual's ethnic identity and sense of belonging to his or her ethnic group. For both first- and second-generation Indians, greater family cohesion predicted less acculturation to the mainstream American culture.

Empirical research on South Asian acculturation and ethnic identity seems consistent with the theoretical literature on these variables. Research has found significant gender and generational variations for Asian Indian immigrant groups in levels of acculturation and ethnic identity (Prathikanti, 1997; Ramisetty-Mikler, 1993).

Values and Worldview

A second and related area of study among South Asians has been in the areas of values and worldviews. Cultural values affect individuals' socialization by influencing their psychological, as well as social, functioning. Marin (1992) discussed the fact that cultural values are a significant and ingrained part of one's self-definition and typically are the last level to be influenced. Individuals negotiating two value systems, such as the Indian and American, are likely to experience distress given the discrepancy between the two value systems, resulting in negative affect (e.g., guilt, anxiety) and cognitive dissonance (Inman, Constantine, & Ladany, 1999). Several studies have explored the influence of a bicultural socialization among South Asians and the role that cultural values play within the context of acculturation.

Inman et al. (1999) examined the experiences of Asian Indian women within a bicultural context. Results revealed significant differences between first- and second-generation women in terms of their motives and coping styles in the negotiation process, with second-generation women experiencing greater pressures and restrictions. For example, although both groups discussed the need to maintain a compartmentalized identity, the physical distance from their families allowed first-generation women to experience fewer conflicts compared to second-generation women who had to deal with issues on a day-to-day basis. Second-generation women also perceived greater restrictions in family relations and stronger pressures to maintain an "Indian" ethnic/cultural identity compared to first-generation women. Finally, with regard to dating/premarital sexual relations, a need to fit into the dominant cultural norms created greater pressures to engage in these behaviors for second-generation women.

Having noted the potential for cultural value conflicts, Inman, Ladany, Constantine, and Morano (2001) developed and validated a scale assessing the cultural value conflicts of South Asian women focusing on cultural value conflicts in two areas, namely, intimate relations and sex role expectations. The scale discriminated between first- and second-generation women and suggested a positive relationship between the cultural value conflicts and measures of anxiety and cultural adjustment difficulties. Their study also suggested that social desirability may play a role in the self-representation of South Asian women.

In light of the importance of ethnic identification and prejudicial experiences experienced by South Asians, Inman (2001) examined the relation between cultural value conflict and racial and ethnic identification. Her results suggested that when South Asians experience racism or discriminatory practices owing to their appearance, they are likely to experience greater sex role conflicts. On the other hand, a stronger immersion into their own culture is likely to result in greater intimate relations conflicts. She also found that South Asian women with stronger internal and external ethnic identification experienced greater conflict with intimate relations and sex role expectations; however, stronger external ethnic identification resulted in lesser sex role expectations conflict.

Ghosh, Bufka, Jensen, and Patel's (1999) study examined a similar theme of attitudes between first- and second-generation Asian Indian Americans toward arranged marriages as well as other values considered important in relationships (e.g., obedience, freedom, equality, and romantic versus mature love). Results revealed that first-generation Asian Indians were more open to arranged marriages than second-generation individuals. Both generations valued equality in relationships; however, the second generation placed an equal value on romantic and mature love. Obedience was not an important value despite the duty toward family and the hierarchical structure typical in Asian Indian families, nor did the second-generation Asian Indian Americans rank freedom higher than the first generation.

Empirical research has focused on acculturation, ethnic identity, and the challenges that South Asian Americans face in negotiating their values. A common theme has been the struggle of balancing the customs and traditions of the Indian and American cultures. Finding comfort with one's sense of self regarding personal choices—including education, marriage, and parental/familial relationships—has been paramount. Thus, it becomes relevant to examine how these struggles manifest themselves as psychological concerns among South Asians.

COMMON PSYCHOLOGICAL CONCERNS AND MENTAL DISORDERS AMONG SOUTH ASIANS

Although there is anecdotal evidence that South Asian Americans may seek therapy at community mental health centers and university counseling centers, with psychiatrists, psychologists in private practice, and traditional or spiritual healers in the community, very little empirical literature exists regarding South Asian-American help-seeking behaviors in response to emotional and psychological difficulties. Some recent efforts have been made to address this limitation. Researchers (Almeida, 1996; Inman & Tewari, in press; Tewari, 2000) have provided some clinical and empirical evidence toward addressing this situation. These authors present specific concerns related to South Asians encountered in their clinical practice (Almeida, 1996; Inman & Tewari, in press) and through archival data (Tewari, 2000).

Tewari (2000) assessed the utilization rates of clients within 13 ethnic groups (including South Asians) over a 14-year period (1985–1998) at a large Southern California university counseling center. Her data indicated that South Asian-American clients underutilized counseling services in proportion to their representation on campus. Furthermore, Tewari (2000) conducted a qualitative content analysis on the presenting concerns listed on intake forms and the treatment session summaries for South Asian-American clients seeking therapy at the same university counseling center. On the intake forms, clients were found to present with general psychological concerns, such as interpersonal problems, school-related problems, mood disorders, sense of self issues, coping difficulties, and anxiety disorders. However, session summaries revealed that several general problems such as interpersonal problems or school-related problems manifested themselves culturally for almost every individual. How these specific issues manifested culturally for the South Asian Americans is discussed in the following sections.

Dating and Arranged Marriages

Tewari (2000) and Inman and Tewari (in press) have noted that a major dilemma facing many South Asian-American clients seeking therapy has involved dating. Clients struggle with the desire to date and explore their sexuality while experiencing distress over not wanting to betray the prohibitions against casual, open dating. Clients often feel pressure from parents to marry individuals of their descent and from the same geographical region in India. Such pressure leads to secret dating practices where many Indian Americans feel compelled to hide their dating experiences from their parents; this results in internal and parental conflicts as parents wish for their children to marry someone of their own race, religion, region, and/or *jati* (caste). In extreme cases, Tewari (2000) found that parents cut off emotional and financial support to their children if they married someone of non–South Asian ancestry.

Sexual Issues

Qualitative data from intakes and therapeutic contacts have revealed that South Asians struggle with sexual and sexuality issues (Tewari, 2000). Specifically, when sexually involved, South Asians have been noted to experience conflicts at different levels because of the fact that sexuality or sexual involvement is not openly discussed in families. Sexual involvement is perceived as a consequence of dating; thus, dating is strongly discouraged within the South Asian community, leading to conflictual feelings surrounding sexuality (Jayakar, 1994; Prathikanti, 1997). However, sexual issues such as sexual abuse and assault, pregnancy, and concern about premarital/extramarital involvement were discussed in therapy sessions. With regard to sexuality issues, few clients discussed homosexual or bisexual concerns; however, a lack of discussion does not indicate a lack of such concerns in the South Asian community.

Autonomy

Other related cultural conflicts and acculturation issues have included struggles with autonomy and independence issues. A common desire for many first-generation South Asian parents is to have their children take responsibility at home and contribute to the family unit emotionally, physically, and sometimes financially. For example, in Tewari's (2000) study, one of the clients who lived at home reported her parents as being traditionally Indian. This client struggled with wanting to move to campus and experience college life, but on the other hand feeling pressured to fulfill her family duty and responsibility to care for her parents and/or siblings. This client was one of many where self-sacrifice for family members was a concern.

Ethnic Identity

Additional acculturation and ethnic identity challenges that seem to manifest themselves have included challenges with physical image and looking physically different than mainstream America. For example, Tewari (2000) found that more than one Sikh male client struggled with the expectation that he wear a turban; if he did not, his father threatened to disown him. These clients were concerned about their physical appearance (e.g., hairiness, wearing a turban), felt pessimistic, and feared never being in a relationship with a non–Indian woman. Many Indian-American students felt the insecurity of being "an outsider" and struggled with such cross-cultural differences. Several clients also experienced racism, discrimination, and sexism; and some experienced homophobia owing to their physical appearance.

Academic Expectations

Data revealed that parental pressure related to career path expectations (e.g., pursuing a science/medical career), with a focus on academics to the exclusion of social or extracurricular activities were important components of academic problems for many Asian Indian-American clients (Inman & Tewari, in press; Tewari, 2000). Often, South Asian-American students struggled with fulfilling their parent's academic expectation versus meeting their own personal desires in academic choices (e.g., pursuing a "non–hard science" career such as a majoring in social sciences, psychology, or the arts). It was not uncommon that such conflicts between parents and children resulted in the threat of withdrawal of support when cultural expectations (related to school and other values) were not met.

Abuse

Unfortunately, sexual, physical, and emotional abuse by family members and/or significant others has been evident in the South Asian-American community. Experiencing abuse was ranked as one of the top five problems that Indian American clients faced in Tewari's study (2000). Clients reported being molested by family members, so-called friends, and in one case a religious leader. Almeida (1996) also has spoken about the increasing frequency of date rape among women, and noted that domestic violence and child abuse have been among the most common mental health problems that Asian-Indian and Pakistani families present in counseling. This was further evidenced in Tewari's (2000) study, where clients reported being date raped and inappropriately touched, but struggled to discuss such issues with their parents. Parents often told them to "forget about it" and blamed them for being victimized and bringing shame to the family. Clients reported difficulty with their parents and yet felt guilty when they disobeyed by exerting their own independence. Many clients also struggled with wanting to maintain a positive relationship with their parents regardless of the conflicts and abuse they were experiencing. Tewari (2000) notes that a large number of clients experienced emotional abuse because their parents were controlling, argumentative, and authoritarian, with many clients specifying problems with their fathers in particular. Almeida (1996) substantiates this in her descriptions of family therapy case studies illustrating controlling, authoritarian parents, and the resultant domestic violence and physical abuse in the homes of Asian-Indian families.

With regard to other mental health concerns, it appeared from Tewari's (2000) study that although suicidal ideation and attempts, somatoform disorders, anxiety, eating disorders, substance dependence and abuse, and personality disorders were also evident in the counselors' case notes, major depression was one of the most common psychological disorders present. Thus, in addressing these clinical issues, it becomes important to understand the therapeutic interventions and healing methods that might benefit this group.

THERAPY AND INTERVENTION STRATEGIES

Although a wide variety of treatment modalities have been used with South Asian Americans, it is important to note that treatment needs to be provided with a cultural context. Thus, a counselor working with South Asians should be familiar with the issues, cultures, and traditional healing methods (e.g., use of horoscopes) of South Asian Americans in order to be culturally sensitive (Murthy, 1998). In terms of counselor preference, South Asian-American clients may wish to see a counselor of their ethnic background depending on their level of comfort and racial/ethnic identity development. Some may be concerned that their issues may be revealed in their communities; therefore, they may prefer a non–South Asian-American counselor. Others who are more comfortable with their ethnic identity may prefer an ethnically similar therapist to explore more deeply what it means to be a South Asian American in the United States.

Conceptualization of South Asian-American individuals may begin with an assessment of their initial presenting problem, their acculturation level, ethnic identity, values, and relationships with parents and/or other family members and friends. Other considerations may include parental reasons for immigration, level of intergenerational conflict prior to immigration, immigration status on entry to the United States (voluntary or involuntary), current immigration status, length of stay in the United States, exposure to Western values prior to immigration, level of community and familial support, degree of contact between own and dominant culture, extent of communal homogeneity or heterogeneity, educational and skill levels, socioeconomic status/social class in the country of origin and in the United States, and religiosity (Almeida, 1996; Inman, Rawls, Meza, & Brown, 2002).

Physical health, eating habits, and school/work/career satisfaction should also be considered. Because of the discomfort or the ambiguity that often comes with being in therapy, feelings and beliefs about counseling and previous counseling experience must be discussed. For new, shy, and/or ambivalent clients, directive therapy may be beneficial until the client is comfortable, trusting, has faith in the counselor's authority, and has developed an understanding of the counseling process. Individual therapy with South Asian-American clients is most effective when the counselor is flexible in the modalities used.

Moreover, since the family is an important source of support for South Asians, whether a client comes in for individual therapy or family therapy, issues need to be examined within a familial context (Inman & Tewari, in press). A useful intervention is the use of a genogram to understanding the immigration history, family structure, and alliances that exist among extended family and friends (McGoldrick & Gerson, 1985). In using the genogram, patterns of communication, gender role socialization, levels of acculturation/ethnic identification, religious affiliations, and an indication of socioeconomic and educational levels can often emerge in a nonthreatening manner (Hardy & Laszloffy, 1995). The South Asian family system is typically patriarchal in its structure, with males and females maintaining their traditional gender roles. Thus, if a family seeks therapy it would not be unusual for the father to be the spokesperson, with his wife sitting beside him and their children sitting next to each other when in a room together. In order to get a thorough conceptualization of the families issues, it may be helpful to have an individual therapy session with each family member periodically to provide opportunities for them to express their thoughts and feelings. Also, because of a sense of diffuse boundaries between parents and children, cultural sensitivity and care should be used when addressing parental need to know about their children's thoughts and behaviors.

Relational, emotional expression is commonly kept to a minimum among South Asians because there is an emphasis on showing modesty in behavior and emotions in therapy (Das & Kemp, 1997). Furthermore, emotional restraint may be seen as strength rather than weakness within this community. A helpful tool here is the use of self-disclosure on the part of the therapist to increase trust levels in the South Asian client–counselor relationship. A silent counselor who expects the client to reveal his or her darkest secrets and fears may be perceived as voyeuristic and distant from the client.

Therefore, sharing of personal challenges that might have been similar to the ones experienced by the client can prove beneficial. This allows the client to not only develop trust, but also feel more comfortable with the therapeutic process. With increased comfort with the therapeutic process, theoretical approaches such as Cognitive-Behavioral, Psychodynamic, and Gestalt therapies may be used. Interventions such as two-chair techniques, journaling, art therapy of feelings, role playing with the therapist, and cognitive reframing of cultural issues are some suggested options. Cognitive reframing of cultural issues may help the client to understand the acculturation process, generational differences with family members, and differences in value systems resulting from living in America as an ethnic individual.

Another therapeutic intervention that has proved helpful is the use of narratives (Inman & Tewari, in press). Because of the difficulty in disclosing personal emotions openly, first-generation South Asians might typically present their challenges through narratives, stories, and metaphors (Almeida, 1996). Therefore, encouraging clients and families to share their experiences and struggles related to immigration through the use of stories or narratives can be a beneficial tool for families negotiating intergenerational conflicts and challenges. This allows immigrant parents not only to acknowledge their own losses that may have occurred through the immigration process (Mehta, 1998), but also to explore their expectations and relationships with their children within this context.

Group therapy is especially useful for South Asian-American clients if the group has a specific focus on South Asian-American issues. For example, groups that are successful in providing support to these individuals are led by group leaders who introduce topics for discussion, such as: acculturation, dedication/responsibility to family versus self, integration into the South Asian/Indian community, religious views, views on dating/arranged marriage/intimacy, sexual orientation, and gender role differences. Also, group members need to feel a level of trust that the other South Asian-American members will not "gossip" regarding the issues discussed in therapy. Overall, group leaders providing therapy to South Asian-American members are probably more successful if they take on more of a directive, facilitative role.

Use of bibliography or psychoeducation can be another important therapy supplement for both first- and second-generation clients. Literature helps to provide some objectivity and distance to the concerns while normalizing what may be seen as shameful or self-stigmatizing issues (Inman & Tewari, in press). Finally, as professionals working with this ethnic group, it is important to note that all therapeutic interventions should be tailored within the context of the client's acculturation level and cultural adherence and credence should be given to traditional healing methods.

CONCLUSION

The focus of this chapter was on highlighting specific characteristics of the groups subsumed under the umbrella of "South Asians." We did this through identifying some similarities and differences between South Asians and other Asian-American groups and providing key empirical and theoretical research conducted on South Asian Americans. A special focus was placed on common psychological concerns presented by this population. Various treatment modalities and intervention strategies were identified in hopes of assisting counselors working with the South Asian and South Asian-American population. It is recommended that psychological treatment focus on providing counseling within a cultural context as issues of acculturation, ethnic identity, and family systems are explored and addressed in therapy.

REFERENCES

Agarwal, P. (1991). *Passage from India: Post 1965 Indian immigrants and their children: Conflicts, concerns and solutions.* Palos Verdes, CA: Yuvati Publications.

Almeida, R. (1996). Hindu, Christian, and Muslim families. In M. McGoldrick, J. Giordano, & J. K. Pearce (Eds.), *Ethnicity and family therapy* (pp. 395–423). New York: Guilford.

Berry, J. (1980). Acculturation as varieties of adaptation. In A. M. Padilla (Ed.), *Acculturation: Theory, models and some new finding* (pp. 9–24). Boulder, CO: Westview.

Bufka, L. F. (1998, August). *Family factors, acculturation and identity in second generation Asian Indians.* Paper presented at the 106th Annual Meeting of the American Psychological Association, San Francisco, CA.

Daniel, A. (2001). *Religions in India.* Accessed: http://adaniel.tripod.com/religions.htm [December 11, 2001].

Das, A. K., & Kemp, S. F. (1997). Between two worlds: Counseling South Asian Americans. *Journal of Multicultural Counseling and Development, 25,* 23–33.

Dasgupta, S. D., & Dasgupta, S. (1996). Public face, private space: Asian Indian women and sexuality. In N. B. Maglin & D. Perry (Eds.), *Bad girls, good girls: Women, sex, and power in the nineties* (pp. 226–243). New Brunswick, NJ: Rutgers University.

Durvasula, R. S., & Mylvaganam, G. A. (1994). Mental health of Asian Indians: Relevant issues and community implications. *Journal of Community Psychology, 22,* 97–108.

Ghosh, S., Bufka, L. F., Jensen, J., & Patel, M. (1999, August). *A contrast between first and second generation Indian Americans: What does each feel about arranged marriages?* Poster presented at the 107th Annual Meeting of the American Psychological Association, Boston, MA.

Gupta, S. (1999). *Emerging voices: South Asian American women redefine self, family and community.* New Delhi, India: Sage.

Hardy, K. V., & Laszloffy, T. A. (1995). The cultural genogram: Key to training culturally competent family therapists. *Journal of Marital and Family Therapy, 21,* 227–237.

Ibrahim, F., Ohnishi, H., & Sandhu, D. S. (1997). Asian American identity development: A culture specific model. *Journal of Multicultural Counseling and Development, 25,* 34–50.

Inman, A. G. (2001, June). *Racial/ethnic identity and its salience to the experience of cultural value conflict for South Asians women.* Poster presented at the 32nd Annual International Conference for the Society for Psychotherapy Research, Montevideo, Uruguay.

Inman, A. G., Constantine, M. G., & Ladany, N. (1999). Cultural value conflict: An examination of Asian Indian women's bicultural experience. In D. S. Sandhu (Ed.), *Asian and Pacific Islander Americans: Issues and concerns for counseling and psychotherapy* (pp. 31–41). Commack, NY: Nova Science.

Inman, A. G., Ladany, N., Constantine, M. G., & Morano, C. K. (2001). Development and preliminary validation of the cultural values conflict scale for South Asian women. *Journal of Counseling Psychology, 48,* 17–27.

Inman, A. G., Rawls, K. N., Meza M. M., & Brown, A. L. (2002). An integrative approach to assessment and intervention with adolescents of color. In R. F. Massey & S. D. Massey (Eds.), *Comprehensive handbook of psychotherapy, Vol. III (interpersonal, humanistic, existential approaches)* (pp. 153-178). New York: Wiley.

Inman, A. G., & Tewari, N. (in press). The power of context: Counseling South Asians within a family context. In G. Roysircar, D. S. Sandhu, & V. S. Bibbins (Eds.), *A guidebook: Practices of multicultural competencies.* Alexandria, VA: American Counseling Association.

Jayakar, K. (1994). Women of the Indian Subcontinent. In L. Comas-Diaz & B. Greene (Eds.), *Women of color: Integrating ethnic and gender identities in psychotherapy* (pp. 161–184). New York: Guilford.

Kim, B. S. (1998, August). *Kim Asian Values Adherence Scale (KAVAS): Development and psychometric properties.* Paper presented at the 106th Annual Meeting of the American Psychological Association Conference, San Francisco, CA.

Krishnan, A., & Berry, J. W. (1992). Acculturative stress and acculturation attitudes among Asian Indian immigrants to the United States. *Psychology and Developing Societies, 4,*188–212.

Lott, J. T. (1998). *Asian Americans: From racial category to multiple identities.* Walnut Creek, CA: Altmira.

Marin, G. (1992). Issues in the measurement of acculturation among Hispanics. In K. F. Geisinger (Ed.), *Psychological testing of Hispanics* (pp. 235–251). Washington, DC: American Psychological Association.

McGoldrick, M., & Gerson, R. (1985). *Genograms and family assessment.* New York: Norton.

McLean, A. (2001, August). *The assimilative self: Implications for cross-cultural therapy with bicultural Indians.* Paper presented at the 109th Annual Meeting of the American Psychological Association, San Francisco, CA.

Mehta, P. (1998). The emergence, conflicts and integration of the bi-cultural self: Psychoanalysis of an adolescent daughter of South Asian immigrant parents. In S. Akhtar & S. Kramer (Eds.), *The colors of childhood: Separation-individuation across cultural, racial and ethnic differences* (pp. 129–168). Northvale, NJ: Jason Aronson.

Murthy, K. (1998, August). *Implications for counseling Asian Indians: Second generation perceptions of the American milieu.* Paper presented at the 106th Annual Meeting of the American Psychological Association Conference, San Francisco, CA.

Prathikanti, S. (1997). East Indian American families. In E. Lee (Ed.), *Working with Asian Americans: A guide for clinicians* (pp. 79–100). New York: Guilford.

Ramisetty-Mikler, S. (1993). Asian Indian immigrants in America and sociocultural issues in counseling. *Journal of Multicultural Counseling, 21,* 36–49.

Sandhu, D. S. (1997). Psychocultural profiles of Asian and Pacific Islander Americans: Implications for counseling and therapy. *Journal of Multicultural Counseling and Development, 25,* 7–22.

Sandhu, D. S., Kaur, K. P., & Tewari, N. (1999). Acculturative experiences of Asian and Pacific Islander Americans: Considerations for counseling and psychotherapy. In D. S. Sandhu (Ed.), *Asian and Pacific Islander Americans: Issues and concerns for counseling and psychotherapy* (pp. 3–20). New York: Nova Science.

Shankar, L. D., & Srikanth, R. (1998). Introduction: Closing the gap? South Asians challenge Asian American studies. In L. D. Shankar & R. Srikanth (Eds.), *A part, yet apart: South Asians in Asian America* (pp. 1–22). Philadelphia: Temple University Press.

Sodowsky, G. R., & Carey, J. C. (1987). Asian Indian immigrants in America: Factors relating to adjustment. *Journal of Multicultural Counseling and Development, 15,* 129–141.

Sodowsky, G. R., & Carey, J. C. (1988). Relationship between acculturation-related demographics and cultural attitudes of an Asian Indian immigrant group. *Journal of Multicultural Counseling and Development, 16,* 117–136.

Sodowsky, G. R., Kwan, K. K., & Pannu, R. (1995). Ethnic identity of Asians in the United

States. In J. G. Ponterotto, J. M. Casas, L. A. Suzuki, & C. M. Alexander (Eds.), *Handbook of multicultural counseling* (pp. 123–154). Thousand Oaks, CA: Sage.

Tanaka, J. S., Ebreo, A., Linn, N., & Morera, O. F. (1998). Research methods: The construct validity of self-identity and its psychological implications. In L. C. Lee & N. W. S. Zane (Eds), *Handbook of Asian American psychology* (pp. 21–79). Thousand Oaks, CA: Sage.

Tewari, N. (2000). *Asian Indian American clients presenting at a university counseling center: An exploration of their concerns and a comparison to other groups.* Unpublished doctoral dissertation, Southern Illinois University, Carbondale, IL.

Tewari, N. (1998, Summer). Where do South Asians fit in? A Bharatiya (Asian Indian) perspective. *Asian American Psychologist Association Women's Division Newsletter*, 3.

Tiwari, N. (1995). *The relationship between acculturation and self-esteem.* Unpublished master's thesis, Southern Illinois University, Carbondale, IL.

United States Census Bureau, Census (2000). *Table DP-1 Profile of general demographic characteristics: 2000 Census of population and housing (May 1, 2001).* Washington, DC: U.S. Department of Commerce.

CHAPTER 12

American-Indian Mental Health Service Delivery

Persistent Challenges and Future Prospects

JOSEPH P. GONE

As early as the Community Mental Health Movement of the 1960s, psychologists have recognized that conventional mental health services have failed to reach a significant segment of the American population who might truly benefit from appropriate support and assistance while experiencing profound psychological distress (Albee, 1968). Although this observation continues to characterize service delivery with regard to many troubled persons in today's society, it would be difficult to identify a more underserved group of people than this country's small population of American Indians and Alaskan Natives (Nelson, McCoy, Stetter, & Vanderwagen, 1992). The cultural, political, and economic isolation of Native Americans from adequate mental health services is even more remarkable when one considers that the federal government is legally and morally obligated to provide such services, given the unique political status of tribal groups in their historic government-to-government relationship with the United States (LaFromboise, 1988; Pevar, 1992). This chapter reviews the principal challenges confronting mental health researchers, professionals, and policymakers as they seek to most effectively address the mental health needs of American Indians before suggesting alternatives to conventional mental health service delivery. It is the firm conviction that Native American people deserve fully accessible, culturally appropriate, and demonstrably effective mental health services during times of psychological distress that motivates this chapter's commitment to re-envisioning mental health service delivery in American-Indian communities.

THE INSTITUTIONAL CONTEXTS OF MENTAL HEALTH SERVICE DELIVERY IN INDIAN COUNTRY

Any valid assessment of the status of mental health services for Native American communities must begin with a basic understanding of tribal sovereignty and the U.S.

federal Trust Responsibility, which provides the requisite political and legal contexts for re-envisioning Indian mental health service delivery.

Tribal Nations

The United States currently maintains government-to-government relationships with some 560 federally recognized tribes of American Indians or Alaska Natives. These tribal groups are the surviving remnants of a pre-Columbian U.S. indigenous population of over 5 million individuals comprising over 400 cultures prior to the American colonial holocaust (which reduced the population to just 250,000 by the close of the 19th century). Even today, the cultural diversity of Native America renders virtually any generalization about American Indians problematic. What most Native Americans do share in common, however, is the legacy of European-American colonization. Owing primarily to a history of treaty-making with the United States prior to 1871, contemporary tribal communities are recognized by the federal government as "domestic, dependent nations" that exercise congressionally limited powers of sovereignty attendant to this status. Moreover, Congress maintains a "general trust relationship" with these federally recognized tribal nations, which is "marked by peculiar and cardinal distinctions which exist nowhere else" in Western jurisprudence, according to the Supreme Court. This trust responsibility "resembles that of a ward to his guardian" and implies a federal "duty of protection." History routinely attests, however, to the failure of the United States to fulfill this obligation of trust and protection to tribal nations. (See Pevar, 1992, for a thorough and accessible overview of federal Indian law and practice.)

The most recent U.S. census (U.S. Census Bureau, 2002) determined that 2.5 million Americans identified solely as American Indian or Alaska Native, with an additional 1.6 million identifying as multiracial with Native American ancestry. Taken together, these individuals comprise 1.5% of the population of the United States. Census identification trends over the past few decades indicate that more Americans are choosing to identify as American Indian or Alaska Native over time because birth rates alone cannot possibly account for the astonishing growth in the self-identified population during this period. Thus, one of the dilemmas confronting American Indian mental health researchers is simply determining who in fact is an Indian for the purposes of their investigations. Inasmuch as American-Indian identity attributions are both complex and contested (Gone, in press), easily confounding the range of simplistic (usually essentialist) conceptual strategies, any particular approach to defining "Indianness" is vulnerable to critique or complaint. Nevertheless, for this chapter, an American Indian or Alaska Native is simply defined as an enrolled member (or "citizen") of a federally recognized tribal nation.

There are many reasons for privileging citizenship as the definitive criterion over self-identified race or ethnicity, degree of ancestry (conventionally measured by "blood quantum"), or cultural affinity or practice, but the single most important reason here pertains to the context in which mental health services are routinely provided to Indian people, namely through the federal programs provided on behalf of tribal nations and their citizens in fulfillment of the federal Trust Responsibility. Thus, in contrast to the 2.5 million Americans who self-identified solely as American Indian or Alaska Native in the most recent U.S. census, this chapter will instead considers the 1.4 million enrolled members of federally recognized tribal nations as the population of Native Americans of interest owing to the significance of the federal services context for the discussion to follow. Once again, however, it is crucial to note that this conservative strategy for defining "Indianness" overlooks many categories of people who might legitimately lay claim to viable American-Indian identities.

The kind, quality, and number of federal governmental institutions and programs that most American-Indian people—especially those residing on reservations—encounter on a daily basis are difficult to adequately convey to mainstream Americans. Fortunately, during the Nixon administration Congress passed Public Law 93-638, the Indian Self-Determination and Education Assistance Act of 1975. This law sought:

> To respond to the strong expression of the Indian people for self-determination by assuring maximum Indian participation in the direction of educational as well as other Federal services to Indian communities so as to render such services more responsive to the needs and desires of those communities.

As a result, modern tribal governments wield substantial influence in their dealings with federal agencies and can even "contract" to directly administer federal programs and services to their own communities using the same federal dollars that would otherwise sustain the programmatic activities of the relevant agency.

The purpose of describing the government-to-government relationship in such detail is twofold. First, it affords the unfamiliar reader with some semblance of the scope and complexity of Indian affairs in the United States. Whether codified in federal law, established through bureaucratic policy, sustained by national moral and ethical obligation, or exacted by modern, politically savvy tribal leaders, the state apparatus designed to regulate and control, support and protect Native Americans—just 1% of the population of the United States—is monolithic. Most important, this distinctively American colonial legacy yields a notion of "Indianness" as not merely another race, ethnicity, or subculture, but instead as an utterly unique *political* status afforded to citizens of tribal nations that traces its origins to the Commerce and Treaty clauses of the U.S. Constitution.

Second, this review illuminates the degree to which government intrusion and control has shaped American-Indian lives historically and renders contemporary reactions of cynicism and suspicion within Indian communities toward such involvement intelligible. That is, the long colonial history endured by American Indians and Alaska Natives has profound psychological consequences for both individuals and their communities, ranging from the idiosyncratic fear and hatred of European-Americans in some instances to a more general (often desperate) pursuit of postcolonial alternatives for grounding personal and communal meaning-making. It is this latter, nearly frantic search for a viable postcolonial source of coherence, connectedness, and continuity that renders the colonial legacy utterly inextricable from contemporary concerns about American-Indian mental health.

The Indian Health Service

Within the federal services context, the principal health care organization entrusted with providing health and mental health services to the enrolled members of federally recognized tribes is that branch of the U.S. Public Health Service known as the Indian Health Service (IHS). Although American Indians and Alaska Natives are technically eligible for health services through the usual venues that provide health care for other Americans (e.g., state and county health clinics, Health Maintenance Organizations, or professionals in private practice), many enrolled tribal members depend primarily on the largely reservation-based IHS for a wide variety of health care services, including mental health services.

Legal Authority and Organization

As one expression of its Trust Responsibility for tribal nations, Congress passed the Snyder Act in 1921 authorizing health services for American Indians to be administered through the Bureau of Indian Affairs (or BIA). In the mid-1950s, Congress established the IHS to assume responsibility for such services. In addition to this early legislative authority, the federal obligation to provide health services to Native Americans was bolstered by Public Law 94-437, the Indian Health Care Improvement Act of 1976. In response to findings that American Indians and Alaska Natives suffered from much poorer health status than other Americans, Congress boldly declared that:

> It is the policy of this Nation, in fulfillment of its special responsibilities and legal
> obligation to the American Indian people, to meet the national goal of providing
> the highest possible health status to Indians and to provide existing Indian health
> services with all the resources necessary to effect that policy.

Thus, the Indian Health Care Improvement Act—reauthorized three times since 1976—remains the modern legal capstone supporting federal provision of health services to Native Americans. Despite this express legal commitment to providing "all the resources necessary" to effect improved health status in tribal communities, however, the Director of the IHS recently commissioned a study that determined that recent Congressional allocations to the IHS represented just 52% of the costs of hypothetically assuring personal health services to a comparable number of federal employees (Federal Disparity Index Workgroup, 2002).

The IHS serves the enrolled members of federally recognized tribes and their descendants, currently comprising a service population (defined as eligible persons residing in geographic areas for which the IHS maintains responsibilities) estimated at 1.5 million (IHS, 2002). Employing a staff of nearly 16,000 from every conceivable health care profession with an annual appropriation of roughly $2.9 billion, the IHS is organized into 12 regional administrative units called Area Offices that are collectively overseen by a Central Office. Within these IHS regional Areas, direct health care services are typically provided by the most basic administrative unit within the IHS, the community-based Service Unit. The Service Unit may include a hospital, clinic, or health station, depending on local need and budgetary considerations, and typically administers a wide range of health programs, including primary medical care, behavioral health, substance abuse treatment, health education, injury prevention, public health nursing, and sanitation facility services. As of October, 1998, the IHS directly administered 66 Service Units, while tribal governments had "contracted" (through the Self-Determination Act) to directly administer 85 Service Units. In sum, the IHS provided health services to American Indians and Alaska Natives through 59 health centers, 44 health stations, 37 hospitals, and four school-based health centers, while tribal governments contracted to provide their own health services through 155 health centers, 76 health stations, 12 hospitals, three school-based health clinics, and 160 Alaska village clinics. In addition to these reservation-based health programs, the IHS also funded 36 urban Indian health projects (IHS, 1998–1999) for Native Americans who have relocated to large urban centers. Approximately 80% of all IHS Service Units maintain mental health (or "behavioral health") programs tasked explicitly with meeting the mental health needs of Indian country.

Indian Health Service Mental Health

The first IHS Office of Mental Health was established in 1965, with an annual appropriation of $500,000. More recently, the coordination of mental health and substance abuse services throughout Indian country has been assigned to the Mental Health Programs Branch and the Alcoholism/Substance Abuse Services Branch of the IHS. The Congressional allocations for these services appear as separate line items in the IHS budget, totaling $47 million for mental health services and $135 million for substance abuse services, respectively, during fiscal year 2002. Together, these allocations represent less than 7% of the total IHS budget this year.

Within its mental health programs specifically, IHS employs over 300 full-time staff, including more than 20 psychiatrists, 60 psychologists, and 110 social workers (J. Davis-Hueston, personal communication, June 22, 2001). Because of a hiring policy that emphasizes Indian preference, the IHS mental health staff is largely American Indian, although the most highly trained professional staff is largely European-American (with only two Indian psychiatrists and 17 Indian psychologists employed in the system). This trend among doctoral-level mental health professionals employed by the IHS no doubt reflects the fact that only 0.1% of clinically trained psychiatrists and .6% of clinically trained psychologists in the United States are American Indian or Alaska Native (West et al., 2000). In the context of these resources, the IHS anticipates providing mental health services at the annual rate of 208,000 "client contacts" (i.e., assessment or treatment sessions) during the current fiscal year. Although systematic information is difficult to obtain, anecdotal sources indicate that the majority of these client contacts involve *individual psychotherapy* spanning a range of theoretical orientations. Although psychopharmacological treatment is not uncommon either, it would appear that much of the responsibility for monitoring psychotropic medications falls to general practitioners within the service system owing to the shortage of psychiatrists. Given the estimated size of the service population, the IHS currently employs

roughly two psychiatrists and four psychologists per 100,000 population (in comparison to general U.S. rates of 14 psychiatrists and 28 psychologists per 100,000 population [see West et al., 2000]). Assuming an arbitrary three "contacts" per client annually,
the IHS thus is prepared to address the mental health needs of less than 5% of the
eligible Native population.

Finally, it should be noted that many American Indians and Alaska Natives journey beyond the IHS service area in pursuit of education, employment, and other opportunities. In fact, a significant proportion of the American Indian population at any
given time resides in the nation's urban centers. Even though these individuals are
entitled to mental health care at IHS facilities, many cannot readily access IHS treatment without traveling long distances to a nearby Service Unit (unless they happen to
live in one of the exceptional metropolitan areas with an IHS urban health project).
Thus, urban Indians—many of whom are impoverished and uninsured—are even less
likely to obtain accessible and appropriate mental health services than their reservation kin, owing to financial constraints, transportation issues, uninformed service providers, etc. Thus, service delivery issues related specifically to urban Native American
mental health needs are even more convoluted than those described in the remainder
of this chapter. (See Witko, in press, for the specific issues pertaining to American
Indian mental health in urban settings.)

FORMIDABLE CHALLENGES CONFRONTING MENTAL HEALTH
SERVICE DELIVERY IN INDIAN COUNTRY

The obstacles to delivering appropriate, accessible, and effective mental health services for American-Indian and Alaska-Native communities are manifold and complex. This section concentrates on two especially formidable challenges that warrant
closer scrutiny in this regard: (a) the infinite insufficiency of conventional mental health
resources in Indian country; and (b) the inevitable cultural incongruence of conventional mental health interventions in Indian country.

Infinite Insufficiency

The first formidable challenge to delivering appropriate, accessible, and effective mental
health services to American Indians represents a simple extension of a more general
national quandary. The most recent, representative, and thorough national epidemiological survey of the prevalence of mental illness in America revealed that nearly half
of the U.S. adult population suffered from a diagnosable mental disorder at some
point in their lifetimes. More specifically, the National Comorbidity Survey (or NCS;
see Kessler et al., 1994) determined that the lifetime prevalence of any *DSM-III-R*
disorder was 48% in the adult population, including major depressive episodes (or
clinical depression) among 17% of the population and alcohol dependence among
14% of the population. In addition, 29% of the adult population suffered from a diagnosable *DSM-III-R* disorder within the previous 12 months. Furthermore, comorbidity

among mental disorders was high, in that over 50% of those reporting diagnosable distress qualified for more than one lifetime diagnosis. Most importantly, only 40% of those with a lifetime mental disorder reported ever obtaining professional treatment for their problems.

The quandary evident in these statistics is not the higher-than-expected rates of psychiatric distress afflicting much of the adult American population, but the comparison of such rates to the actual availability of qualified mental health service providers to treat them. Consider that the entirety of clinically trained (although not necessarily *clinically active*) mental health professionals in the United States (including psychiatrists, psychologists, social workers, psychiatric nurses, counselors, marriage and family therapists, psychosocial rehabilitation specialists, and school psychologists [see West et al., 2000]) totals just over 400,000 service providers for a national population of 280 million—a rate of approximately 150 mental health professionals per 100,000 population. If roughly one-third of America's citizens required mental health care in any given year (as the NCS results suggest), then each provider (ignoring the differences in professional role for the moment) would need to treat 200 clients annually—not including care provided to the same individuals by different professionals or service systems—to meet the nation's mental health needs. The implications of these comparisons are far from trivial, and have been a source of consternation for several decades as clinical researchers have noted that the production of mental health professionals (especially doctoral-level psychologists and psychiatrists) is so gradual that the cadre of practicing professionals will *never* be sufficient to meet the mental health needs of the nation (Albee, 1968).

As one extrapolates these realities to American-Indian and Alaska-Native communities, there can be little question that the disparity between needs and resources in Indian mental health is even more alarming. With regard to Indian mental health needs, compelling data are unusually difficult to obtain owing to the relatively small population and its wide geographic dispersion. Nevertheless, it seems indisputable that American Indians and Alaska Natives are poorer and less healthy than the U.S. population at large, with evident implications for their mental health status. According to the U.S. Census Bureau (2001), the median household income (averaged over 1998 to 2000 to allow for greater statistical stability) for Native Americans was less than $32,000, in comparison to $45,500 for White Americans, and the poverty rate was over 25% in comparison to less than 8% for White Americans. Native people die from alcoholism (627% greater), tuberculosis (533% greater), diabetes (249% greater), accidents (204% greater), suicide (72% greater), pneumonia and influenza (71% greater), and homicide (63% greater) at much higher rates than the U.S. "all races" population (Indian Health Service, 1998–1999). Finally, Indians are much less likely to maintain health insurance coverage (23% uninsured) than White Americans (14% uninsured), and are thus less likely to afford quality health care in times of need (Brown, Ojeda, Wyn, & Levan, 2000).

Unfortunately, there are no published studies of psychiatric epidemiology in Native communities that even begin to approximate the sophistication and rigor of the National Comorbidity Survey (Kessler et al., 1994)—the existing community-based studies

(Roy, Choudhuri, & Irvine, 1970; Sampath, 1974; Shore, Kinzie, Pattison, & Hampson, 1973) relied upon unconventional methodologies or outdated measures. Nevertheless, these studies collectively suggest that the prevalence of psychiatric distress—especially substance dependence and mood disorders—are unusually high in these Native communities (but see O'Nell, 1989, for a review and critique). In a report to the Senate Select Committee on Indian Affairs, Congress' Office of Technology Assessment (1990) reported that American-Indian adolescents were more likely to encounter problems related to developmental disability, depression, suicide, anxiety, alcohol and drug abuse, poor self-esteem and alienation, running away from home, leaving school prematurely, and possibly posttraumatic stress disorder in comparison to non-Indian adolescents. The trends in these studies clearly support the conventional wisdom among IHS mental health professionals that American-Indian and Alaska-Native communities generally experience higher rates of distress than their mainstream counterparts. Nevertheless, mental health researchers are persistent in their call for more sophisticated, rigorous, and culturally appropriate studies to provide more conclusive information regarding mental health status within Native communities.

For now, the best available evidence reveals a key tension in Indian mental health, with overwhelming community need on the one hand and a limited professional base within these communities on the other. More specifically, if mental health experts are willing to stipulate that conventional mental health services are essential for the effective and humane treatment of distress in American-Indian and Alaska-Native lives, then it follows that the anticipated production of mental health professionals (especially at the doctoral level) who serve these communities, when compared to the evident levels of distress that confront them there, is so discordant that it recommends despair. This infinite insufficiency of mental health resources in Indian country gives rise to an important question: Given that available resources will never be adequate to meet the needs of Indian communities under existing mental health service delivery conventions, how might researchers, practitioners, and policymakers effectively cultivate and multiply these limited resources such that they become more widely available for meeting the vast mental health needs of Indian country?

Inevitable Cultural Incongruence

There can be no question that the long search by mental health researchers for effective psychological therapies, treatments, and interventions has generated a variety of techniques that are clinically proven to reduce psychological suffering, impairment, and distress in the lives of individuals struggling with "mental illness" (see, e.g., Chambless & Ollendick, 2001). In fact, mental health professionals now command an arsenal of empirically supported treatments specifically developed to assist people suffering from nearly every major category of disorder classified in the *DSM*. Nevertheless, there is not a single, rigorously controlled outcome study that has assessed the efficacy and/or effectiveness of a conventional psychological intervention with American-Indian and Alaska-Native clients. It remains an empirical question, then, as to whether—and under what conditions—state-of-the-art mental health interventions are likely to benefit Native persons in distress. In the absence of valid scientific data, professional claims regarding the effects of conventional mental health treatments for American-Indian clients or patients remain highly speculative. Therefore, I must leave the question of whether established interventions are effective and efficacious with Indian people to the realm of empirical investigation. But there are clear reasons to suspect that conventional psychological interventions might be detrimental to American-Indian "mental health" *even if* they could be proven to reduce symptoms and improve functioning for particular individuals, owing to the thorny postcolonial context in which American mental health professionals find themselves vis-à-vis Native people. More specifically, the history of European-American colonization renders the provision of conventional mental health interventions to Native people a potentially detrimental encounter, resulting from the inevitable cultural incongruence of such interventions with the extant cultural traditions of many tribal nations.

Cultural contradictions emerge at more fundamental levels than the relatively superficial (albeit deeply significant) characteristics of various intervention technologies, of course. For example, there is an evident epistemological divergence insofar as psychology as an academic discipline is grounded in Western ways of knowing. That is, psychologists routinely adopt methodological conventions premised on a hypothetical-deductive framework (the unlikely synthesis of Western rationalist and empiricist traditions) for testing hypotheses about psychological phenomena. In principle, the theoretical viability of disciplinary constructs depends upon the foundation of evidence mustered to their support. Nevertheless, especially in professional psychology, ideas and concepts that in some cases are simply not amenable to scientific inquiry can retain widespread influence. Consider the Freudian legacy of the tripartite mind, defense mechanisms, or the role of unconscious emotion in the etiology of psychopathology that shapes both public and professional discourse on human psychology in the West despite its inherent unsuitability for scientific refutation. The point here is simply that these influential (albeit often untested and untestable) concepts, models, and orientations comprise a Western ethnopsychology with all manner of implications for the construction of Western minds, selves, and persons, as well as the pathologies that afflict them and the interventions that heal them. And the problem here is simply that these influential Western ethnopsychologies—which quite naturally inhabit conventional mental health practices owing to the latter's Western origins—are discordant with most tribal ethnopsychologies with regard to emotional experience and expression; norms governing kinds and qualities of acceptable communication; the nature of distress, disorder, and its treatment; and the meanings of personhood, social relations, and spirituality.

In the context of cross-cultural mental health service delivery, then, the dominant treatment paradigms typically employed by mental health practitioners are suffused with concepts and categories, principles, and practices that are culturally alien to most indigenous ways of being in the world. For example, Western ethnopsychologies of the person typically embrace the traditions of dualism, individualism, and modernity, conceptually separating mind from body, prioritizing the individual self over social relationships, and often excluding attention to spirituality. One implication of these deep cultural assumptions is the organizational segregation of "mental health" from the rest of biomedicine within Western health care systems. In contrast, most Native cultures conceptualize the person in holistic terms without fragmenting selves into physical, mental, and spiritual components. Furthermore, most illness is understood in Native cultures to result from disrupted spiritual and social relationships. Finally, and most importantly, healing in Native communities is modally understood to require access to sacred power. (For a more detailed review of such cultural contrasts, see Trimble, Manson, Dinges, & Medicine, 1984.) And yet, the Western cultural assumptions exported through conventional psychotherapeutic practices are not merely mundane ideological alternatives—instead, they emerged historically in the context of a brutal U.S. colonialism. Thus, any particular instance of an American-Indian client or patient seeking assistance from a Western mental health professional is inherently shaped by a colonial tradition of power relationships, the troubling implications of which have been widely unexamined within mental health research.

Given the inevitable cultural incongruities of Western mental health interventions with American-Indian and Alaska-Native ethnopsychologies in the historical context of U.S. conquest and colonialism, the disturbing possibility arises that conventional mental health practices may actively undermine the stated commitment of most contemporary tribal communities to cultural preservation and revitalization by surreptitiously displacing key facets of the local ethnopsychology with those of Western ethnopsychology. Thus, it would seem that providers of conventional mental health services must directly confront the distinct possibility that their therapeutic practices represent a nearly invisible (but ongoing) "cultural proselytization" of distressed Native clients in their most vulnerable hour. Based on this potential for subtle cultural proselytization (which follows, of course, from the inevitable cultural incongruence of conventional mental health services in Indian country), I suggest that embracing and disseminating Western mental health concepts in Native communities—particularly when there is no compelling empirical reason to do so—is not only counterproductive to cultural preservation and reproduction but also a clear extension of European-American ideological hegemony.

In one sense, then, this volume's concern with resistance to multiculturalism in mental health service delivery is somewhat ironic, for it is the mental health professional as credentialed therapeutic expert—even when explicitly dedicated to cross-racial sensitivity and multicultural competency—who typically manages to "resist" the unsettling cultural implications of the deep Western ethnopsychological foundation on which the "talking cure" born in Vienna over a century ago ultimately rests. Even as American-Indian and Alaska-Native mental health professionals—having invested a great deal of time, energy, and money in our own training—we are reluctant to consider the neocolonial ramifications of our conventional practices within Native communities. In fact, when Indian psychologists actively resist the conventions of our training, we are most likely to disparage and dismiss the scientific foundations of disciplinary psychology while retaining a vast collection of concepts, categories, and practices that supposedly depend on scientific validation for their legitimacy. In any case, such ironies point to a second key tension in Indian mental health, with the promise of empirically supported interventions on the one hand and the dangers of Western cultural imperialism on the other. This inevitable cultural incongruence of professional mental health practices with extant Native cultural tradition gives rise to a second important question: Given that even our empirically supported treatments have not been assessed with Indian people and depend on Western ethnopsychological theories of self, mind, and personhood, how might researchers, practitioners, and policymakers develop and assess interventions for Native communities that are culturally appropriate, demonstrably effective, and "empowering" in the American postcolonial context?

RE-ENVISIONING MENTAL HEALTH SERVICE DELIVERY IN INDIAN COUNTRY

This, then, is the crucible of mental health service delivery in American-Indian and Alaska-Native communities: The mental health needs of Indian country require a great deal more of the kinds of professional services that do not yet exist. That is, the infinite insufficiency of mental health resources in Indian country requires that mental health researchers, professionals, and policymakers find innovative opportunities to cultivate underdeveloped resources in Native communities that will promote wellness and prevent dysfunction with much greater efficiency than established professional conventions currently afford. In addition, the inevitable cultural incongruence of Western clinical interventions (and their implicit Western ethnopsychology) with extant tribal traditions requires that mental health researchers, professionals, and policymakers sponsor innovative efforts to construct culturally local alternatives to the more conventional and familiar helping services. Finally, any call to innovation in the absence of an explicit commitment to systematic outcome assessment serves no one—the measured application of scientific methodology ensures that associated claims are disciplined by the evidence at hand. Taken together, these commitments provide the impetus for re-envisioning therapeutic intervention in American-Indian and Alaska-Native communities.

CULTIVATING UNDERDEVELOPED RESOURCES

Having observed that Indian country requires a great deal more of the kinds of mental health services that do not yet exist, I should quickly clarify that the lack of appropriate services in no way implies the lack of a well-established means of developing them. With specific regard to the project of cultivating underdeveloped helping resources in Native communities, the enduring legacy of *community psychology* affords a sophisticated approach to undertaking innovation of the kind required in Indian country. Established in the 1960s as a critical alternative to conventional clinical psychology, community psychology (Rappaport, 1977) has sought to integrate its professional commitments to human resource development, progressive political activity, and rigorous psychological science in the context of a paradigm that explicitly embraces cultural relativity, diversity, and ecology. With regard to the conventions of mental health service delivery, community psychologists have long advocated for community-based education and consultation (as opposed to clinic-based psychotherapeutic services) emphasizing collaborative and empowering relationships (as opposed to expert–client relationships) toward the development of strengths-focused (as opposed to deficit-focused) preventive (as opposed to rehabilitative) interventions. (See Rappaport & Seidman, 1983, for a thorough overview.)

The relevance of community psychology for helping to resolve the crucible of Indian mental health service delivery by cultivating underdeveloped resources depends on three closely related strategies. The first strategy promoted by community psychologists involves the reconfiguration of the professional psychologist's role beyond the provision of extended individual psychotherapy in community-based service systems. In support of this vision, community psychologists cite an extensive scientific literature that has thus far remained unable to link doctoral training and experience with enhanced psychotherapeutic outcomes despite 25 years of investigation into the matter. (See Christensen & Jacobson, 1994, for a recent review.) Such provocative scientific findings, combined with the serious economic burden of supporting individual psychotherapy by doctoral-level practitioners (i.e., psychologists and psychiatrists) within the context of an underfunded health care system, raises the question of whether the doctoral-level psychotherapist should retain any role whatsoever within American-Indian mental health service delivery settings. In fact, these findings suggest that in order to most efficiently sustain and extend the existing helping resources within American-Indian or Alaska-Native communities, doctoral-level psychologists in particular (since psychiatrists in Indian country already forego extended psychotherapy) must assume new professional roles. Instead of the direct delivery of conventional mental health services, then, psychologists must be prepared to engage in creative administration, program development, outcome evaluation, research, grant writing, training, and supervision. That is, the professional psychologists serving Native communities most effectively act as creators and facilitators of service systems oriented toward both the cultivation of helping resources already present within these communities as well as the procurement of new resources from outside the communities.

The second strategy promoted by community psychologists for cultivating underdeveloped helping resources involves the enlistment of a variety of nonprofessional "natural" helpers already active in the community into partnership with community-based service systems. These partnerships should furnish the professional psychologist with welcome insights into the culturally salient interventions already practiced in the community, while allowing for the reciprocal contribution of additional resources, professional legitimacy, and helpful organizational structures toward the wider availability and success of local therapeutic practices. The range of potentially valuable nonprofessional helpers presumably varies from community to community, but in general it seems useful to collaborate with recognized medicine persons and tribal healers who retain cultural authority in ritual matters. Given that wellness and healing in so many Native cultures involves appropriate relationships to spiritual beings, the participation of ritual leaders in service system outreach and activity is ideal.

Beside the obvious ceremonial leaders, however, there are undoubtedly other classes of existing natural helpers. For example, most federally recognized tribal nations contract to administer the federal Community Health Representatives (CHR) Program. This program employs and trains paraprofessional health aides who travel to the homes of the elderly and sick to deliver medications, check blood pressure or blood sugar, assist in limited home care, provide transportation to health care appointments, etc. Naturally, CHR providers regularly "counsel" those in their care by expressing empathic support or offering helpful advice. In addition, they are frequently the first to know when struggling community members encounter crisis. As a result, the CHR providers within tribal communities remain an obvious mental health resource that is largely underutilized in the sense that they receive very limited training with regard to assisting persons in psychological distress—even a very modest education and support structure within the local mental health service system could enable CHR providers to help community members cope more effectively with distress or refer community members to more experienced helpers in appropriate situations.

Additional examples of natural helpers who might substantially extend the reach of community-based service systems include tribal college students and key family members. On many reservations, tribal governments operate locally controlled community colleges that enroll a significant number of community members as students. In most tribal colleges, students pursue associate's degrees in vocational curricula such as Human Services. Such students might benefit substantially from structured Human Services practica that could be coordinated jointly by the tribal college and the mental health service system. Indeed, the establishment of a college-based Mental Health Worker's Program could provide a regular supply of talented and energetic community members available to staff a crisis hotline or run a youth prevention program in exchange not for scarce financial resources but for course credit toward their degrees. Beyond tribal college students, certain key members of large extended family networks—often respected elders—already serve as helping resources in Native communities for others to turn to in times of crisis or distress. Such natural helpers routinely advise, counsel, and support their relatives in accordance with tribal kinship traditions, but may nevertheless encounter occasional situations (e.g., a suicidal family member) in which they become overwhelmed by dire circumstance. Informal partnerships between the mental health service system and such helpers may ensure that these resourceful individuals obtain the knowledge, skills, and support to more effectively serve their families in times of need.

A final strategy promoted by community psychologists for cultivating underdeveloped helping resources involves the professional facilitation and support of community-based self-help programs. Once again, a fledgling scientific literature has begun to attest to the therapeutic power of self-help efforts (Gould & Clum, 1993). These kinds of interventions represent one approach to extending the availability of therapeutic resources in the context of a community-based service system. More familiar to mental health professionals in Indian country, however, are the 12-step groups such as Alcoholics Anonymous (AA). Although the philosophy and values of groups like AA distinguish them from professional service delivery in key ways, there can be no question that professional encouragement and support of such groups remains a cost-effective way to multiply the helping resources available to struggling community members. Additionally, many Native communities welcome and celebrate various Christian practices that resemble self-help. For example, several northern Plains tribal communities with long histories of Catholic missionary involvement participate in the Cursillo movement in which adherents gather for emotionally and spiritually intense weekend retreats for cleansing and renewal. Finally, it should be clear that traditional participation in Native ceremonies represents an additional healing resource that might benefit from professional referral and support in the context of a service system's commitment to extending help as widely as possible within the community.

Nevertheless, merely extending the reach of helping services within American-Indian and Alaska Native communities in and of itself is no solution to the crucible of American-Indian mental health service delivery unless such efforts take seriously the call to construct alternative helping interventions that overcome the dangers of subtle Western cultural proselytization in the guise of aiding those in distress.

Constructing Alternative Interventions

The strategies described in the preceding undoubtedly assist the mental health professional in offering a great deal more to Native communities, but before acceptable progress can be made the development of services that do not yet exist is required. The process of actively constructing appropriate alternative interventions depends first and foremost on the systematic exploration of the cultural foundations of such interventions. More specifically, the first stage of program development in Native communities requires the formulation of a reasonably sophisticated ethnopsychology in order to ensure that newly created interventions avoid reproducing the colonial legacy. Such exploration will undoubtedly proceed in interdisciplinary fashion insofar as scientific psychopathology (Millon, Blaney, & Davis, 1999), psychiatric anthropology (Kleinman, 1987), community psychology (Rappaport & Seidman, 2000), sociolinguistics (Hymes, 1974), and the philosophy of social science (Fiske & Shweder, 1986) bear obvious relevance. Nevertheless, the most prominent interdisciplinary tradition of interest here is the re-emerging field of cultural psychology (Shweder & Sullivan, 1993).

Cultural psychology takes as its conceptual point of departure the co-constitution of culture and mind (Shweder, 1990). Its central locus of inquiry therefore concerns the semiotic (i.e., symbolically mediated) nature of human experience, which implies several fundamental commitments. The first of these commitments is the empirical elucidation of human "psychic diversity" across cultures. A second commitment is its focus on human *action* (or cultural practice) that, in this context, implies situated and meaningful human behavior. A third commitment of cultural psychology is the privileging of interpretive methods in an effort to understand cultural meanings inherent to such action. A fourth commitment of cultural psychology is the careful analysis of discourse (or situated communicative practices). The analysis of discursive practice typically focuses on language usage as fundamental to human experience, where language is seen as the primary symbol system by which human beings construct and communicate meaning in embodied action.

The formulation of a local ethnopsychology within the framework of cultural psychology encompasses multiple relevant content areas, including culture, language, and mind; self and personhood; emotional experience and expression; concepts of health, illness, and healing; and research reflexivity (i.e., attention to how the knower constructs the known). For instance, one area of inquiry with obvious relevance for the design of mental health interventions concerns the local construction of emotion. For in marked contrast to academic psychology's reigning assumptions regarding the universality of the so-called "basic" emotions (Ekman, 1984), affect across cultures can differ markedly in terms of the interpretations ascribed to otherwise merely physiological impulses as well as in terms of the salient practices surrounding its communication to other social beings (Harre, 1986; Lutz & White, 1986). As a result, the development of truly appropriate interventions necessarily requires that professionals working in Indian country attain some form of limited competency in the conceptualization and exploration of culture in human activity. Obviously, such competency also requires expertise with interpretive methods in addition to the variable-analytic methods that are most familiar to psychologists (see, e.g., Denzin & Lincoln, 2000). Furthermore, I have already observed that effective mental health professionals in Indian country must learn to solicit the involvement of cultural experts, spiritual leaders, and natural helpers in order to develop a culturally appropriate mental health service system, recognizing that the end results of such collaboration may bear little resemblance to conventional clinical intervention. Finally, it bears restating that Native communities deserve a scientific assessment of efficacy for any new interventions developed in collaboration with local authorities.

Although examples of the kinds of alternative interventions envisioned here are unprecedented in the literature, the process of developing such interventions is rather intuitive. Recall that the ultimate goal of such programmatic efforts is to commence a collaborative, sustained, and empowering relationship with a designated tribal community whereby innovative programs designed to facilitate wellness and prevent dysfunction within the community might be developed, refined, and scientifically assessed in close consultation with local community members. Of course, the precise contours of any intervention developed collaboratively with community members are difficult to predict in advance, but the steps taken toward realizing effective alternative mental health interventions would likely include the following. First, the professional psychologist acting in her flexible role as administrator of the local service system needs to identify and engage a variety of local community members, agencies, and institutions in order to forge relationships that sustain the development, implementation, and assessment of the intervention. Second, the psychologist (or her research collaborators) need to conduct initial ethnographic work with community members in order to better understand the local cultural discourse regarding emotional and psychological health and wellness, as well as community conceptualizations of disordered experience and its treatment. Third, building on these ethnographic findings, the psychologist determines with involved community members what the focus of the intervention should be (e.g., to promote prosocial behavior among troubled community youth, to facilitate effective support and advocacy by individuals on behalf of distressed family members, to consolidate and extend treatment/healing resources within the community, etc.). Fourth, the psychologist would consult with community members to design a specific intervention with careful attention to targeted participants, required resources, desired outcomes, and assessment methodology. Fifth, extramural funding from government agencies or private foundations should be pursued to fund the project. Sixth, the psychologist implements the intervention in close collaboration with community members. Seventh, intervention outcomes are assessed. Finally, results, revisions, and modifications to the program are disseminated in both scientific and grass roots circles. The emphasis here is thus on the development of demonstrably effective, culturally grounded interventions that directly addresses the pressing "mental health" concerns of the communities of interest.

CONCLUSION AND SUMMARY RECOMMENDATIONS

No contemporary culture exists in a vacuum, and in the postmodern era of rapid globalization, cultural transformation is inevitable and sometimes even desirable. But in the context of postcolonial America, it is essential that Native communities be afforded the opportunity to negotiate cultural transformation explicitly and on their own terms. Indeed, the dilemma posed by conventional mental health services in Indian country is not that cultural transformation might occur, but that it might occur without the explicit awareness of either tribal members or the mental health professionals who treat them. My suspicion is that the greatest opportunities for formulating and implementing culturally grounded alternative interventions lie in the arena of community psychology, which has sought over three decades now to explicitly de-emphasize the resource-intensive practice of individual psychotherapy in favor of commencing collaborative, sustained, and empowering relationships with communities of citizens (in this instance, tribal communities) whereby innovative, culturally grounded interventions may be developed, refined, and scientifically assessed in close consultation with local Native people. Such efforts will ultimately depend on the conceptual and methodological approaches of cultural psychology insofar as ascertaining the character of local ethnopsychologies is essential to the success of these endeavors. In sum, the development of such novel, community-based interventions holds the greatest promise for overcoming the crucible of American-Indian mental health service delivery.

As mental health professionals working to cultivate strategies of intervention that proactively assess and surmount the dangers of subtle "cultural proselytization" in cross-cultural contexts and encounters, four principles must guide our fledgling efforts. First, we must always keep *culture* in mind. That is, we must never forget that our professional concepts and categories, and tools and techniques are cultural products or artifacts whose mechanisms and meanings emerge from and depend upon the cultural intelligibility of their operations to both "practitioner" and "client." As cultural artifacts, these interventions must be understood in terms of their historical origins and evolution within the West as just one example of how humans might conceptualize therapeutic intervention more broadly. Second, we must always keep culture in *mind*. That is, we must never forget that the foundations of mind, self, and personhood (i.e., the "psyche") are themselves cultural and therefore vary in remarkable ways across communities around the world. As fundamental constituents of the psyche, cultural meanings and practices must be examined as they pertain to key facets of the local ethnopsychology in order for professional helpers to proceed most appropriately. Third, we must develop, implement, and evaluate innovative, culturally appropriate interventions collaboratively. That is, the local enlistment of a variety of active healers and other "natural" helpers would afford a degree of insight into the culturally salient interventions already practiced in the community, while concurrently allowing for a joint analysis of the validity, viability, and effectiveness of novel forms of intervention in unfamiliar cultural contexts. In fact, close collaboration with community members may be the only means to determine which cultural transformations that accompany conventional techniques are welcomed in the interest of help and healing, and which are seen as undesirable or inappropriate in local cultural contexts. Finally, we must assess process and outcome more comprehensively. That is, given the kinds of innovations that result from collaborative program development, the assessment of effects—both therapeutic and countertherapeutic—throughout the course of an intervention must be both extensive and rigorous. More specifically, in addition to searching for the desired outcomes of such novel efforts, professionals must also attend more comprehensively to the miscommunications, standoffs, breakdowns, and failures in the course of implementing services because such mishaps may signify subtle and implicit incommensurabilities between therapeutic models and the local ethnopsychology.

In considering the foregoing elaboration of my commitment to re-envisioning mental health service delivery in American-Indian and Alaska-Native communities, many may quickly dismiss this approach as too idealistic in the context of the realities of mental health service delivery in the 21st-century United States. Were I constrained by the realities of conventional service delivery in the modal health care system, I would agree with such critiques. The point of reviewing the institutional context of IHS mental health service delivery in such detail, however, was to make clear that federally recognized tribal governments retain the authority under present federal law and practice to contract for local administration of services and programs using congressionally allocated federal monies. This unique right of sovereign tribal governments extends even to the assumption of control over the entire local mental health service system. Thus, the possibilities for reconfiguring such systems in direct response to the extensive mental health needs of the community are constrained only by the imaginations of tribal leaders and the expertise of the mental health professionals they employ. In short, I remain cautiously optimistic that a handful of visionary tribal governments will ultimately recognize the crucible of mental health service delivery and, in response, take measures that will actively facilitate the creation and establishment of a great deal more of the kinds of professional mental health services that do not yet exist.

REFERENCES

Albee, G. W. (1968). Conceptual models and manpower requirements in psychology. *American Psychologist, 23,* 317–320.

Brown, E. R., Ojeda, V. D., Wyn, R., & Levan, R. (2000). *Racial and ethnic disparities in access to health insurance and health care.* Los Angeles: UCLA Center for Health Policy Research and The Henry J. Kaiser Family Foundation.

Chambless, D. L., & Ollendick, T. H. (2001). Empirically supported psychological interventions: Controversies and evidence. *Annual Review of Psychology, 52,* 685–716.

Christensen, A., & Jacobson, N. S. (1994). Who (or what) can do psychotherapy: The status and challenge of nonprofessional therapies. *Psychological Science, 5,* 8–14.

Ekman, P. (1984). Expression and the nature of emotion. In K Scherer & P. Ekman (Eds.), *Approaches to emotion* (pp. 319–343). Hillsdale, NJ: Erlbaum.

Federal Disparity Index Workgroup. (2002). *2002 IHCIF: FY 2001 FEHBP disparity index and application of findings to allocate the FY 2002 Indian Health Care Improvement Fund.* Accessed: http://www.ihs.gov/nonmedicalprograms/lnf/IHCIF2002/2002%20IHCIF%20Report.pdf [May 25, 2002.]

Fiske, D. W., & Shweder, R. A. (1986). *Metatheory in social science: Pluralisms and subjectivities.* Chicago: University of Chicago Press.

Gone, J. P. (in press). Mental health, wellness, and the quest for an authentic American Indian identity. In T. Witko (Ed.), *No longer forgotten: Addressing the mental health needs of urban Indians.* Washington, DC: American Psychological Association.

Gould, R. A., & Clum, G. A. (1993). A meta-analysis of self-help treatment approaches. *Clinical Psychology Review, 13,* 169–186.

Harre, R. (Ed.). (1986). *The social construction of emotions.* Oxford: Basil Blackwell.

Hymes, D. (1974). *Foundations in sociolinguistics: An ethnographic approach.* Philadelphia: University of Pennsylvania Press.

Indian Health Service. (1998–1999). *Trends in Indian Health.* Accessed: http://www.ihs.gov/PublicInfo/Publications/trends98/trends98.asp [April 28, 2002.]

Indian Health Service. (2002). *Indian Health Service fact sheet.* Accessed: http://www.ihs.gov/.asp [April 28, 2002.]

Kessler, R. C., McGonagle, K. A., Zhao, S., Nelson, C. B., Hughes, M., Eshleman, S., Wittchen, H., & Kendler, K. S. (1994). Lifetime and twelve-month prevalence of DSM-III-R psychiatric disorders in the United States. *Archives of General Psychiatry, 51,* 8–19.

Kleinman, A. (1987). Anthropology and psychiatry: The role of culture in cross-cultural research on illness. *British Journal of Psychiatry, 151,* 447–454.

LaFromboise, T. D. (1988). American Indian mental health policy. *American Psychologist, 43,* 388–397.

Lutz, C., & White, G. M. (1986). The anthropology of the emotions. *Annual Review of Anthropology, 15,* 405–436.

Millon, T., Blaney, P. H., & Davis, R. D. (1999). *Oxford textbook of psychopathology.* New York: Oxford University Press.

Nelson, S. H., McCoy, G. F., Stetter, M., & Vanderwagen, W. C. (1992). An overview of mental health services for American Indians and Alaska Natives in the 1990's. *Hospital and Community Psychiatry, 43,* 257–261.

O'Nell, T. D. (1989). Psychiatric investigations among American Indians and Alaska Natives: A critical review. *Culture, Medicine, and Psychiatry, 13,* 51–87.

Pevar, S. L. (1992). *The rights of Indians and tribes: The basic ACLU guide to Indian and tribal rights* (2nd ed.). Carbondale, IL: Southern Illinois University Press.

Rappaport, J. (1977). *Community psychology: Values, research, and action.* Fort Worth, TX: Holt, Rinehart, & Winston.

Rappaport, J., & Seidman, E. (1983). Social and community interventions. In C. E. Walker (Ed.), *The handbook of clinical psychology: Theory, research, and practice* (pp. 1089–1123). Homewood, IL: Dow Jones-Irwin.

Rappaport, J., & Seidman, E. (2000). *Handbook of community psychology.* New York: Kluwer Academic/Plenum.

Roy, C., Choudhuri, A., & Irvine, D. (1970). The prevalence of mental disorders among Saskatchewan Indians. *Journal of Cross-Cultural Psychology, 1,* 383–392.

Sampath, H. M. (1974). Prevalence of psychiatric disorders in a southern Baffin Island Eskimo settlement. *Canadian Psychiatric Association Journal, 19,* 363–367.

Shore, J. H., Kinzie, J. D., Hampson, J. L., & Pattison, E. M. (1973). Psychiatric epidemiology of an Indian village. *Psychiatry, 36,* 70–81.

Shweder, R. A. (1990). Cultural psychology—What is it? In J. W. Stigler, R. A. Shweder, & G. Herdt (Eds.), *Cultural psychology: Essays on comparative human development* (pp. 1–43). New York: Cambridge University Press.

Shweder, R. A., & Sullivan, M. A. (1993). Cultural psychology: Who needs it? *Annual Review of Psychology, 44,* 497–523.

Trimble, J. E., Manson, S. M., Dinges, N. G., & Medicine, B. (1984). American Indian concepts of mental health: Reflections and directions. In P. B. Pedersen, N. Sartorius, & A. J. Marsella (Eds.), *Mental health services: The cross-cultural context* (pp. 199–220). Beverly Hills, CA: Sage.

U.S. Census Bureau. (2001). *American Indian/Alaska Native Heritage Month: November 2001.* Accessed: http://www.census.gov/Press-Release/www/2001/cb01fff15.html [May 5, 2002.]

U.S. Census Bureau. (2002). *The American Indian and Alaska Native population: 2000* (Census 2000 Brief). Washington, DC: Author.

U.S. Congress, Office of Technology Assessment. (1990). *Indian adolescent mental health* (OTA-H-446). Washington, DC: U.S. Government Printing Office.

West, J., Kohout, J., Pion, G. M., Wicherski, M. M., Vandivort-Warren, R. E., Palmiter, M. L., et al. (2000). Chapter 20. Mental health practitioners and trainees. In R. W. Manderscheid & M. J. Henderson (Eds.), *Mental health, United States, 2000.* Rockville, MD: U.S. Department of Health and Human Services.

Witko, T. (in press). *No longer forgotten: Addressing the mental health needs of urban Indians.* Washington, DC: American Psychological Association.

CHAPTER 13

Not Just Black and White

Interracial Relationships and Multicultural Individuals

CHRISTINE C. IIJIMA HALL

This chapter provides professionals with a brief background of the sociological and psychological research and counseling of mixed race couples and multiracial individuals.

HISTORICAL ISSUES OF INTERRACIAL UNIONS/DATING/MARRIAGES

Tragic stories and tales of forbidden sexual unions have filled bookshelves for centuries. Most literature and media depiction of intercultural/racial relationships is in the form of a tragedy. Shakespeare's *Romeo and Juliet* (in Hosley, 1954) is a story where two teenaged lovers make a pact to be together eternally despite the efforts of their two feuding families. Although this may not be viewed as the classic mixed marriage, the issues are similar—two people forbidden to be together on punishment of death. Many years later, the authors of *West Side Story* (Bernstein, 1958) interpreted the Romeo and Juliet tragedy to help us understand the interracial perspective. The opera, *Madame Butterfly* (Puccini, 1961) and the stage show, *Miss Saigon* (Boublil & Shonberg, 1990) show war bringing unlikely matches and the tragedy of taking part in forbidden relationships.

Although *Romeo and Juliet, West Side Story, Madame Butterfly,* and *Miss Saigon* depict mixed relationships, the interracial union most discussed in the United States is one between a Black person and a White person. This began when slaves were brought from Africa in the 1700s. They were viewed as cargo—property to be bought and sold—to do with as the owners desired. Similar to other livestock, slaves were mated to produce additional slaves (Wyatt, 1997). Many of these offspring were fathered by White slave owners. Female slaves were utilized to satisfy the sexual desires of their masters. Slave women were raped, abused, and many killed in the process (Wyatt, 1997).

Although sex between White men and their Black female slaves was common-place, the sexual union between a White woman and a Black male slave was not. The reason was as much capitalistic as moral. That is, if a White man and Black female slave produced a child, the child stayed with the mother, was raised as a slave and considered additional property. However, if a Black male slave fathered a child with a White woman, the child could be raised by the mother, integrated into White society, educated, and own property (Bennett, 1965). To discourage White women from inter-racial mixing, they were told that African men were sexual savages who would rape and physically damage them because their penises were so large (Clark, 1965). Rather than discourage contact, some White women became curious about Black men. In addition, some Black men saw White women as a group to conquer as part of revenge.

Interracial unions were also forbidden because many believed mixed race off-spring were unnatural and against the laws of God and nature. In fact, the term "mulatto," a pejorative for a mixed race person, is derived from the word "mule," which is a sterile creature produced by a donkey and a horse. Ultimately, White society primarily wanted the White population to remain "pure" and "racial pollution" was a major fear (Henriques, 1975).

In order to keep the White race from being diluted, mechanisms were established to deter interracial relationships. Segregation laws established boundaries that deterred interracial contact. That is, Children of Color were not allowed to attend White schools until 1954 (*Brown v. Board of Education*, 1955) and People of Color were not allowed to work and live together until the Civil Rights Act of 1964. It was not until 1967 that the United States formally allowed interracial marriages (*Loving v. Virginia*, 1967). Thus, the United States is fairly young in allowing the integration of schools, work, society, and relationships but many social stigmas still exist.

Discrimination is not solely in the domain of Whites. Although most segregation laws were established to keep Whites from mixing with minorities, many minorities have negative history and feelings toward each other. For example, Americans of all colors may have issues toward sexual relations with Southeast Asians because of the Vietnam War. Marriage between Koreans or Chinese to Japanese may cause consterna-tion because of the history of fighting among these groups. Thus, marriage between two racial minorities in the United States may be as problematic as marriage between a minority person and a White person. Understanding why different ethnic groups view interracial unions negatively is important when working with mixed couples or individuals.

STATISTICS ON INTERRACIAL RELATIONSHIPS

With the stigma, prejudice, and complications of interracial relationships, it would seem the majority of people in the United States would avoid them. In fact, they do. Within the general population, only 5% of marriages in the United States are interra-cial (U.S. Census, 1998). This is up from 2.2% in 1980. In 1980, 165,000 marriages were Black-White. This number tripled to 330,000 in 1998. Although the majority of these interracial marriages are Black-White marriages, many other groups are interracially marrying. Only "White-other" and "Black-other" marriages are reported by the Census. The White-other interracial marriages more than doubled from the 1980 statistic of 450,000 to 975,000 in 1998. The Black-other races marriages increased only slightly from 34,000 in 1980 to 43,000 in 1998.

Several factors may be affecting this increase—more liberal beliefs, increased socioeconomic status of minorities, and generational issues. (The longer an immigrant group is in the United States, the higher the probability of outmarriage.) With integration and socioeconomic improvement of ethnic minorities, Whites and People of Color are living and working in close proximity and having more interaction, which increases the probability of romance.

One particular group experiencing a rapid increase in interracial dating and marriages is the Asian-American group. For example, in the 1980s in Los Angeles County, Asian outmarriages ranges between 11% and 52% (Fujino, 1997). By the 1990s, 54% to 80% of Asian women in the United States were involved in outmarriages (Kitano, Fujino, & Takahashi, 1998). The high outdating/outmarriage rate of Asian females may be due, in addition to those reasons listed in the preceding, to the stereotypical image of Asian women—demure, passive, nondemanding, subservient, small framed, —that may make them more attractive to American men (Hall, 1995). However, Asian-American male outdating and outmarriage rates are also increasing. This is perhaps owing to Asian males being perceived as more successful and emotionally stable (Pan, 2000). In addition, the Asian man's masculinity factor may be increasing because of the changes in the media image of the stronger, more virile, martial arts expert. However, overall, Asian men primarily marry Asian women. If they outmarry, they usually marry White women (Fujino, 1997). Asian women, on the other hand, have the greatest tendency to marry White men followed by Asian men. Both Asian men and women have a low probability of marrying Blacks or Hispanics.

WHAT ARE THE OVERALL REASONS WHY INDIVIDUALS INTERMARRY?

As it is for most marriages, the primary reason people intermarry is love. Several factors contribute to this love. Fujino (1997) and others found these factors to be the following:

1. *Propinquity (location/physical closeness).* That is, the more interaction with a group, the greater the greater for a relationship or marriage. Because of the upward social mobility of ethnic groups, affirmative action, and other legal and social mores, more ethnic groups are living and working closely with Whites and other minorities.
2. Similarity in worldviews. Contrary to the adage that opposites attract, similarity is more attractive (Byrne, 1969). People with similar goals, values, politics, and the like are more likely to associate. This association may lead to a deeper relationship. As ethnic groups and Whites begin to have similar socioeconomic and political

234

backgrounds, there is a likelihood of similar worldviews.
3. *Generation in the United States.* Research has shown that the greater number of generations a family has resided in the United States, the greater the likelihood of someone in the family marrying outside the culture of origin (Kitano et al., 1998).
4. *Group size.* Fujino (1997) found a tendency for individuals from the ethnic group with fewer numbers to marry into the group with larger numbers. Perhaps this results from having more people from which to choose. Another reason may be the more dominant or larger group controlling the culture and economics. Because Whites tend to have larger numbers and more political and economic power, it is more likely that a minority woman would marry a White man; women tend to "marry up" economically.
5. *Physical attractiveness.* Physical attraction is a major factor that initially draws one individual to another (Allen, 1976). No single criterion for dating choices has proven more salient than perceived physical attractiveness.

These factors have been found to increase interracial marriages, but individuals also may fall into the trap of marrying for inappropriate reasons. Some individuals may marry outside their culture or race for reasons of curiosity; rebellion; upward mobility; stereotypes (sexual and racial); or escape from a family, town, or lifestyle. However, it should be pointed out that interracial couples do not have a monopoly on wrong reasons for marriages.

WHAT ABOUT THE CHILDREN?

As stated, society has attempted to discourage interracial mixing through legal and social avenues. One social avenue not yet discussed is guilt. Many have heard the question, "What about the children?" Society has said to mixed couples, "You may want to ruin your lives but if you really cared you'd think about your children. What kind of life will they have?"

This belief of the problematic mixed-race child was prevalent prior to 1980. Primarily, the negative perspective of mixed-race individuals was depicted in the media. One of the most common depictions was the "tragic mulatto." *Imitation of Life*, a film made in the 1934 (Stahl, 1934; remade by Sirk, 1959) was a classic where a mixed race White-Black woman tries to "pass" as White and lives a life of lies, deceit, and tragedy. Decades later, in the 1960s, even half-human and half-Vulcan Mr. Spock on the space-age television series *Star Trek* (Roddenberry, 1966) was torn between two worlds, cultures, lifestyles, and beliefs.

Social science and medical researchers and theorists jumped on the bandwagon to show that interracial offspring were doomed. Stonequist (1937) developed the "Marginal Man" theory where he hypothesized that individuals born to a marginal world (e.g., two races, religions, cultures) lived a marginal status (torn between two cultures, whether religious, cultural, racial, etc.) and would inevitably develop a marginal personality (psychological impairment). This theory was proven multiple times with research conducted on individuals expressing difficulty in functioning in a marginal world. However, the research was conducted on mixed-race individuals who were already experiencing extreme adjustment difficulty and were either incarcerated or committed to mental institutions. (It is questionable whether the difficulty these individuals were experiencing was solely based on their marginal status or other factors such as racial discrimination, poverty, oppression, etc.) These earlier studies did not include individuals who had experienced a marginal status but not a marginal personality—that is, the experiences of normal populations were virtually unknown.

In the late 1970s, a few pieces of research conducted on normal mixed-race populations began to surface. Chang (1974) noticed that military children who were mixed race had excellent coping and intellectual skills. In 1978, Strong interviewed mixed-race adults in Japan to understand their experiences. He found the discrimination of these individuals left behind after the World War II occupation of Japan by the United States to be great. However, the strength developed by those who survived was phenomenal. Ramirez and Castaneda's (Ramirez, 1998) work on biculturalism was also emerging in the 1970s as part of the Chicano movement. They researched the positive aspects of bilingualism and biculturalism at a time when it was believed that bilingualism was seen as a negative attribute and that Mexican Americans in the United States must release all ethnic ties and become 100% American. Although bilingual, bicultural, and biracial issues may have been new in the United States, these were not new to the Hispanic culture. Research and writings on "mestizos" (mixed race) have existed for many decades (Ramirez, 1998).

The early 1980s saw an emergence of research conducted on "normal" mixed-race populations. Hall (1980), Kich (1982), Murphy-Shigematsu (1986), and Thornton (1983) were among the earliest researchers. These social science students were working on their dissertations simultaneously across the country. They began to hear of each other's research through the ethnic grapevine and supported each other in their endeavors. They shared the same stories of the lack of support from traditional researchers and the public in their research. Later, they began to experience an inability to publish their works in professional journals because their academic disciplines felt the topic to be esoteric, not considered scientific, not appropriate research for the discipline, and of no interest to their readers. It was not until the 1990s when Root (1992) contacted these researchers and others and asked them to contribute to her edited book that the beginning of the biracial research movement began in force.

MULTIRACIAL IDENTITY

Root's (1992) first book, *Racially Mixed People in America*, contained data-based research by these aforementioned individuals plus numerous others on issues of mixed race identity. The book is divided into four parts: (a) a background on the issue of race in America; (b) a background on the history of racial mixing in America; (c) research on mixed race individuals; and (d) the social and political future of race in America. The reader is encouraged to refer to this book and to her later book, *The Multiracial Experience: Racial Borders as the New Frontier*, for more detailed understanding of the issues.

The most common aspects of mixed-race culture that have been researched and discussed are the developmental processes of identity formation, factors influencing identity choices, ethnic knowledge, experiences, life satisfaction, and mental health. These are discussed further here.

IDENTITY FORMATION

The ethnic identity choices available to biracial/multiracial individuals are to choose: (a) one race over another; (b) a combination of the races; (c) none of the biological races she or he is born to; (d) none of traditional racial choices. Hall (1980, 1992) investigated the ethnic/racial identity choices of 30 mixed Black and Japanese adults. She presented her respondents with the classic choice of racial categories (Black, White, Asian, Hispanic, Native American) with the instruction to "Please choose one." She found the majority (*N* = 17) chose Black, 10 chose "Other" (with seven specifying Black-Japanese), one identified as Japanese, and one refused to identify himself racially. Thus, Hall's respondents ran the gamut of relevant choices.

Most researchers are finding biracial/multiracial people comfortable with their biracial/multiracial status. For example, Cooke (1997) found the majority of her minority-White respondents referred to themselves as biracial. In addition, Hall (unpublished data) asked her 1980 sample if they felt like a continuation of the Black race, and continuation of the Japanese race or a new people/new race. She found 21 (70%) of her respondents felt like a new people/new race. Root (1990) also found mixed race people felt like a new race. Many groups have developed terms for themselves that reflect a new group. For example, the term "Hapa Haole" (half White) is one used in Hawaii for people who are part White.

In addition to asking her respondents to "choose one," Hall asked her sample to rate themselves, on two separate continuums on how "Black" and "Japanese" they felt. Hall found 26 of her 30 respondents felt both Black and Japanese. Hall analogized this to Bem's (1974) androgyny theory. That is, when given a forced choice (male versus female) an individual will most likely choose the more socially acceptable category (male for men, female for women). However, when asked how masculine or feminine a person is on two separate continuums, individuals may rate themselves high on both. Thus, in Hall's study, the majority chose the more socially acceptable racial group (in the 1970s, this was Black). However, when asked to rate their Blackness and Japaneseness independently of each other, they chose to identify as both. This was one of the first measures of multiculturality/multiraciality for mixed race individuals.

Cross (1991) felt that "personal (racial) identification" may be different from "referent group orientation"—the group with which one feels affinity. Field (1996) studied the relation between Personal Identification (PI) and Referent Group Orientation (RGO) with 31 Black-White biracial individuals. She studied four aspects of an RGO—global self-worth, social acceptance, physical appearance, and romantic appeal. To measure PI, she asked several subjective questions which included questions "regarding their comfort level with their racial heritage, which race they most identified with, which group they felt and thought like, which background they would choose to be, and which racial group they most resembled" (p. 220). Of Field's 31 biracial respondents, 14 had a Black RGO, 12 had a biracial RGO, and 5 had a White RGO. Of those 14 with a Black RGO, nine chose a Black identity label and five chose a biracial identity label. But ultimately they reported mostly identifying with, and feeling, biracial.

Of those who chose a White RGO ($N = 5$), most were more comfortable with White than Black peers. These five used a biracial label to identify their race. The responses of those who chose a biracial RGO ($N = 12$) were extremely varied and difficult to interpret. Equal numbers ($N = 6$) chose to label themselves either biracial or Black. Field discussed that overall, biracials could apply monoracial label to themselves but live a very biracial lifestyle.

Whether the choice is multicultural/multiracial or the traditional monoracial, the choices are different for each mixed-race individual depending on his or her racial composition. That is, an individual who is mixed with two minority backgrounds (e.g., Black-Japanese) may have different life experiences and choices than someone who is mixed minority-White (e.g., Black-White or Japanese-White). New research on comparing the ethnic identity of minority-minority versus minority-majority individuals is emerging (Cooke, 1997; King & DaCosta, 1996; Mukoyama, 1998). Although the research does not give definite data that the ethnic identity of a minority-majority person is more or less difficult than and individual with a minority-minority background, personal interviews have shown some differences in their experiences. For example, minority-minority individuals may "share in common the rejection of White values in order to appreciate minority values" (Root, 1990, p. 197), whereas a person who is part minority and part White may have an "inherent difficulty in rejecting 'whiteness' if one is part white" (p. 197).

In addition, mixtures, whether White-minority or minority-minority, who have a history of conflict may have more difficulty in their being accepted by both ethnic groups. For example, historical conflict may exist between African Americans and Koreans in Los Angeles, Japanese and Chinese, or Indian and Pakistani.

The development of an ethnic/racial identity may be long and progress through social, racial, and emotional developmental stages. Kich (1982, 1992) found three major stages—initial awareness (age 3 to 10), struggle for acceptance from others (age 8 to adolescence/early adulthood), and acceptance of bicultural/biracial self (late adolescence to young adulthood). Very few studies have tried to distinguish among these stages. Field (1996), however, did compare the results of her study on ethnic identity development of adolescents with Hall's (1980) research on adults and commented that a "failure to find a pattern between the various components of racial identity may also reflect a developmental process in which the adults in Hall's study had progressed further" (p. 222).

One of the newest issues in multiracial research is "situational ethnicity or identity."

Researchers have found that multiracial individuals are able to move back and forth between the cultures as needed (Hall, 1980; Root, 1996; Williams, 1992). "This changing of foreground and background does not usually represent confusion, but it may confuse someone who insists that race is an imperturbable fact and synonymous with ethnicity" (Root, 1996, p. 11). Outside critics may think the person is changing personality but in reality Root goes on to say, "the essence of who one is as a person remains the same" (p. 11). This has been a stance that Root (1990) has maintained over the years, as she asserted that ". . . experience would need to be tremendous to compel the individual to change their internally perceived racial identity" (p. 199). I usually explain this phenomenon to others by stating, "If you act differently with your parents, your friends, or in class then you also exhibit situational identity or multiculturality."

OTHER FACTORS AFFECTING ETHNIC IDENTITY

In addition to racial composition, many other factors have been found to influence the ethnic/racial identity choices.

Cultural Knowledge

A belief that mixed race individuals culturally "dilute" the race has been a prevalent one. On the contrary, Hall (1980) found that 27 of her 30 Black-Japanese respondents had knowledge of both Black and Japanese cultures and also identified as being both African American and Japanese. Mass' (1992) excellent research on cultural/ethnic knowledge found that individuals of mixed Caucasian and Japanese heritage had less knowledge of Japanese culture than those who were monorace Japanese but still strongly identified as being Japanese. Thus, Hall found that cultural knowledge and identity were correlated, whereas Mass found this not necessarily true. Regardless, both Hall and Mass found their mixed-race samples to identify with their cultures. In Mass' case, although the knowledge of culture may diminish slightly, the affiliation with the group(s) remains strong. These types of research results reinforce the need to expose children to, and teach them about, the aspects of their cultures. Although the identity and affiliation may be strong, an understanding of the culture may be important when interacting with the different cultural groups for acceptance by the groups, and reinforcing the pride and identity to the groups.

Parental Influence

Parents have a major influence in shaping the lives of children. However, does the minority parent in a White-minority child play a larger role? Is a mother's influence stronger than a father's? Is there an interaction between the sex and race of the parent in the ethnic identity of a mixed-race child?

Prior to 1980, research showed that Black-White families had a higher probability of living in Black neighborhoods because, historically, Blacks were more accepting of mixed-race children. Thus, the children were more exposed to the Black culture, had more Black friends, and thus had a higher probability of identifying as Black. However, times have changed and many Black-White families now are living in Black, White, or mixed neighborhoods. Also there has been an increase in families now where the mother is African American (U.S. Census, 1998), whereas in the past, most Black-White families had African-American fathers. Thus, the research and their findings are more complicated.

Social science research has stated that mothers are the primary the conveyor of culture (Miller & Miller, 1990). However, what happens if the mother is White in a minority-White family? What happens if the mother is the minority component of a minority-minority or minority-White marriage?

Research on mixed race identity has found various results. Mukoyama (1998) surveyed 54 Japanese-White and 32 Japanese-African American individuals. She found that the Japanese parent (regardless of whether it is the mother or father) of Japanese-White individuals had a strong influence in communicating culture. Thus, it appears the minority parent communicated the culture more than the White parent; sex of parent was not the key factor. Mukoyama further found that parents of Japanese–African-American respondents promoted a higher sense of ethnic identification than did parents of Japanese-White individuals. Thus, the mixed individuals may have been receiving double encouragement to identify as minority with minority-minority parents as opposed to minority-White parents.

Cooke (1997) studied 56 minority-White individuals (22 Asian-White, 23 Black-White, 11 Hispanic-White) using a revised version of Phinney's (1992) Multigroup Ethnic Identity Measure (MEIM) called the Cooke-Hall Biracial Identity Attitude Scale (BIAS). The BIAS asks respondents how each parent's racial/ethnic group affected their ethnic identity. Cooke found that biracial identity is highly correlated with the minority parent's racial group.

Further, Hall and Turner (2001) compared the identity development of 22 Asian-White and 12 Asian-minority adults. They found the Asian-minority respondents identified as biracial, whereas the Asian-White respondents did not report biracial identification as frequently. However, in delving further, it appears that most of the Asian-White individuals who did not identify as biracial identified with their mother's racial group rather than their father's. That is, 14 of these 22 Asian-White respondents had Asian mothers and identified more with their mothers. Those with White mothers had no significant difference between identification with their mothers or fathers. Thus, it appears that a mother's influence is even stronger when she is the minority parent. For mixed couples that wish to promote biracial or minority identity, extra care may need to be taken to ensure culture is conveyed and ethnic identification is reinforced when the mother is White. Whether the minority influence is stronger for different minority-majority mixtures is unknown. Also unknown is the weighted parental influence in a minority-minority family.

Gender Differences

Mukoyama (1998) found a sex difference in the ethnic identity of her respondents. She found 51.7% of her male respondents identified as monoracial, whereas only 28.1% of the females did. She concluded that biethnic men may have more societal pressures to be monoethnic than biethnic women. Being mixed race may be more difficult for men than women in today's society. In fact, Root (1990, p. 196) stated:

> It is hypothesized that mixed race men will have a more difficult time overcoming social barriers than mixed race women; they will have to work harder to prove themselves and experience an oppression, which while shared by other minority group men, may exist also within their minority reference groups toward them. On the other hand, because women in general are less threatening to the mainstream culture than men, mixed race women may not experience as much direct oppression as mixed race men. Biracial women may in fact be perceived as less threatening than monoracial women of color.

The Minority Experience

Are mixed race people subjected to more, less, or equal amounts of discrimination than monoraced minority individuals? Poussaint (1975) stated many years ago that light-skinned Blacks are perceived as experiencing less discrimination. This possible preferential treatment by White society of light-skinned Blacks and "guedo" (light/White) Hispanics has caused dissention within these groups. But research has shown that African Americans—regardless of skin color—experience discrimination (Poussaint, 1975). In fact, Cauce, Hiraga, Mason, Aguilar, Ordonez, and Gonzalez (1992) further found that mixed race people with at least one minority parent experience similar discrimination and the resulting stress and anger that result from discrimination. The one-drop (hypodecent) rule may be acting here. That is, society may treat the mixed race individual as a minority regardless of light skin and other features. The research described throughout this chapter has shown the majority of mixed-race people see themselves as minority. A minority-minority individual is certainly a minority but may have less distinct ethnic features. Discrimination is discrimination and it is difficulty to say whether one type is worse than another. "Microaggressions" or "minor" everyday discriminatory acts still cause psychological damage to an individual.

Racial discrimination does not solely emanate from White society. Mixed-race people are also subjected to discrimination from monoracial people of color. Most research and other publications point to the fact that mixed-race people report they are not totally accepted by the groups to which they belong. Many have even stated mistreatment. For example, many mixed-Black individuals discuss that African Americans may not accept them because they are light-skinned or "don't act Black." In addition, Asians and Blacks do not have a history of a positive relationship in the United States; therefore, a mixed Asian-Black individual may receive discriminatory treatment from both groups. "Mixed race persons from two minority groups are likely to experience oppression from the racial group of heritage which has higher social status" (Root, 1990, p. 188).

Geographic Influence

A factor that needs more study is geographic influence on ethnic/racial identity. The racial composition, size, and political climate of communities in which mixed-race couples and their children live have been found to have an affect on the individuals (Root, 1990). That is, a community with similar racial/ethnic groups as the biracial individual aids in learning about the culture. In addition, a community with diverse ethnic composition or a sizeable number of mixed couples may lead to better acceptance of the mixed couple and their children. Root (1990) states, "Biracial people growing up in more racially oppressive parts of the country are less likely to have freedom to choose their racial identity" (p. 199). Further, Spickard (1997) says that Amerasians (Asian-White) are more likely to be harassed in East Coast cities than in West Coast cities but he also believes that, even on the West Coast, acceptance varies by Asian group. For example, he says Japanese interracial marriages and children are more likely to be included in the Japanese-American communities, whereas multiracial Chinese Americans in Chinese communities are "more likely to be treated with suspicion and are less likely to be included in Chinese community institutional life" (p. 54).

Physical Appearance

Physical cues are important when "categorizing" individuals (Mitchell, 1990; Salgado de Snyder et al., 1982). Cooley's (1902) "looking glass self" theory postulates that how a person is perceived by the world is how the person perceives him- or herself. That is, if an individual is perceived as being African American, Asian, Hispanic, Native American, or White by society, society will treat him or her accordingly and the individual will have a strong tendency to identify as such. Although this appears to be true for many mixed-race individuals, it also appears that mixed-race people do not always follow this postulate. Mixed-race people also appear to be identifying with their racial/ethnic groups, whether or not they resemble those groups. For example, an Asian-White woman in Cooke's (1997) study is continually mistaken for Chicana but still strongly identifies with both her Asian and White cultures. The same issue was reported by an East Indian-Black female in Cooke's study. Hall (1980) also found this similar phenomenon. Many of her respondents felt they looked Polynesian but still identified as both Black and Japanese. Williams (1992) found physical appearance was not necessarily the key factor in determining racial identification. She found many Black-Asian and White-Asian participants did not identify with the group they resembled.

Because of the ambiguous and ubiquitous (Hall, 1997) physical appearance of mixed-raced people, multiracial people are constantly asked, "What are you?" (Gaskins,

1999; Williams, 1996). Many mixed race individuals are mistaken for Russian, Ethiopian, Egyptian, Polynesian, and Arab (Williams, 1992). Although this may seem exotic or interesting, acceptance or nonacceptance into one's racial group may depend on physical appearance. Williams' (1992) Asian-White and Asian-minority respondents said that although neither Blacks nor Whites made an issue of their physical differences, Japanese noticed the "slightest physical deviation from them" (p. 290) and were either envious or disgusted. However, acceptance or nonacceptance did not appear to be ". . . the decisive factor in why he or she would choose a certain reference group" (p. 291). Respondents indicated that the social effects of their physical appearances on their ethnic identity choices were important, but not definitive.

How do mixed-race people feel about their appearance? Hall (1997) measured the body satisfaction of her biracial respondents and found the respondents liked what they saw in the mirror. However, this acceptance may have occurred over time. Just as young people may go through a time when they do not like their hair, ears, body, etc., multiracial people appear to have a similar transition period that may be exacerbated by the fact that very few people look like them. Feelings of belongingness are very important to body image and satisfaction. For example, in 1980, Hall met with a young Japanese-American mother whose 5-year-old daughter was mixed Black and Japanese. The daughter was enrolled in a predominantly Japanese private school in the Los Angeles area. The daughter began expressing concern over her looks and asking why she had "meatball hair" (frizzy) rather than "spaghetti hair" (straight) like the rest of her friends. The solution was to enroll the child in a more racially diverse school where meatball, spaghetti, and other types of hair abound. The child showed immediate improvement in her self-esteem and body image.

Divorce

The posttraumatic stress of divorce may exacerbate the difficulty of choosing an ethnic identity. The acceptance (personal, ethnic, social, or otherwise) of the absent parent may be compromised. Many divorced couples have negative feelings toward each other and convey these feelings to the children. Some of these negative feelings may have racial overtones. For example, a White mother of a Black-White child may express anger toward African-Americans, speak harshly of the group, and not approve of the child developing friendships and romantic relationships with African-American peers. The divorce situation may also result in a family moving into the ethnic neighborhood of the primary care parent. Thus, the child may lose role models and cultural understanding of the other parent's ethnic group.

PSYCHOLOGICAL ISSUES

As stated, most research prior to the 1980s found major psychological weaknesses in mixed-race people. Although "the integration of biracial heritage into a positive self-concept is complicated and lengthy" (Root, 1990, p. 186), most post-1980s research found a positive self-esteem or at least one similar to monorace individuals. Hall (1980) found that the majority of her respondents had a good self-esteem and were satisfied with life. In addition to positive scores on a happiness and life satisfaction scale, she also found that when asked "if they were to be born again, would they want to be born Black-Japanese," all but one respondent said yes. Cauce et al. (1992) also found no self-worth and adjustment differences between her biracial and monoracial sample.

Cooke (1997) is one of the few researchers to find self-esteem differences. She found that Black-White biracials had significantly lower self-esteem scores than Asian-White and Hispanic-Asian biracials. Cooke made no definite hypotheses of why this occurred. She cited past research that showed Blacks less likely to feel good about themselves, thus, mixed Black individuals may also have a lower self-esteem. She also noted that her Asian-White and Hispanic-Asian respondents may have been more test-savvy on the self-esteem instrument and answered toward the positive. This is definitely an area of research that needs to be pursued.

A factor that may also affect self-esteem is one of referent group orientation. Many have believed that ethnic identification must be the same as RGO or self-esteem would suffer. To study this, Field (1996) looked at the relationship between ethnic/racial identification and referent group orientation to see if it affected self-concept/self-esteem. She found of her 31 Black-White biracials, those with Black or biracial RGOs had more positive self-esteem than those who chose a White RGO. She also found no significant difference between Black, White, and biracials in their self-concept (measured by social acceptance, physical attractiveness, and romantic appeal).

As with any group, life is not always perfect. Though Gibbs and Hines (1992) found no significant behavioral problems and a good self-esteem in the majority of their biracial sample, they found coping mechanisms to be "more extreme, less flexible, and dynamically related to issues of race and ethnicity" (p. 225). They do say that research results vary in reports depending on research design and sampling. Research in the more nonclinical setting show more positive self-concept and adjustment. "Positive outcomes are associated with supportive families, cohesive social networks, and integrated schools and neighborhoods" (p. 226).

It is important for researchers, mental health practitioners, teachers, parents, etc., not to assume that personal or psychological problems develop in mixed-race people primarily because of their mixed-race status (being a marginal person does not necessarily lead to a marginal personality). As with any individual, many factors affect his or her well-being. Economics, family dynamics, and social influences are just some of these factors.

WHAT HAS CHANGED OVER THE PAST 20 YEARS

In the years when very few biracial children existed, mixed-race children tended to feel like anomalies. Because differences are not well tolerated by children, their lives tended to be difficult. However, with the birth of more interracial children, there has been a better understanding and acceptance of mixed-race individuals of themselves and by others.

Support groups began to emerge around the United States to aid families and individuals with multiracial identity and to provide an opportunity to be with other mixed-race families (Brown & Douglass, 1996). Some of the first groups were I-Pride in the Northern California Bay Area in 1979, the Biracial Family Network in Chicago in 1980, the Interracial Family Circle of Washington, DC, in 1984, and the Multiracial Americans of Southern California (MASC) in 1987. Later, groups such as The Amerasian League, Multiracial International Network, and University of California Berkeley's Hapa Issue's Forum arose (Houston & Williams, 1997).

Language has also changed to meet the needs of this new group of people. For example, the hyphenated version of "bi-racial" appeared in dictionaries as early as 1932 (*Oxford English Dictionary*, 1989) but did not appear in its nonhyphenated form in the *Webster's Dictionary* until 1985. The term "interracial" did not appear until the 1990 edition of *Webster Dictionary* (1990). I had difficulty writing her dissertation during the late 1970s because I had to construct such terminology as "multiracial," "multiraciality," and "Japaneseness" and was questioned on the appropriateness of the terms. However, I was not alone in developing new terminology. Many mixed-race individuals have developed terms to describe themselves, such as Tiger Woods' "Cablinasian" (Caucasian, Black, American Indian, Asian). Other terms I have heard include "JafroAmerican," "Nigganese" (Black-Japanese), and "PortaJap" (Portugese-Japanese). (It should be noted that using a derivative of the pejorative terms "Jap" or "Nigga" were not intended as an insult to the Japanese or African-American cultures, but rather used as endearing and humorous slang.)

THE POLITICAL ASPECTS OF MULTIRACIAL IDENTITY

During the 1990s in the United States, one of the newest ethnic movements began. The movement stressed the importance of personal and social acceptance of multiracial individuals—the human rights of multiracial individuals (Root, 1996). Many fought to validate their existence and show ethnic pride by lobbying the U.S. Census Bureau to incorporate a multiracial category in some manner (Fernandez, 1996). This allowed people the right to declare a mixed-race status without having to choose between one race or another. Two major groups lobbied for this change—Project RACE (Reclassify All Children Equally) and Association of MultiEthnic Americans (AMEA). The result of this movement was the ability of individuals to designate more than one racial category on the 2000 U.S. Census form.

Sadly, this movement—as with other ethnic movements—was fought by some. Opposition from individuals from Black, Hispanic, and Asian groups argued that mixed-race people simply wanted to separate or deny membership in these groups. They feared federal funding and other services would be jeopardized by the lessened "headcount" in these groups by mixed-race people abandoning the "appropriate" race. These fears are dependent on how the United States tallies the data. If the U.S. reports numbers of people in the United States with African-American heritage, White heritage, etc., the individual races will not lose numbers. However, if the United States chooses to aggregate the data in another way, the races could lose representation. It is the responsibility of these groups to ensure the appropriate depiction of the data.

The opponents of mixed-race categories say they understand the need of mixed-race people to convey a mixed-race identity but they believe the Census should not be the conduit. Individuals should pick one race over the other and that identity is not measured by categories on the Census. If, however, the Census nomenclature is not a political statement, then why did African Americans argued for years that "Black" should replace "Negro," or that "African American" should also be included; why did Asians argue to replace "Oriental" with "Asian"? These are all identity and political issues similar to that of the multiracial categories.

Opponents of the multiracial Census identification ultimately fear that mixed-race individuals will choose their White race over their minority race. They believe that mixed-race people who are part White can and will pass as White to strive for "maximum social power and to escape the oppression directed toward people of color" (Root, 1990, p. 187). If this were true, then mixed minority-White individuals would have been doing this for years on the forced-choice Census form, and therefore, the mixed-race category will not make a difference except to perhaps gain numbers in the monoracial categories. This fear is unwarranted because research shows mixed-race minority-White individuals tend to identify more with the minority group than with the White group. This, of course, is true only for those mixed minority-White individuals. I have heard no discussion about mixed-race individuals who are of two ethnic minority groups. Opponents of the mixed-race category tend to think "Black-White" or "minority-White." The minority-minority individual, again, seems to get lost in the discussion. Many anxiously await the myriad interpretations based on the release of the 2000 Census data to observe the results!

CONCLUSION

This chapter has reviewed the historic background of interracial relationships and their offspring. The mental health practitioner should be aware that the issues of mixed-race relationships and multiracial individual issues are complicated. When working with a family or individual, it is important to seek an understanding of the experience, identity, and issues that confront or affect these individuals. The issue is not just Black and White.

REFERENCES

Allen, B. (1976). Race and physical attractiveness as criteria for white subject's dating choices. *Social Behavior and Personality, 4,* 289–296.

Bem, S. (1974). The measurement of psychological androgeny. *Journal of Consulting and Clinical Psychology, 42,* 155–162.

Bennett, L. (1965). Miscegenation in America. In C. Larsson (Ed.), *Marriage across the color line* (pp. 5–28). Chicago: Johnson Publishing Company.

Bernstein, L. (1958). *West Side Story*. New York: Random House.

Boublil, A., & Schonberg, C. (1990). *Miss Saigon*. New York: Geffen.

Brown v. Board of Education, 349 U.S. 294 (1955) (USSC).

Brown, N. G., & Douglass, R. E. (1996). Making the invisible visible: The growth of community network organizations. In M. P. P. Root (Ed.), *The multiracial experience: Racial borders as the new frontier* (pp. 323–340). Thousand Oaks, CA: Sage.

Bryne, D. (1969). Attitudes and attraction. *Advances in Experimental Social Psychology, 16*, 157–165.

Cauce, A. M., Hiraga, Y., Mason, C., Aguilar, T., Ordonez, N., & Gonzales, N. (1992). Between a rock and a hard place: Social adjustment of biracial youth. In M. P. P. Root (Ed.), *Racially mixed people in America* (pp. 207–222). Newbury Park, CA: Sage.

Chang, T. S. (1974). The self-concept of children of ethnically different marriages. *California Journal of Educational Research, 25*, 245–252.

Clark, K. (1965). *Dark ghetto*. New York: Harper & Row.

Cooke, T. (1997). *Biracial identity development: Psychosocial contributions to self-esteem and racial identity*. Unpublished doctoral dissertation, Arizona State University, Tempe, AZ.

Cooley, C. H. (1902). *Human nature and social order*. New York: Scribner.

Cross, W. E. (1991). *Shades of Black: Diversity in African-American identity*. Philadelphia: Temple University Press.

Fernandez, C. A. (1996). Government classification of multiracial/multiethnic people. In M. P. P. Root (Ed.), *The multiracial experience: Racial borders as the new frontier* (pp. 15–36). Thousand Oaks, CA: Sage.

Field, L. (1996). Piecing together the puzzle: Self-concept and group identity in biracial Black/White youth. In M. P. P. Root (Ed.), *The multiracial experience: Racial borders as the new frontier* (pp. 211–226). Thousand Oaks, CA: Sage.

Fujino, D. (1997). The rates, patterns, and reasons for forming heterosexual interracial dating relationships among Asian Americans. *Journal of Social and Personal Relationships, 14*, 809–828.

Gaskins, P. F. (1999). *What are you? Voices of mixed-race young people*. New York: Henry Holt.

Gibbs, J. T., & Hines, A. (1992). Negotiating ethnic identity: Issues for Black–White biracial adolescents. In M. P. P. Root (Ed.), *Racially mixed people in America* (pp. 223–238). Newbury Park, CA: Sage.

Hall, C. C. I. (1980). *Ethnic identity of racially mixed people*. Unpublished doctoral dissertation, University of California, Los Angeles.

Hall, C. C. I. (1992). Please choose one. In M. P. P. Root (Ed.), *Racially mixed people in America* (pp. 250–264). Newbury Park, CA: Sage.

Hall, C. C. I. (1995). Asian eyes: Body image and eating disorders of Asian and Asian American women. *Eating Disorders: The Journal of Treatment and Prevention, 3*, 8–19.

Hall, C. C. I. (1997). Best of both worlds: Body image and satisfaction of a sample of Black-Japanese biracial individuals. *Amerasian Journal, 23*, 87–97.

Hall, C. C. I., & Turner, T. I. C. (2001). The diversity of biracial individuals: Asian-White and Asian-minority biracial identity. In T. Williams-Leon & C. Nakashima (Eds.), *The sum of our parts* (pp. 81–91). Philadelphia: Temple University Press.

Henriques, F. (1975). *Children of conflict: A study of interracial sex and marriage*. New York: E.P. Hutton.

Hosley, R. (Ed.). (1954). *Romeo and Juliet* (by William Shakespeare). New Haven, CT: Yale University Press.

Houston, V. H., & Williams, T. K. (1997). No passing zone: The artistic and discursive voices of Asian-descendent multiracials. *Amerasian Journal, 23*, 69–86.

Kich, G. K. (1982). *Eurasians: Ethnic/racial identity development of biracial Japanese/White adults.* Unpublished doctoral dissertation. Wright Institute of Graduate School of Psychology, Berkeley, CA.

Kich, G. K. (1992). The developmental process of asserting a biracial, bicultural identity. In M. P. P. Root (Ed.), *Racially mixed people in America* (pp. 304–317). Newbury Park, CA: Sage.

King, R. C., & DaCosta, K. M. (1996). Changing face, changing race: The remaking of race in the Japanese American and African American Communities. In M.P.P. Root (Ed.), *The multiracial experience: Racial borders as the new frontier* (pp. 227–244). Thousand Oaks, CA: Sage.

Kitano, H., Fujino, D., & Takahasi, J. (1998). Interracial marriages: Where are the Asian Americans and where are they going? In L. C. Lee & N. W. S. Zane (Eds.), *Handbook of Asian American psychology* (pp. 233–260). Thousand Oaks, CA: Sage.

Loving v. Virginia, 388, U.S. 1. (1967)

Mass, A. I. (1992). Interracial Japanese Americans: The best of both worlds or the end of the Japanese American community. In M. P. P. Root (Ed.), *Racially mixed people in America* (pp. 265–279). Newbury Park, CA: Sage.

Miller, R. L., & Miller, B. (1990). Mothering the biracial child: Bridging the gaps between African–American and White parenting styles. *Women and Therapy, 10,* 169–179.

Mitchell, A. (1990). *Cultural identification, racial knowledge and general psychological well-being among biracial young adults.* Unpublished doctoral dissertation. California School of Professional Psychology, Berkeley, CA.

Mukoyama, T. H. (1998). *Effects of heritage combination on ethnic identity, self-esteem, and adjustment among American biethnic adults.* Unpublished doctoral dissertation, California School of Professional Psychology, Los Angeles, CA.

Murphy-Shigematsu, S. L. (1986). *The voices of Amerasian: Ethnicity, identity and empowerment in interracial Japanese Americans.* Unpublished doctoral dissertation, Harvard University, Cambridge, MA.

The Oxford English Dictionary. (1989). Oxford: Clarendon Press.

Pan, E. (2000, February 21). Why Asian guys are on a roll. *Newsweek,* pp. 50–51.

Phinney, J. (1992). The Multigroup Ethnic Identity Measure: A new scale for use with diverse groups. *Journal of Adolescent Research, 7,* 156–176.

Poussaint, A. (1975). The problems of light-skinned blacks. *Ebony, 30,* 85–88.

Puccini, G. (1961). *Madame Butterfly* (sound recording). United States: Angel.

Ramirez, M. (1998). *Multicultural/multiracial psychology: Mestizo perspectives in personality and mental health.* Northvale, NJ: Jason Aronson.

Roddenberry, G. (Producer). (1966). *Star Trek.*

Root, M. P. P. (1990). Resolving "other" status: Identity development of biracial individuals. In L. Brown & M. P. P. Root (Eds.), *Complexity and diversity in feminist theory and therapy* (pp. 185–205). New York: Haworth.

Root, M. P. P. (1992). *Racially mixed people in America.* Newbury Park, CA: Sage.

Root, M. P. P. (1996). *The multiracial experience: Racial borders as the new frontier.* Thousand Oaks, CA: Sage.

Salgada de Snyder, N., Lopez, C. M., & Padilla, A. M. (1982). Ethnic identity and cultural awareness among offspring of mixed interethnic marriages. *Journal of Early Adolescence, 2,* 277–282.

Sirk, D. (Director). (1959). *Imitation of life.* [film]

Spickard, P. (1997). What must I be? Asian Americans and the question of multiethnic identity. *Amerasian Journal, 23,* 43–60.

Stahl, J. M. (Director). (1934). *Imitation of life.* [film]

Stonequist, E. V. (1937). *The marginal man: A study in personality and culture conflict.* New York: Russell & Russell.

Thornton, M. C. (1983). *A social history of a multiethnic identity: The case of Black Japanese*

Americans. Unpublished doctoral dissertation, University of Michigan, Ann Arbor, MI.

U.S. Bureau of the Census. (1998). *Statistical Abstract of the United States.* Washington, DC: Government Printing Office.

Webster's New World Dictionary (1960). The World Publishing Company: International Copyright Union.

Williams, T. K. (1992). Prism lives: Identity of binational Amerasians. In M. P. P. Root (Ed.), *Racially mixed people in America* (pp. 250–264). Newbury Park, CA: Sage.

Williams, T. K. (1996). Race as process: Reassuring the "What are you?" encounters of biracial individuals. In M. P. P. Root (Ed.), *The multiracial experience: Racial borders as the new frontier* (pp. 191–210). Thousand Oaks, CA: Sage.

Wyatt, G. (1997). *Stolen women.* New York: Wiley.

SECTION 3

DIVERSE NONETHNIC POPULATIONS

Although many individuals equate cultural diversity and multiculturalism with ethnicity, our definition of multiculturalism is broader than just focusing on ethnic minority populations. As such, we have chosen to include chapters that focus on diverse nonethnic groups. This section of the book highlights the mental health history and issues of very diverse cultural groups. The mental health literature for some groups (e.g., women) is quite extensive. On the other hand, mental health research on cultural issues such as the role of religion and spirituality have more recently become popular and of interest to clinicians and researchers.

In their review of the mental health research on women, Iwamasa and Bangi summarize the history of how women were initially viewed in terms of psychopathology—often compared to the "standard" of men, both physically and psychologically. The current research on major disorders and how they affect women are reviewed. Finally, suggestions for areas in further need of examination are outlined, including the need for researchers to begin examining the mental health of culturally diverse women such as Women of Color, older adult women, and poor and incarcerated women.

Because of its impact beyond individuals, Mio et al. focus specifically on domestic violence issues among women. Domestic violence negatively affects not only the woman being abused, but also her children, partner, and ultimately, the community at large. Mio et al. discuss three major areas of domestic violence against women: partner or intimate violence, rape, and sexual harassment. Mio et al. also discuss cultural factors such as ethnicity, socioeconomic status, and sexual orientation in the prevalence of violence against women.

Hancock's chapter focuses on the mental health research on lesbians, gays, and bisexuals (LGB). She outlines the developmental progression of the research, from initially portraying LGB individuals as mentally ill to research that challenged the idea that homosexuality was pathological, and to more recent research that is descriptive and exploratory in nature, which has provided rich information about the lives of LGB people. Hancock also discusses gender differences, the role of race, ethnicity and culture, bisexuality, relationship, family, and parenting, issues related to LGB youth and older adults, and transgender and identity issues.

Crowther and Zeiss' chapter focuses on the fastest-growing cultural group in the United States—older adults. They discuss how the range of who are considered to be older adults continues to expand, resulting in the group of individuals falling into this category being very diverse with varying social experiences, health issues, and different long-term care needs. In addition, this also has resulted in the need for mental health researchers to take age cohorts into consideration. They also report on the changing demographics of older adults, and the role of ethnicity and minority status among the elderly. Finally, Crowther and Zeiss discuss the need for clinicians to be proficient in clinical geropsychology as a result of the changing demographics among older adults.

Leigh focuses on a group of individuals largely neglected in the mental health literature, those who are deaf. Given the history of discrimination and ignorance of deaf people, the incidence of psychological sequelae related to marginalization and discrimination should not be surprising. Leigh summarizes the paradigms of deaf people as having disabilities and of deaf people having their own culture and how such paradigms have influenced deaf identity. She further examines the role of ethnicity among deaf people and mental health issues.

A growing area of interest in the mental health literature is the interface between mental health and religion/spirituality. Dudley-Grant explores these issues among the major ethnic groups. She notes that for many People of Color, religion and spirituality have always played a major role in their psychological lives. She summarizes many traditional health practices as well as innovative culturally consistent approaches to intervention.

CHAPTER 14

Women's Mental Health Research

History, Current Status, and Future Directions

GAYLE Y. IWAMASA
AUDREY K. BANGI

According to the 2000 U.S. Census, 50.9% of the population was female (U.S. Census Bureau, 2001). Women (defined by the Census Bureau as age 18 years and over) comprised 38.4% of the population, as compared to men, who comprised 35.9% of the population. In terms of older adults (age 65 years and over), 7.3% were women and 5.1% were men. Census projections indicate an increase in the percentage of women age 65 and over for the next 100 years (U.S. Census Bureau, 2000). Thus, women comprise the majority of the adult population, and over time will continue to increase in both numbers and age. The 2000 Census also indicated that a female householder with no partner headed 12.2% of all U.S. households. A total of 7.2% of total households were headed by a single mother with children under the age of 18 years. At press time, data on employment and marital status, educational attainment, disability, income, and other demographic characteristics of U.S. women were not yet available.

Of those individuals who reported one race, 25% of the population was ethnic minority (U.S. Census Bureau, 2001). However, this figure is likely an underestimate, because Hispanic/Latinos were assessed separate from the other "race" categories, yet comprised 12.5% of the population. At press time, a breakdown of race by gender census statistics was not yet available. Thus, the percentage of women among the various ethnic minority groups was yet to be determined.

In addition to older women and ethnic minority women, other groups of women—such as lesbians and bisexuals, disabled women, single mothers, immigrant women, and incarcerated women—are more likely to experience stressors and difficulties in addition to those typically experienced by women who do not possess these characteristics. Discrimination, poverty, and lack of access to mental health services are just a few of the additional problems these women may face. Although it is beyond the scope of this chapter to provide in-depth analysis of the experiences of these groups, information on the mental health of these women is included whenever possible throughout the chapter.

Given that women comprise the majority of the adult U.S. population, it is imperative that mental health practitioners understand the experiences of women and the diverse contexts in which they live. The purpose of this chapter is to provide a summary of the history of mental health research on women, summarize the current status of mental health research on women, and make recommendations for future research on women's mental health. Detailed descriptions of specific research studies are beyond the scope of this chapter. Rather, this chapter provides an overarching review of the literature. However, because violence against women is such a major issue for women's mental health, a separate chapter is dedicated to this issue (see Mio et al., this volume).

HISTORICAL PERSPECTIVE
OF WOMEN'S MENTAL HEALTH

Although women have comprised the majority of the population for many years, there is a long history of neglect of women's mental health in the psychological literature. In reviewing the history of women's physical (and then mental) health, the social and cultural context of what is considered to be appropriate, typical, and "normal" over time must be considered (Sechzer, Pfafflin, Denmark, Griffin, & Blumenthal, 1996). For example, a century ago, women were not supposed to be strong and competent, but instead, often had the role of being the "patient." Given that the medical model typically accepted in the United States has been based on the male body, women were considered to be imperfect (Sechzer et al., 1996). As such, women's health care has always maintained a secondary place in research and treatment, which has contributed to the subordination and oppression of women. This has been particularly problematic because of the assumption that, unless specific to women, the etiology, symptomatology, and treatment of disorders for men and women should be the same (Sechzer, Griffin, & Pfafflin, 1994).

However, in the latter part of the 20th century, women's mental health began receiving more attention. There was movement away from using the male as the model of health, and a gender-comparative model is now more accepted (Blumenthal, 1996; Sechzer et al., 1996). Clearly, the focus on the male as the epitome of mental health has been detrimental to women and has slowed the progression of scientific research on the mental health of women. Recently, national efforts have been established in addressing this inequity. For example, in 1991, the Public Health Service Office on Women's Health (OWH) was created by the U.S. Department of Health and Human Services (DHHS), and in 1993 a Deputy Assistant Secretary for Women's Health was established. The OWH collaborates with other DHHS agencies, federal agencies, researchers, practitioners, consumers, and health profession organizations to promote the emphasis on women's issues in research, training, service delivery, education, and policy.

GENERAL PREVALENCE OF PSYCHOLOGICAL DISORDERS AMONG WOMEN

Although women have longer life expectancies as compared to men, women have higher morbidity and poorer health outcomes, with higher prevalence of certain problems as compared to men (Blumenthal, 1996; National Institutes of Health, 1992). Historically, it was frequently asserted that women suffered from psychiatric disorders at disproportionately higher rates as compared to men (Dohrenwend & Dohrenwend, 1974). However, more recently, according to Rosenfield (1999), although the total rates of psychopathology indicate no gender differences, men and women suffer from different psychological disorders. Blumenthal (1995) reported that women are more likely than men to be diagnosed with mood disorders (including depression and rapid cycling bipolar disorder), eating disorders, somatization disorder, anxiety disorders such as panic disorder and phobias, dissociative disorders, and borderline and histrionic personality disorders. They are also more likely than men to attempt suicide. Rosenfield (1999) suggested that women tend to suffer more from internalizing disorders related to loss, fear, hopelessness, and helplessness, whereas men tend to experience more difficulties with externalizing disorders and express their problems in terms of negative behaviors toward others.

Currently, the interaction between biological and psychosocial factors is believed to explain the differences in prevalence of mental disorders among men and women (Blumenthal, 1996). Gender differences in biological factors such as hormones, brain structure/function, and circadian rhythms point to biological etiology. On the other hand, behavioral and gendered social roles among boy and girls, parental reinforcement of gender roles, peers and society, family environment, and experiences of traumatic events cannot be ignored as etiologic factors.

According to some studies on brain function, women outperform men in terms of cognition, aging, and threat from congenital brain problems (Andreason, 1994). In addition, the fact that women live longer points to some biological "protection" from some psychological problems. However, according to Blumenthal (1996), given that women may have better biological protection from mental disorders, it is highly possible that the life experience of being a woman may account for the higher rates in mental illness among women. For example, she indicates that "inferior social status . . . sexual abuse and sexual discrimination, lack of economic equity, and constricted educational and occupational opportunities" (p. 7) are all possible contributors to the development of mental illness among women.

Women also experience difficulties because of lack of access to appropriate mental health services. For example, many women are among the working poor and do not have health insurance coverage for mental health problems. In addition, lack of knowledge about mental health and coping skills is problematic. Women are also more likely to be subject to interpersonal violence such as rape, domestic violence, and other physical crimes than men, and the resources and social context often do not support women for addressing the psychological sequelae of these traumas (Peplau, DeBro, Veniegas, & Taylor, 1999).

RESEARCH ON RATES
OF SPECIFIC PSYCHOLOGICAL DISORDERS

In writing this section, we are aware of the controversies regarding gender bias in the *DSM* classification system. Some of the controversies include some of the personality disorders, premenstrual dysphoric disorder, and factitious disorders such as Munchausen by Proxy Syndrome. A review of these controversies is beyond the scope of this chapter and will not be covered. However, we encourage readers interested in reviewing these controversies to consult Allison and Roberts (1998), Caplan (1992), Figert (1996), Gallant and Hamilton (1988), Lerman (1996), Tavris (1992), and Widiger (1998). Although not a comprehensive list, these readings will familiarize readers with the various arguments pertaining to the political issues surrounding the role of gender in psychiatric diagnoses. Instead, we present a summary of the research on some of the major psychological disorders affecting women.

Mood Disorders

Depression

Women have consistently been found to be diagnosed with depression significantly more than men, and reported gender differences have ranged from two to four times higher (Kornstein, 1997; Sprock & Yoder, 1997). Many readers are likely familiar with Nolen-Hoeksema's (1987) seminal article on sex differences in unipolar depression. She suggested that the sex differences in depression may result from differences in how women and men respond to their depressive symptoms. More recently, Nolen-Hoeksema (1995) provided an updated review of theories of sex differences in depression that indicated that explanations that biological and personality factors account for the differences have not been supported. She again indicated that women and men have different coping styles and are more likely to experience problems such as discrimination and interpersonal violence, which clearly increase the risk of depression. Kornstein (1997) echoed these assertions and also suggested that gender differences in the presentation, course, and response to both medication and psychotherapy indicate that gender-specific assessments and treatments for depression should be developed. Sprock and Yoder (1997) also suggested that methodological issues and sex bias in the research on depression in women must be examined. Furthermore, in focusing on Puerto Rican women, Koss-Chioino (1999) pointed out that culture and ethnicity must be taken into consideration in assessing the etiology and experience of depression of Women of Color.

Not surprisingly, research also has indicated that rates of depression are higher among women with a history of heavy alcohol use (Dixit & Crum, 2000), binge eating disorder (Telch & Stice, 1998), domestic violence (Watson, Barnett, Nikunen, Schultz,

Randolph-Elgin, & Mendez, 1997), poor and/or homeless mothers (Bassuk, Buckner, Perloff, & Bassuk, 1998), and marital problems (Bruce & Kim, 1992). Interestingly, Bruce and Kim also found that the prevalence of depression among women who rated themselves as happily married was 3.7 times greater than for happily married men. In terms of age, in an epidemiologic study of depression, Wu and Anthony (2000) also found that the prevalence of depression among women appears to peak in young adulthood and then again after age 60, which suggested implications for societal contexts in which women live across the lifespan. Additionally, some researchers contend that Asian Americans may somatize their distress (Zheng, Lin, Takeuichi, Kurasaki, Wang, & Cheung, 1997), thus, ethnic group differences among women likely exist across the lifespan.

Depression During and After Pregnancy

Altshuler, Hendrick and Cohen (1998) reported that factors such as prior history of depression, younger age, lack of social support, living alone, more children, relationship conflict, and ambivalence about pregnancy increase the risk of depression during pregnancy. It has been suggested that the experience of mild affective distress following giving birth, commonly known as postpartum blues, is fairly common and temporary (O'Hara, 1987). Postpartum depression is more severe and affects a smaller percentage of women, as is postpartum psychosis. The prevalence rates of postpartum depression in the literature have varied, and in community samples rates of 9.3% (Campbell & Cohen, 1991) to 18.7% to 23.3% (Stuart, Couser, Schilder, O'Hara, & Gorman, 1998) have been reported. However, in a recent meta-analysis, O'Hara and Swain (1996) found a 13% prevalence rate of postpartum depression in 59 studies.

Kumar (1994) argued that maternity blues, postpartum depression, and postpartum psychosis do not vary across cultures or ethnic groups, and reported that incidence rates have not changed in 150 years. Nonacs and Cohen (1998) argued that despite its prevalence, assessment of postpartum depression is often overlooked. Altshuler et al. (1998) reported that women with preexisting psychological problems are at most risk for developing postpartum depression and the risk factors are similar to the risk factors for depression during pregnancy.

Bipolar Disorders

Leibenluft's (1996) review of the literature on bipolar disorder found that rapid cycling of episodes is more common among women; women with bipolar disorder have more depressive episodes and less manic episodes, and may be more likely to experience mixed episodes as compared to men. Leibenluft (1996) reported that besides research on postpartum mania and depression, there is little research on the effects of other female reproductive system events on the course of bipolar disorder. In a critique of Leibenluft's review, Zibin, Nolet, and O'Croinin (1997) emphasized the need to also examine social issues faced by women such as custody hearings and physical abuse on the development of bipolar disorder.

Anxiety Disorders

Yonkers and Gurgis (1995) reviewed the literature on the prevalence of anxiety disorders among women and found that women have higher rates of the following disorders: specific phobia, social phobia, panic disorder with agoraphobia, and generalized anxiety disorder. In addition, they reported that the course of illness of many anxiety disorders, particularly obsessive-compulsive disorder, is longer and has greater morbidity in women. They further reported that women have higher risk for developing posttraumatic stress disorder (PTSD) and are more likely to experience trauma as a result of sexual abuse or incest.

More recent research, such as Howell, Brawman-Mintzer, Monnier, and Yonkers (2001) supports the findings that generalized anxiety disorder is more prevalent in women. Furthermore, there is some indication that although women and men do not differ in the lifetime prevalence of exposure to traumatic events, women are more likely to develop PTSD when experiencing a traumatic event (Breslau, Davis, Andreski, Peterson, & Schultz, 1997) and are more at risk of developing depression and alcohol use disorders following the onset of PTSD (Breslau, Davis, Peterson, & Scultz, 1997).

Substance Abuse

Wilsnack and Wilsnack's (1991) review of the literature on women's drinking found that women's pattern of drinking was somewhat stable and that regardless of age and ethnicity, men's drinking exceeded that of women's. However, the researchers also noted that, among the heaviest drinkers, women reported the same high level of alcohol consumption as men. These women also reported higher levels of fighting with both spouse and non–family members. Several within-group differences were noted— women between the ages of 21 and 34 years reported more drinking problems than women who were older, and engaged in heavy episodic drinking (i.e., 6+ drinks/day). Women between the ages of 35 and 49 who had drinking problems were more likely to report chronic drinking problems. Their review also indicated that research on women's drinking must reflect the complexities of subgroups of women, such as age cohorts, ethnic minority women, employment status and setting, and marital status.

El-Guebaly's (1995) review indicated that women have a higher physical vulnerability to alcohol and are more likely to report a traumatic event associated with the onset of substance abuse. However, women are more likely to receive treatment earlier than men. Intravenous drug use also affects women's risk of HIV infection and attributed to approximately 35% of AIDS cases diagnosed among women between July 1999 and June 2000 (Centers for Disease Control and Prevention [CDC], 2000).

Regarding other illicit drug use, Lex (1995) reported that women typically use marijuana, cocaine, and heroin at rates lower than men. Similar to men, drug use and crime are also associated for women. Lex reported that incarcerated women reported major drug use (39%) and intoxication (34%) at the time of arrest. Also, many women reported beginning drug use, particularly marijuana and heroin, because their partners and/or friends were users. Thus, drug use in women is often initiated in the context of social relationships. Room (1996) also emphasized the need for more research on the roles of contextual variables such as courtship; sexuality; parenthood; peer relationships; work roles; social control by spouse, relatives, or friends; and the role of violence and abuse as gender-specific predictors of substance use.

Regarding treatment, many researchers note that problems such as bias toward conceptualizing alcohol and drug use as a "male" problem has interfered with the development of appropriate assessment and treatment for women. Researchers have noted client variables such as helpseeking (Weisner & Schmidt, 1992), social context (Bushway & Heiland, 1995), patterns of abuse (Yaffe, Jenson, & Howard, 1995), and treatment variables such as predominantly male treatment providers (Abbot, 1994) and lack of gender-sensitive treatment environments (e.g., lack of child care; Schober & Annis, 1996) affect the success, or lack thereof, of substance abuse treatment for women. Furthermore, issues such as pregnancy (Grella, 1996) and rural populations (Booth & McLaughlin, 2000) are often not considered in substance abuse treatment.

Eating Disorders

Woodside and Kennedy's (1995) review of the literature indicated that diagnosis of eating disorders among men is rare. Their review also indicated that the prevalence rate of eating disorders ranges between 0.3% and 6.0% among women and 0.02% and 4.0% among men. Preliminary data suggest that the age of onset is in early adulthood, typically between 18.6 and 21 years of age. In summarizing potential sources of etiology of eating disorders, Woodside and Kennedy discuss genetic, biological, and social factors such as the meaning of puberty and media attention regarding weight loss, and conclude that the etiology is likely multidetermined.

Binge eating disorder has received increasing attention in the psychopathology literature. Recent data from a community study suggest that women diagnosed with binge eating disorder were more likely to have comorbid psychopathology, particularly depression, and also any Axis I and Axis II disorder (when collapsed across disorders) as compared to control group participants (Telch & Stice, 1998). However, some of the rates found were no different from other epidemiologic studies. Additionally, Bulik, Sullivan, Carter, and Joyce (1996) suggested that early-onset anxiety disorders may be a precursor to bulimia nervosa, because presence of an anxiety disorder was related to a history of anorexia nervosa and early onset of drug or alcohol abuse.

Researchers also have begun to examine the role of ethnicity and culture in eating disorders. In a study of college women, Mullholland and Mintz (2001) found that although none of their 413 African-American women participants were classified as having anorexia nervosa or bulimia nervosa, 2% were classified as having an eating disorder NOS and 23% reported symptoms of eating disorders. The authors suggested that these rates were an underestimate and that additional research is needed. Geller and Thomas (1999) reviewed the literature on immigrant women to Western countries and suggested that the rates of eating disorders among immigrant women were higher than women in their native country. Geller and Thomas reviewed issues such as parental separation, the role of culture such as values and intergenerational conflict, country of origin, and religious adherence in the development of eating disorders among immigrant women. Clearly, more research is needed on the prevalence of eating disorders among this growing group of women.

PROBLEMS WITH PSYCHOLOGICAL SEQUELAE

Sexual Abuse

Finkelhor, Hotaling, Lewis, and Smith's (1990) national survey indicated that 27% of the women and 16% of the men participants reported some form of victimization. Median age of abuse was similar (9.6 years for girls and 9.9 years for boys). However, girls were more likely to be abused by a family member (29% as compared to 11% for boys). Perpetrators of abuse for both boys and girls were more likely to be men (98% for girls and 83% for boys). Most participants reported that the experience was a one-time event, whereas 11% of girls and 8% of boys reported that sexual abuse lasted more than a year. Finkelhor et al. (1990) reported that risk factors for sexual abuse included unhappy family life, being raised in the West Coast/Pacific geographical region, and missing one natural parent.

In a study based on the Epidemiologic Catchment Area (ECA) study, Stein, Golding, Siegel, Burnam, and Sorenson (1988) found that over 75% of the women respondents who reported childhood sexual abuse reported at least one psychological symptom, with anxiety, anger, guilt, and depression being the most commonly reported symptoms. Wyatt (1991) reported that sexual dysfunction is a frequent problem among childhood sexual abuse survivors. Gleason (1993) found high prevalence for sexual dysfunction, depression, PTSD, generalized anxiety disorder, and obsessive-compulsive disorder among a sample of 62 battered women.

Wyatt (1991) also summarized the difficulties of defining childhood sexual abuse in the research literature. Additional areas receiving increased attention have focused on ascertaining why some women do not develop PTSD or other severe symptoms following abuse. Williams (1994) conducted an interesting prospective study on memories of childhood sexual abuse and in a sample of 129 African-American women abused approximately 17 years earlier, 38% did not recall the abuse. Williams found that women less likely to recall the abuse were younger at the time of the abuse and were molested by someone they knew. More research is needed to identify both risk and protective factors for the development of distress following abuse.

HIV/AIDS

One of the most pressing health concerns affecting women is HIV/AIDS, reflected by the rise in the proportion of all AIDS cases reported among adult and adolescent women from 7% in 1985 to 23% in 1998 (CDC, 2001). Rates among Women of Color are particularly alarming, with Latina and African-American women accounting for approximately 78% of the total reported AIDS cases among women through 2000 (CDC, 2000). In fact, research indicates that a range of contextual factors promotes risk of HIV infection in the economically disadvantaged and marginalized communities within which many of these women live. Such influences on women's sexual behavior include gender roles, religious norms, cultural values associated with sexuality and sexual expression, and relational barriers to HIV protection (Sherr, 1996; Wingwood & DiClemente, 2000).

HIV/AIDS also significantly complicate the mental and physical health of women. Women living with HIV/AIDS face possible isolation and stigma upon disclosure of their status, conflicting interpersonal demands, and challenges related to their multiple roles as caregivers and partners (Lamping & Mercey, 1996). Difficulties in service utilization and culturally distinct conceptualizations of health care needs further impact treatment of the consequences of HIV infection (Stoller, 1997). HIV/AIDS influence a woman's decisions regarding pregnancy as well, especially in her views of the effectiveness of medications in reducing the risk of mother–child HIV transmission and in her expectations of motherhood in the context of managing a chronic illness (Siegel & Schrimshaw, 2001). Women living with HIV/AIDS also may confront issues of suicide, existential dilemmas, multiple losses/grief, AIDS dementia, and neurological diseases affected by psychiatric symptoms (e.g., toxoplasmosis and psychosis, dementia and depression, cryptococcal meningitis, and mania; Uldall, 1997).

Homelessness

The mental health of the homeless population is understudied (Banyard & Graham-Bermann, 1998). Even more understudied are women, who represent a growing number among those who are homeless. Our knowledge about these women often comes from surveys of social service providers or from women in shelters (DiBlasio & Belcher, 1995). This literature suggests that many homeless women are single parents who face difficulties accessing affordable childcare services and meeting gynecological and prenatal health care needs in addition to confronting poverty and the scarcity of affordable housing (Buckner, Bassuk, & Zima, 1993). These mothers as well as single women who are homeless, however, are vulnerable to family disruption, domestic violence, violent crimes, rape, and sexually transmitted diseases (Buckner, et al., 1993; DiBlasio & Belcher, 1995).

Given this background, it is not surprising that homeless women generally suffer from disproportionately high rates of psychological distress and mental health problems, including depression, posttraumatic reactions, sexual problems, and drug and alcohol abuse (Buckner, et al., 1993). Homeless women also may be diagnosed with disorders such as schizophrenia or antisocial personality disorder, or be dually diagnosed (Brunette & Drake, 1998). Yet, regardless of whether the mental health problems predate the homelessness or are sequelae resulting from becoming homeless, the need for treatment remains both imperative and challenging.

TREATMENT ISSUES

Help-Seeking and Service Utilization

It is generally well-accepted that regardless of rates of psychological distress, women are more likely to seek mental health services than men. However, gender issues in help-seeking and utilization of services is much more complex than a simple assessment of usage. For example, in examining a portion of the ECA data, Leaf and Bruce (1987) found that women were more likely than men to seek help from a primary care physician; they found no gender differences in use of mental health services. Furthermore, they found that among those individuals diagnosed with a disorder, women with positive attitudes toward services and men with negative attitudes toward services had higher rates of service utilization. Rhodes and Goering (1994) emphasized the need to assess social roles and behaviors of men and women in examining gender differences in helpseeking and service utilization. Finally, Padgett, Patrick, Burns, and Schlesinger's (1994) review of insured participants found that African-American and Hispanic women had lower utilization of mental health services.

Pharmacotherapy

Hohmann's (1989) review of data from the 1985 National Ambulatory Medical Care Survey found that women were more likely to be prescribed antianxiety and antidepressant medication in primary care settings as compared to men. Furthermore, this sex difference in prescription of psychotropic medication appears to be global (Ashton, 1991; Linden, Lecrubier, Bellantuono, Benkert, Kisely, & Simon, 1999; Silverstone, 1998). In recent years, many researchers have noted the problems associated with the lack of research on pharmacokinetics of psychotropic medications (e.g., Dawkins, Rudorfer, & Potter, 1993; Lewis-Hall, 1999). For example, researchers have noted sex differences in side effect profiles, medication response, and dosage requirements (Pigott, 1998; Smith & Lin, 1996). The need for research on the effects of psychotropic medications among women is particularly important given potential differences owing to age, sex/gender, culture, race, ethnicity, or socioeconomic status (Ackerman, 1999).

Mental Health Services

Levin, Blanch, and Jennings' (1998) book, *Women's Mental Health Services: A Public Health Perspective* is an excellent review of the issues related to women's mental health services and includes chapters that focus on specific subpopulations of women, such as women with severe mental illness (Blanch, Nicholson, & Purcell, 1998; Mowbray, Oyserman, Saunders, & Rueda-Riedle, 1998), incarcerated women (Veysey, 1998), and older women (Padgett, Burns, & Grau, 1998). The book demonstrates the movement of infusing the needs of women into mental health service delivery.

Feminist Therapy

Treatment issues for women would not be complete without mentioning the significant literature on feminist therapy. Since its emergence in the 1970s, this field has contributed perspectives that mark a distinct departure from the traditional focus on internal causes of psychological problems such as on an individual's deficits and flawed beliefs (Travis & Compton, 2001). Stemming from a framework rooted in diversity, activism, and empowerment, feminist approaches to research and therapeutic interventions strive toward changing the oppressive systems within which women live and interact (Liss, Hoffner, & Crawford, 2000). These approaches not only critically address the influence of socioculturally constructed gender roles and the imbalance of power, but also suggest proactive solutions to these problems.

Although significant strides have been made in promoting the health of women by looking through a feminist lens, additional efforts are required to help ensure that the changing needs of women are adequately met. For instance, Russo and Vaz (2001) emphasize that the complex issues affecting Women of Color must continue to be addressed, given the multitude of social ills (e.g., racial and ethnic discrimination, unemployment, insufficient housing, violence) that they often face and that impact their sense of self. Indeed, the issues of culturally diverse women are often left out of discussions of feminist approaches to therapy. Comas-Díaz and Greene's (1994) groundbreaking book *Women of Color: Integrating Ethnic and Gender Identities in Psychotherapy* remains one of few resources available that focuses on the roles of ethnicity among women in psychotherapy.

IMPLICATIONS

Implications for Clinical Practice

Depending on the setting and environment in which clinicians work, the practitioner is often very busy, with little time in between sessions to review notes and recollect prior sessions. Additionally, in the context of managed care, many practitioners are unduly burdened with paperwork. Thus, it is particularly important that practitioners put concerted effort into understanding the context of their women clients. Clearly, services should be tailored to the specific needs of women (Padgett, 1997).

Clinicians must be aware of how their own personal worldview affects their clinical judgment, and that client characteristics such as gender, ethnicity, age, and social class have strong stimulus value to all of us. Being cognizant of one's own biases and perceptions about women and beliefs about roles of women should be a priority of all clinicians who work with women. Sechzer et al.'s (1996) book *Women and Mental Health* contains several chapters that summarize the unique experiences of Latinas (Gil, 1996), Asian-American women (Shum, 1996), African-American women (Chisholm, 1996; Greene, 1996), and older women (Nadien, 1996). It would behoove practitioners unfamiliar with the heterogeneity among women in these groups to review these chapters.

Implications for Future Research

Certainly, the growing literature and the availability of research funding on women's mental health is a positive indication of the progression and development of rigorous research on women. The existing literature provides a strong base and direction for continuing research on women's mental health. Future research must continue to focus on the role of biological and social risk factors in the development of psychological distress among women. In particular, the impact of life stressors faced disproportionately by women such as interpersonal violence, competing role demands, low socioeconomic status, and societal expectations, on the development of distress must be examined.

Researchers must continue to examine treatment issues such as accessibility, helpseeking, and form and structure of treatment for women. Research on psychopharmacology for women must continue. How the mental health "system" treats girls and women also must be examined. The effects of clinician values and perceptions of girls and women on their treatment of girls and women must be examined. This is particularly important, because many health care providers are faced with requirements to save costs by third parties (Padgett, 1997).

In achieving the goals of the Decade of Behavior (a movement sponsored by the American Psychological Association and a number of other organizations to emphasize the role of behavioral science in problem-solving issues of national significance) it is also important to bridge the gaps between scientific research related to the well-being of women and practical applications of the findings in community and clinical settings (Worell, 2001). Furthermore, Travis and Compton (2001) insist that a more contextual understanding of the issues affecting women's experiences of health is integral to improving their access to and quality of care.

Finally, as with the general mental health research literature, researchers must move beyond studying predominantly middle-class, middle-aged, White women and seek to understand the complex lives of Women of Color, homeless women, aging women, lesbian and bisexual women, and women living in rural areas. Just as mental health models of men are not appropriate for women, models of mental health for middle-class, middle-aged White women are frequently not appropriate for women not sharing those demographic characteristics.

Implications for Training Mental Health Practitioners

One may argue that practitioners who provide treatment to women are only as good as their training. If this is the case, it is incumbent on educators and supervisors of those who will engage in applied practice with women to be aware of the multitude of women's issues such that they can provide appropriate supervision and training to both women and men who will be providing treatment to women. Given that the training and supervisory relationship itself is a power hierarchy (Kaiser, 1997) and gender of both supervisor/trainer and supervisee/trainee obviously affects the supervisory/training relationship, we have yet to know how such issues affect treatment outcome for women.

Munson (1997) provided an excellent review of some of the issues related to gender in supervision and noted that the literature on gender issues in supervision has not kept up with the changing feminization of clinical practice. Banks (2001) echoed this problem and called for the need to examine the European-American perspective of training that predominates supervision given the growth of feminist therapy and the changing demographics of the United States. Feminist therapy supervision emphasizes ethical issues, collaboration, personal disclosure by the supervisor, discussions of power and authority, and advocacy (Porter et al., 1997). Such discussions are promising and must be followed by outcome data on the types of training practitioners receive and the quality of mental health services that women receive.

SUMMARY AND CONCLUSION

In general, an impressive literature on the mental health of women has developed over the past few decades. Acknowledgment of the need to move beyond a "male" model of mental health has spurred a plethora of research on a wide variety of psychological disorders and treatment. Although still in its relative infancy, the research accumulated thus far indicates that the context of women's lives and the resulting psychological experiences of women are complex and warrant further investigation. Researchers and funding agencies are finally acknowledging that there exist unique issues and experiences specific to women (e.g., sexual abuse and assault, pregnancy and maternity, physiologic and hormonal, etc.) which must be examined. As the field of women's mental health continues to grow, clinicians and researchers are urged to continue examining the complex lives of *all* women, and not continue to focus solely on the lives of middle-class, middle-aged White women.

REFERENCES

Abbott, A. A. (1994). A feminist approach to substance abuse treatment and service delivery. *Social Work in Health Care, 19,* 67–83.

Ackerman, R. J. (1999). An interactional approach for pharmacopsychologists and psychologists: Gender concerns. *Journal of Clinical Psychology in Medical Settings, 6,* 39–61.

Allison, D. B., & Roberts, M. S. (1998). *Disordered mother or disorders diagnosis?: Munchausen by Proxy Syndrome.* Hillsdale, NJ: The Analytic Press.

Altshuler, L. L., Hendrick, V., & Cohen L. S. (1998). Course of mood and anxiety disorders during pregnancy and the postpartum period. *Journal of Clinical Psychiatry, 59,* 29–33.

Andreason, N. (1994). Gender differences in the normal brain: Implications for mental illness. *Journal of Women's Health, 3,* 495.

Ashton, H. (1991). Psychotropic-drug prescribing for women. *British Journal of Psychiatry, 158,* 30–35.

Banks, A. (2001). Tweaking the Euro-American perspective: Infusing cultural awareness and sensitivity into the supervision of family therapy. *Family Journal-Counseling & Therapy for Couples & Families, 9,* 420–423.

Banyard, V. L., & Graham-Bermann, S. A. (1998). Surviving poverty: Stress and coping in the lives of housed and homeless mothers. *American Journal of Orthopsychiatry, 68*, 479–488.

Bassuk, E. L., Buckner, J. C., Perloff, J. N., & Bassuk, S. S. (1998). Prevalence of mental health and substance use disorders among homeless and low-income housed mothers. *American Journal of Psychiatry, 155*, 1561–1564.

Blanch, A. K., Nicholson, J., & Purcell, J. (1998). Parents with severe mental illness and their children: The need for human services integration. In B. L. Levin, A. K. Blanch, & A. Jennings (Eds.), *Women's mental health services: A public health perspective* (pp. 201–214). Thousand Oaks, CA: Sage.

Blumenthal, S. J. (1995). Improving women's mental and physical health: Federal initiatives and programs. *American Psychiatric Press Review of Psychiatry, 14*, 181–204.

Blumenthal, S. J. (1996). Women's mental health: The new national focus. In J. A. Sechzer, S. M. Pfafflin, F. L. Denmark, A. Griffin, & S. J. Blumenthal (Eds.), *Women and mental health* (pp. 1–16). New York: New York Academy of Sciences.

Booth, B. M., & McLaughlin, Y. S. (2000). Barriers to and need for alcohol services for women in rural populations. *Alcoholism: Clinical and Experimental Research, 24*, 1267–1275.

Breaslau, N., Davis, G. C., Andreski, P., Peterson, E. L., & Schultz, L. R. (1997). Sex differences in posttraumatic disorder. *Archives of General Psychiatry, 54*, 1044–1048.

Breaslau, N., Davis, G. C., Peterson, E. L., & Schultz, L. R. (1997). Psychiatric sequelae of posttraumatic disorder in women. *Archives of General Psychiatry, 54*, 81–87.

Bruce, M. L., & Kim, K. M. (1992). Differences in the effects of divorce on major depression in men and women. *American Journal of Psychiatry, 149*, 914–917.

Brunette, M., & Drake, R. E. (1998). Gender differences in homeless persons with schizophrenia and substance abuse. *Community Mental Health Journal, 34*, 627–639.

Bulik, C. M., Sullivan, P. F., Carter, F. A., & Joyce, P. R. (1996). Lifetime anxiety disorders in women with bulimia nervosa. *Comprehensive Psychiatry, 37*, 368–374.

Buckner, J. C., Bassuk, E. L., & Zima, B. T. (1993). Mental health issues affecting homeless women: Implications for intervention. *American Journal of Orthopsychiatry, 6*, 385–399.

Bushway, D., & Heiland, L. (1995). Women in treatment for addiction: What's new in the literature? *Alcoholism Treatment Quarterly, 13*, 83–96.

Campbell, S. B., & Cohen, J. F. (1991). Prevalence and correlates of postpartum depression in first-time mothers. *Journal of Abnormal Psychology, 100*, 594–599.

Caplan, P. J. (1992). Gender issues in the diagnosis of mental disorder. *Women & Therapy, 12*, 71–82.

Centers for Disease Control and Prevention. (2001). *HIV/AIDS among U.S. Women: Minority and young women at continuing risk.* Accessed: http://www.cdc.gov/pubs/facts/women.html [December 15, 2001].

Centers for Disease Control and Prevention. (2000). *HIV/AIDS Surveillance Report, 12*, 1–45.

Chisholm, J. F. (1996). Mental health issues in African-American women. In J. A. Sechzer, S. M. Pfafflin, F. L. Denmark, A. Griffin, & S. J. Blumenthal (Eds.), *Women and Mental Health* (pp. 161–180). New York: New York Academy of Sciences.

Comas-Díaz, L. & Greene, B. (1994). *Women of Color: Integrating ethnic and gender identities in psychotherapy.* New York: Guilford.

Dawkins, K., Rudorfer, M. V., & Potter, W. Z. (1993). Comments on gender differences in pharmacokinetics and pharmacodynamics. *American Journal of Psychiatry, 150*, 678–679.

DiBlasio, F. A., & Belcher, J. R. (1995). Gender differences among homeless persons: Special services in women. *American Journal of Orthopsychiatry, 65*, 131–137.

Dixit, A. R., & Crum, R. M. (2000). Prospective study of depression and the risk of heavy alcohol use in women. *American Journal of Psychiatry, 157*, 751–758.

Dohrenwend, B. P., & Dohrenwend, B. S. (1974). Sex differences and psychiatric disorders. *American Journal of Sociology, 81*, 1447–1454.

El-Guebaly, N. (1995). Alcohol and polysubstance abuse among women. *Canadian Journal of Psychiatry, 40,* 73–79.

Figert A. E. (1996). *Women and the ownership of PMS: The structuring of a psychiatric disorder.* Hawthorne, NY: Aldine de Gruyter.

Finkelhor, D., Hotaling, G., Lewis, I. A., & Smith, C. (1990). Sexual abuse in a national survey of adult men and women: Prevalence, characteristics, and risk factors. *Child Abuse and Neglect, 14,* 19–28.

Gallant, S. J., & Hamilton, J. A. (1988). On a premenstrual psychiatric diagnosis: What's in a name? *Professional Psychology: Research and Practice, 19,* 271–278.

Geller, G., & Thomas, C. D. (1999). A review of eating disorders in immigrant women: Possible evidence for a culture-change model. *Eating Disorders, 7,* 279–299.

Gil, R. M. (1996). Hispanic women and mental health. In J. A. Sechzer, S. M. Pfafflin, F. L. Denmark, A. Griffin, & S. J. Blumenthal (Eds.), *Women and Mental Health* (pp. 147–160). New York: New York Academy of Sciences.

Gleason, W. J. (1993). Mental disorders in battered women: An empirical study. *Violence and Victims, 1,* 53–68.

Greene, B. (1996). African-American women: Considering diverse identities and societal barriers in psychotherapy. In J. A. Sechzer, S. M. Pfafflin, F. L. Denmark, A. Griffin, & S. J. Blumenthal (Eds.), *Women and Mental Health* (pp. 191–210). New York: New York Academy of Sciences.

Grella, C. E. (1996). Background and overview of mental health and substance abuse treatment systems: Meeting the needs of women who are pregnant or parenting. *Journal of Psychoactive Drugs, 28,* 319–343.

Hohmann, A. A. (1989). Gender bias in psychotropic drug prescribing in primary care. *Medical Care, 27,* 478–490.

Howell, H. B., Brawman-Mintzer, O., Monnier, J., & Yonkers, K. A. (2001). Generalized anxiety disorder in women. *Psychiatric Clinics of North America, 24,* 165–178.

Kaiser, T. L. (1997). *Supervisory relationships: Exploring the human element.* Pacific Grove, CA: Brooks/Cole.

Kornstein, S. G. (1997). Gender differences in depression: Implications for treatment. *Journal of Clinical Psychiatry, 58,* 12–18.

Koss-Chioino, J. D. (1999). Depression among Puerto Rican women: Culture, etiology and diagnosis. *Hispanic Journal of Behavioral Sciences, 21,* 330–350.

Kumar, R. (1994). Postnatal mental illness: A transcultural perspective. *Social Psychiatry and Psychiatric Epidemiology, 29,* 250–264.

Lamping, D. L., & Mercey, D. (1996). Health-related quality of life in women with HIV infection. In L. Sherr, C. Hankins, & L. Bennett (Eds.), *AIDS as a gender issue: Psychosocial perspectives* (pp. 78–98). Philadelphia: Taylor & Francis.

Leaf, P. J., & Bruce, M. L. (1987). Gender differences in the use of mental health-related services: A re-examination. *Journal of Health and Social Behavior, 28,* 171–183.

Leibenluft, E. (1996). Women with bipolar illness: Clinical and research issues. *American Journal of Psychiatry, 153,* 163–173.

Lerman, H. (1996). *Pigeonholing women's misery: A history and critical analysis of the psychodiagnosis of women in the twentieth century.* New York: Basic Books.

Levin, B. L., Blanch, A. K., & Jennings, A. (1998). *Women's mental health services: A public health perspective.* Thousand Oaks, CA: Sage.

Lewis-Hall, F. (1999). Gender differences in psychotropic medications. In J. M. Herrera & W. B. Lawson (Eds.), *Cross-cultural psychiatry* (pp. 315–312). Chichester, England: Wiley.

Lex, B. W. (1995). Alcohol and other psychoactive substance dependence in women and men. In M. V. Seeman (Ed.), *Gender and Psychopathology* (pp. 311–358). Washington, DC: American Psychiatric Press.

Linden, M., Lecrubier, Y., Bellantuono, C., Benkert, O., Kisely, S. & Simon, G. (1999). The prescribing of psychotropic drugs by primary care physicians: An international collaborative study. *Journal of Clinical Psychopharmacology, 19*, 132–140.

Liss, M., Hoffner, C., & Crawford, M. (2000). What do feminists believe? *Psychology of Women Quarterly, 24*, 279–284.

Mowbray, C. T., Oyserman, D., Saunders, D., & Rueda-Riedle, A. (1998). Women with severe mental disorders: Issues and service needs. In B. L. Levin, A. K. Blanch, & A. Jennings (Eds.), *Women's Mental Health Services: A Public Health Perspective* (pp. 175–200). Thousand Oaks, CA: Sage.

Mullholland, A. M., & Mintz, L. B. (2001). Prevalence of eating disorders among African American women. *Journal of Counseling Psychology, 48*, 111–116.

Munson, C. E. (1997). Gender and psychotherapy supervision: The partnership model. In C. E. Watkins (Ed.), *Handbook of psychotherapy supervision* (pp. 549–569). New York: Wiley.

Nadien, M. (1996). Aging women: Issues of mental health and maltreatment. In J. A. Sechzer, S. M. Pfafflin, F. L. Denmark, A. Griffin, & S. J. Blumenthal (Eds.), *Women and Mental Health* (pp. 129–146). New York: New York Academy of Sciences.

National Institutes of Health, Office of Research on Women's Health. (1992). *Report of the National Institutes of Health: Opportunities for research on women's health.* (NIH Publication Number 92-3457). Washington, DC: U.S. Government Printing Office.

Nolen-Hoeksema, S. (1987). Sex differences in unipolar depression: Evidence and theory. *Psychological Bulletin, 101*, 259–282.

Nolen-Hoeksema, S. (1995). Epidemiology and theories of gender differences in unipolar depression. In M. V. Seeman (Ed.), *Gender and Psychopathology* (pp. 63–87). Washington, DC: American Psychiatric Press.

Nonacs, R., & Cohen, L. S. (1998). Postpartum mood disorders: Diagnosis and treatment guidelines. *Journal of Clinical Psychiatry, 59*, 34–40.

O'Hara, M. W. (1987). Post-partum 'blues,' depression, and psychosis: A review. *Journal of Psychosomatic Obstetrics and Gynecology, 7*, 205–227.

O'Hara, M. W., & Swain, A. M. (1996). Rates and risk of postpartum depression: A meta-analysis. *International Review of Psychiatry, 8*, 37–54.

Padgett, D. K. (1997). Women's mental health: Some directions for research. *American Journal of Orthopsychiatry, 67*, 522–534.

Padgett, D. K., Burns, B. J. & Grau, L. A. (1998). Risk factors and resilience: Mental health needs and service use of older women. In B. L. Levin, A. K. Blanch, & A. Jennings (Eds.), *Women's mental health services: A public health perspective* (pp. 390–413). Thousand Oaks, CA: Sage.

Padgett, D. K., Patrick, C., Burns, B. J., & Schlesinger, H. J. (1994). Women and outpatient mental health services: Use by Black, Hispanic and White women in a national insured population. *Journal of Mental Health Administration, 21*, 347–360.

Peplau, L. A., DeBro, S. C., Veniegas, R. C., & Taylor, P. L. (1999). *Gender, culture, and ethnicity: Current research about women and men.* Mountain View, CA: Mayfield.

Pigott, T. A. (1999). Gender differences in the epidemiology and treatment of anxiety disorders. *Journal of Clinical Psychiatry, 60*, 4–15.

Porter, N., Vasquez, M., Fygetakis, L., Mangione, L., Nickerson, E. T., Pieniadz, J., et al. (1997). Covision: Feminist supervision, process, and collaboration. In J. Worrell & N. G. Johnson (Eds.), *Shaping the future of feminist psychology: Education, research and practice* (pp. 155–171). Washington, DC: American Psychological Association.

Rhodes, A., & Goering, P. (1994). Gender differences in the use of outpatient mental health services. *The Journal of Mental Health Administration, 21*, 338–346.

Robins, L. N., Helzer, J. E., Weissman, M. M. Orvaschel, H., Gruenberg, E., Burke, J. D., et al. (1984). Lifetime prevalence of specific disorders in three sites. *Archives of General Psychiatry, 41*, 949–958.

Room, R. (1996). Gender roles and interactions in drinking and drug use. *Journal of Substance Abuse, 8,* 227–239.

Rosenfield, S. (1999). Splitting the difference: Gender, the self and mental health. In C. S. Aneschensel & J. C. Phelan (Eds.), *Handbook of the Sociology of Mental Health* (pp. 209–224). New York: Kluwer Academic/Plenum.

Russo, N. F., & Vaz, K. (2001). Addressing diversity in the Decade of Behavior: Focus on Women of Color. *Psychology of Women Quarterly, 25,* 280–294.

Schober, R., & Annis, H. M. (1996). Barriers to help-seeking for change in drinking: A gender-focused review of the literature. *Addictive Behaviors, 21,* 81–92.

Sechzer, J. A., Griffin, A., & Pfafflin, S. M. (1994). Women's health and paradigm change. In J. A. Sechzer, A. Griffin, & S. M. Pfafflin (Eds.), *Forging a Women's Health Research Agenda: Policy Issues for the 1990s* (pp. 2–20). New York: New York Academy of Sciences.

Sechzer, J. A., Pfafflin, S. M., Denmark, F. L., Griffin, A., & Blumenthal, S. J. (1996). Women and mental health: An introduction. In J. A. Sechzer, S. M. Pfafflin, F. L. Denmark, A. Griffin, & S. J. Blumenthal (Eds.), *Women and Mental Health* (pp. vii–x). New York: New York Academy of Sciences.

Sherr, L. (1996). Tomorrow's era: Gender, psychology and HIV infection. In L. Sherr, C. Hankins, & L. Bennett (Eds.), *AIDS as a gender issue: Psychosocial perspectives* (pp. 16–45). Philadelphia: Taylor & Francis.

Shum, L. M. (1996). Asian American women: Cultural and mental health issues. In J. A. Sechzer, S. M. Pfafflin, F. L. Denmark, A. Griffin, & S. J. Blumenthal (Eds.), *Women and Mental Health* (pp. 181–190). New York: New York Academy of Sciences.

Siegel, K., & Schrimshaw, E. W. (2001). Reasons and justifications for considering pregnancy among women living with HIV/AIDS. *Psychology of Women Quarterly, 25,* 112–123.

Silverstone, T. (1998). Women and pharmacological therapies. In S. E. Romans (Ed.), *Folding back the shadows: A perspective on women's mental health* (pp. 219-230). Dunedin, New Zealand: University of Otago Press.

Smith, M., & Lin, K. (1996). Gender and ethnic differences in the pharamacogenetics of psychotropics. In M. F. Jensvold, U. Halbreich, & J. A. Hamilton (Eds.), *Psychopharmacology and women: Sex, gender, and hormones* (pp. 121–136). Washington, DC: American Psychiatric Press.

Sprock, J., & Yoder, C. Y. (1997). Women and depression: An update on the report of the APA Task Force. *Sex Roles, 36,* 269–303.

Stein, J. A., Golding, J. M., Siegel, J. M., Burnam, M. A., & Sorenson, S. B. (1988). Long-term psychological sequelae of child sexual abuse. In G. E. Wyatt & G. J. Powell (Eds.), *Lasting Effects of Child Sexual Abuse* (pp.135–154). Newbury Park, CA: Sage.

Stoller, N. E. (1997). Responses to stigma and marginality: The health of lesbians, imprisoned women, and women with HIV. In S. B. Ruzek, V. L. Olesen, & A. E. Clarke (Eds.), *Women's health complexities and differences* (pp. 451–472). Columbus, OH: Ohio State University Press.

Stuart, S., Couser, G., Schilder, K., O'Hara, M. & Gorman, L. (1998). Postpartum anxiety and depression: Onset and comorbidity in a community sample. *Journal of Nervous and Mental Disease, 186,* 420–424.

Swanson, J. W., & Holzer, C. E. (1991). Violence and ECA data. *Hospital and Community Psychiatry, 42,* 954–955.

Tavris, C. (1992). *The mismeasure of woman.* New York: Simon & Schuster.

Telch, C. E., & Stice, E. (1998). Psychiatric comorbidity in women with binge eating disorder: Prevalence rates from a non-treatment-seeking sample. *Journal of Consulting and Clinical Psychology, 66,* 768–776.

Travis, C. B., & Compton, J. D. (2001). Feminism and health in the Decade of Behavior. *Psychology of Women Quarterly, 25,* 312–323.

Uldall, K. K. (1997). The role of psychiatry in HIV care. In M. G. Winiarski (Ed.), *HIV Mental Health for the 21st Century* (pp. 98–115). New York: NYU Press.

U.S. Bureau of the Census. (2000). *National population projections, III. Population pyramids, Total resident population of the United States by sex, middle series.* Accessed: http://www.census.gov/population/www/projections/natchart.html [July 31, 2001].

U.S. Bureau of the Census. (2001). *Profile of general demographic characteristics: 2000 Census of population and housing: United States.* Accessed: http://www.census.gov/prod/cen2000/dp1/2kh00.pdf [July 31, 2001].

Veysey, B. M. (1998). Specific needs of women diagnosed with mental illness in U.S. jails. In B. L. Levin, A. K. Blanch, & A. Jennings (Eds.), *Women's Mental Health Services: A Public Health Perspective* (pp. 368–389). Thousand Oaks, CA: Sage.

Watson, C. G., Barnett, M., Nikunen, L. Schultz, C., Randolph-Elgin, T. & Mendez, C. M. (1997). Lifetime prevalences of nine common psychiatric/personality disorders in female domestic abuse survivors. *Journal of Nervous and Mental Disease, 185,* 645–647.

Weisner, C., & Schmidt, L. (1992). Gender disparities in treatment for alcohol problems. *Journal of the American Medical Association, 268,* 1872–1876.

Widiger, T. A. (1998). Sex biases in the diagnosis of personality disorders. *Journal of Personality Disorders, 12,* 95–118.

Williams, L. M. (1994). Recall of childhood trauma: A prospective study of women's memories of child sexual abuse. *Journal of Consulting and Clinical Psychology, 62,* 1167–1176.

Wilsnack, S. C., & Wilsnack, R. W. (1991). Epidemiology of women's drinking. *Journal of Substance Abuse, 3,* 133–157.

Wingwood, G. M., & DiClemente, R. J. (2000). Application of the theory of gender and power to examine HIV-related exposures, risk factors, and effective interventions for women. *Health Education & Behavior, 27,* 539–565.

Woodside, D. B., & Kennedy, S. H. (1995). Gender differences in eating disorders. In M. V. Seeman (Ed.), *Gender and Psychopathology* (pp. 253–268). Washington, DC: American Psychiatric Press.

Worell, J. (2001). Feminist interventions: Accountability beyond symptom reduction. *Psychology of Women Quarterly, 25,* 335–343.

Wu, L., & Anthony, J. C. (2000). The estimated rate of depressed mood in U.S. adults: Recent evidence for a peak in later life. *Journal of Affective Disorders, 60,* 159–171.

Wyatt, G. E. (1991). Child sexual abuse and its effects on sexual functioning. *Annual Review of Sex Research: An Integrative and Interdisciplinary Review, 2,* 249–266.

Yaffe, J., Jenson, J. M., & Howard, M. O. (1995). Women and substance abuse: Implications for treatment. *Alcoholism Treatment Quarterly, 13,* 1–15.

Yonkers, K. A., & Gurgis, G. (1995). Gender differences in the prevalence and expression of anxiety disorders. In M. V. Seeman (Ed.), *Gender and Psychopathology* (pp. 113–130). Washington, DC: American Psychiatric Press.

Zheng, Y., Lin, M., Takeuichi, D., Kurasaki, K., Wang, Y., & Cheung, F. (1997). An epidemiological study of neurasthenia in Chinese Americans in Los Angeles. *Comprehensive Psychiatry, 38,* 249–259.

Zibin, T., Nolet, C., & O'Croinin, F. (1997). Bipolar women. *American Journal of Psychiatry, 154,* 441.

CHAPTER 15

Violence Against Women

A Silent Pandemic

JEFFERY SCOTT MIO
MARY P. KOSS
MICHELE HARWAY
JAMES M. O'NEIL
ROBERT GEFFNER
BIANCA CODY MURPHY
DAVID C. IVEY

Battering by an intimate partner is the single most common cause of injuries to women requiring medical intervention, accounting for more injuries than automobile accidents, muggings, and rape combined. An estimated 1 million women each year seek medical assistance for injuries resulting from such battering. . . . Injuries vary widely, and can include black eyes, cuts, bruises, concussions, bites, burns, bone fractures, damage to hearing and vision, and knife and bullet wounds (Russo, Denious, Keita, & Koss, 1997, p. 319).

National survey data reveal that 76% of the physical assaults and rapes on women were perpetrated by intimate partners—the very people whom we trust to help keep us safe and secure (Tjaden & Thoennes, 2000). The present chapter examines three major areas of violence against women: partner or intimate violence, rape, and sexual harassment. Despite the alarming incidence of these forms of violence against women, they are markedly underreported and represent a silent pandemic in our society. This chapter is greatly influenced by a landmark book in this area, *No Safe Haven: Male Violence Against Women at Home, at Work, and in the Community* (Koss, Goodman, Browne, Fitzgerald, Keita, & Russo, 1994).

PARTNER VIOLENCE

The opening quote for this chapter underscores how prevalent a problem violence against women is in our society. This section examines the prevalence of partner violence, the resistance against reporting such violence, cultural factors regarding partner violence, and consequences of partner violence. We distinguish "partner violence" from "domestic violence" because domestic violence includes violence against children and elderly adults, whereas the focus of this chapter is on violence against adult women, of which partner violence is a subset. Partner violence refers to the physical acts of aggression that occur in relationships, ranging from punching and slapping to escalated beating and even murder. Physical violence may occur alone, but more typically is expressed together with an ongoing pattern also consisting of psychological abuse and acts of marital/partner rape.

Until recently, most studies of partner violence have been almost exclusively of heterosexual partners, with only limited information about prevalence/incidence of partner violence among gay, lesbian, bisexual, and transgendered people. There is a growing body of evidence that suggests that same-gender partner violence is as common as heterosexual partner violence (Farley, 1996; Renzetti, 1992). The dynamics and types of violence in same-gender relationships are similar to heterosexual partner violence (verbal threats, public humiliation, destruction of property, abuse of children, sexual abuse, and life-threatening acts). Many people do not recognize same-gender partner violence because partner violence is often portrayed as male violence against women. Estimates of the prevalence of abuse in lesbian relationships vary widely as researchers have used different methods and questions to measure abuse. We do not have statistics about intimate partner violence for transgendered individuals in either heterosexual or same-gendered couples, although there is anecdotal evidence that it does occur.

Prevalence Statistics

Physical Violence

Statistics regarding partner physical violence are somewhat elusive in that many people are reticent to report such violence to the police. Moreover, different studies collect data differently, and the way in which the questions are asked have a profound effect upon the prevalence revealed (Koss et al., 1994). Moreover, there is often a distinction between *incidence* versus *prevalence*. Incidence refers to the number of new cases in a fixed period, typically 1 year, whereas prevalence is the cumulative number of people affected over a long period of time, typically the lifetime. Whereas there may be fewer incidents of partner violence occurring in a particular year or from year to year, because the effects of such violence last a long time, prevalence may better capture the full impact of partner violence.

In the National Violence Against Women Survey (Tjaden & Thoennes, 1998, 2000), 51.9% of the female respondents reported a physical assault in their lifetime, compared with 66.4% of the male respondents. However, the picture dramatically reverses when the focus is limited to acts perpetrated by an intimate partner. In their lifetimes, 22.1% of women and 7.4% of men have been physically assaulted by an intimate partner, defined as current and former dates, spouses, and cohabiting partners of both opposite and same sex. Thus, most of the violence experienced by men is at the hands of strangers, whereas women are at greatest danger from their intimate partners. However, although this 3:1 ratio of female-to-male victimization may seem like an important difference, the discrepancy is even larger when seriousness of violence is taken into account. According to the Bureau of Justice Statistics (1997), over 35% of victimized women versus less than 5% of men who have been abused are treated for partner violence–related injuries in hospital emergency departments. "In the United States, women are more likely to be killed by their male partners than by all other · categories of persons combined" (Koss et al., 1994; p. 73).

Partner violence against women occurs early on in relationships as well among established couples. For example, Ellis (1989) and Stets and Pirog-Good (1989) found that the incidence of violence in cohabitating and dating couples is even higher than in marital couples. Supportive of this, White and Koss (1991), in a survey of 2,602 college women, found that 32% of those surveyed on 32 campuses reported physically aggressive behavior from a date or intimate partner. In a recent study of high school students, one in five girls had experienced sexual and/or physical assault by a friend or boyfriend (Silverman, Raj, Mucci, & Hathaway, 2001).

Whereas partner violence is highly prevalent in dating and married couples, it is even more prevalent in couples undergoing a divorce. Although there are some socioeconomic differences, this form of violence cuts across social groups. Frasier (1986) found that 40% of women from lower socioeconomic backgrounds and 25% of women from middle SES backgrounds who were filing for divorce reported that they were victims of physical violence from their partners. Among women who had experienced intimate partner assaults, 77.6% were attacked both before and after the relationship ended (Tjaden & Thoennes, 2000).

Finally, intimate partner violence not only occurs during pregnancy, but pregnancy may increase a woman's chances of being attacked. Around the world, as many as one in every four women is physically abused by the father of her child during her pregnancy (for a review see Heise, Ellsberg, & Gottemoeller, 1999).

Sexual Violence

Prior to the 1970s, laws governing rape across the United States contained an exception clause that precluded men from being charged for rape by their wives. However, since that time these laws have been modified, and most states permit charges of marital rape (Koss et al., 1994; Mio & Foster, 1991). Because this term has not been used until the last couple of decades, many women may not categorize sex forced by their partners as rape. Therefore, statistics for marital rape are difficult to determine. Russell (1982) conservatively estimated that 14% of ever-married women were raped by their husbands or ex-husbands. However, marital sexual assault is rarely reported to law enforcement authorities, and societal sanctions against marital sexual assault are rarely applied, despite the fact that marital rape laws exist in 35 states (cf., Bergen, 1996).

Interestingly, there is evidence that Latinas have adopted more modern conceptualizations of marital rape. Ramos, Koss, and Russo (1999) found that many of their research participants in a focus group format accepted the notion that sex within the context of marriage can be nonconsensual and therefore considered to be rape. They told of incidents in which they did not want to have sex with their husbands but they did so anyway because they thought it was their duty. Nevertheless, in their minds they believed they were being raped by their husbands. These participants were relatively mature (mean age of 31.8 years) and they were generally not acculturated to the United States (16 of the 17 participants were born in Mexico, and 16 of the 17 were monolingual Spanish). Overall, Ramos et al. (1999) concluded that these research participants reflected a mix of traditional Mexican values of sex within marriage, where they are expected to be subservient to their husbands' advances, and modern conceptions of rape, where marital rape is an acceptable categorization of unwanted sex.

Rape also occurs in relationships prior to marriage or cohabitation. College women who were surveyed reported a high incidence of forced sexual intercourse (20%) by age 18 (Brener, McMahon, Warren, & Douglas, 1999). This figure was confirmed by a recent study released by the U.S. Department of Justice that estimated one in five college women would be raped during her educational career (Fisher, Cullen, & Turner, 2000). Among women who have been raped, 32.4% indicate that the first rape was when they were between the ages of 12 and 17 years, the period of time during which sexual interest develops and dating begins (Tjaden & Thoennes, 1998). These figures may be underestimates, because there are personal and societal resistances against reporting rape and other forms of sexual violence when the perpetrators are known.

Resistance Against Reporting Partner Violence

In addition to surveys, there are a number of other sources of information on sexual and physical violence. One source is crimes reported to the police, that the U.S. Department of Justice and the Federal Bureau of Investigation publish yearly under the title *Uniform Crime Reports*. It is estimated that only approximately 16% of rapes and physical assaults by intimates are reported to police. Among the major reasons for not reporting were that the victim was a minor (20.3%), fear of the perpetrator (21.2%), shame and desire to keep the incident private (16.1%), and the belief that the police would not believe the victim and could not do anything about the rape (20.3%; Tjaden & Thoennes, 2000). Another source of statistics in this area are reports from hospitals and primary care physicians. However, such reports appear to be an underestimate of the true problem. According to Ruddy and McDaniel (1995), although a relatively high percent of emergency room visits are precipitated by domestic violence as determined by surveys of victims (10% to 25%), only a small percent are identified by attending physicians (2% to 8%).

Many make a distinction between domestic violence *prevalence* versus *detection*. For example, Rose, Peabody, and Stratigeas (1991) found that despite the fact that 71% of intensive case management patients reported physical abuse histories and 43% reported sexual abuse histories, *none* of the patients reported that they had been asked about their abuse experiences. Hamburger, Saunders, and Hovey (1992) found that despite the fact that there was a high incidence of partner violence (39% prevalence, with 25% lifetime injury rate), of the 394 women involved in a study at a community-based clinic, only six were every asked about partner violence by their physicians. Such questioning is important because patients tend not to report abuse on their own. O'Leary, Barling, Arias, Rosenbaum, Malone, and Tyree (1992) found that whereas only 1.5% of husbands and 6% of wives spontaneously reported domestic violence when seeking marital therapy, 67% reported domestic violence when asked via a structured measurement scale.

Part of the detection problem results from the lack of training on the part of primary care physicians, and part of it results from the fear of discovery of such violence. For example, Sugg and Inui (1992) found that 61% of the primary care physicians they interviewed reported no training on partner abuse at *any* point in their lives (from medical school through continuing education), whereas only 8% reported having good training. According to Brown, Lent, and Sas (1993) and Sugg and Inui (1992), physician resistance to inquiring about partner violence include: (a) not wanting to open up a "Pandora's box"; (b) time constraints, both in inquiring about the abuse and in the aftermath (referrals, follow-up appointments, etc.); (c) feeling awkward about asking; and (d) a sense that because there are no effective treatments for partner violence, it would be futile to inquire about a problem for which there were no treatment.

In most jurisdictions, mental health practitioners are not mandated reporters in cases of partner violence and their ethical code precludes them from breaking confidentiality except in instances where reporting is mandated. Like physicians, however, psychotherapists have a duty to provide the highest standard of care to their clients. Unfortunately, in cases of partner violence, this standard is seldom the case because most psychotherapists—even well-trained ones—do not know how to assess for relationship violence. Without making a proper assessment, mental health professionals are seldom aware that they are treating couples who are experiencing violence, because couples seldom volunteer this information at intake. Ehrensaft and Vivian (1996) indicate that this is because those involved in violent relationships are fearful, feel ashamed, and do not expect to be believed. Moreover, couples often do not consider the violence a problem. The violence is seen as unstable, infrequent, and secondary to other problems.

Because those affected are unlikely to volunteer the information, it behooves the clinicians to make the appropriate assessment. However, there is evidence that mental health clinicians only rarely do so. In an early study, Goodstein and Page (1981) reported that battered women in emergency rooms who had consulted psychotherapists did not return for a second session because the psychotherapist never asked about the violence. Hansen, Harway, and Cervantes (1991) and Harway and Hansen (1993), in two different studies, found that a majority of therapists were unable to recognize even very blatant examples of relationship violence and as a consequence suggested inappropriate interventions. Finally, Holtzworth-Munroe, Waltz, Jacobson, Monaco, Fehrenbach, and Gottman (1992) reported on their efforts to recruit martially distressed but nonviolent couples for a comparison study. Five different samples yielded 55% to 56% of the martially distressed but supposedly nonviolent couples actually included men who reported that they had been violent toward their wives. This latter study is often cited as evidence that many unreported cases of relationship violence are being treated for other clinical presentations.

Cultural Factors

"Cultural factors" can take in a number of different meanings of "culture." Here, we will discuss socioeconomic status (SES), ethnic minority factors, and lesbian issues.

Socioeconomic Status

Partner or intimate violence occurs at all levels of socioeconomic status (SES) (Bachman, 1999). However, there does seem to be a relation between SES and the incidence of intimate violent acts. For example, women with family incomes of less than $10,000 per year were more likely to have reported experiencing violence at the hands of intimate partners than those whose family incomes are greater than $10,000 (nearly 20% versus about 10% for other categories). Although this $10,000 figure is an important cut-off point, in general, as family income goes up, the number of intimate partner violence reporting goes down. Only 4.5% of those coming from families with incomes $50,000 or over report intimate partner violence. Thus, one can speculate that as the stressors of poverty go up, the probability of there being intimate partner violence also goes up. (An alternative interpretation is that intimate partner violence is reported more in lower SES families, whereas it is kept more hidden in higher SES families.) It is possible that both adulthood poverty income and adulthood victimization are linked to prior victimization in childhood and its aftereffects. Living in poverty further exacerbates the burden of a harsh childhood by placing people in dangerous neighborhoods and low-income jobs that may entail nighttime working hours, use of public transportation, and increased vulnerability to substance abuse. These are all factors linked to increased rates of victimization (Heise et al., 1999).

Ethnic Minority Factors

As Bachman (1999) put it, "There is a paucity of research exploring violence against women of color" (p. 117). Part of the explanation of this paucity of research is that there is a greater need to keep victimization silent in these communities (Barnett, Miller-Perrin, & Perrin, 1997; Sanchez-Hucles & Dutton, 1999). Thus, the prevalence of intimate partner violence within ethnic minority communities is an unknown quantity. Factors that may contribute to the silence in ethnic minority communities regarding partner violence include: (a) economic disadvantage, thus fewer options to leave relationships (e.g., in inner city African Americans); (b) rural isolation (e.g., in American-Indian populations); (c) stoicism and feelings of shame (e.g., in Asian populations; Lum, 1998; Wiehe, 1998); and (d) degree of acculturation (e.g., in Latino populations; Browne, 1997; Sorenson & Telles, 1991).

Browne (1997) and Sorenson and Telles (1991), in independent studies examining Mexico-born versus America-born Mexican Americans, found that Mexico-born

Mexican Americans had a lower rate of partner violence than their America-born coun- terparts. Thus, it seems that acculturation into the American culture was associated with greater partner violence. At this point, it is unclear what contributes to this in- crease. It could be that spousal abuse is simply more accepted in America than it is in Mexico. However, it could also be that America-born Mexican Americans may be less tolerant of such abuse and are more willing to report it. Alternatively, cultural prohibi- tions about discussing such a personal matter with strangers may be stronger among respondents born in Mexico, leading them to withhold relevant information from the interviewer. Yet another reason could be that America-born Mexican Americans (as well as other ethnic minorities) are more inculcated into a society that still struggles with racism, and that the feeling of powerlessness as an ethnic minority within a ra- cially difficult environment leads to a greater propensity to be violent. Because inti- mate partners are the most available target, they carry the brunt of the violence. Harway and O'Neil (1999) suggest that such broader institutional forms of oppression (e.g., racism, also sexism, classism, homophobism, etc.) create a context within which part- ner violence may occur.

Allen (1990) found violence against women and children to be abhorrent in tradi- tional American-Indian populations. However, contact with White populations and, significantly alcohol, seemed to change such attitudes:

> Allen contended that abuse of Native American women and children by Native American men was almost unknown until the introduction of alcohol and of patri- archal beliefs that sanction subservience of women to men. Before the influence of Westernization, Native Americans feared violations against women because respect for women was tied to their beliefs about women's powers over life and death. (quoted in Koss et al., 1994, p. 56)

In contemporary times, prevalence rates of partner abuse for American-Indian women are at least as high as those for White women of similar economic levels.

Examination of intimate rape lifetime prevalence rates reveals that Asian-Pacific Islander women have a rate (3.8%) that is about half of the rate for Whites (7.7%), African Americans (7.4%), and mixed-race people (8.1%). In contrast, the rate for American Indian/Alaska Natives was about twice as large (15.9%; Tjaden & Thoennes, 2000). For partner assault the figures are 21.3% among Whites, 26.3% among African Americans, 27% among persons who describe themselves as mixed race, 12.8% among Asian Pacific Islanders, and 30.7% among American Indian/Alaska Natives. The rates among Whites not of Hispanic ethnicity for rape and physical assault are 5.7% and 22.1%, respectively, compared to 7.9% and 21.2% among those of Hispanic ethnicity. However, these figures must be interpreted in light of the challenges of collecting valid data on intimate violence among ethnic and minority populations as described in the preceding.

Regarding the SES issue, the best predictors of risk of intimate partner violence for women were: cohabiting, being African American or American Indian, having an education level higher than one's partner, having been previously assaulted as a child, and having a jealous or possessive partner who was verbally abusive and denied access to family, friends, or income (Tjaden & Thoennes, 2000). White and Asian ethnicities were "protective" against intimate partner violence. The best predictors of being injured by an intimate were being Hispanic; between 18 and 25 years old; and having a partner who threatened to harm or kill, who used a weapon, who was using drugs or alcohol, and who was a spouse. Cohabiting partners did not escalate their violence to the extent that married partners did (Tjaden & Thoennes, 2000).

Russo et al. (1997) cautioned about investing too much in differences in violence rates by ethnicity because it is highly correlated with social class in the United States. They examined a set of 439 African-American protocols from a larger nationwide study examining violence against women. Of the 439 women interviewed, 195 were either married or cohabiting with a man. Of these 195 women, 37 (19%) reported partner violence. Consistent with the SES relations discussed in the preceding, as income went down, partner violence went up. They found that 18.9% of African American women with lower household incomes as compared with 9.8% with higher household incomes reported minor partner violence, and 13.2% from lower income levels as compared with 4.5% from higher income levels reported severe partner violence.

Lesbian Issues

Like ethnic minority populations, the lesbian population is often silent with respect to same-sex violence (Russo, 1999). Russo (1999) suggests that this results from the broader homophobic context within which such abuse occurs:

> The differences between lesbian and heterosexual battering, we have argued, are the homophobic context that lesbian batterers use as an additional strategy of control and the heterosexism of the social institutions (police, courts, social services) that perpetuate battering because they are inaccessible or hostile to lesbians. (p. 84)

Lundy (1999) concurs, "[E]ven where state law covers same-sex as well as heterosexual domestic violence, the chances are that the laws are not enforced equally and that same-sex litigants are treated with less dignity, sympathy, and respect than their straight counterparts" (p. 43).

Another factor to consider with respect to partner violence within the lesbian community is the fear of "outing," the practice of revealing publicly the homosexuality of an individual who has tried to keep her sexuality private (Renzetti, 1997a, b; Russo, 1999). Outing may result in the loss of family and friends, jobs, and other forms of discrimination; therefore, the abused partner may remain silent to protect herself from such negative outcomes. Within ethnic minority populations, there may be even less acceptance of lesbian lifestyles than in the broader community; therefore, there may be even more reticence by an abused partner to report her abuse (Lum, 1998; Toro-Alfonso, 1999; Wiehe, 1998). There are also issues related to reporting, such as the fact that police records are public and that police officers may arrest both parties because they do not know how to identify the primary aggressor among two women. There are also shelter issues: A lesbian woman may be the object of hate speech by other residents, and because the partner is a woman, she may gain admission to the shelter by claiming to be abused by *her* partner.

Consequences

Intimate partner violence can produce a number of negative consequences. Such consequences include fear and posttraumatic stress disorder (Barnett et al., 1997; Koss et al., 1994). Fear is perhaps the most common reaction for victims of partner abuse (Russell, Lipov, Phillips, & White, 1989). Such fear is both in staying and being beaten again, and leaving and being stalked and beaten even more severely or even killed.

Partner violence can cause stress, leading to both physical and mental illness (Barnett et al., 1997; Koss, Koss, & Woodruff, 1991). Moreover, Stark and Flitcraft (1996) found that partner violence is a *causative* factor for psychological problems as opposed to merely a concomitant effect. They examined battered and nonbattered women who were comparable on all measures in medical charts before the first reported incident of injuries for the battered group. After this first reported incident, battered women had much higher incidents of mental health problems, including psychiatric disorders, substance abuse, and suicide attempts.

Koss et al. (1994), however, caution against focusing too much on women's reactions to violence. They contend that such focus tends to diagnose the victims' responses and decontextualize the source of the abuse and the societal context within which the abuse occurred. Hence, the partners tend not to be the focus of this form of diagnosis, and sexism within society that tolerates such violence is ignored. They prefer to focus upon the root causes of intimate partner violence as opposed to diagnosing the almost predictable reactions that *anyone* would have after traumatic experiences.

There are consequences of partner violence that go beyond the reactions of the victims. Such violence, of course, can destroy the marital relationship. Rosenbaum and O'Leary (1986) compared violent and nonviolent discordant couples and found lower marital/partner satisfaction among those whose discord was caused by violence. Giles-Sims (1998) found evidence that partner violence can lead to less satisfying parental relationships. Ultimately, partner violence can lead to the dissolution of the relationship.

Intimate partner violence also has a profound effect upon children who are exposed to such violence (Geffner, Jaffe, & Sudermann, 2000; Koss et al., 1994; Lehmann, 1997). For example, Lehmann (1997) and found a greater preponderance of posttraumatic stress disorder (PTSD) or PTSD symptoms exhibited by children exposed to violence. Moreover, boys exposed to such violence are more likely to abuse their partners as adults, and girls are more likely to become victims of abuse (Kalmuss, 1984; Koss et al., 1994). More recently, Kerig (1999) found that girls exposed to partner violence may also be violent themselves as adults.

RAPE

Warr (1985) pointed out that men are more likely than women to be victims of violent crimes outside of the home if one does not count rape. However, the addition of rape increases the likelihood of women being victimized, and it is the *most* highly feared crime by women under the age of 35. One of the reasons for this fear is that the effects of rape can last for such a long time. In their groundbreaking work in this area, Burgess and Holmstrom (1979) examined the aftereffects of rape. They found that 37% of victims of rape felt recovered within months, 37% felt recovered after several years, and 26% did not feel recovered even after several years.

Rape can have both medical and psychological consequences. Medical consequences of rape include genital injuries, nongenital physical injuries, sexually transmitted diseases, HIV transmission, and pregnancy. Psychological consequences include anxiety, depression, sexual dysfunction, PTSD, and interpersonal difficulties (Koss, 1988; Koss et al., 1994).

Koss, Gidycz, and Wisniewski (1987) found that 14.8% of women college students had been raped since age 14. Brener et al. (1999) found that 15% of college women in a national sample had been raped since age 15, and Fisher et al. (2000) reported that one woman in five would be raped during her college career. Thus, the rate of rape among college students appears to have been stable, or even to be increasing. The two most recent studies did not measure rape through incapacitation with drugs and/or alcohol.

Figures about rape are very sensitive to the way they are measured. Koss (1996) has severely criticized the National Crime Victimization Survey for underestimating rape, pointing to features of question wording, context of the survey, lack of rapport, gender matching, and privacy that contributed to underdetection. Fisher et al. (2000) did a direct comparison of the behaviorally specific approach to rape questioning advocated by Koss and the National Crime Victimization Survey standard rape items. Behaviorally specific questioning resulted in the identification of 11 times more rape than the standard questions.

In addition to the approach to questioning, there are other reasons that rape is not detected. Rape often engenders feelings of being "damaged goods;" therefore, women may be reluctant to report having been victimized. Also, women fear being accused of falsely reporting rape in order to retaliate against a particular male or gain sympathy from others. Still others may not want to re-experience the trauma that the rape caused and thus prefer to remain silent. They may not view their forced sex as qualifying for the term "rape," and do not respond if that word is used in probing. Finally, male partners or family members of rape victims may feel powerless because of the rape, and they may feel blamed for not being able to protect the victim. As such, the anger, outrage, and feelings of powerlessness of these family members may not be experienced as support for the rape victim herself, and problems may result from these feelings of nonsupport. Although Ramos et al. (1999) found that even very traditional Mexican-American women are changing in their views, some still may hold a "blame the victim" attitude toward rape. Part of this attitude may owe to the parable of Saint Maria Goretti, who chose death over rape. Her choice of death over rape resulted in her being canonized in the Catholic faith but held as an unrealistic standard for those women faced with the same choice. To the extent that the women did not measure up to the standard of Saint Maria Goretti, they may choose silence so that no one knows their choice. Again, we want to emphasize that Ramos et al. (1999) found that this had been held as a standard within traditional Mexican lore, but this standard has been changing in recent times, and this parable has less and less influence in today's culture.

Still, rape is a problem for ethnic minority women and also for lesbians (Koss et al., 1994; Wyatt, 1992). Koss et al. (1994) wrote:

> On the street, [women] face the risk of crimes such as purse snatching, mugging, stalking, frottage, shootings, and rape by a stranger. Such street crime disproportionally plagues ethnic minority and poor women. . . . Lesbian women may be additionally targeted for antigay violence that include verbal epithets, physical assault, and even rape. (p. 157)

This form of violence against Women of Color occurs within a context of historical racism. From the earliest days of Spanish conquistadors, Native American women were seen as slaves and sexual relations and rape were commonplace (Clinton, 1998). "Sexual abuse was one means of controlling slaves. Owners asserted their authority by subjecting women to rape or sexual coercion and by forcing men to give sexual favors; slave men were also degraded by their inability to protect their female kin" (Clinton, 1998, p. 796). The rape of Black slaves in Colonial times was legal. This tradition continued when the colonies broke away from England: "The rape of a female slave by a white man would be assault and battery only if her owner had any objection—which he never would if he was the rapist" (Clinton, 1998, p. 797).

Sexual violence against Asian women also has its roots in history. When gold was discovered in California, the West needed laborers. Chinese men were encouraged to immigrate to the United States to make their riches on "Gold Mountain." However, they ended up being entrapped as laborers who worked for others and did not have enough money to return to China. Also, legally, they could not bring their wives, because anti-Chinese immigration laws only permitted men to immigrate. Most of the women—who only constituted about 5% of all Chinese immigrants in the United States—were prostitutes (Lee, 1997; Wong, 1988). Thus, the early Chinese women who immigrated to the United States were seen as sexual objects for the purposes of domination. Although the early Japanese women did not have this history, there is a cultural value, called *gaman,* which roughly translates into persevering or enduring hardships (Homma-True, 1997). Thus, should any Japanese woman be raped, the rapist would likely not be caught, because the woman's notions of *gaman* would prevent her from reporting it.

SEXUAL HARASSMENT

Although some may not feel that sexual harassment is at the same level as domestic violence or rape, it still has profound psychological effects on its victims. Certainly, domestic violence and rape are severe physical assaults on women, and may even cause death. However, sexual harassment may lead women to feel trapped and psychologically immobile. Thus, as Koss et al. (1994) pointed out, if women are assaulted at home, in the community, and at work, there truly is no safe haven for them to feel secure.

In the fall of 1991, America was gripped by the explosive testimony of Anita Hill in her allegations to the Senate Judiciary Committee that U.S. Justice nominee Clarence Thomas sexually harassed her over the course of a number of years. Thus, America became aware of the problems of sexual harassment in the workplace. Before this time, although there were laws against such behavior, allegations of such behavior tended not to be taken seriously (Koss et al., 1994). Until this time, early views of sexual harassment were that it was misguided romance, or romance gone astray. This view influenced court cases as recently as the 1990s (Bravo & Cassady, 1992; Castellow, Wuenisch, & Moore, 1990). For example, an Alabama judge ruled that a plaintiff's accusations could not be believed because she was not as attractive as the defendant's wife (Bravo & Cassady, 1992).

However, at its core, sexual harassment is about dominance and is perpetuated by a context of societal sexism. Koss et al. (1994) asserted:

> Research has also begun to confirm what has long been suspected, however, and that is the intertwining of sexuality, dominance, and misogyny in those men who are most likely to harass. . . . It is not necessary to argue that harassment has nothing to do with sexuality to demonstrate that it has everything to do with violation. (p. 113)

Francis (2001) sees sexual harassment as a violation of three areas: (a) *legal*, as it involves sex discrimination; (b) *moral*, as it violates appropriate standards of conduct; and (c) *social*, as it crosses lines of expected conventions of civility. She sees harassment as a legal violation because it violates one's state and federal civil rights. A moral violation occurs because harassment typically involves differential statuses of power, and the harasser uses this power differential to his advantage. Finally, a social violation occurs to the extent that one has an expectation of typical behaviors, and harassment violates these expectations.

Sexual harassment is an underreported crime. Mink (2000) uses the cases of Anita Hill versus Clarence Thomas and Paula Jones versus President Bill Clinton as examples of how the accusers were viciously attacked for their accusations. Consequences of reporting can include being fired, forced to quit, made to feel uncomfortable in other areas, and fear of rape. Thus, many women opt to merely put up with the harassment or to seek to transfer away from the offender. As a result, although sexual harassment is experienced by 50% or more by some accounts (Koss et al., 1994), less than 5% of the victims ever reported their experiences, and an even smaller percent file formal complaints. Lesbians are not immune from sexual harassment. Those who are not out may be assumed to be single heterosexual women and at a higher risk for harassment. Those who are out may be at a higher risk for harassment owing to prejudicial and homophobic reactions by their coworkers (Koss et al., 1994).

Sexual harassment had theoretically been illegal since the passage of the Civil Rights Act of 1964. However, it was not codified until 1980, when the Equal Employment Opportunity Commission (EEOC) identified two types of harassment: *quid pro quo* and hostile environment. The *quid pro quo* form of harassment involves extortion of sexual cooperation in exchange for job-related consequences (advancement or threats for penalties). These threats either can be explicit or subtle. The hostile environment form of harassment involves unwelcome or offensive sex-related behavior. Till (1980) further subdivided sexual harassment into five areas: gender harassment, seductive behavior, sexual bribery, sexual coercion, and sexual imposition. These five areas clearly create a hostile environment, although sexual bribery and sexual coercion seem to be more directly related to the *quid pro quo* criterion.

As compared with men, women have broader definitions of sexual harassment and more readily identify sexual harassment occurring in the workplace. This is particularly true for subtle forms of harassment and the identification of hostile environments. These findings were supported by analogue studies. In reviewing a large body of literature on this topic, Koss et al. (1994) concluded:

> [W]omen are more likely to believe that harassment is a serious problem, to hold perpetrators responsible for their behavior, to believe that reports of harassment are likely to be true and should be taken seriously, and so on. Men, on the other hand, are more likely to disbelieve reports, to hold the woman responsible for the situation, and to blame the woman for its occurrence or for not handling it properly. (p. 119)

Koss et al. explain these differences because: (a) women are much more likely to be victims, and men are much more likely to be perpetrators; and (b) men are much more likely to hold traditional sex-role attitudes and beliefs. Past research has found that belief in traditional sex roles contributes greatly to victim-blaming attitudes in sexual harassment cases. When traditional beliefs are held constant, gender differences disappear.

When victims report the harassing behavior, in general things get worse, not better. Rather than having negative consequences for the perpetrator, a significant percentage of the victims ended up changing jobs through quitting, firing, transferring, or being reassigned. Other consequences include decreased job satisfaction, increased absences, negative performance evaluations, and strained interpersonal relations. Gutek and Koss (1993) found a variety of health-related consequences of sexual harassment, including gastrointestinal disturbances, headaches, inability to sleep, and crying spells. They felt that the diagnostic category of PTSD was a useful framework to understand postharassment reactions, because such behavior tends to be traumatic for the victims.

PREVENTION AND INTERVENTION

As we have implied throughout this chapter, the underlying link among all forms of violence against women is how underreported all of these forms of violence are. Intimate partner violence is underreported because it may put the victim in more danger, it may not be supported by family and friends, and there are not enough societal supports for the victims (women's shelters, legal protections, etc.). Rape is underreported because it may cause the victim to relive the rape, because there may be an element of shame in being raped, and because reactions from family members may not be seen as supportive of the victim, instead being reactions to the family members' own sense of powerlessness. Sexual harassment is underreported because it may put the accuser in more serious trouble than the accused, the accuser may not be believed, and of the sometimes nebulous circumstances of the event (e.g., differences in interpretation of interactions, "he said–she said" arguments). Thus, perhaps the *most* therapeutic thing we can do as a society is to educate the public about these issues.

As an example of public education addressing these social problems, Foshee and colleagues (Foshee et al., 1996; Foshee, Bauman, Arriaga, Helms, Koch, & Linder, 1998) proposed a Safe Dates project. This is a primary prevention program for adolescents, which includes discussions of caring relationships, dating abuse, communication skills, and anger management. Foshee et al. (1998) documented the effectiveness of this Safe Dates program. It was introduced in 14 Southeastern U.S. schools, and it led to a decrease in self-reported perpetration of psychological abuse, sexual violence, and violence against dating partners.

Although the preceding findings are encouraging, in their review of programs educating university students about rape, Bachar and Koss (2001) found that results were mixed. For example, some of the programs reported immediate effectiveness in rape-supportive attitudes, but these changes did not persist over time. Some programs that targeted men found that only some aspects of the program seemed to be effective (e.g., rape-supportive cognitions), but other aspects (e.g., victim empathy) were counterproductive. Some programs that targeted women also produced mixed results. For example, one program designed to reduce the risk of sexual assault was found to be effective for women who had never been victimized, but this program had no effect for women who were previously victimized.

With respect to partner violence, Ashur (1993) recommends early detection by primary care physicians. To the extent that such physicians do not know exactly how to inquire about domestic violence issues, Ashur presented exactly how to inquire about these issues via a SAFE question format. SAFE stands for Stress/Safety, Afraid/ Abused, Friends/Family, and Emergency plan. For example, one can ask about stressors in the marriage or if one feels safe in the marriage, if they feel abused or afraid to be with their partner at times, if any family or friends know about the abuse and if they could provide any support, and if they had a plan to go somewhere in case of an emergency, such as at a friend's house or a domestic violence shelter. From these assessment questions, a treatment plan can be developed. Also, the questions in the SAFE regime imply treatment, for if one has not told family or friends about the abuse, asking about this implies that they should be told. This way, they can be prepared to be involved in the emergency plan. Moreover, Ruddy and McDaniel (1995) suggest that one way to help primary care physicians to understand domestic violence is to present it as a chronic illness. This will help them to understand that although there may not be an overnight "cure" for the problem, one can make incremental steps.

Geffner and colleagues (Geffner, Barrett, & Rossman, 1995; Geffner, Jaffe, &

Sudermann, 2000; Geffner & Mantooth, 2000) have discussed the advocacy approach to partner violence and also the reconstruction approach. The advocacy approach is where the therapist sees the couple separately. The wife is presented with the cycle of violence model developed by Walker (1979), and her abuse trauma is addressed, while the husband is taught anger management and takes responsibility for his actions. The couple is seen separately, because conjoint sessions can further traumatize the wife. The reconstruction approach is done in conjoint format, where the cycle of violence is discussed with both members of the couple and the husband learns to take responsibility for his violence. Geffner et al. (1995) suggest that an effective treatment plan is to use a combination of the advocacy and reconstruction approaches, where the advocacy approach is used first; when the couple seems ready to be seen together, the reconstruction approached is used. This method is effective if the couple is firmly committed to staying together.

A caveat to the aforementioned interventions is that they were not designed for ethnic minority populations. One of the major barriers to treatment or services of any kind for Latinas and Asian women is the dearth of linguistically relevant interventions. Still, with the development of empirically demonstrable efficacious interventions, linguistically relevant services are sure to follow.

CONCLUSION

Violence against women in all its forms is a serious problem that is even more serious when the issue of underreporting is taking into consideration. This issue cuts across all cultural and socioeconomic groups. It is incumbent on mental health professionals to educate the public about this problem, help the public identify the various forms of such violence, and be able to treat victims of such violence. The final section of this chapter suggested educational and intervention programs that seem promising. It is hoped that chapters such as this help to reduce the threat of violence that influences women's underlying feelings of safety and poses a substantial threat to the physical, social, and emotional health of women. In so doing, we can perhaps turn the silent pandemic of violence against women in all its forms into a sad but historical chapter in this country.

REFERENCES

Allen, P. G. (1990). Violence and the American Indian woman. *The speaking profits us: Violence in the lives of women of color.* Seattle: SAFECO Insurance Co.

Ashur, M. L. C. (1993). Asking questions about domestic violence: SAFE questions. *Journal of the American Medical Association, 269,* 2367.

Bachar, K., & Koss, M. P. (2001). From prevalence to prevention: Closing the gap between what we know about rape and what we do. In C. M. Renzetti, J. L. Edleson, & R. K. Bergen (Eds.), *Sourcebook on violence against women* (pp. 117–142). Thousand Oaks, CA: Sage.

Bachman, R. (1999). Epidemiology of intimate partner violence involving adults. In R. T.

Ammerman & M. Hersen (Eds.), *Assessment of family violence: A clinical and legal sourcebook* (2nd ed., pp. 107–123). New York: Wiley.

Barnett, O. W., Miller-Perrin, C. L., & Perrin, R. D. (1997). *Family violence across the lifespan: An introduction.* Thousand Oaks, CA: Sage.

Bergen, R. K. (1996). *Wife rape: Understanding the response of survivors and service providers.* Thousand Oaks, CA: Sage.

Bravo, E., & Cassady, E. (1992). *The 9 to 5 guide to combating sexual harassment.* New York: Wiley.

Brener, N. D., McMahon, P. M., Warren, C. W., & Douglas, K. A. (1999). Forced sexual intercourse and associated health-risk behaviors among female college students in the United States. *Journal of Consulting and Clinical Psychology, 67,* 252–259.

Brown, J. B., Lent, B., & Sas, G. (1993). Identifying and treating wife abuse. *The Journal of Family Practice, 36,* 185–191.

Browne, A. (1997). Violence in marriage: Until death do us part? In A. P. Cardarelli (Ed.), *Violence between intimate partners: Patterns, causes, and effects* (pp. 48–69). Needham Heights, MA: Allyn & Bacon.

Bureau of Justice Statistics. (1989). *Criminal victimization in the United States, 1987.* Washington, DC: U.S. Department of Justice.

Bureau of Justice Statistics. (1997). *Violence related injuries treated in hospital emergency departments.* NCJ–156921.

Burgess, A. W., & Holmstrom, L. L. (1979). Rape: Sexual disruption and recovery. *American Journal of Orthopsychiatry, 49,* 648–657.

Castellow, W. A., Wuenisch, K. L., & Moore, C. H. (1990). Effects of physical attractiveness of the plaintiff and defendant in sexual harassment judgments. *Journal of Social Behavior and Personality, 6,* 547–562.

Clinton, C. (1998). Sexual exploitation. In P. Finkelman & J. C. Miller (Eds.), *Macmillan encyclopedia of world slavery* (Vol. 2, pp. 796–798). New York: Simon & Schuster Macmillan.

Ellis, L. (1989). *Theories of rape: Inquiries into the causes of sexual aggression.* New York: Hemisphere.

Ehrensaft, M. K., & Vivian, D. (1996). Spouses' reasons for not reporting existing marital aggression as a marital problem. *Journal of Family Psychology, 10,* 443–453.

Farley, N. (1996). A survey of factors contributing to gay and lesbian domestic violence. In C. M. Renzetti & C. H. Miley (Eds.), *Violence in gay and lesbian domestic partnerships* (pp. 35–44). New York: Harrington Park.

Fisher, B. S., Cullen, F. T., & Turner, M. G. (2000). *The sexual victimization of college women.* NCJ 182369, U.S. Department of Justice Office of Justice Programs.

Foshee, V. A., Bauman, K. E., Arriaga, X. B., Helms, R. W., Koch, G. C., & Linder, G. F. (1998). An evaluation of Safe Dates: An adolescent dating violence prevention program. *American Journal of Public Health, 88,* 45–50.

Foshee, V. A., Linder, G. F., Bauman, K. E., Langwick, S. A., Arriaga, X. B., Heath, J. L., McMahon, P. M., & Bangdwala, S. (1996). The Safe Dates project: Theoretical basis, evaluation design, and selected baseline findings. *The American Journal of Preventive Medicine, 12,* 39–47.

Francis, L. P. (2001). *Sexual harassment as an ethical issue in academic life.* Lanham, MD: Rowman & Littlefield.

Frasier, M. (1986). Domestic violence: A medicolegal review. *Journal of Forensic Science, 31,* 1409–1419.

Geffner, R., Barrett, M. J., & Rossman, B. B. R. (1995). Domestic violence and sexual abuse: Multiple systems perspectives. In R. Mikesell, D. Lusterman, & S. McDaniel (Eds.), *Integrating family therapy: A handbook of family psychology and systems theory* (pp. 501–517). Washington, DC: American Psychological Association.

Geffner, R., Jaffe, P. G., & Sudermann, M. (2000). *Children exposed to domestic violence: Current research, interventions, prevention, & policy development.* New York: Haworth.

Geffner, R., & Mantooth, C. (2000). *Ending spouse/partner abuse: A psychoeducational approach for individuals and couples.* New York: Springer.

Giles-Sims, J. (1998). The aftermath of partner violence. In J. L. Jasinski & L. M. Williams (Eds.), *Partner violence: A comprehensive review of 20 years of research* (pp. 44–72). Thousand Oaks, CA: Sage.

Goodstein, R. K., & Page, A. W. (1981). Battered wife syndrome: Overview of dynamics and treatment. *American Journal of Psychiatry, 138,* 1036–1044.

Gutek, B., & Koss, M. P. (1993). Changed women and changed organizations: Consequences and coping with sexual harassment. *Journal of Vocational Behavior, 42,* 28–48.

Hamburger, L. K., Saunders, D. G., & Hovey, M. (1992). The prevalence of domestic violence in community practice and rate of physician inquiry. *Family Medicine, 24,* 283–287.

Hansen, M., Harway, M., & Cervantes, N. (1991). Therapists' perceptions of severity in cases of family violence. *Violence and Victims, 4,* 275–286.

Harway, M., & Hansen, M. (1993). *Spouse abuse: Assessing and treating battered women, batterers, and their children.* Sarasota, FL: Professional Resource Press.

Harway, M., & O'Neil, J. M. (1999). *What causes men's violence against women?* Thousand Oaks, CA: Sage.

Heise, L., Ellsberg, M., & Gottemoeller, M. (1999). Ending violence against women. *Population Reports, 27 (Series L, Number 11),* 1–43.

Hotzworth-Munroe, A., Waltz, J., Jacobson, N. S., Monaco, V., Fehrenbach, P.A., & Gottman, J. M. (1992). Recruiting nonviolent men as control subjects for research on marital violence: How easily can it be done? *Violence and Victims, 7,* 79–88.

Homma-True, R. (1997). Japanese American families. In E. Lee (Ed.), *Working with Asian Americans: A guide for clinicians* (pp. 114–124). New York: Guilford.

Kalmuss, D. S. (1984). The intergenerational transmission of marital aggression. *Journal of Marriage and the Family, 46,* 11–19.

Kerig, P. (1999). Gender issues in the effects of exposure to violence on children. *Journal of Emotional Abuse, 1,* 87–105.

Koss, M. P. (1988). Women's mental health research agenda: Violence against women. *Women's mental health occasional paper series.* Washington, DC: National Institute of Mental Health.

Koss, M. P. (1996). The measurement of rape victimization in crime surveys. *Criminal Justice & Behavior, 23,* 55–59.

Koss, M. (2000, August). Blame, shame, and community: Responses to violence against women. *Invited Address: 2000 Distinguished Contribution to Research in Public Policy.* Presented at the 108th Annual Convention of the American Psychological Association, Washington, DC.

Koss, M. P., Gidycz, C. A., & Wisniewski, N. (1987). The scope of rape: Incidence and prevalence of sexual aggression and victimization in a national sample of higher education students. *Journal of Consulting and Clinical Psychology, 55,* 162–170.

Koss, M. P., Goodman, L. A., Browne, A., Fitzgerald, L. F., Keita, G. P., & Russo, N. F. (1994). *No safe haven: Male violence against women at home, at work, and in the community.* Washington, DC: American Psychological Association.

Koss, M. P., Koss, P., & Woodruff, W. J. (1991). Deleterious effects of criminal victimization or women's health and medical utilization. *Archives of Internal Medicine, 151,* 342–357.

Lee, E. (1997). Chinese American families. In E. Lee (Ed.), *Working with Asian Americans: A guide for clinicians* (pp. 46–78). New York: Guilford.

Lehmann, P. (1997). The development of posttraumatic stress disorder (PTSD) in a sample of child witnesses to mother assault. *Journal of Family Violence, 12,* 241–257.

Lundy, S. E. (1999). Equal protection/equal safety: Representing victims of same-sex partner abuse in court. In B. Leventhal & S. E. Lundy (Eds.), *Same-sex domestic violence: Strategies for change* (pp. 43–55). Thousand Oaks, CA: Sage.

Lum, J. L. (1998). Family violence. In L. C. Lee & N. W. S. Zane (Eds.), *Handbook of Asian American psychology* (pp. 505–525). Thousand Oaks, CA: Sage.

Mink, G. (2000). *Hostile environment: The political betrayal of sexually harassed women.* Ithaca, NY: Cornell University Press.

Mio, J. S., & Foster, J. D. (1991). The effects of rape upon victims and families: Implications for a comprehensive family therapy. *The American Journal of Family Therapy, 19,* 147–159.

O'Leary, K. D., Barling, J., Arias, I., Rosenbaum, A., Malone, J., & Tyree, A. (1992). Assessment of physical aggression in marriage: The need for a multimodal method. *Behavioral Assessment, 14,* 5–14.

O'Neil, J. M., & Harway, M. (1999). Revised multivariate model explaining men's risk factors for violence against women: Theoretical propositions, new hypotheses, and proactive recommendations. In M. Harway & J. M. O'Neil (Eds.), *What causes men's violence against women?* (pp. 207–241). Thousand Oaks, CA: Sage.

Ramos, L. L., Koss, M. P., & Russo, N. F. (1999). Mexican American women's definitions of rape and sexual abuse. *Hispanic Journal of Behavioral Sciences, 21,* 236–265.

Renzetti, C. (1992). *Violent betrayal: Partner abuse in lesbian relationships.* Newbury Park, CA: Sage.

Renzetti, C. M. (1997a). Violence and abuse among same-sex couples. In A. P. Cardarelli (Ed.), *Violence between intimate partners: Patterns, causes, and effects* (pp. 70–89). Needham Heights, MA: Allyn & Bacon.

Renzetti, C. M. (1997b). Violence in lesbian and gay relationships. In L. L. O'Toole & J. R. Schiffman (Eds.), *Gender violence: Interdisciplinary perspectives* (pp. 285–293). New York: New York University Press.

Rose, S. M., Peabody, C. G., & Stratigeas, B. (1991). Undetected abuse among intensive case management clients. *Hospital and Community Psychiatry, 42,* 99–103.

Rosenbaum, A., & O'Leary, K. D. (1986). The treatment of marital violence. In N. S. Jacobson & A. S. Gurman (Eds.), *Clinical handbook of marital therapy* (pp. 385–405). New York: Guilford.

Ruddy, N. B., & McDaniel, S. H. (1995). Domestic violence in primary care: The psychologist's role. *Journal of Clinical Psychology in Medical Settings, 2,* 49–69.

Russell, D. E. H. (1982). *Rape in marriage.* New York: Macmillan.

Russell, D. E. H. (1998). *Dangerous relationships: Pornography, misogyny, and rape.* Thousand Oaks, CA: Sage.

Russell, M. N., Lipov, E., Phillips, N., & White, B. (1989). Psychological profiles of violent and nonviolent martially distressed couples. *Psychotherapy, 26,* 81–87.

Russo, A. (1999). Lesbians organizing lesbians against battering. In B. Leventhal & S. E. Lundy (Eds.), *Same-sex domestic violence: Strategies for change* (pp. 83–96). Thousand Oaks, CA: Sage.

Russo, N. F., Denious, J. E., Keita, G. P., & Koss, M. P. (1997). Intimate violence and Black women's health. *Women's Health: Research on Gender, Behavior, and Policy, 3,* 315–348.

Sanchez-Hucles, J., & Dutton, M. A. (1999). The interaction between societal violence and domestic violence: Racial and cultural factors. In M. Harway & J. M. O'Neil (Eds.), *What causes men's violence against women?* (pp. 183–203). Thousand Oaks, CA: Sage.

Silverman, J. G., Raj, A., Mucci, L. A., & Hathaway, J. (2001). Dating violence against adolescent girls and associated substance use, unhealthy weight control, sexual risk behavior, pregnancy, and suicidality. *JAMA: Journal of the American Medical Association, 286,* 572–579.

Sorenson, S. B., & Telles, C. A. (1991). Self-reports of spousal violence in a Mexican American and non-Hispanic White population. *Violence and Victims, 6,* 3–15.

Stark, E., & Flitcraft, A. (1996). *Women at risk.* Thousand Oaks, CA: Sage.

Stets, J. E., & Pirog-Good, M. A. (1989). Patterns of physical and sexual abuse for men and women in dating relationships: A descriptive analysis. *Journal of Family Violence, 4,* 63–76.

Sugg, N. K., & Inui, T. (1992). Primary care physicians' response to domestic violence. *Journal of the American Medical Association, 267,* 3157–3160.

Till, F. J. (1980). *Sexual harassment: A report on the sexual harassment of students.* Washington, DC: National Advisory Council on Women's Educational Programs.

Tjaden, P., & Thoennes, N. (1998, November). *Prevalence, incidence, and consequences of violence against women: Findings from the National Violence Against Women Survey* (Research in Brief). Washington, DC: U.S. Department of Justice.

Tjaden, P., & Thoennes, N. (2000). *Extent, nature, and consequences of intimate partner violence. Findings from the National Violence Against Women Survey* (NCJ–18167). Washington, DC: U.S. Government Printing Office.

Toro-Alfonso, J. (1999). Domestic violence among same-sex partners in gay, lesbian, bisexual, and transgender communities in Puerto Rico. In B. Leventhal, & S. E. Lundy (Eds.), *Same-sex domestic violence: Strategies for change* (pp. 157–163). Thousand Oaks, CA: Sage.

Walker, L. (1979). *The battered woman.* New York: Harper & Row.

Warr, M. (1985). Fear of rape among urban women. *Social Problems, 32,* 239–250.

White, J. W., & Koss, M. P. (1991). Courtship violence: Incidence in a national sample of higher education students. *Violence and Victims, 6,* 247–256.

Wiehe, V. R. (1998). *Understanding family violence: Treating and preventing partner, child, sibling, and elder abuse.* Thousand Oaks, CA: Sage.

Wong, M. G. (1988). The Chinese American family. In C. H. Mandel, R. W. Habenstein, & R. Wright (Eds.), *Ethnic families in America* (3rd ed.). New York: Elsevier Science.

Wyatt, G. E. (1992). The sociocultural context of African American and White American women's rape. *Journal of Social Issues, 48,* 77–91.

CHAPTER 16

Lesbian, Gay, and Bisexual Psychology

Past, Present, and Future Directions

KRISTIN A. HANCOCK

For over a century, homosexuality was treated as mental illness by practitioners who employed a variety of therapeutic approaches to "cure" it. The psychological research of Hooker (1957) challenged this position by demonstrating that there were no differences between nonclinical samples of homosexual males and heterosexual males on projective test responses and that experts on these measures could not tell them apart. Other such studies followed and these studies formed the basis for what is now referred to as lesbian, gay, and bisexual (LGB) psychology. In 1973, the American Psychiatric Association (APA) removed homosexuality from its list of mental disorders (American Psychiatric Association, 1974). In 1975, the APA adopted a resolution stating that "homosexuality per se implies no impairment in judgment, stability, reliability, or general social or vocational capabilities" (Conger, 1975, p. 633).

The generations of research that led up to and followed these changes have created a new area of study in psychology—one based on empiricism instead of pretense. This chapter summarizes research on LGB people from the ground-breaking work that challenged the view of homosexuality as mental illness to the descriptive studies of the present that not only provide more refined information about subgroups of LGB people but shed light on various aspects of their lives and experiences in society. The chapter also discusses directions for future research in LGB psychology. The impetus for the development of empirical literature about LGB people comes primarily from the pathologizing of homosexuality. Therefore, this chapter focuses on the literature most relevant to mental health professionals.

LESBIAN, GAY, AND BISEXUAL RESEARCH
HISTORY AND HIGHLIGHTS

Generally speaking, there have been three generations of research related to LGB mental health issues. The first generation focused upon homosexuality as psychopathology and the second on depathologizing homosexuality. LGB psychology then turned its attention to the exploration of the similarities and differences among LGB people, the ways in which they are similar to and different from heterosexual people, and the exploration of the unique issues of LGB populations.

Homosexuality as Psychopathology

Prior to 1973, the literature on homosexuality was based on the presumption that homosexuality was a mental disorder. The perception of homosexuality as mental illness coincided with advances in medicine toward the end of the 19th century and prevailed for at least half of the 20th century. The challenge for this medical model was to discover the etiology of homosexuality and to then develop a treatment for it. Theories were generated regarding faulty resolution of the Oedipal complex (Freud, 1922, 1923), repression (Stekel, 1933), and phobic reactions to members of the other sex (Rado, 1949; Socarides, 1978). The so-called "reparative" or conversion therapies were developed to change the individual's homosexual orientation to a heterosexual orientation. However, the empirical basis for the notion of homosexuality as psychopathology has been viewed as methodologically flawed (Gonsiorek, 1991; Haldeman, 1991).

When homosexuality was removed from the official diagnostic nomenclature, it was removed because there was no empirical basis for it as mental illness or as an indicator of psychological disturbance. Gonsiorek (1991) reviews the research that supposedly supports the notion of homosexuality as psychopathology and describes a number of problems, including lack of clarity in terminology, inaccurate classification of participants, inappropriate comparison groups, faulty sampling procedures, ignorance with regard to confounding social factors, and questionable outcome measures. Similarly, in his consideration of the research on sexual orientation conversion therapies, Haldeman (1991) concludes:

> Perhaps conversion therapy seemed viable when homosexuality was still thought to be an illness; at this point, it is an idea whose time has come and gone. At no point has there been empirical support for the idea of conversion; indeed, the methodological flaws in these studies are enormous. It now makes sense to discontinue focusing on conversion attempts and focus instead on healing and educating an intolerant social context. Some will say that an individual has the 'right to choose' conversion treatment. Such a choice, however, is almost always based on the internalized effects of a hostile family and an intolerant society. As long as we focus on homosexuality itself as the problem, we miss the point. (pp. 159–160)

Efforts continue to be made to develop treatments for homosexuality by those who continue to believe that it should be changed—for religious reasons. Once a leading proponent of conversion therapy for homosexuality, Davison (1991) observes that "change-of-orientation therapy programs are ethically improper and should be eliminated. Their availability only confirms professional and societal biases against homosexuality, despite seemingly progressive rhetoric about its normalcy" (p. 148).

SECOND-GENERATION
(OR "PSYCHOLOGICAL ADJUSTMENT") RESEARCH

The decision to remove homosexuality from the list of mental disorders was based on a generation of research that found that individuals with a homosexual orientation were no more or less psychological impaired than their heterosexual counterparts.[1] This second-generation literature began with the work of Hooker (1957) mentioned in the preceding. Her research found no difference in nonclinical samples of heterosexual and homosexual men on projective test responses. Following this, a substantial body of research emerged that essentially found no significant difference between heterosexual and homosexual individuals on a wide range of variables related to mental health. This generation of research revealed no significant differences between heterosexual, homosexual, or bisexual individuals on indices of psychological functioning (Pillard, 1988; Rothblum, 1994; Weinberg & Williams, 1974). No differences were found in other studies, including those on cognitive abilities (Tuttle & Pillard, 1991), psychological well-being (Herek, 1990), and self-esteem (Savin-Williams, 1990). Fox (1996) also noted that he found no indication of psychopathology in nonclinical studies of bisexual men and women.

The second-generation research, however, did not put the issue of the relationship between homosexuality and psychopathology entirely to rest. In what may be a new and critically important line of inquiry, Cochran (2001), in her review of recent studies of mental health morbidity and its relationship to sexual orientation, has noted that lesbians and gay men seem to manifest higher rates of stress-related disorders than their heterosexual counterparts. Gilman, Cochran, Mays, Hughes, Ostrow, and Kessler (2001) found that a homosexual orientation appears to be related to an increased risk of anxiety, mood, and substance use disorders.[2] Such findings point to an important question: If lesbians, gay men, and possibly bisexual individuals are somewhat more likely to manifest psychological disturbances, what is the reason? Those who wish to do so might be tempted to revisit the "homosexuality = psychopathology" position. However, with so much literature available to counter this position, the answer may lie elsewhere. The mental health consequences of societal stigmatization must be more fully addressed in order to settle the issue. In fact, the research has shown that LGB may be at increased risk for mental health problems and distress because of the discrimination and negative experiences they undergo in a heterosexist society (DiPlacido, 1998; Meyer, 1995). These problems, however, are associated with the way LGB people are treated in society (D'Augelli & Grossman, 2001)—not with their sexual orientation per se.

DESCRIPTIVE STUDIES IN LESBIAN, GAY, AND BISEXUAL
PSYCHOLOGY: THE THIRD GENERATION OF RESEARCH

The most interesting and informative research has developed beyond challenging the mental illness model of homosexuality. An entire generation of literature that might be referred to as descriptive research is exploring the lives of lesbian, gay, and bisexual people in greater detail and has brought much needed refinement to our understanding of these populations. This section describes some of the major areas examined by this research.

Gender Differences

Until the 1980s, literature on homosexuality ignored gender differences and focused primarily upon gay men. This "androcentric" approach tended to treat observations and research findings on gay men as though they pertained to all homosexual people—including lesbians. However, as the descriptive research developed and the societal awareness of gender differences grew, the literature found that there were important differences between lesbians and gay men. One the most consistent observations is that lesbians tend to exhibit more fluidity with regard to their sexual feelings, behaviors, and identity than gay men (Dempsey, Hillier, & Harrison, 2001; Gonsiorek, 1991). Gay male couples appear more sexually active than lesbian or heterosexual couples and less partner exclusivity has been noted by authors such as Blumstein and Schwartz (1983), Kurdek (1995), and Peplau (1991). Differences regarding money and its association with power in relationships have been found more often in gay male relationships than in lesbian relationships (Blumstein & Schwartz, 1983). Although differences such as these might lead to the conclusion that gender and gender role socialization are important factors in understanding the identity development and relationships of lesbians and gay men, it is also important to be aware of the ways in which the dynamics of gay men and lesbians do not reflect gender role norms. Green, Bettinger, and Zacks (1996) describe lesbians and gay men as being more androgynous and therefore less influenced by gender role programming than their heterosexual counterparts. However, it is also too simplistic to say that gay men and lesbians merely manifest cross-gender attitudes and behaviors. Gay men and lesbians draw from both masculine and feminine attitudes and behaviors in their relationships with greater freedom than their heterosexual counterparts (Hancock, 2000). Furthermore, the issue of gender and gender roles and the particular ways in which LGB people manifest/utilize them continues to be the focus of attention and debate.

Race, Ethnicity, and Culture

Following the issue of gender, research in LGB psychology turned its attention to the impact of race, ethnicity, and culture—particularly as they pertain to LGB identity development. As was the case with gender, many of the conclusions made from early research on LGB people were based on studies of White people—particularly gay men (Chan, 1989, 1992; Greene, 1997). Even when the descriptive research literature began to examine gender differences, findings pertaining to identity development, antigay prejudice, and other important topics were insensitive to the unique issues experienced by LGB People of Color. Thus, generalizations were made about these issues in the lives of LGB people that did not apply to LGB People of Color.

The 1980s saw a dramatic increase of writing and research involving LGB People of Color. Much of this literature targets clinical psychology and the issues relevant to assessing and treating LGB People of Color. This work has challenged psychology to conceptualize identity with more sensitivity and complexity. Race, ethnicity, and culture precede the development of a lesbian, gay, or bisexual identity and impact the experience of that identity in a number of ways (Garnets & Kimmel, 1993; Greene, 1997). Greene (1997) describes the areas in which race, ethnicity, and culture can influence the development and/or expression of a lesbian, gay, or bisexual identity. These areas include gender roles and the part played by reproductive sexuality in a particular culture, the importance of family and familial roles, and the importance of religion as a source of community and support. LGB People of Color grapple with the difficult and often painful task of negotiating multiple stigmatized identities (Chan, 1989, 1992; Croom, 2000; Martinez & Sullivan, 1998; Mays & Cochran, 1988).

Experiencing racism in the White LGB communities and antigay prejudice to various degrees within their own ethnic communities, LGB People of Color may be forced to choose between two cultures that may be antagonistic to one another, sometimes prioritizing one over the other or relinquishing one altogether (Croom, 2000). Chan (1989) notes that since "identity development is a fluid, ever changing process, an individual may choose to identify and identify more closely with being lesbian or gay or Asian American at different times depending on need and situation factors" (p. 383).

With some notable exceptions (Cochran & Mays, 1994; Mays & Cochran, 1988; Peplau, Cochran, & Mays, 1997), the empirical work on race, ethnicity, and culture in LGB psychology has suffered from the omission of people of color from LGB research samples and, when the work specifically includes People of Color, small sample sizes (Croom, 2000). Moreover, the context and method of measurement also may have an important impact upon the results of a given study when researchers do not account for cultural bias in themselves and the tools employed in their work. It is difficult to make valid and reliable observations/conclusions about any given population under these circumstances.

Bisexuality

Bisexuality, defined as a capacity to experience sexual attraction toward and/or sexual behavior with persons of both genders, has been documented by cross-cultural research for many years (Fox, 1996). However, until fairly recently, it has not been regarded as a valid sexual orientation. Rather, theorists who support a dichotomous model of sexuality have viewed it as a transitional or transient state. The dichotomous category model proposes that human beings are either heterosexual or homosexual and, traditionally, heterosexuality has been regarded as the healthy outcome of psychosexual development.

The removal of homosexuality from diagnostic nomenclature has facilitated recognition of bisexuality as a viable sexual orientation for some individuals. However, even this poses significant problems. The use of discrete categories of sexual orientation is now viewed as inadequate to address the complexity of human sexual experience. The problem is that research shows that sexual behavior, identity, and desire are not highly intercorrelated (Firestein, 1996; Rothblum, 2000). Although psychological research on bisexuality poses major challenges to researchers in such areas as conceptualization and operational definition (cf. Paul, 1996), it becomes increasingly clear that pursuing this line of inquiry will clarify our understanding of human sexuality.

Authors (Dworkin, 2000, 2001; Fox, 1996; Ochs, 1996) acknowledge the difficulties bisexual people have as a result of the negative attitudes they experience from the heterosexual and homosexual communities and note that these attitudes adversely affect the psychological well-being of bisexual men and women. To treat these clients means accepting that human sexuality is not an "either/or" phenomenon in human nature and it involves a need for approaching the sexual, relational, and identity experiences of clients with respect for the complexity of each.

Relationships, Families, and Parenting

A great deal of information has emerged in third-generation research about LGB relationships, families, and parenting. Studies on lesbian and gay couples have shown significantly shorter relationships than their heterosexual counterparts and higher rates of dissolution during the first 10 years (Blumstein & Schwartz, 1983; Kurdek, 1995). Green, Bettinger, and Zacks (1996) suggest that heterosexual married couples experience greater social support for their relationships, are more likely to be raising children together (providing a strong incentive to stay together), face greater legal and economic barriers to separation (particularly when children are involved), and are more likely to harbor more conservative value systems that keep them together even when couple members are unhappy. The literature has also found that gay men and lesbians form relationships with issues that are both similar to and different from heterosexual couples (Peplau, Veniegas, & Campbell, 1996). The differences, according to Garnets and Kimmel (1993), involve sexual behavior, gender role socialization, and the societal stigmatization of LGB relationships. Ossana (2000) observes that LGB couples seek psychotherapy regarding issues related to homophobia and coming out, differences in identity development, stigma, and exclusion from socially sanctioned rituals. Most of this research has been conducted with populations of White lesbians and gay men. More studies on lesbian and gay couples from other races and ethnicities are needed as are additional studies on the relationships of bisexual men and women in couples.

The family issues of LGB people also tend to be more complicated because LGB people do not often share the sexual orientation status of the rest of their families. This can cause difficult conflicts within the family of origin. In some instances, LGB family members are rejected once the LGB individual's sexual orientation is known. However, research has indicated that the "coming out" to one's family of origin is a long-term process (Ben-Ari, 1995; Mattison & McWhirter, 1995) and that the initial period of rejection sometimes seen is short-lived (Laird, 1996; Mathews & Lease, 2000). Authors such as Dahlheimer and Feigal (1994) describe the family of origin's process in coming to terms with its member's homosexual or bisexual orientation as a loss—particularly on the part of the parents. Dreams of a traditional marriage, lifestyle, and possibly grandchildren are no longer appropriate and the family requires time to adjust to the loss and accommodate the new information about its LGB member.

Although much has been written about the coming out process in LGB people, not enough information yet exists on their families of origin. Of particular interest would be information regarding the factors that enable some families to process the coming out of one of its members with relatively little conflict and harm, explorations of the impact of religion, religiosity, race, and ethnicity on a family's response to a member's revealing a lesbian, gay, or bisexual orientation.

The term "families of creation" encompasses various familial structures. Most LGB families (headed by LGB people) are the result of heterosexual relationships in which one or both LGB couple members have children (Patterson, 1996; Patterson & Chan, 1996). Lesbian and gay people are also creating families through donor insemination, adoption, and foster parenting in increasing numbers (Mathews & Lease, 2000). Patterson (1996) reviewed the research on the children in these families and notes that, in response to traditional concerns about LGB parents, these children are no more likely to be LGB than children with heterosexual parents. She also observes that there have been no differences found in the gender identity and peer relationships of the children of LGB parents. There are some indications, however, that the children of LGB parents express more concern about being stigmatized because of their parents' sexual orientation. Patterson (1996) suggests that more research is needed about this and about other aspects of parenting such as the factors contributing to the choice to parent and the impact of the sociopolitical climate upon LGB parenting.

Another kind of created family is referred to as a "family of choice." "Family of choice" is a term used to describe the nonbiologically related individuals who come together and form a supportive group or network that performs many or all of the functions a family of origin serves. Families of choice are sometimes created to fulfill the functions that a family of origin would serve (Dahlheimer & Feigal, 1994; Mathews & Lease, 2000) when acceptance is not forthcoming from the family of origin. Mathews and Lease (2000) note that these families of choice may be sources of protection for their members as well as sources of socialization, support, and self-esteem. Members of these families of choice may include LGB couples and individuals as well as supportive heterosexual friends and couples and may be more important to the LGB person than his/her family of origin (Weston, 1992). Little is actually known about the specific circumstances that contribute to the creation of these families of choice or the extent to which members may change over time. Nevertheless, they serve important functions in a social context that is sometimes harsh.

Lesbian, Gay, Bisexual, and Questioning Youth

The literature on LGB youth reveals serious problems and highlights the need for greater attention to the mental health needs of this population. Hershberger and D'Augelli (2000) observe that LGB youths do not share their sexual orientation status with their family of origin and are therefore not likely to be able to rely upon their family's support. In fact, as youths come to terms with a LGB orientation, the need for secrecy may prevail. Savin-Williams (1998) reported that anywhere from 25% to 84% of LGB youths had revealed their sexual orientation to their families—depending on which study was being considered. Hershberger and D'Augelli (2000) summarize research that supports the need for concern regarding familial responses to disclosure of an LGB sexual orientation. Initial reactions of parents, siblings, and friends are frequently negative (Robinson, Walters, & Skeen, 1989; Rotheram-Borus, Hunter, & Rosario, 1994). The victimization of LGB youths is also a major concern (D'Augelli & Dark, 1995; D'Augelli, Hershberger, & Pilkington, 1998). Hershberger and D'Augelli (2000) note that lesbian and gay youths are, in fact, more likely to be physically or sexually abused than their heterosexual counterparts. When compared to LGB adults, LGB youths are more apt to be victimized and the mental health problems that stem from this victimization may be more severe (D'Augelli, 1998). High-risk behaviors and suicidality have been shown to be significant problems among LGB youths (Hershberger & D'Augelli, 2000). Programs that assist LGB youths with counseling and support are needed to help address the difficulties revealed by third-generation research.

Sexual Prejudice

One of the most important areas in LGB research is the study of homophobia and sexual prejudice. Once defined as a one-dimensional construct involving an irrational fear of homosexual people, the term "homophobia" (with its original definition) has been examined and criticized for its failure to adequately and accurately address the phenomena associated with negative attitudes toward individuals with a nonheterosexual orientation, which Herek (2000a) refers to as "sexual prejudice." Heterosexism, an important component in understanding sexual prejudice, is defined as "the ideological system that denies, denigrates, and stigmatizes any non-heterosexual form of behavior, identity, relationship, or community" (Herek, 1995, p. 321) and has dominated the theory, language, research, and clinical interventions of psychology (Anderson, 1996; Brown, 1989) and the education of psychologists (Glenn & Russell, 1986; Hancock, 2000; Pilkington & Cantor, 1996). Sexual prejudice and its psychological, behavioral, and institutional manifestations have been closely studied in third-generation research. Sexual prejudice and victimization is also likely to take a significant toll upon the mental health and well-being of LGB individuals (DiPlacido, 1998; Greene, 1997; Herek, Gillis, & Cogan, 1999; Meyer, 1995). Negative attitudes toward LGB people are related to gender (Herek, 2002), gender identity (Herek, 2000b), religiosity (Herek & Capitanio, 1995; Plugge-Foust & Strickland, 2000; Schope & Eliason, 2000). On the other hand, more positive attitudes are related to personal contact with LGB people (Herek & Capitanio, 1995, 1996).

It is important to note that, when LGB people internalize negative societal attitudes, they may be at higher risk to suffer from a variety of mental health problems (Gilman et al., 2001). These problems may include lowered self-esteem (Gonsiorek, 1993; Herek, Cogan, Gillis, & Glunt, 1998), depression and suicidality (Garofalo,

Wolf, Wissow, Woods, & Goodman, 1999; Herek et al., 1998; Meyer, 1995; Shidlo, 1994), alcoholism and other substance-related problems (Cochran, Keenan, Schober, & Mays, 2000), sexual dysfunction and other relationship problems (Meyer & Dean, 1998), and stress (Cochran, 2001). Because LGB people utilize mental health services in greater proportions than their heterosexual counterparts (Cochran, 2001; Jones & Gabriel, 1999), these findings are important. Also important is the level of familiarity that mental health service providers have with the issues of LGB people (Hancock, 1995, 2000) and the sensitivity and respect the providers bring to their work with LGB clients (American Psychological Association, 2000; Morrow, 2000).

NEW TRENDS AND FUTURE DIRECTIONS

The descriptive information about LGB people produced over the past 25 years is impressive. Third-generation literature raises new questions. As our knowledge increases, new areas of inquiry appear as well. This section highlights some of these questions and areas.

The Issues of Older Lesbian, Gay, and Bisexual People

The "post–World War II baby boomer" generation is now middle-aged. Greater numbers of people will soon reach old age. The political force of this group and organizations that lobby for it will be major. However, whether the unique concerns of LGB older adults are included in the agenda of the various lobbying efforts remains to be seen. The issues of older LGB people have not been given nearly the same attention in the literature as those of their younger LGB counterparts. What research has been done was conducted using rather small samples of White, middle-to-upper income lesbians and gay men (Fassinger, 1997; Jacobson & Grossman, 1996). Thus, any further research will need to include samples with more diverse populations of LGB older adults (Baron & Cramer, 2000).

There are, of course, a number of myths about older LGB adults regarding loneliness, isolation, being "closeted," and being generally dissatisfied with life (Jacobson & Grossman, 1996). However, what research is available defies these myths. An intriguing observation has been made by some researchers (Berger & Kelly, 1996; Vacha, 1985) regarding what is referred to as "mastery of stigma," that requires more investigation and may have some interesting implications for aging in other stigmatized groups. "Mastery of stigma" involves better coping skills on the part of older LGB adults attributed to skills developed as a result of living with sexual prejudice most of their lives (Vacha, 1985). Are these findings replicable? If so, do other oppressed groups develop such skills and for the same reasons?

Family of Origin Issues

As noted, more research has been conducted on the coming-out process of LGB individuals than has been conducted on their spouses and families of origin. Research on these populations would certainly yield important information. Are there stages in the responses of the family of origin? What elements contribute to an outcome in which family members maintain a close and loving relationship with their LGB member following that member's disclosure of a homosexual or bisexual orientation? Because LGB individuals are not the only individuals impacted in the coming-out process, this research would provide important information to mental health professionals who may be treating a family who is dealing with coming out. Similarly, there has not yet been much research generated on the heterosexual spouses of individuals who come out while they are married.

Lesbian, Gay, and Bisexual Affirmative Psychotherapy and the Education of Psychologists

In February 2000, the American Psychological Association (APA) approved a set of Guidelines for Psychotherapy with Lesbian, Gay, and Bisexual Clients in an effort to provide psychologists with more current information and a nonpathologizing approach to working with such clients. These guidelines begin to articulate what Malyon (1982) referred to as "gay affirmative" treatment. Basically, affirmative treatment was viewed as an approach that did not pathologize LGB people. However, the concept of LGB affirmative psychotherapy has not been developed to any great extent. APA's guidelines represent a significant step in this direction. They provide general suggestions for practice in the areas of attitudes toward homosexuality and bisexuality, relationships and families, diversity, and education. Israel, Ketz, Detrie, Burke, and Shulman (2000) provide further assistance to psychologists by attempting to develop an empirical definition of psychotherapeutic competence with LGB clients. This kind of research not only serves clinicians but academicians and supervisors who teach and supervise psychotherapists as well because it provides specific and empirically supported information for training.

Gender and Transgender Issues

One of the most important and controversial issues to surface in recent years involves gender, gender identity, and their relationship to sexual orientation. As noted, gender, gender roles, and their manifestations/utilization are not completely understood. Explorations in this area are beginning to prompt psychology to take a profound look at some very old assumptions about gender, gender identity, behavior, and sexual orientation. Historically, the stereotypes regarding LGB people have included the simplistic notion that, on some level, gay men really want to be women and lesbians wish to be men. Although there does appear to be some relationship between cross-gender behavior in children and homosexuality in adulthood, the relationship does not appear to account for adult homosexuality and bisexuality entirely. Golombok and Fivush (1994) conclude that the relationship is complex and not completely understood:

> it is important to remember that simply because an association exists between cross-gender behavior in childhood and homosexuality in adulthood, or because differ-

ences have sometimes been found in the patterns of parenting experienced by homosexual and heterosexual men and women, this does not mean that all or even most adults who identify as homosexual were unconventional in their gender role behavior as children or were raised by dominant mothers and distant fathers. The retrospective studies show that a substantial proportion of homosexual adults report no or few cross-gender behaviors as children, and that many had good relationships with their parents. (p. 143)

Moreover, studies are still needed to address the fact that "tomboy" behavior in childhood appears to be less related to adult bisexuality or lesbianism than feminine behavior in little boys is to adult bisexuality or male homosexuality (Bailey, 1996; Peplau & Garnets, 2000).

Understanding the relationship between gender, gender identity, and sexual orientation presents an opportunity for psychologists to explore the most fundamental aspects of human nature. However, it presents quite a challenge as well. First, there is the problem of classification. Gainor (2000) describes a number terms—each depicting a different group of individuals and requiring separate definitions—under the broad heading of *transgender*. For example, she observes that, although "transgenderist" individuals are those who live full or part time as the other gender and may even take hormones, "transsexual" individuals are people who experience more profound gender dysphoria and who wish to fulfill a desire to live out their lives as members of the other gender. Transsexual persons are the most uncomfortable, identify as the other gender, and are the most interested in cross-living, obtaining hormones, and seeking genital reassignment surgery (GRS). "Transvestites," also included in Gainor's (2000) listing of groups, dress in clothing of the other gender for erotic pleasure and/or emotional satisfaction. Although transvestite individuals can be LGB, most are heterosexual and male (American Psychiatric Association, 2000; Docter & Fleming, 2001). "Androgynous" persons are those who tend to manifest gender role characteristics of both genders and who may choose not to be identified as a member of either gender. Finally, there are "intersex" individuals. According to Gainor (2000), these individuals have "medically established physical or hormonal attributes of both the male and female sexes" (p. 141). A review of this list and the associated literature confronts researchers with a complicated picture—one that challenges our definitions of gender.

Second, the issue is raised as to whether or not classifications of this nature are accurate or useful (Rothblum, 2000). Examination of the preceding listing presents us with a very basic question: Is our understanding and definition of gender adequate? Rothblum (2000) writes "the transgender movement is beginning to underscore the fact that an understanding of sexual orientation needs a better framework for thinking about gender itself" (p. 202). We are now clearly beginning to explore realms in human nature where the dichotomous categories "male" and "female" are difficult to discern. People depend on these basic categories. Demonstrating that they may, in fact, not be distinct and reliable is not likely to be well received or supported.

Embaye (2001) states that the treatment issues of transgendered persons may include relationship, family, and occupational problems, victimization and harassment, depression, issues related to "presentation," posttransition issues, and other psychiatric difficulties. Although psychologists nowadays may be exposed to information pertaining to gender, gender roles, and gender identity in such courses as social psychology or psychology of women, very little is presented about transgendered issues. Some information may be obtained in psychopathology courses but this information may be of limited value and does nothing to further our understanding. Psychologists in practice are not adequately prepared to deal with the issues presented by transgendered clients.

Sexual Orientation

Just as our notion of gender is evolving away from the comfortable categories of "male" and "female," new and more complex frameworks for understanding sexual orientation are also on the horizon. The recognition of bisexuality as a valid sexual orientation as well as a transitional state challenged the dichotomous heterosexual/homosexual model of sexual orientation. Authors (Firestein, 1996; Peplau & Garnets, 2000; Rothblum, 2000) have more recently urged psychologists to discard this older perspective in favor of paradigms that account for what actually occurs and describe the different ways in which individuals identify themselves and behave sexually. Multidimensional models of sexual orientation have been proposed in an effort to account for the complexity researchers continue to find and conceptualize sexual orientation with a number of variables that must be considered (e.g., sexual attraction, sexual behavior, fantasies, identity, emotional preference, relationship status, and comfort with one's own orientation) (Coleman, 1990; Klein, Sepekoff, & Wolf, 1985)—some of which may not necessarily be consistent with the others. Factors such as culture, race, ethnicity, social class, education, and religiosity also have been mentioned as important influences on sexual orientation (Greene, 2000; Peplau & Garnets, 2000).

Another layer of complexity has been introduced with research that shows that sexual orientation in women is fluid, responsive to social context, and may change over time (Peplau & Garnets, 2000), suggesting that biological determinants of sexual orientation may not be as important as once thought—at least for women. The literature pertaining to men reveals sexual orientation that appears to be more biologically determined and less fluid that it seems to be in women (Bohan & Russell, 1999). Basically, the picture regarding sexual orientation is not only multidimensional and may have very different dimensions, manifestations, and meanings according to the gender and the personal experience of the individual (Haldeman, 1999). Separate models for men and women may be necessary to understand the nature of sexual orientation as it exists today.

From Categories to Complexity: Sexual Orientation, Identity, and the Whole Person

Not only have three generations of literature on LGB psychology produced a great amount of information, they have painted a very complicated picture of identity, sexual orientation, and human behavior. Current literature in LGB psychology challenges simpler notions of gender, gender identity, sexuality, sexual orientation, relationship, and family. Psychology has depended, in large measure, upon categories—increasing in number and specificity over time—to explore and explain sexual orientation, identity, and LGB people. In the process of categorizing and organizing characteristics such has sexual orientation or identity, research has attempted to increase our understanding of human nature by studying its parts without realizing what this does to the accuracy of that understanding. However, this methodology has become cumbersome and is beginning to reveal its limitations. As we begin a new millennium, we find that an approach that examines parts apart from their whole is one that warrants critical attention and revision.

END NOTES

1. In most research prior to the 1980s, participants were not asked about bisexual orientation. Thus, results of earlier research did not officially pertain to bisexuality. However, it is likely that many of the studies that included samples of gay and lesbian individuals also included bisexual individuals.
2. In this study, "homosexual" is defined as having same-sex sexual partners. It is important to note that there is some debate regarding the role a lesbian, gay, or bisexual identity plays. Rothblum (personal communication, September 2, 2001) has observed that studies on LGB self-identified people have found that lesbians do not differ from their heterosexual counterparts with regard to self-esteem and mental health. Sampling women-who-have-sex-with-women (as opposed to self-identified lesbians), therefore, may yield groups who are more prone to exhibit mental health problems.

REFERENCES

American Psychiatric Association. (1974). Position statement on homosexuality and civil rights. *American Journal of Psychiatry, 131,* 497.

American Psychiatric Association. (2000). *Diagnostic and statistical manual of mental disorders* (4th ed. text rev.). Washington, DC: Author.

American Psychological Association. (2000). Guidelines for psychotherapy with lesbian, gay, and bisexual clients. *American Psychologist, 55,* 1440–1451.

Anderson, S. (1996). Addressing heterosexist bias in the treatment of lesbian couples with chemical dependency. In J. Laird & R. Green (Eds.), *Lesbians and gays in couples and families: A handbook for therapists* (pp. 316-340). San Francisco: Jossey-Bass.

Bailey, M. (1996). Gender identity. In R. Savin-Williams & K. Cohen (Eds.), *The lives of lesbians, gays, and bisexuals: Children to adults* (pp. 71–93). Fort Worth, TX: Harcourt Brace.

Baron, A., & Cramer, D. (2000). Potential counseling concerns of aging lesbian, gay, and bisexual clients. In R. Perez, K. DeBord, & K. Bieschke (Eds.), *Handbook of counseling and psychotherapy with lesbian, gay, and bisexual clients* (pp. 207–223). Washington, DC: American Psychological Association.

Ben-Ari, A. (1995). Coming out: A dialectic of intimacy and privacy. *Families in Society: The Journal of Contemporary Human Services, 76,* 306–314.

Berger, R., & Kelly, J. (1996). Gay men and lesbians grown older. In R. Cabaj & T. Stein (Eds.), *Textbook of homosexuality and mental health* (pp. 305–316). Washington, DC: American Psychiatric Press.

Blumenfeld, W., & Raymond, D. (1988). *Looking at gay and lesbian life.* Boston: Beacon.

Blumstein, P., & Schwartz, P. (1983). *American couples: Money, work, sex.* New York: Morrow.

Bohan, J., & Russell, G. (1999). Implications for psychological research and theory building. In J. Bohan & G. Russell (Eds.), *Conversations about psychology and sexual orientation* (pp. 85–105). New York: New York University Press.

Brown, L. (1989). Lesbians, gay men, and their families: Common clinical issues. *Journal of Gay and Lesbian Psychotherapy, 1*, 65–77.

Chan, C. (1989). Issues of identity development among Asian-American lesbians and gay men. *Journal of Counseling and Development, 68*, 16–20.

Chan, C. (1992). Cultural considerations in counseling Asian American lesbians and gay men. In S. Dworkin & F. Gutierrez (Eds.), *Counseling gay men and lesbians: Journey to the end of the rainbow* (pp. 115-124). Alexandria, VA: American Association for Counseling and Development.

Cochran, S. (2001). Practice implications of recent research on psychiatric disorders among lesbians and gay men. In D. Haldeman (Chair), *Presidential initiatives on expanding opportunities for psychologists in practice—Lesbian, gay, bisexual, and transgender issues: Innovations for the new millennium.* Symposium conducted at the annual meeting of the American Psychological Association, San Francisco, CA.

Cochran, S., & Mays, V. (1994). Depressive distress among homosexually active African American men and women. *American Journal of Psychiatry, 151*, 524–529.

Cochran, S., Keenan, C., Schober, C., & Mays, V. (2000). Estimates of alcohol use and clinical treatment needs among homosexually active men and women in the U.S. population. *Journal of Consulting and Clinical Psychology, 68*, 1062–1071.

Coleman, E. (1990). Toward an understanding of sexual orientation. In D. McWhirter, S. Sanders, & J. Reinisch (Eds.), *Homosexuality/heterosexuality: Concepts of sexual orientation* (pp. 267–276). New York: Oxford University Press.

Conger, J. (1975). Proceedings of the American Psychological Association for the year 1974: Minutes of the annual meeting of the Council of Representatives. *American Psychologist, 30*, 620–651.

Croom, G. (2000). Lesbian, gay, and bisexual People of Color: A challenge to representative sampling in empirical research. In B. Greene & G. Croom (Eds.), *Psychological perspectives on lesbian and gay issues: Volume 5. Education, research, and practice in lesbian, gay, bisexual, and transgendered psychology: A resource manual* (pp. 263–281). Thousand Oaks, CA: Sage.

D'Augelli, A. (1998). Developmental implications of victimization of lesbian, gay, and bisexual youths. In G. Herek (Ed.), *Psychological perspectives on lesbian and gay issues: Vol. 4. Stigma and sexual orientation: Understanding prejudice against lesbians, gay men, and bisexuals* (pp. 187–210). Thousand Oaks, CA: Sage.

D'Augelli, A., & Dark, L. (1995). Vulnerable populations: Lesbian, gay, and bisexual youth. In L. Eron, J. Gentry, & P. Schlegel (Eds.), *Reason to hope: A psychosocial perspective on violence and youth* (pp. 177–196). Washington, DC: American Psychological Association.

D'Augelli, A., Hershberger, S., & Pilkington, N. (1998). Lesbian, gay, and bisexual youths and their families: Disclosure of sexual orientation and its consequences. *Journal of Orthopsychiatry, 68*, 361–371.

D'Augelli, A., & Grossman, A. (2001). Disclosure of sexual orientation, victimization, and mental health among lesbian, gay, and bisexual older adults. *Journal of Interpersonal Violence, 16*, 1008–1027.

Dahlheimer, D., & Feigal, J. (1994). Community as family: The multiple-family contexts of gay and lesbian clients. In C. Huber (Ed.), *Transitioning from individual to family counseling* (pp. 63–74). Alexandria, VA: American Counseling Association.

Davison, G. (1991). Constructionism and morality in therapy for homosexuality. In J. Gonsiorek

& J. Weinrich (Eds.), *Homosexuality: Research implications for public policy* (pp. 137–148). Newbury Park, CA: Sage.

Dempsey, D., Hillier, L., & Harrison, L. (2001). Gendered explorations among same-sex attracted young people in Australia. *Journal of Adolescence, 24*, 67–81.

DiPlacido, J. (1998). Minority stress among lesbians, gay men, and bisexuals: A consequence of heterosexism homophobia, and stigmatization. In G. Herek (Ed.), *Psychological perspectives on lesbian and gay issues: Vol. 4. Stigma and sexual orientation: Understanding prejudice against lesbians, gay men, and bisexuals* (pp. 138–159). Thousand Oaks, CA: Sage.

Docter, R., & Fleming, J. (2001). Measures of transgender behavior. *Archives of Sexual Behavior, 30*, 255–271.

Dworkin, S. (2000). Individual therapy with lesbian, gay, and bisexual clients. In R. Perez, K. DeBord, & K. Bieschke (Eds.), *Handbook of counseling and psychotherapy with lesbian, gay, and bisexual clients* (pp. 157–181). Washington, DC: American Psychological Association.

Dworkin, S. (2001). Treating the bisexual client. *Journal of Clinical Psychology, 57*, 671–680.

Embaye, N. (2001, January). *Transgender identity: Implications for practice, training, and research.* Poster session presented at the biannual National Multicultural Conference and Summit II: The Psychology of Race/Ethnicity, Gender, Sexual Orientation, and Disability: Intersections, Divergence, and Convergence, Santa Barbara, CA.

Fassinger, R. (1997). Issues in group work with older lesbians. *Group, 21*, 191–210.

Firestein, B. (1996). Bisexuality as a paradigm shift: Transforming our disciplines. In B. Firestein (Ed.), *Bisexuality: The psychology and politics of an invisible minority* (pp. 263–291). Thousand Oaks, CA: Sage.

Freud, S. (1922). Some neurotic mechanisms in jealousy, paranoia and homosexualiy. *Standard Edition, 18*, 223–232.

Freud, S. (1923). The ego and the id. *Standard Edition, 19*, 3–66.

Fox, R. (1996). Bisexuality in perspective: A review of theory and research. In B. Firestein (Ed.), *Bisexuality: The psychology and politics of an invisible minority* (pp. 3–50). Thousand Oaks, CA: Sage.

Gainor, K. (2000). Transgender issues in lesbian, gay, and bisexual psychology: Implications for clinical practice and training. In B. Greene & G. Croom (Eds.), *Psychological perspectives on lesbian and gay issues: Vol. 5. Education, research, and practice in lesbian, gay, bisexual, and transgendered psychology: A resource manual* (pp. 131–160). Thousand Oaks, CA: Sage.

Garofalo, R., Wolf, R., Wissow, L., Woods, E., & Goodman, E. (1999). Sexual orientation and risk of suicide attempts among a representative sample of youth. *Archives of Pediatrics and Adolescent Medicine, 153*, 487–493.

Garnets, L., & Kimmel, D. (1993). Lesbian and gay male dimentsions in the psychological study of human diversity. In L. Garnets & D. Kimmel (Eds.), *Psychological perspectives on lesbian and gay male experiences* (pp. 1–51). New York: Columbia University Press.

Garnets, L., Hancock, K., Cochran, S., Goodchilds, J., & Peplau, L. (1991). Issues in psychotherapy with lesbians and gay men: A survey of psychologists. *American Psychologist, 46*, 964–972.

Gilman, S. E., Cochran, S. D., Mays, V. M., Hughes, M., Ostrow, D., & Kessler, R. C. (2001). Risk of psychiatric disorders among individuals reporting same-sex sexual partners in the National Comorbidity Survey. *American Journal of Public Health, 91*, 933–939.

Glenn, A., & Russell, R. (1986). Heterosexual bias among counselor trainees. *Counselor Education and Supervision, 25*, 222–229.

Golombok, S., & Fivush, R. (1994). *Gender development.* New York: Cambridge University Press.

Gonsiorek, J. (1991). The empirical basis for the demise of the illness model of homosexuality. In J. Gonsiorek & J. Weinrich (Eds.), *Homosexuality: Research implications for public policy* (pp. 115–136). Newbury Park, CA: Sage.

Gonsiorek, J. (1993). Mental health issues of gay and lesbian adolescents. In L. Garnets & D. Kimmel (Eds.), *Psychological perspectives on lesbian and gay male experiences* (pp. 469–485). New York: Columbia University Press.

Greene, B. (1997). Ethnic minority lesbians and gay men: Mental health treatment issues. In B. Greene (Ed.), *Psychological perspectives on lesbian and gay issues: Volume 3. Ethnic and cultural diversity among lesbians and gay men* (pp. 216–239). Thousand Oaks, CA: Sage.

Greene, B. (2000). Beyond heterosexism and across the cultural divide: Developing an inclusive lesbian, gay, and bisexual psychology: A look at the future. In B. Greene & G. Croom (Eds.), *Psychological perspectives on lesbian and gay issues: Volume 5. Education, research, and practice in lesbian, gay, bisexual, and transgendered psychology: A resource manual* (pp. 1–45). Thousand Oaks, CA: Sage.

Green, R. J., Bettinger, M., & Zacks, E. (1996). Are lesbian couples fused and gay male couples disengaged? Questioning gender straightjackets. In J. Laird & R. J. Green (Eds.), *Lesbians and gays in couples and families* (pp. 185–230). San Francisco: Jossey-Bass.

Haldeman, D. (1991). Sexual orientation conversion therapy for gay men and lesbians: A scientific examination. In J. Gonsiorek & J. Weinrich (Eds.), *Homosexuality: Research implications for public policy* (pp. 149–160). Newbury Park, CA: Sage.

Haldeman, D. (1999). The best of both worlds: Essentialism, social constructionism, and clinical practice. In J. Bohan & G. Russell (Eds.), *Conversations about psychology and sexual orientation* (pp. 57–70). New York: New York University Press.

Hancock, K. (1995). Psychotherapy with lesbians and gay men. In A. D'Augelli & C. Patterson (Eds.), *Lesbian, gay, and bisexual identities over the lifespan: Psychological perspectives* (pp. 398-432). New York: Oxford University Press.

Hancock, K. (2000). Lesbian, gay, and bisexual lives: Basic issues in psychotherapy training and practice. In B. Greene & G. Croom (Eds.), *Psychological perspectives on lesbian and gay issues: Volume 5. Education, research, and practice in lesbian, gay, bisexual, and transgendered psychology: A resource manual* (pp. 91–130). Thousand Oaks, CA: Sage.

Herek, G. (1990). Gay people and government security clearance: A social perspective. *American Psychologist, 45,* 1035–1042.

Herek, G. (1995). Psychological heterosexism in the United States. In A. D'Augelli & C. Patterson (Eds.), *Lesbian, gay, and bisexual identities over the life span: Psychological perspectives* (pp. 321–346). New York: Oxford University Press.

Herek, G. (2000a). The psychology of sexual prejudice. *Current Directions in Psychological Science, 9,* 19–22.

Herek, G. (2000b). Sexual prejudice and gender: Do heterosexuals' attitudes toward lesbians and gay men differ? *Journal of Social Issues, 56,* 251–266.

Herek, G. (2002). Gender gaps in public opinion about lesbians and gay men. *Public Opinion Quarterly, 66,* 40-66.

Herek, G., & Capitanio, J. (1995). Black heterosexuals' attitudes toward lesbians and gay men in the United States. *The Journal of Sex Research, 32,* 95–105.

Herek, G., & Capitanio, J. (1996). "Some of my best friends": Intergroup contact, concealable stigma, and heterosexuals' attitudes toward gay men and lesbians. *Personality and Social Psychology Bulletin, 22,* 412–424.

Herek, G., Gillis, J., & Cogan, J. (1999). Psychological sequelae of hate crime victimization among lesbian, gay, and bisexual adults. *Journal of Consulting and Clinical Psychology, 67,* 945–951.

Herek, G., Cogan, J., Gillis, J., & Glunt, E. (1998). Correlates of internalized homophobia in a community sample of lesbians and gay men. *Journal of Gay and Lesbian Medical Association, 2,* 17–25.

Hershberger, S., & D'Augelli, A. (2000). Issues in counseling lesbian, gay, and bisexual adolescents. In R. Perez, K. DeBord, & K. Bieschke (Eds.), *Handbook of counseling and psychotherapy with lesbian, gay, and bisexual clients* (pp. 225–247). Washington, DC: American Psychological Association.

Hooker, E. (1957). The adjustment of the male overt homosexual. *Journal of Projective Techniques, 21,* 17–31.

Israel, T., Ketz, K., Detrie, P., Burke, M., & Shulman, J. (2000, August). *Developing an empirical definition of counselor competence with lesbian, gay, and bisexual clients.* Paper presented at the 108th annual meeting of the American Psychological Association, Washington, DC.

Jacobson, S., & Grossman, A. (1996). Older lesbians and gay men: Old myths, new images, and future directions. In R. Savin-Williams & K. Cohen (Eds.), *The lives of lesbians, gays, and bisexuals: Children to adults* (pp. 345–373). Fort Worth, TX: Harcourt Brace.

Jones, M., & Gabriel, M. (1999). Utilization of psychotherapy by lesbians, gay men, and bisexuals: Findings from a nationwide survey. *American Journal of Orthopsychiatry, 69,* 209–219.

Klein, F., Sepekoff, B., & Wolf, T. (1985). Sexual orientation: A multivariate dynamic process. *Journal of Homosexuality, 11,* 35–49.

Kurdek, L. (1995). Lesbian and gay couples. In A. D'Augelli & C. Patterson (Eds.), *Lesbian, gay, and bisexual identities over the life span: Psychological perspectives* (pp. 243–261). New York: Oxford University Press.

Laird, J. (1996). Invisible ties: Lesbians and their families of origin. In J. Laird & R. Green (Eds.), *Lesbians and gays in couples and families: A handbook for therapists* (pp. 89–122). San Francisco, CA: Jossey-Bass.

Malyon, A. (1982). Psychotherapeutic implications of internalized homophobia in gay men. *Journal of Homosexuality, 7,* 59–69.

Manalansan, M. (1996). Double minorities: Latino, Black, and Asian men who have sex with men. In R. Savin-Williams & K. Cohen (Eds.), *The lives of lesbians, gays, and bisexuals: Children to adults* (pp. 393–415). Fort Worth, TX: Harcourt Brace.

Martinez, D., & Sullivan, S. (1998). African American gay men and lesbians: Examining the complexity of gay identity development. *Journal of Human Behavior in the Social Environment, 1,* 243–264.

Mathews C., & Lease, S. (2000). Focus on lesbian, gay, and bisexual families. In R. Perez, K. DeBord, & K. Bieschke (Eds.), *Handbook of counseling and psychotherapy with lesbian, gay, and bisexual clients* (pp. 249–273). Washington, DC: American Psychological Association.

Mattison, A., & McWhirter, D. (1995). Lesbians, gay men, and their families: Some therapeutic issues. *Psychiatric Clinics of North American, 18,* 123–137.

Mays, V., & Cochran, S. (1988). The Black Women's Relationship Project: A national survey of Black lesbians. In M. Shernoff & W. Scott (Eds.), *A sourcebook of lesbian/gay healthcare* (2nd ed., pp. 54–62). Washington, DC: National Lesbian and Gay Health Foundation.

Meyer, I. (1995). Minority stress and mental health in gay men. *Journal of Health and Social Behavior, 7,* 9–25.

Meyer, I., & Dean, L. (1998). Internalized homophobia, intimacy, and sexual behavior among gay and bisexual men. In G. Herek (Ed.), *Psychological perspectives on lesbian and gay issues: Vol. 4. Stigma and sexual orientation: Understanding prejudice against lesbians, gay men, and bisexuals* (pp. 160–186). Thousand Oaks, CA: Sage.

Morrow, S. (2000). First do no harm: Therapist issues in psychotherapy with lesbian, gay, and bisexual clients. In R. Perez, K. DeBord, & K. Bieschke (Eds.), *Handbook of counseling and psychotherapy with lesbian, gay, and bisexual clients* (pp. 137–156). Washington, DC: American Psychological Association.

Ochs, R. (1996). Biphobia: It goes more than two ways. In B. Firestein (Ed.), *Bisexuality: The psychology and politics of an invisible minority* (pp. 217–239). Thousand Oaks, CA: Sage.

Ossana, S. (2000). Relationship and couples counseling. In R. Perez, K. DeBord, & K. Bieschke (Eds.), *Handbook of counseling and psychotherapy with lesbian, gay, and bisexual clients* (pp. 275–302). Washington, DC: American Psychological Association.

Patterson, C. (1996). Lesbian mothers and their children: The findings from the Bay Area Families Study. In J. Laird & R. Green (Eds.), *Lesbians and gays in couples and families: A handbook for therapists* (pp. 420–437). San Francisco: Jossey-Bass.

Patterson, C., & Chan, R. (1996). Gay fathers and their children. In R. Savin-Williams & K. Cohen (Eds.), *The lives of lesbians, gays, and bisexuals: Children to adults* (pp. 371–393). Fort Worth, TX: Harcourt Brace.

Paul, J. (1996). Bisexuality: Exploring/exploding the boundaries. In R. Savin-Williams & K. Cohen (Eds.), *The lives of lesbians, gays, and bisexuals: Children to adults* (pp. 436–461). Fort Worth, TX: Harcourt Brace.

Peplau, L. (1991). Lesbian and gay relationships. In J. Gonsiorek & J. Weinrich (Eds.), *Homosexuality: Research implications for public policy* (pp. 177–196). Newbury Park, CA: Sage.

Peplau, L., & Garnets, L. (2000). A new paradigm for understanding women's sexuality and sexual orientation. *Journal of Social Issues, 56,* 329–350.

Peplau, L., Cochran, S., & Mays, V. (1997). A national survey of the intimate relationships of African American lesbians and gay men: A look at commitment, satisfaction, sexual behavior, and HIV disease. In B. Greene & G. Croom (Eds.), *Psychological perspectives on lesbian and gay issues: Volume 5. Education, research, and practice in lesbian, gay, bisexual, and transgendered psychology: A resource manual* (pp. 11–38). Thousand Oaks, CA: Sage.

Peplau, L., Veniegas, R., & Campbell, S. (1996). Gay and lesbian relationships. In R. Savin-Williams & K. Cohen (Eds.), *The lives of lesbians, gays, and bisexuals: Children to adults* (pp. 250–273). Fort Worth, TX: Harcourt Brace.

Pilkington, N., & Cantor, J. (1996). Perceptions of heterosexual bias in professional psychology programs: A survey of graduate students. *Professional Psychology: Research and Practice, 27,* 604–612.

Pillard, R. (1988). Sexual orientation and mental disorder. *Psychiatric Annals, 18,* 51–56.

Plugge-Foust, C., & Strickland, G. (2000). Homophobia, irrationality, and Christian ideology: Does a relationship exist? *Journal of Sex Education and Therapy, 25,* 240–244.

Rado, S. (1949). An adaptational view of sexual behavior. In P. H. Hoch & J. Zubin (Eds.), *Psychosexual development in health and disease* (pp. 159–189). New York: Grune & Stratton.

Robinson, B., Walters, L., & Skeen, P. (1998). Response of parents to learning that their child is homosexual and concern over AIDS: A national survey. *Journal of Homosexuality, 18,* 59–80.

Rothblum, E. (1994). "I only read about myself on bathroom walls": The need for research on the mental health of lesbians and gay men. *Journal of Consulting and Clinical Psychology, 62,* 213–220.

Rothblum, E. (2000). Sexual orientation and sex in women's lives: Conceptual and methodological issues. *Journal of Social Issues, 56,* 193–204.

Rotheram-Borus, M., Hunter, J., & Rosario, M. (1994). Suicidal behavior and gay-related stress among gay and bisexual male adolescents. *Journal of Adolescent Research, 9,* 498–508.

Savin-Williams, R. (1998). The disclosure to families of same-sex attractions by lesbian, gay, and bisexual youths. *Journal of Research on Adolescence, 8,* 49–68.

Savin-Williams, R. (1990). *Gay and lesbian youth: Expressions of identity.* New York: Hemisphere.

Schope, R., & Eliason, M. (2000). Thinking versus acting: Assessing the relationship between heterosexual attitudes and behaviors towards homosexuals. *Journal of Gay and Lesbian Services: Issues in Practice, Policy, and Research, 11,* 69–92.

Shidlo, A. (1994). Internalized homophobia: Conceptual and empirical issues in measurement. In B. Greene & G. Herek (Eds.), *Psychological perspectives on lesbian and gay issues: Vol. 1. Lesbian and gay psychology: Theory, research, and clinical applications* (pp. 176–205). Thousand Oaks, CA: Sage.

Socarides, C. (1978). *Homosexuality.* New York: Jason Aronson.

Stekel, W. (1933). *Bi-sexual love.* Brooklyn: Physicians and Surgeons Book Company.

Tuttle, G., & Pillard, R. (1991). Sexual orientation and cognitive abilities. *Archives of Sexual Behavior, 20,* 307–318.

Vacha, K. (1985). *Quiet fire: Memoirs of older gay men.* Trumansburg, NY: Crossing Press.

Weinberg, M., & Williams, C. (1974). *Male homosexuals: Their problems and adaptations.* New York: Oxford University Press.

Weston, K. (1992). *Families we choose.* New York: Columbia University.

CHAPTER 17

Aging and Mental Health

MARTHA R. CROWTHER
ANTONETTE M. ZEISS

In the United States the population of persons age 65 years and older is experiencing a remarkable growth. Older adults currently comprise 16% of the population, but by the year 2020, the elderly population is expected to increase to approximately 22% (U.S. Census Bureau, 2000). Current estimates are that over the next 40 years, the number of persons who are 65 years and over will double and persons 85 years and over will triple (U.S. Census Bureau, 2000). In the United States, there is differential longevity between men and women. The average lifespan in 1993 for men was 72 years and for women 79 years, up by almost 6 years since 1970 and almost 30 years since 1900. For those who have managed to make it to age 65, the figures are even more promising: men of 65 years can expect to live on average to age 77; women can expect to live on average to age 81.

As a result of increased life expectancy, family structures within the United States are changing. There are currently many three-, four-, and five-generation families. However, fewer persons are born into each generation, subsequently family trees have become smaller. Qualls (1996) describes the change in family structures as "tall, skinny, family trees."

At least two generations are included in the older adult cohort, with different experiences and historical perspectives, the young-old and the oldest-old (Berger, 1994). The phrase "oldest-old" refers to adults aged 85 years and over. The division between young-old and old-old has helped with viewing older adults as a diverse population with varying social and health problems and long-term care needs. Some researchers have been concerned, however, that the distinction may cause stereotyping in the oldest-old group (Binstock, 1992). This is an important consideration, given that chronological age is not the only factor that determines how persons adjust to aging. State of mind, health habits, and general social and psychological outlook on life also determine adjustment to old age.

Ethnic minority elderly will account for a significant proportion of the projected increase in the older adult population; their rates of growth are expected to exceed those of Caucasians over the next 50 years. Similar growth in the older population is also occurring in other parts of the world. Worldwide, the population growth of persons 65 years and over has increased by 2.5% per year. This is contrasted with the world annual population growth of 1.7%. Currently, the United States, Europe, and Japan have the highest percentages of older persons (World Health Organization, 2001).

Looking more closely at how the ethnic composition of older adults is changing, the U.S. 2000 Census data project a decrease in the percentage of elderly Caucasians and an increase in the percentage of ethnic minority elders. In 2000, 84% of people aged 65 and older were Caucasian, 8% were African American, 6% were Hispanic, 2% were Asian and Pacific Islander, and less than 1% were American Indian and Alaska Native. In 2050, it is estimated that Caucasians will decline 20% (from 84% in 2000) to 64%. In contrast, by 2050, it is projected that the Hispanic population will account for 16% of the older population, 12% of the population is anticipated to be African American, and 7% of the population is expected to comprise Asian and Pacific Islander (U.S. Census Bureau, 2000). Although the older population will increase among all ethnic minority groups, Hispanic elderly are projected to grow the fastest, from about 2 million in 2000 to over 13 million by 2050. This process is expected to occur in a linear fashion, and by 2028, older Hispanics are projected to exceed the number of older African Americans (U.S. Census Bureau, 2000).

AGEISM AND THE CHALLENGE OF THE NEW DEMOGRAPHICS OF AGING

Traditionally, Americans have viewed older adults as a homogenous population and held negative attitudes and stereotypes toward older adults and aging. Unfortunately, professionals in the area of gerontology have sometimes unwittingly propagated those negative attitudes and stereotypes with a focus on problems of aging, as opposed to the strengths and stabilities of older adults. For example, much of the early research on aging studied older persons in nursing homes, retirement communities, and/or those who are chronically ill. Fortunately, the trend has changed and the spectrum of current research on older adults encompasses their strengths as well as their weaknesses thus helping to change perceptions of aging and the aged.

Multiculturalism and Aging

Research on aging and ageism also has been limited in that it has largely focused on Caucasian older adults. Even without the projected increases in older adults from other ethnic and cultural groups, it would be essential to expand the field of geropsychology to include attention to the full multicultural range. The projected population figures make this need even more urgent; to begin to address this need, it is important to start with an overview of the concepts of "culture" and "ethnicity" and how they could be more fully incorporated into research on aging.

Culture has been defined in a variety of ways. Betancourt and Lopez (1993) examined the study of culture in American psychology and found that over 100 definitions of culture exist. Shiang and colleagues (1998) define culture as "a shared belief system, a set of values, a common his/herstory, symbols, as well as preferred ways of behaving." Culture is passed to us through family and community. Culture shapes how we see others and ourselves. There are multiple cultural layers from the influences of our immediate environment, which includes family, to the larger society in which we live. Bronfrenbrenner's ecological developmental theory (1989) addresses the multiple layers of culture that influence our thoughts, feelings, and actions. Culture is the foundation that allows us to make sense out of world.

Ethnic Minority Status and Aging

The term "ethnicity" involves aspects of culture, but it is not the same as culture. It is a multidimensional construct that encompasses cultural norms and values, along with experiences and attitudes associated with ethnic minority status in America.

The phrase ethnic minority elders is deceptive, in that the reader can have the illusion that ethnic minorities comprise a discrete number of groups and can be discussed in a clear and concise manner. According to the U.S. Census (2000), White, African American, American Indian, and Asian and Pacific Islander are considered racial groups, whereas Hispanic is considered an ethnic group. For the purposes of clarity in this chapter we will use the term "ethnic minority" to encompass African Americans, Hispanic Americans, Asian and Pacific Islander Americans as well as American Indian and Alaska Natives. Within each minority group, there is a tremendous amount of variability. For example, there are over 30 Asian American/Pacific Islander ethnic groups that comprise the category Asian American. Likewise the term Hispanic comprises persons with heritage from Mexico, Puerto Rico, Cuba, El Salvador, the Dominican Republic and other Latin countries. American Indian and Alaska Natives comprise 530 distinct tribes, of which the United States government recognizes 478. Lastly, African Americans traditionally encompass persons of African descent that include individuals from Africa, the Caribbean, and those born in America.

It is also important to note that there also is diversity within the Caucasian group, although clinicians and researchers often ignore the variability within this population. The ethnic groups that comprise the classification Caucasian originate from different countries (e.g., Germany, Italy, Ireland, Poland, Russia, and Israel). Older Caucasian adults may strongly identify with their ethnic classification. Thus, thinking of this group as homogenous may cause mental health professionals to ignore important cultural components.

Ethnic minority groups differ in general status, acculturation level, language, religion/spiritual beliefs, cultural traditions and values, and gender roles. Based on the heterogeneity that exists both between and within each ethnic minority group, it is important to consider not only the racial designation of the individual but his or her specific ethnic identification. Additionally, individual differences become a crucial part of the mental health profile (Whitfield & Baker-Thomas, 1999). Examining an older adult from an individual perspective does not shift the focus away from his or her ethnic identification. On the contrary, it allows the mental health practitioner to understand the traits and qualities that exist within a culture and how those traits and qualities are manifested in an individual by examining the interactions among cultural, social, biological, environmental, and psychological factors.

PROFICIENCY IN CLINICAL GEROPSYCHOLOGY

Clinical geropsychology is the field that specifically focuses on studying older adults and developing empirically supported skills for psychological assessment and treatment of them; particularly older adults with psychopathology or whose quality of life is negatively influenced by psychosocial factors. Given the increasing population of older adults detailed in the preceding and the complex life experiences and changing demographics of the population, it is important for more mental health professionals to be prepared to assess and treat older clients, and it is important for clinical geropsychologists to be prepared to work with a culturally and ethnically diverse population. Aging is a psychological, biological, and social process. Therefore, psychologists working with this population should have knowledge of a broad array of topics that encompass work with older adults. As a reflection of and in reaction to the increasing number of older adults and their growing diversity, practitioners and researchers in the area of mental health increasingly emphasize issues that concern aging and the aged. For example, the most recent Surgeon General's Report included, for the first time, a chapter on older adults and mental health (USDHHS, 1999). The U.S. Department of Health and Human Services Administration on Aging recently issued a companion to the Surgeon General's Report that focused on the issues and opportunities of Older Adults and Mental Health (USDHHS, 2001). The research on aging and mental health comprises a wide variety of topics, which include psychology and aging (Birren & Schaie, 1996); cognition (Baltes & Staudinger, 1996; Hess & Blanchard-Fields, 1999), caregiving (Gallagher-Thompson, Coon, Rivera, Powers, & Zeiss, 1998; USDHHS, 1998; Zarit, Gaugler, & Jarrott, 1999), retirement (Floyd et al., 1992), widowhood (Thompson, Gallagher-Thompson, Futterman, Gilewki, & Peterson (1991), spirituality and religion (Armstrong & Crowther, 2002; McFadden, 1996), advanced care directives (Smyer & Allen-Burge, 1999), mental disorders (Gatz, Kasl-Godley, & Karel, 1996) and service delivery (Gatz & Smyer, 1992). Overall, research indicates that older adults are a diverse population encompassing both community dwelling elderly who are still socially and physically active, as well as the aged who are sick and frail. Older adults, and in many cases their families, are becoming a larger part of the mental health care system. Findings such as these have drawn attention from health care providers, researchers, and social scientists interested in mental health and aging. However, most studies on older adults do not take racial and/or cultural distinctions into account in the manifestation of disease.

Until recently, outpatient mental health care services have been underutilized by older adults, despite 1975 legislation mandating specialized services for mentally ill older adults within community mental health centers. The majority of older adults who receive mental health services are seen as inpatients during a hospitalization in a psychiatric hospital or a nursing home. Possible explanations for this phenomenon include the idea that there is stigma attached to receiving mental health services within this cohort, but this concern has not been supported in research (Landreville, Landry, Baillargeon, Guérette, & Matteau, 2001; Rokke & Scogin, 1995). Another explanation for underutilization of mental health services by older adults is that many mental health professionals have historically displayed "professional ageism" dating back to Freud, who was pessimistic about psychological change or the benefits of therapy in later life (Freud, 1924). Finally, Medicare reimbursement for psychological services in the United States is very limited. The majority of the money spent goes toward psychopharmacology as opposed to psychotherapy, reducing the availability of mental health services.

However, patterns of usage of mental health services by the elderly are changing. Successive cohorts of older persons have higher levels of education and a greater acceptance of psychology. Rokke and Scogin (1995), for example, showed that older adults considered cognitive therapy to be more credible and acceptable than drug therapy for depression; this finding was replicated and expanded by Landreville and colleagues (2001). It is likely that mental health professionals could be much more active in reaching out to older adults to provide service, and that when this is done, they can expect an increasingly positive welcome.

As more older adults seek or accept mental health services, mental health providers must be prepared to meet this need. To address issues of responsibility and competency in providing such care, the American Psychological Association (APA) has approved Clinical Geropsychology as an area of special proficiency. Suggested guidelines addressing the needed competencies for proficiency in clinical geropsychology have been drafted and widely promulgated (APA Interdivisional Task Force, 1999), although they are not yet approved as an official document by APA. The 13 areas of knowledge and skills needed to be proficient in clinical geropsychology are outlined in Table 17.1.

Highlighting some of the aspects of competency, clinical geropsychologists should be familiar with the continuity and change processes, such as normal and abnormal changes in adult cognition; variability in rates and trajectories of change; and the effects of biopsychosocial factors on cognitive achievement and performance. Additionally, biological aspects of aging are important considerations, including the normal biological aging changes and disease; lifestyle and behavioral factors in health; chronic and terminal illness as well as pharmacological issues. Geropsychologists must know about health as well as illness, about normality as well as abnormality. If memory problems are reported, are they normal for age or a result of dementia? Do changes in sleep pattern and changes in appetite indicate depression, failure to thrive, or "normal" aging?

The geropsychologist also should be aware of psychosocial issues older adults face, which include problems in daily living, losses from a variety of sources (e.g., deaths and the end of employment), facing limitations in functioning, financial problems, and environmental and contextual issues. Understanding relationships in later life is also important, including the roles of intergenerational acquaintances, lifelong

TABLE 17.1. Clinical Geropsychology Competency Areas

Competency Area	Specific Content of Each Competency Area
Research and theory in aging	Concepts of aging and development, research methodology relevant to aging, cohort differences
Cognitive psychology and change	Normal and abnormal changes in adult cognition; variability in rates and trajectories of change; effects of biopsychosocial factors on cognitive achievement and performance
Social/psychological aspects of aging	Demographics of aging; intergenerational issues; relationships in later life; cross-cultural and minority issues; environmental and contextual issues; perceptions of aging; adapting to typical age-related changes; personality; developmental issues; reminiscence; late life loss and bereavement
Biological aspects of aging	Normal biological aging changes; abnormal changes and disease; lifestyle and behavioral factors in health; chronic and terminal illness; pharmacology issues
Psychopathology (issues relevant to aging)	Epidemiological and diagnostic aspects of major mental health problems of late life; behavioral problems of late life
Problems in daily living	Deficits in social and daily living skills; coping with stressors; decision-making capacity; level of care; elder abuse and neglect
Sociocultural and socioeconomic factors	Individual factors influencing health and psychological problems in late life, such as gender, ethnicity, age cohort, education, socioeconomic status, religion, sexual orientation, changes in social status and living situation
Assessment: 1. Methodology of assessment of the older adult	1. Methods of assessment and their use over time and age; use of interdisciplinary assessment to determine interrelationships among problems
2. Specific issues in assessment of older adults	2. Problems with testing norms, adaptation for frailties and sensory impairment, special factors in interpretation and communication of assessment findings
3. Assessment of therapeutic and programmatic efficacy	3. Assessment at individual, group, program, and systems levels of intervention
Treatment: 1. Individual, group, couples, and family psychotherapy interventions and environmental modifications	1. Emphasis on treatments with established efficacy
2. Specific applications of psychotherapy interventions for the aging	2. Emphasis on special approaches such as reminiscence, grief therapy, developmental issues of late life, therapy for those with communication difficulties, enhancing cognitive function, psychoeducational programs
3. Issues in providing services in specific settings	3. Outpatient and inpatient mental health settings, medical settings, nursing homes, community-based and in-home care settings

TABLE 17.1. Continued

Competency Area	Specific Content of Each Competency Area
Prevention and crisis intervention services	Outreach, referral and early intervention, providing health promotion resources
Consultation	Consultation to families and other caregivers, other professionals, self-help and support groups, institutions, agencies and community organizations; staff training; program development
Interface with other disciplines	1. Appropriate referral to other disciplines 2. Work within interdisciplinary teams and across a range of sites
Special ethical issues in providing services to the aged	Informed consent with cognitively impaired elders; existential issues; patient autonomy and self-determination; competing interests between older adults and family members; elder abuse; role conflicts in nursing homes; confidentiality issues in working with families and teams

friendships, intimate relationships, and other social relations. On the negative side of relationships, mental health providers for older adults must content with elder abuse and neglect. Psychologists working with older adults must be aware of the ethical responsibilities associated with confidentiality, informed consent, and relationships with family members, collaborative relationships, and goals and value conflicts.

Covering all of these topics in full detail is beyond the scope of this chapter. Therefore, the next section focuses on how the proficiencies may be differentially affected by ethnic minority status.

HOW PROFICIENCIES MAY BE DIFFERENTIALLY AFFECTED BY ETHNIC MINORITY STATUS

Older adults are a heterogeneous group in terms of values, motives, social and psychological status, and behavior, as well as a quickly growing population. The needs for mental health practitioners to be more informed about work with this diverse population of older adults have been summarized in the definition of proficiency in clinical geropsychology. That definition emphasizes broad-based knowledge of aging as a biological, psychological, and sociocultural experience. The proficiencies review adaptations of assessment and treatment for older adults, and they emphasize the need for mental health providers to work as part of interprofessional teams to meet the broad biological, social, and psychological needs of older adults. In all of these areas, attention must be paid to the way in which the older adult's experience is influenced by his or her membership in specific cultural and ethnic groups.

General Principles

As diversity issues are incorporated into conceptualizations of psychological phenomena, the category of "aged" is considered a special population and thus differences within the older adult population often have been ignored. The growth in the number of ethnic minority elders suggests that mental health practitioners and researchers must become culturally competent. Cross-cultural and minority aging issues require special knowledge, including how to interact with older minorities to convey respect and create a positive working relation. For example, in working with older adults there may be social role expectations based on age and minority status. The literature focused on mental health differences among older adults has found that race/ethnicity can play a large role in conceptualization of mental health. Variables to consider in ethnic minority case conceptualization include environment, time orientation (past, present, future), relations, communication style, and beliefs regarding how to interact with health care providers (Matthews & Peterman, 1998).

The length of time the older adult has been in the United States along with the level of acculturation must also be taken into account in case conceptualization and treatment planning. Mental health professionals working with older adults who are originally from other countries need to understand what brought the individual or his or her family to the United States, how long the person has been in the United States, the subsequent culture change, and the level of acculturation. For example, recent research has found that Mexican-born Mexican Americans had significantly lower prevalence rates across a wide range of mental health disorders than did U.S.-born Mexican Americans (Hansen, Pepitone-Arreola-Rockwell, & Green, 2000).

Providing Diagnostic Services and Individual Therapy to Ethnic Minority Older Adults

Members of ethnic minority groups are less likely to seek treatment for mental health concerns (Wyckle & Musil, 1993), and older ethnic minorities require special assessment and treatment attention. There has been progress in developing culturally valid and reliable diagnostic measures (Iwamasa & Hilliard, 1999), but continued efforts are needed in this area.

Ethnic minority status may play a role in determining the manifestation of mental disorders (e.g., Gray-Little, 1995), so the incorporation of specific cultural beliefs and behaviors into standard clinical treatments is greatly needed (Shiang, Kjellander, Huang, & Bogumill, 1998). For example, Hilliard and Iwamasa (2001) found that Japanese-American older adults conceptualized anxiety differently from the traditional psychiatric conceptualization of anxiety. As a possible explanation they suggest that somatic symptomatology may be perceived as encompassing particular forms of mental distress in the Asian culture. The *DSM-IV* addresses ethnic and cultural issues, including the role of culture in the expression and evaluation of symptoms, as well as the impact of culture on the therapeutic relation, but the information included is based on insufficient research and is not widely used (APA, 1998).

There is also a dearth of culturally competent mental health professionals. This is a major problem because the literature suggests that therapist–client match in language and ethnicity is related to the success of the treatment. The increasing diversity of the older adult population requires that we train a cadre of mental health professionals sensitive to the impact of ethnic minority status and age on case conceptualization, diagnosis, and treatment.

Families and Caregiving

Increases in longevity and multigenerational households have focused attention on families and caregiving. There are two types of caregiving often involving older adults. One type of caregiving involves older adults as the *care recipient.* The other type of caregiving refers to older adults as the *caregiver.*

Families are often involved in the health care of older adults ranging from providing transportation and sitting in on medical examinations to caregiving in the home (Zeiss & Steffen, 1996). Families play an integral part in caregiving. Approximately 13 million caregivers provide care to older relatives (Biegel, Sales, & Schultz, 1991). They provide varied types of care to older adults ranging from financial assistance to hands-on (Cohen, 1995; Gatz, Bengston, & Blum, 1990; Sussman, 1985). There are several stressors associated with providing care to an older adult. The caregiving literature indicates that many caregivers are at risk for mental and physical disorders as a result of caregiving. Many caregivers also experience increased rates of depression, anger, and anxiety (Schultz, O'Brien, Bookwala, & Fleissner, 1995).

Older adults frequently have primary caregiving responsibilities for a relative (most typically a spouse); thus, increasing the strain of caregiving tasks, in particular providing hands-on care (Zarit et al., 1999). In addition to providing care for an elderly relative, many older adults are providing care for their disabled children, those who are chronically mentally ill or mentally retarded (Bengston, Cutler, Mangen, & Marshall, 1985; Eggebeen & Wilhelm, 1995; Gatz et al, 1990).

Additionally, older adults are increasingly providing care for their grandchildren (Fuller-Thomson, Minkler, & Driver, 1997). Grandparents caring for their grandchildren are often referred to in the literature as custodial grandparents or surrogate parents. Nationally, 3.9 million children under the age of 18 lived in homes maintained by their grandparents, representing 5.5% of all children (Bryson & Casper, 1999). Of the children living with their grandparents, 1.4 million had neither parent present, representing 37% of children who live in grandparent maintained households (Casper & Bryson, 1998; Lugaila, 1998). There is a growing body of literature in the area of grandparents who have taken on a parental role for their grandchildren (Crowther & Rodriguez, in press). Such grandparents struggle with setting priorities and deciding how to divide their time, energy, and financial resources. The research addressing the health status of grandparents who are the primary caregivers for their grandchildren has identified a number of problems, including depression, insomnia, hypertension, and mobility loss as a result of the physical demand of child care.

Any of the caregiving roles described in the preceding may vary as a function of ethnic minority status, age, or the relation between caregiver and care recipient. There are strong sociohistorical beliefs and roles that govern how families provide care. However, many of those beliefs and norms are interfacing with mainstream society, creating changes in how caregiving was once performed. For example, Chornesky (2001) interviewed social workers to discuss major intergenerational issues in Native American communities. Two major issues are elder care and older adults who are providing care for their grandchildren. In terms of elder care, many older adults provided care for their children with the expectation that their children would provide care for them in their old age, in accord with cultural traditions. Given the impact of mainstream culture on the lives of many caregivers and structural changes in the family, which require adult members to work outside the home, caring for elders becomes difficult if not impossible. Adult children often feel enormous guilt when they are not able to care for family elders, and there is often discord among the children. Barriers to care outside the home include transportation difficulties and the lack of sensitivity and responsiveness by professionals regarding cultural definitions of disease and healing.

Viewing families and caregiving from a multidimensional perspective sheds light on the complexity of multigenerational relations and the external forces that impact on them. It is important to keep in mind that older adults can be care recipients as well as caregivers. Regardless of who is providing care, many caregivers need access to information and resources regarding how to manage their caregiving role. Additionally, mental health professionals should be sensitive to cultural definitions of wellness and disease to better facilitate the needs of intergenerational families.

SUMMARY AND RECOMMENDATIONS FOR FUTURE RESEARCH

This chapter has provided an overview of issues related to mental health and aging. Older adults are a heterogeneous population. They vary in personality, health status, cognitive status, and lifestyle. The percentage of older adults is increasing in the United States and throughout the world. Additionally, in the United States the number of older ethnic minorities is growing. Given the increase in the aged population, it is important to consider mental health services and policies along with the resources and infrastructure needed to support the mental health needs of the elderly and their families. This chapter was not meant to be a comprehensive review of the field of mental health and aging. Rather, the overview was intended to stimulate interest in issues that affect older people, their families, and the health professionals with whom they interact. In response to the "graying of America" there has been an increase in the field of clinical geropsychology. Persons interested in mental health and older adults must have a broad understanding of the psychological, biological, and social aspects of aging as proposed in the biopsychosocial model, as summarized in the review of the areas of proficiency in clinical geropsychology.

The areas of proficiency provide a valuable summary of the highlights of what is currently known about providing mental health services to older adults; however, much of what we currently know is based on research with the current cohort of older adults, particularly those who are Caucasian Americans. That research does not fully represent the heterogeneity within older adults now and will be less representative of future generations of older adults. In particular, there is considerable speculation that the large number of children born after World War II (now nearing older adult status) may age differently. Three issues have been raised.

First, it is often suggested that this cohort of elders may be more open to psychological interventions, escalating needs for research on assessment and therapy with older adults and for enhanced training of all clinical psychologists regarding work with older adults. On the other hand, coming generations of older adults may be healthier and more functional (Waidmann & Liu, 2000), reducing depression and other psychological sequelae of disability, thus reducing the need for psychological interventions. Finally, the increasing proportion of ethnic minority elders also will create challenges; as current generations of minority Americans age they will carry with them salient features such as a continuing imbalanced sex ratio, segregated distribution, and proportion in poverty. In addition, the aging of individuals from multiple cultural traditions, racial backgrounds, and ethnic perspectives must be recognized, studied, and findings incorporated into strategies for assessment of mental health concerns, prevention of mental health problems in late life, and treatment for those who do have clinical concerns. With this in mind, Iwamasa and Sorocco (in press) in their chapter on research methodology with ethnic minority older adults discuss the need to be more creative and culturally appropriate in the selection of research methodology. Clearly, researchers and clinicians in the field of gerontology need to be guided by research to date but open to dramatic shifts in the field.

REFERENCES

American Psychiatric Association. (1994). *Diagnostic and statistical manual of mental disorders* (4th ed.). Washington, DC: Author.

American Psychological Association Interdivisional Task Force on qualifications for practice in clinical and applied geropsychology. (1999). Qualifications for practice in clinical geropsychology, Unpublished Working Draft #7. Bethesda, MD: Division 12, Section II and Division 20.

Armstrong, T., & Crowther, M. (2002). Spirituality among older African Americans. *Journal of Adult Development, 9,* 3–12.

Baltes, P. B., & Staudinger, U. (1996). Interactive minds. Cambridge: Cambridge University Press.

Bengston, V. L., Cutler, N. E., Mangen, D. J., & Marshall, V. W. (1985). Generations, cohorts and relations between age groups. In R. H. Binstock & E. Shanas (Eds.), *Handbook of aging and social sciences* (2nd ed., pp. 415–449). New York: Van Nostrand Reinhold.

Berger, K. S. (1994). Late adulthood. *Developing through the life span.* New York: Worth.

Betancourt, H., & Lopez, S. R. (1993). The study of culture, ethnicity, and race in American psychology. *American Psychologist, 48,* 629–637.

Biegel, D. E., Sales, E., & Schultz, R. (1991). Family caregiving in chronic illness. Newbury Park, CA: Sage.

Binstock, R. H. (1992). The oldest old and "intergenerational equity." In R. M. Suzman, D. P. Willis, & K. G. Manton (Eds.), *The oldest old* (pp. 394–417). New York: Oxford University Press.

Birren, J. E. & Schaie, K. W. (1996). *The handbooks of aging: Handbook of the psychology of aging* (4th ed.). San Diego, CA: Academic Press.

Bronfrenbrenner, U. (1989). Ecological systems theory. In R. Vasta (Ed.), *Annals of child development: Vol. 6. Six theories of child development: Revised formulations and current issues* (pp. 187–249). Greenwich, CT: JAI Press.

Bryson, K., & Casper, L. M. (1999). Coresident grandparents and grandchildren: May 1999. *U.S. Bureau of the Census Current population reports.* (Series P-23 No. 198). Washington, DC: U.S. Government Printing Office.

Casper, L. M., & Bryson, K. R. (1998). *Co-resident parents and their grandchildren: Grandparent maintained families.* Population Division Working Paper No. 26. Washington, DC: U.S. Bureau of the Census.

Chornesky, A. (2001). Elders as primary caregivers of grandchildren. *New Mexico Geriatric Education Center,* 3–4.

Cohen, G. D. (1995). Intergenerationalism: A new "ism" with positive mental health and social policy potential. *American Journal of Geriatric Psychiatry, 2,* 185–187.

Crowther, M., & Rodriguez, R. (2002). Stress and coping model of custodial grandparenting among African Americans. In B. Hayslip & J. Patrick (Eds.), *Working with custodial grandparents* (pp. 145–162). New York: Springer.

Eggebeen, D. J., & Wilhelm, M. O. (1995). Patterns of support given by older Americans to their children. In S. A. Bass (Ed.), *Older and active: How Americans over 55 are contributing to society* (pp. 122–168). New Haven, CT: Yale University Press.

Floyd, F. J., Haynes, S. N., Doll, E. R., Winemiller, D., Lemsky, C., Burgy, T. M., Werle, M., & Heilman, N. (1992). Assessing retirement satisfaction and perceptions of retirement experiences. *Psychology and Aging, 7,* 609–621.

Freud, S. (1924). On psychotherapy. In *Collected papers,* Vol. 1. London: Hogarth.

Fuller-Thomson, E., Minkler, M., & Driver, D. (1997). A profile of grandparents raising grandchildren in the United States. *The Gerontologist, 37,* 406–411.

Gallagher-Thompson, D., Coon, D., Rivera, P., Powers, D., & Zeiss, A. (1998). Family caregiving: Stress, coping, and intervention. In Hersen, M. & Van Hasselt, V. (Eds.), *Handbook of Clinical Geropsychology* (pp. 469-494). New York: Plenum.

Gatz, M., Kasl-Godley, J. E., & Karel, M. J. (1996). Aging and mental disorders. In J. E. Birren & K. W. Schaie (Eds.), *The handbooks of aging: Handbook of the psychology of aging* (4th ed., pp. 365–382). San Diego, CA: Academic Press.

Gatz, M., & Smyer, M. (1992). The mental health system and older adults in the 1990s. *American Psychologist, 47,* 15–25.

Gatz, M., Bengston, V. L., & Blum, M. J. (1990). Caregiving families. In J. E. Birren & K. W. Schaie (Eds.), *Handbook of the psychology of aging* (pp. 404–426). San Diego, CA: Academic Press.

Gray-Little, B. (1995). The assessment of psychopathology in racial and ethnic minorities. In J. N. Butcher (Ed.), *Clinical personality assessment: Practical approaches* (pp. 141–157). New York: Oxford University Press.

Hansen, N. D., Pepitone-Arreola-Rockwell, F., Greene, A. F. (2000). Multicultural competence: Criteria and case examples. *Professional Psychology: Research and Practice, 31,* 652–660.

Hess, T. M., & Blanchard-Fields, F. (1999). *Social cognition and aging.* San Diego, CA: Academic.

Hilliard, K. M., & Iwamasa, G. Y. (2001). The conceptualization of anxiety: An exploratory study of Japanese American older adults. *Journal of Clinical Geropsychology, 7,* 53–65.

Iwamasa, G. Y., & Sorocco, K. H. (in press). Aging and Asian Americans: Developing culturally appropriate research methodology. In G. N. Hall & S. Okazaki (Eds.), *Asian American psychology: The science of lives in context*. Washington, DC: American Psychological Association.

Iwamasa, G. Y., & Hilliard, K. M. (1999). Depression and anxiety among Asian American
elders: A review of the literature. *Clinical Psychology Review, 19*, 343–357.

Landreville, P., Landry, J., Baillargeon, L., Guérette, A., & Matteau, E. (2001). Older adults'
acceptance of psychological and pharmacological treatments for depression. *Journal of
Gerontology: Psychological Sciences, 56B*, P285–P291.

Lugaila, T. (1998). *Marital status and living arrangements: March 1997. Current population
reports, population characteristics*. Series P-20 No. 514 Washington, DC: U.S. Government Printing Office.

Matthews, A. K., & Peterman, A. H. (1998). Improving provision of effective treatment for
racial and cultural minorities. *Psychotherapy: Theory, Research, Practice, Training, 35*,
291–305.

McFadden, S. (1996). Aging and mental disorders. In J. E. Birren & K. W. Schaie (Eds.), *The
handbooks of aging: Handbook of the psychology of aging* (4th ed., pp. 365–382). San
Diego, CA: Academic Press.

Qualls, S. H. (1996). Family therapy with aging families. In S. Zarit & R. Knight (Eds.),
Psychotherapy and aging (pp. 121–137). Washington, DC: American Psychological Association Press.

Rokke, P. D., & Scogin, F. (1995). Depression treatment preferences in younger and older
adults. *Journal of Clinical Geropsychology, 1*, 243–257.

Schultz, R., O'Brien, A. T., Bookwala, J., & Fleissner, K. (1995). Psychiatric and physical
morbidity effects of dementia caregiving: Prevalence, correlates, and causes. *Gerontologist, 35*, 771–791.

Shiang, J., Kjellander, C., Huang, K., & Bogumill, S. (1998). Developing cultural competency
in clinical practice: Treatment considerations for Chinese cultural groups in the United
States. *Clinical Psychology: Science and Practice, 5*, 182–210.

Smyer, M. A., & Allen-Burge, R. (1999). Older adults decision making capacity: Institutional
settings and individual choices. In J. C. Cavanaugh & S. K. Whitbourne (Eds.), *Gerontology: An Interdisciplinary Perspective* (pp. 391–413). New York: Oxford University Press.

Sussman, M. B. (1985). The family life of old people. In R. H. Binstock & E. Shanas (Eds.),
Handbook of aging and social sciences (pp. 415–449). New York: Van Nostrand Reinhold.

Thompson, L. W., Gallagher-Thompson, D., Futterman, A., Gilewki, M. J., & Peterson, J.
(1991). The effects of late-life spousal bereavement over a 30-month interval. *Psychology and Aging, 6*, 434–441.

U.S. Census Bureau. (2000). *Population projections of the United States by age, race, Hispanic
origin, and nativity: 1999 to 2100*. Washington, DC: U.S. Government Printing Office.

U.S. Department of Health and Human Services. (1998). *Informal caregiving. Compassion in
action*. Washington, DC: U.S. Department of Health and Human Services, Office of the
Assistant Secretary for Planning & Evaluation.

U.S. Department of Health and Human Services. (1999). Mental health: A report of the Surgeon General. Rockville, MD: U.S. Department of Health and Human Services, Substance Abuse and Mental Health Services Administration, Center for Mental Health Services, National Institutes of Health, National Institute of Mental Health.

U.S. Department of Health and Human Services, Administration on Aging. (2001). *Older
adults and mental health: Issues and opportunities*. Washington, DC: U.S. Department of
Health and Human Services & Administration on Aging.

Waidmann, T. A., & Liu, K. (2000). Disability trends among elderly persons and implications
for the future. *Journal of Gerontology: Social Sciences, 55B*, S298–S307.

Whitfield, K., & Baker-Thomas, T. (1999). Individual differences in aging minorities. *International Journal of Aging and Human Development, 48*, 73–79.

World Health Organization. (2001). *Global movement for active ageing—background information* (pp. 1–3). Accessed: http://www.int/hpr/globalmovement/background.htm [April 9, 2002].

Wyckle, M. L., & Musil, C. M. (1993). Mental health of older persons: Social and cultural factors. *Generations, 17,* 7–12.

Zarit, S., Gaugler, J., & Jarrott, S. (1999). Useful services for families: Research findings and directions. *International Journal of Geriatric Psychiatry, 14,* 165–181.

Zeiss, A.M., & Steffen, A. (1996). Treatment issues with elderly clients. *Cognitive and Behavioral Practice, 3,* 371–389.

CHAPTER 18

Deaf

Moving from Hearing Loss to Diversity

IRENE W. LEIGH

Ethnicity alone does not define diversity, as this book clearly demonstrates. Diversity encompasses the variety endemic to humanity. What many fail to realize is that deaf people are part of the diversity spectrum as well (Leigh, Corbett, Gutman, & Morere, 1996). People react to "deaf" as a "difference," a difference that is rarely welcomed or celebrated by mainstream society. Not hearing, in the eyes of many, equates being cut off from the world of sound, language, and life. In this respect, "deaf" becomes "not able" or, in other words, disabled, in comparison to hearing counterparts (Biderman, 1998; Corker, 1998; Davis, 1995; Humphries, 1993, 1996). And, as we know, people with disabilities have been marginalized; pitied; and rejected from jobs, housing, and social situations, among others. In fact, deaf people have been the victims of discrimination throughout history (Jankowski, 1997; Van Cleve, 1993). What is all too often overlooked is the resiliency of many deaf people and their ability to function as mentally healthy individuals, able to manage their lives independently. This chapter outlines the differences between the paradigms of deaf people as people with disabilities and deaf people as people with a culture, specifically Deaf culture. Next, how these paradigms have influenced deaf identity constructs is explored. The ethnic dimension and its interface with deafness is taken into account. Following this, mental health considerations are addressed.

First, a review of population statistics helps to define the people who are the focus of this chapter. There are approximately 28 million people with hearing impairments in the United States (National Institute on Deafness and Other Communication Disorders, 1996, as cited in Niparko, 2000). For most of them, hearing loss emerges as part of the aging process. This number is expected to grow dramatically because of increased life expectancy. Based on a review of various studies, Blanchfield, Dunbar, Feldman, and Gardner (1999) estimated that within this group of people with hearing impairments there are approximately 464,000 to 738,000 severely to profoundly deaf people.[1] Out of this number, roughly 400,000 may be connected to the deaf community (Schein, 1989), although the figure may well be higher. Before explaining what the deaf community is, it is important to explore how deafness typically has been conceptualized by the majority hearing society and by many deaf people themselves.

DEAF AS DISABILITY

In the minds of most people, the word "deaf" means not hearing. Therefore, to be deaf is to have a disability. Specifically, the sense of hearing is nonfunctional for the purpose of auditory orientation to the immediate environment in general and spoken communication in particular. The etiology of hearing loss tends to be genetically based, disease based, age based, or caused by environmental hazards. Because essentially hearing is based on biological functions, the medical approach typically is the first resort for those concerned about the possibility of hearing loss. Medicine essentially is about preventing or curing disease, treating symptoms, and improving or maintaining one's functional ability (Jonsen, Siegler, & Winslade, 1998). This perspective therefore encourages the conceptualization of deafness as a pathological condition that needs to be corrected or repaired in order to enhance one's ability to receive sound. Without this correction, deafness tends to be viewed as a tragedy, the ultimate consequence being that: "Beyond sound are no human relationships, no government, no equality of existence, no inkling of knowledge" (Brueggemann, 1999, p. 106).

In order to provide access to sound, and therefore to spoken language, communication, and a "normal life" for those who are diagnosed as deaf, medicine focuses on cure. For problems related to the middle ear, correction is more likely to be effective. However, in the case of severe to profound deafness (most often related to inner ear dysfunction), cure typically is not possible. Subsequently, the next step is to create a pathway to sound with the use of technology, such as hearing aids and cochlear implants[2] or other assistive listening devices. These tools, together with intensive auditory and speech training to enhance comprehension and production of spoken communication, are meant to facilitate access to the auditory environment. In this way, the hope is that the disability of deafness may be overcome and deaf people can function "just like everyone else."

For those who lose their hearing after they have mastered spoken language, the disability of hearing loss can lead to social and psychological effects such as withdrawal, isolation, and depression (Meadow-Orlans, 1985). Interpersonal relationships and career trajectories can be negatively affected by communication difficulties. The ability to maximize use of assistive listening devices and learn to lip read or use sign language varies according to individual characteristics. Visual aids such as closed captioning of television programs facilitate access to auditory-based information. Individuals learn to cope depending on the effectiveness of technology, their resiliency, and the presence of social support systems.

The medical and audiological establishments play a critical role in the diagnosis of deafness during the early years of life. After diagnosis, infants and young children receive hearing aids or cochlear implants and are referred to specialized education programs that will facilitate access to language. Different programs have different philosophies about communication and language. Some emphasize auditory avenues to learning language with the aid of assistive devices; some focus on listening and visual cues such as lip reading, whereas others encourage the use of varied signed English systems (in which signs follow English word order), Cued Speech (which uses handshapes to make speech sounds visible), or American Sign Language (ASL), a visual language with its own grammar and syntax (Moores, 2001; Paul & Jackson, 1993). Hearing families have to adjust to the communication needs of their deaf children, who would otherwise typically feel left out within family interactions because they cannot hear what is going on. For many families, the diagnosis of deafness is unexpected, and the adjustments that need to be made tend to be basically in terms of making language accessible to the deaf child in order to encourage communication and social intercourse. Deaf persons who grow up, succeed in the world of work, and mingle with hearing peers are often described as having "overcome their deafness" in order to achieve a "normal" life that approximates hearing ways of functioning. Crossing the bridge to such normalcy requires perseverance, dedication, and hard work to minimize the impact of being deaf.

DEAF AS CULTURE

In contrast to those who see themselves as audiologically deaf, many deaf people do not minimize the implications of being deaf. Rather, they revel in being deaf. For them, "deaf" is not an audiological condition per se, but rather a "normal" state of affairs. Specifically, deaf, as in Deaf culture, forms their way of life, communication, daily routines, and socialization (Padden & Humphries, 1988). Many deaf persons have gravitated toward each other based in large part on shared experiences and the need for a communal sense of belonging. Out of these connections, deaf communities have evolved throughout the world (Higgins, 1980; Lane, Hoffmeister, & Bahan, 1996; Neisser, 1983; Schein, 1989).

In the United States, deaf communities have been around for over two centuries (Schein, 1989; Van Cleve & Crouch, 1989). The foundations of these deaf communities were created by graduates of residential state schools and day schools for the deaf all over the country where the majority of deaf children were educated up until the mid-20th century. These graduates, who shared common experiences growing up, formed deaf clubs, deaf associations such as the National Association of the Deaf, deaf religious organizations, and deaf sports organizations, among others. All of these contributed to the structure and existence of the deaf community.

The notion of a Deaf culture is of more recent origin, having emerged out of the recognition that ASL does contain linguistic properties that make it a bona fide language (Lane, Hoffmeister, & Bahan, 1996; Padden & Humphries, 1988; Paul & Jackson, 1993; Schein, 1989). As Humphries (1996) points out, deaf people have begun to define themselves, not as based on disability or "handicapped" paradigms, but rather as a group of people who have a language of their own (ASL) and function in specific ways. These include, for example, the ways they relate to others in a visual medium, such as waving hands to get the attention of others, the ways in which they prefer to get together, and their sharing of common stories and jokes about their lives as deaf people. Deaf people who view themselves as culturally Deaf have minimal interest in how well they hear from an audiological perspective, because hearing and speaking English are not prominent aspects of their culture. They do see the importance of reading and writing English in relating with their network of hearing people and obtaining employment.

Even though the concept of a Deaf culture is increasingly accepted in the literature, those such as Stewart (1992) have questioned its foundation. In his eyes, the phrase "Deaf culture" and its minimization of the disability of deafness was developed for political purposes, in order to provide greater legitimacy to the opinions of a group of deaf people increasingly resistant to the notion that they were "disabled." Nonetheless, deaf people who claim ASL as their language have taken the Deaf culture frame to heart. The widely publicized 1988 Deaf President Now movement (which developed as a protest against the appointment of a hearing president to run Gallaudet University, the world's only liberal arts institution of higher learning for deaf students, and culminated in the installation of Gallaudet's first deaf president) reflects a visceral collective reaction to the legitimacy of Deaf culture and the rights of deaf people to control their own institutions and destinies (Christiansen & Barnartt, 1995; Gannon, 1989).

Although deaf children (and hearing children) of culturally Deaf parents grow up within the culture, most deaf children have hearing parents (Moores, 2001); therefore, they become aware of the deaf community and Deaf cultural ways of behaving mostly during school years and beyond. They find out about deaf-sponsored events. When they attend these events, they are exposed to deaf people. The excitement at connecting with them because of shared experiences and shared understanding of how it is to live as deaf persons in a hearing environment facilitates the connections to the deaf community, and the shared ways of behaving that is part of Deaf culture.

Nowadays, deaf children are increasingly educated in mainstream public school settings and in specialized day schools or programs (Holden-Pitt & Diaz, 1998). Correspondingly, the number of deaf children attending residential schools has significantly declined. Because of advances in telecommunications such as the Internet and teletypewriters (TTYs) that function as telephones, thereby bringing deaf people geographically far apart closer together, deaf people are now relying less on physical places such as deaf clubs and specific places for the sense of community. As Padden and Rayman (2000) explain, occasional events in various places provide the new venue for deaf community interactions. The boundaries that separated deaf events from the hearing community are no longer as firm, becasue deaf events take place in hotels, convention centers, and sports arenas where hearing people mingle as well. More hearing students are taking ASL classes and learning about the deaf community in Deaf Studies programs. All these are contributing to the changes in the deaf community now taking place.

Among the new innovations in technology that are changing the face of the United States, there are two that impact the deaf community, specifically the advent of cochlear implants (see end note 2), and advances that permit the identification of genes.

The cochlear implant issue has drawn passionate responses from various factions (Christiansen & Leigh, 2002). Advocates of cochlear implants see the implant as a miracle cure with the potential of eradicating deafness because, for a good number of users, such instruments provide improved access to the world of sound in comparison with hearing aids. The effectiveness of these instruments has improved over the years, and the age of implantation has dropped to the point where infants 12 months of age or even younger are now being implanted. Because the vast majority of implanted children have hearing parents, the push for spoken English is strong. One critical caveat related to cochlear implants is that access to sound does not equate understanding of sound without intensive auditory or listening training.

A number of deaf activists, on the other hand, see cochlear implantation as the specter of genocide, the goal being to eradicate sign language and Deaf culture. Many members of the culture up until recently rejected any deaf adult who even ventured to consider the possibility of getting a cochlear implant. This rejection has now changed to grudging acceptance as it becomes apparent that those culturally Deaf adults who decided to get the implant in order to experience sound still held on to Deaf culture values such as maintaining ties with deaf peers and continuing to use ASL. Also, among the increasing number of young people who have grown up with cochlear implants, many continue to see themselves as deaf, cherish ties to the deaf community, and express the desire to keep on using ASL or learn it (Christiansen & Leigh, 2002). Such young people will ensure that the deaf community maintains its vibrancy in the face of new advents in technology. Additionally, this increased acceptance of cochlear implants is reflected in the National Association of the Deaf position statement on cochlear implants (National Association of the Deaf, 2000). Specifically, cochlear implants are now accepted as one of a variety of options to be considered for the deaf child, rather than rejected outright.

As the technical potential for identifying the genes that cause deafness increases, deaf persons may be increasingly confronted with the possibility of genetic manipulation to eliminate deafness. The implications for the deaf community are only now beginning to be recognized (Arnos, 2002).

DEAF IDENTITY

As we know, people have multiple identities, depending on their environment and what is most salient at any given point in time. These identities, which help individuals define who and what they are, tend to be forged through perceptions of differences and classificatory structures such as gender, ethnicity, educational levels, career classifications, sexual orientation, and so on, that highlight these differences (Corker, 1996; Woodward, 1997). Identities play a critical role in self-understanding and psychological adjustment (Waterman, 1992). Increased awareness of cultural diversity has fueled research into cultural identities and their role in facilitating mental health. Because of the recent recognition of Deaf culture, researchers have started exploring deaf identity, how it develops, and its role in the psychological health of deaf individuals.

Exactly what constitutes a deaf identity and how does one acquire it? The audiological connotation for a deaf identity can be expressed by the following: "I do not hear; therefore I am deaf and not hearing." The cultural connotation is based on one saying something like, "I am deaf. I use ASL. I connect with deaf people."

In exploring how these different deaf identities develop, Glickman (1996) developed a model based on cultural and racial identity development models. In this model, he lists four different stages of deaf identity. Stage 1 is labeled as the culturally hearing stage. In this stage, deafness is understood as a medical condition, not as a cultural state of being. Medicine and technology are seen as a means for ameliorating the disability of deafness. To be "normal," the deaf person needs to mimic hearing ways of speaking, understanding, and behaving. Overcoming the need for support services is seen as a means of facilitating integration into hearing society. Glickman views this stage as most relevant to individuals who lose their hearing in adulthood, but also applicable to those deaf individuals who use spoken English, interact primarily with hearing peers, and who may belong to organizations advocating the teaching of spoken language to deaf children. His basic assumption is that this stage tends not to be a healthy one emotionally for those growing up deaf, because they are essentially "denying their deafness."

In Stage 2, which reflects cultural marginality, deaf persons do not fully identify with either Deaf or hearing culture. They tend to have difficulties in maintaining intimate relationships in either deaf or hearing groups, and exist on the fringe of both groups. Glickman theorizes that this category is applicable to deaf children born into hearing families who initially are naive to deafness. These children start off with limited exposure to deaf groups, and are not fully part of the hearing environment because of limited access to sound and spoken language.

Deaf individuals in Stage 3 have moved toward immersing themselves in the Deaf-World. They embrace a positive and uncritical, idealized identification with Deaf culture and act the way they believe authentic "deaf" people are supposed to. Hearing values are denigrated, and hearing people are attacked, as are deaf people with "hearing minds" who speak English. Culturally Deaf people can do no wrong. As deaf people start to recognize the strengths and weaknesses not only of deaf people, but also of hearing people, and more fully integrate the values of both hearing and Deaf cultures, they enter the fourth stage, which is the bicultural stage. In this stage, both ASL and English are respected. For deaf individuals starting off in the culturally marginal stage, Glickman sees the bicultural stage as the final one in the process of deaf identity development. Deaf children of deaf parents, who usually reflect pride in being deaf as well as comfort in dealing with both deaf and hearing worlds, tend to demonstrate a bicultural identity early on.

Glickman (1996) developed the Deaf Identity Development Scale (DIDS) in order to assist mental health professionals in understanding their clients' deaf identity. The DIDS is a 60-item measure that consists of four scales, each reflecting one of the described stages. The Hearing Scale has items such as "I only socialize with hearing people" (Glickman, 1996, p. 149). "Neither deaf nor hearing people accept me" (p. 149) is found in the Marginal Scale, whereas the Immersion Scale has items such as

"Deaf people should only socialize with other deaf people." Lastly, "I enjoy both Deaf and hearing cultures" (p. 150) reflects items in the Bicultural Scale.

Even though Glickman demonstrated acceptable reliability for each of the four scales, as well as construct validity, follow-up studies have indicated problems with the bicultural scale (Fischer, 2000; Friedburg, 2000; Leigh, Marcus, Dobosh, & Allen, 1998). In these studies, the Bicultural Scale did not discriminate well among subjects, including hearing subjects having little contact with deaf people. One possible explanation is that this scale includes bicultural attitudinal items that may have pulled for social desirability in the eyes of both deaf and hearing respondents. As a case in point, Padden (1996) notes that individuals identifying with Deaf culture are increasingly recognizing the need to assume a more bicultural stance owing to current technology and work settings that offer more opportunities for interaction with hearing peers.

In contrast to Glickman's (1996) approach, Maxwell McCaw (2001) turns to the acculturation model as a basis for understanding deaf identities. In this model, the ultimate patterns of acculturation for immigrants often vary in terms of the level of psychological (or internalized) identification with each culture (the culture of origin and the new host culture), the degree of behavioral involvement in the two cultures, and the level of cultural competence in these cultures. By the same token, acculturation patterns for deaf and hard-of-hearing individuals can vary in terms of the level of psychological identification with Deaf culture and with the culture of their hearing society, the degree of behavioral involvement in the two cultures, and the level of cultural competence in these cultures.

To test this idea, Maxwell McCaw (2001) developed the Deaf Acculturation Scale (DAS), which consists of two acculturation scales: a Deaf Acculturation Scale and a Hearing Acculturation Scale. Each scale contains five subscales (five deaf subscales and five hearing subscales) that are parallel to each other and measure acculturation across five domains. The Cultural Identification Subscales measure psychological identification with other deaf/hearing people, use of self-labels, and level of comfort within each culture (e.g., "I call myself Deaf," and "I call myself hard of hearing or hearing-impaired"). The Cultural Participation Subscales were designed to measure cultural behaviors. These scales examine the degree to which deaf and hard-of-hearing people participate in various cultural activities (e.g., "How much do you enjoy attending deaf parties, gatherings, events?" and "How much do you enjoy attending hearing parties, gatherings, events?"). The Cultural Attitudes Subscales were designed to measure preferences for friends, lovers, spouses, educational and work colleagues to be either deaf or hearing (e.g., "I would prefer my spouse/partner to be deaf" and "I would prefer my spouse/partner to be hearing"). The remaining two subscales were designed to measure cultural competence, which in this case includes both language competence and overall knowledge of each individual culture such as knowledge of the structure of social networks and knowledge of the collective history. Therefore, items in the Language Competence subscales measure expressive and receptive competence in American Sign Language (ASL), as well as competence in spoken and written English (e.g., "How well do you sign in ASL?" and "How well do you speak in English, using your voice?"). The Cultural Knowledge subscales measure knowledge of the deaf and hearing worlds (e.g., "How well do you know favorite jokes about deaf culture?" or "How well do you know popular nursery rhymes and children's stories in English?").

Based on a median-split of the Hearing and Deaf Acculturation scales, the overall scale produces four kinds of acculturation in Deaf people: hearing acculturated (high scores in hearing acculturation and low scores in deaf acculturation), marginal (low scores in both hearing and deaf acculturation), deaf acculturated (high scores in deaf acculturation and low scores in hearing acculturation), and bicultural (high scores in both deaf and hearing acculturation). Reliability and validity were demonstrated to be in the acceptable range.

Maxwell McCaw (2001) also explored the relationship between psychological well-being and DAS acculturation styles. Her results indicated that for deaf and hard-of-hearing subjects, deaf acculturation and biculturalism were equally associated with a healthy sense of well-being, more so than for those who were hearing acculturated. Marginalism was found to be the least adaptive of the four acculturation styles. In essence, being comfortable with one's deafness is as critical for psychological well-being as is the ability to comfortably switch between deaf and hearing environments.

Corker (1996) takes a different approach in conceptualizing deaf identity. She argues that deafness is not necessarily a core identity for those who do not grow up within deaf families. Rather, she perceives the integration of deafness to be an additional developmental task, which depends considerably on environmental variables and family and school situations. For example, the experience of stigma or feelings of difference when with hearing persons can heighten the salience of a deaf identity, whereas the absence of both stigma and feelings of difference will minimizes the need to focus on deafness as an integral part of one's identity. Corker recognizes ethnic or racial identity as more of a critical key determinant in core identity construction, with ethnic identity taking precedence over the integration of deafness because of the influence of family in the early years. That is not to deny the existence of an interactive effect between ethnicity and being deaf, which is the subject of the next section.

THE ETHNIC DIMENSION

Although the meaning of deafness is a common bond for deaf community members, in fact the deaf community is a microcosm of the larger community within which it is nested. The surrounding social, cultural, ethnic, linguistic, religious, political, and regional entities will impact on the deaf experience and the deaf connection (Corker, 1996; Humphries, 1993; Lane, Hoffmeister, & Bahan, 1996; Leigh & Lewis, 1999). The deaf community is not immune to the increasing ethnic diversity in the United States. The most recent statistics for deaf and hard-of-hearing children and youth, which are based on reports from schools and programs throughout the United States that educate deaf children (Holden-Pitt & Diaz, 1998), indicate that ethnic demographic patterns are very similar to the projections made by the U.S. Bureau of the Census (1996, as cited in Delgado, 2000). Specifically, the numbers of White deaf and hard-of-hearing children have decreased from 71% in 1977–1978 to 58% in 1996–

1997, whereas the numbers of Latino and Asian/Pacific Islander deaf and hard-of-hearing children have doubled, with Latinos increasing from 9% to 18% and Asian/Pacific Islanders from 1% to 4%. The numbers for African Americans and Native Americans have remained constant at 17% and 1%, respectively.

As those who consider themselves part of Deaf culture move toward a more bicultural stance in relating to both the Deaf world and the hearing environment, there is increased recognition that to speak of the bicultural deaf person may in fact be limiting. When the Deaf person is African American, Vietnamese, Cuban, Native American, or White, to speak of this deaf person as multicultural may be a more accurate reflection of reality. Such an individual is likely to be a member of at least three communities: the larger deaf community, his or her ethnic hearing community, and his or her ethnic deaf community (Corbett, 1999; Leigh, Corbett, Gutman, & Morere, 1996). To be mentally healthy, multicultural deaf people need to integrate these community memberships and their "Americanness" into their ethnic/cultural identities rather than being limited to one aspect to the detriment of the others (Wu & Grant, 1999). As part of the acculturative process, they need to be able to adapt communication and behavior appropriately suited to the cultural milieu in which they find themselves, whether it be within their American or ethnic deaf community, or their ethnic hearing community, and to switch easily when cultural milieus change. This fits the alternation model of LaFromboise, Coleman, and Gerton (1993), which postulates that one's behavior can be altered to fit the social context as appropriate without essentially compromising his or her sense of ethnic cultural identity. Similarly, the Deaf culture identity, or the "Americanness" need not be compromised by ethnicity.

Although multicultural deaf individuals, whether immigrants or born in the United States, do work toward achieving some measure of American identity and American Deaf culture connections, there is a clear sense of "coming home" when they connect with other deaf people who share their ethnic identity (Corbett, 1999; Eldredge, 1999; Hernandez, 1999; Wu & Grant, 1999). This phenomenon has given rise to organizations such as the National Black Deaf Advocates and the Asian American Deaf Congress. These organizations provide deaf members with the opportunity to share ways in which the process of integrating a multiplicity of identities, including the deaf dimension, can be facilitated. The National Association of the Deaf, founded over a century ago by White deaf men (Van Cleve & Crouch, 1989), provides opportunities for interacting with the larger deaf community and access to American Deaf values.

In thinking about the impact of multiculturalism, an additional consideration is that social perceptions about deafness vary according to culture as well as level of education and socioeconomic factors (Christensen & Delgado, 1993; Yacobacci-Tam, 1987). Some societies or cultures view deafness as a disability or a stigma that needs to be hidden away to minimize shame; others see it as a punishment for past sins or as an act of God that they must accept. Fatalistic views of the implications of deafness are often present, meaning that the deaf person is seen as one who needs care, and who is limited in assuming the typical responsibilities of adulthood. Those with more education are less fatalistic and more able to consider the possibility that deaf persons can achieve their potential and rise to meet life challenges. Although these varying perceptions are culture-specific, confronting American attitudes that emphasize the potential of deaf individuals to grow in ways previously not thought possible sets in motion a process that changes self-perceptions of what one can do as a deaf person in the United States. Hernandez (1999), in her moving description of a Latino deaf adolescent immigrant group, illustrates how the process of immigration and exposure to both ethnic deaf peer support and American Deaf culture values profoundly alters what it means to be a Latino deaf person in the United States as opposed to the country of origin.

Dealing with the interface between deafness and ethnicity is no simple matter. To provide effective mental health services to this population, professionals need to be attuned to cultural issues related to being deaf and being a member of varied ethnic groups. This is a task not easily accomplished, considering that deaf people in need of mental health interventions have typically been underserved because of difficulties in communication and the lack of service providers who can communicate with them in their preferred language or communication system (Steinberg, Loew, & Sullivan, 1999). The addition of the ethnic component serves to add new complexity in considering the best means of providing services. The next section covers issues that are critical in the area of mental health service delivery to this specialized population.

IMPLICATIONS FOR MENTAL HEALTH SERVICES

Specialized mental health services for this population continue to be very limited. Available services tend to be scattered mostly throughout the East and West Coasts of the United States (Morton & Christensen, 2000). In addition, deaf persons receiving public mental health services, including psychiatric hospitalization, are less likely than hearing persons to be from racial/ethnic minority groups (Pollard, 1994; Trybus, 1983).

What are the typical perspectives of the deaf consumer regarding mental health services? Steinberg, Loew, and Sullivan (1999) present findings from a 2-year study in which deaf adults were interviewed about their knowledge, attitudes, and beliefs about mental health and mental health services. Participants overwhelmingly maintained that mental health problems in any one individual stemmed not from the deafness, but rather from external aspects such as upbringing, family problems, and, in particular, communication problems. Deafness was not seen as pathogenic. Rather, communication issues were seen as central to the mental health of deaf individuals. In other words, deaf people in general, and deaf people from various cultural backgrounds, present with unique and often unmet communication needs, ranging from ASL or signed English to pantomime and gesture, from using spoken language to writing back and forth. Sophistication in written or spoken languages, or in some form of sign language, varies greatly from individual to individual, whether American or from homes where other languages are used. Many of these individuals expect that communication barriers are present.

Although signing clinicians were preferred for direct communication, respondents expressed willingness to work with sign language interpreters who could facilitate interaction with service providers. However, concern was expressed regarding the ability of such interpreters to understand the deaf client and convey all the nuances required for diagnostic and therapeutic purposes. Many respondents had limited information on mental health resources for deaf clientele, which attests to the infrequency of such services in various locales.

Additionally, there was a pervasive perception that deaf persons in need of mental health intervention are at the mercy of hearing authorities who may or may not understand them. Hearing authority figures need to be familiar with the deaf community and its diverse components in order to facilitate effective mental health service delivery. In fact, mental health professionals naive to deafness have all too often mislabeled typical behavioral characteristics of deaf persons as reflecting symptoms of psychopathology (Pollard, 1992). For example, many clinicians are not necessarily aware that the average reading level for this population is roughly fourth grade (Moores, 2001). Therefore, they may be prone to mistakenly diagnose a thought disorder based on the deaf person's written communication in English, which may in actuality indicate limitations in the ability to use English rather than psychopathology. Additionally, clinicians can misattribute markedly diminished interest in daily activities to the presence of a major depression when the deaf person is in a setting such as a group home or hospital where staff members do not know ASL and there is minimal opportunity for conversational dialogue. In essence, assumptions about observable behavior often are based on the mental health professional's perspective that is typically grounded within the dominant culture, one that does not take deaf behavioral norms or needs into account. As Phillips (1996, p. 138) aptly puts it:

> In any culture, such as the dominant Anglo-American culture or the culture-within-a-culture of a hospital setting (with its own language-within-a-language and its own unique customs and rituals), culturally syntonic ideas and values are given preferential status. As a result, the viable ideas and values of cultural minorities may be devalued, discredited, and marginalized, thus becoming twice removed from the dominant culture and its norms.

Within this context, it makes inherent sense that many members of the deaf community may at some level express mistrust of the hearing community and particularly of hearing mental health professionals with limited understanding of the lives of deaf people.

According to Phillips (1996), if mental health professionals could agree on one thing, it would be most likely that it is best to start where the client is. This basic understanding of the client requires that the professionals place the client's daily cultural realities at the center of the treatment process rather than making treatment decisions based on *a priori* assumptions about what the client needs. For example, if a Chinese-American deaf woman is referred for individual psychotherapy, is that in fact the most culturally appropriate intervention, when the standard procedure is for Chinese-American families to be involved in the treatment process? Also, is the therapist sensitive to the interface between Chinese culture, American culture, and Deaf culture, and how these may possibly play out in this individual? Does the therapist understand the communication needs of this person? In the case of a Native American person who is deaf and whose family believes in consulting with a medicine man, how does the therapist respect this cultural dictum and simultaneously maintain a relationship with the client, who may be also be part of the local Deaf culture? Such complexities mandate that mental health service providers take all these varied cultural realities into account.

Today, we know that psychopathology incidences for deaf people parallel those for their normally hearing counterparts, even taking into account reports of exacerbated stress experienced by many deaf individuals dealing with the effects of a society that does not always accommodate their communication needs (Robinson, 1978). In a study of public mental health service and diagnostic trends for deaf and hard-of-hearing individuals based on public mental health records in the city of Rochester, NY, home to a large deaf population, Pollard (1994) confirmed that *DSM-IV* Axis I diagnoses for the deaf and hard-of-hearing sample were roughly comparable to those for the comparison sample. This includes adjustment disorders, mood disorders, organic mental disorders, schizophrenia, unclassified psychotic disorders, and anxiety disorders. The proportion of Substance Use Disorders and "All other mental disorders" was significantly lower for the deaf and hard-of-hearing sample. Additionally, categories covering deferred, missing, or no diagnoses were significantly more frequent for the deaf and hard-of-hearing sample. In the Axis II category, the most noteworthy finding is that of greater frequency in mental retardation diagnoses for this sample. This comes as no surprise considering the impact of limitations in English fluency on verbal measures of intelligence (the use of which is inappropriate for most deaf persons) as well as the increased risk of mental retardation associated with some etiologies for deafness. However, it is important to keep in mind that many etiologies of deafness do not necessarily include mental retardation.

Pollard (1994) concludes that his findings indicate a restricted range of *DSM-IV* diagnoses for the deaf and hard-of-hearing sample. Since the mental health and deafness literature does not support the presence of this restricted range, he ascribes the findings to communication barriers that make it difficult for clinicians to do thorough diagnostic interviews despite their skills. Confronting individuals who rely on sign language for communication can easily be discomfiting for experienced clinicians, and even more so when no sign language interpreter is present.

Considering that psychiatric services for this population were nonexistent before 1955 (Altshuler, 1969), the growth in service delivery, albeit limited as indicated earlier, is a positive sign. However, accessibility to services continues to be an issue. Pollard (1994) provides statistics to illustrate that in Rochester, NY, deaf clients tend to receive services at small, specialized community mental health centers where access in the guise of signing clinicians, onsite sign language interpreters, and TTYs is readily available. However, deaf clients, whatever their needs may be, are therefore dissuaded from going to larger facilities with a broader range of services such as staff psychiatrists, day treatment programs, an array of therapists, and so on, because of lack of access. Pollard considers this to be discriminatory and in violation of the equal access concept for all, both hearing and deaf. Leigh (2000) illustrated accessibility issues at a conference for mental health agencies throughout New York state that was set up with the goal of improving equal access in areas without specialized services for deaf people. Standards of care issues for deaf patients in the mental health system have been addressed by Myers (1995), who identifies detailed methods of access, even including visual emergency alert signalers, in order to achieve functional equivalence with hearing clientele who can call the centers any time, hear emergency warning signals on site, and communicate readily with service providers.

In order to provide functional equivalence and optimal accessibility, training of mental health service providers is a prerequisite. Training programs have increasingly focused on the importance of diversity and sensitivity to cultural and ethnic differences (Leigh et al., 1996; Yutrzenka, 1995). The diversity spectrum cannot exclude persons with disabilities, including those who are deaf. However, this focus has yet to be consistently reflected in training programs despite the fact that disability crosses all racial/ethnic boundaries (Davis, 1995). This is clearly an issue that will become increasingly salient in the coming years. Although there are a few psychology, social work, and mental health counseling programs throughout the United States that provide specialized training to serve deaf persons with mental health needs (Leigh & Lewis, 1999), improved awareness about the needs of deaf persons and sign language interpreter issues provided in more generic training programs will go a long way toward assuring the accessibility of mental health service programs for deaf clientele.

The new area of telehealth affords a promising avenue that will enhance accessibility of mental health services for individuals not within easy reach of mental health services (Jerome & Zaylor, 2000). Because signing clinicians are few and far between in many areas of the United States, the utilization of computer technology and videoconferencing holds great promise for providing services without the necessity of dealing with geographical unavailability. Deaf clients will be able to receive signed communication from service providers who appear on screens and can provide one-on-one communication. Telepsychiatry services for deaf clients are currently being provided in the state of South Carolina (Critchfield, Afrin, & Bateson, 1999). The years ahead may very well see rapid expansion of this new means of service provision.

CONCLUSIONS AND RECOMMENDATIONS

As we move further into the 21st century, the diversity within the United States deaf community is now growing to encompass deaf people who have or do not have cochlear implants, who espouse or do not espouse a strong deaf identity, who are increasingly from diverse racial/ethnic backgrounds and less often from White backgrounds, and who adopt various ways of communicating with the world at large in addition to ASL or who do not use ASL. The acceptance of ASL as a formal language has led to the expansion of ongoing research into the properties of nonspoken languages. Deaf identity development recently has emerged as an area of study. Institutions of higher education are increasingly supporting Deaf Studies programs, which were nonexistent 30 years ago. Thanks to the Internet and other technological innovations, the deaf community is less constrained by geographical boundaries. To provide this changing community with optimal mental health service, clinicians need to understand the community itself; the various ways in which deaf people live their lives; the communication needs of deaf people; as well as the influence of diverse cultural forces, technology, and genetics on their lives. Given that, deaf people will be well served in the mental health arena.

Those clinicians who are interested in learning more about the deaf community can contact local universities and check out course offerings in Deaf Studies or Psychology and Deafness. ASL courses are offered in many facilities. However, as with any foreign language, it takes years to achieve full competency, keeping in mind that ASL is a visual-spatial language that renders it different from spoken languages. In areas where ASL-proficient clinicians are lacking, the use of interpreters is viable only when they are properly certified and knowledgeable about mental health issues. The National Registry of Interpreters for the Deaf (www.rid.org), which certifies interpreters, provides contact information to locate interpreters in various areas.

If deaf persons are referred to clinicians who may need consultation on treatment approaches or referral information, it is possible to contact various organizations such as the American Deafness and Rehabilitation Association (www.adara.org), American Psychological Association (www.apa.org), National Association of Social Workers (www.naswdc.org), or the American Psychiatric Association (www.psych.org) and request specialists knowledgeable about mental health and deaf people.

ACKNOWLEDGMENT

I wish to thank John Christiansen and Deborah Maxwell McCaw for their contributions to this chapter.

END NOTES

1. As opposed to a mild or moderate loss, severe to profound deafness typically means that one has little or no functional hearing ability for the ordinary purposes of life (Paul & Jackson, 1993).
2. The cochlear implant is a hearing device that is surgically implanted behind the ear. It enhances the ability to perceive sound but does not provide normal hearing.

REFERENCES

Altshuler, K. (1969). New York State program of mental health services. In K. Altshuler & J. D. Rainer (Eds.). *Mental health and the deaf: Approaches and prospects* (pp. 15–23). Washington, DC: U.S. Department of Health, Education, and Welfare.
Americans with Disabilities Act of 1990, 42 U.S.C.A. & 12101 et seq. (West, 1993).
Arnos, K. S. (2002). Genetics and deafness: Impacts on the deaf community. *Sign Language Studies, 2,* 150–168.
Biderman, B. (1998). *Wired for sound: A journey into hearing.* Toronto, Canada: Trifolium.

Blanchfield, B., Dunbar, J., Feldman, J., & Gardner, E. (1999). *The severely to profoundly hearing impaired population in the United States: Prevalence and demographics*. Bethesda, MD: Project HOPE Center for Health Affairs. Available online: http://www.projhope.org

Brueggemann, B. J. (1999). *Lend me your ear: Rhetorical constructions of deafness*. Washington, DC: Gallaudet University Press.

Christiansen, J., & Barnartt, S. (1995). *Deaf president now! The 1988 revolution at Gallaudet University*. Washington, DC: Gallaudet University Press.

Christiansen, J., & Leigh, I. W. (2002). *Children with cochlear implants: Ethics and choices*. Washington, DC: Gallaudet University Press.

Christensen, K., & Delgado, G. (Eds.). (1993). *Multicultural issues in deafness*. New York: Longman.

Corbett, C. (1999). Mental health issues for African American deaf people. In I. W. Leigh (Ed.), *Psychotherapy with deaf clients from diverse groups* (pp. 151–176). Washington, DC: Gallaudet University Press.

Corker, M. (1996). *Deaf transitions*. London: Jessica Kingsley.

Corker, M. (1998). *Deaf and disabled, or deafness disabled?* Bristol, PA: Open University Press.

Critchfield, B., Afrin, J., & Bateson, T. (1999). *Telepsychiatry and deaf people: A forward leap into effective service delivery*. Presentation, ADARA Conference, Washington, DC.

Davis, L. (1995). *Enforcing normality: Disability, deafness, and the body*. New York: Versace.

Delgado, G. (2000). How are we doing? In K. Christensen (Ed.), *Deaf plus: A multicultural perspective* (pp. 29–40). San Diego: DawnSign Press.

Eldredge, N. (1999). Culturally responsive psychotherapy with American Indians who are deaf. In I. W. Leigh (Ed.), *Psychotherapy with deaf clients from diverse groups* (pp. 177–201). Washington, DC: Gallaudet University Press.

Fischer, L. (2000). *Cultural identity development and self concept of adults who are deaf: A comparative analysis*. Unpublished doctoral dissertation, Arizona State University, Tempe.

Friedburg, I. (2000). *Reference group orientation and self-esteem of deaf and hard-of-hearing college students*. Unpublished doctoral dissertation. Washington, DC: Gallaudet University.

Gannon, J. (1989). *The week the world heard Gallaudet*. Washington, DC: Gallaudet University Press.

Glickman, N. (1996). The development of culturally deaf identities. In N. Glickman & M. Harvey (Eds.), *Culturally affirmative psychotherapy with Deaf persons* (pp. 115–153). Mahwah, NJ: Erlbaum.

Hernandez, M. (1999). The role of therapeutic groups in working with Latino deaf adolescent immigrants. In I. W. Leigh (Ed.), *Psychotherapy with deaf clients from diverse groups* (pp. 227–249). Washington, DC: Gallaudet University Press.

Higgins, P. O. (1980). *Outsiders in a hearing world: A sociology of deafness*. Beverly Hills, CA: Sage.

Holden-Pitt, L., & Diaz, J. (1998). Thirty years of the annual survey of deaf and hard-of-hearing children and youth: A glance over the decades. *American Annals of the Deaf, 142*, 72–76.

Humphries, T. (1993). Deaf culture and cultures. In K. M. Christiansen & G. L. Delgado (Eds.), *Multicultural issues in deafness* (pp. 3–15). White Plains, NY: Longman.

Humphries, T. (1996). Of deaf-mutes, the strange, and the modern deaf self. In N. S. Glickman & M. A. Harvey (Eds.), *Culturally affirmative psychotherapy with Deaf persons* (pp. 99–114). Mahwah, NJ: Erlbaum.

Jankowski, K. (1997). *Deaf empowerment*. Washington, DC: Gallaudet University Press.

Jerome, L., & Zaylor, C. (2000). Cyberspace: Creating a therapeutic environment for telehealth applications. *Professional Psychology: Research and Practice, 31*, 478–483.

Jonsen, A., Siegler, M., & Winslade, W. (1998). *Clinical ethics* (4th ed.). New York: McGraw-Hill.

LaFromboise, T., Coleman, H., & Gerton, J. (1993). Psychological impact of biculturalism: Evidence and theory. *Psychological Bulletin, 114,* 395–412.

Lane, H., Hoffmeister, R., & Bahan, B. (1996). *A journey into the Deaf-World.* San Diego, CA: DawnSign Press.

Leigh, I. W. (2000). *Mental health access for deaf and hard-of-hearing consumers.* Presented at Access Is the Issue: Access to Mental Health for Deaf and Hard-of-Hearing Persons, Training Conference, New York City.

Leigh, I. W., & Lewis, J. W. (1999). Deaf therapists and the deaf community. In I. W. Leigh (Ed.), *Psychotherapy with deaf clients from diverse groups* (pp. 45–65). Washington, DC: Gallaudet University Press.

Leigh, I. W., Corbett, C., Gutman, V., & Morere, D. (1996). Providing psychological services to deaf individuals: A response to new perceptions of diversity. *Professional Psychology: Research and Practice, 27,* 364–371.

Leigh, I. W., Marcus, A., Dobosh, P., & Allen, T. (1998). Deaf/hearing identity paradigms: Modification of the Deaf Identity Development Scale. *Journal of Deaf Studies and Deaf Education, 3,* 329–338.

Maxwell McCaw, D. (2001). *Acculturation and psychological well-being in deaf and hard-of-hearing people.* Unpublished doctoral dissertation. Washington, DC: The George Washington University.

Meadow-Orlans, K. (1985). Social and psychological effects of hearing loss in adulthood: A literature review. In H. Orlans (Ed.), *Adjustment to adult hearing loss* (pp. 35–57). San Diego: College-Hill Press.

Moores, D. (2001). *Educating the deaf: Psychology, principles, and practices,* 5th ed. Boston: Houghton Mifflin.

Morton, D., & Christensen, J. N. (2000). *Mental health services for deaf people: A resource directory.* Washington, DC: Department of Counseling, Gallaudet University.

Myers, R. (Ed.). (1995). *Standards of care for the delivery of mental health services to deaf and hard-of-hearing persons.* Silver Spring, MD: National Association of the Deaf.

National Association of the Deaf. (2000). "NAD position statement on cochlear implants." Available online at: http://www.nad.org/infocenter/newsroom/papers/CochlearImplants.html.

Neisser, A. (1983). *The other side of silence: Sign language and the deaf community in America.* New York: Knopf.

Niparko, J. (2000). The epidemiology of hearing loss: How prevalent is hearing loss? In J. Niparko, K. Kirk, N. Mellon, A. Robbins, D. Tucci, & B. Wilson (Eds.), *Cochlear implants: Principles and practices* (pp. 88–92). Philadelphia: Lippincott Williams & Wilkins.

Padden, C. (1996). From the cultural to the bicultural: The modern deaf community. In I. Parasnis (Ed.), *Cultural and language diversity and the deaf experience* (pp. 79–98). New York: Cambridge University Press.

Padden, C., & Humphries, T. (1988). *Deaf in America: Voices from a culture.* Cambridge, MA: Harvard University Press.

Padden, C., & Rayman, J. (2000). *The future of American Sign Language.* Unpublished manuscript, University of California, San Diego.

Paul, P., & Jackson, D. (1993). *Toward a psychology of deafness.* Boston: Allyn & Bacon.

Phillips, B. (1996). Bringing culture to the forefront: Formulating diagnostic impressions of deaf and hard-of-hearing people at times of medical crises. *Professional Psychology: Research and Practice, 27,* 137–144.

Pollard, R. Q. (1992). 100 years in psychology and deafness: A centennial retrospective. *Journal of the American Deafness and Rehabilitation Association, 26,* 32–46.

Pollard, R. Q. (1994). Public mental health service and diagnostic trends regarding individuals who are deaf or hard of hearing. *Rehabilitation Psychology, 39,* 147–160.

Robinson, L. (1978). *Sound minds in a soundless world.* Washington, DC: U.S. Department of Health, Education, and Welfare.

Schein, J. (1989). *At home among strangers.* Washington, DC: Gallaudet University Press.

Steinberg, A., Loew, R., & Sullivan, V. J. (1999). The diversity of consumer knowledge, attitudes, beliefs, and experiences: Recent findings. In I. W. Leigh (Ed.), *Psychotherapy with deaf clients from diverse groups* (pp. 23–43). Washington, DC: Gallaudet University Press.

Stewart, L. (1992). Debunking the bilingual/bicultural snow job in the American deaf community. In M. Garretson (Ed.). *Viewpoints on Deafness: A Deaf American Monograph, 42,* 129–142.

Trybus, R. (1983). Hearing-impaired patients in public psychiatric hospitals throughout the United States. In D. Watson & B. Heller (Eds.), *Mental health and deafness: Strategic perspectives* (pp. 1–19). Silver Spring, MD: American Deafness and Rehabilitation Association.

Van Cleve, J. (Ed.). (1993). *Deaf history unveiled.* Washington, DC: Gallaudet University Press.

Van Cleve, J. V., & Crouch, B. (1989). *A place of their own: Creating the Deaf community in America.* Washington, DC: Gallaudet University Press.

Waterman, A.S. (1992). Identity as an aspect of optimal psychological functioning. In G. R. Adams, T. P. Gullotta, & R. Montemayor (Eds.), *Adolescent identity formation* (pp. 50–72). Newbury Park, CA: Sage.

Woodward, K. (1997). Concepts of identity and difference. In K. Woodward (Ed.), *Identity and difference* (pp. 7–50). Thousand Oaks, CA: Sage.

Wu, C., & Grant, N. (1999). Asian American and Deaf. In I. W. Leigh (Ed.), *Psychotherapy with deaf clients from diverse groups* (pp. 203–226). Washington, DC: Gallaudet University Press.

Yacobacci-Tam, P. (1987). Interacting with the culturally different family. *Volta Review, 89,* 46–58.

Yutrzenka, B. (1995). Making a case for training in ethnic and cultural diversity in increasing treatment efficacy. *Journal of Consulting and Clinical Psychology, 63,* 197–206.

CHAPTER 19

Perspectives on Spirituality and Psychology in Ethnic Populations

G. RITA DUDLEY-GRANT

Faith is the ultimate essence of intellect. Through the practice of correct faith, the intellect comes to shine. Intellect without correct faith lacks a firm anchor in the soil of life and eventually becomes disordered. This prompted the first Soka Gakkai president, Tsunesaburo Makiguchi, to remark that many modern thinkers were suffering from what he termed "higher psychosis." Faith without intellect, meanwhile, leads to blind faith and fanaticism. Faith or intellect alone—one without the other—is unhealthy.

Ikeda, 1999, p. 361

This quote from a leading contemporary Buddhist scholar and current president of one of the largest Buddhist sects in the world encapsulates the essence of the difference between Western psychology, and psychology as it has been practiced throughout the rest of the world. Spirituality has long been recognized as a key component of emotional and psychological well-being in multiethnic communities. People of Color around the world have maintained much closer ties to their spiritual beliefs and practices than is common in the more scientifically oriented values and practices of Western society (Bankart, 1997; Boyd-Franklin & Franklin, 2000). From the primacy of the spiritual leader in addressing familial and emotional issues, to collaborations with spiritual healers, spirituality has maintained its place as essential to the overall health and well being of individuals and communities of non-European descent.

More recently, it is gratifying to see that psychology has begun to recognize and validate the role of spirituality in the psychological well-being of all individuals (Farley, 1996). Books and articles on psychology, therapy, and spirituality have burgeoned in recent times (Budd, 1999; Chirban, 1996). Indeed, Bullis (1996) has described how a clinical social worker can take a spiritual history, and clarify the client's beliefs, and prayer and meditative practices as an important part of growth in therapy.

Psychology and religion has an old and respected tradition within psychology, including the Division of Religion and Psychology within the American Psychological Association (APA). However, the focus has been largely from the Judeo-Christian perspective. Practitioners interested in the less mainstream, or more multicultural approaches to the integration of spirituality and psychology have only recently begun to have a voice within the wider psychological community. Most recently, Richards and Bergin (2000) in their book on psychotherapy and religious diversity included a chapter on spirituality and ethnicity that investigates the impact of ethnicity on religious practices and also considers indigenous beliefs, often a significant part of ethnic minority culture.

Clearly then, for People of Color, spiritual practices of all kinds maintain a place of centrality in the functioning of the individual and the community. Boyd-Franklin and Franklin (2000) have emphasized this essential component, devoting an entire chapter to spirituality and religion in their book on raising African-American teenage sons. Within medicine, it has been recognized that traditional healers have actually provided for the health of mankind for centuries (Anduze, 1993). However, like psychology, traditional medical practices have focused more on Western medicine than the totality of the healing arts. He suggests that the image of Hippocrates has long signaled the rightness of Western civilization's (White) medicine and the exclusion of Imhotep's Afro-Eastern medicine. In former times, mental illness was perceived as a form of spiritual possession, particularly in the African and Hispanic cultures, but treatment and cure for such illnesses were seen as the purview of traditional healers, such as curanderas, witch doctors, or shamans.

With the continued integration of cultural awareness into mainstream psychology, there has been a growing and steady acceptance of the potential benefit, and need for collaboration between psychologists and faith healers. A prime example is the personal experience of this author, who over the past 4 years has presented yearly symposiums at the APA annual conventions on spirituality and psychotherapy to standing room only audiences. The topics have included a variety of types of collaboration, both with traditional healers (Dudley-Grant, 1999, 2001a), and with Buddhism and psychotherapy (Dudley-Grant, 1998, 2000, 2001b). It is fascinating to see the diverse composition of the audiences, who range from younger psychologists seeking new approaches, to seasoned psychologists who have engaged in this kind of collaboration over a number of years, and are finally finding like-minded persons within the profession.

The need for such collaboration is essential, as there remains stigma attached both to the use of natural healers as well as the use of mental health services. Nevertheless, a significant portion of the population seeks out natural healers in their attempt to address issues ranging from personal problems to larger scale community problems.

Traditional collaborations have occurred primarily on an individual level. However, in some societies, such as Native American culture, spiritual healing is also a major part of community ritual (Fleming, 2001). An essential aspect of this work is the understanding of the belief system, which will inform the types of interventions that will be acceptable to the individual, group, or community. Traditional community structures are continually evolving, particularly with the advent of telecommunication. Coping with the pressures of modern life continues to strain every level of society.

The challenge for the psychologist is to integrate modern and traditional approaches in assisting on all levels to cope with the new realities.

This chapter addresses some of the traditional and more innovative approaches to intervention and collaboration that are presenting in our current times. Some considerations on culturally consonant approaches to spirituality from the African-American, Hispanic, Native American, and Asian-American perspectives are made. Such a broad approach to this topic prohibits a detailed analysis of each of the traditions. There are some generalities that cut across the traditions, however. These, the author attempts to present. Most significantly, the importance of the continued recognition and forward movement of the integration of spiritual considerations into the mainstream of psychology, particularly when working with multiethnic populations, are explored.

PSYCHOLOGY AND SPIRITUALITY
IN HISTORICAL PERSPECTIVE

Psychology has traditionally sought to identify itself as a science. The birth of the discipline was based on the experimental and research method and in an effort to explain human behavior in scientific terms (Coon, 1992). Moncayo (1998) suggests this is in part owing to its basis within empiricism. Empiricism or science, presents itself as the presupposed superior form of knowledge, the sole arbiter of truth. He attributes the misleading assumption of the modern and current dualistic distinction between modern scientific facts and traditional mythological beliefs to this misassumption and takes issue with the notion that anything that cannot be empirically and atheoretically demonstrated is false or an error. With the growth of the practitioner movement has been the closer connection to the treatment of mental illness. However, Western psychology continues to emphasize the role of research and the importance of measuring outcomes of interventions. The scientist practitioner is seen as the epitome, with greatest respect and validity given to those interventions and outcomes that are the most measurable.

Thus, psychology like medicine has been no less rejecting of the notion of "faith healers." Those exhibiting emotional distress, changes in personality, loss of weight, and who believed themselves to be possessed by spirits, were diagnosed as being delusional or frankly psychotic. Even worse, practitioners, the witch doctors, Espiritistas or Spriritists, or Obeah men or women, were viewed as mentally ill at best or charlatans at worst (depending on one's perspective), particularly when in a trance state or speaking with the spirits. Yet these traditional healers have saved many lives, healed illnesses, rescued marriages and relationships, counseled community and world leaders, and brought hope to many. One example of this comes from medical science as related by Anduze (1993).

> As the story goes . . . there was once a Nigerian prince attending a prestigious London university. He became quite ill and all the top English doctors and scientific minds failed to diagnose or cure him. The family sent home for the local tribal

doctor who came with a bunch of rauwolfia roots to cure the 'moon madness' (mental
illness). After receiving the appropriate dosage, the prince was up and around and
none the worse in no time. The English quickly seized the remaining roots and
upon analysis 'invented' the first synthetic tranquilizer, Reserpine—the basis for
many antihypertensives. (p. 1)

This story characterizes how Western medicine has taken the knowledge of traditional
healers without crediting or legitimizing its source.

SPIRITUALITY, PSYCHOLOGY, AND
THE AFRICAN-AMERICAN EXPERIENCE

Within the African Diaspora, spirituality has remained a fundamental aspect of community life, as spirituality was completely integrated in African culture (Nobles, 1980).
As slaves were moved around the world, and as European colonialism modified the
cultures within the tribes and peoples on the continent, the practices changed. Christianity became, and remains, the dominant spiritual practice within the African culture. However, the mutual interchange modified the ways in which it was practiced.
The Christian religion as practiced by people of African descent incorporated traditional African practices (Black, 1996). For example, the African tradition of storytelling
was integrated into the preaching of the Baptist and Methodist missionaries sent to
work with the slaves, and developed into the strong oral tradition and dramatic narrative
style found in many Black churches today (Frazier, 1963). The strong African
connection to one's ancestors, who were seen as protectors of the village and very
much a part of the living world, could be seen in the attraction of the Charismatic
Christian practices of speaking in tongues, also a major factor in Black worship.

In the Caribbean, another major location of the African Diaspora, three primary
practices are identified as those of indigenous healers, although there are many more
subgroups and branches within the three main areas. These are Espiritistas, Spiritists,
or Curanderos, primarily found in the Spanish-speaking Caribbean. There are the Obeah
practitioners primarily of the Black, Eastern Caribbean. And perhaps most well known,
and most maligned, the voodoo or witch doctors who originate in Haiti (Black, 1996).
The Spanish-speaking indigenous beliefs will be taken up in a latter section of this
chapter. However, within the theology and practice of voodoo found in Haiti, Obeah
from the English Caribbean, and other traditional spiritual practices found throughout
the Caribbean are included many African Gods in the pantheon of traditionally Catholic deities (Dudley-Grant, 1999).

Metraux (1959) characterized voodoo as a conglomeration of beliefs and rites of
African origin intermingled with Catholic practice and rituals which are now the religion of the greater part of the Haitian peasants as well as middle and upper classes. It
serves the same function as other religions, including remedy of ills, satisfaction of
needs, and the hope of survival. One could suggest that the difference between prayer
to saints and spirits is simply a matter of class and culture rather than a true distinction
of experience.

It is important to note that these indigenous faiths are practiced concomitantly with active participation in traditional Christian religions. Thus, in this author's collaboration with an Espiritista, it was revealed that several members of the prominent middle- and upper-class members of the community, quite active in the church, also came regularly to her for guidance on problems ranging from relationships to success in political careers (Dudley-Grant, 1999). What is extremely interesting is when one considers the rituals of the Catholic and High Anglican or Episcopal Church, the worship of this or that patron saint is very akin to homage paid to the voodoo gods. And the priests of each sect or practice may be held in the same awe and reverence, with the expectation of a closer connection with God, however that may be conceptualized.

African Americans also practice other faiths such as the Nation of Islam, and other Muslim groups, the Soka Gakkai International of the United States (SGI-USA) and other Buddhist sects, as well as the practice of African traditions such as the Yoruba from Nigeria and the religions of Ancient Egypt (Boyd-Franklin & Franklin, 2000; Dockett & North-Schulte, in press). Indeed, the Nation of Islam is credited with the saving of lives, particularly inside America's prisons, so overpopulated with Black American males. Most prominent among those saved is Malcolm X, who renounced his self-centered life of drugs and other antisocial behavior to become a leader of the Black empowerment movement of the 1960s.

Religiosity has served a number of purposes within the African-American community. Jenkins (1995) suggested that religious experience has guided the adaptation of Black people to life in America. He cites several researchers who have both documented the high involvement of the Black community with religion, both organized and personal, and made the distinction between this involvement as a source of strength rather than an avoidance of the realities of racism and discrimination in our society. He concludes that active involvement in religious activity has helped African Americans sustain their sense of competence and agency in the context of humanistic psychology. Spirituality as a central aspect of psychological well-being also has served to minimize the stigma of mental illness. It is much more acceptable to seek out the assistance of a pastoral counselor than that of a psychologist or psychotherapist. Within these communities, the first person to be consulted when an emotional crisis arises within the individual, family, or community is the pastor or religious leader. It has been suggested that the "growth-wholeness model" of pastoral counseling is more culturally consonant with African Americans and other minority groups than the more traditional psychodynamic or cognitive behavioral approaches to psychotherapy. Nevertheless, even pastoral counselors can encounter difficulties when they lack adequate knowledge of the subcultures of their counselees (Wimberly, 1993).

Spiritual beliefs are cited as a necessary if not the most essential ingredient in developing values in young people, most especially the vulnerable adolescent Black male population. Indeed, Boyd-Franklin and Franklin (2000), exemplified the primacy of faith in their own lives when describing their move from New York to New Jersey. They emphasized the importance of maintaining close ties to a positive Black community and a healthy environment, particularly for their son. They discussed their dilemma in trying to ensure that their youngest son would have strong Black role models in his life. In selecting a new community when they decided to move from

New York City, their priority was to find a "church home" or "church family," which preempted the decision based on more commonly accepted factors such as neighborhood, architecture, or even educational facilities. On a more personal note, it was striking to this author to learn as a young adult that my father, a pillar in our church who raised my brother and me strictly within the Episcopal faith, considered himself to be an atheist. When I asked this incredibly warm, intelligent, and deeply spiritual man why he insisted on our virtually daily practice of Christianity, he explained that he felt that it was by far the best way to teach human social values to children.

Na'im Akbar (2000) has created a "rites of passage" ritual, steeped in spiritual traditions which he promotes for Black teens, particularly boys to develop their sense of self, self-esteem, and appreciation for Afrocentric values, protective factors in managing what can be perceived as the toxic environment of the Western culture.

Research has now begun to codify and validate these long-known practices and beliefs. Spirituality has been effectively used to frame treatment approaches with multiethnic populations. For example, Frame, Williams, and Green (1999) report on the utilization of spiritual metaphors from the African-American culture, such as the "Balm in Gilead" exercise to address a broad range of issues that African-American women bring to treatment, including emotional isolation and low self-esteem. In a review of the special issues associated with the use of Cognitive-Behavioral Therapy (CBT) with Women of Color, Lewis (1994) emphasized the multifaceted and unique needs of these women. She characterized family (nuclear and extended), community, spirituality, and respect for authority as key elements of those needs and suggested that they were essential in understanding Women of Color. She illustrated her emphasis on spirituality in a case study utilizing CBT where the individual's use of prayer as a coping mechanism is strongly reinforced. As Boyd-Franklin (1989) has emphasized, spirituality is so interwoven into Black society that a practitioner seeking to successfully intervene with this culture must be cognizant and respectful of the multiple roles that it plays.

HISPANICS AND FAITH HEALING

The Hispanic community differs from other ethnicities in one singularly unique way, that being a group defined more by culture than by biology. Indeed, Pinderhuges (1989) has pointed out that the same individual can go from being White in Puerto Rico, to being mulatto in Mexico, to being Black in the United States. Since culture can be seen as the defining factor, the values of that culture take even more primacy in understanding group members. Jenkins, De La Cancela, and Chin (1993) suggested that ethnospecific religious beliefs and practices also influence the meaning of ethnicity for Puerto Ricans. These beliefs are a blend of African religious rites that contain a variety of faiths, both traditional and nontraditional, such as Catholicism, *Espiritismo,* and folk healing to name but the few most central and widespread.

The Latin culture is a deeply spiritual and religious one. Most closely identified with Catholicism, Latino spirituality is also heavily influenced by its African roots in the Caribbean, and its heritage from the Mestizo and other Indian tribes from South America. Cervantes (2001) developed a model that incorporates spirituality as an integral part of treatment. He suggests that the integration of spirituality is essential to fully appreciate the psychohistorical and sociocultural aspects of the Latino culture. That culture is heavily influenced by a psychospiritual belief system incorporating Mesoamerican Indigenous roots (Cervantes, 2001; Fukuyama & Sevig, 1999). He emphasized the intercultural nature of the "Mestizo" heritage with its mixture of European and Indian influences resulting in a unique blend of spirituality, traditionalism, and modernity.

There are some overarching values that appear to cut across much of the Latino subculture. The primacy of the family is a distinctive Latin characteristic in the sense that family commitments supercede all others. A popular stereotype is the "machismo" of the Latin male. However, Vasquez (1994) and others have found that the myth of male dominance in the Latino culture is often exaggerated. She distinguishes between healthy families, and those with dysfunction. In healthy families, the traditional role of working father and homemaker mother does not exclude equality in decision-making and conflict resolution. Dysfunctional families may be more male dominant, with oppressive, even abusive expression of power differentials and women's voices being subverted. She emphasizes that in therapy it is important not to negate the strong value of family and support for same, nor to pathologize the woman who places family first over self. Nevertheless, Latina women can be seen as more vulnerable to abuse because of this cultural value. For example, in the United States Virgin Islands, the court system has found a preponderance of Latin women in the domestic violence courts, despite the Black population being the largest (personal communication, Judge Patricia Steele, Judge Family Court in the Territorial Court of the Virgin Islands, Dec. 4, 2001).

Another consistent value that cuts across subcultural lines is the dedication to religion. Whether it is practiced traditionally in the formal church setting, or through private, often daily practices in their homes, Latinos tend to be very dedicated to their religious beliefs. The practice is open and well-integrated into daily life. An example of this dedication may be experienced by anyone traveling by air to a Latin country. Upon landing, prayer and clapping is routine, as is making the sign of the cross and praying to the Virgin Mary on take off.

Equally as prevalent, though not as visible, is the adherence to "traditional" practices. The "Espiritista," or "Curandera" (depending on the subculture), are consulted as readily as the parish priest. Comas-Diaz (1981) has written about the efficacy of collaboration between such traditional practitioners. She has argued for an inclusion of such collaboration and an acceptance of these practices in the lives of Latinos. Key in the collaboration is the development of trust, both with the client and with the native healer. It is essential that any provider engage in a self-study and values clarification to ensure that he or she is approaching the native healer from the perspective of collaboration with a colleague of equivalent status and training, rather than the disingenuous stance of one who is merely curious or attempting to "humor" the client.

Remarkably, I was struck in my own collaboration with an Espiritista, in working with a mixed-marriage couple of Puerto Rican and Caucasian-American background, at the extensiveness of the traditional healer's training. There were many similarities to other more traditional professions. Once the talent is identified in the individual, he or she must go through an extensive apprenticeship with a seasoned practitioner. Upon "certification" he or she does not simply carry on a practice but must return yearly for further training either with the original teacher or with other senior practitioners. The community affords many of the same checks and balances, as well as some level of monitoring, much as our ethical principles and boards guide the practice of psychology.

Ultimately, cure, improvement, or recovery stems as much from the individual's belief in the validity and potential benefit of the treatment, as from the intervention itself. The goal remains the strengthening of the individual to combat one's difficulties, however defined. Delgado and Humm-Delgado (1982), and Rosado and Elias (1993) have shown that Latin communities are more likely to seek help for emotional and family problems from a spiritual leader than from a psychologist. Therefore, for the psychologist practitioner, once a relationship with such individuals has been established, referrals in each direction can occur for the ultimate benefit of the client.

SPIRITUALITY, PSYCHOLOGY, AND NATIVE AMERICAN CULTURE

The Native American cultural experience is perhaps the one most closely identified with active and ongoing engagement in spiritual practices. Although spirituality has been identified as one of five life tasks that additionally include work, social relations, intimacy, and one's identity, researchers have used this tool to identify differences between Native American and mainstream American cultures (Kawulich & Curlette, 1998). From the Shaman to the Medicine Man, these individuals have historically and currently served as leaders in their communities, blessing and protecting their tribes. In addition, the culture of the American Indian is one that originates in the spiritual connections of its members to each other, to all peoples and nature (Sutton & Broken Nose, 1996). Spiritual belief patterns appear to permeate every aspect of the culture. These include experiences as diverse as that of one's ancestors as active participants in one's daily life, to the determination of where one can live. For example, the concept of culturally related anxiety can be seen in the Navajo tribe who try to educate their people in both traditional and "Western" practices. The Navajo reservation is located within a sacred geographic region, bounded by the holy mountains where they believe they were created in and meant to live in. Anxiety may occur when a Navajo attempts to use his or her Western training as a springboard into greater acculturation by moving out of the area to better educate him- or herself or to build on the very Westernization taught by the tribespeople.

McNeil, Kee, and Zvolensky (1999) studied the relationship between ethnic identity and culturally related anxiety in a group of Navajo college students. They found that the two concepts were separate and distinct, but that there could be many sources of culturally related anxiety including the cognitive dissonance created between traditional beliefs, including those that were spiritually based, and the more Westernized value structure. In fact, Native Americans have gone to great lengths to protect their culture and values, including their spiritual practices. For example, it was reported in their chapter on American Indians that the Tlingit Indians requested baptism into the Eastern Orthodox Christian Church so that they could worship in their own language and thereby communicate with the Great Spirit in a more personal and effective manner (La Framboise, Berman, & Balvindar, 1994).

An essential aspect of the Native American experience is the wholesale genocide and destruction of the indigenous Indian culture by the European immigrants. From the earliest days of Columbus, the Indian peoples and culture were denigrated. Tafoya and Del Vecchio (1996) give a particularly moving account of what they characterize as the "Native American Holocaust Experience." They describe three skills required by all tribes for their children to be accepted by an adult member of the tribe. These include: "(1) knowledge of cultural heritage; (2) spiritual/religious practices; and (3) economic survival skills" (Tafoya & Del Vecchio, 1996). The authors target the missionary boarding school system, designed to make the Indigenous Indians into "good American citizens," as perhaps the most cruel and pernicious attempt by the United States government to destroy the Native American culture. Children as young as 5 years old were removed from their families, taken to boarding schools, and prohibited access to family visits because of cost and distance. The students were forbidden to speak their native language, their hair was cut, and their native dress was confiscated. They were stripped of their cultural practices, resulting in Indian tribal ways and belief systems being decimated. Mental health sequelae resulting from this barbarous treatment include low self-esteem, posttraumatic stress disorder, substance abuse, poor parenting practices, and suicidal depression. The authors strongly recommend that mental health professionals attempting to treat Native Americans become sensitized to this tragic history as well as other very positive aspects of Native American culture.

Psychopathology is seen not solely as a psychobiological process, but a disruption in the harmony between the Native American individual and his or her sociocultural community and spiritual world (La Framboise et al., 1994; Tafoya & Del Vecchio, 1996). Mental health interventions must understand and respect this reality. La Framboise et al. (1994) explain the difference between Indian spirituality and Christianity in terms of their continued connection to and support from the spirit world through medicine men and women. An essential aspect of service provision must be some familiarity with and appreciation for the Native American culture and the role that spirituality plays. It is noteworthy that recently many of the professional psychological gatherings of People of Color have started and/or ended with a ceremonial Native American blessing and cleansing of the proceedings. Richard M. Suinn, the 1999 President of the APA, successfully introduced this experience to the general psychology community. The ceremony, carried out during the opening ceremonies of the 1999 Annual Convention has been acknowledged as one of the most spiritually moving in the history of the Association. The growth in appreciation of the Native American approach to spirituality as one that encompasses, and is welcoming to, other cultural beliefs and practices can be seen as a reflection of the Native American culture, so very tied to the ecology and the environment. Thus many American Indians view development as being circular, in that we move from our oneness with the "Great

One," into the separateness of rebirth, live and die to be reunited again in the never-ending circle of life. It is fascinating to see these themes of circularity and unification of life and death repeated through the seemingly disparate subcultures under consideration. So too, then, the eternality of life, reflected in the Native American tradition, is a central aspect of belief systems in the East as well, as explicated next, when considering Asian aspects of spirituality and psychological theory.

ASIAN AMERICANS AND SPIRITUALITY

Consideration of Asian cultural spirituality is perhaps the most daunting in that the monolith that is typically characterized as "Asian American" is possibly the most diverse of all American ethnic minority groups. People that fall into the census categories of Asian come from places as far-flung and disparate as Mainland China to Guam, to Asian India and Pakistan. Bradshaw (1994) cogently indicated in her excellent review of Asian and Asian American women that the Eurocentric use of the term "Asian" illustrates two points: the irrational nature of racial categories and the ignorance it encourages. Given the vast geographic regions designated as "Asian" clearly the designation is not based on cultural similarity. If the term "Asian" lacks both physical and cultural homogeneity, it is essentially meaningless; thus, she strongly encouraged the use of geographic markers when discussing various Asian subcultural groups.

Of the major groups in the United States, the two largest are the Chinese with close to 2 million, closely followed by the Filipinos, and then the Japanese, with well over 1 million each. Other cultural groups include Vietnamese, Koreans, Asian Indians, Cambodians, Laotians, Hmong, Mien, and other Asians for a total that is well over 5 million by the end of the 1980s. Today it is estimated that there are over 11 million Asian Americans, considered the fastest growing minority in America (Separate Hour, 2002). The communities that formed in the United States are significantly different than those left behind. The two major organizing forces have been economic/political, or more socially oriented based on kinship ties, religious affiliation, and/or common locality or dialect (Chan, 1991). These communities and belief systems have existed despite tremendous oppression, most notably during World War II with the internment of Japanese Americans. Virtually the entire population was treated as prisoners of war, and while in the concentration camps were prohibited from practicing Shintoism and other indigenous religions. Many renounced their citizenship and were repatriated in protest over the way they had been treated. Nevertheless, the many disparate Asian populations have survived and thrived with a significant growth in the migration to the United States after the introduction of the 1965 Immigration Act.

The cultural heterogeneity also makes it considerably more difficult to speak to an "Asian" approach to spirituality per se. Nevertheless, some overarching values in existence over centuries have continued to underlie the value system of the various Asian subcultural groups. One important aspect of this value is that of the connection to one's ancestors manifested in the ancestor altars. These physical symbols, which vary according to the culture and acculturation of the particular individual, represent a deeply held belief in the presence, influence, and necessity of honoring one's ancestors. The value, significant of the eternity of life, can stand along side the variety of religious practices found in the Asian communities. Nevertheless, ancestors play a major role in the internal emotional functioning and well-being of significant portions of the Asian-American community, an essential element not to be overlooked in therapy (Chao, 2000).

Christianity has become a dominating force in the Asian-American community with about one-fourth of the population being evangelical Christian. The remaining three fourths are Roman Catholic, Buddhist, and atheist. Christian pastors of Asian-American descent seeking to integrate the congregation have encountered racism still so prevalent in the religious community. Even those pastors who actively reach out to Caucasian or other ethnic minority groups have only met with limited success. The difficulty primarily ascribed to the lack of success of such efforts may be the cultural differences inherent in language, food, and lifestyle expectations (Separate Hour, 2002).

It has been suggested that Confucianism and Buddhism are the two prevalent spiritual orientations that have played the dominant role in the Asian cultural values and practices, particularly those from Mainland China, Japan, and Korea (Bradshaw, 1994). At the same time, the Filipino culture has been greatly influenced by the European-Christian domination introduced by Spanish Catholicism. Confucius has been characterized as expounding a strongly patriarchal philosophy that proscribed specific behaviors for men in society. Buddhism, less chauvinistic, although originating in India, spread to China and Japan, where Buddhist teachers such as Tien Tai from China expounded philosophies of life that have spread to the West and created a rapidly growing Buddhist community beyond the confines of the Asian-American community. His concept of *ichinen sanzen* or 3,000 life experiences in a single moment, spoke to the unity of all phenomena contained in each moment of life. This philosophy highlights the Asian appreciation for a present moment orientation or attempting to be fully present to one's life experiences.

When working with Asian Americans in therapy, it is important to assess the impact of their belief systems on their psyche. It has been suggested that the philosophies of Confucianism, Buddhism, and Taoism have resulted in great emphasis on certain values including those of harmony; humility; and respect for family, authority, and tradition. The family (extended family and the group) often take precedence over the desires or needs of the individual with that precedence inclusive of past and future generations. Other values include interpersonal style of expression valuing restraint of self-expression and high achievement partially out of a sense of duty and obligation. Morita therapy, developed by a Japanese clinician, Shoma Morita, emphasizes the recognition and acceptance of feelings while focusing on behavior change, and has been likened to rational-emotive therapy and existential therapy. Thus, issues of harmony and respect are essential, as well as one's spiritual beliefs about family and community as well as self, when attempting counseling interventions with Asian clients (Lee, 1999).

Of all of the spiritual belief systems inherent in the ethnic minority communities, Buddhism appears to have generated the most interest within mainstream psychology

(Epstein, 1995; Molino, 1998; Thurman, 1998). This phenomenon may have occurred because of Buddhist philosophy, which has been presented as, in part, the study of the psychology of mankind, along with methods of addressing the suffering as identified as an ingrained part of the human condition. The rest of this section further considers the types of Buddhism, as they present in relationship to various psychological theories.

PSYCHOLOGY AND BUDDHISM

Buddhism is not a monolithic religion, philosophy, nor way of life, any more than is Christianity. As Buddhism spread into various parts of the world, so too did the various aspects of its theory. Early Buddhist thought, known as Theravada Buddhism, focused primarily on the strictures and guidelines for daily life propounded during the early writings of Shakyamuni. Shakyamuni, the person who first expounded Buddhism, was moved to abdicate his princely life and engage in his Bodhisattva practices by his despair over the suffering of his people in India. Shakyamuni or Gautama Buddha had first practiced in India and recognized that all suffering came from attachments to delusions of permanency in life. He saw that the four poisons—birth, old age, sickness, and death—were inherent in the human condition, and the major cause of all suffering. It was his desire to relieve the suffering of his people by coming to understand it at its most basic level, which ultimately led to his enlightenment. His teachings were aimed at sharing his insights and philosophies with the rest of humanity (Erricker, 1995).

A basic tenant of Buddhist philosophy is that suffering comes from attachment to transient aspects of life. It is posited that our vision is deluded and that it is this delusion that results in our clinging to certain aspects of life, although rejecting others (Leifer, 1999). Ultimate enlightenment is insight into the true and transient nature of all things (Ikeda, 1999). The meditative practices can be seen as seeking to enable one both to concentrate and use insight to achieve a deeper level of understanding and awareness (Epstein, 1995) as a means of achieving enlightenment. Nichiren Daishonin's Buddhism charges one with taking ultimate responsibility for one's life and following a path of faith, practice, and study that allows one to move ever-forward on the path toward enlightenment or absolute happiness.

Shakyamuni, having become awakened to his mission to help humanity overcome these sufferings, taught many "sutras" or teachings, principles of living that would enable individuals to move beyond their attachments to the deep joy that comes from the living of an enlightened life. His teachings over many years were in stages that initially prepared individuals to grasp and understand his teaching. These early teachings formed the basis for Theravada Buddhism, also sometimes characterized as the "lesser vehicle" (Bankart, Dockett, & Dudley-Grant, in press). In the last 7 years of his life, he expounded the Lotus Sutra, sometimes known as the King of all Sutras. The title of these sutras is "Myoho Renge Kyo," which means devotion to the mystic law of cause and effect. In thirteenth-century Japan, a Buddhist priest named Nichiren became enlightened to his own life as the original Buddha and taught that Nam Myoho

Renge Kyo was the law, which could lead the common people to enlightenment. This law is the fundamental principle of the simultaneity of cause and effect, which assists all individuals to recognize their ability to achieve their own freedom and happiness and their responsibility for their fellow man, living the way of the Bodhisattva (*The Winning Life*, 1998).

From a psychological perspective, Buddhist philosophy presents a vision that cuts across theoretical orientations. From the strictest Freudian psychodynamic theories, to the cognitive behavioral approaches to behavior change, Buddhist theory reveals its deep insights into the processes of the human spirit and behavior change (Claxton, 1986; Molino, 1998). Indeed

> The wisdom of the Buddha's revelation is that the answers to life's most perplexing and persistent dilemmas are not outside our selves. The therapist cannot cure; God is unlikely to rescue you. Love is a gift that is offered—it can no more be seized, contained, controlled, or consumed than air. There is no meaningful distinction between you and me. Age, gender, skin color, infirmity, flags of nations—none of these constructs for you a different world than the one I inhabit. Our tears are the same; our children are the same; our fears, our hopes, and our minds are the same. Every atom that divides us is an illusion. Every perception, attitude, sensory impression is arbitrary; every distinction, every category, every drawn line in the sand is meaningless. There is no fixed point that is the center of the universe, no more than there is a fixed trait that is the center of a human being. Life is never static. All life is *process*; it is not in any way, shape, or form a fixed entity. Life is an ever-moving stream of atoms, molecules, energy fields, beings, becomings and, yes, even extinctions. (Bankart et al., in press)

Some of the most popular forms of Buddhism in America include Zen, Tibetan, and Nichiren. Each of these schools takes a somewhat different approach to the practice, reflective of their philosophy (Prebish & Tanaka, 1998). However, some overarching values are the understanding of life as eternal, the importance of adherence to the "middle way," and two major philosophical understandings of "karma" and "dependent origination." Similar to the belief system of Native Americans, Buddhist philosophy views life as eternal, with death simply as another manifestation of life. This philosophy permeates the Asian-American cultural value system that teaches that one's life is deeply connected to one's ancestors for seven generations past and future (Ikeda, 1977).

Various aspects of Buddhist philosophy have had a profound impact on Western psychology. Within the broad field of psychoanalysis, Zen Buddhism is acknowledged to have greatly influenced the work of Carl Jung. Less known is the Buddhist influence on Freud's thinking with strong linkages between the goal of humanistic psychoanalysis and Zen Buddhism (Erricker, 1995). There are also aspects of cognitive behavioral theory that also align with Buddhist philosophy, particularly using chanting, and taking full responsibility for one's actions as a form of "stress inoculation" as taught in Nichiren Buddhism (Dockett, 1993). Young and Lee (1997) have proposed three approaches to therapy that use Chinese Buddhist teachings. Conceptual therapy uses a cognitive behavioral approach incorporating concepts such as reincarnation or compassion to alleviate suffering by enabling the individual to reconceptualize their problems and enhance their ability to manage them. Practical therapy takes a more behavioral approach, suggesting activities such as meditation or chanting, which reinforce improved physical functioning such as lowering bodily responses to stress. As mentioned, with African Americans, storytelling is an important therapeutic tool. Buddhist parables, another use of storytelling in therapy, can effectively be utilized to assist the development of problem-solving skills while reducing anxiety.

A particularly well-known theoretical model that has extensively used Buddhist applications is Dialectical Behavioral Therapy or DBT. DBT is a manualized, empirically supported treatment approach for individuals who meet criteria for borderline personality disorder. Developed by Linehan, it defines this severe personality disorder as a pervasive disorder of the emotion regulation system. Significant therapeutic interventions include many mindfulness exercises, and meditations to assist the individual in developing consciousness, competence, and agency when managing their responses to situations (Linehan, 1987; Sanderson, 2000).

The United States continues to increasingly embrace and popularize Buddhist practice, as has the psychological community. Nevertheless, racism remains, distinguishing "White Buddhism" from "ethnic Buddhism" (Fields, 1998). Thus, Buddhism in the United States faces some of the same challenges found throughout the religious/ spiritual world regarding the social ills that have plagued the ethnic minority community for centuries.

SPIRITUALITY AND RECOVERY—A MODEL FOR INTEGRATION

One area of mental health functioning where spirituality has taken a central role is in the field of substance abuse treatment and recovery. A consideration of how spirituality functions within this field may serve as a model for the most effective integration of spirituality into one's practice, from Christian and Buddhist perspectives.

Drug addiction has grown into one of the leading mental health problems around the world. Two major Western psychological theories of addiction, psychodynamic and cognitive-behavioral, currently provide the foundation for much of addiction research and intervention and its relationship to spirituality, a long-standing aspect of recovery is recently gaining attention from the research community. Spirituality and addiction have been linked for many years, as exemplified through the growth and acknowledged success of Alcoholics Anonymous (AA) and other 12-step programs (Green, Fullilove, & Fullilove, 1998). In 2000, the National Institute on Alcohol Abuse and Alcoholism, in conjunction with the Fetzer Institute, a nonprofit foundation, released a Request for Funding (RFA) to research the role of religiousness and spirituality in the prevention, treatment, and recovery from alcoholism and alcohol-related diseases (NIAA, Feb. 18, 2000). Although there has been a concerted attempt to distinguish religion from spirituality (Green et al., 1998), spirituality has most frequently focused on belief in an external being or process, "power greater than ourselves to restore us to sanity" (AA, 1976), following a Judeo-Christian theology.

Buddhism also has addressed issues of addiction, from spiritual and theoretical perspectives (Groves & Farmer, 1994). Buddhist doctrines address craving and attachment, indicating that an appreciation of the impermanence of all things can inform our understanding of the causation and mechanics of addictions. Buddhist theories of the 12-fold chain of interdependent origination have been used as a model for understanding addiction (Metzner, 1996). Recently, the concept of the presence of the Ten Worlds, where the world of hunger or insatiable desire as found in addiction is one of the four lower worlds leading to the destruction of the human spirit, has been considered in relationship to addictions (Dudley-Grant, 2000). Buddhism focuses inward on the individual, rather than outward toward an external force to address suffering in one's life. From this perspective, it can be difficult to resolve Buddhist spirituality with the traditional understanding of the role of spirituality in addiction and recovery.

However, research has shown that the most effective approach to treatment is a combination of therapeutic interventions, along with participation in group processes such as AA (Alford, 1980). The concept of a spiritual connection that is essential to and supports the addiction recovery has been supported by the outcome literature on the efficacy of 12-step programs. Research further documents that a multipronged approach to treatment, utilizing individual as well as group interventions, appears to be the most effective in achieving long-term recovery (Sheeren, 1988). The clinicians' support of their clients' participation in 12-step or other group programs assists the clients to create the most comprehensive approach to recovery, while having a unified sense of the illness a recovery from same (Khantzian & Mack, 1994).

SPIRITUAL/PSYCHOLOGICAL INTEGRATION IN PRACTICE

This chapter has attempted to examine spirituality as it manifests in various aspects of psychology with ethnic minority populations. It is clear that spirituality has a growing acceptance within the field of psychology (Smith, 2001). In addition, research on cultural consonance has shown that each U.S. ethnic minority group places a high value on one's spiritual life and spiritual connection. It is apparent then that the effective, culturally consonant practitioner must have an awareness of and willingness to engage with the ethnically diverse client in a discussion of the understanding of the client's belief system. It is also essential that the practitioner understand that the client's belief system may be very complex in that socially acceptable beliefs and practices such as Christianity may exist along with more "traditional" or ethnocultural practices such as Espiritista or voodoo.

This awareness is particularly important as it can frame the client's understanding and definition of the cause of emotional suffering, which greatly affects the treatment. Traditional "talking therapy" whether insight-oriented or behaviorally based will not achieve the greatest level of efficacy if the client believes he or she has been "possessed," that a spell has been put on him or her, or if he or she is living out of harmony with one's higher power, however defined, whether that be God or the universal law. While it is neither practical nor desirable for the therapist to become a native healer, nor even to attempt to utilize their methods, a respectful appreciation for the client's belief system, as well as knowledge of the other interventions, is an essential component of treatment. Some ethnic minority psychologists have suggested that the therapist's knowledge should extend to the point where he or she is able to assist the client in distinguishing between the truly competent native healers and charlatans (Garcia, 1999). This level of knowledge may not always be possible; however, it is a noteworthy goal to strive for, and encourages the practitioner to extend one's knowledge beyond the boundaries of traditional psychological theory and practice found in texts, classrooms, and the office. Certainly, a key component of effective therapy with ethnic minorities is the willingness to seek out information of cultural relevance and to be nontraditional in one's approach to the therapeutic intervention and relationship (Comas-Diaz & Griffith, 1988; Garrett-Akinsanya, 2001). The integration of spiritual knowledge in working with ethnic minority populations can be seen as an extension of this innovation, in keeping with a field that appears to be poised to embrace these considerations within the broader scope of clinical practice. Undoubtedly, the practitioner will be enhanced by efforts in this area of practice, and may well embark on a personal journey of discovery, which may spark positive changes in every aspect of life, as well as enhancing effective psychological practice with people of all ethnicities.

REFERENCES

Akbar, N. (2000, March). *From miseducation to education: Who says that Black History Month is in February only.* Invited address presented to Grand Rounds at University of the Virgin Islands, St. Croix, USVI.

Alcoholics Anonymous. (3rd ed.). (1976). New York: Alcoholics Anonymous World Services.

Alford, G. S. (1980). Alcoholics anonymous: An empirical outcome study. *Addictive Behaviors, 5,* 359–370.

Anduze, A. (1993, May). *Controversy in the use of non-conventional medicines in the Caribbean.* Paper presented at 18th Annual Conference of the Caribbean Studies Association, Jamaica.

Bankart, P. (1997). *Talking cures: A history of Western and Eastern psychotherapies.* Pacific Grove, CA: Brooks/Cole.

Bankart, P, Dockett, K., & Dudley-Grant, G. R. (in press). On the path of the Buddha: A psychologists' guide to the history of Buddhism. In K. Dockett, P. Bankart, & G. R. Dudley-Grant (Eds.), *Psychology and Buddhism: From individual to global community.* Amsterdam: Kluwer.

Black, L. (1996). Families of African origin: An overview. In M. McGoldrick, J. Giordano, & J. K. Pearce. *Ethnicity & family therapy* (2nd ed., pp. 57–65). New York: Guilford.

Boyd-Franklin, N. (1989). *Black families in therapy: A multisystems approach.* New York: Guilford.

Boyd-Franklin, N., & Franklin, A. J. (2000). *Boys into men: Raising our African American teenage sons.* New York: Plume.

Bradshaw, C. K. (1994). Asian and Asian American women: Historical and political considerations in psychotherapy. In L. Comas-Diaz & B. Greene (Eds.), *Women of Color: Integrating ethnic and gender identities in psychotherapy* (pp. 72–113). New York: Guilford.

Budd, F. C. (1999). An Air Force model of psychologist-chaplain collaboration. *Professional Psychology: Research & Practice, 30,* 552–556.

Bullis, R. K. (1996). *Spirituality in social work practice.* Washington, DC: Taylor & Francis.

Cervantes, J. (2001, August). Mestizo spirituality: Counseling model for Chicano/Latino; Native/Indigenous peoples. In G. R. Dudley-Grant (Chair). *Working with spiritual healers: Challenges and opportunities.* Pod conducted at the 109th Annual Convention of the American Psychological Association, San Francisco, CA.

Chao, C. M. (2000). Ancestors and ancestor altars: Connecting relationships. In J. L. Chin, (Ed.), *Relationships among Asian American women.* Washington, DC: American Psychological Association.

Chan, S. (1991). *Asian Americans: An interpretive history.* Boston: Twayne.

Chirban, J. (1996). *Personhood: Orthodox Christianity and the connection between body, mind, and soul.* Westport, CT: Greenwood.

Claxton, G. (1986, reprinted 1996). The lights on but there's nobody home: The psychology of no-self. In G. Claxton (Ed.), *Beyond therapy: The impact of Eastern religions on psychological theory and practice* (pp. 49–70). Dorset, England: Prism Press.

Comas-Diaz, L. (1981). Puerto Rican espiritism and psychotherapy. *American Journal of Orthopsychiatry, 5,* 636–645.

Comas-Diaz, L., & Griffith, E. E. H. (1988). *Clinical guidelines in cross-cultural mental health.* New York: Wiley.

Coon, D. J. (1992). Testing the limits of sense and science: American experimental psychologists combat spiritualism, 1880–1920. *American Psychologist, 47,* 143–151.

Delgado, M., & Humm-Delgado, D. (1982). Natural support systems: Source of strength in Hispanic communities. *Social Work, 27,* 83–89.

Dockett, K. (1993). Resources for stress resistance: Parallels in psychology and Buddhism. *The Philosophy and Practice of the SGI, SGI-USA Culture Department Booklet Series, 3.* Santa Monica, CA: Soka Gakkai International-USA.

Dockett, K., & North-Schulte, D. (in press). Transcending difference: Mahayana principles of integration. In P. Bankart, K. Dockett, & G. R. Dudley-Grant (Eds.), *Psychology and Buddhism: From individual to global community.* Amsterdam: Kluwer.

Dudley-Grant, G. R. (1998, August). Individualism and collectivism: Psychodynamic theories and commonalities with Buddhist thought. In A. Marsella & G. R. Dudley-Grant (Co-Chairs), *Buddhist and Western psychological thought: Conceptual foundations and assumptions.* Symposium conducted at the 106th Annual Convention of the American Psychological Association, San Francisco, CA.

Dudley-Grant, G. R. (1999, August). Psychologists and Indigenous Healers in the Caribbean. In M. A. Garcia (Chair), *Collaboration between traditional healers and psychologists.* Symposium conducted at the 107th Annual Convention of the American Psychological Association, Boston, MA.

Dudley-Grant, G. R. (2000, August). Buddhism, addiction theory and recovery in psychotherapy. In A. Marsella & D. K. Pryor (Co-Chairs). *Healing for the Millennium I: Buddhist application for western psychotherapy.* Symposium conducted at the 108th Annual Convention of the American Psychological Association, Washington, DC.

Dudley-Grant, G. R. (2001a, August). Indigenous spirituality and psychology in the Caribbean. In G. R. Dudley-Grant (Chair). *Working with spiritual healers: Challenges and opportunities.* Pod conducted at the 109th Annual Convention of the American Psychological Association, San Francisco, CA.

Dudley-Grant, G. R. (Chair). (2001b, August). *Healing the person, family, society and planet: Buddhism and psychotherapy.* Symposium conducted at the 109th Annual Convention of the American Psychological Association, San Francisco, CA.

Erricker, C. (1995). *World faiths: Buddhism.* Chicago: NTC/Contemporary.

Epstein, M. (1995). Thoughts without a thinker: Buddhism and psychoanalysis. *Psychoanalytic review, 82,* 391–406.

Farley, F. (1996). From the heart. 102nd Annual Convention of the American Psychological Association: Presidential address (1994, Los Angeles, California). *American Psychologist, 51,* 772–776.

Fields, R. (1998). Divided Dharma: White Buddhists, ethnic Buddhists and racism. In C. S. Prebish & K. K. Tanaka (Eds.), *The faces of Buddhism in America* (pp. 196–206). Berkeley, CA: University of California Press.

Fleming, C. (2001, August). Working with spiritual healers: The Native American experience. In G. R. Dudley-Grant (Chair). *Working with spiritual healers: Challenges and opportunities.* Pod conducted at the 109th Annual Convention of the American Psychological Association, San Francisco, CA.

Frame, M. W., Williams, C. B., & Green, E. L. (1999). Balm in Gilead: Spiritual dimensions in counseling African American women. *Journal of Multicultural Counseling & Development, 27,* 182–192.

Frazier, E. F. (1963). *The Negro church in America.* New York: Schocken.

Fukuyama, M. A., & Sevig. T. D. (1999). *Integrating spirituality into multicultural counseling.* Thousand Oaks, CA: Sage.

Garcia M. A. (Chair). (1999, August). *Collaboration between traditional healers and psychologists.* Symposium conducted at the 107th Annual Convention of the American Psychological Association, Boston, MA.

Garrett-Akinsanya, B. (2001). Looking for an open door: Improving access for ethnic psychologists serving ethnically diverse populations. *The Independent Practitioner, 21,* 223–227.

Green, L. L., Fullilove, M. T., & Fullilove, R. E. (1998). Stories of spiritual awakening: The nature of spirituality in recovery. *Journal of Substance Abuse Treatment, 15,* 325–332.

Groves, P.G., & Farmer, R. (1994). Buddhism and addictions. *Addiction Research, 2,* 183–194.

Ikeda, D. (1977). *Buddhism, the first millennium.* Tokyo: Kodansha International.

Ikeda, D. (1999). *For today and tomorrow: Daily encouragement.* Santa Monica, CA: World Tribune Press.

Jenkins, A. H. (1995). *Psychology and African Americans* (2nd ed.). Boston: Allyn & Bacon.

Jenkins, Y. M., De la Cancela, V. & Chin, J. L. (1993). Historical overviews: Three sociopolitical perspectives. In J. L. Chin, De La Cancela, & Y. M. Jenkins (Eds.), *Diversity in psychotherapy* (pp. 17–43). Westport, CT: Praeger.

Khantzian, E., & Mack, J. (1994). How AA works and why it's important for clinicians to understand. *Journal of Substance Abuse Treatment, 11,* 77–92.

Kawulich, B. B., & Curlette, W. L. (1998). Life tasks and the Native American perspectives. *Journal of Individual Psychology, 54,* 359–367.

La Framboise, T. D., Berman, J. S., & Balvindar, K. S. (1994). American Indian women. In L. Comas-Diaz & B. Greene (Eds.), *Women of Color: Integrating ethnic and gender identities in psychotherapy* (pp. 30–71). New York: Guilford.

Lee, W. M. L. (1999). *An introduction to multicultural counseling.* Philadelphia: Accelerated Development.

Leifer, R. (1999). Buddhist conceptualization and treatment of anger. *Journal of Clinical Psychology, 55,* 339–351.

Lewis, S. (1994). Cognitive-behavioral approaches. In L. Comas-Diaz & B. Greene (Eds.), *Women of Color: Integrating ethnic and gender identities in psychotherapy* (pp. 223–238). New York: Guilford.

Linehan, M. M. (1987). Dialectical behavioral therapy: A cognitive behavioral approach to parasuicide. *Journal of Personality Disorders, 1,* 328–333.

McNeil, D. W., Kee, M., & Zvolensky, M. J. (1999). Culturally related anxiety and ethnic identity in Navajo college students. *Cultural Diversity and Ethnic Minority Psychology, 5,* 56–64.

Metraux, A. (1959). *Voodoo in Haiti.* Translated by Hugo Charteries. New York: Schocken.

Metzner, R. (1996). The Buddhist six-worlds model of consciousness and reality. *The Journal of Transpersonal Psychology, 28,* 155–166.

Molino, A. (1998). *The couch and the tree: Dialogues in psychoanalysis and Buddhism.* New York: North Point Press.

Moncayo, R. (1998). Cultural diversity and the cultural and epistemological structure of psychoanalysis: Implications for psychotherapy with Latinos and other minorities. *Psychoanalytic Psychology, 15,* 262–286.

National Institute on Alcohol Abuse and Alcoholism (NIAA), (Friday, Feb 18, 2000). RFA: AA-00-002, retrieved 2/24/00 from the World Wide Web: ScienceWise.Com

Nobles, W. (1980). African philosophy: Foundations for Black psychology. In R. Jones (Ed.), *Black psychology* (2nd ed., pp. 23–36). New York: Harper & Row.

Pinderhughes, E. B. (1989). *Understanding race, ethnicity, and power.* New York: Free Press.

Prebish, C. S., & Tanaka, K. K. (Eds.). (1998). *The faces of Buddhism in America.* Berkeley: University of California Press.

Richards, P. S., & Bergin, A. E. (2000). *Handbook of Psychotherapy and Religious Diversity.* Washington, DC: American Psychological Association.

Rosado, J. W., & Elias, M. J. (1993). Ecological and psychocultural mediators in the delivery of services for urban, culturally diverse Hispanic clients. *Professional Psychology: Research and Practice, 24,* 450–459.

Sanderson, C. (2000). Dialectical behavior therapy. Continuing Education workshop conducted at the 108th Annual Convention of the American Psychological Association, Washington, DC.

Separate hour: Church integration not easy for Asian Americans. (2002, January 17). *The Avis, St. Croix, USVI,* pp. 14–15.

Sheeren, M. (1988). The relationship between relapse and involvement in Alcoholics Anonymous. *Journal of Studies on Alcohol, 49,* 104–106.

Smith, T. B. (2001). [Review of the book *Handbook of psychotherapy and religious diversity*]. *Cultural Diversity and Ethnic Minority Psychology, 7,* 399–400.

Sutton C. T., & Broken Nose, M. A. (1996). American Indian families: An overview. In M. McGoldrick, J. Giordano, & J. K. Pearce. *Ethnicity & family therapy* (2nd ed., pp. 31–44). New York: Guilford.

Tafoya, N., & Del Vecchio, A. (1996). Back to the future: An examination of the Native American Holocaust. In M. McGoldrick, J. Giordano, & J. K. Pearce (Eds.), *Ethnicity & family therapy* (2nd ed., pp. 45–56). New York: Guilford.

Thurman, R. (1998). *Inner revolution: Life, liberty and the pursuit of real happiness.* New York: Riverhead Books.

Vasquez, M. J. T. (1994). Latinas. In L. Comas-Diaz & B. Greene (Eds.), *Women of Color: Integrating ethnic and gender identities in psychotherapy* (pp. 114–138). New York: Guilford.

Wimberly, E. P. (1993). Minorities. In R. J. Wicks, R. D. Parsons; et al. (Eds.). *Clinical handbook of pastoral counseling, Vol. 1* (Exp. ed., pp. 300–317). Mahwah, NJ: Paulist Press.

The winning life: An introduction to Buddhist practice. (1998). Santa Monica, CA: The Sokka Gakkai (SGI-USA).

Young, W. H., & Lee, E. (1997). Chinese Buddhism: Its implications for counseling. In E. Lee (Ed.), *Working with Asian Americans: A guide for clinicians.* New York: Guilford.

Index

Older adults (*continued*)
usage patterns of mental health services by, 313;
young-old, 309
O'Leary, K. D., 273, 277
Omnibus Personality Inventory (OPI), 176
O'Neil, J. M., 275
Onwughalu, M., 134
Ordonez, N., 240
Organizational cultural competency, 85
Organizational diversity initiatives:
basic assumptions about resistance to, 88–89;
context for, 86;
definition of terminology, 86–87;
premises of, 87–88;
resistance to, 90–94, 103
Organizational resistance to multiculturalism, 83–89, 103:
defense mechanisms, 90–91;
ethnocentrism and racial identity models, 94–95;
internal/external persona model, 93–94;
loss and change model, 91–93;
minority identity development model, 95;
paradigms of resistance, 90
Ossana, S., 294
Ostrow, D., 291
O'Sullivan, M. J., 182

Padden, C., 326, 329
Padgett, D. K., 260
Padilla, A. M., 168
Page, A. W., 273
Paniagua, F. A., 167
Parham, T. A., 123–124, 127, 132–133, 135
Patel, M., 201
Patrick, C., 260
Patterson, C., 295
Peabody, C. G., 272
Peplau, L., 292
Perry, William, 21, 23
Pharmacotherapy, gender differences in, 260
Phillips, B., 333
Phinney, J., 126–127, 134
Pinderhuges, E. B., 346
Pirog-Good, M. A., 271
Pollard, R. Q., 334
Posttraumatic stress disorder in Asian/Pacific Islander Americans, 178
Poussaint, A., 240
Prathikanti, S., 198, 302
Principled activistic disposition of White racism:
characteristics of, 25–26;
recommendations for dealing with, 34

Principled disposition of White racism:
characteristics of, 24–26;
recommendations for dealing with, 32–24
Project RACE, 244
Psychological dispositions of White racism, 34–35:
affective-impulsive, 20–22, 25–26;
liberal, 22–25, 30–32;
principled, 24–26, 32–34;
principled activistic, 25–26, 34;
rational, 21–22, 25, 28–30
Psychology:
collaboration with faith healers, 342–344;
focus on Western spiritual traditions in, 342;
historical perspective of spirituality and, 343–344;
interest in Buddhism, 351–353;
use of Buddhist teachings in, 353–354
Psychotherapy:
cognitive match between client and therapist, 184;
effects of ethnic similarity-dissimilarity between client and therapist, 183–184
Pure race ideology, 59–62:
privilege based on, 62–63

Qualls, S. H., 309

Race:
as a construct in the service of racism, 74;
defined, 58;
meanings of, 75;
measures of, 127;
one-drop rule, 55, 60–62, 69–70;
resistance to inclusion by minority groups, 62;
scientific classification of, 60–61;
social construction of, 57–58, 62
Racial discrimination, 240–241
Racial Identity Attitude Scale (RIAS), 127
Racial identity development models, 119, 125–127
Racism:
aversion, 6–7, 11;
counseling for dealing with, 28–31, 33;
covert, intentional, 8–9;
covert, unintentional, 8–11;
effect on African-American couples, 146;
frustrated idealism regarding, 24–25;
in mental health profession, 17–20, 23–26;
in response to civil rights, 4;
institutional policies against, 27;
modern forms of, 1, 4–6, 14–15;
overt, intentional, 8–9, 21;
stimulating behavioral responsivity to, 31–32;